RETAIL SECURITY:

Controlling Loss For Profit

BOB CURTIS

BUTTERWORTHS
Boston • London

All references in this book to personnel of male gender are used for convenience only and shall be regarded as including both males and females.

Library of Congress Cataloging in Publication Data

Curtis, Bob.
Retail security.

Includes index.
1. Retail trade—Security measures. 2. Shoplifting. 3. Inventory shortages. I. Title
HF5429.27.C87 1982 658.8'7 82-14740
ISBN 0-409-95066-1

Published by Butterworth Publishers
10 Tower Office Park
Woburn, MA 01801

10 9 8 7 6 5 4 3 2 1

Printed in the United States of America

TABLE OF CONTENTS

ACKNOWLEDGEMENTS

This book, obviously, has been enriched by the knowledge and experience of many people. George Callahan, the father of modern retail security, made substantial contributions to the ideas contained here. In addition, Edward Tubman, Ken Galston, Philip Schaeffer, George Bell, Norman Lenox, Donald Eugene, Peter Kuntz, Dick Groberg, Charles Bernstein, Belden Menkus, and William Clark provided experience and input into this work.

I owe a special debt to Harriet and Norman Felder, who guided my writing and encouraged me as personal mentors throughout the years. Dr. Fabian L. Rouke, one of the nation's leading criminologists, trained me in abnormal psychology and for fifteen years acted as counselor and friend.

Many store security directors provided information that has been included in this book, and to name them all would be an impossible task, but I am especially indebted to Edward Wetton, Larry Glass, Glen Dornfeld, and Nelson Carrick.

Retail executives outside the security field also provided many of the concepts found in these pages. I am indebted to Joseph Walters, Morris Moss, Stanley Landon, Joseph Miller, Newton Hamblet, and many others.

My thanks as well to the valuable guidance and personal help I have received from Dave Karstens, whose loyalty, understanding, and guidance have made him a wise counselor over the years and a close friend. I also want to thank Rick Newman, whose experience, ideas, and interest have encouraged me and provided valuable insights to this field.

Raymond C. Farber is one of the men whose genius has given the security field its first recognition as an important profession. I am indebted to him and to Louis Camin for their personal support and encouragement and for the opportunities to work closely with other leaders in the security field.

A special word of thanks to my editor, confidant, and close personal friend, Jan Reber. One of the young giants in today's field of business security, I am grateful to Jan Reber not only for his editorial help, encouragement, and insights, but also for his creativeness in originating the concept of such a book and his urging that I be the person to write it.

The dirty work in writing a book of this length, or of any length, is that of retyping and reshaping draft after draft until the paper shuffling becomes a literal nightmare of chaos and confusion. For all her solid support, constructive suggestions, and tremendous energies I am grateful to my Girl Friday, Pat Martin. But in addition to all these important qualities and contribution, the one I most treasure is her enthusiasm for getting the book done, an enthusiasm that often bolstered the frustrated writer and overcame those low points when it always seemed as though the work could never be completed. I also want to give a word of thanks to her sidekick Phyllis Sharp who did so much by taking on some of the arduous typing chores.

Last, my thanks to my wife and my sons for their interest and enthusiasm throughout this apparently never ending project.

Bob Curtis
Dayton, Ohio

Chapter 1

WHAT IS RETAIL SECURITY?

Let's Look at a Modern Retail Security Office

Behind the security office door a lot of interesting activity is taking place. The secretary is on the phone. She says, "Go to the fifth floor right away. There is a stray dog barking at people in the sportswear department. See Mr. Johnson and hurry!"

Hardly has she hung up when the phones are ringing again with new problems. Nearby a man and woman are looking over several register tapes. The woman says, "We have three violations on him. I think we ought to pull him."

On the other side of the room a customer is talking to a young man. He makes notes on a pad as she says, "I laid the purse down while I examined some stockings and when I went to pick it up it was gone. It had my car keys, license, checkbook, and over $80 in it. What will I do?"

Behind a closed door can be heard the muffled voice of an excited woman, "It's the first time I ever stole anything in my life! I swear it! Please don't send me to jail! What will my husband do when he finds out?"

Every day a great variety of problems come to the security office for some type of action. In no part of a store is there more variety of activity than in the security department. The security person never knows when he goes to work in the morning what will happen before the end of the day—a buyer's desk has been rifled—a carton of flat irons is missing from the warehouse—a customer package has been torn open and the contents stolen—a clerical worker needs protection in getting home from the store because her estranged husband is threatening to beat her up—smoke seeps out into an upper floor and a search has to be made for a fire—two boys are causing alarm on the street floor with a trained white mouse; they are playfully putting the mouse onto the arms of unsuspecting customers.

Incidents like these and hundreds of others occur day in and day out.

Because security work is complex, we need to step back a few paces to see what it is all about. What are the aims of the security department? How does it accomplish them? Let's take it from the beginning and see if we can tie all of this unrelated activity into a logical pattern.

Security Department Objectives

Security is a department set up to protect the store properties, personnel, and customers from loss or injury. It operates 24 hours a day, every day of the year.

There are *five* basic categories that are of concern to security.

1. Malefactors. This is a broad heading that covers some of the most time-consuming and important parts of the department's operation. Security deals with the *detection* of malefactors and the *prevention* of loss caused by malefactors. This includes thefts by shoplifters and dishonest employees, and also involves such problems as pickpockets, bad check operators, refunders, impostors, prowlers, drunks, and perverts.

2. Carelessness. At the root of almost all loss is carelessness. The fire that breaks out in the warehouse paint shop, for example, may have been caused by a person who carelessly left oily rags in the corner. The theft of a $4,000 mink stole in the fur department may have been caused by a careless department manager who did not have sufficient salespeople assigned to cover the department during the lunch hour. Carelessness as related to store security is a problem that must be detected and corrected.

3. Error. Errors affect store losses, and therefore they are of interest to security. The possible types of errors in a store operation are so numerous it would take pages to list them. There are pricing errors, errors in writing saleschecks, errors in counting money, and many,

many others. Many errors that lead to loss can be detected and corrected as a result of security work.

4. Lawsuits. Because of the nature of security work, there is always the danger of lawsuits. Such lawsuits may be for false arrest, defamation of character, libel, or similar charges. This is a constant threat to a store. Because settlements in such cases can be substantial, Security has to operate with good judgment to protect the store from lawsuits.

5. Fires or Other Calamities. Security also serves the store in the detection and prevention of fires, waterflow damage, and similar emergencies that are a constant threat to any company.

Responsibilities increase during the hours in which the store is closed. Throughout the long nights, holidays, and weekends when most people are away from the store, security keeps its vigil. Security people are alert for smoke, flames, or flowing water. They check on windows being left open during cold weather. A sudden freeze may open a sprinkler head. A flat iron left on in the tailor shop can start a fire. These and many other small things may lead to major disasters.

Organization of the Security Department

Who carries out the work required for these five problems mentioned in the preceding paragraphs?

Security is a relatively small department. All of its people have to be flexible; there is an overlap of duties. In a crisis anyone available handles the problem. For purposes of organization, however, we can divide security into *seven* areas.

1. Administration. This includes the supervisors of different departments within security. Supervisors handle the routine problems of scheduling and assigning work as well as other details that are the normal functions of supervision. But because security work in itself is not routine, because no two days are the same, the administrative people have to go beyond routine planning.

The security manager must do a continuous job of analyzing, planning, and deputizing. He must have long-range objectives and he must also see that daily problems are being well handled.

It is vital that Mr. Jones in yard goods gets a detective right away when he phones for help. It is also important that a long-range study be made of the return goods operation to see what loopholes can be plugged to prevent future losses.

In security work, long-range plans have to be meshed with day-to-day activities. There is a need for the security head to be flexible. He must keep all of his cases, problems, and projects moving forward at once. He must be able to judge between the important and the unimportant problems. His job is interesting, often exciting, and always challenging. Only people with energy, enthusiasm, and imagination need apply.

2. Investigators. Some stores have several security investigators. In other stores this job might fall on the security head, a floor detective, or even the secretary. Everyone in security is an investigator at one time or another. But in the well-planned security department there will be people who spend most of their time in investigative activities.

Investigators work on problems of detection and prevention. They interview people on departmental losses, or a shoplifter on his methods of theft. They talk with the dishonest employee to find out how he stole. They listen; they dig; they seek out facts, opinions, and ideas. They build plans for constructive action to prevent future losses. Often, by picking up a small lead, they can pull in a thread that is tied to a dishonest person. Like all people who work in security, their job is an important part of the final results.

3. Floor Detectives. Most good floor detectives are women. Some stores today find it hard to employ capable women and instead use men as floor detectives. There is a need for both men and women in floor work, however, for women can go into the fitting rooms, which is forbidden to men.

More important, some women seem to have an intuitive knack for finding a shoplifter.

The floor detective is a basic part of security. The work is, first, the detection of thieves, but it can also be the prevention of many thefts. The detective is also called on to do investigations. This employee can be an effective aid in reducing losses.

4. Honesty Shoppers. Some stores have their own honesty shoppers. Others use an outside agency. In either case the honesty shopper is an important member of security. For the time, effort, and cost involved the "shopper" will detect more dishonest employees than can be done by any other method.

This shopper checks the honesty of your store's selling areas. Although his job is to find dishonest salespeople, a shopper's work can help to prevent theft if violations of store policy are reported (such as failure to give a sales receipt). Such reports are turned over to the store personnel office for a correctional interview. The warning interview may stop borderline people from theft.

A shopping staff also acts as a psychological barrier to theft for many employees. If people know they will be tested from time to time this can keep them honest.

Honesty shoppers can prove their value by the number of cases they develop. It has been found that in most stores shopping pays for itself in money recovered from the people apprehended. Its greatest value, of course, is in the prevention of future thefts by the malefactors who are caught.

5. **Guards and Watchmen.** These men control employee exits, the movement of people in and out of the building, and the employee package system. They also patrol the building during the hours in which the store is closed. They are alert to the dangers of fire, water damage, or other calamities. Their work is primarily preventive, although they may detect a prowler or find a dishonest employee or other kinds of malefactors. In many ways their job is the most routine of any job in security.

If a crisis occurs, these men are called upon to use their resourcefulness, experience, and judgment. The guard at this time can often save hundreds or thousands of dollars of loss to the store. He may have to act courageously, decisively, and with good judgment at this time of need. It is at the moment of crisis that his value becomes most apparent.

6. **Undercover Detectives.** Little is said openly about this phase of security work. Many stores employ detectives who work in various nonselling areas as regular employees of that area. These undercover detectives can be effective in finding the dishonest employee if they are capable observers and are located in a spot with specific theft problems.

The undercover detective must be able to win over other employees. He must be able to judge the important from the unimportant. It is also important that he be able to conceal his identity. It's a tough job that requires special skills, and when such detectives are well placed they become valuable to store security.

7. **Office Staff.** This group of people is often the key to success or failure in a large security department. Communication must be rapid and accurate. The central control is the security office. The secretary who handles the phones and assigns detectives to emergency calls is a vital post in the security organization. Her judgment, that is, her ability to decide rapidly and report accurately, can be the difference

between a case and confused, useless action. In addition, the office people who handle records, case histories, statements, files, and similar tasks are important to a smoothly running department.

How security people handle incoming phone calls is important. Their attitude can result in good public relations, which in turn gets other store people to help security. A poor attitude can cause other store people to be indifferent or even hostile toward security.

On the shoulders of the office staff rests a great responsibility. They are the people who back up the investigators, floor detectives, guards, shoppers, and employee observers. Their cheerfulness, positive attitude, cooperation, and enthusiasm can be a stimulant that makes the whole system work. Their ability to communicate and to keep good records can be a vital link in the chain between a lead and an arrest.

It is important that each group within the security network be able to function together as a team.

Outside Groups

There is another group of people not included in our analysis because they do not work directly for the store. Outside law enforcement people, the city, county, and state police departments, are also important to store security. Without their aid, store security would find the prosecution of cases difficult.

Now let's look at how all of these people get the job done. What methods do they use in their security work? We can divide them into *seven* types of activity.

Security Department Methods

Investigations. No plans can be made, or no goals intelligently set until you first make an analysis of your problem. You need facts to make decisions. Investigations furnish these facts, for they are the foundation of all security work. It is through investigation that analysis is made. The results help us to set objectives and make plans.

Investigation may lead to the arrest of a malefactor. It may lead to changes in store systems to cut future losses. Investigations set the course for action.

Where should you locate your floor detectives? Investigation of your records will show where they are needed. What should you do to prevent losses in delivery? First, you need to find out how the system is being operated. Does your inventory shortage sheet show losses in the cosmetic department? First, you must find out where the losses are occurring and what type of things are being stolen. First come the questions; then investigations follow to find the answers.

Interviews. Are case interviews merely routine? No, interviews can be valuable. They can help you by closing up loopholes in your store's systems and controls. Interviews can lead to the recovery of stolen merchandise, and they can also teach us why certain people steal. There is no other job in security work that requires more skill. Only a few people can be outstanding interviewers. Interviewing is one of the highest developments of human communication and the most important talent an investigator can have.

Systems and Controls. A store with good systems and controls prevents many losses. Good systems can detect thefts and may lead to the culprit. Security helps the store to develop better systems and controls.

Almost every system put into a retail store was initially placed there to prevent loss, to be guardians of store goods or money. Security looks for loopholes in store systems. Sometimes the problem is not in the system but in the supervisor who fails to operate the system properly.

Whenever people are caught stealing security attempts to learn whether the theft could have been prevented by a better system. Systems and controls are the best means for cutting losses that your store has. Security is concerned with how well your systems are operated and where new controls may be needed.

Scientific Devices. Security uses scientific devices to aid in the fight against crime. Most devices are used to find malefactors, but some are used to prevent losses. They act as a physical or psychological barrier to theft. A tape recorder for recording interviews of dishonest people is used to prevent a possible civil lawsuit against the store. A lie detector can be used to find out from a thief the names of other people who are stealing from the store. It may also be used to learn how much money a thief has taken. Alarm systems are used to warn off intruders.

Today many scientific devices are important to retail security.

Reports and Records. Your security reports and records are another means of reaching security objectives. Reports reveal things that will improve systems. They may suggest ways of extending the security department coverage.

Records are often vital in the development of a case. There are many uses for security reports and records.

Educational Programs. Another approach to the problems of loss is that of the educational program. Educational programs can be used for training new employees. All of the methods used by the training department are applicable: visual aids, such as films or photographs; talks; memos; conferences; and meetings.

The educational program keeps store personnel alert to the problems of loss. It can stimulate an award program and lead to the arrest of important criminals. It can improve the store operation of controls that prevent loss. Most important it can also set up psychological barriers in the minds of store personnel to prevent them from stealing.

Physical Layouts. Good physical layout can help cut loss. Security must be alert to the location of cash registers. They may find that the receiving room should be partitioned off and made inaccessible to people outside of the receiving area. Fitting rooms need to be designed with a single entrance aisle. The fur department should not be located near an exit stairway. These and many other security problems are affected by layout.

Security can help the store when an area is being redesigned. The store that considers security whenever it makes a change in physical layout soon finds that a little advance thought about security needs can prevent thousands of dollars in future losses.

Security has three objectives:

1. To prevent future loss.
2. To apprehend malefactors.
3. To recover stolen merchandise or money.

These goals, in turn, lead to the ultimate goal: increasing your store's net profit.

Increasing the net profit is the final objective. This is why we have a retail security department, why we work at loss problems. The security department is concerned with preventing losses, apprehending malefactors, and recovering goods or money. *The result is a larger net profit.*

Chapter 2

HANDLING SHOPLIFTER PROBLEMS: PART I

During the past few years much has been learned about methods of combating shoplifting. If properly applied, these techniques can go a long way toward reducing losses. Still the problem is a serious one. A former security head of Marshall Field & Co. in Chicago has said, "Unfortunately, we know from experience that dishonest employees can be a source of large losses. What isn't realized is that the professional shoplifter also causes large losses. There are professional shoplifters who will steal six to seven hundred dollars worth of merchandise from your store in a single day."

Many of our present shoplifting problems result from our narrowing profit margins, which have caused most stores to use fewer salespeople. This reduction of retail staffs has been possible because of new merchandising techniques. Among them is the trend to "self-service." As the owner of one self-service store put it, "In self-service we ask our customers to help themselves. They sure do!" Open displays and self-service are methods of merchandising that are here to stay. We can't turn the clock back, but we must work in terms of present problems.

In the old days we could hide things under glass or lock things in cases. Today, this is not possible. We must develop new techniques to combat these new shoplifter risks. We want customers to handle merchandise, to feel it and to try it on. We know this helps to sell it. To reduce shoplifter losses we must see that our employees are adequately trained. They require a constant reminder about the dangers of shoplifting thefts. Within budget limits, stores also need more security specialists.

The Law

"The taking without consent, of any article of value, from the possession of a store with intent to deprive that store of its ownership" is considered larceny in many states. In some states the value of the goods may determine whether the crime is first or second degree larceny.

In most cases shoplifting is now considered a *felony*. Taking possession of an article even for a moment is considered "taking," but the matter of *intent* is vitally important. At times intent is difficult to prove. The merchant who apprehends a dishonest person *must* be able to prove that this person intended to steal.

Intent is the purpose or design of the person who has the merchandise in his possession. It is the "why" of his act. You may never be able to prove what was in his mind and the law does not always require it. Intent may be inferred by the things the suspect does, such as his physical actions. Let's assume that a customer picks up a handbag, puts it over her arm, and turns away from the counter. She then walks toward the front door. She may have either the intent of stealing the bag or the honest intent of seeing its color in daylight. As she goes toward the door, it would not be wise to assume that she intends to steal the bag. On the other hand, if she were observed taking the handbag and stuffing it into her shopping bag, her intent to steal would be pretty well established and an apprehension would be in order.

In a Michigan case, two men took coats from a rack and concealed them under their own coats. The clerk did not see them take the coats, but he did see the suspects conceal the coats. The department manager was summoned, and as he approached the suspects he saw them put the coats back on the rack. The court held that the larceny was completed when these men took the coats from the rack with the *intent* to steal them. Their *intent* to steal was demonstrated by the concealment. Discarding the coats before leaving the store did not correct the problem of crime. The Michigan Supreme Court upheld the conviction. These legal points bring out the fact that it is important to catch and arrest guilty shoplifters, but it is a job for specialized people. Trained experts are aware of the laws relating to this type of theft. In many stores it is best to prevent thefts before they occur.

Need for Larger Security Staffs

Theft losses vary from store to store. Professional thieves know a well-managed store from a store that is not. They know, better perhaps than you do, whether your clerks are asleep. They know if you take unnecessary risks in merchandise displays. They are aware of the factors in your operation that allow a thief to steal with little fear of detection.

Generally, however, stores have been unwilling to spend money on needed security department personnel. Yet the professional thieves are seldom caught by casual observers such as salespeople. They are caught by trained security detectives, and it is the professional thieves who cause the big shoplifting losses.

Employee education programs are important and should be continued, but stores seriously interested in reducing losses should bring their security personnel up to a strength suitable for handling the store's theft problems.

Some stores have no security department, and even larger stores with security departments are almost without exception *understaffed* in relationship to the crime problems faced today. It has been estimated by the security head of a large retail store in Chicago that only one out of every two hundred shoplifters is apprehended. An analysis done by a New York store in which shoplifter apprehensions were related to known thefts such as pickpockets and handbag thieves showed that, at least, *eighty-five* shoplifters stole undetected for each shoplifter apprehended.

The average shoplifting case runs from $3.50 to $64. The amount of theft depends upon the area in which your detectives work as well as the general price range of your store merchandise. When you analyze the number of missed apprehensions, in relation to the known shoplifter recoveries, it becomes immediately apparent that some stores lose as much as $2,000 to $4,000 in a single day from shoplifter thefts. This, of course, is small compared to what dishonest employee losses can be, but shoplifting still represents an important part of any store's theft problem.

Selecting Detectives

Good detectives are hard to find. Stores who have capable detectives seldom let them go unless there is a major problem in connection with the person's work or personality.

Since Macy's, for example, hires and trains its own detectives, the store needs to be aware of some of the problems involved in selecting detectives. First, there is the always present danger that a person with criminal tendencies will attempt to get onto the security staff. (This is a common problem in hiring people for retail security.) Experienced security directors know of many instances in which people with previous criminal records have attempted to get jobs as store detectives. Because people of this type are drawn to retail security work, a careful screening of job applicants is vital.

Newspaper Advertisement. It has been found that by putting ads in the paper to attract people interested in retail security work, the criminal element and psychologically maladjusted people usually reply. Seldom can a suitable retail security person be found as a result of direct advertising. The best detectives are people who have never requested security work and who are "sold" on joining the security staff.

Other Store Areas. Some successful security directors have been alerted to find store personnel who have detective talent. They draw their security people from cashiers, packers, salespeople, and office help.

They look for people with a lot of energy who are used to hard work. They also seek people with good eyesight, stamina, and an inquiring mind.

The director tries to find people who get along well with others. They feel this encourages help from store personnel on security problems. It has been found, however, that many times good floor detectives are not good human relations experts. Outstanding detectives quite often have a subconscious hostility toward people. They channel this hostility in a drive against dishonest people. Such people are apt to be less tolerant and less understanding in dealing with people than people who are good in human relationships. Where the combination of natural detective talent and good human relations ability exists, you have a valuable person. There are many detectives of this type, but there are also many more who are capable detectives but not very successful in getting along with others.

Award Winners. Some security directors select detectives from the group of store employees who consistently win awards for spotting shoplifters. We must inject a word of caution here. Studies of award winners have been made to see if they have a tendency toward dishonesty. In a survey in a New York store, for example, it was found that 45 percent of all people who won awards for spotting thieves were themselves dishonest. Because of this potential danger, an award winner should be checked carefully before being accepted for your store's security department.

Shoplifter as Detective. At least one store has experimented with the theory that "it takes a thief to catch a thief." They employed a shoplifter as a floor detective. This woman has worked for two or three years successfully as a floor detective. The fact that she was previously a shoplifter has not been revealed to the rest of the security staff. If it were ever known that she had been previously arrested as a shoplifter, the morale of the department would be impaired.

I don't feel this principle can be completely justified. It may work in an individual case, but people who steal from a retail store are usually maladjusted, and they are solving personality pressures through a pattern of theft. Placing such a person in a position where merchandise is easily available is unfair to that person. They often do not have the psychological barriers to theft that are developed in normal people. Putting someone with a tendency toward dishonesty into a security department is tantamount to placing this person in a position of undue temptation to steal. This is not wise.

Need for Various Types

There should be a wide range in the ages and types of people employed in the security department. If a store puts only one type of person in its floor detective group, professional shoplifters soon learn to spot the store detective.

Any peculiarities that set your detectives apart as a group should be avoided. For example, in one store all of the floor detectives wore their coats over their shoulders. This mannerism became a signal to professional thieves. In another instance, all floor detectives wore shoulder strap handbags. This again had to be discontinued because thieves were soon able to spot the detective in any of the store areas. This same identification problem will exist if you hire people all of one age or one type.

Need for Enthusiasm

The most important factor in the success of floor detectives is their enthusiasm for the job. Good detectives invariably have great enthusiasm. If you listen to them talk as a group you will discover that they talk shop before they go on the floor in the morning, they talk shop during their lunch period, they talk shop during their relief period, and they will tell you that they dream at night of following thieves.

Probationary Period

In choosing floor detectives, there should certainly be a 90-day probationary period. This probation should be enforced to the letter. If a floor detective has not shown at least standard case productivity by the end of 90 days, there is usually little chance that such a person will later develop into a satisfactory case producer.

Stores have consistently found that people who don't produce cases in the first month or so seldom prove to be effective detectives in the long run. To learn whether people can be "trained" to be a case producer, as an experiment one store kept a floor detective for over a year to see if she would develop. After a year she still had not made a single apprehension. In other instances, stores with no standards of production have employed floor detectives for as long as 15 years without the detective ever producing an average number of cases.

Rating the Detective

No matter what other assets a floor detective has, such as investigative ability, human relations skill, interest, or enthusiasm, there is still only one way of judging floor detectives; that is, on the basis of their apprehensions. They must be rated on the number of apprehensions and the value of the merchandise involved.

Today, with reduced selling staffs and "self-service," there is a greater need than ever for adequate floor detective staffs.

One large store has 160 floor detectives. Compare this with other large stores who employ staffs of eight to twelve floor detectives and mistakenly feel they are doing a good security job. A common sense ratio of floor detectives would run at least two floor detectives for every $3 million gross annual sales.

A detective should produce twenty-five to thirty cases a month, and a minimum average (three months) for any detective is twelve cases per month.

Training Detectives

Training detectives is important. They must know the law, store procedures, and the policies of your security department. It is a fallacy, however, to believe that training will go very far toward improving a detective's skill at finding thieves. People with no previous training whatsoever, but with a "knack" for detection, will get eight to twelve

cases their first month on the floor. A person with only average detective ability will usually average one or two cases a month for the first two or three months. At the end of three months, every detective should be producing the average number of cases found in the department.

Floor. In training detectives, there is no substitute for floor work with an experienced operator. Most stores put a new detective with their best operator for the first week of training. After that they have the new detective work with one operator after another on a day-to-day basis until all operators have had some experience with the new detective. After a couple of weeks of this type of direct supervision, the new detective is put out alone with a warning not to make any apprehensions. If the detective sees a suspect, a call must be made for experienced help.

To the store, the training period of a new detective is a delicate time. There is a real danger of an inexperienced person making a false arrest. To prevent this, care must be taken to emphasize again and again that the new detective is not under any circumstances to make an apprehension without the permission of an experienced detective.

Manual. In addition to the floor training, new detectives should receive some instruction on material in the detective manual. (A copy of a detective manual appears at the end of the book.) Because floor work during the morning hours is apt to be slow, some stores have the new detective study the detective manual in the morning, and spend the afternoon with a floor detective.

Films. There is another approach to speeding up detective training, which is the use of movie training films. The newly hired floor detective who is working with an experienced person on the floor learns from observing actual thefts. In some stores, however, thefts may not be frequent. The number of thefts seen by the new detective will determine the new person's rate of development. By using movie films that reenact different methods of theft in many locations throughout the store, the new detective gets a visual experience similar to working on the floor with an actual detective. It is true that there is not the emotional excitement of an actual theft. This excitement, of course, helps to impress the method of theft on the mind of the new person. Still there is an opportunity to observe methods of theft in the departments seen in the film.

In a few minutes of movie film several weeks of floor experience can be condensed. By showing such films over and over again, the new detective can become conditioned to the point where similar theft situations are recognized. The detective can recognize them on the floor after having seen them in the training films.

Training Branch Detectives. Training of branch store detectives or operators for smaller stores poses a problem. The best solution is to have such people trained in a larger store where there are frequent thefts so they can gain experience rapidly and shorten the length of training. In New York City, for example, some stores make arrangements with a larger department store to have their people trained by working with the floor detectives of the larger store. This has worked out successfully.

In one case a store management wanted to replace its entire security department. To do this they hired eight detectives and had them trained in a larger store. When these eight people had been trained, they moved the entire group into the store. At the same time they discharged the incumbent group. This grafting of an entirely new group of people into the store security operation was done smoothly and effectively. The new group immediately produced twenty times the number of cases of the group they replaced. It was an overnight transformation of an entire department. It proved that detectives trained in one store can be moved successfully to another store. Branch store security people can often be trained in the parent store, since there is often more customer traffic and more opportunity to observe shoplifter techniques in the downtown unit.

Assigning Detectives

In addition to training detectives, a major factor in case production is detective assignment. Detectives who have been trained almost exclusively on street floor type of thefts are almost never successful in detecting fitting room thieves. It is important that in the first stages of training your new detective be placed in fitting room operations. The new detective can usually learn floor thefts after working in fitting rooms, but can seldom learn fitting room techniques after open floor training.

When a store assigns most of its detectives to watch for open floor thefts, recoveries are low. This is because of the small unit value of the goods involved. By having detectives concentrate in fitting rooms and higher priced departments, the store will get less shoplifting cases, but more recoveries. A woman stealing a suit for $150 in a fitting room is a more important loss problem than a woman stealing a $15 pair of gloves from a street floor counter. By intelligent assigning of detectives you can improve your store's recoveries.

Some stores have their detectives work in pairs. Being a floor detective is a lonely job and a partner works out well if the two people are compatible.

There are extremes in detective assignment. For example, one store will let their detectives go anywhere in the store they choose. This leaves assignment up to the detective. In this case, if a detective has been successful in the first few cases by getting apprehensions from the inexpensive jewelry department, this will be where that detective will work 75 percent of the time. On the other hand, if the detective has been very successful in getting the first few cases out of the expensive dress department, this will be the area in which the person will work the major part of the time. The weaknesses of this approach are immediately apparent. A lot of the store would not get any coverage, and the detective's application in certain departments will not be logical but will be entirely dependent upon individual experience. The store does not usually get the best coverage from this type of assignment.

At the other extreme is the store that assigns the detective to a specific counter. One large store in New York assigns a detective to the glove counter—for eight hours a day. The detective's only job is to watch hands handling the stacks of gloves in the glove bins. When a pair of hands pulls off a price ticket or folds a pair of gloves, the detective then looks up to see the face that goes with this particular pair of dishonest hands. Undoubtedly, this technique can produce cases, but the question is for how long? Can case production be maintained if the detective becomes stagnant and bored? Reducing floor detective work to a production line operation does not usually work well. Good detectives are creative, and they should be encouraged to use their imagination. A detective's natural curiosity can often lead to detection of important thieves.

The right answer to detective assignment lies between the two extremes of allowing a detective too much freedom or pinning a detective down to a limited area.

Supervising Floor Productivity

Next to a detective's instinctive ability, no other factor affects productivity as much as the quality of detective supervision. If the supervisor creates a good working climate, productivity will soar. The principles of good supervision that apply in any department apply equally to security. Floor detectives need to be treated as individuals. They want recognition as a person. They need attention and acknowledgment of their personal worth.

Principles of Prevention

There are many things stores can do to prevent shoplifter thefts. Most important of course is a program of employee education. In stores that are too small to have security departments, the alertness of store personnel is the only protection the storeowner has against customer thefts. Salesclerks, buyers, supervisors, and all the other people who work on the selling floors are your main line of defense.

Some of the ways of preventing shoplifting are as follows:

- Observe carefully and constantly what is going on in any department. This means keeping an eye on the customer, the employee working there, the price tickets on the merchandise, and the arrangement of displays as well as the handling of cash transactions and all other details that are constantly going on in any selling area. By making a point of such observation, you are in a position to notice immediately when anything is out of order. It takes both purpose and practice to become a good observer and there is no better means of deterring shoplifting or detecting it when it does appear.

  One of the best ways of observing customers is to *watch their hands.* If they have picked up and are holding merchandise, this does not always mean that they are ready to make a purchase. Salespeople should be sure to let these customers know that they have been seen and will be helped as soon as possible. Prompt service is important not only because it is good for customer relations but also because the lack of it may sometimes provide a temptation to steal.

  If you see a customer take merchandise, she can be approached in a pleasant fashion and asked, "May I wrap that for you?" Sometimes you may wish to say to someone who has wandered far afield, "Are you looking for a salesperson?" If you suspect that a customer is on the verge of stealing something, watch her openly and courteously. *Watching* is a particularly effective way of dampening a shoplifter's ardor for theft.
- Keep your department neat. Shoplifters like to operate in disorderly surroundings; they feel there is less likelihood that the merchandise they steal will be missed. Dissarranged stacks of goods on counters or empty hangers in dressing rooms obscure the fact that a shoplifter may have taken merchandise. Keep your department orderly.

  Neatness of stock is an important element in preventing shoplifter thefts. As one saleslady said, "I am very particular about my stock," and then added, "a neat stock is not only easier to watch and keep track of, but it is also a great help in selling. When I show my merchandise, especially the expensive pieces, I place those the customer is not interested in on the ledge in back of me until I have completed my sale. I then put them away. That way I can take more interest in my customer because I do not have so many articles to watch."

Another salesclerk stated, "I have been successful in recognizing shoplifters because I study the habits of my customers. I have learned that the habits of shoplifters are not the same. I have noticed that the shoplifter may approach the counter slowly and when I look, will often turn around and walk away. She may return in a few minutes and fondle an article, hold it for a while, then drop it if someone approaches. Just before she is ready to take it she will usually put her hand on the article and give a quick look around before taking it."

"Once I recognize the actions of a shoplifter, I never look directly at her. I excuse myself to my customer, then I phone the security department or quietly ask another employee to call for me. I try not to show my suspicion. If the person does not steal, there is no harm done, but I try to remember that person so that I can watch for her if she comes in again."

- Plan department layouts to minimize opportunities for shoplifting. When possible it is helpful to have merchandise so arranged that the prospective purchaser or thief must pause briefly in picking up an item and not be able to merely take it or push it into a bag as he walks along the counter. Keep all selling structures low enough so clerks can see over them.
- Arrange your counter displays in *patterns* so that small objects are arranged in groups of set numbers. This makes it possible for a salesperson to see when one of the items is missing. Thieves may be reluctant to disturb pattern displays because they know the arrangement was placed there for the purpose of detection. For example, handbags can be displayed in groups of six.
- Keep things like costume jewelry on a stand so that an item must be unhooked to be removed. This again makes it necessary for a thief to stop and attract attention, the one thing the shoplifter does not want to do.
- Fasten the plugs on electrical appliances securely so that a person would be conspicuous if he attempted to remove them.
- When displaying pairs of things like shoes or earrings, display only one item.
- Arrange mirrors in each department to provide a view of spots that would otherwise be hidden.

- Another important point in preventing losses is to encourage *good service.* Remember that a lot of courteous attention will usually discourage a thief. Shoplifters do not like attention. A greeting by a busy salesclerk such as, "I'll be with you in a moment," may send a shoplifter away.
- Fitting rooms have long been a problem to retailers because they offer a convenient, hidden room in which the thief can operate. Fitting rooms in which merchandise has been left carelessly by a salesgirl after a customer has gone are an ideal setup for the professional thief. A professional thief with a store suit box can steal hundreds of dollars of expensive suits or dresses in a single trip into your store. A continuous campaign should be conducted to see that your salespeople keep fitting rooms cleared of merchandise. It is also important that fitting rooms be left clean at night. If this isn't done porters and people who work at night will find the fitting room a secluded spot ideal for thefts.

  Build your fitting rooms with a single aisle entrance so that people have to leave the way they came in. There should be no fitting rooms with doors. Walls of the fitting rooms should be at least a foot off the floor and curtains should be no longer than the walls.

  Some stores have found fitting room checkers useful in controlling fitting room areas. Other stores feel that checking is good only on a seasonal basis. It has been noted that professionals will often steal from fitting rooms controlled by checkers because they know there are no floor detectives covering the area. It is relatively simple for the professional thief to fold one or two pieces of merchandise between hangers and get it past the checker unobserved. When this happens the fitting rooms with checkers become more of a liability than an asset. The checker unknowingly helps the professional steal.

Clinics Needed

There are many more methods that can be used to discourage shoplifting. Study each of your departments with this thought in mind: HOW CAN I MAKE THIS DEPARTMENT LESS VULNERABLE TO SHOPLIFTING THEFTS?

Regular clinics should be held with salespeople to instruct them about shoplifter operations. (A word of caution is needed here. As noted in the employee education chapter, it is wrong to teach people methods of theft unless you incorporate into their training some material about the penalties of stealing. Failure to do this means that your educational program may very well create thieves in your organization.)

Salespeople Need the Facts

Management should explain to employees the hazards of conducting a retail business. They should know the store's shortage figures. They should be told that thefts are committed in other ways beside hold-ups and burglaries. Acquaint them with the fact that there are professional thieves who shoplift. Tell them about the amateur thieves who compulsively steal from the stores. Give them some idea as to how these shoplifters work and instruct them carefully in what to do if they have a suspect.

Salespeople should not be allowed to make arrests, but they should be encouraged to prevent losses by being alert and offering good service to customers who look suspicious. Explain to your people that the theft of a $40 dress from a fitting room costs the store its profit on fifty dresses. Get them to think in terms of protecting the store properties as they would their own belongings.

Criminal Behavior Pattern

You need to teach your personnel that honest people act honestly and dishonest people do not; they act *nervous.*

One large store in Chicago trains its detectives by putting them on the floor for two weeks to do nothing but study the actions and activities of "normal" customers. Once they understand the pattern of normal customer behavior, they then become aware of any customer who is acting in an "abnormal" manner. This training method has given the store a high apprehension record.

This same technique can be used in training salespeople. By making them alert as to how regular customers act, thereby giving them a standard for normal behavior, they will then recognize any customer who is not acting in the normal fashion.

Surprisingly enough, some management people feel that clerks will naturally be able to tell the difference between the dishonest customer and the normal customer. This is not the case. Unless you train your people by calling their attention to the differences between the two types of "shoppers," they will not ordinarily spot the thief. This is proven by the fact that some salespeople who have worked for as long as twenty years in a high-theft department such as costume jewelry will never have seen a single customer shoplift during this entire period even though such thefts occur in this department daily.

Your salespeople and other employees should be told that people act differently when they are frightened. People who steal usually have a fear of being caught. This fear shows up in nervousness, unusual watchfulness, uncommon methods of handling merchandise, and other mannerisms that are different from the actions of the normal customer.

It is important to let your employees know that security is their individual responsibility and that it is part of their job. Also tell them they will be rated on their ability to prevent and detect dishonesty just as they are rated on their sales ability.

Awards

Cash awards are also a form of recognition for employees. Many employees respond to incentives. Cash awards stimulate a certain group of people in your organization to work hard at the problem of finding the thief.

Analysis of cash award programs in stores usually shows a return of $10 in recovered merchandise for every dollar invested in awards. There is also the additional value of taking a thief out of circulation, which prevents future losses. In addition to the cash awards there should also be recognition in the form of memos of commendation for employees who give suggestions for improving displays or anything else that improves store security. A good technique is to tell the employee that the memos of commendation will be reviewed again at the time of the person's annual appraisal.

Need for a Continuous Program

A single big meeting on retail security after each inventory has very little lasting value. What is needed in any store is a continuing stimulation of interest in the problem throughout the year. A single big meeting can start off a drive against theft, but this should be followed up by weekly department meetings, posters, memos, and other reminders.

A lot can be done to help reduce shoplifting losses by training new employees during orientation training. Your store's news bulletins or other employee publications can carry articles on award winners and similar material on shoplifter problems. Bulletin boards can also be used to keep alive interest in reducing store losses.

Involve the Entire Store Organization

Everyone in your store from stockboy to store president should be alert to the problems of theft and should be trained to try and prevent it wherever possible.

The president of a large auto parts company, in a talk on inventory control, said, "The process of enlightment via education begins with the lowest paid worker and ends with top management, or even better, with the firm's directors. The executive who spares a few moments from his other duties to look into a stockroom is by his very presence adding importance to the seemingly mundane job of placing materials in racks. Even the presence of a public accountant, peering into bins or checking records, has the salutary effect of demonstrating that management is very much interested in inventory control."

The attitude or climate for security control is set at the top level of management. If the president, vice president, and other members of the top echelon show the salespeople, stock people, and other workers their interest and concern over losses, this attitude will soon be reflected by equal concern in the rest of your store's personnel.

The controller of a large company in Washington put it this way: "The first and most important fundamental upon which all other controls are completely dependent is the long-range attitude of management. It must be one that does not permit a loose, weak operation subject to individual whims. It is an attitude that permits some risks to be planned and calculated, but does not dignify with a fancy title 'calculated risk' situations that have deteriorated or have become uncalculated hazards." This company includes all supervisory personnel with general store employees in all loss prevention programs.

One store instituted an inventory shrinkage program that was designed "In order to educate all store people on the special problem of inventory shrinkage due to shoplifting through temptation." The program was designed to show in a vivid way how the store suffers every time a single item of merchandise is stolen. As an executive from this store said, "Shoplifters, like termites, eat at the well-being of material success which our employees are striving for."

We all have a stake in the problems of crime. Crime is not a problem that solely concerns the mayor, the chief of police, and the criminal courts of our cities. The problem of crime lies squarely in the laps of the people who work in any business in any city. Crime is our mutual problem, at home, in the schools, in the stores and where we work.

Tricks of the Trade

Professionals. Professional thieves sometimes have special clothing that is designed to help them steal. They sometimes wear overcoats with large pockets sewn in the lining. They may use hooks sewn under their garments to hold stolen merchandise. Some professional women shoplifters still use "booster skirts," which are usually large bloomers that are tied around the legs. They can stuff three or four suits into them and walk out of the store. A topcoat with slit pockets is often used for theft.

Some professional shoplifters operate in rings. They have "schools" in which young shoplifters are trained before going into the stores. Many times these rings steal merchandise on order. They have a group of "customers" who steal the items requested. In these schools the thief learns by practicing with various types of merchandise and various methods of concealment.

Early and Late Shoplifters. There are shoplifters who make a specialty of stealing as soon as a store opens. Usually at opening time employees go to the store cafeteria or restaurant for a cup of coffee. Professional thieves know that the store is not fully staffed until at least an hour after opening. These shoplifters find this an ideal time in which to steal.

Another favorite time of day for thieves is at store closing time. Shoplifters hide in washrooms until they hear the closing bell ring. They know that most employees are on their way home the minute the bell sounds. They take advantage of the late hour confusion to help themselves to goods as they leave the store.

Clouters. There are thieves that detectives call "clouters." They come into a store at any time of the day and *grab* a quantity of merchandise off a rack or counter. Once they have secured the goods, they run out of the store without any attempt at concealment.

Clouters are often successful because they are hard to catch. If you chase them they throw the merchandise down. They then have no merchandise in their possession when they are caught. They often beat the store when brought to court.

Good clouters work on the assumption that stores are afraid to arrest them because of the possibility of a lawsuit for false arrest if the store fails to convict them.

Stockroom Thieves. Another type of thief who causes serious loss to stores is the stockroom thief. All stores, regardless of size, have stockrooms. And many small stores don't realize that it is possible to steal large quantities of goods from stockrooms. Stockroom thefts represent a far greater source of loss than many stores realize.

Analysis of Shoplifter Cases

Shoplifter cases take out of circulation malefactors that cause severe losses for your store. Interviewing these people can be helpful to improving your store systems and controls. Discuss with the suspect the method of theft, why the theft was from a certain department, what were the plans for succeeding with the theft, and so on. From such questions you will learn a great deal about floor coverage, salesclerk alertness, displays, fitting room controls, and more. Important things can also be learned about weaknesses in the store operation by studying loss reports.

To determine the amount of shoplifting activity in any given area is a difficult, but important, undertaking.

Control Committee

Some stores fight losses by appointing a shortage control committee. This group consists of representatives from all major store divisions.

The committee meets every month to review the store's security problems. Special studies of all store procedures and systems are conducted on a year-round basis, to determine what to discard or how to modernize those that might be unusually vulnerable to theft.

Outside Agency

If your store is too small to employ a permanent security staff, it is advisable to employ occasionally a few professional detectives from a detective agency to test your store for a few weeks. In this way you can determine from time to time how serious the problem is. Such sampling will, on occasion, uncover large-scale thefts.

Merchant Group Campaigns Against Shoplifting

Not to be overlooked in any educational approach to shoplifting problems is the practice of having local campaigns against shoplifting. They are conducted by local merchant groups and chambers of commerce. Many communities across the country have successfully conducted such campaigns. They have proven successful in reducing losses from shoplifter thefts.

The merchant groups plan the programs, coordinate activities, and contact news sources. They are the sparkplugs of the operation.

Success in the campaign benefits the community in general and the stores in particular. These programs take a lot of time and effort. They require the work of many people, but the results are very worthwhile.

An outline for such a program follows:

1. Select two days for the concerted campaign.
2. Prepare warning posters signed by the chamber of commerce or retail group for each and ALL the stores, not just a few. The poster warning issued by an association does not hurt a store's *individual* customer relationships. These posters might deal with the anti-shoplifting law or emphasize the penalties of shoplifting.
3. The community group brings the local newspaper editors and radio and television executives into their planning. These media people welcome the opportunity to serve their advertisers, and they contribute an important public service by participating in the campaign.

   Shoplifting, of course, is *news* and arrangements are made with these news agencies and communication media to cover the problems of shoplifter loss to the local stores. Methods of theft should not be shown or discussed. The campaign should attempt to set up psychological barriers to theft. Articles discuss the personality adjustment problems of shoplifters and the penalties to the individual who is caught stealing.
4. The campaign is then taken into the schools. Superintendents are usually eager to cooperate. Meetings can be arranged to discuss the shoplifting problem with students and the merchants' group can supply the speakers. Enlist the aid of student government bodies, teachers, and members of parent groups. It is helpful to have school principals and student counsel leaders present to help plan the drive.
5. Take the campaign to churches and other civic groups. Include the Boy Scouts, Kiwanis, YMCA, YWCA, and similar service organizations. Leaders in these groups are a potent force in the community.
6. Ask all local and state retail associations to issue bulletins and give other help through publicity aids.

It is also important to enlist the help of business and industry in general. Banks, insurance companies, railroads, manufacturers, and others should be asked to use their employee publications to help publicize the drive.

Judges and police officials should be included in all phases of the campaign planning. Not only is their participation helpful because of the information they provide, but also it encourages their interest in the problem. Their support also gives the campaign official leadership, which favorably impresses the public.

In some cities where the program has been put into effect, police departments have put special plain clothes officers in the stores for the duration of the program. Prosecutors have also assigned special assistants to aid the merchants in shoplifter prosecutions during this period.

Because the campaign is designed to aid the merchant, he should make the greatest contribution. A campaign of this type would fail without the concentrated effort of *all* merchants. Each store must assist in the drive by giving whatever time and effort is needed to make the program a success.

Part of each store's program should be to educate their employees on how to prevent losses. Although the program may result in the arrests of malefactors, its real value lies in theft prevention.

The follow-up to the campaign is most important. One big, splashy event lasting two days is dramatic and draws attention to the loss problems, but lasting benefits require weekly and monthly follow-up keeping people alert to the problem until it becomes a habit of thought. The objective should be to make the anti-shoplifter idea a permanent attitude of the community.

Preventive security programs are a never-ending job, because the time will probably never come when merchants are free from the dangers of shoplifter thefts.

Self-Service Means New Problems

Stores operating with turnstiles and self-service counters can be protected by slots or viewing "peepholes" that allow detectives to observe the selling areas from behind the scenes. If such peepholes are reasonably apparent they will often act as a psychological barrier to theft. As one executive put it, "We find that peepholes have eliminated a lot of shoplifting by professionals. They survey the store and when they see a peephole they just turn around and walk out. We have also found that putting one stock clerk in every aisle reduces shoplifting."

Checking Customers Can Cause Legal Problems

The legal problems of checking customers can be very delicate. An example was described by a branch comptroller of a supermarket in Chicago, "A woman came into one of our stores and purchased four packages of frozen food. They were put into a bag and she paid for them. Then she walked back to the frozen food case and deposited the bag inside the food case. She looked furtively over her right and left shoulders and then proceeded to take each package of frozen food out of the food case and put it into her shopping bag. Remember, the bag containing her original purchase was in the frozen food case. All anyone could see if they were observing her was that she was taking merchandise out of the frozen food case and putting it in the shopping bag."

The woman was stopped and taken to the manager for questioning. She said, "You have no right to question me. I paid for the food which I bought." She was able to give a full and accurate description of the person to whom she paid her money. This salesgirl corroborated her statement.

"The woman was highly indignant. She said that we had humiliated her and forcibly detained her and she threatened to sue us. It just so happens that we have signs in our stores reserving the right to inspect shopping bags. We were very careful in our handling of this woman in asking that she give us an opportunity to examine her shopping bag. We accused her of nothing. We told her that we thought a mistake had been made, that we would like to have the opportunity to look in her bag."

The woman obtained an attorney and the store was able to convince him they had done nothing illegal. The case was kept out of court by making a small settlement.

This situation illustrates the dangers of assuming that what you see will be sufficient to prove intent to steal.

Problems of Arrest

The problems of arrest or detention should be discussed with your city's prosecuting attorney and your store's legal counsel. Legal definitions are included in a chapter on mercantile laws. There are, however, some other points that should be brought up in regard to shoplifter apprehensions.

Retailers are often reluctant to apprehend shoplifters. They have heard of many lawsuits in which heavy damages were levied for false arrest, false imprisonment, libel, slander, and defamation of character as well as for assault and battery. Apprehensions can, however, be made. The point is to be certain that the people making the apprehensions are well versed in the laws of arrest and the rights of the citizen.

In any security plan it is important to decide who is going to make arrests. These people should be given a thorough training in the law of arrest and subsequent procedures including court appearances. Any person authorized to make arrests needs to be trained and retrained in the techniques of shoplifter apprehensions.

Unfortunately, facts and circumstances in one situation can make an arrest legal, while the same facts in another situation can make an arrest quite wrong. It would be impossible to give just a few broad principles and expect that they could be applied properly. For example, it is difficult to say what amount of force would be "excessive" or "proper" or how long you could detain a person and still have a court say that the detention was for a "reasonable" time.

Rules of Arrest

Basically the rules of arrest in a shoplifting case are as follows:

1. The detective must see the whole operation.
2. More than one article should be stolen. (This is not always necessary but it strengthens your case.)
3. The detective should have a witness. This does not require the detective to have a witness to the whole theft but to at least part of it, particularly the part that shows intent to steal. Intent is proved by such things as the thief tearing off a price tag, concealing the merchandise, or moving stolen merchandise from one bag to another and so on.
4. The *intent* to steal must be *proved*. The *intent* to steal can't be proved when a customer puts a belt around her waist because this is where she normally wears a belt. Neither can the intent to steal be proved when she carries a handbag out of the store over her arm because this is where she normally carries a handbag. To prove intent to steal it is necessary to prove that the thief *intended* to defraud the store. The best method of proving intent is concealment. Concealment in itself, however, is hard to define. Certain things can be thoroughly hidden from the eye and yet not be concealed in the legal sense. If a man puts a wallet into his hip pocket, that is not legal concealment because that is where a man usually carries his wallet.
5. The detective should know exactly where the articles that have been stolen are located on the person of the malefactor. The detective should, of course, recover these articles immediately after making the apprehension.

6. In most cases, the detective should wait until the subject leaves the store before making an arrest. A suspect may be apprehended as soon as you can prove intent to steal. But there are advantages if you can let the thief leave your store before the apprehension is made. First, your court case is strengthened. Second, if a fight develops during the apprehension you are not as likely to inconvenience your customers by creating a disturbance on the selling floor.

Legal Definition

It may be helpful if you understand the legal definition of shoplifting. There are two elements in the act of shoplifting (a form of stealing known in legal language as *larceny*): (1) taking the merchandise and (2) carrying the merchandise away with the intention of theft.

You must be able to prove in court that both of these occurred. There is no need to fear making an apprehension if you *know* you can substantiate these *two* points. *Did the person take the merchandise? Can you prove he or she intended to steal it?*

Law Protects the Innocent

In our country laws are set up to protect innocent people from false accusations. Any mistakes that occur when cases are improperly handled may be very costly to your store. Lawsuits may result from charges of mental anguish, false arrest, false imprisonment, defamation of character, and so on. Professional shoplifters and their lawyers know how to take advantage of the law. This places the responsibility on your store to be sure you have sufficient evidence in order to win your case.

Remember these vital points:

1. You must have SEEN the person take the merchandise.
2. You must know where the merchandise is and that it is still in the possession of the person who stole it.
3. You must be able to prove that the person *intended* to steal this merchandise.
4. You must be able to identify the stolen article.
5. The goods must be identified as the property of your store.

Making the Arrest

Assuming that you have observed these precautions, your next step is the arrest. Often it is best to wait until the subject leaves the store. Then approach him with the question, "Is this the first time you have ever done this?" Usually the shoplifter will answer, "Yes." The person making the arrest should then say, "Don't you know it's wrong to steal?" The shoplifter will usually answer, "Yes." You can now bring the suspect back to the security office for further questioning.

This arrest method keeps the shoplifter calm and achieves an admission of theft at the point of arrest. It strengthens your case legally and often prevents a long, wrangling interview in the security office.

Getting possession of the stolen goods at once and getting an admission of guilt at the time of apprehension are both helpful when you later conduct your shoplifter interview. It also gives you a better case if you decide to prosecute.

After you have the subject identify herself, you should make a thorough search of her person. In the case of a woman, check her handbag carefully for locker keys, refund receipts, and so forth. Next question the person about the theft that just occurred and also about previous thefts. Obtain a statement in regard to ALL pertinent matters.

The shoplifter's statement is usually a prepared form (see Chapter 16). It may, however, be a narrative type of statement, in which case you detail all the shoplifter's operation. Tell when the suspect came into the store; where the suspect went; what the suspect did, and so on. All statements should be signed in duplicate. They should always be signed in the presence of a witness. It is also advisable to have the subject read her statement aloud and ask her if the statement just read is true. If the subject agrees that it is true, have her write on the bottom of the statement, "I have read this and it is true," before signing it.

Arrest Precautions

Other things to remember when apprehending a shoplifter:

1. Be sure that the person making the arrest is authorized to make such an arrest. Is this person thoroughly familiar with the laws of arrest? Don't forget that apprehending any person, no matter what age or what social or economic position, means taking away a person's liberty. Liberty of the individual is a constitutional right and to take it away unlawfully is a major crime.
2. Do not arrest anyone unless you yourself have actually seen the theft of merchandise. You should have seen the person enter the selling department.
3. Do not let the suspect out of your sight from the time you see her steal the merchandise until you make the arrest. This is the only way you can be certain that she still has the goods in her possession.

4. Ask the suspect quietly, but firmly, to accompany you to one of the store's offices. Watch her closely to prevent escape or disposal of the stolen goods. Keep asking her questions, so she doesn't have time to plan an escape.
5. It is desirable to have a woman store detective present when a female shoplifter is being interviewed by a man.
6. Decide on the basis of store policy what the disposition of the case should be.

Reasons for Prosecution

In many cases it will be necessary for you to take the shoplifter into custody and, after the interview, turn the suspect over to the police.

Reasons for prosecuting are as follows:

1. The person has a previous criminal record.
2. The person is obviously a professional thief and is stealing in order to sell the merchandise.
3. The person refuses to sign a statement admitting the theft of the goods.
4. The person has no identification and can't be identified. (An unknown person may have a serious criminal background and therefore such a person must be prosecuted.)
5. The person assaulted the arresting detective during apprehension.
6. The person's attitude is hostile and uncooperative.
7. The value of goods stolen is high.
8. The person is a vagrant.
9. The person needs physical, mental, or welfare help.

Once deciding to prosecute, there are certain things to be kept in mind in regard to your appearance in court.

The Complaint

The heart of your store's case against the accused person is contained in a statement called the *complaint*. This complaint is issued by a complaint clerk. Later it is signed by a judge if he is satisfied there is sufficient evidence to indicate that a crime has been committed. The complaint forms are filled out in the complaint clerk's office at court. They must be made out and signed by the person who saw the actual theft take place and made the arrest. The usual procedure is to dictate the complaint to a clerk in the complaint office. The complaint clerk types the case story onto the complaint form. As a complainant, always READ very carefully the final copy of the complaint before signing it. Be sure that it is complete and *accurate*. Failure to do this has many times caused cases to be thrown out of court. This can result in serious lawsuits against the store.

Caution your people *never* to sign a blank complaint. Impress on your detectives the necessity of reading the complaint before signing it. Tell them to be sure that all details are accurate.

When the accused person first arrives in court a *preliminary* hearing may be held. This is an informal proceeding at which a judge determines whether or not there are reasonable grounds to believe that a crime has been committed. If the judge decides that the accusation is a reasonable one and that the case is of a substantial nature, the accused person may be held for a grand jury hearing or the person may be released on bail. If the amount involved is small the judge may have the necessary jurisdiction to conduct an immediate trial. (This is sometimes true of peace officers who conduct trials on misdemeanors. However, the accused person may request a jury trial or a postponement.)

Testifying as a Witness

If the case goes to trial before a judge or a jury, your part in the trial will be that of a witness. Here are some suggestions to make you a good witness:

1. Prepare your testimony carefully in advance. Know what you are going to say well enough that you do not need to refer to notes. Make sure that you have *all the facts* and that your information is *accurate.*
2. Do not volunteer information. Answer the questions as they are asked and as briefly as possible. Many times, by volunteering information, a witness creates complications for the prosecutor.
3. Be sure you know precisely what was taken. Be able to describe each item, its color, its size, and its value.
4. Be factual and precise and tell the court exactly what happened. Include details such as when the price tags were removed from the garment, where they were discarded, where the merchandise was concealed, and how it was rolled up or folded. Remember the judge is seeking the facts that can help him to determine whether or not the person is guilty. Have the date and the time of day,

the department, and all of the narrative facts of your shoplifting story in accurate and related detail.

5. Be able to prove the store's ownership of the stolen goods. This may seem like a technicality and it may not be required but a court *can* request it.
6. Bring the stolen goods into court unless they have been retained by the officer making the arrest. Be sure that you can identify these goods as being the same merchandise taken off the person at the time of arrest.
7. If possible, have witnesses available who were present when the suspect was being questioned; also have available witnesses who saw the actual theft. These witnesses can verify the subject's confession and any other conversations. Remember that witnesses are a help in verifying facts.
8. Be able to report accurately any conversations that may have occurred during the case. This may help to establish the suspect as an experienced shoplifter. Write out at the time the case is being prepared exactly what the suspected person said to you. This may be important evidence.

It should be noted here that ALL facts of the case should be written down *on the same day the case occurs if the case is being prosecuted.* This will provide an important written record to refresh your memory at the time of trial. Several days or even weeks may elapse before the case goes to trial and with all of the other matters that come up in retail security work, the specific facts needed for the trial may become confused or may be forgotten. So let me repeat, *write the facts down while they are still fresh in your mind.*

9. Always remember the necessary legal components of larceny are:
   a. To take and carry away personal goods.
   b. With the intent to steal.

Here are some further thoughts about testifying in court.

Direct Examination

1. Answer all questions in a clear, concise manner.
2. Pitch your voice loud enough so that your testimony can be clearly understood by the judge or jury.
3. Your narration should be limited to *only* the facts of the case. Omit unimportant details. Avoid making inferences, but report all important actions. Be brief.

4. Conduct yourself in a fair, frank manner at all times.
5. Avoid such speech mannerisms as, "I can truthfully say."

Cross Examination

1. Answer questions with a "Yes" or "No" when possible.
2. If this is not possible, modify your reply by saying, "Under certain circumstances. . . ."
3. If you don't know, say you don't know!
4. Think before you answer any question.
5. Answer the questions put to you. Don't argue and don't lose your temper.
6. Admit all previous discussion of the case without hesitation.
7. Listen carefully to every question put to you and be sure you understand the question before attempting to answer it.
8. Some questions may require multiple answers. Before answering such a question, make sure that you understand what is being asked and then answer each part of the question separately.
9. Do not volunteer *anything* beyond what the question calls for.
10. Witnesses are not expected to know everything, particularly unimportant details.
11. If you don't recall something, say that you do not recall it.
12. The witness should avoid any appearance of bias, either for or against the defendant. His role should be completely *neutral.*
13. If the witness does not understand a question, have the stenographer repeat it back or ask the lawyer to rephrase it before answering.
14. Be careful of questions like, "Do you want the jury to understand. . . ." "Are you as positive about this as the rest of your testimony. . . ."
15. Never try to be "smart." Simply tell your story and then stop!

Shoplifting Legislation

Today with retailers emphasizing "self-service," the number of thefts from shoplifters is increasing. It is estimated that annual merchandise losses from shoplifting range upward of $750 million.

Shoplifting is a peculiar type of crime because it is an uninsurable risk. This is largely because it is virtually impossible to determine exactly what part of the stock shortages could be charged to this type of theft. The high frequency of the losses and the small amount involved in such incidents would cause the expense of investigating and making reimbursement so excessive that insurance can't be considered.

One of the problems of shoplifting is the fact that people can steal from retail stores with very little risk of arrest and prosecution. Many merchants and police realize that we are trying to combat shoplifting with unwieldy and outmoded laws. These laws badly hamper their ability to handle the problem.

Most larceny laws require that the thief must take the article and start to remove it from the premises. The most essential element of the theft, as we have mentioned, is that there must be proof of INTENT. Often such proof has to be inferred from an elaborate attempt to conceal the goods on the thief's person. Another proof of intent is the fact that the thief carried the goods out of the store without paying for them.

Professional Shoplifters

Arrests of professional shoplifters are important because these professional thieves steal a large amount of merchandise. Professionals are a small group of thieves but their forays are frequent and selective. The expert professional may go many years without being arrested. Arresting this type of thief is important not only because it gets a thief out of circulation and protects the storeowner's property, but also under police questioning the veteran store thief may supply vital information that illuminates other areas of organized crime.

The professional thief invariably is connected with one or more receivers of stolen goods. These receivers purchase the goods stolen by the professional at about one-fourth of their retail value. Such "fences" are often part of an intercity network. They provide the profit motive underlying store larceny and other types of professional theft.

Often these fences outline theft campaigns. They even create barriers to arrest and prosecution by a wholesale bribery of public officials. If you catch one receiver you may put numerous professional shoplifters out of business. By eliminating the fence you destroy the source of their instructions as well as their sales outlet.

By arresting the professional shoplifter you may also put a kink in the local narcotics traffic. The incidence of drug addiction among store thieves is high in certain cities. A narcotics addict must, of course, maintain periodic contact with the drug peddlers. The peddler realizes the addict needs methods of raising funds to support an expensive habit so they suggest shoplifting to their customers. If you arrest a professional shoplifter who is also a drug addict, you effectively hit hard at the illicit trade in narcotics.

Few Shoplifters Prosecuted

In spite of police and community need for prosecution of professional thieves, only a very small fraction of the total offenses are reported.

And little is known about what is being done to rehabilitate the high percentage of malefactors being released by the stores. If no rehabilitation takes place to help shoplifters return to a normal pattern of life, then we are creating a dangerous group of potential criminals.

Juvenile Shoplifters

It is sometimes true that law enforcement people find juvenile shoplifters on their first experiments in crime. If you catch the juvenile early and give him proper help, such young people can sometimes be guided back into a normal life. This is often impossible if their early criminal activities go undetected.

Legal Problems

One reason merchants don't prosecute many shoplifters is because of restrictive legal rules that protect the criminal as well as the innocent citizen.

Arrests of petty thieves who steal $15 to $30 worth of merchandise must be handled as misdemeanors. In most states there are serious legal restraints on such misdemeanor apprehensions. For example, neither a peace officer nor a private citizen may arrest someone for a misdemeanor without a warrant . . . even though the crime was committed in his presence. Some states have adopted "larceny laws" (laws that make any theft from a retail store grand larceny) or "anti-shoplifting laws" as a means of offsetting these restrictive legal provisions.

Chapter 3

HANDLING SHOPLIFTER PROBLEMS: PART II

Guides to Shoplifting Arrests

The penalty for misjudgment when arresting a shoplifter can be costly. Not only can the suspect claim false arrest, but also the lawyers usually throw in charges of defamation of character, assault, invasion of privacy, and so on. Cases are settled daily both in and out of court for anywhere from $200 to several hundred thousands of dollars.

Naturally, these risks do not mean stores should stop apprehending shoplifters, but it does mean that store personnel who handle such arrests should learn how to make a legal arrest.

Elements of Legal Arrest

Two elements are required before a legal larceny arrest can occur. First *there must be a "taking away" of something of value.*

Such a taking away is not, in itself, sufficient evidence to prove a larceny. A second element must also be present.

A legal larceny also requires that the person making the arrest must be able to prove in court that: *The taking away of property of value was done with INTENT to steal.* It is this second element that is often overlooked and may cause serious repercussions in court. Unless you can prove the INTENT to steal, you may have a false

arrest. Later the person arrested may bring a lawsuit against the store and the person making the apprehension.

Let's review these two elements again because they are vital to EVERY larceny apprehension you will ever make.

To establish that a larceny has been committed, the complainant must prove, beyond any reasonable doubt, that two elements were present at the time of arrest:

1. *The taking away of store property of value by the suspect. . . .*
2. *done with INTENT to steal.*

Before you make ANY larceny arrest be sure you are in a position to prove *both* of these elements.

Proving Intent

How do you prove "intent" to steal? The most common way of proving intent to steal is by showing that the suspect *concealed* the item taken from the store. To prove legal concealment, however, the item must be carried in a place or manner in which such merchandise is *not normally* carried.

A woman who tries on several belts and then leaves one of them on and closes her coat over it has not *legally* concealed the belt. True, it is concealed—but not *legally* concealed. Why? Because that is where a belt is normally worn—around the waist. The suspect can claim in court that she "forgot" she had a store belt on when she left the store, and the court may dismiss the case because there appears to be a reasonable doubt the suspect *intended* to steal the belt.

Let's say a woman drops a store lipstick into her handbag; again the store could not use "concealment" to prove the woman intended to steal the lipstick. The lipstick cannot be seen because it is in her handbag and thus it is concealed—but it is not legally concealed because that is where a lipstick is normally carried.

On the other hand, if a shopper removes a handbag from a display and shoves it up under the arm of her coat, this *is* legal concealment and proves intent to steal because a handbag is not usually carried in this manner.

Another way of proving intent to steal is when a shopper tears off the price tag or removes store wrappings or other identifying materials. This is evidence of intent to steal and no matter where the item is later concealed for removal from the store, the intent to steal has been established.

If a suspect takes the merchandise out of a pocket or shopping bag and looks at it and then replaces it or moves it to another pocket, the intent to steal is established. These actions show the shopper is fully aware of possessing store merchandise.

Another valid proof of intent to steal can be established if you overhear a conversation between two thieves intent on shoplifting and their words reveal a plan to steal from the store.

Not all shoplifters can legally be apprehended. Some must be allowed to leave the store. Apprehending a suspected thief when you have a doubtful case is unwise, for it may lead to a costly false arrest lawsuit. The results of such a lawsuit will be far more costly than the merchandise lost by letting the shoplifter get away.

The top retail detectives put the situation in these words: "*If in doubt—let it out!*" This is good advice that should be followed by all retailers.

Arrest Criteria

Obviously it is best to make sure a larceny situation meets certain criteria before a store employee apprehends a malefactor. To that end, I have developed a series of standards to be met before an arrest can be undertaken. These "Rules of Arrest" have been used by several hundred client-stores for many years. For the seven years I was the Security Director of the J.L. Hudson Company, in Detroit, we used these rules for all shoplifting apprehensions and 10,000 shoplifter apprehensions were made during this period without a single claim of "false arrest."

If these rules are followed by the people in your store trained to know the elements of a legal larceny, you can forget about the headaches of a false arrest case. (*Note*: Before you use these rules, be sure to check with your store's legal counsel to make sure that they meet all local legal requirements)

Rule 1. The Person Making the Arrest Must Witness the Entire Theft.

The person making the arrest must see the suspect walk up to the display rack, showcase, counter, gondola, or shelf. This person must *themself* see the merchandise being removed. *Never* rely on others to tell you about a supposed theft. The arresting person must witness the theft.

The law requires the person making the larceny apprehension to see the theft occur.

If you don't see the suspect approach the display, put off making the arrest (the customer may be making an even exchange and you may have arrived too late to see the purchased item being replaced before the exchanged item was taken), keep your eye on the subject, and see if something else is taken before the customer leaves the store.

Rule 2. The Person Making the Arrest Must Have Continual, Unbroken Surveillance of the Subject from the Moment of Theft to the Moment of Arrest.

This means following the footsteps of the suspect. Go down the same aisle as the suspect. Don't go down a parallel aisle as you will lose sight of the suspect and the thief may realize you are following him and he may throw down the stolen merchandise before leaving the store without your realizing it. When you arrest the suspect you'll come up empty handed.

Rule 3. If Possible, the Person Making the Arrest Should Have a Witness.

The best kind of witness is an employee who has observed the actual theft of merchandise. If an employee has not seen the actual theft but has observed proof of intent to steal, such as tearing off a price tag or removing merchandise wrappings, he is also a good witness.

Even a witness to the apprehension who can later testify to seeing you remove the stolen goods from the shoplifter's person, and has overheard the shoplifter admit to stealing, can help substantiate your case in court.

Try to have a witness with you when leaving the store to make the arrest. Without such a witness, proceed with extreme caution.

Rule 4. The Shoplifter Must Show, by Some Overt Act, the Intent to Steal.

The person making the arrest must witness a legal concealment of the stolen property, or the tearing off of the price tag, removal of wrapping, the moving of stolen goods, or some other equally specific proof of the person's intent to steal.

Rule 5. Usually, More Than One Item Should Be Stolen.

Although this rule need not always be followed because it is often not practical, it does strengthen the store's case and should usually be applied. Don't risk a costly lawsuit for a single, inexpensive item.

Rule 6. The Stolen Merchandise Should Have a Minimum Value of at Least $2.

Many stores today set a minimum value on a shoplifter case of $2, $3, or $5. The risk of a possibly expensive lawsuit must be balanced against the value of your recovery. Such a risk is unwarranted for a 69¢ lipstick. Judges often resent giving time to criminal cases involving a minor theft. If the store decides to prosecute and loses its case in court, the false arrest penalty can be devastating.

Rule 7. The Stolen Property Should Be in the Possession of the Suspect at the Moment of Arrest.

Do not carry out the arrest unless you are sure the suspect has the property on him. You should also know the value of the stolen items and where they are located on the shoplifter when you make the arrest.

Rule 8. The Arrest Should Be Made Outside the Store.

Some states require that a suspected shoplifter leave the store before an arrest is made. In other states it is permissible to apprehend a shoplifter at any time, as long as you can prove intent to steal.

Nevertheless, it is usually best to wait until the suspect leaves the store before making an arrest. This strengthens the case and avoids disrupting customers and store operations.

Arrest Alternatives

Inside every large problem is a small problem struggling to get out. With the "Rules of Arrest" they can end the nightmare fear of lawsuits from false arrest. Yet playing it safe by following these rules can be frustrating at times. A situation will occur when you "know" a shoplifter has stolen an item of store merchandise but you don't have a situation that meets all the rules of arrest. You would be wise to leave the matter alone.

Still, all of us hate to see this kind of thief take advantage of us. Perhaps the value of the merchandise stolen doesn't meet Rule 6, or you are "nearly" sure the sticky-fingered customer has slipped a wrench up his sleeve, but you don't have a witness. Perhaps you aren't sure what kind of a tool the thief took.

When these types of incidents occur, do you really have to follow the rules of arrest? Do you have to let the culprit off scot free? Should you let this thief take away store merchandise? It is infuriating to think about it!

When these "almost" larcenies occur, aren't there some alternatives to this list of rules?

Sometimes you can act, but you need to be careful. One technique to use when you are *sure* you have seen a customer steal an item of merchandise is to follow the suspect out of the store and when you are a distance away from the store, approach the subject with a friendly manner and use a *face-saving question* to recover the store's merchandise.

Say, in a most pleasant way, to the errant customer: "Pardon me, but don't you have something you'd like me to return to the store for you?"

Do not touch the suspect; do not physically restrain this person in any way. If your suspicions are correct, the thief is likely to blush and say something to the effect: "Oh my goodness, I completely forgot I had this," pulling the item in question out of its hiding place and offering it to you with profuse apologies.

Usually it is best to respond in a courteous manner and thank the customer for giving you the item to return to the store. If the customer feigns a bad memory and says, "What item?" you can say politely, "The hammer you have under the coat on your arm," or whatever might be appropriate.

At this point, if the customer still insists that he doesn't know what you are talking about, which is unlikely, simply apologize and briefly admit that you must be mistaken and continue walking along toward your car or toward the rear receiving dock of the store. Use this approach *only* in situations in which you are completely sure that the customer has shoplifted.

You may be tempted at this point (particularly if the person confesses regret) to make a shoplifting arrest. *Resist this temptation.* If you would have had a good larceny case, you would have made the usual arrest instead of using this face-saving question. Therefore stay within the recovery game plan and leave the idea of arresting this person alone.

No matter how promising the situation may look at the moment, once the culprit gets a lawyer and you are called to the witness stand in court, you may find the final outcome is an unhappy one. Making an arrest, in violation of the rules of arrest, can be dangerous. Be glad you recovered the merchandise, which is better than making a dubious arrest.

Delayed Contact Method of Arrest

The arrest of a shoplifter can be a problem. What might happen when you try to arrest a thief? The shoplifter may kick and scream, pull a knife, or stick a gun in your ribs.

Without a systematic method of arrest, every shoplifter arrest is a gamble.

A successful method of arrest has two objectives:

1. To reduce the risk of resistance and physical violence.
2. To obtain an admission of guilt as soon as possible.

The method of arrest that minimizes the risk of violence and obtains a confession at once is called "the delayed contact" method of arrest.

This system of apprehension took several years of trial and error to perfect. It is the product of several hundred arrests during which a variety of techniques were tested.

It uses certain psychological strategies to achieve the desired goals. The first contact with the shoplifter is designed to prevent an emotional explosion and then it takes advantage of the thief's immediate emotional shock and mental paralysis. Specific words are used to obtain automatically an admission of guilt.

The delayed contact method of arrest is deceptively simple and easy to use. It arms the employee with a specific, rehearsed plan and allows him to deal with the shoplifter safely and competently.

The Confrontation

Keep in mind that making a shoplifter apprehension has certain psychological problems for both the store employee and the thief. At the moment of arrest the person who has just left the store after shoplifting one or more items of merchandise is wound up tighter than a $2 watch. This fact is often lost sight of by the store employee because of his own fears about the impending confrontation.

The store person making the arrest is just as uptight as the larcenist.

Place yourself in the shoes of the thief for a moment. Let's say you've slipped a small electric drill off the counter and up under a raincoat you are carrying over your arm. You hope, but are not sure, that no one has seen you take the drill. Naturally you keep peering around to see if anyone is watching you. You pretend to glance at other merchandise and edge yourself toward the front door and freedom.

As you near the exit the stolen drill seems to get heavier with each step you take. You are sweating, and you imagine someone's eyes are looking at the back of your head. You swing around abruptly to catch the unseen eyes, but no one is looking at you. But that act of spinning around has increased the pounding of your heart. The store walls seem to be pressing in on you and sweat runs down your neck.

Finally you're at the door. You can't stand the pressure any longer and you suddenly burst out of the store angrily elbowing past slower shoppers.

Now you're in the parking lot and it's only a few more steps to your car and safety. You want to run but you hold yourself in. This is the moment of truth. You are at the peak of your fears and your body is hitting your veins with adrenalin. You have razor blades in your guts.

Meanwhile, what about the store manager who is hot on your heels preparing to make an arrest? He's also churning a lot of adrenalin into his blood in anticipation of catching a shoplifter. His fears are heightened by thoughts about what might happen next. Will the thief pull a knife? Is the shoplifter going to fight or run? Is he going to throw down the merchandise and escape? He looks big and tough!

Suddenly the moment has come for the store manager to move in. He grabs the thief's arm, almost knocking him off his feet, "Give me that drill!" he yells. The crook lashes out at the manager. They roll on the ground kicking and punching each other, and so it goes. . . .

Must an apprehension result in a fight? No, indeed. Not if we recognize that the shoplifter is just as keyed up as we are when we make the arrest. *The cause of most fights is the shock to the nervous system that results from the uptight store employee grabbing an uptight thief.* Like two bottles of nitroglycerine, they will explode if they are handled roughly! A fight results.

How do we avoid a fight? How do we obtain an admission of guilt by the malefactor in the first minute or so of an apprehension? By following the delayed contact method of arrest.

The delayed contact method takes advantage of the momentary disorientation of the thief during the first few minutes of the apprehension. These first few moments of the arrest can result either in a violent reaction by the culprit, or submission and confession. To prevent violence and gain a confession, in making an arrest you must use the exact wording of the questions in the delayed contact method and follow the arrest procedure step by step.

Step 1. In making an arrest you should follow the subject at least 100 feet from the store exit. As you approach the suspect, walk in rhythm beside the thief, but *do not make any body contact*!

Step 2. First, get the shoplifter's attention by saying something like, "Excuse me, may I speak to you a moment?" Keep walking; don't stop walking at any time in the apprehension unless the thief stops walking.

Step 3. When you are sure you have the attention of the subject, move in and *gently*, but firmly, take the subject's arm.

Step 4. Ask the subject—*in these exact words*—"Is this the first time you ever did this?" In nearly every case, the shoplifter will instinctively reply to the effect, "Yes, I don't know why I did it . . . ." This constitutes the first admission of guilt.

Step 5. The first admission of guilt must be tied down, and so you now ask a second important question; "Don't you know it's wrong to steal?" The shoplifter invariably confirms his first answer by saying something like, "Yes, I don't know why I did it, I don't know what got into me today. . . ."

Step 6. Now, while still walking beside the suspect, gently start to shift direction and begin circling back toward the store. At the same time recover *one item* of stolen merchandise. This is important evidence.

Step 7. As you start back to the store, reassure the shoplifter by saying, "Let's go back to the store and see if we can straighten this matter out."

Try to convey to the thief that you are understanding, and help him to believe that by going back to the store peacefully he may be able to talk his way out of the situation.

Step 8. As you walk back to the store ask a series of questions. First, "What is your name?" Get the subject's *first name* and use it frequently during the walk back to the store.

Step 9. Keep the shoplifter's attention occupied all the way back to the store by asking questions that require the thief to think about answers rather than about fighting, running away, or throwing down the stolen merchandise.

"Do you shop in the store often?" "Are you married?" "What does your husband/wife do for a living?" "Do you have any children?" "What are their names?" "How old are they?" and so on.

These questions will keep the shoplifter's attention occupied.

Exceptions

In most instances the delayed contact method of apprehension works as planned. But occasionally (in about 2 percent of all arrests) the thief doesn't respond as expected to the initial question. What then?

When you say to the suspect: "Is this the first time you ever did this?" he or she may look at you as though you've lost your mind and mumble "What are you talking about?" or "What do you mean?" or "Do I know you?" and so on. When and if this happens, you must play it by ear.

If the thief says: "I don't know what you're talking about!" You can respond by saying, "I think you do." But don't try to force a confession at this time. Stay cool. Trying to fight the situation can cause the arrest to come apart at the seams. Don't let this response catch you off guard.

If the shoplifter has failed to respond to the key question, don't let it throw you. But now you *must* change your immediate objective. In a normal apprehension at this point you would be attempting to get a confession, but since you've hit a clinker give up that objective. A more important goal is to get the thief back into the store.

Forget about trying to get a confession now. Later, when you are back at the store, you will have plenty of opportunity to obtain it.

The moment you get the first uncooperative response from a subject, move to Step 7, "Let's go back and see if we can straighten this matter out."

This approach often works. But again, it may not. The hostile subject may try to pull away from you and demand to be released. *DO NOT RELEASE THE SUBJECT*. By stopping this person you have already made an apprehension. You have a legal larceny case against the thief or you wouldn't have made the arrest, so DON'T BACK DOWN NOW.

Try to persuade the thief to come back to the store peacefully. But if the criminal is determined to escape, then take whatever action is required to force the subject to return to the store with you. The law allows you to use whatever force is necessary to make an arrest. The only restraint is that you must not use "*excessive*" force, which is considered force beyond that needed to return the subject to the store.

Sometimes the troublemaker can be brought under control by saying, "If you don't want to go back to the store and talk this over, then we can go directly to the police station." Often this type of comment improves the subject's cooperativeness.

What if the shoplifter is bigger and stronger than you are? That problem does occur and it is wise to have enough help so that you outweigh and outnumber the person you intend to arrest. Gather employee assistance as you leave the store and if a suspect appears formidable make sure you have enough help to subdue him.

Search

What about searching the shoplifter? The rules of search and seizure are complex but one or two points may be helpful. The law allows you to make a thorough search of your subject at the time of arrest.

You should do this as soon as the subject is back in the office. Search for anything the prisoner can use to injure himself or someone else. Naturally, guns and knives should be removed from the malefactor, as well as nail files, scissors, darning needles, razor blades, and anything else that could be used to injure anyone.

Also remove all pills from the subject and do not allow the malefactor to take any pills unless a qualified nurse or doctor is present and authorizes it.

Before starting to search your subject, ask a man to remove everything from his pockets and turn them inside out; a woman should be requested to remove the contents of her handbag and empty them on the desk. Look through these things and select identification documents. A driver's license, birth certificate, union membership card, or other suitable form of identification should be used to establish who the person is.

In addition, have the shoplifter count his or her money after emptying the pockets or purse. Do not touch the money yourself but ask the subject to count it and watch this person do so. Record the total amount of cash on the case history. Also list details of the person's identification (Year, state, and number of driver's license, etc.). Record on the case history the name of the person who searched the subject.

If the culprit has a motel key, locker key, pawn tickets, or other evidence suggesting a professional operation, these items should be turned over to the police who may want to search the motel room or locker for stolen goods.

Play It Safe

A final word of caution; if a shoplifting situation does not measure up to the rules of arrest covered in this chapter, don't be tempted to take unnecessary chances by deciding that this time you'll make an exception. For as surely as you try to skip one of the rules of arrest, you are going to stick your foot in a beartrap. Measure the potential risks against the possible gains you can expect from breaking the rules, and then let common sense prevail. Although you don't like to let a thief get away, don't be too concerned. Experience shows that in most cases when a shoplifter has been allowed to get away the first time, this person will be seen stealing again and this time a legal arrest can be made.

Chapter 4

HOW TO IMPROVE DETECTIVE CASE PRODUCTION

Many store security directors would like to have their floor detectives make more shoplifter apprehensions. In fact, most detectives would also like to increase their proficiency. These are not idle wishes; almost any security department can improve its case production.

Viewpoints Are Barriers to Improvement

Of course, some floor detectives, and even some security directors, say that a detective has only so much ability and it can't be changed. They believe the present shoplifter arrest records are close to the maximum that can be attained. Others argue that they could catch more thieves if more of them came into the store and that they are catching all the shoplifters who do enter the store. Some security directors even insist that if there were more shoplifters around some of their people would be apprehending them, thus showing up the case production records of other staff members.

Some security heads and their detective staff believe that each detective has a limited amount of ability to spot shoplifters and that nothing can be done to improve it. Therefore, they argue, little can be done to improve the department's performance.

In spite of these viewpoints, however, experience shows that in most instances a department's case production record can be improved by a systematic review of the way in which detectives are selected, trained, assigned, motivated, and managed.

Recognizing the Problem

I recently had a store manager ask me: "What can I do to improve my floor detective's shoplifter arrests?"

"Why are you concerned about them?" I asked him.

"To tell you the truth, I was completely satisfied they were producing as many cases in our store as detectives in other similar stores in our city were getting, until last week. . . ."

"What happened to change your mind?"

"Well, my confidence was dented by a conversation I had at lunch the other day with the manager of another store—just like mine—who started talking about a couple of professional shoplifters his people had caught that morning. This led me to ask how many cases his detectives averaged in a normal month. I was shocked when it turned out that with one less detective on his staff than we have, his people are apprehending three times the number of shoplifters my detectives catch."

"Perhaps he was exaggerating his figures to impress you; people have been known to color the facts."

"That thought crossed my mind, but I've known this manager for a long time and he's always been truthful with me. Later his claims were verified by one of my own detectives who is a friend of a detective who works in his store. She asked me if I knew how many cases his people were getting, and when I asked her how many, she gave me the same figures he'd told me."

"Perhaps his store is located in a different type of neighborhood with more crime."

"No, his store is only three blocks away; it sells the same type of merchandise we do and does about the same sales volume."

"And his people get a lot more apprehensions than yours?"

"I'll say! I even have one man on my staff who hasn't caught a shoplifter in three months."

"What does he say when you talk to him about this?"

"Oh, he's got an excuse. He says he's seen some thefts but he claims that he would rather warn the person stealing not to do it anymore than to make an arrest. He says he takes the stolen merchandise away from them, gives them a lecture, and lets them go. I don't even know if that's a good policy.

"I have three women detectives who catch a few shoplifters each month, but they don't get cases like the detectives in the other store.

What am I doing wrong? How can I get my people to produce cases like he does?"

No doubt about it . . . this manager has a problem, but at least he recognizes it. In many stores detectives are not catching as many shoplifters as they should but neither the security director nor the store management realizes it.

First, of course, someone must question the adequacy of present detective performance before corrective measures can be considered. Unless the problem is recognized, nothing can be done to solve it.

Once the need is recognized, practical steps can be taken to improve case production. But before we explore the various factors that need to be considered in order to upgrade apprehensions, let's first look at the detective who is not making arrests but claims he is catching shoplifters.

This detective claims that, rather than arresting the larcenist, he prefers to recover the merchandise, give the thief a warning lecture, and let him go. Such a claim should be carefully examined.

Case of the "Kind" Detective

It may be that this detective is telling the truth, but without verification of his case by an arrest, case history, and signed confession we have no factual way of evaluating his case productivity. We have only his word for the number of thieves apprehended by him.

I have known a few detectives who have been pressed for cases and, being unable to produce them, have claimed they saw a shoplifter steal but the culprit got frightened and fled before they could grab him. They take credit for a so-called case and recovery of store merchandise. This male detective's story sounds a little like a variation on this "thrown merchandise" syndrome. (Let me hasten to add that many detectives *DO* see a shoplifter steal and *DO* recover thrown merchandise when the frightened shoplifter throws it down and runs. I am referring here to the small handful of detectives who claim a phony "recovery" to bolster a sagging record of apprehensions.)

Store Policy

Warning a thief rather than apprehending him is a question of policy. Is this procedure store policy? Or is it the detective's own concept? Has it been cleared with members of management?

We also have to consider not only the lack of accountability for case production in such a policy, but also whether it is sound in terms of protecting store assets.

Has an Arrest Been Made?

It would seem difficult if not impossible for a detective to recover merchandise from a shoplifter and also warn this person not to steal again without directly or indirectly accusing the suspect of larceny. The detective is also "detaining" the person during the time it takes to give his lecture and recover the store merchandise. These actions would seem to indicate an arrest has occurred. (Of course you should clear all legal questions with your company's lawyer.)

If an arrest has occurred, then we must realize that the way this detective is handling it is unwise. Why? Because it's possible that a shoplifter could later sue the detective and the store for false arrest and defamation of character, which is not a pleasant prospect.

Normally, a store has only two shields against a civil suit for false arrest. One is the prosecution and conviction of the larcenist by the store and the other is a properly witnessed confession signed by the thief. One of these two shields against civil lawsuits is needed in every case to avoid a claim of "false arrest."

The detective is placing the store in jeopardy each time he detains a customer and then releases him without taking a written, signed confession.

Increasing Detective Case Production

Increasing detective cases involves a variety of things, including hiring the right people, proper training, sound supervision, rating their work, realistic expectations, intelligent motivation, and high morale.

Keep in mind that as interested as management is in getting top case production, they aren't any more interested than the people doing the job, that is, the detectives themselves. Every store detective I've ever known wanted to catch more thieves.

The Hiring Problem

First, are you hiring the right people for the detective job? *The ability to "see" people steal is both a unique and rare talent.* People who have this ability to a marked degree are very rare.

Desire to Become a Competent Detective Is Not Enough

Oddly enough, the fact that a person wants to be a detective is no indication of his or her ability to be one. I recall a young lady who came to Lord & Taylor's with the strongest drive to be a successful store detective of anyone I've known. Mary Williams was short in height; she had a face no one could remember. Mary blended into a crowd of customers so well that at times I could be standing a few feet away from her and never see her. Her appearance and enthusiasm left no doubt in anyone's mind that one day Mary would become a crackerjack detective.

She began training in the usual way. Mornings, when store traffic was slow, Mary stayed in the office studying the detective manual. Later, as customer traffic became heavier, she went with an experienced detective to work the floor. In the first few weeks on the job Mary observed numerous shoplifting thefts and was involved in trailing, surveillance, and interviewing. She also learned how to do a subject search and how to take a case history. Mary soon became familiar with store policies and the laws related to security work.

Mary did well in all aspects of her training except one. She did not herself spot any shoplifter.

Inability to Spot Shoplifters

At first, the failure to spot shoplifters didn't cause any concern in the department. Everyone figured Mary was just a slow starter. Certainly anyone with her surveillance ability and enthusiasm couldn't fail to start spotting thieves sooner or later.

But as the days and then the weeks went by, the problem became increasingly apparent. This trainee simply couldn't detect shoplifters. Mary did everything else well; she was such a likeable person that the detectives (often hostile to new people) took her under their wing, encouraging her and trying to train her to recognize clues that give shoplifters away.

Mary became more and more frustrated and this drove her to work even harder. She was soon gulping down her brown-bag lunch in the detective's room and taking only 15 minutes to eat before rushing back to the floor. Mary gave up her relief periods to do floor work. She even worked on her day off and stayed evenings after her regular work shift was over. And all this effort, all this determination, all this drive were to no avail. *She simply could not spot a shoplifter!*

How Much Time Is Needed to Train?

The store had a policy that trainees had to get at least one case on their own within the first three months of probationary work or be discharged. But at the end of her 90-day probationary period this determined young lady still had not had a shoplifting case of her own. What was even more astounding, Mary had not seen a shoplifter steal anything except when the thief was pointed out to her by an experienced detective.

At a management conference it was decided that because of Mary's determination and hard work the probationary rule should be waived this one time. Even though Mary had not made an arrest, it was decided to keep her on the staff as long as necessary to let her develop into a producing detective.

The experiment was a noble one. Could a person of talent and drive, if kept long enough and if trained enough, become a satisfactory store detective?

And the answer? Well, after being in training *one full year*, after being handed to every experienced detective on the staff for training, after working lunch hours, relief periods, evenings, and even during her vacation, *after one full year of training and hard work, this trainee had never seen even one shoplifter steal!*

This incident was depressing to the trainee and to all of us in the the department, but it taught us an important lesson: *you either have the ability to spot thieves or you don't.* And if you don't have this unique talent it *cannot* be drilled into you. You *can't* learn it no matter how hard you try.

People with a talent for spotting shoplifters can be trained to sharpen this talent, but unless they have it to begin with, nothing can be done to attain it.

A case-producing detective must first have a unique ability to spot shoplifters. A security staff with people on it who don't have this talent is one reason why some stores have unsatisfactory case production.

Once you recognize the unique talents possessed by "star" detectives, then you have to learn how to select other people with this ability.

Case Required in Three Months

The first step to upgrading a security staff is to recognize that *every detective hired must start producing cases, on his or her own, within three months of employment.* If a trainee doesn't get a case in three months, replace this person with a new trainee. Keep trying out trainees until you find someone who *does* start producing cases within the probationary period.

A year or so after we tried to make Mary into a detective we hired another young lady named Eunice Dietrich.

Eunice had never been a floor detective, and she was also enthusiastic about the work. But she differed considerably from the first trainee. *The first day that Eunice worked on the selling floor she spotted and helped apprehend eight shoplifters!*

Eunice Dietrich went on to become the highest case-producing store detective I have ever known. She proved that when it comes to detective ability; *you've either got it or you don't.*

Selecting Top Producers

Hiring the right people is the first step to improved detective case production.

How do you select people who are most likely to become top case-producing detectives? A detective selection test can identify the case producers at the point of employment. Without such a test, however, you must use the employment interview to verify that the applicant has several characteristics common to outstanding floor detectives.

Characteristics to Look for When Hiring

First, you want a person with *a positive attitude.* Granted, many stores have effective detectives who are by nature grouchy and negative and such people often produce cases, but the value of these cases is often offset by the poisonous criticism and fault finding such detectives scatter throughout the security department.

These troublemakers can cause a lot of staff conflicts. They often have fights with malefactors during apprehensions, and their hostile attitude can cause problems with other store employees. Such detectives may also produce false arrests.

It's prudent to let these openly hostile people seek employment elsewhere. You should look for a person with a positive attitude.

Test for Positive Attitude

You should be able to spot a negative person early in the employment interview. Test the applicant to see how this person responds to suggestion.

For example, suggest to a woman with a handbag in her lap that she might be more comfortable putting the handbag on the desk. If she responds by saying "Thanks" and doing as you suggest, this is a first indication she may be a positive person.

A male applicant about to take one of two chairs in front of your desk may be given the suggestion he will be more comfortable in the alternate chair from the one in which he has selected to sit. How he responds will be a first indication of his attitude. If he agrees with you and sits in the chair you have selected, chances are he is a positive person. If he rejects your suggestion out of hand, chances are he has a negative attitude.

Follow up such initial tests with questions about past jobs, for example, how the applicant feels about past bosses and former employee associates. If the applicant responds with an excess of critical, self-serving remarks, you can safely assume that this person has a negative viewpoint and you should weigh this fact carefully when making your final judgment about hiring this person.

A negative attitude, by itself, should not of course disqualify an applicant. But it should be considered during the evaluation process. A positive attitude can be an important plus for the applicant.

The characteristic of positive attitude (does the person see a tumbler of water as "half-full" or "half-empty"?) does *not* indicate case-producing ability. In fact the person with a negative attitude is sometimes good at catching shoplifters. But a positive attitude is a desirable trait, and it is important in the overall performance of the detective.

Does the Applicant Have a Strong Drive?

The next trait is one that *can* be important in case production. Does the applicant have a *strong drive?* Good detectives must have a high level of energy to get cases.

Determine if the applicant has in the past shown a pattern of behavior indicating a strong drive. You want a person who will not be easily discouraged, one who will break down barriers to achieve his goals.

Has the applicant ever overcome a serious handicap? Did he go to school while at the same time holding a job to help pay for his education? Did he decide to get onto the school football team even though normally he might have been rejected because of his physical limitations?

As you listen to the applicant tell his story, seek out information that shows a strong drive, or the lack of it.

Sleep Needs Can be a Key to Drive

A good question to ask the applicant is, "How many hours sleep a night do you require to feel in top condition?" Experience shows a correlation between the hours of sleep needed to be in peak condition and a person's drive. The individual who requires no more than four or five hours sleep a night usually has a high level of energy.

On the other hand, a person who needs nine or ten hours of rest to feel really good is apt to lack the amount of drive needed in detective work.

The average person requires eight hours of sleep, and the applicant who needs eight hours is all right. Such a person may prove to have adequate drive for the job, but the answer is not revealed by his need for sleep. You must look for the answer in a review of his past achievements.

Top detectives have exceptional energy. They dive into their work and show above average activity both on and off the job.

Steady Persistence

Drive involves not only energy but also determination. You want a person whose past experience shows steady persistence and determination to achieve his goals.

The good detective is tenacious as a bulldog; he doesn't give up easily. Once he has a thief in his sight he goes after this thief with a determination that often astounds the outsider.

A top detective following a suspect is not easily dissuaded. Rarely is the detective shut out of a crowded elevator when he must follow the subject on board. A jam of customers does not block his surveillance path, and a thief that resists arrest is brought back to the store every time.

With conclusive evidence that an applicant has an exceptionally strong drive, chances are excellent he or she will be an effective detective. Certainly without such a drive there is little likelihood the applicant will be a winner.

Detectives Must Have Sound Judgment

Competent detectives must also have *excellent judgment.* A person who gets a lot of cases but also brings back a bad one on occasion is bad news for any security department. A new detective must learn the legal aspects of larceny to know when to make a legal arrest, and he must also have the self-control and judgment to apply what he knows.

Even a single false arrest cannot be tolerated in a well-managed security department. The rules for arrest are firm and require that certain things must be present before an arrest is made. The detective job cannot be done by a person with faulty judgment.

How do we decide whether an applicant has good judgment? One way is to ask questions that indicate the applicant's *maturity.* Look for indications of reliability and realistic thinking. Does the applicant fantasize about the nature of detective work? Does he think it is a James Bond type of job with sexy women on the side? How realistic are the applicant's expectations? What incidents in the past show that this person has good judgment? Get answers to these questions before you make a final decision about the applicant's suitability for security work.

Ability to Get Along Well with Others

A final important quality you want in a detective applicant is *the ability to get along well with others.*

Security work is largely a team operation. It requires cooperative people who enjoy working together. Catching malefactors requires exceptional concentration and any personality clashes within the department can destroy productivity. Anger and conflicts destroy concentration.

Detectives need a personal network of friendly employees, cultivated by the agent, who will tip the agent off whenever a suspect enters their department. To develop an informant network a detective must have a friendly, outgoing personality. This means a marked ability to get along well with others.

Women Often Make the Best Store Detectives

To improve case production it is important to know that usually *women produce far more shoplifter apprehensions then men.* The talent for detection of shoplifters has proven to be one area in which men and women show a marked difference in ability.

In spite of the fact that a few men are good case producers, they are the exception rather than the rule.

Study of Cases

For instance, in a study of 7,000 shoplifter apprehensions at the J.L. Hudson Company, in Detroit, it was found that when the apprehensions of men and women were compared on a pro-rated basis, women detectives outproduced men at the rate of 35 cases to 1, which means that for every shoplifter arrest by a male detective, a woman made 35 arrests.

Case-Producing Men Are an Asset

This does not mean you should exclude men when considering detective applicants. If you can find one of those rare gems, a man who can produce cases on a par with women, grab him. He's worth his weight in gold.

On the other hand, some stores fail to catch a sizeable number of shoplifters because they have unknowingly weighted the detective staff with too many men. I know stores where the only people employed as floor detectives are men. This is unwise.

Apprehension Problems

One reason why some stores use mostly male floor detectives is that they recognize the dangers to a detective when making an arrest. If the store is in an economic area in which assaults and street crimes are common then it is understandable that men as detectives rather than women make more sense. But such situations can often be improved by employing women detectives while backing them up with men. In any store a woman detective should be able to summon male help when needed. This can often be done with a two-way radio carried in the detective's purse.

If a store has hosts on the floor (guards in plain clothes), these men should be easily summoned to help women detectives. In other stores, the assistant store manager, department head, or any other men working in selling departments can be trained to help detectives make apprehensions.

It is not sound strategy for a store to hire men to catch shoplifters (unless a male detective has in the past proven himself to be a top case producer). Often a simple answer to improving case production is to shift from men to women detectives.

Need for Realistic Expectations

Good case production depends upon realistic expectations. If a floor detective has never caught 35 shoplifters in a month, it is unrealistic to set a monthly case quota for such a person at 35 cases.

It is also unrealistic to expect case production from a detective assigned to a location where she cannot get cases. For example, it may be important to have a detective assigned to protect the store's fur department, but there is little opportunity for such a detective to produce shoplifter arrests.

The same situation may arise if a detective is assigned to a particular store. Some stores, because of their size, geographic location, or merchandise carried, may not be susceptible to much shoplifting loss. In such a situation it would be unrealistic to expect a detective to produce as many cases as the detective assigned to a larger store with a high theft rate.

Of course, before a store is designated a "low-case location," it should be screened by the department's better case-producing detectives to make sure that appearances are not deceiving.

Some stores are obviously high-risk locations. But other stores can be deceiving in appearance. A store may be located in a high-income residential area and appear peaceful on the surface, but be a hotbed of shoplifting activity underneath. Because such a store does not appear to be shoplifter-prone, management may be satisfied with relatively low case production. But the true situation is often revealed when a "star" detective hits the store and suddenly produces twenty-five cases a month, whereas the other detectives have been averaging only seven or eight arrests.

Before you dismiss a branch store as not having a shoplifter problem be sure it is vetted by a person of proven detective ability. Otherwise you may be accepting second-best case production and losing your shirt to unseen shoplifters.

Where the detective works in a store can affect the number of cases apprehended and can also affect the recoveries on these cases.

A detective who is assigned fitting room coverage may not produce as many apprehensions as the detective working on the open floor where a lot of small, easily pocketed items are displayed.

But the fitting room detective will usually have a higher average recovery per case. The greater value of fitting room cases will offset the smaller number of apprehensions.

Recoveries are Important in Rating Detectives

The quality of the cases is more important than their number. A fitting room case in which the store recovers $45 worth of merchandise is worth more than the arrest of a child who steals an 89¢ widget from the hardware department. Although both cases appear as a statistic in the monthly summary of cases, in terms of return on investment the 89¢ case is too costly for the store to handle.

Yardstick for Rating Detectives

This brings up the problem of evaluating a detective's case production. Obviously, the *number* of arrests, in itself, is not a sufficient yardstick for measurement.

I have known detectives to build their number of monthly arrests by apprehending not only the child who stole an 89¢ item but also his three companions who were standing with him at the counter. The detective takes credit for *four cases* on a single recovery of 89¢. This sort of thing obviously skews the figures and gives a false impression of the detective's effectiveness.

One way of rating detectives to overcome incorrectly weighted statistics is to find each person's average recovery per case. How is this done? Total the detective's number of cases for the month and then total the recoveries from these cases. Next, divide the total recovery figure by the detective's number of arrests. This provides an average dollar recovery figure per case.

Another rating method is to determine the detective's cost per case. (1) Total the detective's monthly salary; (2) subtract from the total monthly salary the agent's total case recoveries, which gives you an adjusted detective cost figure; (3) divide this adjusted cost figure by the number of arrests made; the answer gives you the detective's cost per case.

For example, say a detective's monthly salary is $640 and this month she made 12 arrests with an average recovery per case of $9. Thus her total recoveries for 12 cases is $108. Subtract the recoveries of $108 from the total monthly detective salary of $640, which gives a net cost of $532. Now divide this net cost of $532 by the number of apprehensions made (12); each arrest cost the store $44.33.

These so-called cost per case averages can then be compared throughout the department to see how one detective is producing compared to another. This is a more equitable way of evaluating detective performance than by simply counting the number of apprehensions.

It is also desirable to make quarterly evaluations of this type because case production should be averaged out over three or four months in order to get a true picture of an individual detective's performance.

Allow for Production Slumps

Every detective hits dry periods in which case production slumps. In some instances a capable detective may go an entire month or longer without an arrest. Similar slumps occur in other professional fields. A top golfer, like Johnny Miller, may win a handful of big golf tournaments and suddenly hit a slump. Johnny Miller's slump lasted for three years, during which time he failed to win a single major tournament.

Similar slumps appear in detective performance. Hopefully, a drop in cases won't extend longer than a few weeks, but every detective can run into periods in which they simply lose their ability to "see" shoplifters. To balance out such slumps, case production should be evaluated not only monthly but also on a quarterly basis.

Increasing Case Recoveries Is Important

The quality of cases is fully as important as the number. To assure cases of value it is good strategy to analyze the store and locate where the most costly shoplifting losses are occurring.

Usually small appliances, women's apparel, men's clothing, auto accessories, power tools, health and beauty aids, and sports equipment are departments with costly shoplifting losses. In training new detectives it is desirable to have an experienced detective work with the trainee in such departments.

Where a new detective gets her first case is vitally important to her future recoveries. If the first case involves a small, inexpensive item like costume jewelry, the detective will not be as likely to get high-value cases as the trainee who gets her first case in a fitting room or another department where expensive merchandise is sold.

Why is the location of her first case so important? When a detective hits a slump in cases and is eager to get a case, she invariably returns to the department where she made her first case. It is not unlike the "imprint" of baby chicks who attach themselves to a "mother" by assuming that "mother" is the first animal they see after being hatched. The detective has an "imprint" from her first case and assumes that the easiest place to get cases is in the department where she spotted her first case.

Make sure the first apprehension of the detective-trainee occurs in a department with high-value merchandise.

Catching the Professional

In training the new detective, emphasize the importance of catching professional thieves (people who steal in order to sell). Such thefts often involve two people stealing in collusion. A professional shoplifting team may often steal $1,500 worth of apparel from a store in two or three hours.

Professional shoplifters have their own techniques of operation and detectives should know their methods. The professional usually scouts the store in order to spot the floor detective before stealing. One thief may set up the merchandise that is to be stolen, with her partner staging a distracting incident such as a fight or argument with a clerk to draw attention away from the person doing the stealing. Although the larceny-minded housewife usually displays her nervousness as she walks through the store, thus giving her intentions away, the professional—once the floor detective has been located—may operate without any outward signs of nervousness. After stealing, the professional may spot a detective following her and realize that her theft was observed. While an amateur thief would show signs of panic, the professional stays cool and doesn't let the detective know she has been spotted. When the opportunity arises the professional deftly throws the stolen merchandise so that if she is picked up outside the store she'll be "clean."

Detectives need to learn the differences between amateur and professional thieves. In trailing a professional, the detective must be especially observant to make sure the merchandise hasn't been thrown before the arrest.

To insure that every arrest is legal often requires close cooperation between detectives. Cases in which shoplifters work in concert always require more than one detective because more than one person must be kept under surveillance. But in every case the detective who acts as witness can help by observing the shoplifter's actions from a different angle. With two detectives on a suspect there is less chance the case will go wrong. This makes it easier to observe the thefts and if the merchandise *is* thrown at least one of the detectives will be in a position to see it happen.

Give Credit for Being a Witness

When evaluating a detective's performance include the person's record as a case witness. If you score detective cases on a point basis, plan to give 80 or 90 percent of the points to the detective originating the case because spotting the shoplifter is the most important element in a case. But also give the witness on the case points for her work. The backup person deserves recognition and this encourages cooperation.

When stores give credit for a case only to the person originating it and the witness receives no credit for her help, cooperation tends to be unsatisfactory. The situation is particularly poor if the security director makes the detective case production competitive. When detectives compete for cases, the detective called upon as a witness to help another agent get a case becomes involved in a conflicting role. On the one hand she is expected to compete with the other detective in getting cases, and on the other she is asked to serve as a helper in getting a case for the rival detective. An unhappy situation.

Bitter rivalry can develop between detectives in competitive situations, and a witness may sometimes secretly destroy the other person's case by allowing the thief to spot her. The witness can do this with little danger of being caught. She simply holds her eyes on the thief until he catches sight of her watching him. This kills the case. The other detective is so intently watching the thief she seldom sees this act of sabotage.

By giving detectives credit for acting as a witness you encourage cooperation and this increases case production.

Is the Detective Playing a Role?

What else can be done to improve case production? If you have a detective who in the past has been an excellent case producer and has now entered a production slump that has extended longer than normal, it is wise to review how the detective is acting on the floor.

"Is the detective acting like a customer while looking for shoplifters?"

Is the detective leaning on a counter? Or is she gossiping with salespeople? Is she looking at customers so openly that she gives herself away? Is she looking at people rather than merchandise? Is she just standing around a department, apparently without purpose, staring off into space?

Or does the detective act like a customer from the moment she steps onto the selling floor until she leaves it?

Has the detective learned how store customers act as they roam about the store? (This is one way of spotting thieves because, once you know how legitimate customers act, the shoplifter stands out like a sore thumb.) If the detective has not learned how customers act, or if she is not acting like a customer, then it's a good idea for her to spend a few hours doing nothing but looking at customers and studying their behavior patterns so she can better play the role of "customer" while on the floor.

Even the amateur thief usually roams a selling floor looking for store detectives before stealing. As you observe a detective suffering a case slump, ask yourself if a thief could easily spot her as a detective because she isn't acting like a customer. If so, coach the detective so that she learns to blend in with the customers.

A primary reason why some detectives fail to get as many cases as they should is because they can be too obviously spotted as a detective when they are on the selling floor. The capable detective disappears before your eyes because she acts like a customer, thus concealing her identity from the larcenist.

How Detectives Reveal Their Identity

Detectives sometimes give themselves away as surely as if they carried a sign on their back saying, "Look, I'm a Store Detective."

Because detectives want their hands to be free to bring back a shoplifter, they often use shoulder-strap handbags. Perhaps one detective can get away with such a handbag, but it is unwise for every woman on the staff to wear a shoulder-strap handbag. This does give the game away.

Because stores are often hot in winter months, some detectives wear light summer coats (which is okay if they are in dark winter colors) *over their shoulders*. A coat worn over the shoulders tells the potential larcenist that the person wearing it is a detective. It soon becomes a mark of Cain as far as the detective is concerned because clever shoplifters tend to give the detective a wide berth. If all the detectives do it, you might as well put them in police uniforms, for professional shoplifters will seldom fall into their hands.

A detective's identity is often revealed to shoplifters because it was thoughtlessly decided that detectives should unlock customer doors at store opening time and man them at closing time. Some shoplifters are known to watch store opening and closing periods because it is easy to spot detectives.

Don't Have Detectives Guard Customer Doors

I know stores where detectives do cash pickups, or get customer descriptions from salespeople on bad checks. Jobs of this type, which take the detective out of her customer role, damage her effectiveness.

Avoid Bright Ornaments

Detectives should be observed periodically by the supervisor to see that they don't stand out when mingling with customers. They must disappear into the crowd.

Pay particular attention to distinctive accessories. Detectives are often stylish dressers and they like to highlight their attire with scarfs or pins, but the detective should *avoid using any bright-colored scarf or pin of an unusual design.* Anything that helps the thief remember the detective is a handicap. It gives the thief an advantage in spotting the detective trailing him.

I recall a professional shoplifter who was caught stealing expensive jewelry. The detective, who often worked in the jewelry department, told the shoplifter she'd seen her there many times, but she'd never seen her steal. "Why did you steal today?" asked the detective.

"Because," said the shoplifter, "you didn't wear your gold ring with the three red stones." Glancing at her hands the detective suddenly realized she'd forgotten to put on her ring that morning. The shoplifter added, "Whenever I was at the jewelry counter and saw that ring I knew a detective was around so I didn't steal. But today I felt safe because I didn't see the ring."

Detectives should also be cautioned about chewing gum. A detective dressed like a teenager can get away with it, but it can be a nervous habit that becomes a warning flag to the knowledgable shoplifter. It is understandable that a detective might like to chew gum to keep her nerves under control, but it isn't wise to do so. Some things become a popular practice among a specific group of people. Baseball players, for example, are associated with chewing tobacco, and many store detectives chew gum. Gum is a security cliché, and detectives should avoid it because it often reveals their true identity.

Detectives should alter their appearance several times each day. Women detectives can change their height with high heels or loafers; eyeglass frames with clear glass can also change a person's appearance. Changes in hairdo and makeup also can make a person unrecognizable.

With a wig, glasses, low heels, and a bit of makeup a young detective can suddenly become a middle-aged shopper. She should of course rehearse the stance, walk, and slope of shoulders to fit the image of an older woman.

Stores I consult with keep a rack of coats to fit all detectives. They are in a variety of designs and colors. The store, in some instances, also furnishes eyeglass frames of different styles with clear lenses, either plain or tinted. Numerous wigs are also supplied in a range of hair colors and styles. Detectives usually furnish their own extra pairs of shoes.

Detectives in these stores freely exchange their disguise paraphernalia with each other, Makeup tables with large mirrors and lights—like those in stage dressing rooms—are provided and this allows the detectives to do a professional job of makeup.

A detective sits down before the makeup mirror as one person and in a few minutes, like magic, she's changed into a different person, one the shoplifter would never identify as the detective he or she spotted in the store a few days ago. Detectives need these simple ways of altering their appearance.

I've known situations in which a detective spotted a known thief entering the store, a thief who knew the detective. To avoid being "made" the detective rushed to the detective's room and quickly changed her hairdo, coat, and shoes to reappear, moments later, on the selling floor completely changed in appearance. She then located the hot suspect and took over surveillance that led to an apprehension.

It goes without saying that detectives who have the resources to change their appearance several times a day will get more cases.

Fatigue Can Hurt Concentration

A detective's concentration and rhythm of work must not be broken if she is to become a high case producer. I have found that by requiring detectives to get off their feet, to sit down 10 minutes out of every hour of floor work, increases apprehensions.

This hourly rest period, sitting in a fitting room or off the sales floor, prevents fatigue that snaps the concentration of many good detectives, thus cutting down their effectiveness.

Training detectives to use auto-suggestion for increased concentration also helps get more cases. The physical senses are more acute when a person is relaxed. This fact is recorded in many psychological studies. Therefore the detective who can be trained to relax on the floor will find her perception sharpened.

In most stores a large number of shoplifting cases are caught by the detective because she spots the suspect while going or coming from lunch. The reason this time of day is the most productive is because *the agent has relaxed* in anticipation of the break from work. As she walks across the floor, in this relaxed state, her senses are sharpened and she spots suspects she might have missed if she were still patrolling the floor.

In fact, when detectives hit a slump and become frustrated because they can't get a case, this condition feeds on itself and becomes worse because they try too hard to locate a suspect

Pushing for a suspect causes the agent to become tense and reduces her perceptive abilities.

In addition, when in a case slump the detective walks too much. The tendency of the frustrated detective is to spot a suspect and to start following him; then the detective often sees what appears to be an even better prospect and so she drops the first one and follows the second. Then she sees a third suspect who looks even better than either of the first two and she follows that one. In this process the detective walks, walks, walks. In her eagerness to get a case, she doesn't stay with any suspect long enough to determine whether they will steal or not.

Detectives in a slump should be taught to stand still more.

To reduce the tendency to walk too much a detective should be told to stand at a counter in a high-theft department such as gloves, health and beauty aids, or hosiery and do nothing but watch customers' hands. Sooner or later a thief will appear on the scene and she will break her losing streak.

Rotating Detectives Between Stores Is Undesirable

Another practice that reduces case productivity is to move detectives around from one branch store to another.

A security director may reason that by rotating detectives between stores they are less likely to become well known and therefore will get more cases. Not so.

In actual tests of this theory I found that detectives have to get into the rhythm of the store they work in. This "feel" for customer activity requires one or two weeks in a different store environment before the detective achieves a unity with the environment that allows her to produce cases. Case production is substantially reduced if detectives are moved from one store to another.

Concentration

Without a high level of concentration a detective can't spot thieves, and without concentration, those that are spotted may escape because the detective's mind may wander and she may lose sight of them while trailing them, or she may miss seeing them steal because she looked away at the wrong moment.

Spotting the suspect, seeing the theft, and trailing the thief are key elements in case production. They depend upon one thing: *concentration.*

Supervisor Floor Tours

Caution detectives about getting enough rest while off the job. Being well rested can do wonders for detective apprehensions.

The supervisor of detectives should make floor tours at least twice a day and contact the detectives while they are on the floor working. The supervisor should watch from a distance to see if a detective is concealing her identity by acting like a customer and also watch for excessive walking (a sign of tension that reduces effectiveness).

Look for signs of fatigue. Watch for detectives who lean on counters, yawn, glance frequently at the clock, or idly stare off into space; usually you can tell by a little patient observation whether a detective is full of drive and energy or is obviously worn out and tired.

When contacting the detective a couple of times a day on the floor, determine whether she is watching a suspect or just standing around doing nothing. Also ask a few questions about what she has seen during the day and in talking with the detective try and evaluate her mood.

The supervisor should be alert to a security person who appears distracted or moody. Often if encouraged to talk the agent will tell the supervisor about any serious problems that are unresolved in her personal life. When a detective is obviously struggling with personal problems she will not get cases. Concentration is destroyed.

To remedy this situation the supervisor would be wise to take the detective to the office for a talk, or better still, invite the person out for a cup of coffee and encourage the agent to spill out her troubles. A sympathetic ear can help the detective gain some insight and work out a solution to her problems.

Counsel Detectives

Nondirectional counseling techniques should be learned by the supervisor so that detectives who become depressed or angry about personal matters can be counseled back into emotional stability and mental health. Happy, well-adjusted detectives get many more cases than distracted, upset agents. Nondirectional counseling can help overcome detective frustrations and increase their productivity.

Early and Late Workers

If your store uses detectives on two shifts, the first during daytime hours and the second starting in the afternoon and going to a night-time closing, you should consider who is an early worker and who is a late worker among your security staff.

The world is divided into two groups of people. Some are early workers. They get up at the crack of dawn every day whether they are working or on vacation. They function best during the morning and early afternoon hours. They often reach their peak between 11 A.M. and 2 P.M., and by late afternoon they begin to taper off; by early evening they are getting tired and are ready for an early bedtime.

Others are late workers. They hate to get up in the morning! Once forced out of bed they are groggy for a time, and they may not become fully awake until after they have had their morning coffee.

Even after late workers arise and start to function, they are slow to raise their body temperature and don't really feel up to snuff until midafternoon. This group will reach their peak of performance from the afternoon until late evening hours. They may still be going strong at midnight, hating to retire even in the early morning hours.

It is easy to determine which detectives on your staff belong to each group. Just ask whether they find it difficult to wake up in the morning.

Early workers will be enthusiastic about their early morning hours, for then they are full of energy and eager to go. Late workers will tell you how it feels to drag out of bed and that they feel fuzzy for several hours after starting their day.

Once you have established whether a detective is an early or late worker, it is wise to try to use your early workers on the day shift. They will be ready to get cases from the minute the store opens until they go off work in the afternoon.

Late workers, naturally, should be assigned the late afternoon and evening hours when they reach the peak of their energies.

You can improve detective performance by simply readjusting your staff's working hours to coincide with their patterns of energy.

Part-Time Versus Full-Time Detectives

Another surprising discovery I made several years ago is that *part-time detectives usually produce as many cases as full-time agents*. Why this is so is not entirely clear, but it is perhaps the result of less fatigue and of normal detective competition between full- and part-time people. It works only if you also have full-time detectives working with the part-timers. The part-timer sees the full-time detective's apprehensions and wants to produce as many cases as the full-timer, and so they do!

I suspect that another reason why part-timers produce a lot of cases for the hours worked is because there is less chance of fatigue robbing the agent of her concentration.

Detectives Can Decide to Get Cases

I have also found that many detectives can catch a shoplifter whenever they want to. This ability can be triggered in two ways.

First, when a shoplifter is apprehended, bring detectives (one at a time) off the floor to look at the subject through a two-way mirror. This serves several purposes. If the detective has seen the subject in the store previously, it may increase the amount of the larceny confession and thus increase the restitution.

In addition, even though the detective has never seen the larcenist before, she will remember the shoplifter's face and will spot the thief if he or she comes into the store in the future.

Finally, the detective is motivated to go out and get a shoplifter too. In fact, I have seen situations where one after another, during the day, detectives have made apprehensions until only one detective had not caught a shoplifter. And I have seen that lone detective go back to the selling floor determined not to be the odd man out . . . and get a case.

The other reason I know detectives can get cases when they want to is based on a successful experiment undertaken at the J.L. Hudson Company. I reviewed three years of apprehensions in the store and found that a detective never caught more than two shoplifters in one day.

I reasoned that a detective who had caught two shoplifters in a day probably would not catch a third, and therefore why should the agent hang around? I made a policy that whenever a detective had made two arrests in the same day, she could have the remainder of the day off. The result was that we nearly doubled our case production.

On occasion a detective would start work in the morning and mention that she had an appointment at the hairdresser for 2 P.M.; she needed a couple of cases so she could take the afternoon off from work. The detective would invariably, before lunch time, have made her two apprehensions.

Group Competition Can Be Imprudent

Unwise techniques of motivation can destroy case productivity. I recall learning this fact the hard way. I dreamed up a scheme for stimulating production of cases through competition. I mounted a large chart in the detective's lounge that listed the number of apprehensions each detective made during the past month. Then I gave prizes to the top three case producers for the month. The rewards were things such as theatre tickets, candy, flowers, and other small gifts.

This competition seemed great at the time, but it proved to be a disaster. Not only did it destroy department cooperation, but also it led to witnesses on cases deliberately allowing themselves to be "made" by the suspect, thus killing another detective's case. Hostility flared up throughout the department and the constant bickering and anger destroyed concentration; the case production dropped.

The chart had the opposite effect from what I had intended. When a detective in the low case-producing group looked at the number of cases the top detectives were pulling in, they were not motivated to improve their own case activity; instead they became discouraged and their production dropped even further.

The "star" case producers also failed to produce as many cases as before because they saw they didn't have to work as hard as before to stay near the top of the list.

After a few months I abandoned the chart and the prizes. I had not only failed to improve case production with my competition, but I had also succeeded in damaging the effectiveness of the staff.

Competition Can Motivate If It Is the Right Kind

Does competition play a part in improving detective case production? Yes, but not competition between detectives, which destroys morale and case production. A detective's case production, however, can be improved if you encourage the detective to compete against her own past performance.

The security supervisor should interview each detective monthly and discuss the past month's apprehensions. If the number of cases is below the department average, it often pays to ask the detective if she thinks she can, in the coming month, increase her number of arrests by *one more case* than she had during the past month. Most detectives don't consider this as unrealistic and readily agree to try and do it. In most instances they do get the extra case; sometimes even a few more cases than they were aiming for.

If the agent is still below par in cases, set the next month's goal one more case above the number caught in the past month. Keep doing this each month, making the goals completely realistic, and you can soon raise an agent's arrests to an acceptable level.

Naturally, some months a detective will not make the new case goal. That's to be expected. But they usually do meet it if you average their cases over a three-month period. This average will often be a pleasant surprise. You may find that a person who seemed hopeless is now meeting her case goals (on the average) every month.

All of us enjoy improving our performance, no matter what job we hold, and competition against our own past performance is motivating and positive. It does not set people at each other's throats the way competition between people does.

Fear of Physical Injury

Sometimes a detective does not respond to self-competition and we must find out what is holding her back. In some instances you may discover she is not producing up to expectations because of *a fear of physical injury* when arresting a malefactor.

This fear of injury is sometimes justified, but it should not be blown out of proportion by a lively imagination. Even the most difficult case isn't like going over Niagara Falls in a Dixie cup.

Of course it is normal to be afraid of the unknown. That is man's nature and the reason for his survival. Naturally, it is always possible the thief may pull a gun or a knife, or perhaps slam a fist into the detective's face. On rare occasions such things have happened. But in spite of the possible dangers that may occur when a shoplifter resists apprehension, overall such violence almost never occurs if the delayed contact method of apprehension is used by the arresting detective.

Since a fear of physical violence may be causing some detectives to avoid making arrests they consider dangerous, it is important to provide your staff defenses against possible violence.

Women detectives particularly need to be backed up with easily available help. These may be men who head up selling departments, the store manager, or his assistant; or in larger stores, it might be male investigators who are also part of the security staff.

Train Backup Men

These backup men should be trained in proper arrest procedures, how to handle themselves in case of malefactor resistance; and they should know the laws relating to the crime of larceny so they won't make any costly mistakes during an arrest. They should be instructed to take their directions from the store detective running the case and not act on their own.

Before an arrest, it is sound policy to be sure that the detective making the arrest has enough help to outweigh the larcenist if the thief should resist arrest.

Judo Training

Store detectives should receive judo training. This should be given by a professional instructor. In addition, the store should make arrangements with the instructor and a local gym so that detectives can retain their judo abilities through at least an hour of judo practice each week after work.

At Hudson's in Detroit, city police cooperated in providing the store not only the services of the department's judo instructor but also the use of the police gym. Some stores arrange judo instruction through the local "Y."

When the store is located in a neighborhood in which holdups, muggings, and other crimes of violence are common, it is a good idea to equip all members of the security staff with tear gas that can be carried in a pocket or purse.

Fear of physical injury may be holding back your staff and making case production substandard. It is a worrisome thing for any detective and you should take steps to alleviate such fears.

At this point you might think we've covered all the ways of improving detective case production. We may have done so, but there is one more vital area to consider and that is home plate.

Management Style

How is the security staff's morale?

What type of leadership is being provided for the detectives?

Studies of security department operations in more than 200 client companies show a remarkable difference in the supervision of security departments with low case production and those with high case production.

In the departments with low case production I found that supervisors are constantly putting pressure on detectives to get more and more cases. This aggressive, relentless style of management soon causes severe frustration in detectives, who are a self-motivated group.

The outside pressure, added to the normal desire of the detective to produce cases, freezes the agent's abilities, and instead of getting more cases the detective invariably gets fewer cases. Fear of retribution by the demanding department head paralyzes the detective so that she cannot produce anywhere near the number of cases she is capable of getting.

Authoritarian Supervisor

The supervisors in these groups also have little interest in the personal problems of subordinates. They are not sensitive to the detective's individual needs. In fact, they have little understanding or interest in people and are more work centered than employee centered.

Productivity in these groups is poor because the supervisor is dictatorial and dogmatic. He gives workers little opportunity to discuss new rulings. In fact, there is little meaningful communication between subordinate and superior and hardly any democratic group discussions.

Heads of security departments with poor detective performance also fail to keep their staff informed about what is occurring in the company. In fact, they are often paranoid in their secrecy about what is occurring not only in the company but even in the security department. Only one or two "favorites" are allowed to know what is happening behind the closed doors of the security director's office.

Emphasis in these departments is also more on the status of the security supervisor than anything else. He usually shows an abnormal need for personal security and spends a lot of his time and effort in holding onto or improving his status in the company. His interests are centered around himself, not his department or his staff.

These low-production supervisors who are on an ego trip also are deaf to any suggestions by their underlings. They brush off suggestions from detectives and have no awareness of things they say and do that damage their detectives' self-esteem.

Low-production supervisors often are overly critical. They have insatiable egos and a high level of personal insecurity that requires blind obedience and often shuts them off from important information. They do not tolerate suggestions from their people. Detectives also don't feel free to discuss with them important things about the job.

High-Producing Departments

Departments showing consistently high levels of case production are directed by supervisors who are quite different from the supervisors of departments with a record of low case production.

In stores where the detectives do a crackerjack job of getting cases, the supervisor is found to be democratic and open with his people. He encourages his staff to join in group discussions. He recognizes the value of employee opinions and seeks them out. He respects the experience, knowledge, and ability of his staff and builds up their self-esteem by recognizing their achievements.

The good security director does a minimum of paperwork and devotes much of his time to working with his staff. He believes employees should have a minimum amount of frustration, should enjoy their work, and have a high level of self-esteem.

To the top supervisors, the superior-subordinate relationship is a "helping" situation. He sees his job as that of *helping* his staff to produce to their fullest capabilities. He wants them to know their position is secure and permanent. He feels his own job is secure, and thus he passes this feeling of confidence and security down to his subordinates.

The best security head helps his people to gain personal job satisfaction. He sees to it that their education and training never end, and that they keep moving ahead with the times.

In top-ranking departments, the supervisor lets employees know where they stand at all times and he tells them what he thinks of their work and how well they are doing.

This type of supervisor obviously likes working with people. He has a strong personal interest in the detectives' problems, and he praises far more than he criticizes.

In addition, the successful security director knows his job, can explain it clearly to his staff, and yet is always interested and willing to listen to constructive suggestions and criticisms.

Self-Esteem Is Important

Every worker, no matter what the job, wants to be proud of the company he works for, proud of his department, proud of his boss, and proud of himself. The successful security director provides this type of working environment. He sets an example, a model the employee can emulate. His management practices are not only modern and humanistic, but also he sets a good leadership example in terms of ethics and human relations. He is concerned for his people, and he also has empathy for malefactors. He provides daily opportunities for his staff to have two-way communication with him. He encourages participation in helping him solve the problems of the department.

He also recognizes the unique abilities of his detectives. And he backs his people with company management.

Up-to-Date Offices and Equipment

The successful security director gives his people self-esteem through status symbols. He provides them with modern, well-located offices, which are well furnished and properly decorated. He would not tolerate the basement closets used by many of the low-producing security directors. The security department not only has excellent offices but the director also provides the latest in security equipment and facilities for the staff.

A successful security director doesn't tolerate lazy or dishonest people on his staff. But he has little need for concern about such problems because his style of management gives his staff a professional standing among their peers. This leads not only to high self-esteem but also to group pride in the department. As a result, the security staff does not tolerate dishonesty, laziness, or poor performance by its members.

Detective as a Professional

In such a department, the security job is viewed as a professional career. The company supports the security director in recognizing the unique talents of top-producing detectives and pays salaries that reflect the judgment and responsibility inherent in the detective's job.

Management recognizes that a mistake in judgment by a detective cannot only cost the firm many thousands of dollars but can cause publicity that can damage the company's image and cause an adverse affect on sales.

The best security directors and the management of the companies they work for know the detective's job is no penny-ante game to be played by someone who is slovenly, careless, or incompetent. Too much is at stake. With false arrest lawsuits against stores today resulting in judgments of as much as $5 million, this is not a minimum wage kind of job.

The enlightened company pays a salary that provides proper compensation for the responsibility involved, which in turn attracts competent, high-calibre people who provide the professional expertise needed by the store.

SUMMARY

At this point it's safe to say we've covered all the ways of improving detective case production. We've even touched home plate.

Here is a summary checklist of suggestions:

1. Detective ability is best judged by case production.
2. First you must hire the right people.
3. The ability to catch shoplifters is unique, not all people possess it.
4. It is a "natural" talent. It cannot be acquired through training.
5. In selecting potentially effective detectives you should look for four important qualities:
   a. Positive attitude
   b. Strong drive
   c. Mature personality
   d. Marked ability to get along with others
6. Strong drive is the most important characteristic for good case performance.
7. Women produce more shoplifting cases then men. Don't weigh down the security department with too many male detectives.
8. Are case expectations realistic in terms of shoplifting in the store and department in which the detective is assigned to work?
9. Rating detectives requires analysis of both the *number* of cases and the *value* of cases apprehended.
10. All detectives have periods when productivity slumps. To evaluate a detective's productivity properly, average results over a period of three or four months.
11. Don't put additional pressure on detectives when they are in a slump as this may paralyze their ability and prolong the length of the slump.
12. The detective-trainee should make her first apprehension in a fitting room or in a department with expensive merchandise.
13. Professional thieves are important; train detectives to understand differences in behavior between professional and amateur shoplifters.
14. Witnesses to the case are important. When evaluating performance give credit for the times a detective helped another as a witness on her case.
15. The supervisor should periodically observe a detective while she is working on the floor to see if she acts like a customer.
16. While working, detectives should avoid shoulder-strap handbags, wearing their coat over their shoulders, chewing gum, or any other mannerisms that make it easy for a shoplifter to pick out the detectives from the customers.
17. Don't give detectives such jobs as locking or unlocking the store's customer doors; and don't have them work in selling departments on investigations, getting bad check descriptions, and so on. Such

jobs betray the detective to the dishonest customer and make the floor detection job more difficult.

18. Make sure a detective's clothing and makeup help her blend in with the customers. Encourage her to carry parcels with printed names of nearby stores on them. For example, if the detective is working in the jeans department, she should dress in jeans. Make sure the choice of clothing fits the profile of the store customers; don't let the detectives over dress for the job.
19. Detectives should avoid distinctive accessories such as a brightly colored scarf, unique pin, or shiny costume jewelry, all of which a thief can easily remember and which help him to identify the detective if he is being followed.
20. Watch that detectives don't give themselves away by leaning on counters, gossiping with clerks, looking off into space, or staring at customers instead of looking at the merchandise. All of these are dead giveaways.
21. Provide a change of clothes, wigs, glasses, and makeup so that detectives can alter their appearance several times a day.
22. To avoid excessive fatigue require detectives to sit down for 10 minutes of every hour they work on the selling floor.
23. Detectives in a slump should learn to stand still and watch the customers' hands at a glove or handkerchief counter.
24. Don't rotate detectives between branch stores; this reduces their productivity.
25. Encourage detectives to get enough sleep and to learn to relax their muscles while working on the floor.
26. Personal problems ruin case production. Watch for signs of a detective with personal problems and use nondirectional counseling to help her resolve them.
27. Assign early workers in the department to day shifts and late workers to afternoon and evening work periods.
28. Use part-time as well as full-time detectives.
29. When a shoplifter is apprehended call the detectives to the security office one at a time to see the malefactor. This stimulates cases.
30. Research the maximum number of cases detectives usually get in one day. Set this maximum as a department standard and whenever a detective produces the daily maximum, reward her with the remainder of the day off.
31. Don't try to increase cases by encouraging detectives to compete with each other for arrests. This destroys morale and hurts case production.
32. Encourage detectives to compete monthly against their own previous month's record of apprehensions.

33. Protect detectives from dangers of physical inury with easily available backup male hlep.
34. Give detectives judo training and furnish them with tear gas weapons.
35. Authoritarian management of the security department results in low case productivity.
36. Security supervisors who use a democratic or participative style of management have excellent case production records.
37. Detective wages should reflect their unique talents and the responsibility they assume when making arrests.
38. Providing detectives with proper offices and modern equipment adds to their self-esteem and attracts competent people to join the company, thus improving security department effectiveness in all phases of its operation.

Chapter 5

DISHONEST EMPLOYEES

Many people who work in stores think of themselves as *honest*, even though they do take a little bit, here and there. They look upon themselves as "amateur" thieves. Insurance companies handling fidelity claims show that these so-called amateurs are today outstealing professional burglars by more than 5 to 1!

These employees—unarmed robbers—took their bosses for more than half a billion dollars annually through embezzlement, forgery, and direct thefts. The trend is growing alarmingly upward. Stealing cash, goods, juggling the books, and other types of employee thefts have skyrocketed in recent years.

Surety Claims Reflect the Theft Problem

Claim amounts filed with surety companies are staggering. In one case a man employed by a bank for 35 years embezzled over half a million dollars. In the same town, less than 30 days later, the president of another bank was caught juggling the books to the tune of $650,000.

Some of the biggest hauls were made by people who did not have access to cash. One store had five men who stole over $100,000 in merchandise from the warehouse. In another store, four stockboys admitted stealing $80,000 worth of goods from the store during the Christmas season.

Eight employees of a railroad, including a captain in the railroad police, got away with six and a half million pounds of scrap brass worth $760,000. Employees of a fuel company stole fuel oil worth more than a million dollars.

Study Results of One Store

A detective agency recently checked a store in the South and found 150 employees were stealing from the store. Think of it! Salesgirls, cashiers, and stockmen were all taking money and merchandise. In a single day 25 fraud refunds were detected. A salesclerk would wrap an expensive item and then hand it to a contact person. The contact would take it to the refund desk and pick up the cash. The money from the refund would be divided later between the salesclerk and the contact.

A man who picked up trash in an Ohio store worked thefts with nine porters. This group stole several thousand dollars worth of goods. The porters concealed high-priced merchandise in refuse cans; the cans were picked up daily with the trash. The stolen things were later sold to a fence.

Male employees working in a packing plant in Iowa were caught with refrigerated meat strapped around their waists. Workers in a Seattle plant took home thousands of dollars worth of tools. Records show that theft-minded men and women steal anything that is not nailed down.

Which Employee Steals?

The average dishonest employee usually has advanced to a position of trust. He is usually above average in ability and is ambitious to get ahead. He has shown himself willing to accept responsibility.

An employee usually begins stealing because of an emergency need for money. He looks on this first misstep as a "loan" that he will repay. Once he discovers it's easier to steal than it is to pay off these so-called loans, he's on the road to large-scale thefts.

What Has Caused the Increase in Employee Thefts?

Why this rise in dishonesty? One reason is the leadership example set by people in high places. As one thief put it, "All those big shots are getting theirs, why shouldn't I get mine?"

A chain store manager says, "The Santa Claus philosophy is at fault. This idea of something for nothing has been eating us ever since we've been told the government owes us a living."

Another cause is the fact that big business has eliminated the personal relationship between boss and worker. Although a person might not dream of taking a cent from an employer he calls by his first name, this same person will often steal, without any feeling of guilt, from an *impersonal* corporation.

The store management that fails to keep personal contact with people at all levels of the business causes many internal theft problems.

Another element is today's rise in prices and taxes. Inflation hits our pocketbooks. People who want to maintain a high standard of living often resort to thefts from their employer.

Four Major Factors

The Chicago Crime Commission looked over the cases of a dozen of the country's biggest bonding companies. They found four major factors in employee theft.

1. **Gambling.** Do you know a person who has been caught in the quicksand of the numbers pool or has bet heavily on the races? Some get involved with cards and indulge in heavy poker games. A man who loses money at gambling has difficulty recouping. Theft is one answer to the gambler's problem.

2. **High Living Standards.** Motivational advertising puts pressures on all of us. Many people want to have luxuries they can't afford. Advertising often overstimulates our working group. They expect to own a Cadillac, a $90,000-house, a swimming pool, and all the other things advertisers make so desirable. This excessive stimulation of new desires in the masses of our population is an important element in today's higher crime rates.

3. **Undesirable Associates.** There are some people in our society who have not found a good personal adjustment to life. Often they become involved with criminal elements. If these people work in a store, they can act as accomplices and the results can be devastating to the store.

4. **Inadequate Income.** Thefts can result from real need. For example, one man had a three-year-old girl who suffered from a rare type of eye cancer. A doctor told this man that his little girl's only chance was an eye

operation. The man, who was a department head in a men's clothing store, asked his boss for a loan. The loan was refused. This man needed money desperately. He started to destroy saleschecks and pocket cash. When finally caught he had taken over $2,500 for his little girl's operation.

In another case a salesman asked for a cost-of-living raise. It was refused. Each week, after the raise was turned down, he stole ten dollars from his sales, the amount of the raise he had requested.

Methods of Employee Thefts

Every cent of cash coming into your store passes through the hands of two or more employees. Unless you have good systems and enforce store controls, the people inside your company will take advantage of your carelessness. Because all the methods that can be used by employees to steal from a store are too numerous to mention, we'll cover only a few basics here.

How Employees Steal

1. Underringing the cash register. A clerk does not give the customer a sales receipt and pockets the difference.
2. Failing to ring up sales. Leaving the register drawer open, putting the money directly into the register without ringing a sale, and taking out the stolen money later in the day.
3. Ringing up "no sale" on the register or voiding a salescheck after the customer has left the department.
4. Giving a cut price to friends. Quoting items below retail value to friends in the store, relatives, or accomplices. In some cases, buying goods with the employee discount and then refunding them at full value.
5. Passing out merchandise across the counter to accomplices, friends, or relatives. To the observer it looks like a routine exchange or sale.
6. Swapping stolen merchandise with friends employed in other departments and in return getting other items stolen by them.
7. Hiding merchandise on her person or in her handbag or parcels. Taking it out of the store at lunch time or during relief periods. Using an unauthorized store exit.
8. Overcharging customers so that these cash overages can be stolen.
9. Stealing cash from a "common drawer" register.

10. Hiding goods in stairways, public lockers, corridors, and trash cans for later theft by the employee or an accomplice.
11. Stealing packages from the delivery truck.
12. Stealing from the warehouse through collusion between the warehouse foreman and/or other warehouse employees. Sometimes such a conspiracy includes a salesperson from the store. A salesperson furnishes a salescheck to an accomplice in the warehouse who uses it to send out stolen goods.
13. Stealing from the stockroom by putting goods on his person or in packages. May also steal from a delivery tank at rest in a hallway. Merchandise is also stolen from the return goods room, the layaway department, the hold room, etc.
14. False entries by the buyer to pad his inventory so that shortages will not be noticed.
15. Cashing bad checks for accomplices.
16. Making false entries in the store's books and records to conceal thefts.
17. Imposting on customer charge accounts. Holding a charge plate after a customer has made a purchase and then later making an imposted charge to this account by using the stolen plate.
18. Hiding small items of merchandise in a regular employee package.
19. Violating employee discount rules by giving "special" employee discounts to friends, accomplices, and contacts.
20. Giving fraudulent refunds to accomplices or putting through fictitious refunds on his own.
21. Putting on jewelry, scarves, or jackets to model while selling and later pretending to forget to take them off. Wearing them home and keeping the merchandise.
22. Shoplifting on lunch hours or relief periods.

Methods of Embezzlement

Employee thefts may range from the simple pocketing of an item of merchandise to the most intricate accounting manipulation. Following is a list of some of the more common methods used by employees to embezzle money:

1. The dishonest employee issues a check in payment of bills for a fictitious supplier. The check is sent to a prearranged address and later it's cashed through a dummy company or by faked endorsements.
2. Employee invoices goods above established prices and gets a cash kickback from the resource.

3. Raising the amount on checks, invoices, or vouchers after they have been officially approved.
4. Issuing and cashing checks for returned purchases not actually returned.
5. Pocketing the proceeds of cash sales and not recording the transaction.
6. Pocketing collections made on presumably uncollectable accounts (bad debts).
7. Pocketing small amounts from incoming payments on accounts and applying subsequent remittances on other items to cover the shortages (similar to bank check "kiting").
8. Forging checks and destroying them when returned by the bank. Then concealing these transactions by forced footings in the cash books or by raising the amounts of legitimate checks.
9. Overcharging customers and pocketing the difference.
10. Padding the payrolls as to the rates, time worked, or number of employees.
11. Failing to record returned purchases and stealing an equal amount of cash.
12. Paying creditors' invoices twice and appropriating the second check.
13. Stealing checks made payable to cash.
14. Increasing the amounts of creditors' debts and pocketing the excess or splitting it with the creditor.
15. Pocketing unclaimed wages.
16. Pocketing portions of collections made from customers and offsetting them on the books by improper credits for allowances or discounts.

What Can Be Done?

There are several things that can be done about employee thefts:

1. Screen all new employees to eliminate the abnormally psychotic person, the person with a criminal record, or the person who appears to be severely maladjusted.
2. Have good systems and controls. See to it that store rules are enforced at all times.
3. See that your supervisors set a good leadership example.
4. Have a tight control on employee packages.
5. Use honesty shopping for testing salespeople.
6. Have "employee observers" work in nonselling areas.
7. Establish before- and after-hour "plants" in high-loss areas.

8. Give special attention to employees who have excessive charges, garnishment on their salaries, are borrowing heavily, or who show any unusual signs of personality or financial weakness.
9. Observe activities of employees with marital difficulties, or those with alcoholic or other severe neurotic problems.
10. Strengthen your internal audit controls.
11. Make your supervisors alert to employee theft problems.
12. Have retraining classes for people who make numerous salescheck errors. Give help to employees who are weak in figures or in weighing or measuring. Where necessary, retrain personnel in proper handling of markdowns, loss reports, and damage and breakage reports.
13. Let the management of your branch stores know of any employees discharged for dishonesty. You don't want this employee to be able later to get a job in the branch store.
14. Check employees who arrive early or who stay after hours when there is no need for such early or late work.
15. Check packages found on delivery platforms, loading docks, and similar places to see that they have correct shipping labels.
16. Be sure you have a strong refund system. Check to see that it is being followed in practice as it is outlined in theory.
17. Be aware of the problems of theft "contamination." If you catch a dishonest employee, check on other people working near this person to see if there are any other employees in the department stealing. Dishonesty spreads; it is like a contagious disease.
18. Have a fixed policy for disposing of all dishonest employees. If any employee is caught stealing, you should have a policy of instant dismissal.

Failure to take decisive action or failure to be consistent in dishonest employee cases can have an adverse effect on your other employees. It can lead to increased dishonesty among all personnel.

Suggestions for Small Stores

Here are some suggestions for small stores in which only one office clerk is employed. This one person often combines all the functions of bookkeeping with the collection and disbursement of funds. Good internal control requires work to be divided so that there is little opportunity for inside theft without collusion.

In small stores the most practical method calls for the store manager to assume some of the duties of an internal auditor. This includes check of transactions, confirmation of items, and investigation of original documents. Where a store owner employs only one bookkeeper, it still is possible to have a program of internal audit to compensate for the lack of internal control. Such a program would have some of the following factors (many of these points apply equally well to larger stores):

1. All cash receipts should be deposited intact daily.
2. All disbursements should be by check, countersigned by the manager.
3. Each month the manager should personally reconcile the bank accounts.
4. On occasion, the manager should verify outgoing customer statements. Check them against the accounts receivable ledger and then mail them personally.
5. During the first few days of each month the manager should receive and open all of the incoming mail.
6. The manager should compare all cash receipts with the store books and with the deposits shown on his bank statement.
7. Someone other than the bookkeeper should do all of the receiving and shipping of merchandise.
8. Journal entries should receive the approval of the manager, especially if they have to do with sales allowances or bad debts.
9. The bookkeeper should be bonded for a suitable amount of money.
10. Be sure your mail is opened by a trusted employee other than the cashier or cash receivable bookkeeper.
11. Have the people who open the mail prepare a list of all mail received. Have it classified as to checks, money orders, and so forth. Compare this list regularly with the cash receipt book ledger.
12. Are your cash registers locked so that the salesperson cannot read the totals and later check her cash against the register total?
13. Are all of your refunds and saleschecks prenumbered?
14. Do you keep a control on all salesbooks and all refund books?
15. Do you record interest payments, rents, and other periodic nonsales income so that failure to get a receipt would be noticed and investigated?
16. Are you sure that someone other than the cashier or accounts receivable bookkeeper directly receives bank debit advices?
17. Be sure that the duties of your cashier, accounts receivable bookkeeper, and general bookkeeper are performed by different people. They are intended to act as a crosscheck against each other.
18. See to it that your cash is physically safeguarded.

19. Does your general bookkeeper maintain a detailed record of negotiable notes and securities and are the actual documents held by another person so that comparisons can be made periodically?
20. Are you careful about petty cash disbursements?
    a. Do you maintain a specific cash fund for small disbursements requiring currency?
    b. Is the fund of a type so that the cash and payout slips balance at all times?
    c. When the petty cash fund is reimbursed are all supporting vouchers examined and cancelled by an authorized person?
    d. Are all petty cash receipts in ink, dated and signed by the person receiving the money?
    e. Are original invoices obtained whenever possible?
    f. Are frequent unannounced inspections of the petty cash fund made by someone other than the usual custodian?

Check Distribution

1. Are all of your bank checks on safety paper, serially prenumbered and accounted for?
2. All of your checks should be written in permanent ink or by a checkwriting machine.
3. Be sure at time of signing that your checks are completed except for your signature and are accompanied by supporting documents on which the check number and payment date appear in ink.
4. You should always prohibit the drawing of checks to cash and also forbid the signing of any checks in advance.

Cash, Payrolls, and Merchandise

1. Are totals of cash disbursement journals periodically verified and compared to general books by people other than the cashier, accounts receivable bookkeeper, or person keeping the general books?
2. You should have an occasional audit of your pay rates and time worked calculations.
3. Occasionally, wages should be distributed to employees by the store manager.
4. Special care should be employed in the handling of your merchandise.
    a. All purchases should be authorized by a responsible person.
    b. All purchase invoices should be approved for payment only upon evidence of receipt of the merchandise.

c. The receipt of merchandise should be in written form and numerically controlled.
d. Your purchasing, receiving, and storeroom functions should all be performed by different people who are held responsible for shortages and overages in their area.

5. Purchases and sales invoices should be checked for the following:
   a. Quantity received or shipped
   b. Prices
   c. Terms
   d. Shipping charges
   e. Additions and extensions
   f. Dates (on purchase invoices to prevent reuse or alterations)
6. All accommodation purchases for employees should be properly billed.
7. Returns to manufacturer should be based on written authorization only and should be properly accounted for.
8. Selling prices should be clearly set. Any exceptions to the standard pricing formula should require special authorization.
9. All credits and return goods should be approved by responsible persons.
10. In addition to perpetual inventories, periodic unannounced counts should be made by employees other than the people operating in the department being checked.
11. Be sure to place responsibility for shortages or overages of inventory. See to it that all adjustments for inventory differences are approved by responsible people.
12. Monthly bank statements and cancelled checks should be reconciled to your general books by people other than the people who keep the cash records.
13. Cancelled checks should be examined for signatures and endorsements and the checks returned to the bank where necessary. Note deposit dates shown on the bank statements as compared to deposit dates shown by your records of cash receipts.
14. Check discount allowances to see if they are contrary to terms of sale as approved by responsible officials.
15. Be sure that all credits to accounts other than those arising out of cash remittances and cash discounts are approved by people in authority other than the cashier or accounts receivable bookkeeper.
16. The writing off of bad debts should be authorized only by one responsible person.
17. Keep careful control of your records of bad debts that are less than three years old.

18. At least once each year you should have a mailing of customer statements that is checked to see that it agrees with the accounts receivable records. This mailing should be under the control of someone other than the cashier or accounts receivable bookkeeper.
19. Be sure that all employees who handle securities or other valuables are bonded for a sufficient amount.
20. Require all employees to take vacations, and have their duties during that period performed by other employees.
21. Be sure all accounting methods, routines, and systems are detailed in manuals.
22. Have physical safeguards for all important records.

Other General Controls

Employee Package Controls. Dishonest employees attempting to steal merchandise will often use an unauthorized exit door. Surveillance should be made of these unauthorized exits from time to time to see if employees are taking out packages either during their lunch or relief period. They may also be leaving 10 or 15 minutes prior to store closing via an unauthorized exit.

By placing people at these doors who know the employees, such a dishonest employee can be spotted and stopped. All packages should be opened and checked. Have a written rule that any employee using an unauthorized exit is subject to dismissal.

Another weak spot in employee package control occurs on nights with late openings. On days when your store is open until late in the evening, a certain number of employees usually work early hours and leave the store around 5:30 P.M. These employees should leave by the authorized exit.

The dishonest employee can use this early hour exit as an opportunity to go out a customer door with stolen merchandise. On nights when the store has late openings, a spot check should be made of customer doors to see if dishonest employees are going out unauthorized exits.

The same early exit problem often applies to maintenance or other employees who work a schedule calling for them to leave the store before regular closing time.

Inventory Shortages. Official inventories are the store's basic shortage control. If an inventory is correctly taken, it shows the results of all actions of security and other store departments during a season. The security manager should be familiar with every record that produces the inventory.

Inventory results should be studied by the security manager as an important phase of his job. He should make comparisons with other stores, department by department, to see what the national trends are and to see in what areas his store is out of line. Inventory figures should also be reviewed with the shortage controller.

Certain departments are known as high-shortage areas, costume jewelry and sportswear, for example. High shortages in such departments can be expected more than in the furniture department or major appliances. By watching the history of shortages in a department over a period of time, the security manager can discover where investigative action is needed.

In departments that appear to have serious theft problems, the security manager, in cooperation with the shortage controller and the head of internal audit, should set up a program of combined effort to reduce these losses. In such a program, every phase of the department's operation should be checked.

This investigation should be carried out on the selling floor, in the stock area, warehouse, delivery, receiving and marking, and so on. There should be temporary controls installed on every part of the department's operation. Such controls may not reveal where the shortage problem is, but they will often bring the high shortages back into line.

Inventory shortages, when caused by theft, are usually the result of internal dishonesty. Therefore, controls should be designed to prevent employee thefts.

It is also helpful in high-shortage departments to shift buyers and other personnel to see if shortages are the result of poor administration. Usually, good shortage results follow good executives. Poor administrators, on the other hand, usually have poor inventory showings no matter what department they operate.

Control of Fitting Rooms. Although we mentioned fitting room controls in another chapter, they are important enough to review here. We think of shoplifters as being people from outside the store, but employees can also shoplift on their lunch hour or during their relief period. Fitting room controls are meant to check shoplifting by employees as well as by outsiders.

During selling hours, many stores employ fitting room checkers. This is a control used according to the nature of the merchandise being handled. A checker monitors every customer entering or leaving the fitting room area. This control can be done with numbered discs or by a tally sheet. However it is managed, the fitting room checker counts the garments the customer has when she enters the fitting room and checks to be sure she has the same number of garments when she leaves.

Some stores use other methods for controlling their fitting rooms. One good method is to assign a maid, hostess, or stock person to continually clear the fitting rooms of excess merchandise.

In some stores security has regular fitting room patrols. Detectives go through the fitting rooms calling attention to garments left in the rooms. They turn these garments over to the department supervisor for follow-up. Such patrols can be done on an hourly basis.

When there is undue carelessness by salespeople, a report of the garments found can be given to the merchandise manager for follow-up. In some stores, salespeople are assigned individual fitting rooms. If garments are left in a fitting room, the salesperson is held accountable. Continued carelessness can result in dismissal.

After selling hours, a check of the fitting rooms can be made by night security to see if they are being used for theft purposes at night.

A fitting room check system known as the "last and the first" is frequently used. A round is made of all fitting rooms in the store by a night watchman or investigator one hour after store closing. At this time anything left in the fitting rooms is taken out. Another patrol is made 30 minutes before store opening to see if the fitting rooms have been used since the last check.

Sometimes such a patrol will discover early hour employees trying on garments in a darkened area. If this occurs, the people should be questioned. Whatever system you choose, some type of fitting room control is essential for cutting losses.

Critical Hours. Crucial hours for store security are the first hour after store closing and the last hour before store opening. Many dishonest employees steal during these periods.

During these times special attention should be given to employees loitering in selling or nonselling areas. This can be done by staggering the work hours of floor detectives and investigators. Have two groups, one scheduled to come in an hour early, the other scheduled to stay a half hour after closing. The late group is assigned to make a complete patrol of fitting rooms during the first hour after store closing. The early morning group makes the same kind of check during the hour prior to store opening. When first tried, these patrols often detect dishonest employee activity.

Daily Cash Bag Overage. As a created systems check, plant an overage of $5 or $10 in the daily cash bag assigned to a suspected salesperson. If she fails to report the overage have her shopped by the honesty shoppers.

An Inventory Shortage Committee. Some stores have found it worthwhile for a committee of executives from several store divisions to review shortage problems each month.

This inventory shortage committee should include the security head, personnel manager, credit department head, internal audit head, inventory shortage controller, merchandise manager, delivery supervisor, receiving and marketing supervisor, warehouse manager, and the wrapping and packing supervisor.

This committee should work year round on special projects to find soft spots in the store's operations that might lead to losses. They should make studies and then suggest methods for improving store systems, controls, and supervision. A good inventory shortage committee can improve the entire store operation.

Special Counts. This is a simple method for checking high-loss departments to see if items are being stolen at night. It can also be used to check departments that are reporting things missing overnight.

Assign a detective to work in cooperation with the department supervisor. Have him select several racks of goods and make a unit count at store closing time. This count is held until the next morning when the racks are rechecked shortly before store opening. If losses show up in the morning count, you may want to ask night security to make one or two unit counts of the same racks during the night to narrow down the time of loss. Once the time of theft is found, a detective can be put in the department as a "plant" during the critical hour to catch the thief.

From Receiving and Marking to Selling Areas. High-shortage departments should check in all goods received from the receiving and marking area. The merchandise should have a copy of the packing slip attached to it showing how many items are being sent to the selling floor. A person in the selling department should count the goods being received to see if the number of units coincides with the number listed on the packing slip.

Goods are often stolen in transit between the receiving and marking room and the selling department, especially smaller items that can be easily concealed. Theft can also occur if the merchandise is desirable to stockboys, porters, and so on. A unit count of merchandise delivered to the selling department will show if any such thefts are taking place.

Control Employee Doors. Every store should have a pass system for checking early and late employees. In one store, failure to have a door control resulted in two former employees (previously stockboys) getting into the store unnoticed at 7:30 in the morning. These two boys stole over $2,000 worth of men's clothing on this one morning visit. They put their loot into suitcases and shopping bags and took them out of the store shortly after the customer doors were opened for business.

No one should enter your store during nonselling hours without a door pass. Any employee leaving your store more than 30 minutes after closing time should also have a pass. If anyone leaving the building after hours has no pass, then this person should be required to show identification. A report should be made to the department manager of any employee staying after store hours without permission. You should have a firm rule that no one may enter your store before regular store hours without an approved pass.

If your store does not have a good control on people who are authorized to come into the store before or after hours, you may find that there are several people staying late or coming in early in the morning without authority. These people may very likely be doing this in order to steal merchandise.

Surveillance of Critical Areas. Make a surveillance of loss areas from time to time. Good spots for surveillance are central wrapping desks, loading docks, stockrooms, and high-shortage departments.

Plants are often long, tiresome, and time-consuming, but they are very successful in detecting dishonest employees.

Controls of Workmen. Quite a few stores have a control on workmen entering and leaving the building. They require all packages brought into the building to be checked into a package checkroom located at the entrance. They also have the men open their tool and lunch boxes for inspection when leaving. Before any store attempts such a check they should consult with union officials, if a union is involved, and it should also be cleared with the store attorneys.

Salespeople Surveillance. This is an excellent way to get leads for shopping tests. This control is based on the theory that if money is to be taken from a register, or if packages of stolen goods are to be prepared for carrying home, there is a likelihood that such activities will take place just before opening and just after store closing.

To detect such activities, observation of a selling department is made just before opening and just after store closing. Such observation produces good results. High-shortage departments should be selected and a good physical arrangement made so that the area can be watched.

Wrapping Department. Created system checks should be made to see if the wrapper will package items without a sales check. Failure to conform to store rules should be followed up vigorously; otherwise you have a loophole for employee theft.

Measuring Yard Goods. Although it is not always meant to be dishonest, some salespeople have a tendency to give liberal measurements of yard goods so that they can attract more customers. Others are simply inaccurate.

Measuring machines themselves often get out of kilter. One store found in a survey that 67 out of a total of 72 yardage measuring machines were inaccurate in measuring yard goods.

As a check on this shortage problem, periodically take all yard goods packages in delivery and make a spot check of the yardage lengths. If errors are found, make a report for the merchandise manager. A periodic check on the accuracy of your yardage control machines is also important. Any clerk who shows a series of careless yardage measurements should have a corrective interview.

Parked Cars and Night Personnel. The checking of parked cars, especially cars parked around the store at night, will often reveal large-scale thefts. This should be handled by your night security head and a detective from the city police department. It should be done without prior notice, and it should occur at different hours of the night.

First learn the identity of cars belonging to store personnel. This can be done by observation or by a check of license plates. Particular attention should be given to parked cars of night watchmen, the night store superintendent, and other supervisory personnel. These people should also be observed when they leave the store to see if the regular package checking procedure is followed.

When a watchman leaves his shift and carries a package with him, it should be checked by another watchman. Actually, there is little reason for people working at night to take packages out of the building. Any packages brought to work should be held at the entrance and be returned when the employee leaves.

If a watchman comes on duty at midnight and leaves early in the morning before the store opens, the mere existence of a package of any kind is highly suspect. One store had two watchmen on the midnight shift who checked each other in and out with stolen merchandise. The thefts of these two men were substantial.

Check of Delivery Trucks. It is expensive and difficult to follow and observe your store's delivery trucks. However, if your store has its own delivery service you need this type of control.

Such an observation will do several things. It gives you a chance to check on the speed and careful driving habits of your truck drivers. It also stops irregularities such as visits to bars, malingering, gathering of drivers in each other's homes, visits to the driver's own home, and other unauthorized stops. Of greatest value to security is the fact it also reveals the delivery of stolen goods.

Markdowns. Markdown checks are important in inventory shortage figures. It has long been felt by security people that a substantial portion of the "book" value of inventory losses is due to the negligent or deliberate failure of buyers to take proper markdowns. A spot check can reduce this source of inventory error.

One method of checking is to make periodic visits to a high-shortage department. Merchandise showing a marked down price tag is taken off the selling floor to the buyer's office. A request is then made to see the actual markdown sheet showing this merchandise. Any failure of these figures to check out indicates a manipulation of markdowns.

Relationship of Flash and Audited Sales Reports. Whenever discussing shortages with a buyer, you should ask, "Are you satisfied that your audited sales figures correlate properly with your flash sales reports?" If there is a wide discrepancy between these two figures, an investigation should be made. The cause of this difference may be any one of several things:

1. Addition errors by sales clerks.
2. Tabulating errors.
3. Refunds and credits going through an audit that the buyer does not know about. (Bureau of adjustment credits, for example, which are perhaps being passed by a dishonest person in the bureau of adjustment.)
4. Refunds and credits going through auditing on days different from the day on which they are deducted on the flash sales.

Check Advertised Items Against Markdown Book. This is another control for spotting a careless markdown operation. Early in the morning on the sale day, make a check of the quantity of items being offered on the selling floor. Check this figure against the number of such items listed in the buyer's markdown book.

Test Sales Price on Nonmarked Goods. A lot of goods are bulk-marked, and individual items don't have price tags. This can cause shortages.

Shoppers should occasionally test contingent and part-time salespeople to see if they are quoting the correct price. The shopper should make a purchase of a nonmarked item and later determine if the price charged was correct.

Test C.O.D. Packages. Send out a C.O.D. package without writing it on the route sheet. Later make a follow-up to see if the driver collected the money and check to see if he paid in the C.O.D. money.

Employee Discounts. Inventory errors can result from failure to take markdowns for employee discounts. Make shopping tests of employees to see if your salespeople are asking for passes that authorize discounts; also see if the clerks are recording the discount amount. Failure to record the sale as a discount will give the department a shortage.

Early Deliveries. Some stores have early morning deliveries of bread, milk, butter, and baked goods to the cafeterias. Some also have dirty laundry picked up; others have trash taken out of the building. In all cases, spot checks of these visits by tradesmen should be made. Surveillances should be made to see if thefts are occurring.

Large-scale thefts have often gone undetected when a delivery person has acted in collusion with a dishonest employee. Merchandise has been stolen by being taken out of the store hidden in trash or in a pile of dirty laundry. In one store a shoe salesman stole $12,000 worth of shoes by working in collusion with a milk delivery man. Each day the salesman put several pairs of new shoes into the cafeteria's empty milk cans. The cans and stolen shoes were picked up by the morning milkman. It was an easy method of theft.

Sacks of dirty linen offer an excellent hiding place for stolen merchandise. Periodically inspect the sacks of soiled linen being taken out of your store. Arrangements for spot checks should be made with the head of the linen supply company and other pickup companies, such as those that handle your trash and garbage. These company managers should advise their employees that they will be subject to occasional inspection whenever they enter your store premises.

Review Allowance Refunds. From time to time it's a good practice to pull all of a department's adjustment and allowance refunds. The very nature of an allowance refund is suspicious; it furnishes an easy way for a dishonest employee to steal.

If the allowance refund is found to be legitimate on investigation, a check should also be made to determine whether a markdown has been taken.

When allowances and adjustments are made in the bureau of adjustment, markdowns are generally taken automatically. However, some stores have a system that permits salespeople to issue such refunds and service managers or buyers to authorize them. In such cases, the system requires the buyer to take the markdown. If action is not taken immediately it is often forgotten, thus causing an inventory shortage.

Credit Union Loans. Special arrangements should be made between the security department and the store credit union so that all employee requests for loans are checked by the security manager. In this way, the credit union will not have an uncollectable loan on its hands if the security department is about to apprehend a particular dishonest employee. It is surprising how many times dishonest employees are found to be indebted to the store or credit union.

The security department should also shop salespeople applying for loans. A spot check of their employee packages is also advisable. People under economic pressure may be tempted to steal.

Furniture Sales. In some stores it is possible for a dishonest salesperson to steal furniture. The salesman sells furniture to an accomplice and has the salescheck stamped "paid." He then changes the warehouse copy of the salescheck by adding a list of additional furniture through the carbon. This "extra" furniture is then delivered without question and, of course, without being paid for. Check your furniture controls for this type of theft.

Bonding Card. Some stores request an applicant to make out a "bonding request" card at the time of employment. In one Milwaukee store, the application asks if the applicant has ever been convicted of any crime.

Stores using bonding request cards claim that this system eliminates many thieves, burglars, and embezzlers at the point of employment.

Packing Error Check. It has been found that an alert packer can catch many types of errors. One store has a "packing error system" in which a packer is given ten cents for each error detected.

Such errors include failure to total the salescheck properly, incorrect number of items listed on the salescheck in relation to the goods given to the packer for wrapping, damaged merchandise, and so forth. This control improves the selling operation, prevents losses, and reduces customer complaints.

Employee Saleschecks. With cycle billing, the control of employee saleschecks can be a problem. In one store, for example, there are more than a hundred employees working in the audit area. All these people have access to the cycle-billing files. In order to overcome the danger of these people destroying their own saleschecks, this store has a periodic control.

Without the knowledge of the employees working in the cycle-billing area, audit periodically takes all the store's saleschecks and removes the charge purchases of the people who work in the cycle-billing area. These saleschecks are photographed on microfilm. After being recorded on film, the checks are put back into the regular flow of salescheck operation. At a later date, a check is made against each employee's account to see if the photographed checks were properly posted.

Many stores have learned too late that cycle billing is wide open to employee dishonesty. An employee who works in the cycle-billing area can go to the selling floor and make charge purchases and then return to the cycle-billing department and wait for her saleschecks to come through. By lingering for a moment at lunch time, or by coming in a few minutes early in the morning, this employee can take her saleschecks out of the cycle-billing file and destroy them. Such thefts have gone undetected for years.

Stores who have cycle billing and do not have a control on the saleschecks of employees working in the area are gambling heavily on human nature. Every store needs some type of control in this area.

Night Audit of Registers. Are the change banks of your salespeople left in cash register drawers overnight? If so, your auditing department should make periodic audits of each drawer to see if there are any shortages. Clerks who have a shortage should be given as leads to the security department for honesty shopping tests.

Sealing Trucks. Many stores today use railroad seals to protect goods in trucks moving between stores or warehouses. To check the effectiveness of your sealing system you should occasionally remove the normal seal after the truck is en route. Replace it with a substitute seal as a created systems check.

If the person who checks the seal at the receiving end does not report the variation in seal number, then you will know that your control system is not being operated as planned. Presentation of the correct serial number is a dramatic method of education. It reminds your people to do a more conscientious job of operating this control.

"Hold" Merchandise. Floor detectives should make regular investigations of hold areas in each selling department. There should be a supporting document on every piece of merchandise being held.

People can be tempted to steal because of a department's sloppy housekeeping. Night security should occasionally go through an entire department, pulling out all merchandise and packages that seem misplaced or questionable. Such checking not only uncovers leads on dishonest employees but also results in better housekeeping.

Alteration Department. Check the alteration rooms. How are garments received? Determine if systems are being followed. One point to be noted is whether employees are altering personal garments without an alteration card or other record.

Alteration procedures should be watched closely because this is an easy way for a dishonest employee to get merchandise out of the store. Careless operation of controls may allow an employee in the selling department to send a garment to the alteration department for alteration and then have it sent to an outside address on a COM (customers own merchandise) salescheck. Cross reference all saleschecks and alteration cards.

Cleaning and Pressing Operations. If your store does cleaning and pressing on the premises, there should be a control to insure that all garments are sent back to the selling department after cleaning or pressing. When a department manager sends dresses with lipstick on them to the cleaning and pressing department for rehabilitation, does he know whether all of these garments come back to his selling area? Have a check-back system. Failure to have adequate controls here opens the way for theft by people in the cleaning and pressing workrooms.

Wrapping Desks. Your wrapping and packing supervisor should occasionally step into a packing area and check wrapped packages to see that all orders have been correctly filled. He should check to see if the merchandise conforms in quantity and price to the salescheck. This spot check can also reveal any irregularities such as the wrapper who sends out unauthorized merchandise. Every package should contain a salescheck copy that matches the contents of the package.

Some stores make this control inspection by picking off packages just prior to their transfer to the delivery department.

Locker Controls. Spot checks should be made of public lockers. A regular inspection should be made by the locker attendant for "left" merchandise with a view to seeing if any of it appears to be stolen.

Have a night security investigator check lockers at closing time to determine which lockers are in use. Another check at midnight and one early in the morning will show if any additional locker keys have been removed. If so, such a locker should be inspected. It has been found that some dishonest night employees conceal stolen goods in lockers to be removed the next day during normal store hours.

Mail Procedures. A created system check should be made by occasionally inserting money into the incoming mail. This is done to see if such money is being properly recorded by people in the mailroom. One method is to insert money in payment of a charge account that is nonexistent. The purpose of this check is to determine if the cash gets from the mailroom to the accounts receivable department.

Management's Obligation

Losses cannot be computed purely in terms of dollars and cents. In many instances—perhaps the majority—an individual would not have become dishonest if reasonable, precautionary methods had been exercised. To take steps that will successfully prevent this kind of dishonesty may save many lives from ruin.

This, of course, is only one reason why stores should have modern, well-staffed retail security departments. A good security department not only protects the store's profits, but also the store's greatest asset, *its people.*

Every employer has a moral responsibility to his employees to remove as much of the temptation to steal as is humanly possible. He should see that employees are decently paid, given reasonable working conditions, and in short, are convinced that their welfare is constantly on his mind.

An elderly banker in Indiana has his own method of coping with the employee theft problem. When he hires a new cashier he hands the newcomer a handwritten note, which says, "Handling other people's money is fraught with peril for the handler—no man is above temptation. But we are all in this struggle for decency and integrity together, and we need one another's help. So if you are ever tempted, come to me and we will talk things over. Always remember that being a person you yourself can be proud of is a thousand times more important than all the money in all the banks in the world."

Correct Employees' Errors

Store management has a responsibility to its people. If a department manager cautions salespeople and nonselling personnel about errors that they make and if he corrects his people when they violate store rules or policies, his personnel will quite often not take the chance of stealing. They would be afraid that they would be caught just as they were caught when violating company rules. As one dishonest employee put it, "My boss never checked up on me and I began to feel that there was no risk involved in stealing from the company, that's why I started to steal."

When I interview anyone about the theft of money I always ask the person to tell me in his own words the reason for the theft. I've found in almost every instance that employees start to steal because of laxity in enforcing store rules on the part of the people who have the responsibility for supervision and enforcement.

If you really want to prevent theft in your store, then you must compel the people who supervise to see to it that the rules and policies of your organization are strictly followed. The reason you have these rules is to prevent dishonesty. When you get the people who are, in reality, their brother's keeper to see to it that the people under them follow the rules, you will not only minimize theft but you will also prevent many good people from becoming thieves and you will enable people to like themselves better.

Correct the Cause

You will never be able to stop theft in a retail store until you correct the cause of theft, and *the cause is carelessness or laxity in supervision.* In each department and in each area of your store someone has the responsibility for supervision. This is the primary thing that keeps most people honest.

For example, when a salesperson fails to give a customer a receipt, a rule of your store has been violated, and unless you insist upon observance of that rule, you are inviting that salesperson to steal.

Determine "How" an Employee Stole

The apprehension of dishonest employees will do little good if each case is not carefully reviewed to find out *how* the employee stole and *why* the employee stole. If the case points up any failure in your store's systems, controls, or supervision, this inadequacy should be corrected.

Many times dishonest employees are taken out of a department, one after the other, week after week, which means that the situation in this department breeds dishonesty. Management failure is *causing* people to steal. Until you change the situation, the people in that department will continue to steal.

The best way to prevent theft from a store is to *remove the opportunity to steal.* The best way to do this is by insisting on strict enforcement of all store rules. One of the big problems we have in retailing today is the fact that we are negligent in correcting employees. We do not enforce the rules and policies. We do not run our systems as they were intended to be run.

Correction of employees has almost stopped in the retail business *because many supervisors haven't the courage to correct the people who are working for them!*

If your store rules are observed at all times, you will have a healthier organization. All your people will feel better about the store and they will feel better about themselves.

Conclusion

In this chapter we have covered some of the many methods that can be used to prevent and detect dishonesty among store employees. You should keep in mind there are three *basic* approaches to the dishonest employee problem:

1. Careful screening of all new personnel at the point of employment.
2. Good systems and controls with adequate checks and follow-up to see that they are operating as planned.
3. High standards of supervisory leadership. Good leadership sets a good example and enforces store rules.

Try applying these three elements. If you do, your problems of internal theft will be greatly reduced.

Chapter 6

SPOTTING THE HIGH-RISK EMPLOYEE

Most of us develop wrong ideas about the type of employee who steals. Too often we feel it is only NEW employees who steal. But the facts indicate this is erroneous.

Which Employee Steals?

A study by Continental Casualty Insurance of their fidelity claims showed that on the average:

> A dishonest employee has worked for a company for 6 years, 5 months, before he starts to steal.
> And how long does he steal before he's caught? 3 years, 2 months.

So there you have it. The average dishonest employee is caught only after working 9 years and 7 months. He began his stealing from the store after he had worked 6 years and 5 months, and he got away with it for 3 years and 2 months before he was tripped up.

It's also interesting to note that the average age of the dishonest employee when caught is 35 (see Figure 6.1). Only 7 percent of those caught are women. Men dominate the picture; 93% of the dishonest employees caught were men.

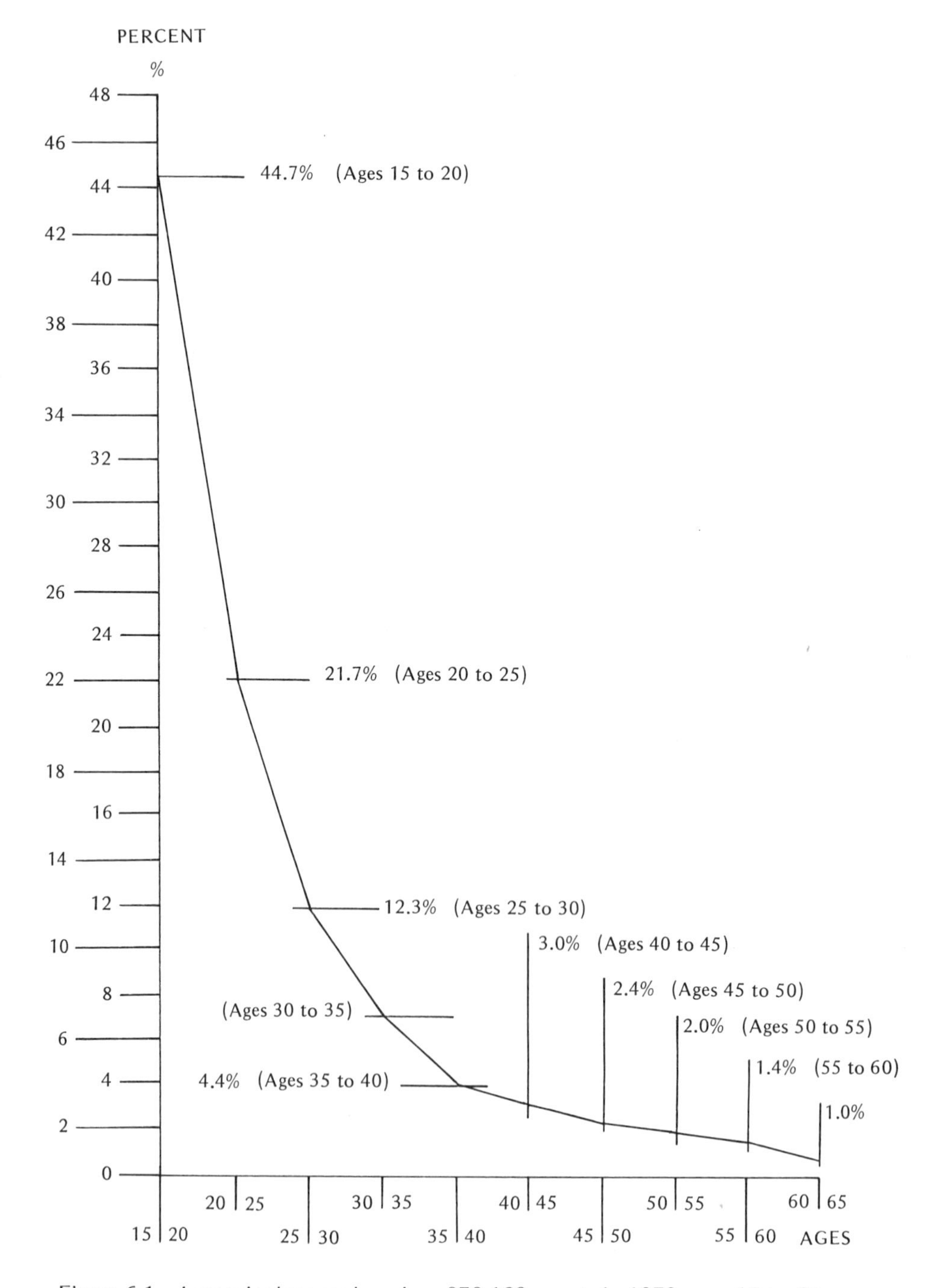

Figure 6.1. Larcenies by age: based on 878,129 arrests in 1978, ages 15 to 65. (From FBI Uniform Crime Report.)

The Seven Clues

The person living above his means is an obvious clue to a high-risk employee. Many other clues are less obvious and therefore likely to be overlooked. Over the years, studies have shown that there are seven clues to high-risk employees:

1. *Living Beyond Means.* Such a person must have some kind of additional income; it may be from your profits.
2. *Serious Debts.* Employees caught in a vice between creditors will often try to satisfy the wolves howling at their door by dipping into the store profits.
3. *Gambling.* Someone has to pay the piper. Every person who is a chronic gambler is more willing to take a chance on horses, numbers, and store merchandise.
4. *Liquor.* People who drink heavily have serious psychological problems and pressures; liquor quiets their nerves and clouds their judgment, thus making stealing easier.
5. *Questionable Associates.* This is self-explanatory. Store merchandise can easily find its way outside to a friendly "fence."
6. *Eager Beavers.* The overeager employees who work early and late may be attempting to assuage a guilty conscience and create an honesty image to cover their thefts.
7. *Award Winners.* A large number of clerks who are able to spot shoplifters are actually stealing themselves.

Why an Employee Steals

The three most common reasons for employee stealing:

1. Living beyond their income
2. Gambling, liquor, and questionable associates
3. Serious debts, illness, and hospital bills

(All of these factors can be misfortunes that put the employee under emotional and financial pressure. Some financial pressures, however, can develop because a person lacks the ability to handle money in a practical fashion.)

Psychopaths

About 18 percent of the dishonest employees caught are found to be psychopathic or "criminal types." These people are the major thieves and their thefts often involve several thousands of dollars. They have one unique quality in common, which makes it possible to spot them and screen them out at the point of employment—*they have an abnormal LACK of fear.* Dr. Harrison Gough, head of the Psychology Department at the University of California, has developed a successful true and false test of 64 questions to screen out these types of delinquents at the point of employment. The test asks questions such as:

"Have you ever wanted to run away and join a circus?"

"Have you any fear of deep water?"

"Have you ever wanted to join a motorcycle club?"

And so on, questions that reveal the person with little normal sense of fear.

An interesting fact regarding the psychopathic type is that they can take a preemployment polygraph screening test and often come through with a clean record, even though they may have served time in prison. The reason, of course, is apparent. Because they have a distorted lack of normal fears, they do not respond on the polygraph test and therefore sometimes slip through such screening tests.

Financial Problems

Financial pressures, of course, come from a variety of causes. Unusual family expenses such as medical bills or some type of personal catastrophe account for 15 percent of the employee theft cases.

Another type of debt is caused by "women trouble." These debts are often the problem of the man who has remarried and is trying to support two families. Or, of course, the married man who is "running around" and has the added costs of jewels, motels, and entertaining expenses.

Then there are debts caused by extravagant living—expensive clothes, jewelry, automobiles, and so on. This is most often a problem with women and accounts for 43 percent of the female dishonesty.

Again, management should not be blind to any woman working for the store who has overly expensive clothes or jewelry. One store manager was unconcerned when the cashier showed up one day at work wearing a new $2,500 diamond ring. A year later and many thousands of dollars poorer he finally discovered that she was stealing cash while working in the money room. If he had been awake when he saw that telltale ring, he would have saved his store many thousands of lost dollars.

Debts can also come from family expenses, particularly for women who are divorced and are struggling to pay for the cost of bringing up and educating children; or the women whose mate is an alcoholic or unemployed because of injury or disability. These family expenses are the cause of 17 percent of the women workers who steal.

The psychopathic personality accounts for about 16 percent of the female cases, and another 13 percent are caused by men who talk women into stealing and who share in the proceeds from their thefts.

Gambling

Not enough emphasis has been placed on the problem of employee gambling as a cause of dishonesty. A store in Florida was suffering a 4.3 percent shortage and a security survey revealed that a porter made a daily tour of the store to pick up bets by employees. In addition, the store's receiving manager took bets on the dog races from employees.

Management knew what was going on, but the manager just shrugged it off. "That ten-cent bet on a number isn't going to lead any employee to steal from us," he said. How wrong he was. As a result of a security study, recommendations were made to discharge employees who were taking bets and all employees were warned that betting on company property and during work hours would be cause for dismissal. With the end of gambling, shortages decreased. In six months shortages had dropped to 1.6 percent and in a year they were below 1 percent.

Crime specialists believe that the cause of employee thefts—in order of their importance—is:

1. Gambling
2. Heavy debts—extravagant living
3. Undesirable associates
4. Low wages

Gambling, as we can see, was cited as the number one cause of employee thefts. Why? Because gambling changes the philosophy of the person who gambles. He no longer believes in earning the things he wants. He comes to strive for "something for nothing."

Gambling leads to an "easy come, easy go" attitude that soon eats away at all parts of the employee's life. He is apt to become a reckless driver, may increase a drinking habit, and is also more willing to "take a chance" and steal merchandise or money. *Gambling makes any employee a high-risk person.*

Eager Beavers

Do you have an employee who always shows up for work a half hour or an hour early? One who pitches right in to straighten out the stock and clean up, long before other employees show up for work? Such a person is a high-risk employee. Why? Because the eager beavers who show up early or work late after the others have started homeward are often trying to salve their consciences, or are trying to build a favorable image in the boss's mind so he won't suspect them of stealing.

It Takes a Thief

Do you have anyone on your staff who has a particular knack for spotting shoplifters?

Recently a store manager told a workshop group about a night porter who had come into work an hour or so early on several evenings and had spotted an errant housewife or two shoplifting. This porter had a great reputation with management; they felt he was a man of great honesty and integrity. In fact once he had turned in a register receipt bag found next to a register where it had been carelessly left by a clerk hurrying home for dinner.

After the manager told the workshop about this porter, who was a paragon of virtue, I advised him to keep an eye on him. The signs indicated he might be stealing.

The manager protested, but finally agreed. A week later I heard from him. He phoned in a shaky voice to tell me that they had caught the porter and his pal taking a car trunk full of merchandise out of the store at 2 A.M. This porter admitted thefts of $4,000.

Years of experience have shown that a large number of employees who are good at spotting shoplifters are themselves stealing from the store.

To catch a thief you have to be thinking about the problem of stealing. The clerk concerned with stocking a shelf or waiting on a customer does not spot a thief because his or her mind is occupied with the job at hand. But the clerk who is stealing from the store is *thinking* about stealing a lot of the time and therefore notices the shoplifter. People who frequently detect shoplifters are themselves high-risk employees.

A Simple Technique

You might not think you could solve some important crimes by using a simple 3 × 5 note card. But you can indeed.

Take a 3 × 5 card and jot down this list of seven "clues" to theft-prone employees;

1. Living beyond means
2. Serious debts
3. Gambling
4. Liquor
5. Questionable associates
6. Eager beavers
7. Award winners

Keep this card as a checklist. Put it in your calendar for the first day of each month, and on that day take it out and look it over before you replace it in the calendar on the first day of the next month. Ask yourself—and take the time to think about it, too—"Do I have anyone on my staff who fits into any of these high-risk categories?"

If you do have such a person on your staff, have him tested several times by honesty shoppers, have his packages checked out at night, or keep him under some type of surveillance; in other words, give him some special supervisory attention. And do it now—before he becomes a serious supervisory headache.

Teenage Employees May Also Be a High Risk

Statistics suggest that many teenagers are poor risks as employees in terms of honesty. The chart showing annual larceny arrests by age group tends to indicate young people from ages 15 through 19 are a higher larceny risk than older people.

Does this mean the retailer shouldn't employ teenagers? Not necessarily. But it does mean that these young people, if they are employed, should not be the major kind of staff people used. They should be part of an age mix that includes sufficient older personnel to help balance the risk of using young people. The statistics also suggest it is wise to have older people supervise teenage workers, and that a wise management won't put teenagers in jobs where they face an excessive temptation to steal.

Frustration

Most important of all, the person hiring store personnel should screen teenagers carefully to insure that the person being considered for employment has a mature attitude and is able to handle normal on-the-job frustrations.

The reason why teenagers dominate the larceny arrest figures is probably because many theft-related crimes result from a person unable to cope with frustration.

Since frustration is the major underlying cause of much employee stealing, it must be kept in mind that teenagers tend to suffer more frustration than do older workers. As people grow older, most of them learn how to handle frustration successfully. In fact the word "maturity" can be defined as "the ability to cope with frustration." Teenagers often have not had enough life experiences to cope with frustration properly and as a result emotional pressure builds up inside the individual that may finally result in antisocial behavior such as vandalism and theft.

Motivation for Theft

Teenagers who steal are motivated by a variety of needs. In some instances it is an urgent need to prove themselves to their peer group—to show how smart they are or how much courage they possess.

The teenager is also tempted to get something for nothing or enjoy the physical and emotional thrill of the theft experience. The objective of the teenage thief is seldom the merchandise itself, but rather the emotional drive and reactions involved in the experience of stealing. Witness to this is the fact that teenagers seldom use the stolen merchandise but tend to hide it in the back of their closet or under the things in their bureau drawer.

Teenage Experiments in Crime are a Passing Phase

This teenage experiment in crime is usually a passing phase that the individual grows out of. As the individual becomes saturated with the emotional experiences surrounding the thefts, the thrill becomes less enticing. And as the individual grows older, new abilities for dealing with frustration are developed. As these people learn to cope with the problems of life, they move on to a mature pattern of behavior leaving their teenage experiments far behind.

The personnel interviewer needs to screen each teenager carefully to try and determine the individual's level of maturity and should not reject young people simply because they are young. True, the statistics about crimes by young people are frightening, but keep in mind they are also more likely to be caught stealing than are adults, which tends to help balance the statistics against them. In addition, we need to realize that immaturity is not confined to teenagers. Many people who are much older also have not learned how to cope with frustration and are just as poor employment risks.

Use Checklist as a Guide

Don't assume that because an employee is on the checklist of high-risk people that this person *is* stealing. Consider the list only as a reminder and a guide. It merely says to store executives that this type of person should be given some special attention. Keep the checklist available and periodically review it. Consider each employee you have in terms of the checklist. Be particularly watchful of the person who suddenly appears to be living above his or her means. But always use it as a guide and a reminder that is its purpose.

Chapter 7

HONESTY SHOPPING

Why Honesty Shopping?

Interviewer:	"You have sold in our store for seven years. You have a good sales record. Now that we have caught you stealing from your cash register we want to know one thing. . . ."
Salesman:	"Yes, what is that?"
Interviewer:	"How much did you steal?"
Salesman:	"You won't believe me."
Interviewer:	"Try me."
Salesman:	"Well, on the average I stole $30 a day."
Interviewer:	"It's impossible! You ran the highest sales in your department."
Salesman:	"That shows you what a good salesman I am."

Thefts of Cash on Sales

These words are from an actual interview with a dishonest employee. It spotlights one of the causes of loss in every store; theft of cash on sales.

One of the major types of theft is cash taken at the point of sale. It is an easy method of theft. The thief is dealing in money itself, and not goods that later have to be changed into cash.

Many talks with dishonest salespeople show that the cash such a person can steal is unbelievable. As much as $40 to $100 a day is not unusual. Some employees have told how they set standards for their thefts, and even though these goals were often high the thief was able to meet them.

The Thief Can't Stop Stealing

A dishonest employee soon becomes used to the higher standard of living made possible by the thefts of cash. We have seen cases in which four people on one sales counter steal cash from their sales. One of these people is caught by honesty shopping and the other salespeople then know that this person was taken off for theft.

It might be assumed that fear would keep the other salespeople from stealing, at least for a while. The fact is, however, that because they are accustomed to a higher standard of living they have new obligations to meet. They find they can't stop stealing. One person is taken and then another. No matter how great the fear, the other people keep stealing until all of them have been caught.

Employee Thefts Spread

Another thing that occurs in many types of dishonesty is contamination. One employee starts to steal merchandise or cash on sales and in a short time she confides in another employee. She tells how easy it is to steal. Or perhaps she is observed stealing by another salesperson. Soon this second employee is also stealing. The "theft disease" then spreads like a virus. Many a "good" person becomes *contaminated.*

Employee's Attitude

We sometimes feel that if a dishonest employee is seen by another employee that he will feel a sense of duty to the company and will report this person to the store. Sad to say this is wishful thinking. The person who learns about another's thefts will take one of two actions.

First, he may say to himself, "What Joe does is his business. I'm not my brother's keeper. If he gets caught that's his tough luck."

This attitude of "hands off" lets the thefts continue. The employee feels no guilt or sense of duty.

Or the person may say to himself, "Well, if Joe is getting his, why shouldn't I get mine?" He then starts to steal and contamination begins.

Finding One Dishonest Employee Often Indicates Others

A study has shown that when you find one dishonest employee in any area there are usually other dishonest employees in the same place. If one salesgirl is caught stealing cash on sales, many times other salesgirls in the same department will also be caught.

The problem of contamination is a serious one. Any dishonest employee is a problem because of her drain on profits. But a worse problem is her contamination of other employees. Dishonesty among your people cannot be contained. This problem is one that you should always be aware of. It means you need a "mop-up" operation when you arrest a dishonest employee.

GOOD LEADERSHIP CURBS EMPLOYEE THEFTS

Your supervisor is important in any case of employee dishonesty. This is especially true when contamination becomes apparent. There is little doubt that good leadership cuts employee theft.

When groups of people steal cash on sales, it can be assumed that there has been a failure in leadership. If your supervisor is authoritarian he may have caused rebellion among his people. By being a dictator he has set himself up as a hate symbol and this hate is transferred to the store.

Some people steal because they are hostile toward the boss. They ease their guilt by reviewing examples of unfairness by the hated supervisor. They may also have the view that "It's a big company and they wouldn't miss the small amount I take."

Take Time for Employee Human Relations

As is true in so many businesses today, stores have a need to take care of immediate things: promotion of goods, customer relationships, budgets, and similar problems. Little time is left for work on employee human relations and the psychology of leadership.

Our failure in this area has aggravated many of the problems that we face daily. It is these failures that cause employees to handle customers poorly, make employees join unions, create a snafu in systems and controls, cause resistance to new ideas, and give us many other problems.

Poor Leadership Causes Security Problems

Your store security is another area where leadership failure can cause trouble. There is the problem of carelessness in enforcing store rules.

Much dishonesty is the result of loopholes left by laxness and poor supervision. If a store does not require its salespeople to give a sales receipt on every sale, the way is soon open for salespeople to steal cash on their sales.

Customer Audit

Educational programs can stop this type of loophole. One store had a "customer contest" in which they told all of their customers they knew their salespeople were accurate. They offered an award of $2 to anyone who found an error on her sales receipt, even if the error was only a penny.

The results were amazing. Every customer insisted on getting her sales receipt from the salesclerks. They looked it over carefully to try and find an error. This store saved many dollars that would have been lost by error or theft.

This contest made the customer do an audit control on the store's salesclerks. Such a program can be effective temporarily, but it can't be kept up indefinitely. Lasting control must, in the end, rest on the store management.

Hold Supervisors Accountable

Do you hold supervisors responsible in the matter of employee dishonesty? Do you tell your supervisor that if dishonesty is found in his area this may reflect on his leadership ability?

In other words, is he told that he will be held accountable for good systems and controls? He should be held accountable, within reason, for the morale of his personnel. You need to make clear that if he has maladjusted people working for him, he has to bring them to the attention of management.

In some stores, when a dishonest salesperson is caught, they go over the case and determine if any store rules have been broken. The case is also examined to see if there is background of maladjustment. Store management, after getting the facts, calls in the supervisor and goes over the case. If the theft resulted from supervisory failure, the supervisor is held accountable. In some cases severe action has been taken against the supervisor.

By holding the supervisor accountable for his leadership failures you can improve the store operation. You can reduce your theft losses.

Train Supervisors to Work with the Security Department

There is always a danger that a supervisor will cover up his people's dishonesty. He may also try to defeat the security department's work. He feels that if dishonesty is found he will be placed on the spot.

This fear can be overcome by training supervisors to work with the security department. Train them to let security know if they suspect any person of dishonesty. By giving suspects to security they help the store. We all benefit when the supervisor finds such a person and brings his crimes out in the open where the matter can be properly handled.

If your supervisor cooperates with security and this help leads to the apprehension of a criminal, he has done your store a real service, which should be recognized by management.

If your supervisor helps security, and a person in his area is caught stealing, there is no disgrace to the supervisor. The poor supervisor is lax in enforcing store systems. He is the one that should be criticized by management.

Is Honesty Shopping a Good Method of Investigation?

This question was answered not so long ago by a well-known security manager who was on a panel discussing security problems. A store vice president asked from the floor, "What do you feel is the best method of investigating internal thefts?"

The security man replied, "If I could have my choice of only one thing, I would not hesitate to choose *honesty shopping*. Dollar for dollar it is the best investment you can make to cut your losses."

"In my experience," he went on, "I have found that your greatest losses are from your dishonest employees. I can assure you that more dishonest employees can be found by honesty shopping than by any other method."

This man shares the view of most security managers. Honesty shopping is a relatively inexpensive way of checking your salespeople. It usually shows a high return for the money invested.

WHAT IS HONESTY SHOPPING?

Honesty shoppers are detectives who act as customers. They shop throughout the store testing the honesty of salespeople by buying items for cash.

In most cases, the shopper pays the even amount of the sale, including tax. A check is made either by observation at the time of the sale or later by looking at the salesperson's register tape, salesbook, or tally to see if she recorded the sale.

This method of checking is based on the policy current in most stores that the salesperson is required to record every cash sale in the correct amount and proper sequence.

By making shopping tests the store can find the salesperson who is stealing cash on sales. It is a good method of investigation because it can be used on a large scale and can be done over and over again with little chance of detection by employees.

What Does Honesty Shopping Do?

Honesty tests do several things. They find the employee who is stealing and they also show management how well his store systems are being operated. Every test shows whether a sales receipt was given the customer. The percentage of receipts to the number of tests made by the shoppers give management insight into the quality of the store operation. Failure to give receipts on sales usually indicates poor supervision.

Also important is the fact that the tests cause psychological barriers to theft. Your employees should be told at the time of employment or during the training period that they will be checked by shopping. You should tell them that people will be testing them for honesty. The fact that they know they will be tested sets up a barrier to theft in the mind of the employee. This leads to better store operation and less theft.

Keep Honesty Shopping a Separate Function

In some stores service shopping and honesty shopping are done in the same test. Some firms who sell shopping services to stores tell about the value of service shopping as well as honesty shopping in their sales pitch.

Store security people have found that an honesty shopper must devote her full time to the honesty problem. When she has to observe service parts of a salesperson's operation she can't do as good a job of honesty shopping. When you combine service and honesty shopping in a single buy, the honesty tests lose their value. Only when honesty testing is a separate function does the store get full value.

Many stores set up one department for service shopping and another for honesty shopping. They are under two different heads within the store. Honesty shopping, of course, comes under store security. When these departments are set up separately, results are far better in both cases.

WHO SHOULD BE SHOPPED?

Imaginative shoppers, a creative shopping supervisor, and an interested management can go far in finding fresh shopping methods. New things will improve the value of honesty shoppings. Let's review some of the ways that have worked in the past to stimulate you in developing new ideas based on these tried techniques.

General Shopping and Specific Suspects

There are two basic ways of finding the dishonest employee when using shopping. First, there is *general shopping*, which uses wide coverage and many tests. Results are based on the law of averages. This method will always uncover some dishonest employees. Returns are related to the number of tests made.

A second and more effective way is to develop *employee suspects.* They can be tested by shoppers on an individual basis. If the suspects are carefully selected, shopping results will show a high case return for the number of tests. This makes for a better shopping operation. The question is how does someone find shopping suspects?

Experienced Shopper Has Clues

Experienced shoppers are very much like any other detective. If she has ability she will get more cases than an average shopper will. A lot of her ability is the result of intuition and ingenuity. She also has accumulated knowledge from her experience in many shopping cases. A good shopper, like a good floor detective, will have a knack for picking out her suspects and will, as a result, get a high number of cases.

She will learn that the salesgirl wearing a suit with pockets can easily take cash. She will be alert to the salesman who asks her if she wants to put the item in the same bag she is carrying. She notes the salesgirl who keeps her handbag behind the counter. Soon she develops a whole group of suspect indications.

Her shopping is better than the shotgun type of general shopping. The experienced shopper gets her own "leads." She should be told to give them as much attention as possible.

Departments with High Shortages

Another way of spotting good suspects is to put shoppers into areas that show high inventory losses. Inventory losses can be caused by many things, and one of them may be theft of cash on sales. Security should plan special tests in high-shortage departments.

Salespeople with Low Average Cash Sales

Another technique for finding the thief is to average out cash sales. Select a department such as cosmetics, gloves, handbags, or jewelry where there are a lot of small cash sales and have the auditing department analyze the cash sales of each salesclerk. If any clerk is running a daily sales tally of $20 or $30 below the department average, she becomes a shopping suspect.

Of course, people who steal cash on sales are not necessarily going to be low in sales when compared with other people in their department. Sometimes the top salesperson turns out to be the one who is stealing. Management people are often amazed when the "best" salesperson is caught stealing. This hurts because it is a blow to their logic.

But it must be remembered that to be a thief, a person has to have a lot of drive and initiative. These characteristics are also common to the person who is a good salesperson. It is not too surprising to find that some of our so-called top salespeople steal.

Supervisors Have Suspects

The alert supervisor can really help store security. She has a chance to know her people. She can often see irregularities that show a salesperson may be stealing. For example, she may catch a salesclerk lying or ringing up "no sales" or leaving her cash register drawer open. If the supervisor is asked about possible suspects, many theft cases can be uncovered. She is a good source of leads.

When a supervisor goes out of her way to tell security about a suspect, this suspect becomes a top lead. In most cases, such a person will be caught by security. Usually a supervisor will not go out on a limb about one of her people unless she has positive indications of theft.

Salespeople with Excessive Overages and Shortages

Checking overages and shortages can develop leads. This can be done by the control division. Most people feel that shortages are worse than overages, but the fact is that people who have *overages* are more apt to be stealing than people who have shortages.

Overages are a warning flag to security. They are a signal that the salesclerk may be stealing by underringing. People who have a lot of overages should be tested by shoppers.

Salespeople with Excessive "No Sales"

Most stores limit the number of "no sales" on a register for the day. The salesperson who is taking cash often has a lot of no sales, so this is a good way of locating a suspect.

The salesgirl who is underringing may become worried about how much money she has in the register. She wants to have a correct balance. During the day she opens the register using the no sale button and counts her money. Overages and no sales can be warning flags.

Employees with Problems

If an employee is known to be living beyond his means, to have unpaid bills, there is a real danger that he will steal cash from his sales. The maladjusted employee is also a prime suspect.

Therefore, people who have personality problems, are in debt, or are living beyond their means are people who should be shopped.

Rule Breakers

The salesperson who often breaks store rules, who sneaks out early without letting her supervisor know she has gone for the day, or who comes into the store earlier than the other employees is a shopping lead.

Any employee who has a record of abusing store policies should be tested by shopping. Failure to live by the rules may show up in the person's lack of responsiblity when handling store cash.

The person who lies is very suspect. Usually you find that a person who steals also lies. This doesn't mean that all people who lie steal, but it does show that when a person is found to lie, that person should be tested for honesty.

Temporary Help

During Christmas and Easter most stores take on large groups of temporary people. Salespeople hired during these periods know that they are temporary. As a result, some of them steal as much from the store as possible.

Analysis of employee cases shows that temporary people make up a large part of the cases. Because this is true your temporary help should be shopped.

Garnishees

When an employee has his salary garnisheed this is a sign of his inability to handle money. It is a warning that should not go unnoticed. If the person whose salary is garnisheed is a salesperson, one of the steps to be taken should be a series of shopping tests.

Salespeople Who Leave Cash Registers Open

In one store a visiting security manager noted that many salespeople were leaving their register drawers open. They were ringing up their sales but failed to close the register drawer. The store made a survey and found that drawers were left open on 40 percent of the registers, so a series of tests were set up to evaluate the salespeople.

It was found that every salesperson who failed to close her register drawer, except two, was stealing cash on sales.

When a salesperson is underringing she may put a sale in the register without ringing any amount at all. She can do this if she does not close her register drawer after the previous sale. Whenever you see a register with one of the drawers not completely closed you should check to see if the person operating that drawer is stealing cash on sales.

Other Methods Worth Noting

The above list covers most methods of finding shopping leads. Others worth noting are the salesclerk who shows hostility to supervision, salesclerks who are observed writing figures on a scrap of paper near the register (an indication the salesperson is underringing), and salespeople who throw register receipts on the floor instead of giving them to customers.

A last group of suspects to be considered are those who have been given awards for detecting shoplifters. We often feel that when a person is alert enough to bring a shoplifter to our attention, this person is not only a good detective but also probably an honest person.

This has proven to be false. Investigation of award winners in one store showed that 45 percent of the award winners were later caught stealing. A person who sees a theft often has stealing on his mind. It is a good rule to shop any person who gets an award.

You will find that other suspects become evident in the normal course of operations. For example, a dishonest employee may implicate other people in his area.

Better shopping results come from shopping specific suspects rather than from random, general shopping because this group is more apt to steal than is the average salesperson.

Suspect Files

A review of these shopping suspects shows the need for a suspect file. The simplest way to keep such a file is to set up a box of 3 × 5 cards. Whenever a person becomes a suspect, his or her name should be put on a card and filed alphabetically. There should also be one section of the box devoted to active suspects. Each time a test is made the date and the results of the test should be put on the card. In this way a regular check of the suspect file will show whether anyone is being neglected. It will also show a cutoff point at which certain suspects can be discarded because enough tests have been made to show that the person is not stealing.

As an aid to the investigator who may be questioning a suspect about thefts of money from the store, it is helpful to put on the back of the index card some reason why the person is a suspect. How was the lead obtained? Such details can lead to a check of theft activities besides cash thefts.

Areas Not Usually Shopped

In setting up shopper coverage the supervisor should have a list of offbeat selling areas, places that would not usually be shopped. These are spots open to theft because they are neglected. For example:

- Shoe repair department
- Barber shop or beauty salon

- Employee cafeteria
- Cut flowers
- Baked goods
- Pantry shop
- Parking lot
- Warehouse store
- Salvage sales
- Employees store
- Hotdog stand
- Popcorn concessions

Other places may come to mind as you review this list. Some places have not been shopped because the items sold are perishable. Some are departments that are service centers without merchandise. Also overlooked are sales areas located away from the main store.

Because these spots are not shopped, the salespeople may feel free to steal. It can be startling to see how much cash can be stolen from a department like shoe repair, or the dollars taken by salespeople in the baked goods shop.

One store found that every person in their shoe repair was stealing cash on sales. In another store it was found that the men in the store's parking lot were stealing cash from parking fees.

Where to Use Shopping Tests

Here is a shopping suspect list in order of importance!

1. People known to be stealing.
2. Specific leads, people who are in a position of theft or are suspects for a variety of reasons.
3. Offbeat sales locations.
4. General storewide coverage. This assures the store that over a given period of time every salesperson has been tested.

To be effective, shopping should be planned. A hit-or-miss type of shopping will uncover some theft, but using a logical method in applying tests gives a higher return. It is also less likely that bad losses will develop over the years from salespeople who are stealing large amounts of cash.

Types of Shopping Tests

There are five basic types of buying tests:

1. Single buy
2. Combination buy
3. Double buy
4. Exchange buy
5. Refund

There are many variations of these five basic types of buys. An imaginative shopper can work out new ways of applying these techniques to make them more effective.

In any of the first four tests listed your shopper can offer "even" or "uneven" money to a salesclerk. In most shopping tests even money is given. There is also a sixth type of buy that is not a test buy. We call this the "identification" buy.

1. **Single Buy.** In this type of test the shopper buys two of the same items at one time. They may be the same price, or they may be different prices. She notes the register reading for the sale prior to the sale she is making. She then selects two of the same items and pays the salesperson even money (the exact amount) for the whole buy. If she does not get a receipt, an identification buy is made at a later time.

The amount spent should not be very common to the department being tested. The sale must be easy to identify on the tape. A single buy may also be made when the shopper buys a single item and gives the salesgirl the exact money for the sale. By buying two or more items, however, the salesgirl is less likely to be suspicious of the shopper.

2. **Combination Buy.** This buy is like the single buy except the shopper buys two or more different types of items at the same time and pays the salesclerk the exact amount for the whole purchase. The salesclerk may record all, part, or none of the buy.

When she makes a combination buy where a register is used the shopper should be sure to note the previous sale on the register. By knowing the amount on the register at the time the shopper makes her buy, it will be easy to check the sale on which she receives no receipt. Your shopper should not purchase the same amount as that shown on the register for the previous sale.

If the shopper does not get a receipt on a combination buy, an identitication buy must be made later. It is never wise to make an identification buy less than 15 or 20 minutes before or after the first buy. If the two are close in time the salesperson may become suspicious.

Your shopper should always be sure of the exact time of any buy she makes. This is true in both honesty tests and identification buys. The time will be a needed factor later in checking the tape.

The shopper should try to spend enough money in testing a salesclerk so that a real honesty test is made. She must keep in mind, of course, the amount the average person would spend in this department. It is also good to have your shopper select items carefully in advance of her purchase. She should be careful of prices and make a point of choosing even-money items so that the salesclerk will not get too much change.

3. **Double Buy.** There are two parts to this sale. The *first part is made for identification.* The shopper buys one or more items after having made a careful selection. She pays the salesclerk an uneven amount of money (more money than the price of the goods). The salesclerk must then give change. To do this she uses her cash register. The result is that the sale is usually recorded and a receipt given to the shopper. This receipt gives the shopper the salesperson's number so that she can later be identified.

The *second part of the double buy is the honesty test.* After the salesclerk has given the shopper her merchandise and change, the shopper decides to buy an additional item. In buying this extra piece of merchandise she pays the salesclerk the exact amount of money needed. She may ask the salesclerk to include the second item in the bag used for the first part of the sale. Sometimes the salesclerk herself will suggest doing this. Often the salesclerk will not give a receipt for this second item. The double buy may, of course, be made in reverse. Even money is used for the first half and uneven money for the second part.

In paying even money on any shopping test, the shopper should make sure that the salesclerk will have a reasonable chance to take all or part of her money.

In a double buy the shopper has to use good sense in price consistency. It would not be normal, for example, to spend 39¢ on the first part of the sale and $10 on the second part. If a real customer knew she needed an item for 39¢ she would probably know her other needs and would not buy a $10 item on impulse. The second part of the double buy should not be started until the first part is completed.

It is helpful if the shopper knows during the first part of the buy what she intends to purchase as the second part. In this way she can control the type of goods in the first part so the bag will be large enough to accommodate the item bought in the second part. She also can decide the amount to be spent on the first part so she can offer part or all of her change for the second half of the buy.

In selecting items for the second part of the double buy the shopper tries to locate goods as far away as possible from the register. Sometimes the salesclerk can be drawn away from a certain spot by a customer's showing interest in things on display. After looking at the display items the shopper pays for her second purchase and leaves the area. It is good, if the merchandise allows it, to buy more than one item on the second part of the buy. This gives the salesclerk a much better chance to keep all the money or to ring up the amount for only one of the items.

It is often possible to wear or take out an unwrapped item that has been purchased on the second part of the double buy. An example of this would be in the jewelry department. The shopper buys a bracelet and a clip on the second part of the double buy. As soon as she has selected the bracelet, she places it on her arm and tells the salesclerk that she wants to wear it out. She then gives the clip to the salesclerk to be wrapped with the first purchase. The shopper then gives her money in such a way that the salesclerk can easily record the amount for one or the other of the two items.

There are many ways to vary the double buy. It is one of the best shopping tests.

4. Exchange Buy. In this test a shopper hesitates between two or more items. She finally decides to take a less expensive one. She gives the salesclerk uneven money. When she gets her change, package, and sales receipt, she tells the salesclerk that she has decided to take the higher priced item. She then gives the salesperson the exact amount for the difference in price.

> *Example*: She has been shown hose at $2.95, $3.95, and $4.95. She decides to purchase the $2.95 hose and gives the salesclerk $5.00. When the salesclerk returns with the package she tells her that she has decided to take the $4.95 hose instead.
>
> She then gives the salesclerk the even $2.00 for the difference.
>
> The shopper must be careful that there is not too much difference in the prices of the articles selected.
>
> It is not likely, for example, that the customer would buy an item for $1.50 and exchange it for something costing $8.50. The exchange buy is good in departments where salespeople wrap their own sales.

It is also a good method to use in departments where it is hard to make a double buy. This would be true in shoes, ready to wear, sportswear, and millinery. It is not likely that a customer would buy two hats at one time, but she might buy one hat and exchange it for another that sells for a higher price.

In any type of test your shopper should try to get a total amount of purchase that will not constitute the ordinary dollar amount of sale. Sometimes a shopping test has been invalid because the amount spent by the shopper appeared to be recorded. We felt the salesclerk stole the money, but because the shopper had used an amount common to the department there were numerous sales on the register tape showing the same amount as the test. There was no clear-cut theft violation.

5. Refund Buy. There are two uses for the refund buy. First, it can be used as a method of honesty shopping; and second, it can be used to test your store's refund system.

In using the refund as a shopping test the shopper brings an item back to the selling department and obtains a cash refund. She then uses the money from the cash refund to make her even money buy. By using a refund the shopper hides her true identity.

A similar thing can be done by using a charge plate. The shopper is given a charge account under a fictitious name and address. She makes a buy with her charge plate, and then she selects another item and says she has decided to also take this but she doesn't want her husband to know that she is spending the extra money, so she wants to pay cash for this extra bit of merchandise.

By using the refund buy as a test of store systems, the shopper tries to get a refund without a salescheck. If the shopper can't get a refund without a check, she "discovers" the salescheck in her handbag and then goes through the normal steps of the refund buy.

Examples: Variations can be worked out on these methods. One male shopper, for example, carries a suitcase of dirty laundry. He buys two ties from a salesman and then says, "Never mind putting them in the bag, I'll just stick them in here with this wash." He opens the suitcase and has the ties put in along with his soiled shirts. These homey elements allay the fear of the dishonest salesman who feels free to take the cash paid for the ties.

Another shopper is an elderly woman who always wears old clothes. A babushka protects her white hair. She gives the appearance of being confused and not too bright. Many a disarmed employee thinks this woman is an easy mark and does not suspect that under her disguise is a shrewd detective. This woman's many cases testify to her effectiveness.

Another ruse has been the "line" of trying to get the salesperson to sell an item below its marked retail value. In one case a shopper approached a sweater salesman and, after looking at a $45 sweater, confided that she only had $40 to spend. The salesclerk made his own "deal." He sold the $45 sweater to the shopper for $40. In this case he rang a "no sale" and later pocketed the full amount of the sale.

A similar test was made in men's clothing. In this case a salesman took the price tag off of an inexpensive suit and placed it on a $150 suit. The shopper in this case paid $85 for the $150 suit.

6. **Identification Buy.** Some honesty shoppers get an identification buy on every shopper test. However, such a buy is not always needed. Some security departments find they can increase their effectiveness if they limit identification buys to tests that have some indication of irregularity. For example, if the salesperson rings the even money sale and the register shows the amount is correct, there is little value in getting an identification buy.

Since the average shopper makes five or six honesty tests an hour identifying buys are expensive. Identification buys should run about 10 percent of total purchases.

Your identification buy can be made before or after an honesty test. But in either case it should not be made too close to the honesty test.

As in anything involving people, the chance of error is always present. To keep error to a minimum, care should go into identifying the person tested. As a safeguard no salesperson should be apprehended on a single theft violation. A minimum of two thefts on different days should be a standard. This prevents an error that could mean accusing an innocent person.

Identifying buys are routine but sometimes a salesperson has to be asked for a receipt. If this is the case a receipt should be obtained because it is needed proof of the identity of the person.

When a store is keeping coverage records to see that all of its people are shopped or to show the patterns of shopping by department, identification buys may be needed on every sale. This increases the cost of shopping, but if the information is needed to improve overall performance the extra cost may be worthwhile.

EMPLOYING AN OUTSIDE SHOPPING SERVICE

Several large firms specialize in honesty shopping for stores. A shopping service is an asset to a small store without a security department.

An outside service can be just as effective as the store's own shoppers, and in many cases it is even superior. However, the outside firm, to be effective, needs the help of a store executive.

Shopping is best when suspects are tested. The location of good suspects is important in getting cases. For an outside firm to get good results an executive in the store must do the work of locating the "specials" for the outside people to shop.

A Store Executive Must Assist

The store must also furnish, on the day that the outside shoppers come in, descriptions of the people to be shopped. This includes specific details on clothing they are wearing. In this way the shoppers will be able to find the suspects in the departments to which they are assigned. Both store shoppers and shoppers from an outside agency have advantages in certain situations. Both are useful and can be of real aid to store management.

Establish a Policy

If you choose to use an outside firm two things should be decided. First, what is considered a violation? A store with a security department usually requires a minimum of two clear-cut thefts before a person is interviewed on an honesty basis, whereas some outside firms persuade management to take a person off for a single policy violation.

A policy violation is defined as the failure to give a customer a sales receipt. This is not a good standard for determining employee honesty, however. In addition, there is the problem of who will interview the dishonest person. Usually the outside firm can do this well because they are specialists with a lot of interview background.

For many stores the outside service is an aid in the problem of checking for dishonest salespeople. They understand the store's theft problems. The store's own shopping department can also be effective, and if money is a factor, the store's own shoppers usually prove to be less expensive.

STORE HONESTY SHOPPING DEPARTMENT

When the store sets up its own shopping department, such a department should come under the head of your security operation and have a full-time shopping supervisor.

Honesty shoppers are usually part-time housewives who work 8 to 12 hours each week. They like to earn extra spending money. Male shoppers can often be found as students in local colleges studying retailing. These college men find the few hours of retail work each week an interesting experience.

Get a Variety of Shoppers

Your balanced shopping staff should include a range of ages, types, and personalities. There should be many kinds of people, and the shoppers should play different roles depending on their background. A store setting up a shopping department should try to have at least 15 or 20 shoppers to draw on. The more shoppers there are the less danger of the shoppers becoming known to your salespeople.

Scheduling Shoppers

The shoppers can be scheduled in two ways. They can be called in weekly for three days and work five hours each day, or a group of shoppers can be called in for a normal work week and then not be called in again for four weeks.

In this type of rotation you have a basic shopping staff. For example, let us say five shoppers are in your basic group. It is rotated every week for four weeks, requiring a pool of twenty shoppers. The idea is that since the shopper would not be in the store for four weeks, it would be less likely that a salesclerk would identify the shopper.

Location of the Shoppers' Office

The office the shoppers work out of should not be located near security. It should, in fact, be in a remote location. It is not good to locate it near employee locker rooms or other areas where many of your people might observe shoppers entering or leaving. Some stores put shoppers in a building away from the store. This is a good precaution.

Training

A training program should be worked out for the honesty shoppers. The supervisor should be a specialist familiar with the problems of shopping. She has to be accurate and conscientious. She needs to have a good concept not only of shopping methods but also of the legalities of her job. She must know the dangers of any arrest situation.

Shopping Manual

You should develop a shopping manual outlining your basic policies. This manual, along with personal training by your shopping supervisor, is followed up with floor experience in which the trainee spends time every day shopping with an experienced shopper.

A Shopper's Bank

A bank should be set up for your shopping area and should be balanced daily. Regular audits should be made every two or three weeks by your internal audit department at which time the merchandise on hand, credits, and cases are totaled to be sure they balance.

Your shoppers should be given money daily for their shopping tests. The amount should be large enough so that each purchase is a good test of employee honesty. Skimping on funds can hurt the value of the tests.

After she gets her bank for the day, each shopper should count her cash. She must be sure that she has enough coins and bills of all sizes to work efficiently. In some stores shoppers list their bills by number. In this way a bill can be checked if an arrest is made of a dishonest employee who puts the money in his pocket. In other stores this type of case arrest is seldom made. Arrests are made on the day after the test. It is based on an audit check that shows the sale was not properly recorded. If your store uses this method there is little reason to list your bills or to mark them.

Shoppers' Reports

Your shoppers should keep complete records of each test. They should also write out a violation report on any person who fails to give a sales receipt.

Your shopper should note the price tag, and then check it against the actual amount charged for the item. Sometimes a salesclerk makes errors, and they show up in shopping tests. Your shopper should carefully check to see whether a receipt was given to her. She should look in the bag containing the item and unfold the merchandise in her search for this receipt. When she says she didn't get a receipt she must be *sure* about it.

Shopping Supervisor's Responsibilities

Your supervisor should keep a full report on the number of purchases made. She should list the departments tested and the violations found. These facts can be given to store management in a monthly report.

It is also the job of your shopping head to balance out each shopper's cash. She should do this before the shopper leaves at the end of the day. This balancing is done by adding her remaining cash to the value of the goods she purchased. The total should equal the original fund given her in the morning.

Your shopping supervisor also has other tasks. In addition to preparing the day's work by locating "specials" and getting descriptions so that shoppers can easily locate people for special tests, she must also see that yesterday's merchandise is returned to stock. The supervisor makes out her refunds for the items bought and sees to it that these refunds and the merchandise are properly processed.

Shoppers' Purchases

In some stores shoppers' goods are returned directly to the selling area. This is a poor method. Salespeople have good memories. They can often remember the customer who purchased an item. Often, if the salesperson sees the merchandise she may identify the shopper. The salespeople can also get a good idea of how much honesty shopping is being done in their area.

To avoid this, two steps can be taken. First, on any theft violation the merchandise should be held a few days before returning it for credit.

In the case of most theft violations, the items should be held until the case is completed. You may need these items as evidence if a court case develops. Second, a good way of returning merchandise to stock is to set up a system with your store's return goods room so that the purchases are fed back into the return goods room. In this way they are processed as though they have been returned by regular customers. By mixing shoppers' items with ordinary return goods, it is possible to cover up the fact that this merchandise is from test shoppings.

Follow-up on Violations

Another duty of the shopping supervisor is the follow-up on violations. When the shopper writes a report showing that no salescheck was received, or that the salesclerk failed to ring the register, or that other irregularities have occurred, the supervisor will obtain from audit the cash register tape, tallies, saleschecks, or other materials pertinent to the salesperson's work for that day. A check of this material will show whether a policy violation or theft has occurred.

If a violation of policy has occurred, and the salesperson failed to give the customer a receipt but recorded the sale, a violation report is sent to personnel. The salesperson is then interviewed by personnel and reminded that it is store policy to give every customer a sales receipt. Some borderline employees can be saved from stealing cash if management does a good job of follow-up on policy violations of this type.

If a theft has occurred, the sales supervisor will plan more tests of the suspect. After a series of shortages have been accumulated, the case is prepared for interview.

Building a Case

Some stores interview an employee after a single shortage. This is often unwise, for there are many ways an error can occur. With only one shortage an innocent person may be falsely accused of dishonesty. A better standard is to see that you have at least two clear-cut shortages before questioning the employee.

Isn't it better to build an even stronger case than two violations? By doing this you can do a better interview. You can often get a more complete statement on the subject's past thefts. In many cases your more detailed pattern of past theft activity encourages the subject to confess. You can then establish a restitution figure to recover some of your losses.

Let's see how this works. If you shop a salesclerk and she steals three times in a single day for an average daily theft of $15, and you continue this shopping for a week, it can then be proven that her thefts are at least $75 for that one week. If she admits that she has been doing this for three months, you are now in a good position to arrange for repayment at an average of about $75 a week for 12 weeks. The shopping department that takes a salesclerk on only two shortages is not in a strong position for getting repayment on previous thefts.

The Shopper's Responsibilities

Your honesty shopper must be alert to many different parts of her job. For example, she should check her merchandise price tags against the sales receipts to see if she has been correctly charged by the salesclerk. She should also notice the date on her sales receipts. Sometimes a dishonest salesperson will save register stubs from a previous day's work. She feeds these stubs to customers who accept them as receipts for their immediate purchase.

Your shopper must, of course, at all times act like a regular customer. The good shopper is careful about revealing her identity.

It is better if she doesn't even tell her friends outside the store what work she is doing. Casual conversations can sometimes be revealing and a shopper's identity can be exposed if she talks too much. A shopper should at all times give the appearance of buying items for herself. She must shop with care and intelligence. She should not make any personal buys during working hours as it is easy to mix her own money with shopping funds, which will cause confusion.

Your shoppers should bear in mind that all the goods they buy are returned to stock for resale. They should, therefore, return shopping merchandise in a saleable condition. Her reports must be accurate because later these reports may be used as court evidence. They have to be complete and factual.

Shopping Carefully

Your good shoppers do not rush their work. They shop slowly and carefully. They take time to examine and discuss the items they are buying in each test. The normal customer wants to know what value she is getting. She wants to know if the merchandise is going to suit her needs. Is the color right? Is the merchandise well made?

When a careless shopper accepts anything the salesperson shows her without being particular, she runs the danger of being spotted. When she buys hosiery she should ask for her size and shade. She then examines them to see if they are perfect. If the salesperson does not have her size the shopper should not make the mistake of taking a smaller or larger size but should buy something else instead.

The shopper, of course, varies her purchases. She uses the single, double, combination, or exchange buys. She should not get into the habit of making only one type of test.

Blending into the Crowd

She learns to blend into the crowd. She doesn't want the salesperson to remember her after she leaves the counter. Excessive makeup, bright colors, or conspicuous jewelry may cause a salesperson to remember her.

Loud talk can also leave an impression. She must be quiet and unassuming in her manner, avoid talking too loudly, or having too long a conversation with the salesclerk. In sum, she should not do or say anything that would attract attention to herself so that the salesperson could identify her at some future time.

When she is not working on "specials," the shopper should be sure that the rest of the store gets shopping coverage. She should not confine her purchases to the street floor or basement but shop the upper floors as well. She should not wander about aimlessly. This wastes valuable time and may result in her being observed and becoming known. The average customer usually knows what she wants.

Shopping Different Departments

A shopper can improve her case production by looking for departments that are not often tested. If she has been in a department before, she should try to test a different salesclerk to increase her coverage. A shopper should not confine her buys to merchandise that is small, such as notions, gloves, and perfume, but should buy large items as well.

She should not purchase soiled, damaged, or perishable goods. In this way she avoids difficulties in returning these items to stock. She should, for example, avoid buying white goods. These become quickly soiled in handling. Only when told to do so should she buy yard goods cut from a bolt. Instead, she should buy remnants. This would also apply to trimmings sold by the yard. It is unwise for her to buy the last of any item. She should try to select items that are fresh and in good condition, and not "sale" merchandise.

Familiarity with the Merchandise

The shopper should be familiar with the goods she buys. If she is buying socks or clothing for a young child, she should give the salesperson the child's age and be sure she knows the correct size for that age. If she is buying things in the radio, hardware, or paint departments where women are not as familiar with the merchandise as men, she should know exactly what she is buying. What is it to be used for? How much will she need? If she is not sure about the item she would be wiser not to make the purchase.

In giving money to the salesperson a shopper should not place the money on the counter but hand it to the salesperson. She should try to ask the price of the merchandise on every buy. She should ask what the total amount of the sale is and be positive that she gives the exact amount of this total to the salesperson.

If a salesperson overcharges the shopper, she should call this to the salesperson's attention and then note it in her report. If she is undercharged, however, she would be conspicuous if she called this to the salesperson's attention. Therefore she simply notes this in her shopping report.

The shopper should be sure she has a good description of the salesperson when she suspects there has been a violation. She can look for special things such as jewelry, facial scars, glasses or anything else that is distinctive.

Protecting Shoppers' Identity

Shoppers can improve their percentage of "hits" by playing the roles of different types of people. For example, by wearing a maid's uniform under her coat or a manicurist's white gown she offsets the salesperson's natural suspicion. She can also carry packages with the names of other nearby stores. This again suggests that she is a customer and not a shopper.

You must take care even in small ways to prevent the identity of your shoppers from becoming known. For example, since shoppers work for the store, they are entitled to the employee discount. If this discount is given, as it is to other employees, they would soon become known. To avoid this you can get set up a charge account for the shopper and then discount the charge account. In this way the discount is still given to the shopper but her identity is protected.

When a store has branches it is good to rotate your shoppers through all of the stores.

Honesty shopping is a specialized field. It requires alert, imaginative people. Your shopping department will be as effective as the imagination, initiative, and thoroughness of your shopping staff.

INTERVIEW

There are two ways in which a shopping case can be brought to a point of interview. One is to have a series of shortage violations that have been checked against the sales tally, cash register tape, and sales triplicates. The other is to have an "in the pocket" cash theft.

In the second type of case the employee is kept under observation for a minimum of an hour before being brought to the security office.

The most complete type of shopping case combines previous violations and the possession of stolen money at the time of arrest.

In most cases, however, it is enough to have a series of theft shortages that have been checked against the register tape and sales tally. (Incidentally, it should be remembered that in a violation involving an underring the salesperson's balance for the day should be examined. If the salesperson underrang $10, for example, and at the end of the day her balance showed that she is over in her cash of $12.60, this would not be considered a clear-cut theft since an overage did occur in her day's work.)

Prepare Case Carefully Before Interview

Before any interview takes place on shopping violations the case should be carefully prepared. There is no other retail case more delicate than the shopping theft case. It cannot be based on an assumption or a careless examination of the test material. The person doing the interview is dependent on the thoroughness of the shopping supervisor and the accuracy of the shoppers. He must, in addition, go over the case himself so that he understands it.

Once the interviewer has a complete understanding of the shortages and is sure in his own mind that these are clear-cut thefts, he is in a position to talk to the employee. The interview is conducted along the lines used for any dishonest employee case.

The Interview

The dishonest employee may not admit to stealing cash from the store. Still the salesperson cannot argue against the facts shown by the register tapes used as evidence. She will be forced to admit that there is no record of the sale.

Occasionally, a salesperson will admit only that she has violated store policy. Such an employee will have to be closed out for violation of store policy and not for dishonesty. This is true, even though the shoppers, the security head, and the store management believe this person stole the money. Because this is true the interviewer must be aware of the legal limitations in these cases.

Security Person Does Not Escort Suspect

A security person should not be sent to the selling department to escort the salesclerk to the security office for interview. Such a security escort could be called an arrest in a civil suit. This might prove embarrassing for the store. A better system is to contact the salesperson's supervisor and ask her to bring the salesperson to the security office. Similar precautions should be taken during the interview so that the store is in a position to close out the salesperson on a violation of policy if she does not admit theft.

Store Policy Aids Dismissal

Incidentally, another aid is to establish the store's sales policy in writing. In most stores it is accepted that a salesperson *must* ring up all sales accurately and in proper sequence. It is also implied that failure to do so can lead to dismissal.

Your store should clarify its policy in this matter by putting it in writing. Some stores put a printed slip of paper on each employment card, which is then signed by the salesperson at the time of employment. It reads, "*I understand that as a salesperson I must ring up all of my sales and record them in the correct amount and in proper sequence. I also understand that failure to do so may lead to dismissal.*"

By having this policy signed by the salesperson and attached to her card, there is no problem later if she must be dismissed for violation of policy.

If the interviewer is successful in gaining admissions of theft, efforts should be made to reconstruct the theft activity of the employee. Try to determine over what period of time the thefts occurred and how much was stolen. It is also helpful to interview the employee regarding possible theft of goods and ask about her knowledge of other employees that might be stealing from the store.

Tape Record the Interview

Some stores record all interviews of cases on tape. This is particularly valuable for cases involving theft of cash from sales. These recordings can be helpful. If the employee is finally closed out on a violation of store policy she may claim she was abused. By having a recording of the interview these charges can be disproved.

It is also a fact that people who steal cash on sales are sometimes tops in sales for their departments. Because of this it is hard for buyers to believe that these people could be involved in theft. The dishonest employee who refuses to admit her dishonesty may often find a sympathetic person in the department manager, buyer, or even in the merchandise manager. She may distort the interview facts. By having the recorded interview available the matter can be clarified if necessary.

Need for Consistent Management Policy

A last thought that applies to all dishonest employee cases is the need for a consistent management policy. You need a policy of standardized disposition on these cases. This should be determined in advance. Failure to treat dishonest employee cases in a consistent manner can undermine the morale of security people and can lead to further dishonesty among rank-and-file employees.

Your management cannot afford to make exceptions in matters of dishonesty. If one salesperson is discharged for theft of money, then any other salesperson who does the same thing should also be closed out. Neither length of service, age, position, or the amount involved can be considered if your policy is to be consistent and effective. A firm attitude by management can help cut the causes of internal theft.

Other employees, who may be tempted to steal, observe with interest the action management takes on each theft case. Management itself is on trial.

Your interviewer must know management's policy before he begins his questioning. His interview must be in keeping with store policies. In times past store management often made up policies as they went along. Today this approach is not acceptable to either store personnel or administrative executives. Such paternalism can hurt a store, particularly if it is applied to matters of employee honesty.

You have three possible dispositions of a case: (1) a closeout based on admission of theft, (2) a court trial, or (3) dismissal from the store because of the violation of store policy. In all three instances the action taken should be based on a consistent store policy.

PROSECUTION

Some stores prosecute all dishonest employee cases. Others prosecute some but not all cases. A lot depends on the store attitude in these matters. Another factor is the state and local laws within which the store must operate. Not only must you know the laws, but also the interpretation of these laws by the courts in which your store will prosecute its cases.

Some stores have prosecuted many dishonest employee cases successfully and then have run up against a case that was dismissed by the courts because the judge decided that the store had failed to prove intent to steal. When this occurs it is almost always a case based on honesty shopping. This fact shows the need for caution and careful preparation in any shopping case you intend to procecute.

Must Have Witness and Cash

If an honesty shopping case is to be prosecuted, the case must be thoroughly prepared to meet the legal requirements. If you do your interviews on the basis of register tapes and sale tallies, you will need more evidence than this for prosecution. To prepare a case for trial there must be a witness to the actual theft of cash. In addition, the stolen cash must be recovered and identified as evidence.

When the salesperson is arrested and brought to the security office the stolen cash must be available, either on her person, in her handbag, or in her personal belongings. There must be a continual observation of this person from the moment of the test through the entire pattern of theft. It helps to have proof of previous thefts.

It is necessary that the cash given to the suspect be marked for later identification. There must be no doubt when the case is tried in court that the money can be identified as the same money handed to the employee at the time of the sale.

After the dishonest employee comes to the security office, the register drawer containing the balance of her money should be audited by the control division. The drawer should then be sealed and held as evidence in case of trial.

If There Is Doubt—Don't Prosecute

If there is any doubt about being able to prove the employee's intent to steal, the store should not prosecute. Closing out the subject on a violation of store policy is a better solution then prosecution if you have any doubt about your evidence.

When taking an employee to court the store risks a lot. Not only are there the serious costs of a civil judgment but also the possible loss of community goodwill. The risks should be evaluated at the time of decision.

ELECTRONIC DEVICES

Little scientific equipment has been found useful in the problem of cash thefts by salespeople. There are, however, three things that have been used on occasion: ultraviolet light, stop-action cameras, and closed-circuit television.

Ultraviolet Light

Ultraviolet light is sometimes helpful. Usually, however, it is only an additional bit of window dressing that serves little actual value.

An ultraviolet pencil is an effective way of marking money for identification. A bill can be marked with the word "stolen" and the date. In ordinary light the markings are invisible. Under ultraviolet or "black" light the markings glow in a luminous fashion. This can be helpful in "breaking" the dishonest employee at the time of interview.

How does this work? Well, let's suppose the employee, while being interviewed in the security office, is told to empty her handbag and place all the money on the desk. She is then asked if all of this money is hers. The average person in this situation says emphatically that all of the money *is* her own personal money.

At this point the interviewer snaps on an ultraviolet desk lamp that causes two of the marked bills to glow with the words "stolen" on them. This has a shock effect on the employee. The result is that she usually admits her guilt without further discussion.

Since the admission of guilt is usually obtained in the shopping case, the ultraviolet method may be more trouble than it is worth. However, if there is any serious doubt about being able to "break" the employee, the ultraviolet can serve a useful purpose.

Stop-Action Cameras

Some stores have experimented with a stop-action movie camera. This is connected by an electrical circuit to a cash register. The camera is located in such a way that the finder takes in the amount rung on the register as well as the open drawer and the salesperson's hands.

The camera starts to operate when a sale is rung on the register. The camera continues for several seconds of motion picture film and then shuts off. In this way the camera can observe the amount recorded on the register and the action of the hands putting the money into the register.

As with many such devices the task of placing the camera in a concealed location, loading it, developing the film, and reviewing the frames becomes an excessive effort for the results obtained.

In stores where the camera has been tried, it has usually been used for only a brief time. It is soon abandoned in a back closet where it gathers dust along with other similar gadgets that have accumulated from time to time.

Closed-Circuit Television

Closed-circuit television serves a similar purpose as the movie camera but it is more practical. It allows continuous observation of the salesperson and her register for an extended period of time. It does not require fresh film daily. It has a mobility that makes it more desirable.

Television application in theft of cash on sales, however, is limited. Such observation is hardly needed since the evidence obtained on a monitor screen would not be admissible in court. Violations determined by examining the register tape do not require this type of observation. There is little value in using a television camera for watching a cash register theft operation.

MASS SHOPPING TESTS

What about the future potential of honesty shopping? Some stores are beginning to experiment with mass shopping tests by bringing in 15 or 25 shoppers at one time. The shoppers may be moved into a high-shortage department as a group. They momentarily take over the department as customers. Within 20 or 30 minutes, most of the customers buying in a department can be honesty shoppers.

This mass approach can be effective. It may give a quick answer to the security conditions of that area in relation to cash sale thefts. Group shopping of this type also makes it more difficult for a salesperson to detect the honesty shopper.

Stores are also experimenting with other projects. In one instance a specific problem department is tested. Every salesperson is tested for a minimum of ten shoppings within a two-week period. This sampling, if done on a large enough scale, can explore the lost potential in any given sales area.

There is an opportunity for future experiments in various ways. The next few years should develop new techniques that will undoubtedly make shopping even more effective than it is today.

New educational training programs also help. In the end, however, there is no real answer except to enforce store systems. If every one of your customers receives a sales receipt for her purchase salespeople will not steal cash on sales.

The answer to prevention lies in the area of strong systems, interested supervision, fair leadership, and a good internal audit follow-up. *Preventing thefts is the best final answer.* Trying to find the dishonest employee *after* the damage is done is a costly method of cutting your profit losses.

Chapter 8

UNDERCOVER AGENTS

The bedside phone buzzed softly but persistently. A hand appeared from under the blankets and pawed the darkness in search of the sound. George Franklin, president of a chain of eleven stores in Northern California, pushed his way up through heavy clouds of sleep and clumsily grabbed at the instrument.

"Yes?" his voice was a sleepy whisper.

"Hello! Hello! I can hardly hear you." The voice in the receiver was a woman's; it had the irritating twang of an untuned guitar string.

Becoming more awake, the president leaned on his elbow, took a breath, and tried again, "Hello, who is this?" His voice trailed off as he squinted at the illuminated clock on the nightstand. "Four o'clock in the morning, what the hell. . . ."

"Is this Mr. Franklin?"

"Yes, yes, who is this?"

The woman's voice was soft and angry, "Listen, Mr. Franklin, I'm only going to tell you once," the voice on the phone became a whisper of intrigue.

"Your truck drivers and your warehouse men are stealing you blind! Do you hear me, Mr. Franklin? Those bastards are stealing you blind!"

With a loud click the phone went dead and the president heard the open line humming in his ear. Carefully he replaced the phone. For a long moment he leaned motionless on his elbow, staring into the early morning darkness. Disturbed and confused, George Franklin's mind spun with questions.

"Who was that on the phone?" The voice sounded familiar, but he couldn't place it. "What was she saying? The truck drivers are stealing?"

Suddenly the president sat up in bed. The woman's message had finally penetrated the fog. Angrily he reached out in the darkness and with a loud snap the night table lamp sprang into life, the glare of its bulb making him blink in momentary pain as he rubbed his eyes.

Later that morning George Franklin called his security director, Harry Markus, to his office.

"We've got trouble, my friend," he told the security man.

"What kind?" asked Markus, patiently lighting his pipe.

The president told Markus about the phone call and then silently waited for the security director to respond.

"Odd, very odd," said Markus, "we haven't had any indications of stealing in either the truck drivers or among the warehouse people."

"Well, something must be going on!" said the president.

"Yeah, an angry woman."

"Some guy's giving her a hard time and she's decided to get even," said Franklin tapping his pencil on the desk blotter.

"It may be a false alarm."

"At four in the morning?"

The security director was thoughtful, "Only one way to find out."

"What's that?"

"Plant an undercover agent in the driver group. Perhaps put another one in the warehouse. Put him in the dock gang."

"But the truckers are union. Isn't it going to be tough to get an undercover into that group?"

"Perhaps," said Markus, "but I think we can work it. We'll say he's a trainee; he can join the union if he has to."

"How long do you think it'll take to find out what's going on?" asked the president.

"Depends how active the group is and how soon the detective can work his way into their confidence. I'd say it'll take several months. Thieves are damn suspicious of new people."

Franklin shifted his gaze from the security man to the calendar on his desk. "How soon can you plant the agents?"

"By the seventeenth of the month, if we're lucky."

"Well, let's do it. We can be really hurting if we've got large thefts in that area."

"I'll start on it first thing," said Markus, standing up and starting for the door.

"Another thing Harry. . . ."

"Yes?"

"Keep this between us, okay? No one else is to know, not the department heads, not Johnny Wallace the warehouse manager, no one, understand?"

"I understand." And with that Markus left.

Within two weeks the security director had placed two agents, one in the warehouse dock operation and the other as a truck driver's assistant.

At first the agents had little to report. They did occasionally observe some whispering at the far end of the dock between the drivers and dock men, but they saw nothing to indicate that a conspiracy to steal was going on.

This initial lack of suspicious activity temporarily reassured the security director. He began to assume that the president's early morning caller had merely been an angry woman making up a phony story to get someone into trouble.

Then suddenly the picture changed. On Tuesday night the undercover man working on the trucks went to a nearby bar with a truck driver with whom he had become friendly. Over several beers, the agent suggested to the driver he'd like to get his hands on an electric handsaw. He explained that he was planning to put up some plywood panels in his basement to make a playroom out of it and he needed the saw to cut the plywood. He asked the driver if he knew anywhere he might get a saw cheap.

"How cheap?" asked the driver, making rings with his beer glass on the bar top.

"I don't know, say ten dollars?"

"I might be able to help you," said the driver, "let me see what I can do."

That was the first break in the case. Two days later the driver left a $69.95 electric handsaw in the back seat of the undercover agent's car.

In a matter of days the detective had worked his way further into the gang, and three weeks after the handsaw was delivered the agent had enough information so that the security department could move in and make arrests.

The upshot was that four truck drivers and three warehouse dock men were arrested for theft. After they were interrogated, they admitted stealing, as a group, more than $1,000 worth of merchandise a day off the transfer trucks. The gang disposed of the stolen goods through a fence, getting about 20 percent of the retail value. They admitted that they had been stealing off the transfer trucks for the past eight years.

The security department recovered more than $35,000 worth of stolen merchandise from the homes of the culprits. The final total of the admitted thefts was $225,000.

The important lesson to be learned from this case is the fact that although the company's security department had a staff of 28 detectives and 5 investigators, they still had no indication that these collusive thefts were occurring. The security department failed to uncover them because, until the angry woman's phone call, they did not have a systematic undercover program. Without undercover agents they couldn't uncover collusive theft rings that often drain away a large part of company profits.

Once the transfer theft case was resolved the company set up a continuing undercover program, and in several months they broke up several other important theft rings in the night porter group and in the shipping and receiving departments.

Security Staff Is Incomplete Without Undercover Agents

As large as the security staff was (33 people for 11 stores), without an active undercover staff the department was still ineffective in discovering and stopping collusive employee thefts. Without undercover agents, retail security is operating with one hand tied behind its back.

In Retailing the Major Problem Is Internal Thefts

Retailers, in recent years, have come to the conclusion that employee dishonesty is the biggest headache. Retailing is vulnerable to employee thefts more than any other type of business. The availability of desirable merchandise and money, when combined with poorly enforced control procedures and limited supervision, sets up a situation in which any employee at one time or another can be tempted to steal.

Of course shoplifting has also been on the increase. The number of customers who shoplift from the stores today is staggering. But the skyrocketing shortage figures being posted by stores of all kinds is more the result of employee thefts than outsiders.

Employee Thefts Are Frequent

The dishonest employee is on the job day in and day out and once he starts to steal his thefts may occur daily, making a constant drain on the store. The shoplifter, on the other hand, can also hurt the store with his thefts, but visits to the store are periodic and the damage a particular shoplifter does is occasional and more limited than that of a thieving worker.

Employees Have More Opportunities to Steal

In addition, store employees have more access to merchandise, and even to cash, than does the shoplifter. In fact, knowledgeable workers may steal without removing any goods from store premises.

These store thieves rip off the store's refund system, work kickback deals with resource salesmen, or steal in collusion with dishonest resource truckers, or a receiving clerk may sign for merchandise never received by the store. Embezzlement is often easier and more profitable than outright physical theft of merchandise.

With today's need to stem the tidal wave of internal stealing, it is little wonder that store managements are concerned with preventing dishonesty with stronger control procedures, better supervision, and more thorough screening of job applicants.

But in spite of all the constructive things done to prevent employees from stealing, stores also need a program to detect internal thefts.

Some Stores Shy Away from Using Undercover Agents

In the war against employee dishonesty the most powerful weapon a store can command is the undercover agent.

Of course some stores resist the use of undercover agents because they have had unhappy experiences with such agents in the past. In some instances the agent's real identity has been discovered causing serious employee morale problems. In other instances, the undercover agent was simply not productive. And executives also tell horror stories about the undercover agent who reported that there was no theft activity in the department where he was assigned, while in actual fact, the agent had joined the malefactors in the department he was assigned to watch and was himself stealing.

Some managements shy away from undercover programs because they feel undercover detectives are too costly to operate. And in some instances a top management executive has objected to undercover strategies on ethical or philosophic grounds, arguing that it is not morally or ethically right to "spy" on workers.

Added to the negative attitudes stemming from unproductive and dishonest agents is the fact that some stores don't use them because the person in charge of security does not know how to obtain, train, or use undercover agents.

Despite Objections, Undercover Agents Are Often Highly Effective

But in spite of all the objections that can arise when the use of covert surveillance is suggested, these programs have proven highly effective in many stores and have chalked up the apprehension of many dishonest employees. Agents have not only stopped large-scale theft activities in store after store, but also often have more than paid for themselves in the recovery of company merchandise and money.

Most complaints about using covert detectives stem from a lack of understanding of how to select, train, and assign such agents. In the hands of a competent security director, the undercover program is as easy to administer as the floor detective program.

Proper screening of potential undercover detectives can improve the quality of agents in terms of skills needed for this work and can also eliminate the risk of hiring people who may turn out to be dishonest or potential troublemakers.

Apprehensions Are Not the Only Objective

The fact that a good agent is not producing cases is not in itself an unhappy situation. When management is concerned about the possible dishonesty of a specific person or group operating in the store, and wants to *know* if these suspects *are* stealing, the undercover detective can be used to find out. If the answer is negative and the suspicions are not justified in view of the facts, store management can be grateful that the matter has been resolved.

Agents Are Worth the Price

Undercover agents *are* expensive but so is the work of any skilled professional person. But in the matter of the undercover detective, a good agent is worth his price many times over. Stores that use agents in a continuing program of covert surveillance of their operations have the apprehensions and recoveries to prove their value.

Use of Agents Is Not Unethical

An executive's ethical concern about using agents is not justified. After all, management has the right to know what is going on in the store. The undercover program is well within ethical boundaries concerned with the professional rules of right and wrong. As long as undercover people restrict their surveillance to company objectives and avoid such illegal activities as "labor spying," the program is not only ethically proper but also can be construed as necessary to protect company assets for the honest people connected with the enterprise.

Honest employees have nothing to fear from undercover agents. But dishonest workers are themselves acting unethically and immorally and therefore management is justified in ferreting them out.

Fears of unfairness are not a justified reason for management to reject the use of undercover agents. The criminal employee who has thrown away moral and ethical standards is the person who is acting unfairly. The thieving employee has adopted the philosophy, "Never give a sucker an even break." Ethics are on the side of store and the undercover detectives because management has a right to know that certain employees are stealing from the company.

Rejection May Be Caused by Fear

Excessive protestations against the use of undercover agents should be questioned. Perhaps the executive who is so strenuously objecting to such a program may be more concerned about being spied upon than about the agents watching others. Fear can be acute if the executive is himself involved in dishonest activities.

Sometimes an executive may insist that the undercover agents be directed from his office rather than from the security department. This decision may also be suspect, perhaps the reason for it has more to do with covering up the executive's own dishonesty than insuring that the program is well administered.

An Undercover Program Can Serve the Company in Several Ways

An undercover program has many benefits for the company. It is an excellent method for detecting thefts that cannot be prevented by control systems or by supervision. Agents are usually more successful when assigned to work in nonselling departments. Nonselling areas have often proven difficult to control. Large theft rings have been uncovered in receiving, delivery, vendor returns, accounts receivable, marking, night porters, and display departments, to name but a few.

In addition, periodic spot checks of after-hour guards, warehouse and distribution centers, and store transfer operations are also at times productive. And stock boys have been a natural for uncovering in-house theft gangs.

Clears the Innocent

An undercover operation can often resolve the question of whether a suspected worker is stealing. In some instances the agent discovers that the rumors of dishonesty are without foundation and a cloud of suspicion is removed.

Agents, if properly trained and directed, can spot breakdowns in control procedures, weaknesses in supervision, lack of employee discipline, and similar management concerns.

In high-shortage departments undercover detectives often spot the causes of these heavy losses. They may discover that a buyer is failing to take markdowns, or there are pricing errors or errors in figuring extensions, and similar problems. Or they may uncover a clerk making fraudulent refunds or a salesperson stealing cash on sales.

In addition to employee dishonesty, undercover agents can be trained to look for the source of many operating problems, such as absenteeism, high turnover rates, inefficiency, low morale, poor employee relations, incompetent supervision, falsified figures, vandalism, inaccurate reports, carelessness, negligence, and so on.

Need for Acting Ability

Undercover agents and floor detectives have a lot in common; both of them pretend to be something they are not. The floor detective pretends to be a customer so as to spot shoplifters. The undercover detective pretends to be a normal employee while trying to locate dishonest employees stealing in the department where he is assigned.

But the undercover agent, playing his dual role, must have considerable acting ability to convince fellow workers that he is just another employee like themselves, and to convince any dishonest employees that he is willing to join them in their thefts.

When selecting an agent, try to find a person who has shown an interest in the theatre and has some acting ability. The applicant who has acted in school plays, been a member of the college drama club, or played in community theatre or in summer stock is a good bet for undercover work. These theatrical interests make it easier for such a person to project an image of himself that is quite unlike his real character.

The detective must be able to sustain his role over a period of time. While a floor detective can step off the floor and have a cigarette or go to lunch and drop his pretense at being a shopper, no such break is given the undercover agent.

The undercover agent must maintain his role of average employee both on and off the job. He plays this role while on lunch hour and while on his relief period. And since he often may have to associate with the suspected workers after hours, he sometimes must sustain his pretense for a long period of time.

An agent gets little relief from tension while on the job. He constantly guards against discovery. Fear of being discovered haunts his waking and sleeping hours. The slightest slip in behavior, words, or actions can blow his cover. Even his own skills may not be enough to protect him from disaster. While out to lunch with fellow workers a friend may spot him and come running to the lunch table, calling him by his real name and asking him how his "undercover work is going these days. . . ." wow!

The agent can't take anyone into his confidence on the job. He has to be a loner, talking only to himself about his worries and his problems. The undercover person has the ultimate need for self-sufficiency. It is a lonely profession and the agent must have the guts to live an isolated life, independent from the normal warm relationships of friends usually developed on the job.

The paradox is that although a loner, the agent must also be sociable, able to get along well with the people he workes with. What a combination! Isolated and secretive and yet gregarious, outgoing, friendly, and persuasive.

The agent has to develop an image that allows workers to trust and confide in him. Without this ability an agent is totally ineffective in detecting criminals.

As the agent works his way into the confidence of the suspected thieves, he becomes part of the grubby backside of scheming and destruction that typifies the world of collusive criminals. To be successful in his job he must get the thieves to cut him in on the action.

Agent Must Play Games

"Come into my parlor," said the spider to the fly. To get the thieves to invite him into their conspiracy, the agent plays games with his protagonists—dangerous games. Working with a theft ring is not easy.

If the agent's false identity is stripped away, he suddenly becomes exposed and vulnerable. A serious beating, perhaps even death, can result. The danger is real for the untrained, inept, or unlucky undercover detective. Any applicant for such work should be well aware of these risks before going into it.

The job the agent takes on is challenging, difficult, and dangerous. It requires skill and intelligence as well as analytical ability. The applicant who has to have above average intelligence must not show this superiority on the job. You must look for it when hiring an agent, however. Also look for acting and analytical ability. If the applicant likes crossword puzzles or scrabble or other similar games it suggests analytical ability.

The Agent Must Appear Vulnerable to Corruption

The agent must be friendly . . . but not *too* friendly . . . and he must appear corruptible.

His actions, statements, viewpoint, and overall tone must not suggest to the suspects that the agent is too honest to steal. They will never take him into their plot if they believe he's uncorruptible.

How does the agent get his availability across? At first he may try to gain acceptance by gossiping with the suspects about his personal problems, showing he has an unusual need for money. This rationalizes why he might be willing to join the gang.

He can explain, over coffee, to a member of the gang that he hates the company, or that he hates his boss because of some action against him. Or he can cry about being a loser on the ponies and owing a bookie a bundle. He may simply explain that his wife has run up bills and he's heavily in debt. Or he can claim he's got an expensive girl friend who is costing him more than he can earn to keep her in gifts.

He may set up a suspect by telling about an expensive watch his girl friend wants him to buy. He explains he can't afford it and the buyer won't sell it to him at cost. The dishonest worker may respond by offering to get the watch for him either free (to make him obligated) or at a cost of a few dollars, which he can easily afford. This opens the door to a full-time partnership with the thieves.

In other words, to get cut into the action the agent must rationalize his willingness to steal because of money pressures or a desire for particular merchandise. Unless he offers the suspects a believable type of bait, they will be slow to accept him into their intimate circle.

The Agent Must Have Unusual Integrity

The temptation for an agent to steal is tremendous. He becomes a partner with the thieves in his department, and he participates in their thefts to get the goods on them; but he must, nevertheless, remain honest.

Personal honesty is a prime requisite for the good undercover agent. On the one hand, he must be a con artist and play the role of a thieving employee. He must appear vulnerable to temptation, weak, and corruptible, but on the other hand, he must, in fact, be morally strong and incorruptible.

The temptation to join the thieves is always a hidden pressure on the agent, but he must have the character to resist it.

Before hiring anyone as an undercover agent be sure to interview this person carefully for signs of character weakness. Also do a thorough screening of past employment, questioning every previous employer carefully for any indications of dishonesty while working for him. Check out all references for dates, salaries earned, and so on. Make sure he did not lie on his application card. Remember that honesty is a vital necessity when hiring an agent. If you have even a shadow of doubt about an applicant's integrity, do not hire this person. Look for someone else. Keep searching until you find exactly the person you want. The position of undercover agent is too valuable to give to just anyone that comes along.

Women Make Equally Good Agents

Many undercover people are men because, until recently, most non-selling jobs such as warehouse or stock help, night cleaning, and receiving and delivery were primarily done by men. But today the employee picture is becoming more balanced, and women are found in many store departments that a few years ago used only men. Certain investigations are best handled by a woman agent.

Women have proven themselves to be top-drawer agents! And they don't have to be terribly tough either. In fact, women have often made their case because they seemed soft and easy to persuade and control. Sad to say, more women are stealing today than ever before, and when women steal in collusion, only a woman agent can gain acceptance into the theft ring.

A woman agent can often discover large-scale thefts by working as one of the store cashiers. Other women have uncovered major cases in the control division, for example, in the accounts-receivable operation where dishonest workers have torn up invoices so neither they nor their families would have to pay for charged merchandise, or they have stolen money by forging bank checks made out to phony firms. In fact, when it comes to embezzlement on a grand scale, the criminal is often a woman.

In all these situations the undercover woman is extremely effective if she has been carefully chosen, has been properly trained, and likes the work.

Good undercover agents, either men or women, are not easy to find; but the return is worth the effort because good agents are like gold dust in your pocket.

Assigning the Agent

Some undercover agents have been successful in selling departments. They have been able to spot dishonest clerks passing out packages of stolen merchandise to outside accomplices, or cashiers stealing cash on sales. Although these are good cases, they usually involve someone working alone; seldom do we find collusive theft gangs in selling departments.

Selling departments can produce cases, but the greatest value of undercover people has been in nonselling departments. This is where the big cases develop. Nonselling areas are often more vulnerable to employee dishonesty because they are inadequately controlled and poorly supervised. They are also difficult areas for security to watch unless an undercover agent is in the department working with the staff.

Agents Effective in NonSelling Departments

Hidden surveillance of nonselling departments can prove useful at times, but it's still not as effective as an undercover agent. The hidden watcher cannot move about with the employees, often his view is blocked, and he constantly faces the danger of getting caught. If dishonesty is suspected in a nonselling department, an undercover person is often the best answer.

If the security department has a tip about a worker or a group of workers stealing in a particular nonselling department, it's wise to assign an undercover agent into that department. When there are no specific suspects, agents can be used to probe the activities of stock boys or the night-time porter group. Porters have, over the years, proven to be particularly susceptible to dishonesty. Other after-hour workers also need to be checked out periodically: display people, night stockers, after-hour computer personnel, and so on. Truck drivers, warehouse people, and receiving room and marking personnel are all good kinds of workers on which to use undercover detectives.

Sometimes you can place an agent in the best location by reviewing the company's operation to see where conditions exist that might lead to employee thefts. For example, where is supervision weak or nonexistent? Where are the workers checking themselves out of the building? Where do after-hour workers receive little attention by management? And so on!

At Hudson's the company executives had not visited the store from midnight to six in the morning for many years, and yet several hundred porters, stock people, and others were in the store working during those hours. These night workers, unsupervised and unattended, were ripe for criminal activities.

Night porters or any after-hour cleaners, particularly if they are from an outside cleaning agency, are often suspect. These cleaning people are seldom properly screened by the agency hiring them. I have known instances in which the agency claimed its people were screened for previous criminal records and polygraphed before hiring, and yet when we caught them stealing, we discovered they had police records for burglary, holdups, assault, and larceny. And we also found they had never been given a lie detector test by the cleaning agency. It is wise for security to do background checks on everyone who works in the store whether they are on the store payroll or that of an outside agency.

Don't rely on agency reassurances about the honesty of after-hour workers. Test them occasionally with an undercover agent.

If you clean out a gang of night workers, such as porters, don't assume that the night security problem is taken care of for a long time. This is probably a false hope.

Professional thieves who prey on retailers are constantly looking for the weak link in the store's employee group. Some of these criminals concentrate on corrupting the receiving clerk, providing him with kickbacks if he signs for goods not received or turns his back to allow a dishonest trucker to throw cartons of goods from the store dock onto his truck. They also persuade after-hour porters to steal.

Professional criminals recognize that the porter group is usually living on a substandard income and that they have access to valuable store merchandise.

Porters are often talked into stealing, passing the goods on to the outside professional thieves. When you finally knock off a theft ring like this, the temptation is to assume that night cleaners won't be a security department problem again for a long time. This may be unwise because the outside criminals who organized this ring of thieves may now go to work to corrupt the new porters. Often within a month or two the new porters are stealing just as much or more than the porters you recently caught.

Truck drivers who work for the company are also contacted by outside criminals, as are warehouse and distribution center workers. Professional thieves see these positions as easy marks for an ongoing theft of store merchandise. A few discussions by the professional criminals with employees, over coffee in the local diner, can lead to the setting up of an elaborate and costly collusive theft ring. And the only known ways that such rings are uncovered is by a "tip" from an employee, by accident (for example, an employee is caught by city police when committing another crime outside the store and the police find large amounts of store merchandise stored in his garage), or by a clever undercover agent who has worked his way into the confidence of the thieves.

Of these three possible ways of locating such major theft rings, it is apparent that the undercover agent is the most reliable method.

Undercover Objectives

When a particular suspect has surfaced, the agent's assignment may be to find out if a certain person is stealing, whether others are stealing with him, how he is stealing, what is being done with the merchandise, and so on. Finally, when he has enough information a legal apprehension is made.

In another situation, an anonymous tip may be received that a certain person working in a nonselling department is stealing. The undercover agent may, in this instance, be directed to determine first whether the tip is true or false. If the agent establishes beyond any doubt that the suspected thief is not stealing—and this often happens—the agent may be pulled out of the department to work somewhere else where known thieves have been located.

At other times agents may be assigned simply on the basis of the inventory shortage records that show that a particular department's shortages have been steadily growing over the past few months and have reached a volume that requires security attention to the department.

In the case of inventory shortage departments, the agent's goal is to find out, if possible, the primary causes of the inventory shortage figures. This may result in uncovering individual or collusive thefts.

But it also may result in uncovering sloppy bookkeeping, failure to take markdowns, or other causes of the high shortage.

In a thorough investigation of a department, security may combine the efforts of two groups of security people. First, undercover agents may work in the department for a few weeks to see if any flagrant theft operations are draining off merchandise. After this intense undercover effort, the security investigators may go into the department and analyze cash register overages and shortages, check out the validity of refunds, review cash register tapes in detail to see if they show excessive voided transactions or an unusual number of "no-sale" transactions, and so forth.

The investigators have the same purpose as the undercover agents in this instance; both of them are charged with locating the causes of the department's high shortages.

When a store develops a group of professional undercover agents, the task of probing a department for dishonest workers can sometimes be combined with looking for possible procedural loopholes that may be causing heavy losses.

Developing the Undercover Program

The store that has never set up an undercover program as a permanent part of the security operation should probably start by using undercover agents furnished by an outside agency. This can get the program under way rapidly and will provide experience in working with such agents. This experience will help later on when you establish your own operation.

Outside detective agencies, however, are not desirable for a long-term program. Often the agencies are found wanting in the way in which they select undercover people, and some fail to properly train the agents sent to their clients.

In addition, the outside agent is far more costly to the store because the agency must make a profit over and above the agent's salary.

Look for a Reputable Detective Agency

On the other hand, a good agent can be worth the price no matter how expensive he is. One case that rounds up an employee theft ring will pay the agency costs many times over. It is also true that many agencies will provide carefully selected, well-trained agents who are as effective as any agents the store may later employ and train.

The primary concern in working with an outside agency is that it be reputable, reliable, and have a proven record of furnishing productive undercover detectives to its clients. All of these points can be checked out *before* deciding on an agency for your store.

Once an agency sends an undercover person into the store for a particular assignment, the security department should ask the agency for a full report on the past record of this particular agent.

Before putting an agent onto an assignment, the store should know what specific cases the agent developed in past assignments, how long he has been with the agency, what his training has been, who investigated his references and work background, and if the agent was polygraphed, who conducted the test.

In other words, don't leave anything to chance. Know as much as you can about the agent before you use him, and if you have even the slightest question about his experience, skill, honesty, or whether or not he will fit into the work group to which you hope to assign him—don't use him. Continue to reject unsuitable agents even if you are offered several in a row who don't meet your screening standards.

Don't let the agency intimidate you or sell you a bill of goods. And if in the end they can't furnish you with an agent you feel is fully satisfactory for a particular job, give up and go to another agency. Don't risk exposure or dishonesty by the agent! Amateurism is dangerous; don't use an unqualified person! This job is too sensitive for you to take chances. It is better to have no agent than the wrong one.

When you have accepted and assigned an outside agency's undercover detective to a department in the company, continue to work closely with the agency involved. Spell out the information you want the agent to develop. You should decide on reporting procedures. Also make it clear that you don't want voluminous reports on trivia. You are only interested in factual information related directly to employee thefts.

The store security director should personally brief the agent on the background of the situation and the objectives of the assignment. Don't depend on the undercover person to get this vital information second hand from an agency representative.

Also provide the necessary training for the agent in any job skills required in the department where he will work. Tell the agent that you don't want reports on extraneous matters or on infractions of minor rules. You should particularly caution the agent against reporting gossip or unimportant matters. Writing about people returning late from lunch, smoking on the job, or badmouthing a supervisor behind his back are not material for a competent undercover agent's report.

In spite of reassurances that the agency might give about the selection, training, and effectiveness of the agent, it is still prudent to question the agent once he arrives in the store. Ask him the length of time he has worked for the agency, the specific type of training he has received, and ask him for examples of successful investigations he has made in past assignments. Hopefully, this information will correlate with that given by the agency. If it doesn't, it is better to delay using the agent until the matter can be properly resolved. This tactic will probably result in future relations with the agency being more factual since they will now realize that you mean business when you ask for information about new agents.

Developing Store's Own Undercover Program

Although it is often best to start with an outside agency to get a "feel" for undercover work and to learn how to assign and work with an agent, in the long run a store is usually better off developing a permanent in-house undercover staff as part of the security department. (Unless, of course, the store has been fortunate enough to hire a productive outside agency that provides top-quality people, works closely with management, and has a good record of apprehensions.)

When undercover detectives are permanent employees, they tend to develop company loyalty. The longer they work for the store, the more they are accepted by the other employees. They also become intimately familiar with company control systems and procedures that help them find irregularities and weaknesses.

The permanent agents also learn the policies and philosophy of the company. They come to know the various employees and supervisors and are thus better equipped to work with them and to develop acceptance from their co-workers.

At the same time the agent is getting to know the company and its personnel, the security director is getting to know the agent. He will soon know what motivates him, how to evaluate his reports, and how he can be used best because of his background or special skills. The supervisor can work with the agent to improve his performance and job satisfaction.

The store agent also can be moved from one job to another, if the need arises, with little suspicion on the part of the other workers. Instead of requiring a long time to learn the job and to become accepted on his new job assignement, he is accepted faster than a stranger; and since he already knows a lot about company procedures and personalities in management, he can adapt to the work rapidly.

Since job survival is no longer at stake for the undercover person, he does not put excessive pressure on his fellow workers to gain their acceptance. He takes his time and lets the relationship develop normally; this reduces the danger of blowing his cover and usually guarantees acceptance by dishonest employees.

Use Care in Selecting Agents

Now that you are hiring your own undercover agents, exercise great care because the wrong choice can prove costly. You are looking for a permanent member of the security department's undercover staff. You are hoping the person selected will prove productive in making dishonest employee cases, and you also expect this person will build his experience on each case, so that one case will train the agent to spot similar cases in the future.

You want a winner. You don't want your selection to turn out to be dishonest himself. (One firm's study of the backgrounds of people applying for undercover work showed that 23 percent had previous criminal records for larceny and other crimes against property.) You don't want an agent who blows his cover and gives himself away to other employees. You want him to have the judgment to make intelligent and objective reports.

In addition, you want the agent to be able to get along well with people and work his way into the confidence of fellow employees. While doing all this he must also have the drive and persistence to do a full day's work on the "regular" job to which he is assigned. Just because he is a detective does not let him off the hook in regard to doing his "cover-up" job. Role playing requires that he turn out as much work as other members of his work group; otherwise, this alone may raise questions by fellow employees that can lead to uncovering his identity. It can be a real headache for the security director if the undercover agent's department supervisor is dissatisfied with the agent's job performance and tries to transfer or discharge him. Since his identity cannot be revealed to the department head, this can cause problems.

How adaptable is the person you are considering for an undercover job? On occasion, the agent must say things contrary to his real beliefs so that he can gain acceptance by the employees around him. If he is an ardent liberal and his work associates are ultraconservatives, the agent must express enthusiasm for the candidates they praise and emphasize support for the qualities they favor in their political heroes.

If the agent is doubtful about his ability to play a particular role, it would be more sensible to admit this rather than trying to bluff it. One agent worked in the restaurant of a large department store but could not fit comfortably into the dining room atmosphere and wisely asked to be transferred to a department more suited to his actual work experience.

Language skills may be vital to successful undercover work. An agent trying to win the confidence of a warehouse work group with Spanish as their native language cannot possibly win the group's acceptance if he doesn't speak or understand Spanish!

To gain the trust of fellow employees, the agent needs to keep in step with them in language, viewpoint, clothing, hair style, economic level, and so on. A serious mistake would be for a stockboy who works with people earning the minimum wage to come to work driving a late model Corvette and wearing a Rolex watch.

He must also know something about the work he will do. He should know the skills required and the job-related vocabulary to avoid arousing suspicion among regular workers.

Good judgment and emotional stability are the result of the agent's being physically well and mature. Only if he has patience and self-control can he avoid moving too fast or letting some remark slip that betrays his identity. It can take as long as six months for an agent to work his way into the confidence of a group who is stealing on a large scale.

Store Should Have a Contract With the Agent About Discharge

Be prepared to discharge the agent without notice. Even though an agent is hired for a long-term job with the company, it is understandable that something may go wrong. Possibly something may have happened to reveal his identity, a situation that neither the security director nor the agent could have predicted and were powerless to prevent. In such a situation, hopefully a rare one, the store must be in a position to discharge the agent instantly. To avoid argument in such an event, all agents used by the store should sign a contract in which they agree to immediate discharge without notice. Usually this contract should be automatically renewable every three months throughout the agent's length of employment.

Don't ever be caught in a situation where you are forced to keep an agent as a permanent employee and where you cannot get rid of him no matter what happens.

Paying the Agent

Paying the agent requires that the undercover person's identity be protected in the bookkeeping department. In fact, no one, not even the personnel manager, should know that an undercover detective is working in the company. The agent should receive his regular wages in the same manner as his associates. The extra money paid for his undercover work is best paid in cash. Submit a voucher to bookkeeping for an innocuous item such as "public relations expenditure." Either meet the agent to give him this money or send a money order to him at his home.

Keep the agent's extra salary off the official payroll and don't let anyone in the control division know about him.

Protecting the Agent's Identity

If the person being hired as an agent has done undercover work in other firms previously, you may find it necessary to develop a substitute identity for him. This requires selecting a fictitious name, background, and personal history. The name selected must be close enough to the agent's real name so that he can easily answer to it without confusion. Often it is best to retain the agent's own first name while selecting a last name with the same initial as the agent's real initial. If he claims to have lived in other cities, the cities used in his background should be places familiar to him so that he can talk to any one who has lived there with not giving himself away.

It must be a firm policy to protect the agent's identity at all times. The legitimate need to know is the criterion for deciding who must know about an agent. Under no circumstances should the head of the department where the agent is assigned be told about the agent. Neither should the head of a segment of the business where the agent works, such as the warehouse manager, know the agent's identity.

An agent's effectiveness is destroyed if people, even trusted employees, know his identity.

Curiosity is part of human nature, and man's best intentions are no protection from it. Once a supervisor knows that a new man in his department is an undercover detective, he can't resist taking a long look at him to see what sort of person he is. He will also try "subtly" to watch his activities. The supervisor may even make the mistake of calling the agent aside and have a whispered conference with him to find out what he's discovered. Without intending any harm, the supervisor can easily arouse the suspicions of his employees and destroy the agent's effectiveness.

It is also true that sometimes a supervisor is concerned about his own position and *will not want the agent to find anything wrong in his department* because he fears this will reflect poorly on him. In this situation the supervisor may take one or two people aside and point out the agent. He may tell them to "keep an eye on him." These supervisors want to prevent the detective from discovering any dishonesty among their staff. I have known situations in which an insecure supervisor destroyed the agent's cover by pointing him out to all of his employees.

Discovery of Undercover Agent Is Damaging

The constant concern of security directors is that an agent will be discovered. This can be a blow to employee morale.

When an undercover detective is revealed in their midst, dishonest employees often panic. This overreaction may turn into disruptive tactics such as slowdowns, complaints, vandalism, and even strikes.

Keeping an agent's identity secret is vital, for the discovery of an agent can be more serious than thefts. It can lead to violence against the agent, and it can mean a breakdown of the relationship between management and its employees—with serious consequences for the company.

The agent should never be involved in arresting the dishonest employee. Instead, the agent should prepare the security department so that security department investigators can observe the crime and make the arrest. To divert suspicion from the agent, it is prudent to also arrest the undercover agent as one of the conspirators along with the other suspects. He should be brought in, questioned, and treated the same as other members of the gang. Once his job is done, the agent should be moved to another department or to a branch store and be given a fresh assignment.

Don't Boast About the Undercover Agent's Work

Management must resist the temptation to relax after a case and boast about the job done by the undercover detective. This is a mistake. Even honest employees will resent having been spied upon by an agent, and no one enjoys the feeling of having been duped by someone who pretended to be one of them while actually he was a detective assigned to keep them under surveillance.

Not only should an agent never make an arrest but he should never appear in court as a witness for the company. His job is purely investigative and should not touch on other aspects of the apprehension or prosecution of the thieves.

Reporting

Pressure for reports can be a mistake. One well-known consultant who furnishes undercover operators to stores requires every agent on his staff to give him a report of some kind of questionable activity every Friday (whether the agent has observed any questionable activity or not). The word to the agents is that if such a report is not turned in each Friday, the agent will be fired.

As a result, in order to keep their jobs, agents make up reports that are sheer fantasy but read with the excitement of a cheap novel. They try to report items that are impossible to prove. For example, one undercover agent, desperate to report something in his Friday report, resorted to claiming he had seen a sexual act between the receiving room manager and a male employee. He said the incident took place in the washroom, and proved the receiving manager was a homosexual. The store took the agent's word for it and a week later the receiving room manager was fired.

Such false reports are obviously undesirable. But if management insists that the agent constantly provide evidence of suspicious activity, to justify his work, the agent will feel obligated to give management what it demands. Such pressure leads to phony reports.

Allow Time for Results

If you use undercover people, be patient. Don't expect instant results. Place yourself in the shoes of a dishonest worker and ask yourself: would you immediately reveal your activities to a stranger who just joined your department? Not likely.

Recognize that it takes time for an agent to win acceptance from fellow employees. The worst thing you can do is to express impatience and pressure him for daily or weekly reports when he has nothing to report.

An agent needs to feel free to work for weeks without producing anything concrete. Usually the extent of a group's theft activities is related to the length of time needed for an agent to win their acceptance. The more active the gang, the more cautious they become and the longer it takes to gain their confidence. Some cases require six months to a year before they can be broken, but the time invested is worth the effort because such theft rings are doing large-scale damage to the company.

Be Cautious About Reporting

Regular communication with the boss is important, but use care in how you set up the reporting arrangements. If there is any physical danger to the agent, then set up a time schedule for his reports so that a failure to receive a report at the proper time will indicate trouble and will call for immediate action on the part of his superior.

Instruct him to keep all reporting to a minimum. Restrict his reports to information on internal thefts. Do not ask for information on petty rule violations, what employees think of the boss, or other nonsense. Tell the agent to stick to the basic problem—internal dishonesty—and if he doesn't have anything to report (and many times he will not), then tell him to say so.

The frequency of reports depends on the assignment. Some cases require daily reports, and others only once a week. The agent needs to remember that the average worker does little letter writing and if he makes frequent trips to the letter box to "mail a letter," a subject's suspicions may be aroused. In some cases agents have written their reports in the post office, which is also unwise.

The return address on the report envelope should NOT be the agent's home address or that of the store. Set up a prearranged address where a letter can be returned without upsetting the operation. The superior should receive his reports either at home or at a post office box purchased specially for this purpose.

Caution the agent *not* to make notes while on the job. If it becomes absolutely necessary for him to write something down, he should do it on a scrap of paper like a matchbook cover or cigarette wrapper. *He should NEVER carry or use a notebook or notepad.*

The agent should also avoid frequent or unexplained absences from the work group.

Personal Reports While Working Should Be Avoided

Discourage any personal reports while on the job, but if such a report cannot be avoided, then caution the agent to use care to see that he is not followed. He should use a pay telephone and have a good story ready in case he runs into an associate somewhere that would call for an explanation.

Be sure the pay phone is located outside the store; *do not trust the call to go through the store switchboard*. The boss should have a private outside number that the agent can use.

The Initial Contact with Subjects Is Critical

Since the agent's objective is to become accepted by the suspects and be asked eventually to join the operation, his initial contact is critical. He should try to work things out so that the suspects approach him rather than him approaching them. Once they do approach him, he should be slow to respond to their initial overtures.

In some stores employees are aware that undercover detectives are used from time to time, and naturally, they are suspicious of any new person coming into their department. The way the agent develops this first contact sets the stage for his acceptance by the group.

The Agent Must Share in the Subjects' After-Hour Activities

No successful agent can be a clock-watcher. His most valuable time is often after hours when he associates with the other employees. It is during these times, when the agent shares the hobbies, interests, and recreations of the suspects, that he will succeed in winning their acceptance.

Avoid Any Undercover Investigation of Union Activities

Both store management and the agent should be aware that laws in many states prohibit the agent from investigating any kind of union activity among employees. Keep your agent focused on the problem of internal theft and *avoid any activities that might be construed as a violation of laws surrounding union activities.*

The Key Word Is—CONFIDENTIAL

Using an undercover agent successfully is based on keeping the operation confidential. The fact that the operation is secret must be kept in mind at all times by both the agent and by his superior. Nothing must be done by action (or by omission) to betray the fact that a confidential probe of a department is being made.

Using undercover agents to investigate internal dishonesty is a practical and useful method of detecting theft.

The following eleven points are useful to keep in mind when selecting, training, and assigning an undercover agent:

1. Select a person with a flare for acting. Remember that he is going to play an assumed role in the department to which he is assigned.
2. Check his background for honesty and integrity, for he will be placed in a situation where there may be great temptation to steal.
3. Assign the agent to a place where usual security methods have failed. This usually works best in a nonselling department.
4. The agent's first purpose is to gain acceptance from the other employees.
5. The agent's goals are to provide management with information on who is stealing, how they are stealing, and where the merchandise is being disposed of.
6. Protect the identity of the agent at all times.
7. Be sure the agent you select has a sharp mind and knows the work environment to which he is to be assigned. Check to see if he will need to know a foreign language.
8. In selecting a substitute identity for the agent, weave facts with fiction. Keep the agent's first name to avoid critical situations. Have the agent avoid expensive possessions or excess money that might give him away.
9. Make sure the agent uses care in reporting. Avoid having him report trivia and have him stick to the purpose of the assignment. He should avoid excessive reporting, and he should use the phone only in emergencies. He should never carry a notebook.
10. The agent should use care in his first contacts with the subjects. He should gain acceptance by mingling with his work associates in their after-hour activities.
11. Avoid having the agent report on union activities.

Chapter 9

CASE ANALYSIS

Whenever a method of theft is repeated, this means that corrective action has not been taken by management to block such thefts. When types of theft are repeated, patterns of employee dishonesty emerge, and unless operating changes are made, and immediately, internal thefts will spread. Normally honest workers will then be contaminated and the store's theft losses will build up.

The answer is to analyze each dishonest employee case systematically to determine its underlying causes and to develop countermeasures that will prevent such a theft in the future. In other words, *these bad employees can teach us how to be good operators—if we learn from our dishonest employee cases.*

Analysis Is the Key

ANALYSIS is the key to solving shortage problems. Case analysis can reveal hidden loopholes in our control systems, unsatisfactory supervision, or other weaknesses that need correcting. Through analysis of our dishonest employee cases we can discover what control barriers are ineffective or missing from our operations. It can help to pinpoint management practices or attitudes that need changing and that can often show us the corrective steps we need to take to cure shortages.

Determine the Essential Elements in the Situation

What does the word "analysis" mean? The dictionary defines it as, "Determining the elements or essential features in a situation." In other words, you separate the whole into its parts so you can study, investigate, and evaluate the situation. It's like taking a clock apart to see what makes it run, separating each spring and gear, laying them out on the table, and then using a magnifying glass to examine them for weaknesses. Are any of the wheels bent? Any gear cogs missing? Is the mainspring broken? Are the parts fouled with grease and dirt? Are there wheels missing?

Define the Real Problem

Until we know what the real problem is it is impossible to take intelligent corrective action. Analysis helps us to separate the SYMPTOMS of a problem from the UNDERLYING CAUSES. Too often we work at correcting the symptoms of trouble and are baffled because the trouble reoccurs. Attacking symptoms is rarely successful. The important thing is to correct the underlying causes.

If you go out to your garage tomorrow morning and your car won't start, you have a problem. But is the problem the car's failure to start or the fact that you are out of gas? The car not starting is a SYMPTOM of the problem, but the CAUSE is being out of gas.

If we receive a copy of the period's inventory shortages and find that they are high, we have a problem. But is the problem the fact that we have high shortages? Or is the problem the fact that we have loopholes in our control procedures, poor company discipline, or unsatisfactory supervision? The shortages are a SYMPTOM of the problem, whereas the CAUSE is unsatisfactory control of our operations.

Take the Elements of the Situation Apart and Examine Them

Once we recognize that our focus should be on the CAUSES of an undesirable situation, not its SYMPTOMS, we are well on our way toward making an intelligent analysis that can lead to worthwhile corrective action.

In the case of the car that won't start, we take the situation apart by perhaps first examining the fuel gauge to see if we have sufficient gas. Next we may test the battery to see if it has lost its charge. Now we may pull the sparkplugs to determine whether they are fouled. Next we may examine the distributor points to see if they have burned shut, and so on, until we are able to locate the CAUSE of our problem. We may find that we need to get some fuel, charge the battery, replace the sparkplugs, separate the points, and so on. Once we are able to correct the CAUSE, the problem is solved.

In the case of high shortages, we review our control systems and procedures, check on the adequacy of our enforcement, look over our supervisory practices, and so on. If we can find the CAUSES of our shortages we will know what needs to be done to prevent shortages in the future.

Shortage Problems Are Often Complex

But when we talk about correcting high shortages by analysis of a departments' total operations, we soon discover that we are faced with such a labyrinth of factors that solution appears impossible. There are over four hundred possible CAUSES of the problem, thus making it seem like an insurmountable task. If we are lucky we may hit upon the answers but it is more likely that we will become discouraged by the very size of the task and give up before anything meaningful has been accomplished.

This is the point at which the analysis of dishonest employee cases becomes such a valuable management tool. By analyzing an actual theft situation we bring the problem of reducing high shortages down to a workable size. This becomes a logical starting point for the review of our controls. By setting up a program of systematic review of each dishonest employee case, we can begin at once to take corrective actions that will materially improve our internal controls and lead to a substantial reduction in store shortages.

ANALYSIS Can Reveal a Variety of Control Problems Requiring Attention

How does analysis of dishonest employee cases work out in actual practice? Well, when Harry Childs studied the case of the checker who gave "special" prices to other employees, he found that his policies for controlling employee purchases were weak. So now he requires ALL employee purchases to be checked either by the store manager or his assistant. In addition, employees may make purchases only when it is time for them to leave for the day; they may no longer make them during working hours.

When Roger Mapes reviewed his problem of theft by night cleaners he came to the conclusion that night cleaning was too much of a risk in his store. The store could not be properly protected because the night cleaners could not be properly supervised and checked. So he changed his procedure and now the cleaners begin work at 8 A.M.

All the cleaning is done during the day when the store manager is on the premises to supervise their work.

A supermarket in Chicago had two employees who made a deal with an outside trucker and the trio stole several hundred dollars worth of merchandise by concealing it in the outgoing trash. A disgruntled employee tipped off the store manager and the gang of thieves were caught. Analysis of the case showed that the store had no controls for policing the trash operation. As a result, corrective action was taken, and now a supervisor inspects all the trash as it leaves the building. Plans are being made to have an incinerator installed in the store.

Thefts of Cash on Sales

In Newark, New Jersey, honesty shoppers caught a checker who was stealing cash on sales. Analysis of the case disclosed that the checker stole only in the late evening hours between 8:00 and 9:00 P.M. It was learned further that she stole at this hour because the store's assistant manager, who was supposed to stay in the store until closing time, was sneaking home at 7:30 each night and the store was left unattended. The company, based on the case analysis, decided that the assistant manager was not qualified for his supervisory responsibility—he lacked leadership responsibility—and therefore they replaced him with a person of proven supervisory ability.

A Farmington, Long Island, supervisor found that several checkers were stealing cash on sales by creating fraudulent "voids." After a customer left they would report a phony void sale, using an excuse such as "the customer changed her mind," or "I hit a wrong key". . . . Analysis made it apparent that the store had weaknesses in its control over voided transactions. Changes were made in auditing so that excessive void sales would have to be reported to the store management, and supervisors were retrained in handling void transactions. Voids were no longer approved unless the customer was still at the checkout counter and could confirm the error.

Poor Key Controls Caused Thefts

In Portland, Oregon, a wiley porter got hold of a key to the store's outside doors. He had a duplicate key made during his lunch hour and then, while cleaning at night after the store was closed, he began to steal merchandise. With the key he was able to unlock one of the store's side doors and take the merchandise out through an alley at the side of the store to his car.

Analysis of the case led the store management to tighten their control over all store keys. In addition, they decided to install perimeter alarms on the building so that the store could not be entered or exited at night without breaking the alarm barrier. The porter was asigned into the store at a specific hour and the alarm was reinstated after he entered and could not be broken until the hour he was scheduled to leave.

Valuable Information Was Revealed by Case Analysis

As we can see, case analysis in these situations brought the following kinds of important information to light:

- Inadequate controls over employee purchases
- Vulnerable night cleaning operation
- Uncontrolled handling of trash
- Poor supervision
- Unsatisfactory key controls
- Store unprotected at night
- Loopholes in handling void transactions

Analysis of each dishonest employee case takes a little time and effort, but it can pay off handsomely in clues for strengthening controls against internal losses. Such studies can reveal inadequate or unrealistic store policies, poorly enforced procedures, unsatisfactory supervision, the need for better auditing controls, and so on. It pinpoints the weaknesses in the store's control environment.

Many stores fail to take advantage of this golden opportunity to turn a negative situation into a positive one. As a result they are repeatedly hit by the same types of internal theft and losses skyrocket.

Set Up a Case Analysis Committee

Initiating a program to take full benefit of analysis of dishonest employee cases is easy and worthwhile.

1. Plan to do such reviews in a systematic way. Start by setting up a specific day and time for a monthly review of dishonest employee cases.
2. Organize a committee to meet and discuss each employee case. Include on the committee the store manager, controller, security head, personnel manager, and in some cases bring in the department head where the case occurred.

3. Start by having the committee chairman read the entire case aloud, or provide a detailed review of the case for members of the committee to review in advance of the meeting.
4. After all members are familiar with the details of the case, including the method of theft, length of time over which the thefts occurred, type of merchandise stolen, and extent of admitted thefts, you are ready for exploratory discussion. This can be sparked by questions from the chairman.

   When did the thefts occur? What time of day? How often did the employee steal? Why this type of merchandise? Why this particular time? Why this specific method of theft? Who was the employee? How was he screened? What did references say about him? Has he been reviewed previously? What were the findings? What did the supervisor feel about him as a person and as related to his job performance? And so on. Each question can be considered as a spade digging into the earth surrounding the case in the group's search for worthwhile information.
5. Next hit hard at the key question: How can such thefts be prevented in the future? In other words, what went wrong in our personnel selection, supervision, control systems, and procedures? Why was this case allowed to happen? What can we learn from it? How can we cure the situation that caused it? How can it be prevented in the future?
6. Finally, arrive at your conclusions and agree upon the recommendations for improving store operations and controls. Decide what you are going to do. Make plans for needed corrective action. Decide who will take the steps decided upon. If necessary, set up a time table for action and determine who and when a follow-up will be made to insure the situations isolated for treatment are being changed as planned.

Use the Problem-Solving Method

Follow the accepted method used by every successful executive for problem solving:

ANALYZE. 1. Analyze and determine the exact nature of the problem, particularly its underlying causes.

PLAN. 2. Decide what has to be done, and make a plan for corrective action based on your analysis.

DEPUTIZE. 3. Deputize and educate the people who will be assigned the job of initiating corrective action.

FOLLOW UP. 4. Follow up to see that your plan for corrective action is being carried out as you intended.

The Rewards

For the small investment of time and effort, this monthly case review can pay off in gigantic dividends in terms of curing internal thefts. It is a tested and proven technique that is easy to use and can substantially reduce inventory shortages.

By dragging each dishonest employee case into the management laboratory for an autopsy, you will not only discover what needs to be done to tighten store security, but you will also gain new insights into management and employee attitudes in your company and you will gain valuable information about the broad process of management in your firm.

Chapter 10

ESTABLISHING EMPLOYEE DISCIPLINE

To understand fully the importance of satisfying the basic emotional job security needs of employees, you must recognize that:

1. The most important job of any supervisor is to motivate his employees properly, because there isn't a single problem in industry that doesn't directly involve people.
2. Everyone, regardless of job or title, is an employee who has basic emotional job security needs that can be satisfied only by direct, personal, face-to-face communications with his boss.
3. The failure of the supervisor to satisfy the basic emotional job security needs of his employees by direct, personal, face-to-face communications creates a sense of job insecurity in his employees that results in a dangerous emotional vacuum.

Why doesn't every boss get the job of supervising done? There are several reasons. First, most supervisors instinctively shy away from dealing with the emotionally highly charged problems of their employees. These problems are usually messy and unpleasant, and supervisors (like other people) prefer to deal with pleasant and factual things. But most important of all, most supervisors simply don't have the tools or know-how to do the job of supervising effectively.

Job Security Needs

Let's spell out the basic emotional job security needs of employees:

1. What do you expect of your employees in the way of work performance and conduct on the job?

2. Are you telling your employees whether or not they are performing satisfactorily on the job? (And this means praise as well as censure.)
3. Are you treating your employees fairly and impartially?
4. Are you judging your employees on the basis of facts rather than opinions and assumptions?

Even though you're a supervisor, you're also an employee. And as an employee don't you have the four basic emotional job security needs described above? And don't you depend on your boss to satisfy those needs? What about your boss? Doesn't he have these four basic emotional job security needs, and doesn't he depend on his boss to satisfy them? And what about your employees? Don't they have these four basic emotional job security needs? And don't they depend on *you* to satisfy them? Just ask your subordinates to list the qualities of the best boss they ever had. You'll find that their answers tie right back into these four basic emotional job security needs we've been talking about.

It is interesting to discover how readily we place on those to whom we report the obligation for satisfying our personal human needs, but at the same time how easily we can overlook, or fail to recognize, the identical obligation that is placed on us by those who report to us.

Child and Parent

The outstanding characteristic of the relationship between the subordinate and his superiors is his dependence upon them for satisfaction of his needs.

Psychologically, the dependence of the subordinate upon his superiors is a fact of extraordinary significance, in part because of its *emotional* similarity to the dependence characteristics of another earlier relationship, that of the child and his parents.

The similarity is more than an analogy. The adult subordinate's dependence upon his superior actually awakens certain emotions and attitudes that were part of his childhood relationship with his parents, and that apparently have long since been outgrown. The adult is usually unaware of the similarity because most of his complex of childhood emotions has been repressed. Although the emotions influence his behavior, they are not accessible to consciousness under ordinary circumstances.

What Is Discipline?

The best way to satisfy the basic emotional job security needs of your employees is through a well-organized program of store discipline.

But before we tell you how to set up such a program, it might be well to clarify what we mean by "discipline."

Few words in the English language have had their meaning as badly twisted by misuse and misunderstanding as the word "discipline." Because of its sinister connotations, it conjures up in the mind of most people pictures of soulless overseers enforcing their cruel demands on helpless slaves, or Nazi stormtroopers goosestepping off to war with the mechanical precision of toy soldiers. Except in the scientific and academic fields, discipline has come to be synonymous with regimentation. If we're going to use this word, we should agree about its definition. Therefore let's see what the dictionary says.

> *DISCIPLINE.*—noun. (Obsolete) Instruction. 2. A branch of knowledge involving research. 3. Training which corrects, molds, strengthens or perfects. 4. Punishment or chastisement. 5. Control gained by enforcing an order, as in a school or army; hence orderly conduct, as troops noted for their discipline. 6. Rule or system of rules affecting conduct or action, especially practical rules as distinguished from dogmatic formulations.

Don't forget that discipline comes from disciple, that is, one who is shown or taught. Thus when we use the word "discipline" we mean:

> Teaching employees to follow and adhere to reasonable and practical rules of conduct. Punishment is a last resort and is used only when all other corrective measures have failed.

How Discipline Works

With the thought in mind that discipline is a means of teaching, how does it work?

Discipline does not mean strict observance of rigid rules and regulations. On the contrary, it means working, cooperating, and behaving in a normal way as anyone would expect an employee to do. For example, discipline means:

- Reporting to work regularly, on time, and without unnecessary absences.
- Doing a fair day's work.
- Respecting the prestige and authority of supervision.
- Cooperating with others.
- In general, conducting oneself in a reasonable and orderly manner.
- Obeying reasonable orders and carrying out job assignments.

The maintenance of discipline in a store is a management responsibility. It is management's inalienable right or prerogative; it is a responsibility; it is a primary part of the job of managing the business.

Management establishes the rules and it disciplines for violations.

Rules

Several basic principles govern the application of these rules.

1. The employee is entitled to know the rules. The rules should be posted in conspicuous places throughout the store. Most stores also include the rules in handbooks given to employees. The rules are written in simple language that can be understood by everyone.
2. Management accepts full responsibility for assessing discipline. It is the supervisor's job to maintain discipline in his department. It is also his job to assess penalties for infractions of rules. He may consult his superiors for advice in some cases, but the final responsibility is his. He may discharge an employee on the spot for a very serious infraction. He often suspends the employee, pending a complete investigation. It pays to have all the facts before the discipline is set, however.

Penalties

There is no mechanical formula for establishing disciplinary penalties. It cannot be done with a slide rule. You need to have a penalty spread for violation of each posted rule. This specifies a minimum and a maximum within which the penalties are set. In arriving at the proper discipline within the spread, the supervisor takes into consideration four factors.

1. Seriousness of the Offense
2. Past record of the employee
3. Circumstances surrounding the particular case
4. Company practice in similar cases

Discipline is for the purpose of correcting improper conduct and obtaining compliance with store rules. It is not punitive in nature.

Discharge is resorted to in two types of situations:

1. Where the offense is of such a serious nature as to make any other form of discipline inadvisable. For example, assault on a member of supervision, theft, or sabotage.

2. In cases of repeated violations where other efforts to bring correction have failed.

Key Questions

Here are the four key questions:

1. *Are you telling your employees what is expected of them?* The employee is entitled to know the rules.
2. *Are you telling your employees whether or not their conduct on the job or work performance is satisfactory?* Discipline is for the purpose of correcting improper conduct and obtaining compliance with the store rules. It is not punitive in nature.
3. *Are you treating all your employees fairly and impartially?* Are you determining in an impartial way whether the action is for just cause and fair in light of all the facts and circumstances.
4. *Are you basing your decisions on facts rather than opinions or assumptions?*

Key Points

Good discipline is a primary part of the job of managing; the key word here is "primary." The dictionary defines "primary" as:

> First in importance, chief, principal. That which stands first in order of rank or importance.

Stated another way, this means that maintaining good discipline is just as important to the success of a business as sales or accounting. Its importance cannot be overemphasized, nor can its function safely be ignored. As we said earlier, this is a job that must be done.

Second, the establishment of good discipline is a management responsibility. The key word here is "management." Management establishes the rules and sets up disciplines for their violations.

Third, but more important, the supervisor has the key role in maintaining discipline. Since the supervisor has the closest personal contact with his employees, he cannot delegate or duck the job of maintaining good discipline. If the supervisor doesn't maintain discipline, no one else will.

Chapter 11

FRAUDULENT CHECKS

Probably few people can comprehend the number of bank checks being cashed in this country annually. It is a gigantic part of the economy. Last year more than 28 billion checks were cashed by American consumers. If they were pasted together, they would form a tent of paper large enough to cover all of Washington, D.C., and its suburbs. Or if they were glued end on end, they would make a giant paper chain to the moon and back, four times.

More important than the number of checks issued is the considerable loss that businesses suffer from bad checks. Bad check losses last year were a staggering half billion dollars. Who can visualize a pile of bills as high as the Empire State Building? Perhaps the elephantine size can be understood if we break the loss down into smaller particles. How much is lost each minute to bad checks? The answer is $2,660 each minute.

Are bad check losses greater than losses from other crimes, say holdups? Yes, by a wide margin. Check losses last year were sixteen times the amount lost to holdups. The man holding a pen is more dangerous than the man holding a gun.

Five Fatal Words

What, for the store manager, are the most expensive five words in the English language? You've heard them many times in the past and you'll continue to hear them often in the future. "Will you cash a check?"

Those five words are costly. They sound innocent enough. But they cost American businessmen 500 million dollars last year.

Does this bad check problem seriously affect your store? How hard hit are your profits by uncollected and uncollectible bad checks? The answer can be determined by you. It depends on how well you train your staff in handling check cashing procedures.

Training

Naturally, the check handling procedures themselves must be sound. Today, however, most stores know HOW checks should be handled to minimize the risk. The problem is rather one of training key people to follow the rules intelligently.

This is not easy. It takes employee cooperation; it requires limiting the number of people handling checks to as few as practical. And it must be a continuous program sustained 365 days each year. It cannot be a one-shot deal. The single hyponeedle in the arm wears off quickly and people return to bad habits and careless ways. The check security problem centers around the effectiveness of your training program.

Don't Coerce Employees

Commanding people to obey check cashing rules will not work. The more threatening a manager or security director becomes the more he plants the seeds of resistance. People resist being shoved, pushed, nagged, and commanded. In fact, the stronger the threats, the more frightening the pictures of dire results you paint, the more the employee will resist cooperating with you.

And of all the store programs, the one that most requires employee cooperation is the control of bank checks. Without cooperation of all employees handling checks, the program won't work no matter how well it is designed.

Commanding people to follow rules sets up a cycle of command and resistance. The person who is overcoerced fights back. If the resistance to commands is substantial, it can result in paralysis of action. The person may slyly resist because he is afraid of retribution if his resistance is out in the open. He appears to be forgetful, is careless, doesn't follow the rules, and blandly faces you when you hand him the returned check and says he "can't understand what happened."

Other employees who are overcoerced will angrily fight back. They may take a stubborn position that when you're around to supervise them they have to obey the rules but the minute you're not there they can openly flaunt your orders.

Persuasion

To gain employee cooperation for your check control program use persuasion. Don't order, command, or threaten anyone because this sets up a command-resistance cycle that is nearly impossible to correct once it is started. Use suggestions, reminder posters, and reminder memos that are light, persuasive, and even have a touch of humor. Don't bear down hard, don't nag, and don't threaten. This approach simply won't achieve the cooperation you need.

Analyze State Laws

Each store should prepare an analysis of the check fraud laws in its own state. These laws are peculiar to each area of the country. In one state (Georgia), the vast majority of all check prosecutions fall under five statutes. As a point of reference, we are listing them here. Perhaps your state has the same or similar laws. By using this list as a checkoff you can prepare an analysis suitable for your own store.

1. *Insufficient Funds Checks*. An insufficient funds check is a check given under a subject's correct name. The bank on which the check is drawn does not have funds or credits in behalf of the person issuing the check on the date it is presented for payment. To be a fraud check the insufficient funds check must be issued with intent to defraud.
2. *Fictitious Name Check*. In this case, the check is negotiated by the subject knowing that the signature he is putting on it is a fictitious name. It is done to defraud.
3. *Possession of a Check Signed with a Fictitious Name*. This statute concerns a person in possession of a fraudulent check. The person who has the check knows that it is signed with a fictitious name. He has it with intent to use it fraudulently. The check must be drawn on a bank in the state in question. (Some states require possession of *several* fraud checks.)
4. *Forgery*.
   a. *Actual Forgery*. This is a person who signs the name of another person to a check. He does this without permission or authority to sign the other person's name. He does it with intent to defraud.
   b. *Alteration*. In this case a person alters the bank check of another person. This alteration may be a change in the cash amount or in the date. He does this without authority or permission of the person who signed the original check. He does it with intent to defraud.

5. *Uttering of a Forged or Altered Check.* Under this statute a person can be prosecuted for negotiating a forged or altered check. This forged or altered check has been made without the authority or permission of the person whose name is used. The person uttering or negotiating this type of check is doing so knowing it to be forged or altered and with intent to defraud.

Limit the Number of Employees Who Handle Checks

In too many stores all the cashiers take bank checks and give out cash over the amount of the sale. This multiplies the problem of training and motivation and increases the difficulty of adequate check controls. If you use twenty-five cashiers, many of whom are part-timers with minimal interest in the store operation, you will find it difficult if not impossible to develop the tight bank check control you require in today's marketplace.

Most stores would benefit substantially by *using a service desk.* In food stores the loss from fraudulent bottle refunds alone, that can be stopped by a service desk, insures it will pay for itself; and when you add the benefits of tighter bank check control, the desk will pay for itself many times over by substantially cutting check losses.

Use a Service Desk

With a service desk you have to train only three or four people in check handling. This means you can select capable, careful people and do an intensive training job.

You can keep an up-to-date file on insufficient and bad check names at the service desk on a rotor file so that the clerk can clear every name before approving a check. By having the customer get her check approved, for up to $50 or $75 or whatever limit you want to set, you take the pressure off the checkout cashiers. Now they have only to accept the check filled in for the amount of the sale or up to the $5, $10, or $15 cash-over-sale limit imposed by the check cashing clerk at the service desk.

Checkout lines move faster, customers grumble less, and the cashiers can operate without worrying about calling a supervisor to approve a check or arguing with a customer who does not have adequate identification after a $60 sale has been rung up and bagged. Returning such merchandise to stock is costly in itself, and often managers approve the check rather than assume the burden of added stock work. Naturally, the check often bounces but it's too late then to salvage either the store's money or merchandise.

Courtesy Cards

Stores with check cashing courtesy cards, if combined with a check cashing clerk at a service desk, cut their check losses substantially and the card insures that the good customer can have her check approved promptly. Again, by centralizing check cashing, it is fast and easy to check the rotor file for lost, stolen, or misused courtesy check cashing card names so that the person attempting to defraud you doesn't slip through your checkout line.

Stores in larger cities and in substandard neighborhoods, where crime rates are higher than average, also benefit from check cashing cameras to photograph the customer and the check. This again can best be handled at the service desk. Keep film in the camera and keep the records and film up to date so you can properly investigate and collect from the insufficient funds deadbeat and can help the police bring the professional paperhanger to justice.

Good Judgment Is an Important Ingredient

No matter how carefully thought out and intelligent a store's check cashing rules, the employee handling a bank check will often have to exercise personal judgment. No rules, no matter how workable, can be a final guideline for handling checks in a competitive store situation. So one of the elements you are dealing with when training the person responsible for handling checks is the necessity for good judgment.

Use Common Sense

Good judgment is required in following check cashing rules as is the employee's intuition based on experience and common sense. Even if all of the conditions set by the rules are met, a check should not be accepted in certain situations.

When a top-notch person handles checks they often develop an intuitive "feel" for customers who hand them a bad check. A nervousness, an uneasiness, or an uncomfortable sidelong glance is intuitively perceived by the cashier and she refuses the check even though the person presenting the check has more than ample identification.

It is wise to keep in mind that a store is never obligated to accept a customer's check. Accepting a check is a service to the customer and it is one you can refuse without any explanation or without any factual evidence that the check is not acceptable.

Rules for cashing checks provide the groundwork, but people have to interpret those rules every day, on the job, in the rush hours of heavy customer traffic.

Common Problems in Handling Checks

What are some of the major problems encountered in handling checks in today's hectic business world? What are some of the basic things to watch for when someone says those five expensive words . . . "Will you cash a check?"

A common saying is that the "pen is mightier than the sword." The truth of that statement is well illustrated in today's bank check society. The pen is not only mightier than the sword but mightier than the gun and knife as well. In fact the bank check holdup man, armed only with his checkbook and pen, gets away with more money than daring bandits exploited in daily newspaper headlines with their armed robberies.

But the interesting fact is that by taking just a few extra moments of care with each check that is handled you can defeat most of these paper and pen bandits. As a matter of fact, 95 percent of all bad check losses are NOT the result of any unusual talent on the part of the forger. Rather, they are the result of careless screening of the check by employees.

Four Categories of Check Control Procedure

Today there's no mystery about correct bank check procedures. They fall into one of four broad general categories: (1) type of check, (2) check inspection, (3) identification, and (4) sizing up the customer.

Sizing up the customer is where the cashier's personal judgment and intuition play an important role. She has to know how to size up a customer and how to use appearance, actions, and conversation as a guide when cashing checks.

TYPES OF CHECKS

Personal Checks

In discussing the various types of checks let's start with the one you'll come across most often, the personal check.

This is a printed check provided by a bank to a checking account customer, and made out by that person to your store.

Blank Checks

A second type is the blank check, a preprinted form sold in stationery or variety stores, on which the customer fills in the name of his bank and branch location. Such checks are seldom used today, and extreme caution should be taken before honoring one.

Traveler's Checks

Next is the traveler's check, which is becoming more and more popular. These checks are sold by banks and other financial institutions. Usually they are valid, but in the past two years major thefts of these checks have occurred. An underworld ring involved in a multimillion dollar traveler's check racket has been uncovered and several leaders are awaiting trial and sentencing. These checks are usually as good as gold, but if you intuitively feel that the person is a possible risk, feel free to refuse the check. The spotless reputation these checks have always had has been somewhat tarnished by the uncovering of the gigantic forgery ring that specialized in traveler's checks.

Government Checks

The government check may be issued by one of hundreds of various government agencies or departments and it may be a federal, state, or local government check. It may be in payment of Social Security benefits, unemployment benefits, tax refunds, or welfare support.

A lot of mailbox thefts of government checks have occurred in recent years and there has been considerable forgery of such checks. Be extremely careful and thorough in verifying such checks before approving them. A study recently showed that last year 54 percent of the stolen old-age benefit checks were forged and cashed in stores by *teenagers.* Unbelieveable! Yes, but it's true. It illustrates the carelessness that has made check handling such a serious loss problem for stores.

Own Company Checks

Sometimes you find a businessman who tries to cash a check made out to his own company by one of his customers. Normally such a check would be deposited in his bank account. Since he is attempting to cash it in the store, chances are he feels that check will bounce.

Such a check should *never* be cashed.

Third Party Checks

A third party check is a check issued by one person to another person who then presents it to a merchant to be cashed for payment of merchandise or money. Because such checks are highly susceptible to fraud, be careful. If the person issuing the check were to stop payment the merchant would get stuck. The store would then be in the embarrassing position of trying to locate someone who may be difficult or impossible to locate.

Payroll Checks

Payroll checks are widespread in food stores. Wives come into the store and do their weekly grocery buying; they then give the cashier their husband's salary check for payment. Usually a substantial amount of cash has to be given to the customer. Food stores have to accept these checks because it generates business, and if they don't, the customers will trade in other stores that do honor payroll checks. But be careful to honor only payroll checks made out on local companies and drawn on a local bank.

Absolutely avoid a payroll check in which the company name is rubber stamped onto the check. Also inspect any suspicious payroll check carefully to be sure the spelling of all printed material is accurate. Sometimes a forged check is caught because the forger has made a spelling mistake in the name of the company printed on the check.

Remember that professional check forgers use the payroll check most frequently. These checks give the crook a substantial amount of quick cash if he can lay a dozen of them around town before moving on to his next victims. These are the checks most apt to be stolen from the company using them or printed fakes.

Forgers steal a book of payroll checks or even a single check, and then they have duplicates printed, which they pass out in food stores. So examine all payroll checks carefully and don't cash them unless you are quite familiar with the company.

Counter Checks

There is also the so-called counter check. This is not really a check at all, but an instrument used by bank depositors to withdraw money from their own account. Such a check is not negotiable and if a customer gives you one it is usually due to ignorance or carelessness. But in any event, NEVER cash it.

(It is suggested that the store make up a book of sample checks as listed in this chapter to show cashiers so that they can familiarize themselves with these different types of checks.)

"Kiting"

From time to time your store cashier should be reminded to be on the lookout for check kiting. Kiting is an informal term applied to a manipulation in which a person cashes checks regularly and immediately deposits most of the money from these checks in the bank to cover checks cashed the previous day.

In this way, they use the three-day clearance period as a method of obtaining money for personal use from the bank or from the store where the checks are cashed. The check passer is, of course, using money that does not belong to him.

It is possible for a kite to run anywhere from a few dollars to thousands of dollars and the earlier a kite is located and stopped, the smaller the final loss will be.

Kiting Is Difficult to Prove

Kiting is a violation of the law and successful prosecution has often been accomplished when a kite is proven. It is hard, however, to prove a kite without admissions from the culprit. No customer should be accused of a kite merely because there are large and frequent cash deposits and many checks used. Suspected check kiters should be reported to the police.

Anyone who regularly cashes checks at your store, especially on a daily basis, may be kiting. It is a simple matter to determine if there is a kite by merely taking these checks to the bank the same day they are presented. You can see if these checks are good before the kiter has a chance to deposit the proceeds of the checks he cashed yesterday.

At least one insufficient funds check should be secured in a suspected kite case before the suspect is questioned. Once you have such a check it is usually a simple matter to secure a confession from the kiter.

Banks are particularly aware of the kiting problem and will cooperate to the fullest degree in disclosing their records when a kite is in operation. The reason for this is that it is very easy for a bank to be defrauded by a kiter and no bank wants the business of a person who is kiting checks. If the kiter suddenly gives up his manipulation and leaves town, the kite falls and the total losses may involve thousands of dollars. These losses are sustained by the store or bank holding the cashed checks.

Handling Bank Checks

Armed with nothing more than a pen and paper, criminals pass bad checks and get away with sixteen times more money than do daring bandits who grab newspaper headlines with their armed robberies.

Since we can't avoid accepting bad checks in a cash-less society, the store must protect itself against illegal and worthless checks.

Centralized Check Cashing

Centralizing the check cashing responsibility is important. It is far easier to train five people to handle checks properly—five who were selected for their good judgment—than it is to expect twenty-five people to handle checks properly. Many stores assign the responsibility for handling all checks to a single person on each shift. This fixing of responsibility goes a long way toward insuring a more cautious acceptance of checks.

A good rule is to have all routine checks handled by the store cashier and unusual checks by the manager or his assistant.

Whoever handles a bank check must never take anything for granted. Many people who are careful in handling bills and coins become sloppy when running a check transaction through the register. Clerks must be trained to examine each check carefully and to reject any check about which they have doubt.

Who Should Approve Checks?

Who should approve checks? Only a person with proven good judgment. Select this person for intelligence, discernment, experience and accuracy. Be sure he or she is a naturally alert and thorough person.

Professional paperhangers stay clear of stores that gain a reputation for carefully screening all checks.

Maintain a Dollar Limit

Tightly control your authorization for cashing checks. Keep authority controlled with dollar limits on approval of checks. Let department managers or cashiers approve checks up to a determined dollar limit and then have the head cashier or store manager approve all checks above this amount.

Keep the names and a sample signature on each person authorized to approve checks. Usually the list should be held in the cash room so checks coming back as "no account" or other types of bad checks can be referred at once to the person who approved them. Keep the dollar limit the person is allowed to approve on the same list so that the returned check can be examined to see if the authorizer stayed within the boundaries for authorization set by management.

How the Store Receives Checks

There are many areas through which checks come into your store and many reasons why a store acquires checks. The following list includes a few of them:

1. *Sales Floor*. These checks are usually for goods but can also be part cash. Most stores are reluctant to cash checks as an accommodation to customers. Such check cashing, if it is done, is not done on the selling floor but by a special cashier. Floor checks should be for the amount of the sale and have the sales clerk's number and the authorizer's name on the bank check.
2. *Cashier Department*. These checks are usually in full or part payment of an account or they may be entirely for cash. The cashier receiving a check at the cashier's window should write the purpose of the check on the back of it. If it is paid on an account, the check should show the account number. The amount paid on the account should be indicated as well as the amount returned to the customer as cash.
3. *Payment on Account*. These checks are often received in the mail or are presented at the cashier's windows and at store service desks. Mailed bank checks to pay charge accounts usually have no authorizing data on them. When a check is received in payment on an account, there should always be a notation showing the

account number and name of the account on which the check is to be paid. Remember that if a check in payment of an account in another person's name is returned as a fraud check there is no way to remove the payment from the account unless this cross reference appears on the check.

4. *Mail Order.* All checks received in the mail order division should be stamped "M.O.D." There is seldom any other authorization. These checks should be cross referenced with the mail order account number.
5. *C.O.D. Payment.* These checks usually end up in the C.O.D. office or the cashier department. They are stamped "C.O.D." The drivers or other people who accept such checks should place their department and payroll number on the back of the check along with their route number.
6. *Layaway Department.* Such checks should be stamped "Layaway." If the name of the maker of the check is different from the layaway account to which it is being applied, the name of the account should be cross referenced on the back of the check in writing.
7. *A Check in Payment for a Check.* Ordinarily, this does not occur. But when it does, a note should be made on the back of the check showing the date of the previous check and the initials of the person handling this transaction. The first insufficient funds check should not be given back to the customer until the new check has been cleared by the bank.
8. *Miscellaneous.* There are other ways, of course, in which checks come into the store, such as refunds from manufacturers, payments on uneven exchanges, and so on. These checks should be handled along similar lines to those listed above.

Identification of Check Casher

As the police so often try to tell business executives who handle checks, "Know your endorser." This is another way of saying that in every instance in which a check is presented for payment you should identify the person giving the check. Unless a person presenting a check is known personally to the department manager or salesperson, then two good kinds of identification should be obtained and noted on the back lower portion of the check.

Almost all stores have a list of acceptable forms of identification for bank checks. Such a list follows:

1. Driver's license (if signatures and photo compare)
2. Downtown credit plate (if signatures compare)

3. Recently paid utility bills
4. Marriage license
5. Birth certificate
6. Current union cards
7. Shop badges
8. University service cards
9. Other types of identification cards showing picture and signature of customer
10. Gasoline credit cards
11. Diner's Club and similar types of credit cards

Other things may be acceptable, but if the salesperson has any doubt he should refer the check to the department manager. In most cases the test of good identification is that it has a customer's signature and description as part of the identifying information or a registration number that could be used for tracing the customer. Be sure the person tendering the check always signs it in the presence of the salesperson.

Obtain a motor vehicle registration when possible and note on the check what model and make of car it is. For checks in large amounts or in a situation where there is a question, a good practice is to observe the person leaving the store. If he gets into a car, record the model and license number. See if they are different from the information given in the store.

Never accept a Social Security card as proof of identity. Social Security cards are obtainable with great ease under any name you want. Many criminals carry several of these cards on them at all times. Do not accept checks issued on a savings account. Do not accept counter checks when written on special checking accounts.

In recording a bank check identification be thorough. Always show the club name and the card if a club membership card is used, the number and company name if it is a credit card, and so on. By being specific you make it possible to later trace the customer. It is not advisable to accept an out-of-state driver's license as the only means of identification. Require additional identification if this is offered. Examine all identification cards to be sure they have been signed by the customer and are of a current date. A person approving a check should be expected to actually see the customer and to examine the identification presented.

How Should You Inspect a Bank Check?

If a systematic method of looking at a bank check is followed, this approach will prove very valuable in tripping up fraud check passers.

Each check presented for approval should be thoroughly examined and the following details carefully checked:

1. *Date*. Each check must be dated. Do not accept checks where the check is more than 30 days old and do not accept checks that are postdated.
2. *Bank*. The check should show the name, location, and the branch of the bank. This is particularly important if the customer is using a store blank check. The writing must be legible. The check should have the following information:
   a. The *customer's name* handprinted unless it appears in very legible form elsewhere on the check.
   b. A *brief description* can also be very valuable. Include height, weight, eyes, and hair color and anything outstanding about the person such as mustache, glasses, etc.
   c. *Current address*. Make sure that it is current by asking the customer for his address rather than copying it from identifying documents. Note any hesitation or groping in his reply.
   d. *"Pay to" space*. This must be your company or an individual's name. Do not accept counter checks when written on special checking accounts.
   e. *Signature*. This must be complete. If the signature is illegible, print the customer's name underneath the signature. Surprisingly enough a bank check will come through now and then that has no customer's signature at all. Be sure that the check is signed and that the customer's name appears legibly on the check.
   f. *"Amount" spaces*. The amount should be written in and the numerical amount on the check must be in absolute agreement with the written amount.
   g. *Endorsement*. This must be exactly the same as the payee. The check must be written and signed in ink and it must not be altered by erasures, amounts written over, etc.

Three Basic Objectives

In approving checks there are three objectives: to see that the check is properly filled out; to verify through means of identification that the person presenting the check is the person he or she claims to be; and to decide whether the check is good or not, based upon the customer's appearance, actions, conversation, and identification.

If there is a reasonable doubt about any of the above factors you should not approve the check.

Your store's cashier offices should have a list of all people authorized to approve checks. This posting should show the approval signatures and the dollar limit.

When you train persons to handle bank checks they need to be taught the following four things:

1. The various types of checks they will be handling.
2. How to examine a check in a systematic manner.
3. How to identify the endorser (customer passing the check).
4. How to "read" the customer's appearance, actions, and other details that may suggest that the check is not a safe risk.

How to Record Check Losses

Your security manager should keep a constant check on the store's complete fraudulent check situation. He should not only be aware of the fraud checks that are turned over to the security department, but he should also know, on a monthly basis, the bad check losses of the store. A general control of this kind should always be maintained by either the security manager or the store credit manager. There should be a statistical report furnished to the security department every month showing all types of fraudulent bank checks coming into the store monthly and their disposition.

Budget Reserve to Cover Losses

The security manager should also be aware that the store controller sets up a reserve for bad check losses. He should relate the store's check losses with the budget reserve set aside to cover these losses.

He should understand the accounts affecting bad checks as set up in the store's general ledger and should know how the store charges off bad checks, monthly, semiannually, or annually.

It has been found that some stores are not fully aware of their actual check losses until a severe situation has developed. The security manager, by being aware of the general ledger accounts and knowing how check chargeoffs are made, can keep a control to see that the fraudulent check situation in your store does not get out of hand.

Returned Bank Checks

In handling bank checks returned to the store, the first consideration is the *reason* for return. For example, in some stores, insufficient funds checks are immediately *redeposited*, thereby creating a reverse entry on the store's accounts. In other stores, arrangements have been made with the bank to redeposit insufficient funds checks on a second day before they are returned to the store. This is a good procedure because it reduces the number of individual checks handled by the returned check investigator.

Following is a list of the usual reasons for bank checks being returned to the store. Such reasons are usually noted on the check by the bank.

Reasons for Return

1. Insufficient funds
2. No account
3. Account closed
4. Wrong form (should be on special checking account form)
5. Must present pass book (indicates a savings account)
6. Forgery
7. Signature does not correspond
8. Payment stopped
9. Endorsement missing or incomplete
10. Account garnisheed
11. Check altered
12. Check postdated
13. Signature illegible

Obviously some of these checks would be given over to security for investigation but many others would be handled in a routine way by the audit department. Security would, of course, get the checks that say *account closed*, *no account*, *forgery*, *signature not authorized*, *signature does not correspond*, *altered*, and *signature illegible*.

The Protested Check Investigator

This person should write an index card for each check returned by the bank noting the date it was received by the security department. This card should show the name and address of the maker, the date and amount of the check, and the reason for its return.

On this card should be kept the record of other bad checks if any are received. Also, any investigative notes, disposition of checks, date they are paid for or date referred to attorney for collection. These cards should be kept as a permanent file because they can be a helpful source of information when a case develops and there is a need for previous background on a specific customer.

When a returned check is turned over to security, the check investigator searches for an existing check card. If none is found he makes one out. The card is then placed in his file.

The principal task of the check investigator is to collect on as many bank checks as possible. This person must be aggressive and energetic, with unusual mental ability; he will make phone calls, send out letters, and make personal contacts with the objective of collecting on these returned bank checks.

Handling of Insufficient Funds Checks

If he handles insufficient funds checks, the check investigator must use judgment in deciding how long to hold such checks. He should also maintain a cross reference on bad checks with the charge account office.

If a customer gives an insufficient funds check on an account, the account should be so noted. If insufficient funds checks are not collected *within a reasonable length of time*, the protested check investigator should charge them back to the accounts on which they were paid. This will make an additional balance on the account. Some stores may want to charge the account as soon as the insufficient funds bank check is returned by the bank. This gives the people in the credit department better control of the charge account.

After 30 days the check investigator should send all insufficient funds checks to the store's collection attorney.

The most important first investigative step is an intelligent study of the check itself. Few people give a bank check the attention it deserves. The investigator should look for misspelled words and examine the general nature of the writing, looking for unusual markings or unusual methods of making figures. In the case of "no account" or "forged" checks, the check investigator should have photostats made.

Unusual Characteristics

Identifying characteristics should be clipped from the photostats and kept together. Each clipping should have the file number of the case. If the check is typed, the typing should be studied.

In this manner, the original study will identify many related checks if the investigator has studied the checks and kept the unusual characteristics properly organized. By making a chain of similarities, the investigator ties together the person who creates a series of fraudulent bank checks.

Charge Plate Identification

If the check shows a charge plate stamp on it, the investigation broadens. There may be a lost plate or a charge account impostor involved. There may also be a customer who is a deadbeat.

There is also the strong possibility that a mistake has been made. If the person's charge account is in good standing and the account customer is available, this can be cleared up. The charge account case history should be examined. The application for the account should be checked to compare the handwriting of the customer with the check bearing the plate stamp.

Who Authorized the Bad Check?

Every time there is a bad check the identification on the back of the bank check should be studied and evaluated. The name of the authorizer should be noted. If the same authorizer appears too frequently on fraud checks, this person should be considered as a possible accomplice. If cleared as a suspect, he should receive a training session on handling checks.

Whatever investigative steps are needed as a result of the study of the check itself, they should be pursued to their logical end.

Check Credit Card Identification

If a Diner's Club identification credit card number has been used for identification, then the investigator should contact the local headquarters of the Diner's Club and find out all he can about the customer who passed the bad check.

Often the identification itself is the lead that locates the culprit. It is also important to find out if the Diner's Club Card has been reported lost or stolen. If so, the next step is to investigate the circumstances of the loss or theft.

Investigations are a chain type of procedure. At any given point it is difficult to know where the investigation will lead. Each step opens up new possibilities for investigation. The imaginative and alert investigator follows each lead to its logical end.

"Stop Payment" Check

The investigator should first contact the person who gave a "payment stopped" check. After being contacted, this person should be told that payment on the check has been stopped. He should be asked the circumstances surrounding a stop notice being placed on the check. He should also be called upon to make the check good. If he does so the check should be returned to him without further attention.

If the person passing the check begins to argue that the maker had no business stopping payment on the check, he should be told that the reason for stopping payment is a matter between that person and himself and that your store is only an innocent holder of the check. The store wants to get paid and the check will then be returned. He can take up the problem of stopped payment with the maker.

Interview Person Passing "Stop Payment" Check

Whatever he says during this interview should be noted and written down after the interview. Your notes should include the exact time of the interview and what took place. It is helpful sometimes to get a signed statement of the circumstances surrounding the stop payment check. Of course, if he immediately pays the check, no such action is necessary.

The person who gave your store this check should be asked when he cashed the check, which means the day of the month and the hour of the day. It must be remembered that all checks are not cashed on the day they are dated. The exact time of day and the day of the month he cashed the check may become very important in establishing whether the check was cashed after payment was stopped or before. Stop payment checks are seldom considered for criminal action but are handled in a civil action.

Check Details of Interview

The investigator should check to see what date this particular check appeared on a deposit slip. The entry on the deposit tape should be checked and the identity of the person who made the tape record should be established. The investigator should also find out the bank in which this particular deposit was made.

The bank on which the check is drawn should be contacted and a statement secured from a bank official as to the exact date and time of day they received the stop order.

You should also find out whether the stop order was given to the bank in oral or written form. If it was oral, find out who received it. If it was written, a copy of the actual stop order should be obtained. If the bank has a time stamped on the stop payment order, the time shown should be noted. The balance in the maker's account should also be learned if the bank will release this information.

Contact Maker of "Stopped Payment" Check

A second basic action that the investigator can take is to contact the maker of the check. This person should be told that your store has his check and are calling upon him to make it good. If the person passing the check refused to make it good, the maker should be told this. However, the maker should not be told what this person said when he refused to make the check good. If the maker indicates he will make the check good, he should be given no more than 48 hours to do so.

In case neither the passer nor the maker of the check can be contacted, the store should send registered letters, return receipt requested, to both parties. The letters should call upon each person to make good on the check in question with currency, a money order, or a substitute "good" check.

Again, the time allowed for this payment should be set at 48 hours. Depending upon the response from these investigative gambits, the store should then decide whether or not to refer the check to its attorney. If it is referred, a report of the information developed up to this point should be sent with the check. Unless unusual circumstances exist, the matter should certainly be referred to the attorney no later than 30 days after the date of the check.

Interviewing Fraud Check Witnesses

Try to obtain an accurate description of the check passer and a detailed description of the merchandise that was purchased with the check. A check should be made to see if there was a possible refund of the goods. This might be known to the salesperson or the service manager. If you have a suspect, then identification of a photograph of the suspect should be considered.

The question should always be asked in this interview, "Was anyone else with the check passer?" The investigator must remember that salespeople do not as a rule voluntarily mention useful information because they are not specialists in security work and are not, therefore, aware what information has value. The investigator should attempt to win the salesperson or the department manager's cooperation in the investigation and should alert them to watch for the malefactor if he should return to the store.

When Suspect Is Observed in the Store

As a result of your store's "stop" list, a salesperson or other employee may spot the check operator in the store. The action that follows may result in a good case or it may also result in a serious problem for your store.

Call the Police

When a suspect has been spotted, the check investigator should contact the Police Department and have a check specialist sent over as quickly as possible to handle the situation.

If the police would always arrive in time to interview a check suspect, there would be little problem with bad check passers. Unfortunately, in most cases security personnel must act on their own because the police do not arrive in time to handle the problem.

The investigator should have one of the previous bad checks in his hand when he approaches the suspect. (You can see at this point that he would be in trouble if the bad check were at the Police Department and the store had no photostat of it in its files.)

The investigator should already have checked with the bank by telephone and also checked the alleged address, if possible, before talking to the suspect. He must have reasonable grounds for believing that the check being presented at the moment is not good. This preliminary investigative action must be taken rapidly since the investigator may find that the check passer has already left the store before he is ready to handle the problem.

Confront the Suspect

When first talking to the check passer, the investigator should confirm that the check being offered belongs to the subject. Once the subject has admitted that the check is his, the investigator should glance at the check and reach a mental conclusion as to whether it is the same handwriting as that on the bad check that he holds in his hand.

He then questions the check passer about the bank check he has in his hand. If the check passer admits that it is his account (when the check has been returned by the bank "no account"), the only problem is to get the man safely to the security office without his escaping. If he denies it is his check or makes an excuse, which if true would establish his innocence, then an apprehension should not be made at this time.

Obtain Suspects' Identification

If the check passer has an explanation, the next step is to get his identification. At this point the investigator is in a crucial situation. Only a specially trained security person is experienced enough to handle this type of problem.

The check passer probably should be persuaded to go with the investigator to the charge office where a further interview can be held and the facts verified. Or the investigator may use other stalling tactics to delay the check passer until the detective from the police department's check squad arrives.

If the check passer leaves before identification can be established, a floor detective should be assigned to follow the check passer to see if his car license can be obtained. If he travels by taxi, the detective can follow him to his ultimate destination. In this assignment a team of two detectives is best. In this way, one person can watch the suspect while the other detective can periodically call the store to keep the security head informed about the results of the surveillance.

When "Not" to Make an Apprehension

A check passer should seldom be arrested unless there already is a bad check in your files. In many areas of the country the attempt to pass a bad check in the passer's own name is not even considered a crime. In addition, there are many chances for error. The bank could have made a mistake in checking the account. The suspect could have opened an account that morning that had not yet been properly cleared. Because of the dangers of error it should be a general rule that no matter how bad the situation looks a store apprehension should not be made on the first passed check.

Records Check

Names and addresses used on bad checks should be checked out with the police department's identification bureau. It is well known that bad check passers are often criminals with long records for forgery. By checking names and aliases it is sometimes possible to tie a bad check into a criminal investigation that involves wanted notices across the entire country.

Inform Police

Early in the investigation of a fraud check, the bank check and the circumstances of its negotiation should be shown and discussed with the police department's bad check bureau. Some stores have members of the check squad drop into the security office regularly. In such instances a review of the current fraud check investigations is in order.

All too seldom do many stores use the valuable assistance of the police department's bad check detectives. They can often help your investigation and can often tie together bad checks passed at several stores.

Handwriting Expert

Your local police check squad members and the check investigator in your store soon become good at identifying handwriting. However, because of the need for expert testimony in courts it is always advisable to have arrangements set up so that a recognized handwriting expert can be secured when needed.

The official handwriting expert used by the police department or the state crime laboratory is usually available. He should be known by name and you should have a procedure set up so that any questionable check can be examined by him when requested.

The FBI Can Help

The FBI facilities must also not be overlooked. There is a federal statute known as the National Stolen Property Act. This act makes it a federal violation for anyone to transport or cause to be transported in interstate commerce any forced, altered, or counterfeit check if the person knows the check to be forged, altered, or counterfeited.

This statute means that if a check is negotiated in one state but is drawn on a bank in another state and is a counterfeit, forged, or altered check, a federal statute is violated. As a result, the FBI can institute an investigation that might result in federal prosecution.

It is a policy of the FBI, based on decisions of the U.S. Attorneys, that "true name" checks will not be investigated. The U.S. Attorneys have concluded as matter of policy that if a person uses his own name in drawing a check that is returned because of "insufficient funds" or "no account," this is not considered to be a forged, altered, or counterfeit check and does not violate the National Stolen Property Act.

Proving a Federal Violation

It is very difficult to prove that a subject has physically transported a completed counterfeit, forged, or altered check from one state to another. However, one type of violation of the National Stolen Property

Act can be easily proven. This is the cashing of a check in one state drawn on a bank in another state. If such a check is forged, altered, or counterfeited and is intended to defraud, the statute has been violated.

Your store should also be aware that the FBI has a National Fraudulent Check File in Washington. Information from this file is made available to all recognized law enforcement agencies. It is suprising how many random checks that are sent in from all over the country are identified in the National Fraudulent Check File when they are checked by the FBI. As a result, the photograph and criminal record of the subject is often available and is given to the law enforcement agency requesting such information.

When the Suspect Is in the Military

When military people are believed to be involved in a bad check scheme the check investigator should make contact with the nearest military establishment. Such a contact can be a great help, especially if the security manager has laid the groundwork for a good relationship with this establishment. One store does this by giving military investigators part-time employment. This can help in the store's security operation and also create a valuable contact in the military installation.

Be sure you can identify the check passer. Try to have a witness. Without a witness, a handwriting expert's identification is essential when you are ready to prosecute.

The check itself should be given to the check squad of your local police department with the detailed information from your investigation. A photostat of the check should be kept in your security files.

If, after thorough investigation, you cannot positively identify the suspect it is still advisable to turn the check over to the police. The police may tie this check into a later case.

Suggestions

The advice most often given by experts in the field of detecting check frauds is to "Know Your Endorser." Other good advice that has often been repeated is as follows:

1. Do not cash out-of-town checks.
2. Demand two identifications.
3. Guard any blank checks, cancelled checks, and your firm's check protective equipment.

4. When there is heavy customer traffic and salesclerks are busy, be especially careful of checks.
5. Never cash checks for juveniles.
6. Do not cash checks written in pencil or checks that show signs of alteration or erasure.
7. Do not cash postdated checks.
8. Never be impressed because a big company name appears on a check.
9. If the person passing a check has been drinking, be especially cautious. (Never cash a check for an unknown person who has been drinking.)
10. Be aware of nonchalant, careless, and nondirected types of purchasing. If a check passer is not concerned about the price or size of the merchandise selected, be careful.
11. Watch anyone who cashes several checks in the same general area with a small amount of cash being returned to the customer out of each check.
12. Notice general nervousness.
13. No personal checks over set limited amounts (say, $75) should be handled by a department manager or salespeople. Such checks should be referred directly to a central location such as the store's credit manager.
14. All *personal* checks drawn on *out-of-town* banks should require special approval.
15. All checks must be *endorsed* by the *customer* exactly as written by the maker. Be sure to get the address of the customer.
16. Any check made out to your store for which cash is to be given when a portion of the check is in payment of a store bill *should be endorsed* by the customer in the presence of the person accepting the check.
17. Watch for bad check names on your "stop" list.
18. Watch for discrepancies on checks being cashed such as:
    a. Wrong date
    b. Postdated checks
    c. Written amount different from numerals
    d. Check made out to someone other than person cashing it
19. Do not cash checks for anyone presenting a *local bank* check but using *out-of-state* identification without careful investigation.
20. The most dangerous time to cash checks is when the banks are closed. Therefore, be more careful on Saturdays, night openings, and on the days preceding a two- or three-day holiday.
21. Although it is important that you be careful in cashing checks, remember that store employees still represent your store. In many cases their attitudes will affect customer goodwill. They

should be discreet in the way they handle bank checks. It helps to always tell the customer, "thank you," very pleasantly after every transaction.

The "Round Robin" System

The head of the police department's store detail squad in a large midwestern city has set up an unusual communications sytem to handle the problems of professional bad check passers, which is called the "round robin" system.

He persuaded 145 stores, such as grocery chains, drugstores, department stores, and others, to put a phone communication chain into operation.

When a member of the police detail squad receives information that a robbery has occurred in which a large number of blank payroll checks have been stolen, he immediately phones the first store in the communication chain warning them to be on the alert for these stolen payroll checks. He gives all the information on the case that he has available.

This first store in turn calls the second store, which calls the third store, and so on, around the complete chain of 145 stores. Within approximately two hours the final store phones the police to report that the chain has been completed. If he fails to receive the call within a specified time, an investigation is made to see where the communication chain was broken.

This chain phone system is used only for major check problems. It has already proven very successful in capturing many important organized professional bad check passers. This is worth investigating for your city.

Prevention

There are basically four methods you can use to help prevent bad check losses.

1. *Training*. Have thorough initial training and regular follow-up training for all people in your store who are authorized to approve bank checks. Such training can go a long way toward preventing your store from being victimized by bad check passers.
2. *"Stop Lists."* Your store should issue "stop lists" on bad check names regularly. Such check lists should be placed at your main cashier department, department managers' desks, and in the security department.

By giving an award for information leading to the apprehension of a bad check passer you can stimulate store people to be alert. Stop lists are the means of creating a web into which many a bad check passer will sooner or later fall.

3. *"Round Robin" System*. Another method of prevention is to use a telephone communication chain. When a prolific check passer is known to be operating in other stores in your community, a telephone chain of information passed through the leading stores can help you to capture the malefactor.
4. *Communication*. Another aid is to arrange for exchange of information regarding bad check passers with other stores in your community, the police department, your stores' protective association, and any retail associations that may exist. By passing along all check information and keeping people in your city alert to bad check passers much can be done to stamp out this problem.

Fraudulent check passers are becoming a national menace. Only if all stores work together and cooperate with city, county, state, and federal police agencies will this costly type of crime be eliminated as a factor in store losses.

Chapter 12

BURGLARY

Burglary is the largest crime by volume in the United States.* And it is growing each year at an appalling rate. Every store needs to make a maximum effort to prevent such attacks.

Most Burglaries Unsolved

The store manager cannot count upon the police to help him recover his merchandise or money if he suffers an attack. Burglary crimes are difficult to solve. Last year more than 82 percent of all reported burglaries were unsolved.

Detection of a burglar is difficult for several reasons. First of all, he is often a loner. He operates on the premise that safety depends upon solitude, and therefore the burglar shuns partners. This means the police seldom can produce a witness even if they have a suspect. It is also difficult, even if a burglar is caught, to identify the stolen property in his possession as goods stolen from a specific store. If the store cash registers are looted the task of identifying cash is even more difficult than tagging the owner of merchandise. As money leaves no trail, it cannot be identified.

Key Is Prevention

Thus the problem of burglary for a store is one of *prevention*. To set up the most formidable barriers for the criminal, we need to consider five areas:

1. Suitable locks
2. An alarm system, properly selected and installed

*1978 FBI Uniform Crime Report

3. Lighting, both inside and outside the store
4. Cash safe
5. Special security for any narcotics stock

In addition to a review of these five aspects of the store's preparations against burglary, when a store is in a high-risk area of a central city or in an isolated suburban location, where break-in crimes are higher than normal, additional measures need to be considered. For example, placing burglar-resistant plate glass in all ground-level windows and steel screening on the doors and windows, using private police patrols and guard dogs, and so on.

Locks Are the First Element of Control

The store must be sure that it is using the right kind of locks on perimeter doors and windows. A lock serves not only as a barrier to unwanted entry onto the premises, but also should be strong enough so that a burglar has to *force* his way onto the premises. Entry by *force* is an important element in burglary insurance. Most burglary insurance policies require proof of *forced entry* before the policyholder can receive indemnity for a burglary attack.

The term "burglary" legally means: "The act of breaking into a building to steal."

What is the best kind of lock for your store? Most security specialists agree that the PIN-TUMBLER CYLINDER LOCK is the best type for maximum security. Although some pin-tumbler locks have as few as three pins, a suitable lock for a store's perimeter door should have five pins or more; otherwise it does not provide adequate resistance against being picked.

Electronic Locks

Today new locks appearing on the market incorporate electronic and magnetic controls rather than the traditional cylinder with tumblers and pins. These locks can be effective but they must be judged individually for their level of security. Before using a magnetic or electronic lock have your local locksmith evaluate it so you will have a professional's objective opinion of its effectiveness.

A good lock for a store's perimeter door is a deadbolt lock. This is a lock that cannot be opened by sliding a piece of plastic between the door edge and door jam. The deadbolt lock does not have a spring. It requires a positive action with a key or a knob to move the bolt.

An even better lock is the DOUBLE CYLINDER DEADBOLT. Once this lock is attached, it means that the door cannot be opened without a key on either side of the door. This provides good security. A double cylinder deadbolt lock is effective on a glass door because the burglar cannot get into the store by breaking the door by reaching in and turning an inside knob on the lock. This lock also defeats the would-be thief who hides in the store until after it is closed and then steals and plans to leave by breaking out of the store.

As a first step toward burglar-proofing the store, take the time to examine all perimeter doors and determine what kind of locks are used. Strengthen your security by replacing any weak lock hardware with double cylinder deadbolt locks.

Lock Installation

Although the lock itself is important in protecting perimeter doors, the proper installation of the lock is equally important.

The best lock is useless if it is not properly installed. Let me explain what I mean. A premium door lock should have a long latch bolt. But to take advantage of the strength of a long latch bolt the lock installation needs to be given attention. For example, I did a security audit of a chain of eight drugstores located in the inner city of a large metropolitan area. The crime rate in this area is skyrocketing and stores have been a prime target of professional burglary attacks. Downtown streets have poor lighting and there is little vehicular or pedestrian traffic after dark.

The company that hired me to do this study had wisely purchased high-grade, ten-pin double cylinder deadbolt locks for all of the doors on the perimeter of each of their stores. These excellent locks had a long latch bolt, five-eighths of an inch in length. When properly mounted, a lock of this type can resist a "forced" attempt to break into the store. But during the security study I discovered that in five of the eight stores, the perimeter doors were poorly constructed and in several instances *the door jamb was as much as a half inch away from the door.*

This half-inch gap between the door and the jamb resulted in reducing the latch bolt, which was five-eighths of an inch long, to an effective length of only an eighth of an inch. With just the tip of the long bolt resting in the door jamb even the rankest amateur criminal could easily pry the door open. This sloppy installation of a premium lock destroyed its effectiveness.

Use a Lock Specialist

The lesson to be learned from this incident is clear; all perimeter locks should be examined to make sure that they are properly installed so that you will receive full benefit from the money invested in them.

It is a good practice to bring in a local locksmith at least once a year to look over the store locks. He should examine the installations and also test each lock to insure that it is operating properly. This professional locksmith can evaluate whether you have the right kind of lock for a particular location and whether or not it is well installed.

When it comes to burglary, the proverbial "ounce of prevention" is indeed worth pounds of "cure." It is not logical to wait until a burglary occurs to look at the quality of your locks and how well they are installed.

FBI Statistics

Today, BURGLARY is the largest crime by volume in the nation; 3,104,496 burglaries were reported to police in 1978 (FBI statistics), of which only 16 percent were cleared by the police. The magnitude of burglary is even greater than that reported by the FBI total. A federal study of 10,000 residents in Dayton, Ohio, showed that more than 50 percent of them did not report known crimes to the police in 1977. Their reason for not reporting these crimes was often given as: "The police can't do anything about it anyway so why go through the hassel of reporting it?"

If we assume that a similar situation of unreported crimes occurs in other communities, it is reasonable to believe that the total number of burglaries in the country may be running as high as six million each year, or an average of one burglary every five seconds.

The size of the burglary problem today is devastating, and because many retailers have not given enough attention to the problem stores have become one of the main targets.

Burglary thefts in 1978 totaled more than $1.6 billion dollars. A profitable crime.

Key Controls

Locks are a vital part of a store's defense against burglary, but the best lock is vulnerable IF keys are not controlled.

A lock is only as effective as the store's key controls.

What can be done to improve key controls? To keep keys from falling into the hands of the wrong people issue as few keys as possible. Keep up-to-date records of all keys issued. The reserve stock of duplicate keys needs to be very carefully protected.

To avoid the risk of keys being duplicated, caution employees with store keys not to leave them on their key ring when parking their car in an attendant parking lot. In fact, they shouldn't have store keys on the same ring as personal keys such as car or home keys. Tell employees not to leave store keys in their topcoat or raincoat when hanging it up in a restaurant, and never to leave store keys lying about in the cash office or stockrooms.

Whenever a key is reported lost, or when a key-carrying employee leaves your employment without turning in his keys, immediately have the locks re-keyed.

Perimeter locks should not be a "master key" type of lock because this limits the number of "pins" that can be used, and it also increases the risk of the locking system being compromised if the master key is lost or stolen or duplicated illegally.

If you want to use a master key system for internal locks such as stockrooms, cash office door, and so on, that is okay. But don't do it with the perimeter locks.

Have perimeter doors individually keyed and don't carry the keys for internal locks on the same ring with perimeter door keys. You can better protect the outside locks if the keys are kept on a separate key ring.

Don't put identifying tags on any perimeter keys. If they should be lost you won't want to provide the finder with the name of the store or the address. Use a numbered code for identifying keys and keep this information within the company.

Stamp "DO NOT DUPLICATE" on all keys so that an employee can't go out on his lunch hour and get the store keys duplicated.

Finally, take a periodic inventory of all keys. Have each employee SHOW the key(s) assigned to him. You want to actually see the key, for you want to KNOW that the employee still has the key and it has not been lost or stolen.

Once a year re-key all perimeter locks whether the keys have been lost or not.

Always invest in the BEST available locks! Don't economize. You usually get what you pay for in locks. A bargain-priced lock is no bargain.

What about duplicate keys? *Don't keep more than ONE duplicate key for any lock.* Destroy all other duplicates.

KEEP THE *ONE* DUPLICATE KEY IN A SAFE.

Alarm Systems

What type of alarm system should you use to achieve maximum security?

If the store is in a large city where central station alarm service is available, this is worth looking into. How far is the nearest central station of the alarm company office? How long will it take for a patrol car to reach your store?

Central alarm systems have advantages if they are properly serviced and backed up with professional guards. The alarm signal at the store is silent when an illegal entry is made. The alarm signal registers *only* at the alarm company headquarters. A patrol car is dispatched to the scene of the break-in. The system does not scare off the burglar and in some instances guards arrive in time to capture the culprit.

Even if the thief gets away, the central station agents may arrive on the premises fast enough to cut the burglar's efforts short so that losses are reduced.

In some cities the central station may not be located near enough to the store to properly protect it. In smaller cities and rural areas central station service often is not available.

Although central station alarms are desirable, the store has some workable alternatives. A proprietary alarm system can be purchased and installed by the store. This type of alarm system is often connected to a large bell on the outside of the building. If the alarm is tripped the bell sounds loudly until the system is turned off.

Proprietary alarms in larger cities are seldom effective. Pedestrians may hear the alarm bell but often hardly glance up at the sound. People on the street usually assume that it is caused by faulty wiring or that someone has accidentally triggered it. And if it is a burglary they don't want to get involved.

Indifference to alarm bells on buildings is why so many false alarms occur. In a proprietary system the storeowner often neglects upkeep of the alarm system, and after awhile neglect leads to the degeneration of the equipment, with the sensing devices failing and false alarms occurring.

Alarm manufacturers make it clear in literature given to purchasers that any alarm system needs at least minimal maintenance and when false alarms occur it is a reminder that maintenance is needed.

Two alternatives to the bell on the outside of the store should be considered. First is the use of an automatic phone dialing system. The store's alarm system is tied into a phone dialing unit instead of to an outside bell. If a break-in is attempted the alarm activates the automatic phone dialer. The dialer can call the local police department and a recording will notify them that the store is being entered illegally.

In many smaller communities the self-dialing unit has often proven effective. Not only can the unit dial and notify police, but it also can call the store manager at his home and in larger stores it can be programmed to phone the security director.

When using a phone dialer tied into the local police department, the store should be sure that it has a rugged and reliable alarm system, professionally installed. It is important that the alarm system receive monthly maintenance. It is important not to get the police out on false alarms.

Obviously, false alarms concern the police, who are already undermanned. In several large cities such as Cleveland, Ohio, police refuse to allow self-dialing phone tie-ins with the police.

Before investing in the automatic dialing unit contact the local police to see whether they will accept calls from this type of installation.

Sirens and Strobes

A second alternative way of using a proprietary alarm system is to put a sound device, such as a loud siren, inside the store instead of using a bell outside on the building.

By installing a loud pulsating siren with flashing strobe lights inside the store, the burglar can often be driven off the premises before he can steal anything. This alarm unit is designed to be physically painful. The siren hurts the criminal's ears while the flashing lights surprise and disorientate him. One company has a system that uses a siren and strobes with infrared sensing units. The alarm system is triggered the moment a person walks into the store. The infrared units are set to the heat of the human body and do not cause false alarms from cats or rodents. The moment a burglar breaks in, the sensors react to his body heat and trip the alarm system. A pulsating siren erupts at an unbearable volume of 120 decibels, going on and off at a pulse rate of 144 beats a minute. Synchronized with this pulsating siren are several strobe lights flashing at 72 flashes per minute. The effect is devastating to the intruder.

The pulse rate of the siren and the frequency of the strobe flashes are designed to cause maximum physical pain to the intruder without causing any permanent physical damage. The combination of siren and lights physically forces the criminal to run out of the building.

Alarm Sensors

Whatever the type of alarm system installed, there are today a number of possible sensors available for tripping up an intruder.

The security equipment industry is one of today's fastest growing fields. It offers everything from simple foil sensors to more sophisticated microwave, infrared, ultrasonic, and radar sensing devices.

In selecting sensing devices use professional advice. Certain situations work best with a particular kind of sensing device. For example, a motion detection device may work well in one store, but if the store has night workers or keeps a cat on the premises, chances are that seleccing a motion detection sensor would be unwise.

Ultrasonic alarms are often less expensive and are excellent in certain settings. But if outside traffic is extremely noisy, or if air conditioner or refrigerator motors are excessively loud, it may be difficult to tune the sensitivity so that it avoids false alarms and yet retains enough altertness to trigger the presence of an illegal intruder.

The store's construction, location, and so on, need to be evaluated by an alarm specialist before making a final decision about the type of alarm sensors to use.

Central alarm companies usually install their alarms and are knowledgable as to the best sensors to use.

Three Elements of Control

A store alarm system has three basic elements for control. First, you need perimeter protection to detect entrance INTO the building from outside.

You can use silver foil-tape, vibration detectors, invisible light beams, infrared heat-sensing devices, and so on.

The second line of defense is inside the store. You need a "trip" alarm that can sense an intruder who has hidden in the store at closing time and who will later move about in the store collecting his loot in preparation for breaking OUT of the building. This internal alarm system can be radar, ultrasonic, infrared, microwave, and so on. The objective is to detect movement inside the store by a burglar who has remained in the store, after closing time. These interior alarms will (hopefully) summon guards or police who can trap the culprit in the store before he breaks out.

Third, the store safe needs special alarm protection, as does any unit containing narcotics and other restricted drugs. The store safe and the vault for special drugs are often protected with a capacitor alarm sensor or a focused infrared unit that detects a human body approaching the vicinity of the safe.

All three types of sensors are needed in most stores. Wherever possible the triggering sensors should be tied into a central alarm station, phone dialer, or directly into the police station.

Obviously, the mere presence of an alarm system can be a deterrent to some burglars who prefer to attack stores without alarm systems.

To prevent initial entry into the building, we turn to the psychology of the burglar to find the best countermeasure. Store burglary is usually a night crime. The burglar prefers to operate alone and under the cloak of darkness.

Many burglars are concerned about being seen when they approach the store. The best countermeasure to attack therefore is *light*. The outside of the store—particularly the sides or back alleys—should be floodlighted from the roof of the building. Mercury vapor lamps with breakage-resistant glass are often used for this purpose.

It is a good plan to leave several lights on *inside* the store so that any person inside the store late at night will be visible to police in passing patrol cars.

Lights on the outside of the building make a protective no-man's path of light that the burglar is often afraid to cross for fear of being seen. The lights inside the store also scare him off because he fears being seen once he is inside the store.

One supermarket manager, who had been burglarized several times, devised a scheme to make outsiders think someone was still working inside the store late at night.

The manager leaves several lights on, and on a checkout counter near the front door, where it is easily visible to an outsider, he leaves a large coffee thermos, a jacket, and a brown paper bag that looks like someone's lunch. He also keeps the store's music system on throughout the night. The suggestion of a night worker on the premises has succeeded in eliminating further burglaries.

Outside floodlights should be designed to withstand vandalism and heavy weather. Some are outfitted with special glass and protective cases that can withstand wind velocities of over 100 miles per hour (hurricane strength). Purchase lights with heat-tempered lenses because such glass can't be broken by a thrown rock or even an iron pipe. They resist even a .22 caliber rifle.

After floodlights are professionally selected and installed, incorporate an automatic photocell switching device so that lights will turn on at dusk and off at dawn.

One more point should be made about indoor lighting. Police patrols can't see intruders inside the store if large advertising signs cover the display windows. Keep such signs to a reasonable size and allow enough open window space so patrols driving by can see into the store.

The store safe can best be protected if it is visible to the street and is lighted by two light fixtures shining directly onto its face. (You need two such lights because when one bulb burns out the other will still light up the safe.)

With this setup, police patrols can monitor the night security of the safe.

Although the safe is heavy, bolt it to the steel work of the building structure. Even safes weighing a ton or more have been carted off by burglars. Don't depend upon its weight alone to protect you; instead, bolt or weld the safe to the building structure.

Cash Is Often the Target

Burglars prefer money to merchandise. Money is the usual objective because it can't be traced and is immediately available for the thief's use.

Stealing large amounts of merchandise is generally a clumsy crime, and difficult to make practical economically for the thief.

In a large-scale theft of merchandise, the burglar has to cart off the goods which, if done in quantity, is a challenge in itself. Then he sells the goods to a fence. Converting stolen merchandise into cash creates a lot of profit slippage. The fence is also a crook and he offers the burglar 10 percent of the retail value of the stolen goods.

Thus if the thief can crack the safe he's better off, for he has cash in hand when he leaves the premises.

Selecting a Safe

Naturally, it can be argued that it's easier to steal merchandise than money because money is better protected. This is often true, but not always.

A lot depends upon the type of safe used. If the money is simply locked into a file cabinet (which does happen in some stores), it's very easy to open the drawer.

Even if the cash is in a safe it may not be well guarded. A lot depends on the kind of safe used and where it's located.

How does a burglar perform his job? He first analyzes the situation. He cases the store and estimates the potential gains against the difficulties of a burglary attack. He tries to estimate how much time he has to break into the building and get in and out with the loot. He wants to know what alarm systems may need to be neutralized, the type of entrance problems he faces, and how difficult the overall job will be. If he decides the barriers are too difficult or the potential for theft is inadequate, he may conclude that a burglary wouldn't be cost effective. He then seeks out another location with better potential. Therefore the need to take sufficient security measures to avoid burglaries is clear.

Avoid Cash Accumulation

Naturally, the store increases its vulnerability to burglary attack if it allows large sums of money to accumulate in the store overnight or over a weekend. Deposit cash daily and minimize the risk of being chosen as a desirable burglary target. Some cash must be left on the premises for daily business, and neither can restricted drugs be removed from the premises of a drug store, so the store can still be a victim of criminal attack.

If the company is located in a substandard neighborhood with a high crime rate, and if local stores are frequently burglarized, then the store should take extra precautions.

In addition to a suitable burglar alarm system and floodlighting of all store exteriors that open onto back or side alleys, the store should consider using burglar-proof glass for its display windows and any other windows at street level. In high-crime neighborhoods alleyway windows can be secured by bricking them up. Bricks can also be used to eliminate any exterior doors that are not used or needed for fire law compliance. The remaining perimeter doors need strong locks and if they open onto back alleys they should have strong barricades. Ground floor windows that face an alleyway should have steel bars.

Burglar-Resistant Money Chest

What kind of safe deters a burglar? Well, certainly a file cabinet with a combination lock on it is NOT a money safe. And it is not suitable for protecting cash.

Cash should be kept in a *burglar-resistant money chest*, as such safes are called. Many boxes with locks that are called safes are not really intended to repel a burglar. These so-called safes are designed to protect company papers from fire damage. A burglar can easily open a "fire-resistant" safe.

Burglar-resistant safes come in several types. Coded symbols are used to indicate the relative security of various safes.

No safe, of course, is completely invulnerable. Various models of safes are rated in terms of security based on the estimated length of time the safe can resist burglary attack.

The better a safe's security, the longer it takes to break into it.

"E" Type Safes

What is a satisfactory level of safe security? Most insurance firms agree that an "E" type safe is adequate for most store risks. They back up this view with lower insurance premiums for stores using an "E" safe. This saving spread out over a few years can offset the added cost of such a safe.

Is the "E" safe *always* adequate? Not always.

Insurance firms do not feel it is sufficient security in certain cities where torch and explosive attacks on safes are common.

If the store is located in a larger city, the insurance carrier can confirm that the "E" type safe is adequate for the store location. If it's not he can also indicate the model of safe needed to protect cash properly and also win a premium reduction in insurance.

Safe Location

Location of the safe is important. Putting it out of sight in some hidden nook in a stockroom or at the back of the store or perhaps upstairs in the manager's office (any place where it is not easily visible to the street) increases the risk of burglary.

Security specialists urge stores to put their safe in a lighted location where it is visible from the street. Passersby can then see the safe at all hours of the night.

Reminders

Don't make it profitable for a burglar to get into your safe. Keep the cupboard bare. Keep only the barest minimum of cash on hand after hours. Bank all excess cash daily.

Keep cash registers empty at night; cash registers should be unlocked and the drawers left open after hours to avoid a burglar breaking into a register and causing several hundred dollars work of damage to the machine.

Have an alarm on the safe.

Closing the Safe

When closing your safe at night, follow these steps:

1. Check to see that everything has been put into the safe.
2. Make a note of the serial numbers on any large bills deposited in the safe.
3. Make sure the safe is locked. Test the door handle.
4. Activate the burglar alarm.

Don't keep the combination to the safe written anywhere on the store premises, for the thief may find it. The first place he looks for it is under the bottom drawer of your desk. Don't conceal it under the desk blotter, write it under the office shelf, or on the wall beside the safe. (All of these have been done!)

Keep the combination to the safe *off* the premises. Protect it very carefully, for carelessness with the combination will neutralize all of your other security measures.

By giving some attention to the measures discussed, you can reduce the possiblity of having your store burglarized.

Since burglary *is* the largest crime by volume in the nation, it's only a matter of time before a burglar will be looking over your store and evaluating it as a possible target for attack. Sound preparation against burglary will make the criminal see that such an attempt carries a high risk and he may cross the store off his list of targets. Keep in mind that even if the store is attacked, the criminal's effectiveness is limited by an alarm system and it may even catch the intruder.

Chapter 13

INVESTIGATIONS

The good investigator must have patience and tolerance. Tolerance particularly with himself. Time must be allowed for events to develop, and failure to understand this can lead to demoralization and frustration.

Investigation is a science and an art. Basically, it is a science that can be learned by any reasonably intelligent and alert person. Higher intelligence, education, and experience may enable one investigator to handle the same case a little better or more quickly than another, and to this extent, investigation becomes an art with practice.

Investigation, however, can be reduced to a systematic course of action that can apply to almost all cases. Any fairly competent person applying such routine actions can produce good results.

The experienced investigator, though he may know from extensive experience everything that should be done in a case, will find a checklist just as helpful as a beginner will. The experienced person will know the vital importance of methodical coverage of the situation being examined. From the following material the investigator can make such a "checklist."

Investigation Defined

Investigation means research and analysis intended to establish the true nature of a situation. It is a step-by-step inquiry, a search for truth. Its chief characteristics are:

1. Patient, step-by-step inquiry
2. Observation
3. Examination and verification of information where possible

Investigation, if correctly applied, will produce an inescapable conclusion in most instances. Like other sciences, investigation involves the observation and the classification of information. When properly employed it leads to the truth about the matter being studied.

Given two investigators of fairly equal intelligence, with both following the same scientific patterns of inquiry in the same matter, each will reach the same conclusion in about the same length of time. There is nothing magical about investigations. They require planning, patience, and analysis, as do all sciences.

The Investigator

In the retail store the investigator, a jack-of-all-trades, is often called upon to make arrests, conduct physical and technical surveillances, prepare evidence, and testify in court. The job often requires inside or outside investigation of losses, or a check on employee backgrounds, surveys of high-shortage departments, and working with internal auditors.

The investigator must understand and be able to use technical equipment such as cameras, recorders, and so on. He must be able to prepare competent reports and also know how to interview criminal cases. A knowledge of retail systems and procedures as well as the store rules and policies is needed. Such a man or woman must be above average in intelligence and have an intelligently aggressive mind. Most important, the good investigator has to have mature judgment. Knowing what is important, what is unimportant, and sifting out the factual from the imaginative are key prerequisites for the job.

In modern retail security the investigator is an important part of the security operation. Contributions are made in many areas such as interviewing suspects, investigating fraud purchases, departmental losses, protested bank checks, questionable refunds, and investigating theft losses caused by dishonest employees.

Characteristics of a Good Investigator

Such a simple thing as the habit of carrying two pens is characteristic of a good investigator. Always prepared in advance, he won't lose a valuable statement for lack of ink in a pen, or spoil it by having it written in two different inks or partly in ink and partly in pencil.

The agent acquires as much general information as possible about the matter to be investigated before going out on the investigation. Every possible modern device is used to save wasted time and effort.

This agent carries credentials at all times, and all necessary equipment such as notebooks, coins suitable for telephone, a Minox camera, and so on.

The agent establishes friendly relationships with people and officials who may be able to help. This includes police and administrative officers as well as the clerks in their offices. Investigators earn and zealously guard a reputation for honesty and reliability. They avoid overstatement. They speak in terms of facts, not opinions. If opinions must be mentioned they are identified as such and are evaluated in terms of source reliability.

The investigator is friendly and direct in manner and tries to establish some common bond of interest with everyone he meets. He knows that compliments evoke more cooperation than criticism.

Conservative in dress and manner except when circumstances may temporarily require the opposite, the agent is also discreet and considerate and never betrays a confidence once he gives his word.

The first step is to get a preliminary summary of the available facts. This is done before starting the investigation. The agent telephones for appointments to avoid wasting time and also keeps an accurate record of all information.

Winning the confidence of the people interviewed is done with friendliness and an obvious desire for truth, even if it is damaging.

People like someone they serve rather than someone who serves them. Knowing this, the agent will borrow a cigarette from a witness rather than offer one.

Secondary as well as primary facts are gathered. The occupation, age, sex, race, character, and physical conditions of a witness are almost as important as the things the witness knows. These things are important in evaluating the witnesses' statements.

Above all the agent knows that the facts and statements he gathers must be able to stand up under close scrutiny in a court of law.

Personal Appearance

Investigators give careful attention to their appearance. They should avoid wearing loud or flashy clothing that will attract attention. Sport clothing is seldom used as it gives a festive air to an interview that is meant to be businesslike.

Cleanliness is imperative for the investigator, both in clothing and personal habits. The investigator's appearance is a tool of the trade and should include conservative dress; he should be clean and neat at all times.

People form quick and lasting impressions of the agent based on appearance, attitude, and manner. The investigator can create a feeling of dislike in a person being interviewed when the agent is sloppy, for example, fails to have clean fingernails, needs a shave or a haircut, or has soiled or disheveled clothing. Such things not only distract the witness's attention but also create a mental barrier that is not conducive to a good interview. There is usually a tendency on the part of witnesses to get the interview over with as quickly as possible when they consider the interviewer to be unkempt.

The lack of consideration by an investigator has somewhat the same effect on people being interviewed as being unkempt. That is, a deliberate failure to be considerate. There are certain common courtesies the agent should avoid such as smoking without permission, loud and offensive language, tracking dirt into a home or office, or failure to remove his hat or other acts of rudeness. The interviewer should be considerate and courteous at all times.

An investigator benefits from having a good vocabulary, a knowledge of practical psychology, an understanding of the laws of libel and slander, and a sympathetic understanding of human nature. These things combined with intelligence, natural curiosity, persistence, a pleasing personality, and the powers of persuasion can make the investigator effective.

Keeping an Open Mind

An interviewer should try and find out as much as possible about the situation before interviewing people. The agent should never enter an interview with preconceived ideas. An open mind is important throughout the interview. However, this should not prevent the interviewer from being alert to detect inconsistencies or discrepancies in the witness's story.

Follow the Investigation Through

Before beginning an interview the investigator should be familiar with all the details of any previous investigation. In this way he will be able to exploit conversational trends as they occur. It is, of course, more efficient for an investigator to follow through on the same investigation in spite of working hours, vacations, days off, or other problems. This isn't always practical, but when possible the person familiar with the case should conduct all interviews.

Often a witness will mention a person, place, or thing that is of significance only to the investigator who has been working on the case. Noting the comment the agent will quickly draw out the witness further on this aspect of the case. If the same comment were mentioned to an uninformed interviewer, it would have no particular meaning and therefore would not be properly developed.

Laws of Libel and Slander

The interviewer needs to have some knowledge of the laws of libel and slander. Every private person or organization engaged in the business of investigating the actions of others is subject to a lawsuit for libel and slander on the slighest provocation. Sometimes such lawsuits are brought when there is no provocation.

For example, a retail investigator suspects that Mr. A. has committed a crime but is never able to prove it. The investigator believes that Mr. B. knows more than he has told about that crime. A and B are good friends. The investigator holds a private conversation with Mr. B. in which he endeavors to find some holes in Mr. A.'s story, while carefully avoiding making any accusations or derogatory statements. The investigator in this case may be sued by A. for slander and find that Mr. B. is prepared to swear that in the private conversation the investigator stated flatly that Mr. A. had committed the crime. The investigator cannot deny that a private conversation took place, and so the case will go to the jury on conflicting testimony as to what was said. It will be Mr. B's word against the investigator's word before the jury. If Mr. B. is a reasonably convincing liar, Mr. A. will more than likely win the case.

This illustration offers a number of points for consideration.

1. It is slanderous to state that a person has committed a crime, unless you can prove it.
2. It is sufficient publication if the statement is heard by one person other than the person about whom the statement is made.
3. It is dangerous for an investigator to be in a position in which only the agent's testimony will be available against the testimony of one or more hostile witnesses.
4. Procedures for dealing with witnesses and suspects that are routine for police and law enforcement officers cannot be employed safely by private investigators.

Place of Interview

Privacy is important during an interview. It helps concentration and clear thinking by everyone. A witness is more inclined to reveal confidences in private. Undesirable and unwanted persons in the place of interview can have an adverse effect on witnesses. They may lose their train of thought, become rattled, or forget pertinent details.

Choose the place of interview with consideration to other factors. For example, the accessiblity of a stenographer, tape recorders, a lie detector, or other equipment.

The nature of the interview and the person to be questioned may affect the interviewer's decision about where to hold the interview. The place selected should not be distracting or upsetting to the subject. It is difficult, for example, to interview a witness in a jail cell, whereas the same witness may be willing to talk freely in a hotel room. However, the hotel room itself might be inappropriate if a woman or a child were being questioned because it could cause uneasiness and concern.

A schoolroom or the principal's office might be ideal places to interview a juvenile but might be an unhappy choice for an adult.

It is usually better to get the witness away from his place of employment or his home. Find a place where the subject can think freely and independently and where he or she will be on neutral ground.

If a person is interviewed at work an attempt may be made to hurry the investigator so that the witness can go back to work before the boss comes along. The subject may become embarrassed and flustered, feeling that a supervisor or co-worker may be curious about what is happening and think that there is some kind of difficulty.

When you interview a witness at home you may lose control of the interview. The person is in his own environment and is apt to be self-confident and sure of himself. Or the subject may be brief and misleading in order to end the interview quickly before the family comes home. If the family is present the witness may feel they are listening and may not want them to be aware of what is taking place. This fear is distracting. The witness will be more inclined to take time and go into detail if the interview is held away from his home or place of employment.

Time of Interview

Careful thought should be given to selecting the right time to interview a witness. Consider the working hours of the witness, family routines, the purpose of the interview, and the ability to time this interview in order to complete it and interview certain other witnesses. Weigh all these elements carefully before selecting a time for the interview.

Time can also have a psychological aspect. Women and juveniles present a difficult problem with reference to the time they are interviewed. Except in rare cases, they should not be interviewed in late hours of the evening or very early in the morning.

Interview One Person at a Time

The number of persons present during an interview of an adult depends on the situation. Two co-interviewers seem to be the ideal number. This provides cooperation and protection for each of the interviewers. If the witness later changes his or her story, the preponderance of proof is on the side of the interviewers. Each witness should be questioned individually. Don't have two witnesses together during an interview.

In any interview efficiency is in reverse proportion to the number of people present. Too many interviewers can hinder the gaining of information. There is also no reason for friends or associates of a witness to be present during the interview.

When interviewing a juvenile, the investigator should consider the advisability of having a juvenile officer, the school principal, a teacher, a church representative, or a social worker or other suitable person (not parents or relatives) present.

When interviewing a woman the presence of another woman representing the interest of the interviewer is helpful. You can justify having this person by using her as a stenographer.

Preserve Interview Information

Each interviewer develops a system of recording details of an interview. Some trust the information to memory. Others take brief notes, complete notes, written or typewritten signed statements, and so on. Some use tape recorders and others use a combination of these methods. The important point is that the witness should not be frightened by the method of preserving interview information.

Some interviewers do not bring out paper and pencil or a tape recorder until they have first heard the entire story of the witness. Other interviewers get the witness talking and then casually begin taking notes.

On the other hand, some interviewers begin taking a complete statement from the witness the moment the interview begins and do it in such a way that the witness is reassured and continues to be cooperative.

Some witnesses will not respond as well when notes are being made in their presence. Others are more careful about what they say when it is being recorded. However, with most witnesses such carefulness is an asset as they are more inclined to be accurate and truthful.

This problem of preserving the interview is one that agents must solve for themselves. It depends a lot on the witness and the situation. When in doubt, get the full and complete facts from the witness and then decide whether to make notes or take a tape recording.

Prepare for the Interview

Certain work should be done before the interview begins. An interviewer should review the facts that are known about the witness, what the agent believes this person can tell, what type of witness the person will be, and then decide on a strategy for the interview. It is wise to prepare some of the key questions in advance.

It may be necessary to make preliminary tentative arrangements for a lie detector operator to be sure that a test can be run immediately if needed. Confronting witnesses one against the other may be required if two contradicting statements must be resolved. If you plan to have witnesses face each other, check to see if they are both available.

Before going into any interview be sure you know your objectives. Have them well defined and have logical ways planned to achieve them, in the form of preplanned questions, confronting witnesses, and so on.

The Interview

The objective of an interview is to obtain information. It is usually a conversation but it is a planned conversation. The interviewer should talk as little as possible, for his job is listening. Remember this interview is *not* intended to be a mutual exchange of information.

Investigators are supposed to interview the witnesses. Too many times investigators give more information than they receive. Interviewers should do three things.

1. *Stimulate the conversation*. Do this by asking questions that are brief and cannot be answered by yes or no. Use "open ended" questions. Be careful that they do not convey information or suggest a desired answer but merely stimulate the flow of information from the witness.

2. *Guide the conversation into productive channels.* After you have stimulated conversation you must guide it. Get complete and detailed answers about the situation you are investigating.
3. *Corroborate the information furnished by the witness.* Refer to previous information and verify anything that can be checked out.

Watch for Discrepancies

When you note misstatements, inaccuracies, untruths, or discrepancies during an interview *hit them again and again*! This may be done by rephrasing your questions and asking them in another form. You can also require the witness to give you a more detailed account of the information than when first questioned. You can check the statement of one person against another. You may even check a person against his own previous statements to learn which of two conflicting facts is correct. Try to determine which statement was in error and whether the error was an honest mistake or an attempt to mislead you.

Positive Approach

Try not to use a negative approach in questioning, not only in the questions themselves but also in asking a witness to sign a statement. The interviewer who says to a witness, "You couldn't meet me at the store this afternoon, could you?" deserves the "No" such an approach will get. The interviewer has unconsciously allowed an easy "out" for the witness.

This same negative approach is in the question, "You didn't see anybody near the counter when the perfume was stolen, did you?" "You wouldn't want to sign this, would you?" Or, "Would you care to sign this?" With such a negative attitude the interviewer losses control of the situation. The witness gains control and feels no need to appear for the interview, no need to answer questions, or no need to sign the statement.

A positive approach is better because the interviewer stays in control. The agent positively sets the time and place of the interview and announces it to the witness by saying, "We have scheduled your meeting in our office at 4:30 this afternoon." This suggests that everything is all set and the interviewer is sure of himself. It will not be easy for a person to evade such a positive approach. The witness usually accepts the appointment and does not consider declining. The positive approach puts the investigator in the driver's seat. If nothing is done to destroy confidence or indicate timidity, the agent will retain control throughout the interview.

The interviewer should put questions in a positive manner when asking for a signature on a statement, such as "Read the statement." "If it is correct, sign it." This kind of approach persuades the person who is being questioned to mentally acquiesce to the positive guidance of the interviewer.

If you are in full control of the interview, the witness will sense it by the confidence you express in your manner of speech and method of questioning. However, if this person is a borderline case you may decide to do something to establish control of the relationship. You may decide politely but firmly to inform the witness that no smoking is permitted, just as he or she takes out a cigeratte. Or you may direct the witness to another chair after the person has selected a chair. Such procedure will vary with the individual being questioned and with the type of interview.

Questions asked at the start of an interview should be friendly and asked in a manner to calm the nervous person and placate an antagonistic witness. To do this, the first questions should be simple and of a noncontroversial nature. The usual procedure is to ask questions pertaining to name, employment, and so on, then lead into other questions about the person's background. Such questions should be inoffensive so that even the most suspicious person will respond. Once you have the witness talking and answering questions you can ask more pertinent questions, but lead into these important questions gradually and naturally. Do not be too abrupt.

Take Time to Develop Information

From the beginning it is important for the interviewer to be friendly but firm. Do a good job of selling yourself to the witness and be sure to take whatever time is necessary in the "getting acquainted" period. Establish rapport with the person being questioned.

A good method is to establish a common interest. This may require the interviewer to study the witness ahead of time to learn the subject's hobbies and interests. Points of common interest that the interviewer uses to get acquainted may include sports, gardening, the high cost of living, a recent newspaper story, or whatever is getting attention on the front pages of local newspapers at the time of the interview.

Once you can get the witness to start talking, regardless of whether or not the conversation has to do with the facts of the case being investigated, you will be in a position to guide the conversation into a productive discussion about the situation you are exploring.

Sometimes it helps to use diagrams and sketches as a means of helping the hesitant witness to "open up." Using the diagram, get the witness to *instruct* the investigator by pointing out the positions and locations of certain happenings. Make the witness an "expert." Whenever we are asked to instruct someone it gives us pleasure because it increases our self-esteem.

Type of Questions

The interviewer should take care in the forming and phrasing of questions. Avoid the common mistake of putting the answer into the question. Don't ask questions such as, "Is your name Robert Smith?" Instead ask, "What is your name?" Let the witness fill in the answer.

Try not to ask questions that can be answered with a "Yes" or "No." Use "open ended" questions such as, "Where were you when the loss occurred?" Then you can prompt the witness and keep him talking by follow-up questions such as, "What did you observe?" "How was the suspect dressed?" "What time was that?"

Try not to ask questions that can be answered with a question. Don't say, "Tom Smith stole the perfume, didn't he?" Your witness may very well answer, "I don't know, did he?" You may suddenly find yourself being interviewed by your own witness. Also avoid statements that sound like questions such as, "Your name is Jack Thompson?" or "You are the girl who found the empty box?"

Female Witnesses

A male investigator has to exercise particular care and discretion when questioning a woman. He must be careful not to allow himself to be placed in an embarrassing or compromising position. He must use discretion in selecting the place to interview a woman. Also be aware of the other people who should be present during the questioning.

Do not question a woman at unusual hours such as late in the evening. The male agent should not be left alone with a female witness. Always try to have another woman present or in the immediate vicinity. Avoid questioning a woman in a hotel room. Try to conduct interviews in your office or other businesslike places in the daytime.

The agent should be courteous and well mannered. If the interview involves a discussion of sex or other delicate questions the interviewer may decide to have all other people leave the room, including a woman secretary, feeling that complete privacy will be less embarrassing and more conducive to getting the facts. Such problems have to be left to the taste and judgment of the investigator. It is important to avoid vulgarity in language at *all* times in interviewing.

Juvenile Witnesses

The young person is another special problem for the investigator. In general the suggestions used for interviewing a woman should also be followed for the juvenile. Be sure that you are complying with the local and state laws regarding the questioning of young people. Try to interview the juvenile in the presence of a school representative or someone else in a responsible position. In some states juvenile officials are required to be present when an interview is conducted, and even if they are not legally required it is often an asset to have them available.

When questioning a juvenile you must usually spend a great deal more time during the "getting acquainted" period. Children are more suggestible than adults and you have to be careful that you do not suggest answers to questions that you may unconsciously want. The juvenile wants to help and may try to do so by trying to give you the answers you want to hear regardless of the truth of the situation.

Diagrams and photographs are valuable assets in certain types of interviews with juveniles. A paternal attitude on the part of the investigator is often successful. Naturally the age of the person being questioned is a factor in the conduct of the investigator. There can be no set rules about how to question young people, but here are some suggestions:

1. Be careful.
2. Be considerate.
3. Be confidential.
4. Avoid frightening the juvenile witness.
5. Don't show anger or irritation.
6. Be patient.

Willing Witnesses

The willing witness is a friendly witness who wants to help. Such a person often has to be guided and kept from rambling on about matters not directly related to the investigation until the pertinent facts have been related. The interviewer often has to persuade the witness to be more specific. This kind of witness is often vague in reporting events.

Such a person should be encouraged to name other people who can verify the information they provide.

From friendly witnesses you can often obtain names of suspects. Be careful that the witness sticks to the facts. Many willing witnesses distort facts in their eagerness to help the investigator and they often state rumors as facts. Be careful to verify the willing witness's story just as though such a person were a reluctant witness.

Willing witnesses are a form of limelight seeker, and although they are honest, they may make inaccurate and untruthful statements because of imperfect observations or the failure to observe and remember all the facts of the situation.

Hostile Witnesses

There are many things that cause a witness to be hostile. It may be that this person has friendly feelings toward the suspect. Some hostile witnesses can become abusive. The interviewer should avoid an argument. The agent must maintain an even temper at all times even if the witness becomes abusive and argumentative. Remember that a man does not think clearly or act sensibly when he's angry. Keep the subject talking and the hostile witness may say things in anger that wouldn't be said otherwise. These things may be important. Soon a hostile witness may talk himself out of his anger. The person may then develop into a talkative, repentant, and informative witness.

If the interviewer feels that this hostile witness is basically an honest person he may decide to spend some time educating him. He may explain that as an investigator he is not trying to persecute anyone but merely trying to get a picture of the situation. The agent may tell the witness that a full and complete disclosure of the facts will help innocent persons, clearing them of suspicion, whereas distortion or withholding of facts will only aid guilty people in escaping detection.

If the hostile witness is not an honest person and is attempting to shield someone else, the interviewer may decide to have this witness questioned under oath and then take a statement complete with falsehoods, misrepresentations, and discrepancies. The investigator may then proceed in the same manner as with a "lying witness."

"Lying Witnesses"

This type of person should be encouraged to talk and encouraged to tell all his lies in complete detail. He should be questioned so that he will have to tell several lies to cover up his original false statements.

Lies multiply like rabbits; one lie begets another and another. Sooner or later he will be caught in his own web and be forced to tell the truth. If the interview can be conducted under oath, the interviewer may be in a position to threaten the witness with a perjury charge if he doesn't tell the whole and complete truth.

Indifferent Witnesses

Such people do not volunteer information because they don't want to become involved. They usually don't want to be interviewed. On the other hand, they are not usually liars and don't attempt to protect wrongdoers.

These people are honest in their fashion. The interviewer may have to drag the information out of them. In this type of interview the investigator has to be very skillful. Questions must be carefully phrased. It often helps to remind the subject that a full and complete statement at this time may save the witness a lot of trouble and bother at a later date.

Suspicious Witnesses

Some witnesses ask a lot of questions. They are very inquisitive. They try to interview the agent. Cooperation may depend upon how much the interviewer already knows. The investigator has to suggest that he knows more than he really does; he has to infer that he already has the story but wants to hear it substantiated.

Ask the suspicious witness a question or two about something you already know. After the answer indicate you already knew the answer. You may ask what school the subject attended and he may answer "high school"; after you have passed on to several other questions, you might pause to summarize and then say, "You stated that you went to Richmond High School from September 1932 until June 1936." Since he never mentioned the full name of the school or the dates of his attendance, he will be surprised and will assume that you have a lot of information you haven't revealed. He will believe that you already have a complete record of his activities as well as knowledge of what has happened. His suspicious nature may lead him to believe that you are trying to trap him by asking questions to which you have the answers and he may decide to trick you by giving you a truthful account of the situation.

Rules of Interview

No set rules can be given for all interviewing. Each situation requires a different preparation, different approach, and different questions. It is also true that each interviewer will develop his or her own style and manner of questioning witnesses. What one person can do successfully, someone else may find a poor procedure because it is incompatible with that person's personality. Here, however, are some suggestions that can be helpful:

1. Prepare carefully for the interview.
2. Choose the best time and place for the interview.
3. Decide who should be present.
4. Try to keep the number of people present to a minimum.
5. Take time for an adequate preinvestigation.
6. Keep control of the interview at all times.
7. Let the person being interviewed do most of the talking.
8. Ask simple, short questions.
9. Avoid asking questions that can be answered, "Yes" or "No."
10. Phrase the questions so that they do not contain information but instead force the witness to supply the information in his answer.
11. Get the witness to talk and keep talking.
12. Guide conversations toward important predetermined objectives.
13. Get the witness to corroborate or disprove his statements.
14. Be thorough and get details.
15. Be sympathetic and understanding.
16. Be friendly but firm.
17. Don't tell the witness all you know.
18. Take special care when interviewing juveniles or women.

Good Investigations

A friendly source of information is the best place to begin an investigation. The scene of the crime should be visited and studied before interviewing witnesses. Ideally, an interview should be held at the scene of the crime.

It is taken for granted that the investigator will follow a plan or a schedule in the investigation. This plan may be subject to change as new information is gathered. In addition to visiting the scene of the crime, the agent will at times draw diagrams or take photographs if needed as evidence. The investigator will personally examine and identify any physical objects involved. He will get whatever reports are needed, make a police check on suspects for criminal records, check doctor and hospital reports if needed, track down ownership of a car through the state motor vehicle bureau, and do anything else that is needed as part of the investigation.

The most important thing will often be the interviews. Signed statements should be obtained from every person involved in the crime and every possible witness. A case may go to trial and the agent must prepare every case accordingly. Whether or not it actually goes to trial is not important from the investigator's point of view. For working purposes it is assumed that the same degree of thoroughness must be used on every case as that required in preparing for trial.

Besides the facts of a particular case, general details that apply to the case must be found, verified, and recorded. You may, for example, need the business history of one of the parties. Such information is easily available from a telephone directory, business directory, or professional register.

Public libraries are a readily available source of investigative information. Old newspaper files, magazines and pamphlets, and a comprehensive index of periodicals provide much information. Technical experts such as lie detector operators, toxicologists, police laboratory specialists, and similar people often can help in an investigation.

Any person who conceivably might know something about the matter being investigated should be consulted. No investigator can know everything about everything. He should know and use the services of experts.

Human memory is short. Investigators should recognize this fact and be prompt to investigate immediately after the event. Memory and interest of witnesses fade with the passage of time. It must never be forgotten that crowded court calendars today often result in long delays between the time of a crime and the time when the case comes to trial and witnesses actually testify.

Statements made spontaneously by a witnesses at or near the time of the crime are very persuasive when used at a trial. They need to be obtained and recorded word for word as nearly as possible. Whether or not they will be admissible as evidence has to be left up to the decision of the legal counsel. Statements made so near to the time of the incident that they can be considered explanatory of the crime itself are usually admissible. Spontaneity at the crime or immediately after it is the test. A mere narrative of a past event is not considered a spontaneous statement and may not be admissible. Admissions made at the time of the crime are considered in court as part of the facts themselves.

The statements of witnesses must always be compared with the physical facts of the event before you can take them at face value. This should be done well before the time of trial. It must be made certain, for example, that if a witness says he saw or heard something that it was reasonably possible for him to actually see or hear whatever it is he claims to have seen or heard.

Before interviewing a witness, the investigator should try, if possible, to find out what sort of person the witness is, such as the person's social position or financial situation. Get a brief history about such matters as tastes, prejudices, and hobbies. These things can help to win the confidence of this person.

The agent's purpose is to obtain information, not to argue with the witness. Don't influence the subject's account of the event. You must accept the facts the way the witness gives them. Only when the witness's story is obviously prejudiced and untrue do you have any justification for trying to induce him to change it. Even this is a questionable practice, because the law provides for the testing of testimony by cross examination and other methods and quite properly frowns on influencing a witness's story. The investigator should record the exact words that show the prejudice of the witness. He can then rely on legal counsel to bring the witness's testimony into perspective at the time of trial.

The investigator should reflect a confidence at all times that decent people cooperate in a search for the truth.

Getting Witnesses to Court

Some types of witnesses are very hard to get to court. Doctors, for example, dislike taking the time needed to testify. They consider their time too valuable to be wasted on matters other than people who are sick. When interviewing witnesses the investigator should impress on them that they may have to appear in court and that they have a duty to testify. This needs to be done with tact and consideration, because most people fear courts.

A frank explanation of the store's need for help from the witness is the most effective inducement. Most people are decent enough not to wish to be the cause of misguided justice. It helps to suggest that the witness would want help too if the situation were reversed.

Threats usually only antagonize a witness. Experience has shown that an appeal for help and fair play works best.

Trial Preparation

Preparing for trial is, of course, the job of legal counselors; but the investigator's work is designed to assist them. Everything an investigator does should be aimed toward the final court test. The investigator seeks information in every case that will stand the acid test of court scrutiny.

Judge Frederick Evan Crane described courts as "*truth hunting institutions*." Getting the *real truth* is the hard part of any investigation. Once you have the facts, and they are validated, the application of law is relatively simple. It is apparent, therefore, that the investigator prepares for trial just as a lawyer does.

Long before time of the trial every statement made by the people involved should be checked against the known facts. If you fail to do this, opposing counsel may rip your evidence to shreds during the trial, often with a devastating effect on your carefully constructed case.

What witnesses first attest to as facts must be examined at the start of the investigation as only possibilities. If these "facts" aren't possible under the known conditions of the situation being studied, they are unreliable and cannot be used. If a witness says he heard a remark by someone, check the distance from the speaker, the carrying power of the witness's voice, the keenness of hearing of the witness and so on. Pin it down!

Personal bias, special interest in the matter under investigation, social or community friendships, and many other factors may destroy the credibility of a witness's story, making it worthless. These possibilities must be reviewed when evaluating a witness's statements.

Interviews

First, introduce yourself and show your credentials. Explain the purpose of the interview. It's a good idea to produce your notebook at this time if you plan to take notes. Do not, however, write down every word the witness says. Try to use "key" words in your notes to aid later recall. Later you can write up a full statement for the witness's signature. Don't let note taking scare off your witness, but if you want to take notes, do so.

The immediate appearance of a notebook establishes its presence in the interview and indicates that you are serious and businesslike. It says that you are attempting to make an accurate report. It has a tendency to cause the person being questioned to also be accurate.

When talking about your statement, refer to it as "the report," "my notes," or "for my files" rather than calling it a "statement." Legally, what you call it is not important.

Be sure that you have plenty of paper and pens. Hopefully, you will have previously studied model statements so that you already have a firm grasp of structure. The beginner, particularly, should study specimens of various types of statements to use as models for composing his own.

The witness, of course, must be allowed to tell his story in his own words. Use of his words and his ways of stating them is important.

He should never be pushed into testifying for any reason other than civic duty or the desire for truth and justice and common decency. Attempts to buy testimony are not only degrading to the witness and the interviewer, but they are also illegal and immoral. They can boomerang in court. It is poor judgment to use such an approach.

Remember that privacy is essential if you want this person to talk freely. When you have other people around and they cannot be eliminated from the interview at least have them sign the statement as corroborating witnesses.

Many investigators don't realize that children can be good witnesses. They must be old enough to know the difference between right and wrong. Children can sign a report and they don't have to be sworn in when making a signed statement.

When they are applicable, sketches or other illustrative aids, such as Polaroid photographs, can be used during the interview and can later be incorporated into the statement if they are helpful in explaining the situation under study.

When you interview public officials or high-level executives you often don't need to write out a full statement, just put it in note form as a matter of record for yourself.

Your notes as an investigator about how your witness acts in making a statement may prove very helpful later on. If he or she shows signs of uneasiness or gives you a feeling of being untruthful, this may suggest that the statement is unreliable. This fact, of course, does not show up in the statement itself. The investigator's evaluation of the reliability of each witness should be recorded and kept in a separate report attached to the statement.

When you have hostile and negative witnesses their facts are just as valuable as those of friendly witnesses. At times they may be more important. Such people should be persuaded to be cooperative, but if their hostility persists, the words of the witness—exactly as they are spoken—should be recorded. Your trial counsel will welcome these details in a hostile witness's statement.

Throughout your investigative activity use the newspaper reporters' guide. When investigating any incident find out Who, What, When, Where, Why, and How the situation came about.

Investigative Report

When you write a report, this is a formal statement of facts, information, observations, and opinions. Label each category as such. The acid test of an investigator's ability to organize and make sense out of details is the way the report is constructed. You need to make a clear, reliable report. The test of your effectiveness as an investigator is the use of the information that you have gathered, how well you understand it and how intelligently you interpret it.

Try to make your reports uniform. This will save you time and effort.

Many reports are written in the chronological sequence the events occurred, which means you start at the beginning and go to the end. Usually it's best to make your reports in the third person. Make them simple and objective. Don't overelaborate; keep the report sharp and lean. The more words used to express an idea the less impact it has. Try for directness, simplicity, conciseness, and good organization of material.

An outline statement or a narrative style can be used, depending on the complexity of your subject matter and your own writing ability. The outline form is favored by many experienced investigators.

Summarize your facts briefly. Identify your sources. Report inadmissible facts if they are important. If in doubt about legal problems, leave such matters to your legal counsel.

Investigators may make suggestions and personal comments, but such remarks should be made in a separate report, not in the formal report document. This report can be kept with the formal report but should not be included in it because the formal report should deal only with objective facts.

When a joint report is made both investigators should sign the completed report. The report should also indicate which person obtained which facts.

The Statement

When you make a statement you are, in a general sense, writing the facts and details of the case. Usually a statement sets forth the words of a witness after discussion with the investigator. It is usually signed. At times a statement is so incriminating that it is wise to have the statement of the witness sworn to.

Sworn statements are very valuable. It is often wise to have an investigator who is a notary public, because then a sworn statement can be obtained when needed. It is recognized, of course, that sometimes a third party notary is more desirable.

In starting a statement, paper should be ready but it is better not to begin writing until after the witness has told the full story and has clarified some of the uncertain factors in his own mind. You can take notes during this period to guide you in the subsequent writing of the statement.

It is possible that your witness may not be able to read. In such a case this fact should appear in your statement together with an acknowledgment by the witness that the statement was read aloud to the witness. If the person being interviewed does not understand English, this fact also has to be noted in the statement. Also tell what was done to be certain that the statement was understood. If you have an interpreter, note this person's qualifications and have him sign the statement as a witness.

After your first discussion with the person being interviewed, you must tactfully explain that a written record must be made. It is well to speak of it as a report or a record, not as a statement.

A separate statement should be taken from each person interviewed. Never take a joint statement. A joint statement is impossible to use in a trial. The source of any information given that is not based on personal observation must also be noted. Handwritten statements are the strongest. If you use typed copies, take all duplicates with you. They may reveal your case to someone who should not know the facts in the matter. All notes and carbon paper should be removed after a statement is taken.

If a statement covers several pages, each page should be initialed by the witness. Sometimes it is a good idea to make one or two deliberate typing errors in a statement and have the witness indicate corrections in his own handwriting along with his initials. This indicates that the statement is authentic because it has obviously been read and corrected by the witness.

If you mention exhibits in a statement, they should be identified by number and tagged with the correct number. The exhibit tag should also be initialed by the witness. In all reports refer to the exhibit by number and other description. This applies to photographs, diagrams, and so forth.

After you have written a statement, have the witness read it aloud before signing it. Ask the witness to write on the bottom of the statement, "I have read this and it is true," and then have the witness sign the statement.

You can help the witness to keep facts in sequence during the interview, but be careful not to plant your own version of the facts in the witness's mind. Such an approach only defeats your objective because the witness later will remember and testify to the events as he actually saw them and they can differ from your concept of what happened. Any differences between a statement you take now and later testimony in court will hurt your case.

In a criminal situation if the person you are interviewing may himself be involved, it is sometimes necessary to warn him of his constitutional rights. You should note that such a warning was given at the beginning or end of the statement.

When writing the statement use the language of your witness. Include bad grammar if this person uses bad grammar. Write the characteristic words that the person uses in discussing the case. If you put your own words in the statement it will lack authenticity.

Remember that a witness has been known to deny his own statement at a trial, and therefore your identification of the statement needs to be as complete as possible. Only facts admissible in evidence should be in a statement. Many times you will have to take out extraneous matters. Tell the witness tactfully to confine the statement to comments directly related to the subject as much as possible.

Sometimes a witness will refuse to sign the statement after it is written. If this happens, you should read the statement back to the witness with a third person present. Then make a subsidary statement and a statement from the third party. Add this statement to your report and have the third party sign it. A small notation should be added to this effect, "This statement contains the facts as told to (name of investigator) and (name of the third party) by (name of witness) at (address) on (date and hour) and was read by (name of witness) who stated to us that its contents are true, but who refused to sign the statement." Have this notation signed by the investigator and the third party.

Sometimes your witness's story will sound false. If this occurs, make every reasonable effort to test the statement while you are getting it. Don't succumb to your eagerness to get a statement even though it later won't stand up in court. A false statement is undesirable.

A device that sometimes gets a reluctant witness's signature on a statement is assuring the witness that you will not compel him to sign but the fact that he does not wish to sign has to be recorded. A subsidary statement can be offered saying: "The above statement is true but I refuse to sign it because I do not wish to be involved in the matter." Date this statement and have it signed by the witness in the presence of a third party who also signs it.

Try not to leave blank spaces in the statement where other material might be written in later.

In most cases witnesses sign statements without objection. The signing should be treated casually and as a matter of course. The best practice is simply to hand the pen to the witness and say, "Now please sign this for me in order to verify the accuracy of this report."

Laws of Evidence

The laws of evidence are a complex subject. They require long legal study. As an investigator you will probably not have the time or inclination to become an expert on this subject but you will find it helpful to have some familiarity with the general principles of the laws of evidence. The following brief notes deal only with a few of the rules of evidence important to the investigator.

1. *Evidence* means everything that tends to prove or disprove a fact.
2. *Proof* is a result of evidence. If the total of all the facts shown to be true by evidence is conclusively believed, the ultimate fact has been proved.
3. *Direct and indirect evidence* must be distinguished. Direct evidence is evidence that itself tends to prove a fact that is at issue. This usually means an eyewitness account. Indirect evidence (*circumstantial evidence*) is evidence of facts that once established, tend to imply the existence of the facts at issue. In other words, "the thing itself speaks," or a situation or a fact by its very nature implies the evidence indicated.
4. *Real evidence* means the thing or object itself.
5. *Material evidence* means effective or convincing evidence.
6. *Relevant evidence* means evidence of a fact so closely related to the fact at issue. *Irrelevant evidence* means that the evidence does not tend to prove the truth of the fact at issue.
7. *Competent evidence* means such evidence as a particular fact at issue needs in order to be proved. Thus, if an injury results from an assault and battery during apprehension, this evidence of injuries is usually competent. Conversely, evidence of the color of the eyes of the suspect usually would be considered *incompetent evidence.*
8. *Judicial notice* means facts already known and accepted by the court without any need for evidence of those facts to be presented. Thus the court takes judicial notice of certain universally known facts, such as the fact that water is a liquid, that the sun rises in the east, and so on.
9. *Admissible evidence* is evidence that a court is bound to allow to be introduced. *Inadmissible evidence* means that the court may not allow the evidence to be introduced.

10. *Hearsay* evidence is evidence not of the truth of a fact at issue of what somebody *said* was the truth about it orally or in writing. It is a statement based on what someone else said, not on what the person who made the statement himself observed. Such evidence is not admissible in court. It is not possible to test it properly by cross examination of the original person who made the statement, the original speaker not being present, or under oath, when he spoke. However, if the fact is to prove whether or not a person said or spoke certain words, anyone who heard him may give testimony as to what he heard. There are some exceptions to the hearsay rule. Among them are the following:
    a. Dying declarations.
    b. Declarations of intention, reason, feeling, or motive.
    c. Declarations against the interest of the speaker, such as admissions of guilt. They must have been against his interest at the time he spoke.
11. *Circumstantial evidence.* Evidence of a factor, not the fact at issue itself, but which tends to prove the fact at issue, is circumstantial evidence. The fact given in evidence must be convincingly shown and it must not be too remote from the fact at issue to be admitted as evidence. Most evidence in most trials is circumstantial evidence.
12. *Admissions.* An admission is some prior act or statement by a party that was an acknowledgment that a certain fact was not as he now claims it was. Any act or statement that conflicts with what he says at the trial is admissible in evidence as an admission.

The investigator should read a text on the laws of evidence, search, and seizure and also be familiar with the laws of slander and libel.

Chapter 14
FUNDAMENTALS OF INTERROGATION

This as well as the next chapter are directed to the security person or the store executive designated to interview malefactors. If we had to select the one skill needed in security, the ability to interview would be our first choice.

Where Do We Find Interview Techniques?

These techniques are often from the work of detectives, lawyers, psychologists, and other people who work with methods of verbal communication. They have tested many gambits. Some are rejected, and others are retained. In the following pages we will try to set forth some of the proven methods used throughout the world.

Various Techniques Are Needed

Are these techniques fixed rules? No, only suggestions. There are no set rules for interviewing. They can be used in many cases, but not in all cases, because there are always two unknown factors: the personality of (1) the person interviewing and (2) the subject. All of the tips given here have been found to work. They will work again in the future, but you may not have equal success in all cases.

Personalities clash; some people do not get along well with other people. This is caused by hidden psychological factors. The suspect may find that the interviewer reminds him of his hated father. Perhaps the suspect sees mannerisms that cause hostile feelings, based on forgotten childhood events.

Since some people clash, you cannot have a good interview with every type of suspect. You must operate by trial and error. Try one method and then another until you find one that works. Even if you are not successful, this does not mean that the suspect can't be "broken." It is possible that another person with a new approach will succeed.

Stress and Empathy

In the next chapter we discuss two theories of interviewing we call "stress and empathy." All questioning centers on these two basic approaches. For many the stress and empathy ideas are all that are needed. Others may need more detailed methods, however, and this chapter is intended to satisfy this need. You will find that these techniques are not an end in themselves but from them you can develop imaginative variations to meet your needs.

No two people question alike. A good interviewer will understand human nature and he will like people. However, he may also be too sympathetic. You need to separate sentimentality from understanding. Do not let sentimentality destroy your effectiveness.

There is no list of methods to solve all interviews. This would require many books. In the end you would be confused rather than helped. Because this is true, we will point up only a few of the better methods.

Interviewing the Noncriminal

Whenever you question anyone, your attitude and manner will be vital to the effect you create. It is important that you place yourself in the shoes of the person being questioned. How would you feel? What would you want and expect from the interviewer?

Understand the Interviewee's Fears

Many people look upon the police person as someone with magical power. They feel that he can put them in jail on a whim. This fear is caused by a lack of knowledge of police power and its limitations.

Because it leads to fear, it also leads to hostility even in the innocent. People feel afraid and so are not inclined to be helpful to police. It is well to keep this point of view in mind when questioning people.

Gaining help from Mr. Average Citizen has become harder to do in recent years. People cheat a bit on their tax returns, drink a little too much at times, keep one eye on the car mirror when they drive too fast, and believe that laws are made to be broken, they feel that only the dumb are caught.

Knowing these things, you can take steps to overcome them. Treat the person being questioned with courtesy and let him see by your attitude that he is important to you. In this way you can often change him from a hostile person to a helpful friend.

The "Complaint" Interview

One type of interview you will handle is complaints. In these cases be attentive, ask logical questions, and be understanding. The person making the complaint should feel you are on his side.

When checking on losses or other complaints, follow these rules:

1. Be attentive.
2. Recognize the importance of the complaint to the person reporting it.
3. Assure him of prompt action.
4. Tell him you appreciate his interest.
5. Reassure him that the matter will be handled tactfully if this is indicated.
6. Get the full facts in detail. Note them down.
7. Be understanding, but reserve judgment.
8. Offer no opinions.
9. Do not argue or refute the complainant's point of view.

Hurdles to Good Questioning

You should remember that the person you are talking to, by reporting a loss, is doing you a favor. It does not matter what his reasons for doing this may be.

Two hurdles to good questioning in noncriminal matters are, first, the dangers of trying to justify your department's position in the matter. Sometimes an investigator is oversensitive when a report is made. He may even try to contradict the person making the complaint.

The second problem is caused by the man who tries to bolster his own ego by offering opinions on what happened. These quick judgments are often wrong and leave a bad impression on the complainant. They hurt a later check of the facts.

A salesclerk may say a compact has been stolen from her counter and that she saw a short, red-faced man near the display at the time of the theft. Later the compact is found in the basket behind the counter, knocked off by a careless salesclerk.

It is good to tell the salesclerk that her first opinion was a logical conclusion and that the red-faced man may still be a good suspect. If you do not let her save face, she may not give you help in the future.

Explain Your Position

When you have to take action contrary to that expected by the person making the complaint, you should explain why. People will accept a rebuff if they know the reason for it, and if it is apparent that you are acting in good faith.

You may explain the law and the facts of arrest under the law to clarify the situation. Your witness to a crime can then understand why you cannot make an immediate arrest.

When talking to doctors or other professional people who have a code that does not permit them to reveal the source of confidential information, it is advisable for you to explain that you are aware of this fact and that you understand the doctor's position.

Be Tolerant

You should handle everyone—complainants, witnesses, informants, or suspects—with courtesy. By using the golden rule, you will find better channels of communication open between you and the person you are questioning.

Only if you consider the interests of the person you are questioning can you anticipate his objections, arguments, alibis, and other barriers that may stand between you and the information you need. Tolerance of human nature, patience, and a desire to listen will make you successful.

Interviewing the Criminal

You may start a criminal interview with little evidence. You may have only a suspicion that something is wrong. By using methods of questioning, you can often make your case. Ingenuity, imagination, and showmanship help you get results.

You have to use applied psychology. The difference between a good and an unsuccessful interview might be the difference between a lawsuit and an admission of guilt.

Criminal interviewing is one of your important tools. It often accounts for at least 60 percent of your case.

Criminal Interview Objectives

1. Establishing guilt or innocence.
2. Discovering method of theft.
3. Learning over what period of time the thefts occurred.
4. Finding out the amount of merchandise or money involved.
5. Discovering the motivation for the crime.
6. Determining the disposition of the stolen money and goods.
7. Learning how much can be recovered?
8. Finding out about the guilty knowledge of others also stealing from the store.
9. Obtaining legal evidence on the present case.
10. Getting a written confession.
11. Determining subject's mental condition.
12. Determining subject's economic, social, and moral status for the purpose of case disposition.
13. Finding out about previous criminal acts.
14. Discovering the first step in how to help the subject.

These are the things to determine before your case is completed. Each case will place more emphasis on certain objectives. But in all cases everything listed above should be explored.

Give Suspect Benefit of the Doubt

Many times a case is circumstantial. Evidence alone may suggest that a suspect is guilty. In any case in which the facts are not proven there is an element of doubt; there is always a possible explanation. These stories are often unusual to the extent that they may seem untrue, but yet when the facts are checked, they may turn out to be true.

Human nature takes complex twists; it is good to give the suspect the benefit of every doubt.

Indirect Accusation

When you deal with a case in which there is any doubt about guilt, your opening question should be an *indirect accusation*, that is general questions about "irregularities" that give the suspect a chance to give an explanation. This does not place the store in danger and is a fair way to treat the person being questioned.

In an indirect accusation, loaded words such as "steal," "thief," "jail," "police," "liar," "courts," and so on, should be avoided. These terms are related, in the subject's mind, with things that may frighten him into silence rather than into admitting wrongdoing.

Point Out That Violations Have Occurred

Point out to the person that you have checked and found that there were violations of store rules. The facts are on file, and you are anxious to clear up the matter.

You are talking to this person to find out what his side of the story is. You point out that the problem is minor. The person should be led to feel that an admission is not of too much importance. This helps him save face.

If the suspect does not admit violating the store rules, then you can warn him that you had hoped the matter could have been handled without such serious consequences for the subject as publicity, expense, shame, and so on. Still make no direct accusation. Suggest only that there has been a violation of rules.

Avoid "Painting a Black Picture"

You should keep in mind that too much fear paralyzes many people. Painting a black picture of what might happen to the suspect if he does not admit his guilt can make him become too frightened to speak. The thefts of this person may be greater than you suspect and if you cause too much fear he will clam up.

Put Suspect's Viewpoint in Perspective

It may be that this person does not see what he has done in perspective as related to the possible consequences. Many times the subject underrates the consequences of his action. A thief may admit stealing thousands of dollars worth of goods and then, blandly ask, when being closed out, "You mean I'm going to be fired?"

At the other extreme is the person who exaggerates what may happen to him as a result of his thefts. In this case he feels that no matter what he says he will be thrown into jail for years. Your job is to learn the subject's viewpoint and refocus it in correct perspective.

A Case of Proven Theft

When you accuse a person directly at the start of a case, the suspect may violently reject your statements. The result is that you both may end up shouting accusations and denials at each other. The subject becomes so set behind his false denials that he cannot later admit his guilt and still save face.

This attack is a poor step to take at any point in an interview and is even worse at the start. When beginning try not to make an issue about innocence or guilt, even if it is a case in which the guilt is already proven by the facts.

How to Begin

Don't start by getting an admission of guilt from the subject. Instead, begin at a point where you assume by words and attitude that the crime is a fact. Indicate that there is no point in arguing whether the subject did or did not commit the crime, for the facts are conclusive, there is no room for doubt about the subject's guilt.

Why do you start with the fact that the subject did commit the crime? Because then you do not get pulled into a losing fight over guilt or innocence. You assume the subject did commit the crime. When he attempts to debate this fact, you can point out there is no need to talk about guilt or innocence; the facts are final.

The Next Step

Now you focus on the questions of how long and why he stole. You offer ideas how he can save face. Finally you ask him what he feels the store should do in his case.

When you start with these points rather than arguing over an admission of guilt, the suspect will usually admit his guilt by his answer to a secondary question. You might ask how long he has been stealing or say, "What have you done with the money?" The subject gives an admission of guilt in his reply.

A Belief Relationship

As pointed out in the chapter on empathy, at first you should just talk until you have a "belief relationship." Do this before you talk about the crime at hand.

Facts in the case history can be used to open your interview—questions about the person's family, hobbies, and work. It is good to give the subject a chance to get the feel of your personality. Give him a moment to reorientate himself to where he is and what is happening to him. Then you can ask about the crime.

Suspect's Guilt Self-Defeating

Do you know what will defeat the criminal in the end? His own feelings of guilt! It is true that you help him talk and that you are a means to getting his admissions. But he really succumbs in the end because of his own knowledge of being guilty. The fact that he *knows* that he is wrong is the key factor in his defeat.

Time Is in the Interviewer's Favor

Time is on your side. A person who is being questioned is fighting two battles. The first is to outwit your questions. The second is to fight off his own feelings of guilt. That is, the pressures of his own conscience. In the end, *time* will cause him to admit his guilt, unless, of course, barriers have been built up during the interview that make it hard for him to reveal himself because he can no longer save face.

If you spend only twenty minutes with him and give up, you have done a shallow and useless interview. You must have patience and tolerance.

You must use *time* as an element in your favor. The ticking clock helps you flush out the true facts that lie deep in the mind of the person being questioned. It may take hours for a person to tell you things that have been stored up in the secret rooms of his mind—some held in the dark a whole lifetime.

The Intelligent Suspect

Don't shy away from the intelligent subject. You may feel that a person with a bright mind can outwit you. This is not true. The smart person with a sharp brain also has a more vivid imagination. As a result you can get your admission by making images in the imagination of your subject. All of his senses will be keener. This includes his conscience fears and his sense of fair play.

When you deal with such a person, do so courteously. Appeal to his sense of fairness. Bring in his responsibilities to his family and to society. You will find, if you do this, that the bright person is the easiest type you will deal with.

Do You Bluff?

If you bluff, be careful. If your subject discovers one bluff you are lost as far as this interview is concerned.

Just as the confidence and belief relationship is fundamental to get the subject to talk, so does any loss of belief destroy your chance of getting at the truth. You may need to bluff, but do so in a calculated way, recognizing that if you fail, you destroy your whole interview.

Be Confident Suspect Is Guilty

One last point should be made. This is your mental attitude when interviewing a person about a crime of *proven* theft. Review all of your facts and be completely satisfied that the person is guilty.

If for any reason at all, either prior to or during the interview, you lose your belief that the person is guilty, you are defeated. Your feelings cannot be disguised. Unless you have a confident attitude, there will be little chance of getting an admission of guilt.

Sometimes you may start out feeling confident that a person is guilty, but then you become sympathetic after talking to him awhile. You may get to the point where you doubt the facts of the case. In your own mind you cannot believe that such a person could be guilty.

When this occurs it is wise for you to turn the case over to another interviewer. If you continue with the case feeling this way, you are unfair to yourself and your interview will fail.

We find from life whatever we *expect* to find. No single thing will go as far toward making an interview succeed as your attitude of confidence throughout all the questioning.

Direct Accusation

Do you ever need to make a direct accusation? Seldom. However, if this should happen, be aware of the possible results.

Disaster will result if your direct approach fails. You must see that the direct accusation commits you to court action. You must be ready to back up your words in a court of law. Before you make any direct accusations, go over every bit of evidence and be sure your case is complete and accurate. Evaluate your facts and see if they will win your case in court.

A Last Resort

As a rule of thumb, it can be stated that you should *never* make a direct accusation until after you have some admission of guilt. When you get to this point and it appears that there is no other place to go, stop, look, and think. Have you applied all the indirect approaches at your disposal?

Even if you are satisfied that this is true, it is good to turn the subject over to someone else for further questioning. Be sure to exhaust all the best methods available before going to the drastic action of direct accusation.

SPECIAL INTERVIEWING TECHNIQUES

The Idealized Image

One of the best means of getting an admission for a suspect is to contrast his mental picture of his idealized self with the reality of the moment.

Most people retain an idealized image of themselves throughout their lives. It comes into being during adolescence. Our lives are spent in the never-ending struggle to be like our idealized selves. Often we do not compare ourselves as we really are with this idealized image because the contrast is unbearable. It is an inner conflict common to all of us, not only to people in trouble.

This conflict can be used by a good interviewer. He uses it after several minutes of talk have established a confidence-and-belief relationship. He may say, "I just can't understand it, I've been listening to you talk and I can see that you're a very fine person. You speak well, you dress in good taste, and I can tell from your words that you have a good mind. I know your parents taught you the difference between right and wrong. Being the type of person you are, I know you feel the importance of goodness. What I can't understand is how a person as fine as you can be in the position you are today, here before me—as a common thief!"

Help Suspect Understand His Situation

When this picture of the subject as a fine person is done with sincerity and then is suddenly contrasted to the image of him as a thief, the impact is tremendous. It is not uncommon for the subject to break down and cry.

As soon as this impact is made, the interviewer, in soft and understanding questioning, draws out the story of his crime. You will, of course, surround such questions with facesaving remarks. Tell him why he betrayed his true self. Help him explain the motives that led to criminal things. Sincerely help him to understand how he came to his present unhappy situation.

It is good to stress the fact that you understand and like this person even though you do not approve of some of the things he has done. Most of us want people to believe in us. We want them to forgive us for our weaknesses. By being understanding and by letting the subject know that you really do like him as a person, you satisfy this need, which is in all of us.

This Method Requires Sincerity

Needless to say this is a method that can only be used by a sincere and mature person. Only when you are really tolerant of people do you have a strong personal philosophy of goodness. You must be a kind person; only then can such a method of interview be successful. In the hands of an experienced person with these attributes, this method of building conflict within the person, between his idealized image and the reality of the moment, can be a most effective means of finding the truth.

Pleasure Versus Pain

People can be led to any pattern of human action by using the principle of pleasure versus pain. All of us will do those things that give us pleasure and avoid those things that give us pain. This principle is an important one to remember. It is a good tool and it can be useful to you.

There are many means of using pleasure versus pain. Using the third degree is an application of this theory, although here we have something else in mind—the creation of *mental* pictures in the mind of the subject. This is done with word pictures. Words can create mental pictures like a movie film.

Form Mental Pictures with Words

To be good at this you must have a way with words. Words are your keys to the human mind. You must carry a large key ring with a variety of keys. You will see different types of locks on the doors of the minds you wish to explore.

A good interviewer is an actor. He writes his own dialogue; he plays different roles. He may play the role of father. He may play the role of hardened judge. He may play the sympathetic role of kind brother. All of these parts he plays for the purpose of creating images in the mind of the subject. These movies will lead to the release of truth.

You are a combination of hypnotist and storyteller. You hold the subject's eyes and focus his mind on your word images. In a way you hypnotize the subject's mind. By your storytelling ability you lead his mind down whatever path you desire.

Storytelling Ability

This technique is your method of applying either pleasure or pain. For example, you may use subtle words that have a deep effect on a sensitive subject.

A question that sounds quite soft such as, "If we do find we need to lock you up, who in your family should be told to come to the policie station this evening to put up your bail?" It is soft, but it stimulates an entire series of responses, like a one-reel movie.

Suddenly in the mind of the subject explodes an image of her husband coming to see her in jail. If you pause long enough, she will go through a whole series of mental scenes. She will live the whole horrifying experience as though it is happening now.

Another impact question is to ask, "If this crime appears in the newspapers with your name and a picture, how will your friends feel about it?" Again the drug has been injected into her mind to create a whole series of make-believe mental images.

By using your creative imagination, you can work out many more of these loaded questions. There is also a more direct use of the pleasure and pain principle based on building two contrasting images.

Two Contrasting Images

You are a fine person. It hurts me to think of you being handcuffed, taken outside and placed in a police car, taken to the police station where you are booked, fingerprinted, photographed, and placed in a common cell overnight. You will be thrown in with prostitutes, drunks, sexual perverts. You'll share a common toilet, have to sleep on a hard straw bed.

There will be no erasing from your mind in the years ahead, the fears, the memory of such an experience. That, of course, is only the start. After that comes your walk into court, the crowds of curiosity seekers, the shame of being found guilty and, of course, your sentence.

These things which you now face are inevitable because of your attitude. But they are needless. They are a needless torture of your family, your friends, your loved ones. You can avoid this if you show your real character.

You know, a person's character is judged in times of crises. You have done wrong, but now, if you are truly a fine person, you will admit it. You will face the music. If you have the courage to do this, good things will result. This can be a turning point in your life. You can decide in the next few minutes whether you're going to spend tonight in a prison cell, with the trash of humanity or, in the next hour be free, outside on the street. You can be breathing free air, walking alone, a free person.

A terrible load of guilt will be off your conscience. You will be ready to make a fresh start, to build a new life for yourself. Which shall it be? Jail and disgrace or freedom and a fresh start? I am here to help you, but in the end you must help yourself.

Other Themes

Mental images can be built up on many other themes. Picture how a man's wife will feel when she finds out what has happened. Picture what it means to go before a judge and be told you are going to jail. These images can be contrasted with pleasant pictures. Pictures showing a person able to lift his head high because he has freed himself of his burden of guilt. Pictures of new freedom, of a chance for a fresh start.

Good Interviewers Are Good Storytellers

Telling a story is one of the magic features of communication. Throughout history man has influenced other men by weaving the magic fabric of stories. This is one of the great arts of persuasion.

You must practice this art of storytelling. When you complete your story, the subject should feel as though he has lived through the experience, has felt it with all his five senses.

The good storyteller paints pictures for the eyes, ears, touch, smell, and taste. He brings reality into the mind of the subject. The subject responds to the make-believe story with *real* emotion. If you are a good storyteller, you will be a good interviewer.

Create Conflicting Mental Pictures

Remember the plot of your stories should create conflicting mental pictures—one road leads the subject into a world of pain, the other one leads him into a good world of pleasure and happiness.

If the story is properly told, he sees no choice except to follow the pleasure image. Once his desire for the pleasure image is strong, he will make sacrifices to achieve it. The price you ask of him is that he tell you the truth.

The Bold Approach

Have you ever started off your interview with a thick folder filled with papers and various report forms? It is a good method. You place this folder where the subject can see it.

Then you tell him that security has made a complete check and you have a full report on his criminal activities. You point out that the interview is only routine. The store, in order to decide what is to be done, wants to hear his side of the case.

You explain that the store wants to give him a chance to be completely honest. If the store feels he recognizes the fact that he has made a mistake and sincerely wants to right the wrong he has done, then we will see what can be done.

This bolder approach often unnerves the subject and he starts to reveal some of his activities.

The interviewer pursuing this method will pretend to check through his papers in the folder. He will act as though he is verifying the facts disclosed by the subject. You should also tell the subject that your investigation is complete. You have all the necessary evidence ready for court action if such action is necessary.

Sometimes the subject will tell about things security was not aware of. Of course, if he fails to touch on known criminal activities, it shows he has not yet told the whole truth.

Pad and Pencil Technique

A variation is to use the "pad." When the subject appears to be willing to reveal all the things he has stolen, you hand him a pad and pencil and explain that you are going to leave the room for a few minutes. During this time he is to write on the pad a list of all the things that he has stolen.

You point out that you have in your possession a complete list of the things he has stolen. If any one of these items does not appear on his list, you will know that he is not telling the complete truth. You will then take action based on that assumption. Since the subject has no way of knowing what you have on your list he will often be amazingly detailed in his list.

Using Scientific Devices

For a long time police have found that telling the criminal his crime has been proven by scientific devices is often an effective method of getting an admission.

In one case, a store found a suit coat thrown in a corner by an employee. The employee had stolen a new jacket to replace it. When questioned later the employee denied the discarded jacket was his.

The detective pointed out that hairs from the jacket had been analyzed by the police crime laboratory and that they were found to be identical to those on his head. Confronted with this apparent scientific proof the thief broke down and confessed.

A security manager in a large Florida store keeps a number of cameras on a shelf behind his desk in open view of the person being interviewed. This device plants in the subject's mind the idea that the cameras have been used to photograph him stealing. This security manager has found that telling the subject that an automatic camera has been recording his thefts often results in an immediate confession.

Sometimes a photograph of a scientific piece of equipment can have the same effect when given to the subject with the comment, "This is the piece of equipment that caught you."

Using One Criminal Against the Other

When two or more people are caught they are usually questioned in separate rooms. Answers are then used for cross-interviewing. Sometimes it is effective to let the subject being questioned believe that the other person has involved him in the theft situation.

This is a tried and true technique that can be built into a situation in which one of the subjects feels he is being made the "goat." Anger at the apparent betrayal by the other person may cause the criminal to make a clean breast of all the facts.

Along the same lines the criminals can be put in an office wired with a microphone. If you leave them alone for a while they will often discuss their interviews and may reveal important facts about the crime. Do you have a good intercom system? You need it for this kind of case.

Using Small Violations

It is sometimes good to open even a small chink in the armour of your subject. The person being questioned who seems confident that he is not vulnerable can sometimes be broken if an admission can be gained on some minor irregularity of the store system.

It is then pointed out that this is a violation of store policy and is sufficient for dismissal. Once he finds that he is on the defensive, it is easy to move from the minor violation to the more serious one.

Almost all employees violate store rules at some time. Pointing up these minor violations is an effective stepping stone to major admissions.

Rotate Interviewers

People respond to other people in many ways. Some people clash, and others get along well. When you are not making any progress, it is wise to change interviewers.

The person being questioned may not respond to a male interviewer, but will answer questions put forth by a woman. Some people build up a hate image of their father and transfer this hate to the male interviewer, who becomes a father symbol. Such a person may respond to the kind approach of a woman. It is good sense to rotate interviewers until a good relationship has been found between the subject and the interviewer.

Good Guy Versus Bad Guy Approach

A similar thing, well known in police circles, is the "good guy" versus "bad guy" technique. This method is so old it's surprising that it still works. It works if the interviewers are good actors.

The so-called good guy makes a strong appeal to the subject and then leaves the room. At this point the so-called bad guy comes in and upbraids the subject, using a loud voice and poisonous words. He calls him a "liar," "thief," "no good," and so on.

After several minutes of this attack by the supposed bad guy, the good guy returns and in front of the subject throws the bad guy out of the office. He then talks to the subject on the basis of needing help to get rid of the bad guy. He points out that if the subject cooperates with him he may be able to use this to show his boss that the bad guy is no good. He shows how the subject can get even with the bad guy. This is the basic formula.

Stress Methods

Another type of interview is to use several interviewers. Each questions the subject rapidly, creating a crossfire type of questioning. This is a stress method and it may be effective. However, it also can produce false confessions because the subject becomes confused.

There are two other stress methods that are used but which I do not recommend. One is a "truth serum" method.

In this situation the interviewer puts a bottle of so-called truth serum on his desk with a hypodermic needle and leaves the subject, returning in a few minutes to question him further. This is an obvious attempt to create fear in the mind of the subject. Sometimes it creates too much fear and causes silence rather than an admission.

The same problem results from too much fear in the "phony beating" technique. The subject is placed in a room and is left alone for a while. During this period two investigators go into a room next to the room in which the subject is seated. They conduct a loud and angry interview.

The interview becomes more violent until these role players reach a point where the interviewer supposedly hits the subject. The real suspect, who is sitting in the other room waiting to be questioned, can hear the crash of bodies against the wall and the sound of fists beating against the "prisoner." The effect is gruesome. It often creates such fear in the subject that he will not be able to reveal his crime.

Stress methods may work on occasion, but in most cases the empathy method will not only be more effective, but it will also leave the interviewer with a clear conscience. He will know that he has treated the subject as a fellow human being, and in this way he can retain his own integrity.

Let the Subject Lie

When a subject tells a lie the poor interviewer may contradict him. This is wrong. Why? Because it is better to let the subject tell his story and make mental notes of his lies.

By accumulating his lies you can then bring them out one at a time. By piling one lie on top of another it is possible to weigh the evidence so heavily against the subject that he finally breaks down and confesses.

Sometimes this method can be used by writing a statement of the subject's story at the start. Then another statement is made including the discrepancies that have occurred between the first story and the second. Later a third one is made. After the third statement is taken the subject is confronted by the three different stories of his activities. The lies are pointed out.

This narrowing down and boxing in of the suspect can be effective. It must be done coldly, however, without anger or emotional fireworks. The cool, methodical way eventually brings the subject to the point where he has no choice except to admit that he is a liar and is now forced to tell the truth.

Set a Time Limit

In business it is effective to place a deadline on work to be done. It is also good to set a time limit on your interview. Tell the subject you have only twenty minutes left. Tell him that you have to stop at 4:20.

You now place him under a new invisible pressure. As each minute of the interview ticks by he watches the moving clock hand closing in upon him. As he approaches the deadline he finds himself in a mental vise. As each minute ticks off, it tightens the vise until he may break at the moment set as the point of no return.

When the time has run out, if the subject has not confessed, the interviewer can say that he has no choice except to take further action. He then asks if he should call the subject's wife or husband to see if they can work with the store in clearing up this matter, and so on.

Use the Rapid-Fire Questioning Technique

Stress requires disorientation of the subject. Here are some things that disorient a person to a limited extent.

Keeping up a constant question-and-answer conversation with the subject during the early part of the interview prevents him from being able to construct excuses. Since the interviewer is usually fortified with information, the subject is put on the defensive and this gives the interviewer an advantage. Each subject should be studied as an individual. Some people will respond to rapid-fire questions. Others respond better to a leisurely approach.

Anger Can Be Used Effectively

Another method of disorientation is the use of anger. If it is applied objectively with correct timing, it can be effective. If the anger, however, is the result of real irritation on the part of an interviewer who is not able to control himself, it can hurt the interview. Incidentally, if an interviewer does not have self-mastery, he will not be good at persuading people.

One man, known by the author, uses anger very effectively. He can rise from behind his desk and create a scene that would do justice to a tirade by King Richard II. He is so convincing that his own people, who may be in the room at the time, often cower for fear that they too will be subject to his wrath.

His face flushes red and his fists are tightly clenched and white. It appears as if he is going to destroy the subject with the heat from his anger. His temper explodes at the malefactor, "If you don't care what happens to you why should I care?" He races on that the subject leaves him no choice but to take *drastic* action.

He makes it clear that the thief must take full responsibility for his next step. The thief will have serious regrets later, but then it will be out of the interviewer's hands. After watching this ranting and raging for several minutes, many subjects decide that they can no longer run the risk of not cooperating, and they begin to talk.

Again the question has to be asked: Is this method the point of no return? What tricks does the interviewer have left if this staged anger scene fails to impress the subject?

The Off-Again, On-Again Method

Another effective way of disorienting the subject is a pattern of off-again, on-again anger. The interviewer starts by talking in a friendly, calm voice. Then he asks a simple question. No matter what the subject answers, the interviewer suddenly slams his fist on the desk and screams, "*Your're a liar!*"

This is completely unnerving because it is completely unexpected and illogical. Almost as though it never happened, the interviewer goes back to his former pattern of soft-spoken kindness. A few moments later he again reacts in the same angry way and then just as quickly returns to his soft words.

When observed in actual practice, this tactic can so upset a subject that he bursts into tears and pleads with the interviewer not to continue this method of interview.

The fact that the kindness and anger are not logically motivated and cannot be predicted upsets the logical world of the subject. The subject is in a new weird world. People are not reacting in a logical fashion. This, of course, falls well within the range of stress interviewing.

Stress Versus Personal Philosophy

The problem of using this or any other stress technique is to decide how it fits into your personal philosophy. If it means a violation of your personal standards, then by no means should you use stress. If, on the other hand, you believe that the end justifies the means and that such tactics are necessary, if not inevitable, you probably will use such methods. However, remember that in the end the interviewer must live with himself.

Latent sadism may exist in any of us, and you must be constantly on guard that you are not being cruel to a subject to satisfy hidden sadistic needs.

"Facesaving" Is a Requirement

Justification or facesaving is needed in all interviews. It is being pointed out here only to bring to your attention the need for allowing the subject to justify his acts.

For example, you can tell shoplifters that you are aware of the overpowering urge all of us have to take property. You can add that it is surprising that more crimes like this are not committed because people are so careless in allowing property to be available where it can be easily picked up.

Other Devices

The same thing can be used in having the subject write a statement. Encourage the subject to include all possible extenuating circumstances. This statement then not only appears fair but the subject also adds further details, which may include damaging admissions.

Another facesaving device is to suggest that his troubles may have been caused by bad company. He may agree and then lie in an attempt to strengthen the truth of this suggestion, but the lie will include some truth.

In using facesaving devices you provide the subject with the reasons that may have led him to commit his criminal acts. You imply that these reasons may get him out of the trouble he is in, or will, at least, be a means of getting him off as lightly as possible.

Don't Make Promises

Caution should be exercised that these statements should in no way contain any promises. They should not be presented in a manner that will allow a defense attorney or jury to believe that promises were made.

The Exaggeration Technique

A subject can be led to believe that he is involved in something much more serious than his actual crime. Let us say he has stolen cash on sales, but it is pointed out to him that the store believes he answers the description of a member of a gang who broke into the warehouse last week.

Many times by pressing the suspect on a more serious crime he will tell the truth about the crime at hand. He is often eager to talk about his own "minor" crime to take the pressure off him in regard to the more serious offense.

The Religious Approach

If the subject is religious he may respond to a religious appeal. You point out to him that he is not only committing a crime against society but also against his religious beliefs. You tell him he can escape punishment from society but not from God.

Care must be taken here to avoid duress. When you feel that religion means something to the person being questioned, discussing the moral aspects of his problem can help him to arrive at a decision to confess his thefts.

The Stubborn Suspect

There will be some cases in which the subject is stubborn. All your methods fail to move him. Doesn't this suspect know that he is hopelessly trapped in lies? He willingly admits that there is a lot of evidence against him and that he has no defense, and yet he still refuses to talk. Such stubbornness may be caused by many things, but three things are most likely:

1. *Personal hostility toward the interviewer.* This problem can be overcome by changing interviewers. If the interviewer doesn't get along with the subject, a deadend may result.
2. *The interviewer may fail to present facesaving devices.* The stubborn subject needs to find a way out of his dilemma. Facesaving is a bridge that can get him out of the quicksand surrounding him. When stubbornness develops, new attempts should be made to offer excuses for his crime.
3. *False pride or a desire for punishment* may cause stubbornness. Sometimes false pride can be handled by emotional appeals that offset the pride. At other times appeals to reason can overcome false pride. Give him a reasonable explanation of how we all make mistakes. Persuade him to abandon his untenable position.

The desire for self-punishment can often be important in stubbornness. A person knows the thing he has done is wrong. He has an exaggerated idea of the importance of the crime he has committed. The result is that, feeling guilty, he wants to be punished.

This martyr complex can be difficult to overcome. One of the best approaches is to point out that it is not fair to his family and loved ones to make them suffer the disgrace that will become public knowledge when he goes on trial. He is told it can be a burden of shame for his whole family. Sometimes, by playing on his sense of responsibility to his loved ones, the martyr complex can be offset.

Recording the Interview

Whenever interviewing, record the interview. This serves many purposes:

1. It acts as a control to check on the methods used by interviewers.
2. It prevents using the third degree in interviews.
3. It helps trap the suspect in lies.
4. It helps develop cases against the criminal's associates.

5. It aids in later questioning of the subject.
6. It helps the interviewer improve his technique by listening to his interviews.

Recorded interviews should be held for a period of time. By having on hand the recorded interviews the store and the security office are protected against any false charges of mistreatment of subjects.

Training the Interviewer

Not all people make good interviewers. The person who becomes outstanding needs special abilities. He must like people. He must be an actor able to play many different roles. He must have the ability to put himself into the shoes of his subject mentally and emotionally. Only if he can develop empathy can he become a really top interviewer.

He must also be able to talk to the criminal on his own level of understanding. This includes the subject's interests and language. He should not, of course, lower himself in any way by using foul language, nor should he lower his own personal standards of good taste.

Above all else he needs imagination. He must be a good storyteller. He must have enthusiasm for his work and feel confident in his relationships with people. By having a mature mind, emotional stability, patience, and self-control, he can take charge of the interview and direct it toward the objectives he has set as goals for the interview.

He must continue to study people. He should read books on psychology. He must be a responsible person of high character and personal integrity.

Methods of Training

He can be trained by doing several things:

1. Studying tape-recorded interviews done by good interviewers.
2. Reading all available material on interviewing and studying the psychology of motivation.
3. Sitting in as an observer on interviews.
4. Doing role-playing interviews with other investigators.

All of these things will help his understanding of interrogation techniques. Probably role playing will be one of the best exercises. From this he can assimilate techniques and make them part of himself.

By experimenting in role playing he can learn how to use ideas in interviews without harming an actual case interview during his learning period. All of the elements of the actual case are present except the danger of making mistakes in a real-life situation.

Even after he has been trained it is good to have review training. It is also a good idea to have each interviewer occasionally listen to one of his recorded interview tapes.

Preparation for the Interview

Preparation before the interview is important. The following things should be checked:

1. Do you have all of the facts in the case available? Have you personally gone through these facts and verified all of the details to your complete satisfaction?
2. Are you familiar with the case history of the subject? If other security people have worked on the case, have you discussed the case in some detail with these people? To be successful in the interview you should have as much information as possible about the malefactor.
3. Are you sure you know as much as possible about this person? Have you studied personnel records? Discussed the subject with his supervisor? Have you obtained all the information possible from every available source so that you have a picture of his background and personality?

You should have access to all necessary forms involved in interviews such as confessions, shopping violation reports, case histories, cash register tapes, tallies, and so on.

If you are an efficient interviewer you will be respected by the subject. If, however, you flounder around, do not have the necessary papers immediately available, don't have a plan for the interview, and so on, you can soon give the subject the impression that you are not well organized and, therefore, your case is a bluff. The methodical, well-organized interviewer has an advantage.

Be Dramatic

In showing proof of the crime to your subject it is effective to conceal the items and present them dramatically at the right moment. For example, if the person to be questioned has written several fraudulent refunds it is good to keep all of them in your desk drawer when the subject first enters your office.

After talking awhile to establish a confidence-and-belief relationship, you then open the drawer and take out a *single* fraud refund. You present it to the subject and ask for an explanation. If he offers an alibi for this refund, then you reach in the drawer and take out a second one. This continues until the weight of evidence becomes overwhelming. As noted earlier, you must be a showman. Presenting your evidence properly can be a dramatic asset to your interview.

While the interview is being conducted you may have other security personnel continue to work on the case. For example, the employee's locker may be searched, the salesclerk's handbag brought down from the selling department, and so forth. These actions, which are going on during the interview, may uncover new material that can be fed to you while you are questioning the subject.

Plan the Time for the Interview When Possible

If the element of time is within your control, consideration should be given to the time of day in which the subject is to be questioned. If possible, start your case as early in the morning as possible so you have a full day to develop your case. By taking a shopping case at 4:00 P.M. you place yourself under a time pressure. It is not advisable to keep employees for questioning after store closing hours.

Know the Suspect's Mental Attitude

At the end of any interview you should be aware of the mental outlook of your subject before this person leaves the security office. Many people who commit crimes against your store are maladjusted. Any interview, even for a well-adjusted person, can be a disturbing emotional experience. Men have been known to leave their homes. Women have attempted suicide rather than face their families. It is your duty to realize fully the seriousness of the interview to the person being questioned.

At the close of the interview check the person's emotional stability. Time should be allowed to help the person regain his composure. Give help and personal guidance as well as constructive suggestions. If more guidance is needed, direct him to his church, his family doctor, or even to a psychiatrist.

We all have a responsibility to the person being interviewed. This person is a human being, and like ourselves, he is subject to fears that can become so great that his personality can be seriously affected.

Before the suspect leaves your office, you must see that this person is in a *safe* mental condition. Be sure that the emotional turmoil caused by the situation is not going to result in disastrous personal actions. It is often a good idea to arrange for a relative or close friend of the suspect to pick him up after the interview.

Points to Consider

The following general points should be considered:

1. When analyzing the facts before an interview, weed out the factors detrimental to your case and concentrate on your strongest points.
2. If possible, arrange the evidence and information in a logical sequence so that the subject can be intelligently questioned.
3. Be sure to have a woman nearby if a female subject is being questioned.
4. When the subject is an employee, it is better to have his supervisor bring the subject to the office rather than have a member of the security staff escort the employee. The supervisor should be instructed not to allow the employee to discard any evidence and to bring the person directly to your office.
5. In most cases it is not good to allow the subject to smoke until after the first admissions of guilt are made. In no case should the subject be allowed to take any medication without approval of your store nurse or doctor. An overdose of a prescription could be very serious.
6. If the subject is faint or complains about any physical symptoms of illness, contact the store hospital and summon a nurse.
7. When having a statement signed, be sure that two people witness the subject's signature and, if possible, have the confession notarized.
8. Obtain a written confession on the first admission of facts as soon as possible. The second detailed confession covering the whole case can be obtained at a later time.
9. Get all of your admissions on the first day of interviewing. Any person allowed to go home and come back on the following day will usually not admit anything of further value. In no case let the subject go home overnight without first getting a written statement of theft.
10. It is helpful to have some knowledge of your subject's physical condition. Some people have bad hearts, for example, and an interview could result in a fatal heart attack.

11. An interviewer should not interview someone if he feels that his evidence is inadequate, that the time is not right, or that he, himself, feels unable to conduct a good interview at this time.
12. Don't make a direct accusation of a subject if you cannot prove your statement in court.
13. Always interview in private. An interview won't be successful if there are distractions.
14. Do not, as an interviewer, ever make private deals, threats, or promises. Never use force.
15. Do not violate the subject's civil rights.
16. If the subject wants to go to the washroom, do not allow him to go there unescorted.
17. Do not deprive a subject of water or refuse any other reasonable request during an interview.
18. Do not allow the subject to ask questions. You, not the subject, should ask the questions.
19. At the end of the interview, obtain a written confession, preferably in the subject's handwriting. If the subject does not confess, a complete statement of the actual facts of the case should be written out and signed by the subject along with any explanations that the subject offers.
20. Do not promise the subject anything that will obligate you or the store.
21. Do not leave evidence where the subject can destroy it.
22. Do not have any loose objects around that could be used by the subject for self-injury or attack on the interviewer. Put away heavy paperweights, sharp letter openers, scissors, and so forth.
23. At the end of the interview try to reassure the subject so that he or she leaves your office in a state of reasonable composure.

The interviewer learns to interview by practicing his art. You have many opportunities to test methods of interviewing when dealing with complainants and witnesses as well as malefactors. You can also practice interviewing on your friends and associates daily. In fact, whenever you are dealing with people you are practicing the fundamentals of interviewing.

What Technique Should Be Used?

As can be seen by reviewing this chapter and the chapter that follows, there are many available interviewing techniques. In selecting the methods you will use, you should be guided by several things:

1. Does the interview technique fit your own philosophy, that is, your standard of human relationships?
2. Is it a method with which you feel completely comfortable? Does it fit your personality like a glove? Awkwardness in interviewing can develop when you try to use a method not suited to your personality.
3. You must analyze the person being questioned and try to determine what type of person he is. By doing some experimental questioning you can discover what appeals are most likely to be effective with this person.

It is only by choosing your methods of interviewing in relation to the person being questioned and to your own personality can you be successful. Even this is not enough if the technique is not also compatible with your personal moral and ethical standards.

Chapter 15

INTERROGATION: ADVANCED CONCEPTS

On the walls of the interior courtyard of the building in Paris housing the Ministry of Justice, headquarters for the French Police, is embedded a marble tablet into which has been carved more than a hundred names of French Police officials who were routinely tortured to death by the Gestapo in the quest for information during the German occupation of Paris.

The infamy of this form of interrogation has stirred the indignation of civilized men everywhere and it is still a matter of concern that similar methods are in vogue in some countries today. In this chapter the techniques employed in this perverted form of interrogation are described and contrasted with interrogation methods developed by a democratic system.

Brainwashing

You have probably heard that in relatively recent years a new method of interview was developed by interrogators in certain foreign countries. It uses new psychological ways of creating mental stress. You may have heard of this method called "*brainwashing*."

Stress methods have often proved effective. When applied by experts, the system produces predictable results. It's as though you pressed a magic button. When cleverly used, the stress method holds considerable interest. This is especially true if you are a law enforcement person. If you face the daily problems of questioning criminals, you are looking for answers to satisfactorily complete your interview. Is stress one of the answers? It may be, but only under certain conditions.

Techniques May Net Questionable Results

It is true that brainwashing techniques can be effective. Their value, however, can be seriously questioned because of certain results. Stress methods may get you a *false* confession. The person under stress takes on a hypnotized response. He acts like a parrot. Wherever the interview question leads, he follows.

The other major problem with stress interviews is control of the stress pressure. At any moment during the questioning you may unknowingly apply too much stress. What happens? You trigger the subject's protective mechanism.

When this trigger is sprung, your interview is ended. The subject can no longer answer even if he wants to. His ability to talk has been frozen by the panic of fear. A protective curtain of amnesia comes down between the outer world and the secrets locked within his mind.

Protect the Human Personality

How do you define a good method of interview? It should at all times protect the human personality. Everyone has basic human rights, and they must be preserved at all costs. Nothing should be done to injure a person's body, mind, or soul.

The American law enforcement officer must observe the rules of fair play. He must uphold the very laws he has been given to enforce.

American law indicates that no duress can legally be used to obtain a confession. Our society long ago denounced the third degree method. We as a people violently reject the third degree methods used by other countries in stress interviews.

Stress Methods Can Go Too Far

Stress methods used in some nations violate the American philosophy of justice. To them the individual has no rights. He is not considered a human being with the innate dignity of the individual. Under stress, they make him a cowering animal. He is brought into submission by coercion of his mind.

Mental tortures deprive the subject of all of his human values. As the screws are tightened, his personality disintegrates. The result is a traumatic experience that scars the soul. It may leave the person in a permanent state of mental idiocy at the mental level of a babbling infant.

Should you destroy justice, compassion, the law itself? You do this and more when stress methods are used.

The person who uses stress sets up around him a strange world in which he plays Mephistophles. He follows distorted standards. To him any means are justified by the end results. He gives vent to his sadistic desires. He learns to enjoy hurting and torturing others. He becomes, often unknowingly, a worse criminal in the eyes of society than the person he straps to his mental torture rack.

Interviewer's Penalty

You cannot escape the personal penalty that results from violating the integrity of another human being. The moment you use stress methods you are setting a trap for your own self-destruction. The person who follows this path will one day find that shadows of ghostly memories haunt him. These guilt feelings will tinge his thoughts, waking and sleeping.

If he is truly a psychotic without fear or conscience, his stress orgies will finally undermine and destroy whatever factors of rationality he may still possess.

The best way to understand the dangers of stress is to see how it works. Once the mechanism is understood, you will, I am sure, reject stress on both practical and moral grounds.

Advantages of the Empathy Method

Totalitarian dogmas have given birth to the stress interview. The American philosophy of human rights has also given us a successful interview method. The modern American method we shall call "empathy." It is better than the stress method in many ways. It is not as mechanical but it gets more relevant and accurate information. It does not result in false confessions.

Empathy protects the person being questioned. It leaves him his human dignity and all of his rights, both God-given and legal. Empathy, by protecting the personality, also follows Christian beliefs. The empathy approach meets the social standards of our times. It is a rational, common-sense way of using new psychological findings in the difficult area of criminal questioning.

You can use empathy without fear of a guilt hangover. It is in conformity with your highest moral and ethical standards.

If you fail to get a confession, no lasting harm has been done to the personality of the person questioned. Unlike stress, there is no sickness afterward, no mental injury, or no permanent damage to the personality.

Two Conflicting Methods

Today's conflict between the American way of life and the ideologies of certain foreign countries is seen in these two conflicting approaches to interviewing.

We have written the following descriptions so that you may study and compare the stress and empathy methods. After thoughtful study, we know you will agree that empathy is the best interview tool available to the modern law enforcement officer.

In studying empathy, remember that it could only have been developed in a democratic society where the rights of each person are held above all others.

THE STRESS INTERVIEW

The use of anxiety and fear to get confessions is well known. Since World War II psychological research has found some new facts about the effect of stress on the human mind. You can judge your interview methods with these findings.

As you study stress, you should consider the ethical implications of using such a method. You must remember that the degree of an act does not change its morality. Personal integrity comes at a high price. You cannot purchase it with the coins of compromised ethics. When you question a person, you attempt to enter into his mind. If stress is your means of achieving this, then you are intruding by force.

The Fragile Mind

When you stretch a rubber band beyond its limit of physical endurance, it snaps. You destroy its ability to resist the pressures put upon it. When you cause emotions of fear, frustration, anger, humiliation, or anxiety in the mind of a person, you may cause his brain to snap like a rubber band. Such a person can no longer resist the pressures put upon him. He becomes submissive to your will. This is the way stress methods work.

Our mind is fragile. It's delicate and vulnerable. A strategy of terror can do amazing things; it can cause our mind to disintegrate. Our sense of values can be distorted. Our habit patterns of behavior can be wiped clean from the memory slate. The desire to resist can become impotent. Our personal integrity can be destroyed.

The effect of stress on the mind has been shown often in modern times. It is seen in such well-documented cases as that of Cardinal Mindszenty and Colonel Schwable. Today brainwashing and menticide are well known, even to the layman. These are modern psychological ways of bringing the mind into a state of enslavement.

Pavlov's Research

The Russian scientist Pavlov began the research upon which today's brainwashing methods are based. His work is of value to the interviewer.

Pavlov found that there are four basic types of people. Each type reacts in a different way to the stress of anxiety, anger, frustration, and fear. Each of these four types of people have a point at which his mind breaks down. In each person the amount of stress needed to cause this breakdown varies.

You can better judge how much stress must be used if you first find out what basic type your subject is. Observation and a few easy questions should help you to do this.

Basic Personality Types

Type A. Is your subject quick to anger? Is he easily upset; Is he a hostile person? If so, then we will label this excitable person Type "A".

You can easily upset his nervous system with fear or anger. However, too much stress will cause him to become wild. He may explode from panic. If this happens, he will become uncontrollable. To obtain your best results, limit your stress.

Type B. Perhaps you have a naturally cheerful person. Is he good natured? Reasonably confident? Is he lively and optimistic? If so, he will fall into Type "B."

This person can withstand an emotional attack better than any other type. If you try to cause fear or anger, you will get an aggressive reaction. But in his case it won't be wild and uncontrolled like Type "A." No, this man will react with a controlled, purposeful aggression.

Type C. Does the person you are to deal with appear calm, undisturbed? Would you say he is sluggish, not easily aroused to action? Is he passive? Calm rather than aggressive? Does he appear placid? If so, he is Type "C," a person slow to respond to any attack.

Like Type "B," he can withstand a lot of stress. He will not fight you as will Type "B." He will take a quiet, observing attitude. It will be hard to get him to participate in the questioning. He will be slow to anger, hard to frighten, and difficult to question.

Type D. Does your man appear to be a gloomy, depressed person? Does he seem melancholy, sad? Does he say everything is hopeless? Is his outlook negative? Classify him as Type "D."

He meets stress by trying to avoid tension. He has no will to fight. He is the most open to emotional pressures. He has the lowest resistance of all four types; he is easily moved by emotional pressure.

Because he is sensitive, he must be carefully handled. If you cause any excess emotional stress on his mind, he will panic. His mind will be gripped by a fear paralysis. His brain will be paralyzed. He will not be able to talk.

Like Type "A," upsetting his nervous system is easy. However, too much fear, anger, anxiety, or frustration can end his ability to communicate. You must spot this type early in the interview before you defeat yourself by putting on too much pressure.

Overall Pattern of the Interview

Now that we have the four types, let us look at the overall pattern of a stress interview. Remember that you may enter a person's mind by either empathy or stress. They are two opposite ways of getting at the brain's hidden secrets. When you use empathy to open the mind, you pick the lock. When you use stress, you hammer the door down.

There are two guards who protect the mind. One guard is his judgment. The other guard is his habit of conditioned behavior.

Conditioned Reflexes

Your judgment always acts to protect you. When you start to cross the street, your judgment decides whether such a crossing is safe. Whenever you have a choice, your judgment acts to protect you. You must get a confession in spite of the subject's judgment.

His judgment, if alert, will tell him that admitting his crimes is not to his best interest. In an empathy interview we gently cradle judgment to sleep. In a stress interview we hit this guardian over the head until it is unconscious.

By eliminating judgment, we get into the mind. However, we still may not get the information we need. We may be rebuffed by his conditioned habits of behavior. An example of this is seen in the automatic responses of a prize fighter. He has been knocked unconscious but he won't fall down. He continues to fight because of his conditioned reflex responses.

These automatic responses may continue to protect the mind against entry even though the judgment sentry has been knocked out. Therefore, our second step will be to disrupt his conditioned behavior habits so that they no longer serve to protect his brain.

We must make them the traitors who help us get inside the mental fort. In an empathy interview we lure these reflexes to our aid with soft words. In a stress interview we clobber the subject's reflexes into submission.

Stages of Stress

In a stress interview your main tool is fear. You may also use humiliation, anger, frustration, and anxiety. You try to inject these responses in your subject. Strong emotions repeated can have a violent effect on the brain and higher nervous system.

You use poisonous emotions to break the person's judgment, confuse his intellect, destroy his resistance. You want him to become submissive, responsive, and pliable.

The normal person's first reaction to any such attack is resistance. It will be aggressive resistance in Types "A" and "B." It may be passive resistance in Types "C" and "D."

There are three parts to the stress interview. *First*, there will be the person's normal attempts to resist attack; *second*, there is a middle period in which his nervous system is disrupted; *third* comes a period of total brain blackout. It is in the middle period that confession is obtained.

The Middle Period of Stress

Since this middle period of stress is the most important, let's go over it in detail. What are the effects of stress on the subject during this stage?

His mental and nervous state can be compared to an imaginary spot of light shining on his brain. When things are normal the light is a bright red. As his resistance to stress breaks down and his system becomes disrupted, this red light suddenly snaps off and a blue light snaps on.

Now he is in a state of hysterical hypnosis. His judgment is dead or asleep. A whirlpool of mental chaos begins. His brain is now in a state of "waking sleep."

The effect is like that of any ordinary hypnosis. The conscious mind is out of commission, and the subconscious mind takes over. In hypnosis the conscious mind is lulled to sleep; in the stress interview the conscious mind is paralyzed by strong inner conflicts. These inner conflicts are caused by excessive emotional pressures.

Suspect Becomes Submissive

Your subject is now submissive; he responds to suggestions very much like that of any hypnotized person. It is during this state that the mind is ransacked for its hidden secrets.

If stress pressures are continued, the blue light deepens. It becomes darker as the mind becomes paralyzed. His judgment is gone. His suggestibility increases. His memory is washed clean of its habitual responses.

Inhibition

Suddenly a point of complete inhibition occurs. The mind's protective mechanism sounds an alarm. The blue light snaps off. There is nothing left but blackness. The mind has taken emergency action to stop personality destruction. It has shut off all contact with the world. His mind now receives no stimulus and gives no response. Later, when his mind comes back to life, it may be permanently injured.

Before his mental blackout, the blue spotlight period, there are three stages of mental action.

The Phases of Mental Chaos

Phase I. The first stage is one of equal reflex response. The effect is like body fatigue. The mind gives up resisting. A stupor sets in, a sleepy condition in which the subject feels the same reaction to any stimulus.

For example, the thrill of getting a $10,000 legacy is no greater than if he got a dime. In this phase his judgment is weak. Since he is now submissive and his judgment poor, he may give in and answer your questions.

Phase II. If stress is continued, your subject will move into the second phase of abnormal behavior. New behavior patterns begin to show. He will now respond to weak stimuli but not to strong pressure. This topsy-turvy effect is because the stronger stimulus starts the brain's protective action. A fear-paralysis stops the mind's reaction. The weaker stimulus still allows a positive response.

His judgment was knocked out in the first phase. Now in the second phase his mind habits are being disrupted.

If you did not know what is happening, his actions would seem irrational. They are irrational, even to himself. If you shout, "Sit down!" This person may want to obey but cannot. His muscles will not do as his mind directs. He remains standing. If you say, "Sit down," in a quiet voice your subject quickly sits down.

Phase III. In the third phase a new phenomenon occurs. Suddenly this person's world is turned upside down. His switches are reversed. Black is white, and white is black. All his yes answers are now no and vice versa.

He may suddenly like you very much, even though he has hated you up to this point. If he liked coffee and hated tea, he now likes tea and hates coffee. Everything is reversed. If he has refused to confess up to this point, he will now beg to confess.

This effect can be seen in events outside of the interview. Such an instance occurred on a television quiz show. A pretty girl from the South was asked to identify a certain tune played by the orchestra. The band played a few stirring strains of *Dixie*. The southern belle's eyes lighted up. Triumphantly she cried out, "I know, I know—*Yankee Doodle*!" The stress of being on television had brought on this phase of reversed response.

All of these four basic personality types, when put under stress, will go through all three phases of mental chaos. They will go from submission to complete brain blackout. In theory you can always get a confession.

Four Methods of Causing Stress

Pavlov found that there were four ways of causing stress. If you understand these basic concepts, then you can invent numerous ways of applying them.

1. Loud Unexpected Noise. First there is a shock action if you increase the strength of the stimulus, shouting at him, banging the desk, making him stand up or sit down. When you yell angry questions at him, it affects his nervous system. This method works on Type "A" and "D." Mental chaos and submission will result from a loud, unexpected noise or a slap. Any exaggerated and excessive direct attack disrupts his nervous system.

2. Delay an Expected Stimulus. The second way you can cause emotional upset requires more ingenuity. You delay an expected stimulus. Anxiety, worry, and fear can be caused by leading your subject to think something terrible is going to happen. You leave him suspended on a thin cobweb of time. He waits nervously for the event to happen. His fear builds up in his mind as he pictures the coming event. He is wide awake but he has a bad dream—a nightmare. By making him wait you can do far more emotional damage than the dreaded event itself would cause.

3. Confuse the Subject. The third way you cause stress is based on confusing the subject. You move forward and backward, and you alternate positive and negative actions. You are kind, then angry. Mental confusion and fear result. Why? Because your changes seem illogical. He cannot understand your motives.

First you ask an unimportant question in a kindly manner. He answers and then suddenly, for no reason, you become angry. You shout, "*Don't you lie to me*!" Immediately your mood changes. You relax, you smile, you go back to soft-spoken, quiet questions.

If you keep doing this, he will soon become completely disoriented. He will be frightened. He cannot understand what is happening. He fears what may happen in the next moment. Sharp questions by two people, one kind and the other angry, can also cause this type of stress.

4. Affect Subject's Physical Condition. The fourth stress method is to tamper with his physical condition. Do not allow him any food or water for a long period of time. Do not give him urinary relief. Exhaust him with strong unshaded lights in his eyes. Make him stand for several hours while being questioned. These things cause stress by weakening his body. Depressants and stimulants can cause mental confusion and physical debilitation.

The Stress Method Can Cripple a Subject

When your subject surrenders, it may be sudden and against his will. It often comes after an unexpected accusation, a shock, or a humiliation that particularly hurts.

This quick change from defiance to submission is unconscious. It results from inner conflict. In his mind he tells himself to resist, but he has a deep inner desire to give in. He wants to end the torment. This inner conflict causes nervous confusion, and suddenly he collapses.

Conclusion

Stress works but it is a method that often causes the subject to make a false confession. There is also a very real danger that you may injure the subject's mind. This crippling can be permanent. I believe you will find empathy is a better approach.

THE EMPATHY INTERVIEW

When you question another human being about a crime, there are important moral and philosophic considerations that you must settle with your own conscience. One problem is to choose the right method for getting a confession.

The search has always been for a way of questioning that gets results but does not violate the integrity of either your subject or yourself. The empathy interview meets these needs.

Empathy Technique is Nontraumatic

Empathy, unlike stress, does not cause new psychological problems for your subject. It avoids the dangers of a major traumatic experience. It leaves the door open for future rehabilitation.

Empathy is valuable because in 80 percent of the cases you handle, you do not deal with professional criminals. Most of your cases are disturbed people who are normal in most respects. Its greatest value, however, is that it does not result in a false confession.

Understand How Suspect Feels

The empathy method was perfected in recent years by psychologists. They use it to persuade their patients to reveal their inner thoughts. In empathy you attempt to look at the situation from the subject's viewpoint. You try to understand how he thinks, how he feels. You try to enter into his mind and look at life through his eyes.

This can be done if you make a bond of understanding between yourself and the malefactor. Before this bond can be made, however, there must be a strong belief relationship. You must gain his confidence. He must believe in you.

The possible steps in an empathy interview are presented below. They are arranged in the order proven most effective. All of them may not be needed in every case.

Empathy works well for some interviewers. Others may find that they get better results with a different method. It is not meant as the one best way, but it is offered here only as a method we have found effective.

Empathy—Not Sympathy

Sometimes you cannot help feeling sorry for the people you question. If you allow this personal feeling to become dominant at the time of questioning, you cannot do a very good job of interviewing.

Empathy means understanding. It does not mean sympathy. During the period of questioning you become an uncritical observer. You are neutral. You neither agree nor disagree with the subject. You do not judge him; instead you try to understand him.

In the empathy interview you must (a) understand your subject's point of view and (b) create a belief relationship in your subject.

A Belief Relationship

Your belief relationship must come before empathy. To build this bond you must be sincere. You must be interested in the subject and his personal problems.

Do not judge or belittle the subject. There should be no criticism of him, no condemning of the person. This does not mean that you have to approve of his criminal behavior. You do not condemn the person—only what he has done. You can like and respect a person but still not approve of his actions. In other words, you must separate his deeds from his personality.

Begin with Neutral Questions

To start your subject talking, ask him neutral questions that make his responses easy. Emotionally loaded questions should be avoided in the early stages of your interview. Don't ask any questions about the crime itself. If he tries to discuss the crime, change the subject by saying, "We'll get around to that later but first let's talk about you."

Try a "You" Approach

Your purpose is to get him to talk about himself. He is a puzzle to be solved. More than anything else at the moment you want to get to know the person behind the crime. You want to understand why he has done this thing.

Ask about his job, where he lives, his hobbies, and his ambitions. These things are a safe neutral ground for your opening questions.

Some areas of his experience may be emotionally charged. Test carefully during the early stages of your questioning to avoid these areas. Queries about his home life, wife, or children may have strong emotional reactions. If so, avoid these questions until he is talking freely about himself.

People like other people with similar ideals and similar opinions. When possible, tell him you agree with him. This is a help in winning his confidence. People are like mirrors; they reflect other people's attitudes. If you are friendly and show a real interest in him, he will respond in the same way.

Explore More Emotional Areas

Move over to the more emotional questions after a few neutral questions. Ask him about his wife, his personal problems. Still stay away from questions about the crime.

Probe for emotional things that may have upset his personality. Ask yourself what things led him to commit this crime. Explore his social relationships and his economic situation. These things may later serve two purposes. First, they may explain why he stole. Second, they may help when you want to offer facesaving reasons for his criminal act.

Approaching an Empathy Relationship

You may have talked ten minutes or a half hour to get him to the point where he feels free to confide in you about his personal problems.

You are now approaching an empathy relationship. The fact is that when he does begin to explain personal things, you have reached the first step in your empathy interview. He now has confidence in you. He believes you are sincerely trying to help.

Now, if he is willing to talk about his innermost thoughts and feelings, you can encourage him to reveal himself even further. This is done by a technique known in counseling circles as "feedback."

The Feedback Technique

The feedback technique is a way of keeping him talking on an emotionally disturbing subject. As he begins to reveal himself, he will show his inner feelings. Whenever he stops talking an emotional block appears, which makes it hard for him to continue. To help him you feed back his own feelings.

In other words, you mirror his last expressed feeling. Your best response is to review his own words—the words that reflected his feelings. For example, he might say, "When Mary left I felt I couldn't go on, I got blue and down in the dumps." He stops and you feed back his last feelings. You say, "You got discouraged and felt you couldn't go on?" He picks it up as though given a stage cue. "Yes, that's right, Mary had been good to me and I couldn't understand why she left."

By reflecting his feelings you reopen the conversation. You remove a block from the channel between you. Now he can release more inner feelings. This feedback principle is important to the empathy interview. It is a thing you must practice until it becomes an automatic response. Try it daily whenever you talk with people.

The Confession

Sometimes you will get a complete confession at this point in the interview. Confession may come at any point. You should be alert for its signs and move into a discussion of the crime at any point where you feel the subject shows signs of wanting to confess.

You must decide how much feedback and emotional response should be allowed before taking the interview into the area of the crime itself. Needless to say, your confidence and belief relationship must be firmly established. Your subject must be showing his inner self before this move is attempted.

Discuss Subject's Motivation for the Crime

When you feel the time is right to move over to the crime itself, you can usually do this by discussing the subject's motivation. Because you have developed an understanding of his outlook, you can try to clarify his motive for the crime. In doing this you lead to an admission of his guilt.

For example, you might say, "Then after Mary left you became depressed and you felt that if you stole this money from the store you might be able to buy new clothes and fix yourself up, so you could win her back, is that right?"

The Admission

"Yes, that's why I did it. I didn't mean to do wrong. I just needed money for new clothes and didn't know how else to get it, so I took it from my sales."

You would then follow up this admission by saying something like, "But in taking the money you knew you were stealing, didn't you?"

Subject agrees, "Yes."

You add, "And you know it's wrong to steal?"

He says, "Yes, I wish I'd used my head. I know it was wrong and I'm sorry!"

In this way you get your first admission and the critical point of your interview has passed.

The Empathy Method Can Be Used in Any Type of Case

The interview as outlined up to this point is intended as a guide for the most difficult type of case you might have to handle. Is this method good for the average situation? For example, your shoplifting case where the stolen goods are on the thief at the time of arrest. This person readily admits his guilt. Or what about the shopping case where the proof of theft is clear-cut?

Empathy is just as useful in these cases. You vary the plan to fit your needs. In the shoplifter case you begin the interview by getting your admission of theft on the immediate items. A signed statement on these items should be taken.

Now move into an empathy approach. Your purpose is to uncover previous thefts. You want to recover these stolen goods or get repayment for them. Empathy can be used in any case.

We are showing how to use it in the most difficult type of case—the one where there is only circumstantial evidence. This case can be made only if you succeed in getting a confession from your subject.

Avoid the Direct, "Did You?" . . .

We have noted that one way to get the first admission is to talk about the reasons for the crime. You could call this a facesaving method. You are using your subject's motives as an excuse for his criminal act.

One of the reasons empathy works is that it sets the stage for an admission of guilt by exploring the *reason* for the criminal act. This avoids one of the pitfalls many interviewers fall into when trying to wrestle an admission from their subject. *You avoid any direct question that asks the subject did he or did he not commit the crime in question.*

Many an interview bogs down in a mucky swamp of repetitious argument when you make the mistake of asking your subject if he committed the crime in question. He will usually give a negative answer and you are then committed to a tug of war. It is now a fight between you and your subject to get an admission of guilt.

Stick to "Why?" Questions

As your subject becomes more entrenched behind his negative attitude, it becomes harder to get an admission. In other cases a grudging admission may finally be obtained after much effort. You are so frustrated and tired out by the struggle that you don't have the patience or energy to make anything but a token attempt at further admissions.

Stick to questions centering on *why* he committed the crime. Ask him how many times he stole before. Ask him how much is involved. Never argue about his guilt or innocence. Reject any attempts on his part to start such a useless debate. Tell him you refuse to review this instance because the facts speak for themselves. Shift again to questions about why he did it and his previous thefts.

Conclusion

The empathy method is a more satisfying technique than methods using stress. A full admission is obtained just as often by using the empathy technique.

You should try to use the empathy approach before resorting to any fear devices. Be sure stress is necessary before you use it. You should always analyze your own motives whenever you use fear tactics. Be sure the situation calls for such an attack and that it is not the result of an unconscious need on your part to hurt the subject.

The fear interview—even though no physical torture is used—can be just as painful as the third degree. There are cases where fear is perhaps the only method that can be used successfully. However, it should not be applied needlessly.

You must be on guard against your own subconscious motives. Sadism wears many masks, not the least of which is the pious one labeled, "I had to do it that way."

If you interview in anger, be careful—you may have personal problems. You must be alert to the possibility that you have a hidden need to injure others. Such a need can lead you to use a stress method of interrogation.

Summary

The principal ingredients of the empathy technique are as follows:

1. Make a belief relationship between yourself and the subject.
2. Keep a neutral attitude.
3. Respect the subject as a person, even though you do not approve of his criminal actions.
4. Ask neutral questions first to get the subject talking.
5. Center the interview on the subject and learn to be a good listener.
6. From neutral questions, go to emotional ones and finally to questions about the crime itself.
7. The "feedback" technique will help you remove emotional blocks.
8. Get your admission of guilt by discussing *why* the crime was committed.

If you want to be a really good interviewer, you will want to experiment with this method. After you work with it a few times, you'll agree that it is a very successful technique.

Chapter 16

REPORTS AND FORMS

The security department should, of course, have complete and accurate records. All forms involving releases should be cleared through your store's legal counsel to be sure that they meet the requirements of your state.

Most security forms are designed by the individual store to meet the specific needs of the store's management. For this reason the present chapter includes only a few examples of the basic forms that are used by most security departments. As in anything else, these forms can undoubtedly be improved upon and can be redesigned to meet any special requirements within your store. The forms we have included are:

- Customer's Report of Illegal Buying
- Shopper's Violation Form
- Preliminary Investigation Report
- Case History
- Check List
- Arrest Forms
- Court Record
- Shoplifter Statement
- Lie Detector Release
- General Release

These forms are, for the most part, self-explanatory. Also included is a sample form used for monthly and annual reports. This monthly report form is only a statistical summary of the security department's activities. For the report to be complete a covering memo of analysis should be attached.

Purpose of Reports

Aside from these sample forms a word should be said about the purpose of summary reports.

Why do we have monthly and annual reports? Some people feel summary reports are needed as a historical record of the security activities. These people glance through it and then file it under "M" for museum piece.

Isn't such a report part of our controls? What do we mean by controls? When we talk about controls aren't we talking about the control of a person. We shouldn't expect it to be a control of activities as such. In the long run no action is carried on or no results attained without the efforts of a person or several people.

To control a person is to stimulate him to action. We may forget this fact in our control systems. The record is not an end in itself. The purpose is to get management people—and through them, other people—stimulated to action.

A control system needs to be geared toward management people at all levels. It is true that a summary record shows whether a job is being done. It picks out the broad areas that are lagging. However, this should not be the main function of the report. The real value of a report is to direct all management people toward corrective *action.* When any report fails to get constructive action, it is not vital to our business. It becomes only a historical record.

CUSTOMER'S REPORT OF ILLEGAL BUYING
(Impostor Investigation)

Name ______________________________

Address ____________ Telephone ____________ Acct. No. ________

Date Opened ____________ High Credit ____________ How Paid ________

The customer is expected to assume a reasonable responsibility for the use of her Credit Plate. Therefore, when the customer has been negligent in the way she uses her Plate and/or fails to report a lost or stolen Plate immediately, there is a possibility that the customer will be held responsible for its use.

This report is, actually, an accusation of fraud buying against persons known or unknown, and eventual investigation may entail police checking of the neighborhood, friends, associates, employees, servants, relatives or guests—any who might come under suspicion.

NOTE: All of the following questions may *not apply . . . answer only those which do.*

Where did you *first* discover that your Plate was lost or stolen? ____________

Did you immediately report its loss or theft? ________ When? ____________

How ______________________________

Do you know *exactly when* the Plate was lost or stolen? ____________

Do you know *where* your Plate was lost or stolen? ____________

Do you know *how* your Plate was lost or stolen? ____________

Exactly *when* and *where* did you last see your Plate? ____________

Where did you keep your Plate at home? ____________

Who knew where your Credit Plate was usually kept? ____________

Has your Plate been recovered? ______ When ______ How ____________

Who has ever been allowed to buy and charge with your Plate? ____________

Was *anyone* with you the last time you shopped with your Credit Plate? ____________

Who ______________________________

Is there any possibility, *even though remote*, that the Plate could have been *stolen* from your home ______ office ______ Place of Employment ____________

Specifically, *who* was in your home on the days just prior to the illegal buying? (guests, friends, relatives, baby sitters, tradesman, etc.) ____________

____

If you still have your Plate, *who could* have taken it from where it is usually kept and returned it? ______________________________

Do you have any *suspicions* at all, *even if unfounded*, as to who might have used your Credit Plate? ______________________________

Do you have burglar insurance? ______________________________

The above information to the best of my knowledge is completely true and accurate, and I have no other knowledge or suspicions other than those previously indicated as to who could have made the purchases billed to me amounting to $ ____________

Witness ____________ Customer's Signature ____________

Date ____________

INVESTIGATION REPORT
of
FRAUD BUYING

Customer's Name ______________________ Account Number ____________

Address ______________________

* 1. Amount of illegal buying $_______ Date of actual buying ____________

* 2. Was Credit Plate reported lost—stolen?________ By Whom ____________

Time of report ____________ How reported? ____________

* 3. Was reported loss of theft properly noted on ledger card? ____________

* 4a. Was the account properly tagged because of the reported loss of theft at the time of purchase? ____________

4b How many more authorized by Unit Operators in spite of tag? ____________

4c. Were any purchases given out by salespeople without authorization? ____________

4d. Were any tips referred to Floor Service or Selling Supervisor? ____________

5a. Was Credit Plate listed on "Stop List" at time of purchase? ____________

5b. Is name now on the "Stop List"? ____________

* 6. Fraud detected by ____________ How ____________ When ____________

7a. Were all purchases take-withs? ________ If not, what was address of delivery? ________

____

7b. How many tips were over the floor limit? ________ How many signed? ________

8a. Number of salespeople interviewed? ______ Can any salespeople identify (give details)

8b. Could salesperson provide any helpful information or description? ____________

* 9a. Has Plate been recovered? ________ Who has it? ____________

* 9b. What is the tag of the account as of this date? ____________

* 9b. Has customer extra or duplicate Plates? ____________

List specifically ____________

*10. If Credit Plate was not used, give details of method of operation:

*11. Any other pertinent facts? Explain:

*To be filled in by Division Credit Manager at initial interview with customer.

RECOMMENDED DISPOSITION

By Division Credit Manager:

Amount Transferred to Collection for follow-up ______________________

Amount transferred to Illegal Account (write-off) ______________________

Approved for Credit Manager by ______________________

SHOPPING REQUEST **SHOPPING DEPARTMENT**

To: Supr.

Please Shop ______________________

Dept. Number ____________ Floor ____________ Register Number ____________

Reason for Request ______________________

____

____

____

Description of Person to be Shopped: ______________________

Color	: ____________	Style Clothes	: ____________
Height	: ____________	Style Hair	: ____________
Weight	: ____________	Other	: ____________
Color Hair	: ____________		
Color Eyes	: ____________		
Color Clothes	: ____________		

Submitted By ______________________

(Any additional information use other side)

____

____

____

____

SHOPPING RECORD:

Dates Shopped	By Whom	Violation (Yes-no)
____________		
____________		
____________		
____________		

DISPOSITION ______________________
(PULLED OR NOT)

SPECIAL SERVICE

SHOPPERS VIOLATION REPORT

Salesperson's Name ______________ Payroll No. ______________ Date ______________

Dept:__________ Register: __________ Salesbook: __________ Floor: __________

Report Checked By: ______________________________

Shopper: ______________________________

Identifying Purchase: Time:

(List and itemize merchandise)

Purchase #	Amount	S. Tax	F. Tax	Total

Money tendered	10.00	5.00	1.00	.50	.25	.10	.05	.01	Total

Violation Purchase: Time: ______________

(List and itemize merchandise)

Purchase #	Amount	S. Tax	F. Tax	Total

Money tendered	10.00	5.00	1.00	.50	.25	.10	.05	.01	Total

Did salesperson give receipt? ______________________________

Was Sale recorded? ______________________________

Remarks:

Case # ____________________

Ref. ____________________

SECURITY DEPARTMENT

PRELIMINARY INVESTIGATION REPORT

Type of Problem: Time Rec'd Date Rec'd

Place of Occurrence: Received by:

Received from: Title Tel. No. Dept.

Details:

Disposition:

Submitted by: Title: Date of Report:

CASE HISTORY—SECURITY DEPARTMENT

Name of subject									Date issued		File No.
Home address									NEE		Reference
City					State		Zip Code		Alias		
Resides with (Name)					Relationship				Apt. No.		Home Phone
Employed by									Occupation		
Employer's Address									How Long?		
City					State		Zip Code		Salary		Bus. Tel. No.
Age	Date of Birth		Birthplace						Citizen		
Sex	Color	Height	Weight	Build	Hair	Eyes	Complexion		Marital Status		No. of Children

Further description

Identification

Personal History – Names, Addresses and Business Connections of Family and Friends

Previous address:

Cash on Person	Searched by	Entered Office	Police Notified	Left Office	Interviewed by

Place and time first observed		Reason given for act	
Observed by	Witness	Previous Record	Checked by
Subject approached (place and time)		Charge Acct. No.	
Name and Shield No. of Police Officer		Purchases made by subject	

SHOPLIFTER STATEMENT

Statement made this ________ day of ____, 19____

By ____

Living at ____ City of __________

That on the _____ day of _______________, 19___, between the hours of _________ M. and _______ M. I took unlawfully from the possession of THE COMPANY and without permission of the Company or any of its representatives and without paying therefor or expecting to pay therefor the following: ____________________________

____

____

____

____ valued at $________

I am fully aware that THE COMPANY is the owner of the property which was taken by me willfully and unlawfully.

I make this statement after having been advised by representatives of THE COMPANY that I am not required to do so, without in any way having been forced or threatened; it is made freely and voluntarily; and I also have promised representatives of THE COMPANY not to again enter any of their premises.

Signed ______________________________.

Witness

____

____

CHECK LIST

SHOPLIFTER

Name: ______________________________

Age: ______________________________

1. Search of Person
2. Case History
3. File of Previous Record
4. Police Records
5. Statement
6. Restitution Form
7. Charge Account Check
8. Interview Parents if Juvenile
9. Arrest Form if Prosecuted
10. Eating Habits
11. Photograph
12. Return to Stock Slip

DISHONEST EMPLOYEE

Name: ______________________________

Age: ______________________________

1. Case History
2. Search of Person
3. Locker Search
4. Statement
5. Restitution Form
6. Charge Account Check
7. Employee Consultant
8. Employee Counselor
9. Credit Union
10. Locker Key
11. Shopping Pass
12. Eating Habits
13. Photograph
14. Return to Stock Slip

Signature of Interviewer: ______________________________

SECURITY DEPARTMENT

ARREST REPORT

Defendant's Name				Defendant's Address
Age:	Race:	Sex:	Charge:	
Defendant's Name				Defendant's Address
Age:	Race:	Sex:	Charge:	
Defendant's Name				Defendant's Address
Age:	Race:	Sex:	Charge:	

Place of Occurrence:	Time:	Date:

Complainant:	Testifies to:
Witness:	Testifies to:
Interviewer:	Testifies to:

Total Value ________ Evidence Listed on Reverse Side Prosecute ________

COURT RECORD
SECURITY DEPARTMENT

Name: ______________________ Date: __________ File No.: __________

Alias: ______________________ Reference: __________

Address: ______________________

Date of Arrest: __________ Violation: ______________________

Name and Address of Complainant: ______________________

Date:	Name of Judge	Disposition

Remarks:

See reverse side for criminal record

GENERAL RELEASE

I voluntarily and freely agree to submit to an examination test, including therein the use of a deception instrument called the Lie Detector.

I do hereby release the   Company and its officers and employees from any and all manner of suits, actions, claims, and judgments and regardless of the results which may result from the examination including therein the use of the Lie Detector. I release the Company from any and all responsibility.

I have read the above and sign it voluntarily.

IN WITNESS THEREOF, I have hereunto set my hand and seal this __________ day of __________, 19__.

Signed ______________________

WITNESSED:

____

____

____

Subscribed and sworn to before me this __________ day of __________, 19____.

RELEASE

For and in consideration of the sum of One Dollar ($1.00) and other valuable consideration, receipt thereof being hereby acknowledged, I, the undersigned, ____________________ ______________ do hereby RELEASE AND FOREVER DISCHARGE The Company, a Michigan Corporation, of Detroit, Michigan, and any and all of its officers, agents, servants and employees, of and from any and all claims of any and every nature, for damages, demands, or actions at law, including any and all claims or possible claims of any and every nature for damages, and/or for false arrest, and/or for false imprisonment, and/or for malicious prosecution.

It is understood that this RELEASE is not limited to those claims or possible claims, but includes all those claims or possible claims of any and every nature now existing or hereafter arising from transactions, relationships, communications or dealings with the above company, its officers, agents, servants and employees between ____________________ (date) and ____________________ (date).

It is further understood that the Company, its officers, agents, servants, and employees, and each of them, do not admit but expressly deny any liability as to any of the foregoing claims or possible claims now or hereafter existing.

____

____

____

____

Dated ____________________ Signed ____________________

In the presence of: Address ____________________

____________________ Address ____________________

____________________ Address ____________________

State of)
County) ss

____________________ did on the above date sign the foregoing release in my presence, and, being duly sworn by me, did state that he had read the above, understood its contents, knew that it was a release of the matters therein set forth, and that the signing by him was his free act and deed in no way brought about by any force or threat of any kind.

____
Notary Public County, Michigan

____
My commission expires

MONTHLY REPORT

SPECIAL SERVICE REPORT

	Downtown	Northland	Eastland	Lincoln Park
Total Cases				
Gross Amount				
Net Recovery				
CASES				
Shoplifters				
Employees				
Misc.				
RECOVERIES				
Case Mer.				
Money				
Restitution				
Recoveries NP				
Other				
GENERAL				
Investigations				
Shopping Pur.				
Prosecutions				
LOSSES				
Customer				
Employee				
Department				

MONTHLY REPORT

RECOVERIES

	DOWNTOWN	NORTHLAND	EASTLAND	LINCOLN PARK
Merchandise SL				
Merchandise DE				
Merchandise NP				
Money				
Restitution Owed				
Collection Recovery*				
Misplaced Mer. NP*				
From Other Stores				
For Other Stores				
Ret. Refund B/C				
Other				
Gross Amount				

*Not included in Gross Amt.

NET RECOVERY

Merchandise				
Money				
Total				

OUTSTANDING

Restitution-Prom. Note				
Restitution-Other				
Total				

INVESTIGATION

Shoplifting				
Imposter				
Refund				
Bad Check				
Losses				
Police Records Checks				
Employee				
Shopping Purchases				
House Searches				
Night Protection				
Other				
Total				

NIGHT PROTECTION

	Cases	Gross Amount	Net Recovery	Prosecuted	Released
Downtown					
Northland					
Eastland					
Lincoln Park					

MONTHLY REPORT

CASES

	No. Cases	Gross Amt.	Net Recovery	Prosecuted	Released	Referred
Shoplifters						
D–						
N–						
E–						
LP–						
Dishonest Emp.						
D–						
N–						
E–						
LP–						
Other Cases						
D–						
N–						
E–						
LP–						

DISPOSITION OF CASES

	Prosecuted	Released	Referred	Totals
	D N E LP	D N E LP	D N E LP	D N E LP
Adult Male				
Adult Female				
Total Adult				
Juvenile Male				
Juvenile Female				
Total Juvenile				
Total All Types				

SHOPPING

Test Purch.	Ident. Purch.	Total Purch.	Policy Viol.	Theft Viol.	Cases–Amts.
D–					
N–					
E–					
LP–					

Chapter 17

PSYCHOLOGY OF THE RETAIL CRIMINAL

Fabian L. Rouke, Ph.D.

The present serious delinquency situation has developed in spite of the heroic labors put forth by educators, sociologists, penologists, psychologists, and psychiatrists, in the form of preventive and corrective programs. Immeasurable study, planning, and observation have been expended on the problem of delinquency by the best minds of our day.

In fact, when we consider how much has been done in this direction, the paucity of results might cause us to stop and ask ourselves, "Why have our efforts not had greater effect? What has been wrong with our methods, skills, techniques, therapies, whatever you prefer to call them? If we had really understood the elements of the problem, should we not have realized a greater degree of success in solving it?"

What is delinquency? A delinquent, in the legal sense, is a person who has been so judged by a court. However, delinquents are human personalities. Many of these personalities have never been apprehended, never come in contact with a court, and they offer the same problems of understanding as those who have met the technical requirements of the law.

The late Fabian Rouke, Ph.D. was formerly Head of the Psychology Department at Manhattan College in New York City. He was a recognized expert in criminal psychology and for many years assisted both state and federal law enforcement agencies.

Wallerstein and Wyle Study

In a study that confirms this point, Wallerstein and Wyle distributed questionnaires listing 49 offenses under the penal law of the state of New York. All of the offenses were sufficiently serious to draw sentences of not less than one year. Replies were received from 1,020 men, and 678 women. Ninety-nine percent of them admitted having committed one or more of the 49 offenses listed.

The delinquent in any group is the one who will not abide by the code of that group, and although the overt act may be quite different, the personal pattern is the same—namely, a failure to recognize or refusal to respect the rights of another.

To help eliminate delinquency, therefore, we must find those factors that result in the absence of unselfish maturity in the personality.

In finding these factors we can be hopeful of progress, for in the final analysis there is only one road that leads to success. *To prevent crime we must prevent criminals.*

Three Types of Criminals

The retail criminal falls broadly into three categories. These three categories apply both to the internal criminal—the dishonest employee—and to the external criminal—the shoplifter.

The first category is the professional or business criminal who steals for profit. It is his life's avocation. He may or may not be part of an organized ring, but this is his means of making a living.

The second category is the casual pilferer. Here we have the person who takes things for his own use or for gifts to give to his friends. The items he steals usually are small things, but they mount up. The most important factor here is opportunity.

The third category is the neurotic thief whose stealing is symptomatic of a deep-seated emotional need. Here again we can break down the various types of needs. We have some who steal as a substitute for the symbolic needs of sexual gratification. We have those who steal because of a desire to be caught and humiliated and punished to alleviate unconscious guilt. Finally, we have those who steal because of a need for gaining status and acceptance. Perhaps these neurotic motives for stealing will become clearer through a discussion of some actual cases dealing with each of these types.

Need for Status and Acceptance

Let us begin with a college girl, home from a midwestern university for the mid-semister holidays. She was picked up with only two items, a sweater and a skirt. The two articles totaled $130 in value. What was her story?

She was home for the holidays. Her parents were in Florida for the winter season, but she was left a generous allowance with permission by her mother to buy a spring outfit. Her mother also suggested that the girl ask her older sister to go with her "because she has such nice taste in clothes." The older sister, busy with her two-month-old baby, couldn't go, but encouraged the girl to go by herself, saying "You can do just as well as I can."

This older sister had always been a bit of a thorn in the side of the younger one, not due in any part to the sister's own attitude or activity, but because of the mother. The shoplifter was not particularly attractive, but she was quite smart. Her school record in grade school and in high school was straight "A." However, she wasn't popular with the other girls in her classes.

Mother Favors Older Child

Typically, when she brought home her report card, the mother would look at it and say, "Oh that's fine. You are good in school, but look what your sister can do with a few dollars for clothes." The sister, who had left school, worked in the garment industry and had very good opportunities to buy clothes at half price. She also had a flair for style.

All during her life, our subject had been unfavorably compared with her older sister for not being able to do what the other sister could do with clothes. Even at this time, with the mother and father away, and with an allowance given her, the instructions had been, "Take your older sister. She's got good taste."

The girl started downtown alone. She had one idea—"I'm going to show them! I'll do some real shopping." She went to 14th Street, knowing the values that someone who knows clothes can get on 14th Street. In the first store she entered, she chose one or two things. There was no salesclerk available and impulsively she walked out with them. The idea hit her, "This is going to be even better than I thought. Look what I will be able to do without spending much money," and she started up Fifth Avenue.

In talking with her, we asked if she had ever stolen before in her life. "No—well, yes, once, only once."

"When was that and what happened?"

"Well, I was in the first year of high school, and I had never been very popular with the girls in grade school, so I hoped when I got to high school that I would be accepted and that they would like me. They had a club, and the initiation for the club was to steal something. So I looked over the list and I picked out the most difficult thing to steal. Then I went to the five and ten, stole it, and got into the club." She had been assigned to steal a dozen balloons.

The only previous occurrence of stealing in her left had served to gain status and acceptance among her friends. This time, when the opportunity presented itself, the pattern was there. "Stealing gets me the acceptance that I have wanted and that I have never had," so she stole.

"Acceptance" Often a Hidden Need

There are variations on this theme. There was another case of a girl in her late teens whose father had died when she was a baby. The mother devoted her life completely to the task of bringing up her daughter and did remarkably well. She managed to maintain the girl in school, not only through high school but also business school, and the two of them were very close emotionally.

When the girl finished business school, she got a job as a secretary in a TV studio at a good salary. The mother felt that now she could lessen the attention paid to her daughter and look to her own life and her own emotional needs. She was still reasonably young, about thirty-eight or thirty-nine, and it wasn't long before she had a boy friend, and this man was thinking of marriage.

The daughter couldn't take it. She couldn't stand seeing her mother lost to her emotionally, but on the other hand, on a reasoning level, she saw that her mother had been very generous with her and that she actually should not complain.

What followed was a pattern of thinking that was not cold or calculating on a conscious level, but which occurred below the level of consciousness and resulted in her shoplifting. It was simply this: "If disgrace and humiliation can be brought to my family, that fellow won't have a thing to do with my mother. He will just drop her like a hot potato. Then my mother will be mine again." For that reason, this girl became a shoplifter.

Compulsive Need to be Caught and Punished

Another need that often results in compulsive crime is the need for punishment. There are two kinds of guilt: moral guilt, which is intellectual, and emotional guilt, which stems from infantile dependency needs.

Emotional guilt arises normally in early childhood when we have done something that puts us in danger of losing parental approval.

In the immature personality the pattern may persist into adult life. In such cases, even when moral guilt is properly handled and even when contrition has been felt and retribution made, the emotional guilt remains.

One woman had stolen a small article, about $7.95 in value, and at the time she stole it she had over $100 in cash in her purse. She had an open charge account in good standing at the store. Why did she steal?

Sexual Guilt

This woman had married originally in the early 1960s. Three days after she was married, her husband, who was an army officer, went overseas. He was gone for two years. She was working in midtown and on her way home each night she and a man who attracted her happened to be on the same ferry boat. The two of them struck up an acquaintance.

He, too, was married, but sooner or later they began to stay in town occasionally for a drink and dinner together. Later he rented a small apartment and they began to spend evenings together. She became pregnant. He arranged for an abortion. She and this new man were apparently in love. He planned to divorce his wife, and she intended to divorce her husband as soon as he returned from Europe so that they could get married.

When her husband got back, she discovered that he had been wounded and he was convalescing for several months in an army hospital. This postponed her plans, because she couldn't bear to divorce him while he was still hospitalized. As soon as he got well, however, she told him her plan, the divorce went through on both sides, and the remarriage took place.

But all the while, the tremendous guilt that she had, first, over the infidelity to her husband when he was away in the service, and, secondly, over the abortion, had never been assuaged. She needed punishment. She looked for it, and by stealing and being caught with the attendant humiliation she achieved it.

Even Sexual Temptation Can Be a Compulsive Cause of Theft

Not all cases are quite as obvious as these. One case concerned a very respectable housewife with two children and a husband who was in a successful business. Again, there was no financial need, but she was apprehended with a $90 jacket.

In her the personality problem was quite severe. There had been previous instances of shoplifting. In looking for a possible common cause, it was brought out that just before each incident she had undergone some form of sexual temptation—some form of approach that would have led to infidelity. She never had been unfaithful to her husband, but felt that she had wanted to be.

In the first case, which was a few years ago, a girl friend wrote her a glowing account of the doctor in the town where she had grown up. He had been a boy friend of hers, and they had almost married. After reading the letter she went into a reverie. She had always wanted to marry a doctor. "What would it have been like to have married him? I should have." Then there was tremendous guilt for this psychological infidelity, and two days later she stole a record album.

On another occasion, the superintendent of the apartment where she lived made a mild approach. Hearing that she was going to be downtown, he simply said, "I am going to be downtown tomorrow. Why don't we meet for lunch?" She immediately read things into his invitation, felt uneasy about it, and on that trip downtown stole a hat.

Nothing happened for several months. Then she received a telephone call from the boy friend of a divorced woman who lived in the apartment across the hall from her. It was a rather obvious proposition. She couldn't say "no" outright; she hedged a bit, but didn't go through with it. Two days later, she stole a handful of costume jewelry.

The last incident concerned one of her husband's relatives who was visiting at their home on his way from New York. One morning, as usual, the children went off to school and the husband went to work. She was still dressed in a housecoat, and the relative, who got up late, was in his pajamas.

She had always liked him. He started to become somewhat affectionate and demonstrative. She did not protest strongly, but when he took her back in the bedroom, she resisted.

Each time she had wanted to do something that she knew was wrong, and each time she had needed satisfaction and didn't achieve it. She still needed it, so she attained it symbolically, symptomatically, in stealing the forbidden fruit.

Interestingly enough, each time the value of the article stolen more or less corresponded to the intensity and the seriousness of the situation.

Why Should We Care About Human Problems?

These cases are of interest because human problems are always interesting. But what bearing do they have on store security?

In the light of cold facts, retail stores have only one reason for existence. They are in business to make money. They are not mental hygiene clinics and they are not welfare agencies, so why be interested in the psychotherapy of shoplifters?

It is because there is a big source of profit that has been overlooked, that has been undeveloped, and, even worse, in some cases unrecognized and unadmitted. That source of profit is the loss that does not occur. In every sense of the word, if you prevent a loss, you have made a profit. It will show in actual figures.

So far, the problems have been stated. This discussion should not be ended without some measure of suggestion as to what to do for a solution of those problems. Some suggestions will be offered briefly and generally, because each retailer will have to tailor them to his own specific needs.

Professional Criminals Require Strong Security

What about the professional criminal? What can the psychologist do to stop him? The answer is "Very little." That is not the psychologist's job.

The way to prevent the professional criminal is store security in the full sense of the word—not the old-time store detective who stood around on the floor and caught one thief a month and then beat him up, but modern security planning and checking that is carried through the entire merchandising operation from the receiving platform to the customer.

External and Internal Thieves Require Different Countermeasures

As for the thief, there are two problems. For the external thief, the easiest chance lies in the opportunities available to him through exposed merchandise. Studying store layout and displays, and determining how best to put obstacles in his way, is the best way to minimize his threat.

A different problem arises with the internal pilferer—the dishonest employee who is not a thief in the full sense of the word, but who steals because he is working in a store with thousands and thousands of dollars worth of things. He may feel a little unhappy because he was docked for a day that he was out, or he may have some irritation against his particular boss.

When the opportunity comes to take a few things, he thinks, "Well, I am really entitled to that." He doesn't feel like a thief. The store, to him, is an omnipotent father. "They won't miss one pair of nylons," he tells himself, "and I can give them to my girl friend."

To focus the point sharply, how many of you have not at one time or another taken some small thing from your office or place of business? You didn't feel that you were stealing, but it was there, nobody had a need for it, so you took it.

There is a little story along this line that illustrates the point. There was a small boy in kindergarten who repeatedly took all the pencils from the other students' desks so that school authorities called the father in to talk to him. The father said, "I can't understand it. I don't know why he steals pencils. He doesn't need them. Every week I bring him a whole box of pencils from my office."

Internal Theft Responds to the Style of Management

The best method of controlling the internal thief is by initiating a style of management that allows employees to participate in solving operating problems.

The person who is not psychologically a criminal, who just takes things because they are there, will not take things if they are involved in helping the company to be successful. Self-esteem is a major factor in preventing internal losses. The more authoritarian the management, the greater the frustration and hidden hostilities of the employees.

Authoritative management tends to substantially increase internal thefts. On the other hand, a participative style of management, in which managers consult with their people on operating problems and listen to the opinions and advise of their personnel, involves employees to the extent that they tend to look on the company as their company and people do not normally steal from themselves.

Clinics Can Help Neurotic Thieves

In the case of neurotic criminals there is only one way to handle them, which is to refer them to clinical sources for help. How does that help the store? It is the surest way to eliminate repetition.

It has been claimed that the neurotic thief never takes a lot of things in the course of his day. In contradition to that claim, there was one neurotic employee who stole 450 items in the course of a year, including many items that were hardly negligible in value—a silver service, china, valuable linens, drapery material, and many other household items. He covered the field. Why would anybody want that much?

One important answer to the maladjusted person who is apprehended in our stores is to refer such an individual to a psychologist or a psychological clinic for personality help and rehabilitation. *To prevent crime we must first prevent the criminal.*

Chapter 18

COMPLETE PROSECUTION — PRO AND CON

Prosecution of retail malefactors is often a controversial question, and there are two aspects to it. Should we prosecute in order to deter criminals? Or should we prosecute for any other reasons?

In theory, prosecuting criminals should prevent other people from becoming criminals. The statement is often made, "If you have tough laws and treat thieves in a tough fashion you will prevent other people from becoming thieves." There is only one catch to this theory, which is that most people do not respond to logical arguments. As human beings most of us react to life in terms of our emotions rather than because of common sense.

Does Prosecution Deter Criminals?

Some people apprehended in stores must be prosecuted, but not for the reasons you might suppose. Certainly not because such prosecution will deter other people from crime. As many years as we have practiced the principle of criminal punishment in this country we have yet to prove that punishment in itself is a deterrent to crime. There is considerable proof to the contrary. For all practical purposes, the solution of reduced retail crime does not lie in the area of increased punishment for retail criminals.

But before drawing any final conclusions on the problem, let's examine the viewpoints of those who believe that stores should prosecute. Not just those cases that might require prosecution but *all* cases. The following statements are from very capable retail executives. They represent the thinking of many key people in stores across the country. First, here is what the vice president and controller of a large store says:

Some Views for Prosecution

> Some few years ago, at the request of our insurance company, we decided to prosecute *all* shoplifters, both customers and employees. In the three years since then we have found—or at least we believe we have found—that it has been a help.
>
> The deterrent effect is, of course, the prime thing we are shooting for. It isn't the individual $1.98 or $5.98 item that is in question, it is the effect of the tremendous cost overall to the stores involved, and the need to find some means of combatting the problem.
>
> Another part of the problem is that if you follow a strict prosecution policy all by yourself, you can create a bad image of your store in the minds of the public. If at all possible it would be advisable to get together with the other stores in your city so that a uniform policy is being followed by all stores.

Next, this is what a general merchandise manager from a large store in the northwestern part of the country says:

> I believe definitely that the shoplifter should be prosecuted, in the states where it is possible to do so. Time after time I have had people, teenagers and older people, brought up to my office in the absence of the store security head. I have been told time and time again that it is very easy to shoplift in our store. That's the answer these people give. There is only one reply to that, and that is to prosecute and to make it tough.
>
> The local prosecutor in our city has cooperated beautifully. When we turn these shoplifters over to the police, they are booked, and we do not withdraw the charges. They are booked and they are sentenced. I believe that to be the best way.
>
> Where an employee is concerned, we have not gone that far, but we do believe that when an employee is caught in a dishonest act he should be discharged without delay, because you are going to have trouble with him if you keep him.

Management as Judge and Jury

Last, this is what an aggressive and successful vice president of one of the country's leading stores says:

Shoplifting is a crime, and as a store owner or other executive in the organization you have no right whatsoever to become judge and jury and decide who is and who is not to be prosecuted for a crime.

When a person steals merchandise in your store he is a criminal. If you decide that you are going to let that person go and not turn him over to the people to whom you pay taxes to decide such matters—such as your judges or other officials—you are just as guilty as if you let a murderer or anybody else go. Only a matter of degree is involved.

You have no right to set yourself up as judge and jury. You have other people to do that. It's their job to decide whether the person should be punished by imprisonment or fine, and I don't see how we can all be judge and jury. Shoplifting is a crime, and it's taking a lot of money out of our pockets.

The Juvenile Problem

The juvenile problem is particularly bad in our city. More than 50 percent of the people who were charged with shoplifting last year were juveniles. I have talked to many of them. It's a lark to them, and they will go back to school and say that they have been 'picked-up'—that's the phrase they use—"but, they let me go."

I have been told of cases where these young people keep things such as leather jackets in school (the kind of things they couldn't possibly get their parents to buy). When they come to school in the morning, they change into the leather jacket (or other items) that make them look important in high school. They change back at the end of the day and go home in the clothes their parents know about. It's part of the juvenile problem that they all become heroes to the people they go around with.

It is our policy, therefore, when we pick up someone who is guilty of an offense against society, a crime, to turn them over—every one of them—to the people who have the responsibility and jurisdiction to decide what should be done with them. We do not act as judge and jury.

Let's Take a Closer Look

As we can see, these executives are seriously concerned about the problem of crime in their stores. Because of their concern they naturally believe that punishment of *all* offenders will reduce this crime. Unfortunately, the facts do not substantiate their beliefs.

Let's look at the first executive's statement, "In the three years since then we have found—or at least we believe we have found—that it has been a help." This man sincerely believes that he has had a reduction in cases as a result of prosecuting all shoplifters.

The Floor Has Less Coverage

It should be pointed out, however, that when you prosecute all of your cases your store detectives spend over 50 percent of their time in the courts handling these prosecutions. This means that such a store has 50 percent less floor coverage than it would normally have. During the periods in which your detectives are in the courts your store is unguarded against shoplifters. It is therefore conceivable that a store's cases will go down when it steps up its prosecutions. But the reason the cases go down is not because the prosecutions deter criminals, but rather because the store is not being covered by its detectives as adequately as it was prior to the all-out policy of prosecution.

Stores Retaliate

Note also how this executive states that the *deterrent effect* is the prime thing he is shooting for. This, of course, is the expressed motivation of all three retail executives. However, if we can judge their statements on the basis of how most people react, it is more logical to suppose that they want to retaliate against the person who has hurt their store. Many prosecutions are the result of management anger and frustration. It is a human reaction to their admitted inability to stop the problems of theft against their store.

Note how one executive justifies his motives by explaining that the individual $1.98 or $5.98 item is not the question, but rather it is the overall cost to the stores involved and *the need to find some means of combatting the problem.* Isn't he saying here that his store is not willing to spend money for an adequate security department? He feels that the courts should solve his problems for him.

"If Everyone Would Prosecute..."

The executive concerned about public opinion should realize that because all of the stores agree to prosecute shoplifters, this does not necessarily maintain a favorable store image in the community. For example, if your neighbor cruelly beats his child, all of the neighbors are apt to look down on him, but if everyone on your street beats his child, this executive reasons, nobody will look down on anyone—all of them will be looked on favorably. Actually, however, even if everyone cruelly beats their children, this will not in any way change the public's attitude toward people who beat their children.

Is Management Accepting Its Share of the Responsibility?

The second executive says that the people who steal tell him that its very easy to steal in his store, and apparently this makes him angry. He feels there is only one reply and that is to prosecute, to make it tough. Is this prosecution based on logic or on an emotional desire for retaliation? *Have he and the other members of his store management considered what could be done so that shoplifting would not be easy in his store*? Does his store have an adequate security staff? Do they take interest in displaying merchandise so that it cannot be easily taken? What constructive actions are being taken by this executive and his management in order to do their part in reducing thefts in their store?

The Maladjusted Employee

He also says that when an employee steals they don't prosecute him, but they do discharge him without delay, "because you're going to have trouble with him if you keep him." Again, here is an apparent failure to understand the problem of crime itself. It is true that you probably should not keep an employee who steals, but the reason is not because you will have "trouble with him," but rather because this employee is probably a maladjusted person who needs treatment. If the store is not willing to help him get treatment, then by all means he should be discharged.

Certain personalities are not well enough adjusted to be placed in retail stores because temptation to the individual is much higher there than in many other kinds of business. The employee who works in an office, for example, has very little opportunity for theft. A person who works in a department that has very desirable merchandise and handles several hundred dollars in cash every day is placed in a position where temptation of the individual is high. A person who succumbs to this temptation is obviously a poor risk in a store job. Such a person needs to be given psychological treatment so that she will be cured of her problems or she needs to be removed from the area of temptation.

100-Percent Prosecution?

Now let's look at the last executive's statement. He is the most aggressive of the three. He tends to see the whole situation in terms of black and white. He points out that "we have no right whatsoever to become judge and jury and decide who is and who is not to be prosecuted for a crime." He also says that "in his store every one of them is prosecuted."

Now people who work in retail security will raise an eyebrow at this statement. There will be considerable question whether, even in a store such as this one, 100-percent prosecution is feasible or even possible. There will always be cases which, from a legal viewpoint, a store cannot prosecute. When this executive makes the claim that his store prosecutes *all* cases, we must look on this with serious doubt.

Everyone's a Criminal

He goes on further to note that when a person steals in his store "*he is a criminal.*" As noted in Dr. Rouke's chapter, "The Psychology of the Retail Criminal," we would find that most, if not all, of the population consists of "criminals," if it were possible to find out what laws each person has broken. It is well within the area of believability that this executive himself has broken laws throughout his lifetime, and therefore, technically, he, too, is a criminal.

The Store's Responsibility

In saying that the person apprehended should be "turned over to the people who we pay taxes to decide such matters," this executive is getting out from under his responsibilities very nicely. He is saying that he, as a person, and his store have no community responsibility. He rejects any responsibility for the problems of crime in his store.

Isn't he saying that although he may place people in positions of undue temptation and fail to protect his store merchandise or money, still he has no responsibility for what results? He is saying that we should let the judges and the people who are paid by our taxes decide what should be done. This is a buckpassing philosophy that I am sure this executive would never allow in other parts of his store operation.

Because security is a highly specialized field and because most management people do not have the opportunity or the time to get into the more detailed aspects of retail security work, there is a natural temptation to generalize and treat security problems in a rigid, unreasoned way.

Is the Store Criminally Negligent?

When a store refuses to accept any responsibility for theft it should be placed in the same category as the person who parks his car and leaves the ignition key in the dashboard. In many states this lack of responsibility is looked on as a crime. It is apparent that the person who parks his car and leaves the key in the dashboard is setting up a situation that can lead to theft. Many states today recognize this and hold such a person responsible along with the thief.

The third executive also says that shoplifting is a crime and is "taking a lot of money out of our pockets." This is a point of view that does not create a good community image for his store. A store that leads a community to believe that the management is more interested in profits than in serving the people of the community will, in the long run, lose the respect and support of the people.

The Juvenile

He also says that the juvenile problem is particularly bad in his city and places the responsibility for juvenile thefts squarely on the shoulders of the juvenile. Today we recognize that the juvenile has not yet reached an age in which he or she can assume adult responsibility. That is why we have the term "juvenile," and it is also why the courts give special consideration to people below a certain age. This executive wants the juvenile to become as emotionally mature and as balanced as an adult, which is not facing life as it is.

We notice that he does not suggest any responsibility for parents in the problems of juvenile delinquency. He insists that the juvenile problem is strictly the responsibility of juveniles and makes no comment about our failure as adults to solve the problems of the juvenile delinquent. He does not ask whether the parents may be at fault, or the community, or even our national way of life. He places the entire burden of responsiblity on the juveniles and demands punishment for their failure to live up to the moral code of adults.

Crime Problem Solved by the Right Action

These viewpoints are typical of a few retail management people. It is certainly understandable why they feel as they do. When people steal from someone it can make this person very angry. If efforts to prevent such thefts do not succeed, the anger can turn to frustration and a need for action. Good executives are action-oriented; they find that action solves frustration. However, the problems of crime can be solved only by the right action. Criminals do not respond to just any action and *they do not respond to vindictive action.*

Motivation Versus Communication

We must also remember there is a difference between communication and motivation. Motivating people requires appeals and human attitudes. People are triggered to action by the emotional part of their being. Communication can deal on the levels of logic but logic will not motivate them.

The people who believe that prosecution of *all* criminals will reduce crime are trying to apply logic to a problem of human motivation that can respond only to emotional appeals.

At this point it may be felt that the author does not believe in prosecution. This is not true. There are many cases that should be prosecuted. However, not *every* case should be prosecuted.

The Purpose of Retail Security

Let's ask ourselves, what *is* the purpose of retail security? Retail security is a department that retailers have had to add to their companies in order to combat the rising problems of crime.

The objective of store security is to increase net profits. It accomplishes this by detecting criminals and by preventing theft. It is not a law enforcement agency. Security is instead another store department intended to serve the best interests of store operation.

Security is an integrated part of the overall store organization. It must be dedicated to results, not activities. Any activities that do not directly or indirectly result in reduced losses and increased profits should be eliminated from the security department operation. Think of your security department in terms of increased profits, not as a moral or ethical force intended to enforce the law.

Who Should Be Prosecuted?

Within this definitive framework let's discuss who should be prosecuted. Basically, most people have a certain amount of psychotic as well as neurotic tendencies. However, some people have an abnormal amount of these neurotic or psychotic tendencies. People with abnormally strong neurotic maladjustments can be cured. Such people can often be prevented from future criminal actions. Study has shown that about 80 percent of the people apprehended in retail store thefts are abnormally neurotic people.

Abnormally Psychotic Criminals

The remaining group usually consists of abnormally psychotic criminals. Psychotic people have no sense of fear and no conscience. The psychotic person believes that the things that he does wrong are the result of the failures of others, not himself. He sees himself at the center of his world and he believes that his own codes of conduct are superior to all others. Such a person may end up in the professional criminal group. Twenty-five percent of all prison populations in the country are made up of such abnormally psychotic people.

Unfortunately, there is not as yet a successful method for curing such abnormally psychotic people. Therefore, such people should be prosecuted and kept away from society as much as possible.

This is not prosecution undertaken to "get even" with the criminal or intended to deter other people from theft. Instead, it is a necessary action designed to remove from society a group of psychologically ill people who cannot at the present time be cured.

The Neurotic

When determining what action should be taken in the cases of the 80 percent who steal because of neurotic compulsion, consideration should be given to the establishment of community clinics for the psychiatric treatment of such people. This does not mean that the store is becoming involved in social service or welfare work; rather, it means that the store is being coldly realistic in taking action to protect future profits.

Repeat Offenders

A survey made of thirty of the leading stores in New York City showed that *one out of every four people apprehended in those stores, whether prosecuted or released, was later arrested again for committing a second retail crime.*

This means that one in every four people apprehended in a store once continued to steal. This finding has considerable significance. It means that if you were able to prevent such repeaters you would eventually eliminate at least 25 percent of all retail crime.

One New York store tried an experiment with this problem of repeaters. They persuaded 200 retail malefactors to accept psychological treatment. These people were all first offenders. They came from a variety of age groups and backgrounds. Some were housewives, businessmen, teachers, or librarians, people from normal walks of life. These people were turned over to a psychologist for help.

A check after seven years showed that *not a single member of this group had been apprehended again in any of the leading New York stores*. This program indicated that people with neurotic maladjustments can be prevented from future thefts by rehabilitation. It was a constructive experiment that indicated a practical method for reducing store crime.

Criminal Correction

Dr. Albert Ellis (Ph.D. in Clinical Psychology), a recognized national authority, discusses the problem of crime:

> The basic problem of morality, it must always be remembered, is not how to punish an individual for doing an immoral act, but how to induce him (a) not to commit this act in the first place and (b) not to commit it again in case he has made a mistake and committed it at first.
>
> The theory of atonement and punishment is that by blaming an individual for his crime and convincing him that he has sinned against God and the established order by committing it, and then making him atone, or be punished (e.g., jailed or electrocuted) for it, will deter both him and other individuals (who see his sad fate) from committing other crimes. This theory, which has been held by most clergymen, jurists, and penologists for thousands of years, has very little objective evidence in its support—since, in practice, its adherents have by no means stopped criminal actions or "sinning" in all the years they have supported it. Although during these years they have literally anathematized, excommunicated, imprisoned, castrated, confiscated the property of, and beheaded "sinners," we, still today have literally hordes of adulterers, blasphemers, thieves, and murderers with us.
>
> The reason why the blame and atonement theory of keeping people moral has probably never worked too well is that it focuses on the past rather than the present and the future. Instead of teaching the criminal or potential criminal that he should try and not commit offenses in the present and future—which he easily could accomplish in most instances—it teaches him that he is a louse, a skunk, a no-good for his past mistakes and

wrong doings. Since he believes this silly theory, the wrongdoer keeps telling himself over and over again what a worthless fellow he is. Naturally he cannot focus too well on the real problem—which is, I repeat, how can he refrain from doing wrong again. Instead, he focuses on telling himself, "look what an awful person I am. Look how I have sinned. Look how worthless I am. God and man can never love me now. Oh what a terrible adulterer (or thief, or murderer, or what you will) I am." With this line of focus he is almost certain to keep thinking of sinning, instead of not sinning; and eventually he will commit more crimes.

Psychologically, therefore, a sane morality must not teach people the sequence of the internalized sentences consisting of:

A. "I have done wrong, therefore

B. What a blackguard I am!"

but must teach them the sequence

A. "I may have done wrong, therefore

B. How can I *not* repeat my mistake today and tomorrow?"

Reeducating

Dr. Ellis believes that part of the rehabilitation process in the personality reconstruction of a neurotic must involve teaching new standards so that the individual does not commit crimes because of "self-interest." He also states that morality can be more effectively used in the training of children and juveniles if the desire *not* to commit crimes is motivated by the fact that it is to the individual's best "self-interest" not to commit such crimes.

In discussing the problems of prosecution most stores make a very distinct division between prosecuting a shoplifter and prosecuting a dishonest employee.

Prosecuting the Dishonest Employee

The prosecution of the dishonest employee requires additional thought by management, because here the problem involves the store's moral and ethical responsibility in relationship to the individual. Did the store, because of its poor operation or because of lack of judgment by a supervisor, create the situation that lead to dishonesty? Was the employee placed in a position of *undue temptation*?

If you or your store placed an employee in the position of *undue temptation* and the employee stole, then you and the store have a responsibility to that person. It is a moral and ethical responsibility and one that cannot be set aside.

For example, if you put a teenage stockboy into a stockroom where there are a lot of very desirable things such as expensive watches, jack knives, and lighters, and if you have this boy work there four or five hours unsupervised, isn't this putting him in the position of undue temptation?

If he steals who is responsible? He and his family are the ones who will carry the scars of disgrace if he is caught. But who had the responsibility for placing this boy in such a position of *undue temptation*? Before you prosecute any employee ask yourself, "Did our store create this dishonesty?"

When to Prosecute

We have touched here on only a few phases of this very complicated problem of prosecution. Let us repeat that it is definitely necessary to prosecute in certain cases.

You should prosecute the shoplifter who is obviously professional and anyone who is stealing in order to resell the merchandise. You should prosecute anyone who assaults a detective, or who has no identification, because a person who cannot be identified may have a serious criminal record. Criminals with prison records must be prosecuted. Prosecution is certainly necessary in many of these cases.

When Not to Prosecute

Many cases, however, should not be prosecuted. Prosecution in some cases does not serve a constructive purpose. In fact, it often defeats the very objective that it is intended to serve. It may increase crime in your community. Only through psychological treatment of the abnormally neurotic criminals can your store and your community reduce the number of retail criminals.

Most executives in retail stores are enlightened people. They are well aware of the gains being made in the treatment of maladjusted people through psychiatry and psychology. There are only a small group of traditionalists left who believe that crime has to be fought by an all-out war of punishment and atonement. It is toward this small group that we have directed this chapter. Most retail executives today know that the problems of crime cannot be solved by prosecution alone.

The Ultimate Solution

To sum up, prosecution is a necessity in many cases. However, the ultimate solution for crime in this country will not be through the prosecution of all offenders. We must turn for answers to other fields besides punishment in order to solve our crime problems. The psychologists offer us hope in the areas of the abnormally neurotic person.

Recent experiments in biochemical research suggest that chemical changes in the body may be used some day to cure the abnormally psychotic person. There is also hope that certain research may get at the roots of crime and reverse the present upward trend of the national crime statistics.

Large-scale research is being done in the fields of air ionization, motivational psychology, medicine, and biochemical therapy. None of the findings is as yet ready for widespread application, however.

At present the best solution to the problem of retail crime is the application of psychological treatment for neurotic offenders. Enlightened store managements should explore the possibility of setting up clinical rehabilitation centers in their community.

Summary

1. Prosecution is a very controversial question.
2. Some retail executives feel that we need tough laws and must treat thieves in a tough fashion if we are to prevent other people from becoming thieves.
3. Facts belie the deterrent effect of prosecution.
4. Some cases must be prosecuted.
5. One out of every four people apprehended in a retail store is apprehended again later.
   a. Psychological rehabilitation has been shown to prevent repeaters.
6. Theory of punishment has not stopped criminal actions.
7. There is a need to teach criminals how not to repeat the same mistake in the future.
   a. The teaching of new standards must be motivated by "self-interest."
8. Who is responsible if the employee is placed in a position of "undue temptation?"
9. Prosecution of all criminals is no answer to crime.
   a. We must turn to other fields besides punishment to solve the crime problem.
   b. Recent experiments suggest biochemical help for abnormally psychotic people. (For neurotic offenders, however, the best present solution to the problem of retail crime is the application of psychological treatment.)

Chapter 19

VERDICT GUILTY — NOW WHAT?

Karl Menninger, M.D.

Since ancient times criminal law and penology have been based upon what is called in psychology the pain-pleasure principle. There are many reasons for inflicting pain—to urge an animal to greater efforts, to retaliate for pain received, to frighten, or to indulge in idle amusement.

Human beings, like all animals, tend to move away from pain and toward pleasure. Hence the way to control behavior is to reward what is "good" and punish what is "bad." This formula pervades our programs of childrearing, education, and the social control of behavior.

With this concept three out of four readers will no doubt concur.

"Why, of course," they will say. "Only common sense. Take me, for example. I know the speed limit and the penalty. Usually I drive moderately because I don't want to get a ticket. One afternoon I was in a hurry; I had an appointment; I didn't heed the signs. I did what I knew was forbidden and I got caught and received the punishment I deserved. Fair enough. It taught me a lesson. Since then I drive more slowly in that area.

"And surely people are deterred from cheating on their income taxes, robbing banks, and committing rape by the fear of punishment. Why, if we didn't have these crime roadblocks we'd have chaos!"

The late Karl Menninger, MD, with his brother was the founder of the world famous Menninger Clinic in Topeka, Kansas. Dr. Menninger authored several well known and popular books including MAN AGAINST HIMSELF, a fascinating discussion of how some people commit suicide by subtle methods of self-destruction such as excessive drinking and overeating. This material originally appeared in Harpers magazine in 1959 and is reprinted here by special permission.

Threats Don't Always Deter

This sounds reasonable enough and describes that most people think—*part of the time*. But upon reflection we all know that punishments and the threat of punishments do *not* deter *some* people from doing forbidden things. Some of them take a chance on not being caught, and this chance is a very good one, too, better than five to one for most crimes.

Not even the fear of possible death, self-inflicted, deters some speedsters. Exceeding the speed limit is not really regarded as criminal behavior by most people, no matter how dangerous and self-destructive. It is the kind of a "crime" which respectable members of society commit and condone.

This is not the case with rape, bank-robbing, check-forging, vandalism, and the multitude of offenses for which the prison penalty system primarily exists. And from these offenses the average citizen, including the reader, is deterred by quite different restraints.

Conscience Controls Behavior

For most of us it is our conscience, our self-respect, and our wish for the good opinion of our neighbors which are the determining factors in controlling our impulses toward misbehavior.

Prison Threat Doesn't Work

Today it is no secret that our official, prison-threat theory of crime control is an utter failure. Criminologists have known this for years.

When pocket-picking was punishable by hanging in England, the crowds that gathered about the gallows to enjoy the spectacle of an execution were particularly likely to have their pockets picked by skillful operators who, to say the least, were not deterred by the exhibition of "justice."

We have long known that the perpetrators of most offenses are never detected; of those detected, only a fraction are found guilty and still fewer serve a "sentence."

Furthermore, we are quite certain now that of those who do receive the official punishment of the law, many become firmly committed thereby to a continuing life of crime and a continuing feud with law enforcement officers. Finding themselves ostracized from society and blacklisted by industry, they stick with the crowd they have been introduced to in jail and try to play the game of life according to this set of rules. In this way society skillfully concerts individuals of borderline self-control into loyal members of the underground fraternity.

Many Criminals Were Unloved Children

The science of human behavior has gone far beyond the common sense rubrics which dictated the early legal statutes. We know now that one cannot describe rape or bank-robbing or income-tax fraud simply as pleasure. Nor, on the other hand, can we describe imprisonment merely as pain. Slapping the hand of a beloved child as he reaches to do a forbidden act is utterly different from the institutionalized process of official punishment.

The offenders who are chucked into our county and state and federal prisons are not anyone's beloved children; they are usually unloved children, grown up physically but still hungry for human concern which they never got or never get in normal ways. So they pursue it in abnormal ways—abnormal, that is, from *our* standpoint.

Why Our Crime Therapy Has Failed

What might deter the reader from conduct which his neighbors would not like does not necessarily deter the grown-up child of vastly different background. The latter's experiences may have conditioned him to believe that the chances of winning by undetected cheating are vastly greater than the probabilities of fair treatment and opportunity.

He knows about the official threats and the social disapproval of such acts. He knows about the hazards and the risks. But despite all this "knowledge," he becomes involved in waves of discouragement or cupidity or excitement or resentment leading to episodes of social offensiveness.

These episodes may prove vastly expensive both to him and to society. But sometimes they will have an aura of success. Our periodicals have only recently described the wealth and prominence for a time of a man described as a murderer.

Konrad Lorenz, the great psychiatrist and animal psychologist, has beautifully described in geese what he calls a "triumph reaction." It is a sticking out of the chest and flapping of the wings after an encounter with a challenge. All of us have seen this primitive biological triumph reaction—in roosters, in some businessmen and athletes—*and* in some criminals.

Successful Criminals Don't Get Caught

In general, though, the gains and goals of the social offender are not those which most men seek. Most offenders whom we belabor are not very wise, not very smart, not evern very "lucky."

It is not the successful criminal upon whom we inflict our antiquated penal system. It is the unsuccessful criminal, the criminal who really doesn't know how to commit crimes, and who gets caught. Indeed, until he is caught and convicted a man is technically not even called a criminal. The clumsy, the desperate, the obscure, the friendless, the defective, the diseased—these men who commit crimes that do not come off—are bad actors, indeed. But they are not the professional criminals, many of whom occupy high places.

In some instances the crime is the merest accident or incident or impulse, expressed under unbearable stress. More often the offender is a persistently perverse, lonely, and resentful individual who joins the only group to which he is eligible—the outcasts and the antisocial.

The Law and Confinement

And what do we do with such offenders? After a solemn public ceremony we pronounce them enemies of the people, and consign them for arbitrary periods to institutional confinement on the basis of laws written many years ago.

Here they languish until time has ground out so many weary months and years. Then with a planlessness and stupidity only surpassed by that of their original incarceration they are dumped back upon society, regardless of whether any change has taken place in them for the better and with every assurance that changes have taken place in them for the worse.

Once more they enter the unequal tussle with society. Proscribed from employment by most concerns, they are expected to invent a new way to make a living and to survive without any further help from society.

Recommended Improvements Were Made Long Ago

Intelligent members of society are well aware that the present system is antiquated, expensive, and disappointing, and that we are wasting vast quantities of manpower through primitive methods of dealing with those who transgress the law.

In 1917 the famous Wichersham report of the New York State Prison Survey Committee recommended the abolition of jails, the institutional system, and treatment program, and the use of indeterminate sentences. How little progress we have made!

In 1933 the American Psychiatric Association, the American Bar Association, and the American Medical Association officially and jointly recommended psychiatric service for every criminal and juvenile, and to assist the court and prison and parole officers with all offenders.

Have these recommendations been carried out anywhere in the United States? With few exceptions offenders continue to be dealt with according to oldtime instructions, written by men now dead who knew nothing about the present offender, his past life, the misunderstandings accumulated by him, or the provocation given to him.

Rehabilitation Occurs If Someone Cares

The sensible, scientific question is: What kind of treatment could be instituted that would deter him or be most likely to deter him? Some of these methods are well known. For some offenders, who have the money or the skillful legal counsel or the good luck to face a wise judge, go a different route from the prescribed routine. Instead of jail and deterioration, they get the sort of reeducation and redirection associated with psychiatric institutions and the psychiatric profession.

Relatively few wealthy offenders get their "treatment" in jail. This does not mean that justice is to be bought, or bought off. But it does mean that some offenders have relatives and friends who *care* and who try to find the best possible solution to the problem of persistent misbehavior, which is NOT the good old jail-and-penitentiary and make'-em-sorry treatment. It is a reflection on the democratic ideals of our country that these better ways are so often—indeed, *usually*—denied to the poor, the friendless, and the ignorant.

Length and Type of Incarceration

If we were to follow scientific methods, the convicted offender would be detained indefinitely pending a decision as to whether, and how and when, to reintroduce him successfully into society. All the skill and knowledge of modern behavioral science would be used to examine his personality assets, his liabilities and potentialities, the environment from which he came, its effect upon him, and his effects upon it.

Having arrived at some diagnostic grasp of the offender's personality, those in charge can decide whether there is a chance that he can be redirected into a mutually satisfactory adaptation to the world.

If so, the most suitable techniques in education, industrial training, group administration, and psychotherapy should be selectively applied.

All this may be best done extramurally or intramurally. It may require maximum "security" or only minimum "security." If, in due time, perceptible change occurs, the process should be expedited by finding a suitable spot in society and industry for him, and getting him out of prison control and into civil status (with parole control) as quickly as possible.

Move Prisoners Out Swiftly

We psychiatrists learned the desirability of moving patients out of institutional control swiftly. At one time, few patients were discharged under two years; now most patients are discharged within the first year. But some patients do not respond to our efforts, and they have to remain in the hospital, or return to it promptly after a trial home visit.

And if the *prisoner*, like some of the psychiatric patients, cannot be changed by genuine efforts to rehabilitate him, we must look *our* failure in the face, and provide for his indefinitely continued confinement, regardless of the technical reasons for it. This we owe society for its protection.

The Civilized Program

There will be some offenders about whom the most experienced are mistaken, both ways. And there will be some concerning whom no one knows what is best. There are many problems for research. But what I have outlined is, I believe, the program of modern penology, the program now being carried out in some degree in California and a few other states, and in some of the federal prisons.

This civilized program, which would save so much now-wasted money, so much unused manpower, and so much injustice and suffering, is slow to spread. It is held back by many things—by the continued use of fixed sentences in many places; by unenlightened community attitudes toward the offender whom some want tortured; by the prevalent popular assumption that burying a frustrated individual in a hole for a short time will change his warped mind, and that when he is certainly worse, he should be released because his "time" has been served; by the persistent failure of the law to distinguish between crime as an accidental, incidental, explosive event, crime as a behavior pattern expressive of chronic unutterable rage and frustration, and crime as a business or elected way of life.

Progress is further handicapped by the lack of interest in the subject on the part of lawyers, most of whom are proud to say that they are not concerned with criminal law. It is handicapped by the lack of interest on the part of members of my own profession. It is handicapped by the mutual distrust of lawyers and psychiatrists.

The Theory of Insanity

The infestation or devil-possession theory of mental disease is an outmoded, pre-medieval concept. Although largely abandoned by psychiatry, it steadfastly persists in the minds of many laymen, including, unfortunately, many lawyers.

On the other hand, most lawyers have no really clear idea of the way in which a psychiatrist functions or of the basic concepts to which he adheres. They cannot understand, for example, why there is no such thing (for psychiatrists) as "insanity."

Most lawyers have no conception of the meaning or methods of psychiatric work. They can take a quick look at a suspect, listen to a few anecdotes about him, and thereupon be able to say definitely, that the awful "it"—the dreadful miasma of madness, the loathsome affliction of "insanity"—is present or absent. Because we all like to please, some timid psychiatrists fall in with this fallacy of the lawyers and go through these preposterous antics.

The Psychiatrist's View

It is true that almost any offender—like anyone else—when questioned for a short time, even by the most skillful psychiatrist, can make responses and display behavior patterns which will indicate that he is enough like the rest of us to be called "sane."

But a barrage of questions is not a psychiatric examination. Modern scientific personality study depends upon various specialists—physical, clinical, and sociological as well as psychological. It takes into consideration not only static and presently observable factors, but dynamic and historical factors, and factors of environmental interaction and change. It also looks into the future for correction, reeducation, and prevention.

Hence, the same individuals who appear so normal to superficial observation are frequently discovered in the course of prolonged, intensive scientific study to have tendencies regarded as "deviant," "peculiar," "unhealthy," "sick," "crazy," "senseless," "irrational," "insane."

The "Excused"

But now you may ask, "Is it not possible to find such tendencies in any individual if one looks hard enough? And if this is so, if we are all a little crazy or potentially so, what is the essence of your psychiatric distinctions? Who is it that you want excused?"

And here is the crux of it all. We psychiatrists don't want *anyone* excused. In fact, psychiatrists are much more concerned about the protection of the public than are the lawyers. I repeat; psychiatrists don't want anyone excused, certainly not anyone who shows antisocial tendencies. We consider them all responsible, which lawyers do not. And we want the prisoner to take on that responsibility, or else deliver it to someone who will be concerned about the protection of society and about the prisoner, too.

We don't want anyone excused, but neither do we want anyone stupidly disposed of, futilely detained, or prematurely released. We don't want them tortured, either sensationally with hot irons or quietly by long-continued and forced idleness.

In the psychiatrist's mind nothing should be done in the name of punishment, though he is well aware that the offender may regard either the diagnostic procedure or the treatment or the detention incident to the treatment as punitive. But this is in *his* mind, not in the psychiatrist's mind. And in our opinion it should not be in the public's mind, because it is an illusion.

Defining the "Criminal"

It is true that we psychiatrists consider that all people have potentialities for antisocial behavior. The law assumes this, too. Most of the time most people control their criminal impulses. But for various reasons and under all kinds of circumstances some individuals become increasingly disorganized or demoralized, and then they begin to be socially offensive.

The man who does criminal things is less convincingly disorganized than the patient who "looks" sick, because the former more nearly resembles the rest of us, and seems to be indulging in acts that we have struggled with and controlled. So we get hot under the collar about the one and we call him "criminal" whereas we pityingly forgive the other and call him "lunatic."

But a surgeon uses the same principles of surgery whether he is dealing with a "clean" case, say some cosmetic surgery on a face, or a "dirty" case which is foul-smelling and offensive. What we are after is results and the emotions of the operator must be under control. Words like "criminal" and "insane" have no place in the scientific vocabulary any more than pejorative adjectives like "vicious," "psychopathic," "bloodthirsty," etc.

The need is to find all the *descriptive* adjectives that apply to the case, and this is a scientific job—not a popular exercise in name-calling. Nobody's insides are very beautiful; and in the cases that require social control there has been a great wound and some of the insides are showing.

The Judges

Intelligent judges all over the country are increasingly surrendering the onerous responsibility of deciding in advance what a man's conduct will be in prison and how rapidly his wicked impulses will evaporate there.

With more use of the indeterminate sentence and the establishment of scientific diagnostic centers, we shall be in a position to make progress in the science of *treating* antisocial trends. Furthermore, we shall get away from the present legal smog that hangs over the prisons, which lets us detain with heartbreaking futility some prisoners fully rehabilitated while others, whom the prison officials know full well to be dangerous and unemployable, must be released, *against our judgment*, because a judge far away (who has by this time forgotten all about it) said that five years was enough.

In my frequent visits to prisons I am always astonished at how rarely the judges who have prescribed the "treatment" come to see whether or not it is effective. What if doctors who sent their seriously ill patients to hospitals never called to see them!

Diagnostic Centers

As more states adopt diagnostic centers directed toward getting the prisoners *out* of jail and back to work, under modern, well-structured parole systems, the taboo on jail and prison, like that on state hospitals, will begin to diminish. Once it was a lifelong disgrace to have been in either.

Lunatics, as they were cruelly called, were feared and avoided. Today only the ignorant retain this phobia. Cancer was then considered a *shameful* thing to have, and victims of it were afraid to mention it, or have it correctly treated, because they did not want to be disgraced. The time will come when offenders, much as we disapprove of their offenses, will no longer be unemployable untouchables.

Capital Punishment

To a physician discussing the wiser treatment of our fellow men it seems hardly necessary to add that under no circumstances should we kill them. It was never considered right for doctors to kill their patients, no matter how hopeless their condition.

True, some patients in state institutions have undoubtedly been executed without benefit of sentence. They were a nuisance, expensive to keep and dangerous to release. Various people took it upon themselves to put an end to the matter, and I have even heard them boast of it. The Hitler regime had the same philosophy.

But in most civilized countries today we have a higher opinion of the rights of the individual and of the limits to the state's power. We know, too, that for the most part the death penalty is inflicted upon obscure, impoverished, defective, and friendless individuals. We know that it intimidates juries in their efforts to determine guilt without prejudice.

Most of all, we know that no state employees—except perhaps some that ought to be patients themselves— want a job on the killing squad, and few wardens can stomach this piece of medievalism in their own prisons.

Capital punishment is, in my opinion, morally wrong. It has a bad effect on everyone, especially those involved in it. It gives a false sense of security to the public. Worst of all it beclouds the entire issue of motivation in crime, which is so importantly relevant to the question of what to do for, and with the criminal that will be most constructive to society as a whole.

Punishing—and even killing—criminals may yield a kind of grim gratification; let us all admit that there are times when we are so shocked at the depredations of an offender that we persuade ourselves that this is a man the Creator didn't intend to create, and that we had better help correct the mistake. But playing God in this way has no conceivable moral or scientific justification.

Verdict Guilty—Now What?

Let us return, in conclusion, to the initial question: "Verdict guilty—now what?"

My answer is that now we, the designated representatives of the society which has failed to integrate this man, which has failed him in some way, hurt him and been hurt by him, should take over. It is *our* move. And our move must be a constructive one, an intelligent one, a purposeful one—not a primitive, retaliatory, offensive move.

We, the agents of society, must move to end the game of tit-for-tat and blow-for-blow in which the offender has foolishly and futilely engaged himself and us. We are not driven, as he is, to wild and impulsive actions.

With knowledge comes power, and with power there is no need for the frightened vengeance of the old penology. In its place should go quiet, dignified, therapeutic programs for the rehabilitation of the disorganized one, if possible, the protection of society during his treatment period, and his guided return to useful citizenship, as soon as this can be affected.

Chapter 20

FIDELITY INSURANCE

Many stores have developed and established sound systems, policies, and rules for the conduct of a stable business. No concern can run itself without a system or the enforcement thereof, but somehow peculiarly in the retail business, because of its flexibility and movement, it is often believed that systems, policies, and rules operate themselves.

All systems need constructive enforcement to insure observation and execution on the part of store management. For the want of a better term, this ingredient can be called discipline. The apparent failure on the part of store managements to have in existence an agency that can probe, check, correct, prevent, and punish is tantamount to management indifference.

Numerous outside professional investigative agencies, specializing in retail losses, have continually warned that system breakdowns create dishonesty that remains undetected because of management unconcern.

Embezzlement

In these days when space and outer-space conquests by rocket-propelled missiles, underwater navigational records set by atomic-powered submarines, and transatlantic air crossings by jet-engine airliners are competing for headlines with news bulletins from the Near East, Middle East, and Far East, it is no wonder that an ordinary everyday crime such as the embezzlement of a quarter of a million dollars is relegated to the back pages of the daily papers.

A Quarter of a Million Dollar Loss

There was an item on one of the back pages of a large metropolitan newspaper stating that the stockholders of a department store were being notified that the recent purchase of another store was being renegotiated. The original purchase price, for the assets of an out-of-town store, was being reduced by approximately $250,000 because a deficit had been discovered in the assets of the newly acquired branch store.

In a special letter to the stockholders, it was stated that "we have discovered that a defalcation extending over a period of years had occurred at the store." The purchasing stockholders can consider themselves fortunate at least in the fact that the loss was discovered in time to permit the renegotiation of the purchase price so as to cover the deficiency in the net worth of the newly acquired subsidiary. The selling stockholders must reconcile themselves to the fact that they are getting $250,000 less than they expected for the sale of their property.

It should make all of us stop and think a moment about the almost incredible situation in which an apparently well-managed and successful business can be subjected to an embezzlement loss of over $250,000 that has been discovered only because the business is being sold to new owners. This was in the face of and despite the usual internal and independent audits that we must assume had been conducted.

Estimated Losses

The annual loss resulting from crimes perpetrated on businessmen has been variously estimated at from $16 billion to as much as $40 billion. The reason there is such a wide range in these figures is that they are little more than informed guesses.

One magazine stated that "Possibly a million businessmen are victimized by embezzlers every year. Business's annual loss from embezzlement is estimated to run between $16 and $40 billion. Nevertheless, half of all embezzlements go undetected or are charged off to some other cause, and only one out of ten discovered defaulters is ever brought to court."

I could go on and on citing figures and facts, all of which reach the same conclusion—crime is taking an increasing toll on the businessman.

Judging from the various comments in business magazines and trade journals as well as the almost daily back page story of embezzlement and fraud, it is high time we devoted some attention to improving and increasing the protection against such losses.

Aids to Minimizing Dishonesty Losses

Three principal safeguards tend to minimize dishonesty losses. None of them is wholly effective, however, without the others.

- *Internal control* is perhaps the most effective preventive method, but even good internal control will not make it impossible for employees to defraud their employers.
- *Independent audits* discourage fraud and often uncover it; but they do not—as is sometimes mistakenly supposed—guarantee disclosure of all irregularities.
- *Fidelity coverage* is the means of recovering what may be lost in spite of management's best efforts to prevent irregularities.

Fidelity Bond Coverage

Fidelity bond coverage is designed to take care of the requirements of commercial concerns no matter how varied the business activities may be or how large the scope of operations and number of employees. Blanket coverage applies to all officers and employees and offers the best protection for the lowest cost.

Despite the attractiveness of these contracts, from the point of view of coverage and of price, we still find concerns suffering from underinsurance or being without any protection whatsoever. Some of the case histories of embezzlement losses read like fictionalized accounts and demonstrate the accuracy of the statement that truth is often stranger than fiction.

While dishonesty and fire are the two major causes of loss to American business enterprises, employee dishonesty in one respect is to be more dreaded than fire. Fire usually makes its presence known immediately and can often be subdued before much damage is done. Dishonesty, however, frequently is discovered only after a substantial loss already has developed. The dishonest employee has in many cases brought his firm to the brink of insolvency by the time his depredations are discovered.

Who Embezzles?

Having employees who are considered trustworthy provides no immunity against embezzlement. Trusted employees, in fact, are in an excellent position to embezzle precisely because they are trusted.

In a typical fraud case, the trusted employee "borrows" some of the company's money for personal use, telling himself that he will pay it back. As he gets in deeper and deeper, it eventually becomes clear he can never repay it all, so he continues to steal until he is discovered.

The average embezzler is said to be about thirty-six years old, married, with two children, and having served his present employer about five years with apparent honesty and diligence and earning a comfortable living wage. There is nothing about this picture to set the average embezzler apart from the average man or woman. Yet, one or more of the following causes of stealing motivate him: gambling, extravagant living standards, unusual family expenses, undesirable associates, inadequate income, and resentment or revenge.

Internal Control Systems Need Annual Review

Many companies that have been defrauded over a considerable period of time thought they had an adequate system of control. What happened was that the system had broken down at some point because of the difference between theory and practice. The lesson to be learned is that any system of internal control requires periodic checking to make sure that the system is working.

There should be a review of the system at least once a year. If the company has an annual audit by a certified public accountant, a review of the internal control system should be a part of his examination. He will often make suggestions for improvement of internal controls. Such suggestions can be disregarded only at considerable risk to the company.

A Dishonest Parts Clerk

Currency and checks are especially tempting to the dishonest employee if he thinks he can put them to his own use without being caught. For example, a parts clerk for an appliance distributor pocketed much of the cash received from buyers of service parts for more than a year. Although he was required to make out sales slips, he simply destroyed the duplicate copies. No one discovered it because the slips were not numbered.

Another chance to detect theft was missed because this same clerk maintained inventory records. This year-end physical inventory of service parts was taken by all employees but it was the same clerk alone who priced, extended, and summarized the inventories.

The discovery finally occurred when the clerk happened to be at lunch one day and the office manager wanted information about the price and quality of a part. While looking through the inventory records he began to suspect the fraud.

The controls against embezzlement of cash receipts in the foregoing situation were poor and such a loss could occur in any similar situations if:

1. Sales slips are not prenumbered.
2. The same person who handles sales also balances the day's cash against sales slips or cash register tape, without being checked.
3. Daily receipts are not always deposited promptly and intact.
4. Records of cash receipts are not checked against duplicate deposit tickets.
5. Bank statements are reconciled by an employee who has access to cash or to records of cash transactions.

The Lapping Technique

A favorite trick of embezzlers is known as "lapping." One firm lost more than $300,000 through the use of this technique by one employee. Here is how it usually works.

The dishonest employee steals from incoming payments by customers. This results in a shortage in one or more accounts. He later covers this shortage with remittances from other customers. The shortage is always there but not in the same account.

When an audit is made, he may try to hide the shortage by having a check drawn for transfer of funds from one bank to another. He deposits the check on the last day of the year, but he carries it on the books as a credit to the short account. The check doesn't clear until the year's end, of course, and when it does he offsets it by "borrowing" again from a customer's account.

Embezzling in Accounts Receivable

The situations that invite fraud in connection with accounts receivable exist where:

1. The same person opens the mail and posts incoming checks to accounts receivable.

2. Statements of customers' accounts are prepared and mailed without independent checking by the accounts receivable bookkeeper.
3. Customers are not asked to confirm their balances to someone other than the cashier or bookkeeper.
4. Customers' questions about their accounts are handled by the same person who posts accounts receivable.

How a Theft Worked in Accounts Payable

Information that we have collected indicates that outgoing payments are as inviting to an embezzler as incoming payments. There are various ways of concealing the theft.

An interesting case involved a bookkeeper who forged a number of checks to his own order. For each forged check, however, he prepared a check in the same amount to the order of a creditor and presented it, with the creditor's bill, to the signing official. The bill was one that had already been paid, but it was slightly altered so that the signing official did not recognize it and the check was signed.

The bookkeeper kept the signed check, forged an endorsement and appropriate bank stamps to cancel the check with a perforation stamp, and kept it until the bank statement came to him. He then substituted this specially prepared check for the one that he had forged to his own order.

This operation was repeated many times until the bank happened to get one of his forged checks on which the amount in words did not agree with the figures. The bank called the treasurer of the company to ask for the correct amount of the check made out to the bookkeeper. The treasurer was astounded that such a check existed. Thus ended a scheme that should have been stopped before it began.

This type of fraud and others are possible if:

1. Blank checks are not prenumbered and carefully safeguarded.
2. Signed checks are returned for mailing to the person who prepared them.
3. Bills and supporting papers are not cancelled by the signing official to prevent their reuse.
4. Bank statements are received by an employee who also handles cash or checks.

Embezzling in the Purchasing Department

Another type of fraud involves purchase transactions. An accountant of a food processing company embezzled more than $25,000 during a three-year period.

He prepared bills on the printed forms of an imaginary company for nonexistent shipments of glass containers. After forging the initials of the purchasing agent, he presented the bill along with a check to be signed by the treasurer.

The signed check went to the address on the bill, a place where the accountant had arranged to pick up mail. When he received the check he deposited it in a bank account he had established for the imaginary supplier. Later he drew off funds to his personal account.

There are many kinds of fraud in connection with purchases, and you may be inviting loss if you allow any of the following situations to exist:

1. Payments are made without proof that goods have been received.
2. Bills are not compared with requisitions and/or purchase orders.
3. Materials purchased are not reconciled with inventory and materials used in production.

Thefts from Petty Cash

Stealing from petty cash can be made difficult if simple precautions are taken. Frequently there are laxities that make it too easy.

A woman who was in charge of a petty cash account in the western regional office of a metal products concern dipped into the till for $100 at a time merely by the stroke of a pencil. When a salesman gave her a slip made out for $75 to be used for travel or entertainment, she turned it into $175 with a single stroke. She handed the salesman his $75 and put $100 in her purse.

Later she began to insert twos instead of ones, increasing her take to $200 on each slip, but the alteration became more obvious and led to her ultimate exposure. Here are some common practices that make it easy for an employee to steal petty cash:

1. Figures only are used, instead of writing the amount in words as on a check.
2. Slips are written in pencil rather than in ink.
3. Slips are not adequately checked before reimbursement and cancelled to prevent their reuse.

Payroll Thefts

Payroll frauds are another source of loss to management. The paymaster of a large food concern stole more than $200,000 from the payroll in a series of frauds over a period of almost fifteen years before being detected.

Two signatures were required on all paychecks, but one signature was the paymaster's and the other was the controller's signature imprinted from a plate in the custody of the paymaster. His technique was to mark "vacation" falsely on a time card, place the two signatures on a vacation check for the employees, and cash the check by forging the endorsement.

Do any of the following circumstances, all of which facilitate payroll fraud, exist in your company:

1. Persons preparing the payroll also handle cash.
2. Attendance records are not maintained independently of the persons who prepare the payroll.
3. Checks are signed by someone who also has a part in preparing the payroll.
4. Cancelled checks are not carefully examined for comparison of endorsements with signatures in the employment records.

Stealing Merchandise

Although cash and checks are especially tempting, the dishonest employee also covets merchandise that can be turned into cash. Small objects are often carried out on the employee's person but larger thefts may be engaged in a highly organized basis.

An eastern manufacturer found that goods worth approximately $10,000 per month were disappearing from stock. It was discovered that the general plant foreman was the leader of a gang of a dozen employees who carried out some of the items on their persons, slipped others into trucks along with the company's regular shipments, and transported still others in a truck that was brought to the plant at night.

There is serious danger of thefts from inventory if:

1. Physical inventories are not taken periodically and reconciled with perpetual inventory records.
2. The same person who maintains perpetual inventory records also takes the physical inventory.
3. An adequate plant security system is not in effect.
4. Employees are allowed to regard "petty" thievery as a trivial matter.

Thefts of Securities

Embezzlement of securities is another form of fraud that plagues management.

More than $800,000 was stolen by a trusted official through the manipulation of securities in this particular case history. He happened to be a bank official who was also the treasurer of a charity but the same thing can happen when a man is an official of more than one organization.

This bank official knew that the bank had purchased certain bonds. He had the charity buy an identical amount of the same bonds, but the bond numbers he reported to the charity were the numbers on the bank's bonds. He then sold the charity's bonds and kept the proceeds.

When the charity was audited he transferred the bonds from the bank's vault to the charity's vault until after the audit. This continued until he died and was no longer able to carry the bonds back and forth.

Among the situations that may lead to embezzlement of securities are as follows:

1. An individual is able to remove securities from their place of safekeeping without another person being present.
2. Securities are not registered by the company.
3. Records of securities are kept by the same person who has custody of them.

Control Plus Fidelity Bond Coverage

Protection against embezzlement requires a good system of (1) *internal control*, which is supplemented by an (2) *independent audit*, plus (3) fidelity bond coverage. Neither one can take the place of the other.

Controls make fraud difficult but not impossible. Therefore, fidelity bond coverage is needed to provide sufficient protection against frauds that may not be detected in time to prevent a loss.

On the other hand, insurance can never replace adequate control. Without adequate control, losses may be undiscovered until they exceed the amount of insurance. Inadequate control may even make the risk uninsurable.

Here are some of the results of a good system of internal control:

1. Fraud is discouraged because the potential embezzler is aware of the greater odds against indefinitely concealing his acts.

2. Fraud is much more likely to be detected in its early stages.
3. The cost of dishonesty insurance will be kept at a minimum through experience rating and overall low loss level.
4. The data you use in making your business decisions will be more reliable.

The last point should not be forgotten while giving our main attention to embezzlement. Without adequate internal control, vital data can be falsified either in connection with embezzlement or in an effort to make a good showing. For example, costs actually belonging to an operation that is causing losses might improperly be charged against more profitable operations. It is easy to see the danger in making business decisions based on erroneous information.

A good system of control for one business might not be good for another. Size and other factors will determine the system best suited to your business. Many of the controls that can be used to good advantage in a large company are not possible in a smaller enterprise. On the other hand, the proprietor of a small business is able to use certain methods of personal observation and checking that would not be feasible in a large concern.

Here is where you must rely on advice from someone who is thoroughly familiar with internal control and is also well acquainted with your business situation. The logical advisor is the certified public accountant who audits your company's financial statements.

Basic Elements of Internal Control

Here are some of the elements of internal control that your auditor will probably suggest whether your company is large or small:

1. A plan of organization that clearly establishes lines of authority and responsibility. One of the fundamental principles is that accounting functions must be separated as much as possible from operational functions.
2. A chart of accounts for the classification of data in a way that will help to produce consistent and meaningful reports.
3. Records and forms designed to be easily understood and to show clearly whether control procedures have been followed.
4. Sound practices, such as division of duties, so that no one person will handle a transaction from beginning to end.

5. Personnel selection and training that will tend to eliminate applicants of poor character and to encourage faithful observances of established procedures.
6. Supervision and enforcement of the plan.

Finally, it must be realized that your system of internal control can make embezzling difficult but not impossible. Although good control will discourage many potential embezzlers and often expose fraud in its early stages, you are still in danger of loss due to collusion or a steal-and-run type of fraud.

Some people steal. They always have, and they always will. There is no absolute deterrent that operates against the human craving for something for nothing. Therefore, in the final analysis, we must see to it that we have protection against the embezzlement loss that may occur despite our efforts at preventing it.

Types of Insurance Coverage

Today, insureds have available to them through the services of their insurance counselors the broadest forms of protection against crime losses at the lowest rates in the history of the insurance business. These coverages are obtainable in individual policies in selective amounts, in combination policies with coverages selected by the insured, and in blanket policies with various coverages included in one uniform or blanket amount.

Loss of any kind of property, real or personal, caused by dishonesty of employees can be covered by either a commercial blanket bond or a blanket position bond. Both forms automatically cover all of the insured's personnel but the insured is given a choice between these forms because there are certain differences in the amount recoverable in the event of a collusion or conspiracy loss caused by a group of dishonest employees.

Loss of money and securities by dishonesty of persons other than employees; destruction or disappearance and loss of property other than money and securities by safe burglary or robbery, inside the premises; loss of money and securities by dishonesty of persons other than employees; destruction or disappearance and loss of property other than money and securities by robbery, outside the premises, are all covered by a *broad form money and securities policy.*

Loss from forgery of the insured's name as maker or alteration of the amount of checks, drafts, and so on are covered by a *depositors forgery bond.*

Loss of merchandise held for sale, furniture and fixtures, and so on, by burglary or robbery of the insured's private watchman and other related coverages are provided by a *mercantile open stock burglary policy*.

Insurance Can Be Tailored to the Company

One or more of these coverages can be combined under either a *comprehensive dishonesty disappearance and destruction policy*, in which the insured can obtain the equivalent of the separate coverages in selective amounts, or a *blanket crime policy*, which provides a single, blanket amount of coverage for all the exposures enumerated in the policy.

In fact, these coverages can be virtually tailored or custom-made to the insured's specific requirements. Accept the advice of your insurance man regarding the amount and type of coverage your business needs. You must agree that it is better to have the coverage and the protection needed before you suffer a loss than to rectify the inadequacy or absence of coverage after a loss.

More and better internal control and more and better insurance coverage are needed to meet the ever-increasing requirements of business enterprises. Keep this mental picture before you. Values and costs of all commodities and services are rising. Crime losses are rising. Businesses are getting caught in this squeeze. They are not only suffering the loss of their money and property that is not adequately insured, but they are also suffering an additional loss through higher replacement costs, which they must assume when they are not insured.

Loss of Time

Another element should enter into your consideration; that is, the loss of profits suffered in addition to the actual loss of property.

Suppose a business realizes a net profit of 2 percent. If an embezzler in the firm steals only $100, the firm must sell $5,000 in merchandise *without profit* to offset the $100 loss. If he steals $1,000 from his employer, the firm must sell $50,000 in merchandise without profit. The higher the embezzlement figure, the longer the businessman must work without profit to offset the loss.

In some cases embezzlements have been so large that the businessman has been forced into bankruptcy. We should do everything in our power to prevent this by acquiring adequate coverage.

Formula for Fidelity Bonds

At one time it was difficult to determine the amount of fidelity bond coverage needed to adequately protect a firm against embezzlement losses. Today, however, there is a simple formula by which this need can easily be filled.

This formula is the result of a careful study for a number of years of employee dishonesty losses of $10,000 or more as reported to the Surety Association of America. This formula is based on the consideration of two principal elements of a firm's exposure to large embezzlement losses: (1) current assets and (2) gross sales or income. These elements produce a "*dishonesty exposure index*," which in turn indicates, within an average range, a firm's minimum honesty insurance needs.

This formula can be used to implement a program for the development of more adequate fidelity bond coverage. Solicit the advice and counsel of your accountants in the preparation of the data and the application of the formula and call in your insurance counselor. Follow his recommendations in the determination of a proper amount of fidelity bond for your particular needs.

Chapter 21

THE CONCEPT OF PREVENTION

All of us have known the basic value of prevention since our childhood when we chanted, "A stitch in time saves nine!"

The importance of prevention has never been better illustrated than in the area of store shortages. Locking the barn door *after* the shortage exists is a costly business. With the pressures of modern competitive business and retailing's narrowing profit margins caused by increased wages, taxes, and other business costs, the problems of preventing store losses are more acute today than ever before.

Shortage Figures Soared

With the battle cry of "calculated risk," store managements have often reduced procedures and cut controls to the barest minimum. Internal audit and security staffs have sometimes been reduced to a point of ineffectiveness. As inventory shortage figures showed mounting losses, these same management people hid behind the claims of "book error" and "paper losses."

A Changing Philosophy

But today there is a changing philosophy. Many enlightened retail executives recognize the crime problem for what it really is—*a serious threat to store profits.*

The search is on for new and better methods of preventing retail crimes.

Why prevention rather than detection? There are two reasons; prevention is less costly and it is more effective.

Our need today is to find the important and practical retail controls that can prevent theft losses. The present business economy forces us to spend our money and efforts on only those controls that are really effective. We will never stop all theft losses, and therefore our need is to prevent continuing losses and major thefts. Controls should flash warning flags when large-scale losses start to develop. Controls should also create psychological barriers to prevent customer and employee thefts.

Education Is Essential

Many other things are just as important as the store's efforts in preventive procedures and controls. First, there are employee education programs. There is a need to train supervisors so they will set a better leadership example. It is also necessary to have supervisors who will see that store procedures operate in reality as they are intended to operate in theory and who understand how to handle the people who work for them.

Adequate Staffing

It is also important to maintain an adequate and capable security staff.

More care should be taken in selecting new employees. Retailing must do a better job of selling itself to young people in search of a career, and it must find new recruiting sources.

Stores also need sound programs for helping the troubled or maladjusted people in their midst. There are often many signposts indicating future trouble if supervisors are trained to recognize them. But recognizing those who are maladjusted is not enough; they must also be prepared to help such people just as they now help employees who become physically ill.

The Crime Problem

Finally, retailers need to encourage and support independent research programs to get at the basic causes and cures of crime in general.

As retail management knows only too well, the constantly rising national crime statistics are costing stores across the country a larger and larger percentage of their profits every year.

Detection of criminals will always be an important part of any store's operation, but if we in retail management really intend to reduce the amount of annual tribute we pay to crime, we must spend more time and money on *crime prevention.* So far we have made only a token effort in this direction.

As soon as retailers recognize the real theft losses they are suffering, they will apply themselves vigorously to the philosophy of prevention. These areas of prevention provide significant potential for increasing store profits by reducing large-scale theft losses.

To paraphrase the childhood chant, "A dollar spent in time will save nine," multiply this by a thousand or a million and the principle is just as sound today as it has always been.

Summary

1. Failure to have prevention procedures is costly.
2. Philosophy on "calculated risk" should be changed.
3. Detection is more costly and less effective than prevention.
4. Controls should be designed to:
   a. Prevent major thefts
   b. Flash a warning signal
   c. Set up psychological barriers to theft
5. In addition to controls, the following is needed:
   a. Education programs
   b. Better supervisory leadership example
   c. Adequate and capable security staff
   d. Care in selecting new employees
   e. Help for the maladjusted
   f. Research to find causes and cures of crime
6. Detection is always needed but more money and effort are needed for prevention.

Chapter 22

SECURITY EDUCATION: PART I

The other-directed child faces not only the requirement that he make good but also the problem of defining what making good means. He finds that both the definition and the evaluation of himself depend on the company he keeps.

Approval itself, irrespective of content, becomes almost the only unequivocal good in this situation! One makes good when one is approved of. Thus all power is in the hands of the approving group. The child learns that nothing in his character, no possession he owns, no inheritance of name or talent, no work he has done is valued for itself but only for its effect on others.

Parents in the groups depending on other-direction install in their children a psychological radar set—tuned to detect the action, and especially the symbolic action of others. Thereafter, the parents influence the children's character only insofar as (a) their own signals mingle with others over the radar, (b) they can locate their children in a certain social environment in order to alter to a very limited degree what signals they will receive, (c) they take the risks of a very partial and precarious censorship of incoming messages. Thus the parents' role diminishes in importance.

So Says David Riesman in *The Lonely Crowd*

Man in the Gray Flannel Suit

The man wore a gray flannel business suit. The time was two o'clock in the afternoon. Slowly, almost casually, he walked into the camera stockroom. In his hand he carried a large blueprint. The stockroom shelves were crowded with high-priced cameras, projectors, film, and lenses.

Suddenly a pert young salesclerk appeared. She walked up to the man and smiled, "Are we going to get more stock space?"

"Possibly," answered the man.

"Do you work for the store?" she persisted.

"Only indirectly," said the man patiently. "I'm with Burton Brothers, a contracting outfit. We do work for your store."

"I see," replied the salesclerk. She shifted nervously from one foot to the other. "May I see your identification?"

"Sure." The man searched through his pockets. He was no longer smiling. Beads of sweat formed around his eyes. It was plain that the salesclerk's questions were annoying to him. "I must have left my wallet upstairs in my coat," he grumbled.

The salesclerk smiled again, "We can phone the building office and get clearance for you."

"Yes—all right." The man's voice showed he was unhappy. "Where's the phone?" he asked.

"Follow me, it's just outside." Briskly the salesclerk walked out of the stockroom.

The man with the blueprint was right behind her. As they came out of the stockroom door the man suddenly bolted, his blueprint still tightly clutched in his hand as he ran across the selling floor and down the crowded escalator. There were gasps and angry shouts as he roughly shoved customers aside. He made his escape good.

This same man was caught two weeks later. City police picked him up. He was a professional thief who made his living by stealing from stores.

The salesclerk who had smiled and asked questions was now a heroine. She had saved her store hundreds of dollars. The thief admitted that he had big plans that day in the camera stockroom. He had intended to steal several beautiful and expensive miniature cameras.

Why is this story important to all retail management people? Because this man would have stolen several cameras if a pert young salesclerk had not asked him some questions. Why did she ask those questions? Because she had been *trained* to question any stranger who entered her stockroom. She had been trained in a class she attended on security education.

There are many other stores where salespeople are trained to fight crime. How about the people in your store? Are they helping you cut losses? They will—if you train them.

Educational Programs Are Profitable

Security training saves stores thousands of dollars a year. Such programs can have an impact, not only on theft, but also on careless attitudes, system failures, and supervisory neglect. To reduce shortages you have to work at *everything*. Security training programs that hit at the many causes of loss are one of our best weapons. Education *can* cut shortages.

You can *talk* a shortage down. If you get everyone interested in your shortage problems, these problems begin to solve themselves.

Security Education Motivates

Ideas have power. They are one of the great motivating forces. Education, as we are using it here, means motivating people with *ideas*.

Psychologists have found that there are words, pictures, designs, and colors that can act as triggers to the human mind. These devices can influence our attitudes and our actions. We call the techniques used for such motivation *education*.

Security Programs Are Needed Today

Several years ago employee security programs would not have worked. Today they do! Why? What is the difference between then and now?

The answer is not simple. It has to do with a change in human motivation. People have undergone a major psychological change. We can see this change. We can evaluate it and even gain some insight into what caused it. But we don't have all the answers, not yet.

Let's examine a question vital to law enforcement people, but which is even more important to every person in the country. Why has crime increased? Why is it that each year's statistics show more crime?

Statistics show juvenile delinquency has become a major crime problem. It has increased in amount and in destructive violence. Why? What's different about today? What has happened? What has gone wrong?

People act because they are *motivated* to act. The question is—where does the motivating force come from?

From Inner to Outer Direction

Whyte in his book, *The Organization Man*, sums up the problem when he says, "Man today has changed. Where a few years ago he was inner-directed, today he has become an outer-directed person." He says, "We no longer have the built-in 'Protestant ethic'."

He means that "outer-directed" people get their motivation from *outside* themselves. Years ago these orders came from *within*. For example, years ago a man in business who liked polka-dot ties wore them. He made his own decisions, he was *inner-directed*. Today the man in business who likes polka-dot ties looks around him to see what the other men in business are wearing. If they are all wearing striped ties, he, too, wears a striped tie. He is *outer-directed*.

If you are "inner-directed" you decide from within yourself what is right and wrong. Nothing that other people do changes your opinion of what is right or wrong. You know for yourself because you depend on the answers within your own mind. You act on this *inner direction*.

But what about the new era? The new generation? How do they decide what is right and wrong? Many of them seek the guidance from the outer world. They look outside themselves for answers to moral questions. Outer-directed people conform to the beliefs and actions of those around them. It is on the basis of this emulation of others that he makes his decisions.

We see this principle illustrated in the modern juvenile delinquent in his black leather jacket. In the gangs that roam restlessly about large cities we see the results of the new outer direction.

The rules are made by the gang leader. The group follows the "code." The gang creates its own standards. The individual juvenile becomes a caricature of a Mafia boss. The juvenile delinquent lives in a weird world of jungle laws. Moral standards of the past are meaningless. There is no inner direction to turn to for answers to right and wrong. Actions of these youths are determined by the leaders' decisions.

Troubled parents feel insecure. Why do children act as they do? Why do they run wild? Will their child become a victim? Will he be a member of the leather jacket, roaring muffler set? What gets into them? Perhaps the parents of these young men have betrayed their trust, have failed in their responsibility toward their son or daughter, have deprived them of a part of their natural birthright—a moral code—have failed to give them the love, understanding, and moral values so much needed in the development and nourishment of a healthy conscience.

Conformity Is Part of the Crime Problem

The sign of outer direction is conformity. The inner-directed person has a moral gyroscope built inside himself. It keeps him on a set moral path. In the new age of the outer-directed man, there is no gyroscope—no inner stability. There is only one basic rule of behavior and that is that you must conform. Lindner in his book on juvenile delinquency, *Must You Conform*?, points out that juvenile delinquency is a pathological disease today. He notes further that it is contagious. It is passed on from the unclean to infect the clean.

A child who unfortunately gets into a delinquent gang becomes a delinquent because he has learned to conform with outside leadership. He has no built-in moral gyroscope for inner guidance.

As you think about this, you will see the direct relationship between outer direction and the national picture of a steadily increasing crime rate. Some men will do a good job of rationalizing the values in modern conformity. They will tell you that this conformity is an indication of a new flexibility, an ability to adapt to life. They will say that a man who conforms shows his ability to be a team worker. There may be some truth in such statements. But also there is no denying that a person who is outer-directed has behavior patterns that are set by those outside of himself.

This change in the country's psychology explains why security educational programs work today. It is because man today is more susceptible to *outside* influences. He can be influenced by training as never before. We can shape his attitudes and beliefs without him being aware of it. He is willing and waiting for us to motivate him. He wants to know what is expected of him. In fact, he wants to conform.

Today educational programs can be important. They are effective. Also important are the leadership roles of supervisors. How they act will determine the patterns of behavior of those who work for them. Theirs is a serious responsibility. Leaders must set an example of honesty for their people.

Supervisor Sets Standards

Study an individual supervisor and you will know the attitudes of his people because people emulate their leader.

Conformity increases the problems of criminal contamination. One dishonest employee infests another employee. Soon, you have several dishonest employees. The disease spreads!

Security educational programs are the answer to furnishing constructive guidance to people in all areas of your store. Such programs are not only a deterrent to crime, but also are a management responsibility.

We have a duty to set up moral standards for our people. If they must conform, let them conform with honesty and integrity.

The individual's inner moral gyroscope no longer operates to protect a store's merchandise and money from theft. We must face this shocking fact. We must assume that there is less individual morality than we have known in the past. Today individual standards are often the result of group conformity. With security educational programs we can prevent losses through constructive motivation of outer-directed people.

Train to Shape Behavior

Master the tools of education and you can shape people's attitudes. For instance, you can get salespeople to act as detectives. This greatly increases the size of your security staff.

One security director has said, "Eighty percent of all shoplifter cases should originate with your salespeople." A good training program can make these words a reality.

Trained people also eliminate false arrests. Your employment office can be trained to use care in selecting new employees. You can improve supervisors' controls. You can tighten store control procedures. With soundly designed security training programs you can stir people throughout your store to security actions.

Mental images can also be used to set up *invisible barriers* to theft. This new field of security education can be one of the most important things a store can do to increase its profits.

Whom Do You Train?

When you talk about such programs do you think of them only in terms of salespeople? True, security programs have been used to train salespeople to watch for shoplifters, but aren't there other ways you can use security training programs? Here is a partial list of groups who can be motivated by a security program:

1. New employees
2. Store supervisors
3. Top management executives
4. Employment department personnel
5. Merchandising executives
6. Departments with high losses
7. General public

Let's look at one or two of these groups and see how we can motivate them to help reduce store losses.

New Employees

When a new person comes into your store, this person usually gets training in things like writing saleschecks and store rules. Wouldn't it also be wise to have a session on retail security problems? It can do two things: encourage the new person to help the store cut losses and build "conditioned responses" to keep this new employee honest.

Let's look at such a session. First, you might sketch a picture of the store security department. You can tell about how your detectives are trained. Tell stories showing their effectiveness in catching thieves. You want the new person to be aware of the fact that your store is alert to theft problems. Emphasize that you have well-trained security people.

Use Words to Paint Pictures

Does your store have scientific detection equipment? Then discuss and show this equipment to the new person. Make it clear that dishonesty will be found out, that punishment will be quick and severe. Tell in strong word pictures what the penalties of crime are.

Use actual cases. Back up descriptive words with pictures or slides showing recovered goods. Get the message across sharply and clearly.

Tell about the salesclerk you caught in jewelry—how she was caught stealing and was prosecuted. Show blowups of another employee who received unfavorable newspaper publicity. Let the new person see these things.

Tell about the dishonest carpenter you caught stealing. He was thirty-six years old. Point out that he has not been able to get a job for two years now as a result of his arrest. Paint a picture of the social disgrace that comes to a person when he is caught. When a thief is discovered this brings sorrow to loved ones.

Don't miss any of the picture—don't soften it and don't compromise it. During these few minutes of training the new person's future life is in your hands. He came into your store free of guilt. You are going to put him in a virtual Garden of Eden surrounded with desirable, wonderful things. He will also handle money. Lots of money, several hundred dollars every day. Now and only now do you have the chance to save him from himself. You want to prevent this person from facing future disgrace. You want him to avoid future unhappiness; now is your chance—you can build into his mind, strong invisible barriers to theft. So do not spare him. Cut him, scar him, frighten him, make the images burn so deep that they will not be easily erased.

Talk about your store's award system. After explaining how awards are earned, be sure to warn about the dangers of false arrest. See that the new person gets the security department's telephone number and instructions about what to do in case he needs help.

Tell the new salesclerk that any customer he waits on may be an honesty shopper. Explain how the employee package system works. Review store rules that tie in with security. Finally, try to get the new employee's help in reducing store losses by following these procedures:

1. Keeping fitting rooms clear of merchandise at all times.
2. Limiting the number of garments a customer can take into a fitting room (usually no more than three articles).
3. Describing the types of people who should get special sales attention.
4. Showing that no one is supposed to take merchandise out of the department without a loan slip.
5. Using care in displaying expensive goods.
6. Telling the salesperson to avoid carelessness of all types (carelessness leads to loss).

Here are the goals for a security training program directed at new employees:

1. Set up psychological barriers to theft. Use words to build walls in the employee's mind with pictures that will not be easily forgotten.
2. Give the new employee an understanding of how the security department operates. Don't forget to tell about your scientific detection devices.
3. Explain how stores need to fight losses. Tell how losses affect profits and how profits affect employee security.
4. Motivate the employees to help in reducing losses.
5. Go over your store's award system (include warnings against false arrest).
6. Explain about honesty shoppers. Point out that salespeople will be shopped regularly.
7. If the clerk needs a floor detective in a hurry, tell him how to get one.
8. Review any store rules related to security. Include an explanation of your employee package system.

Security for Supervisors

When you devise a program for supervisors, of course, you have different goals from those for training new employees. In this program your main theme is supervisory responsibility. As part of his job, the supervisor is expected to detect and prevent dishonesty. Focus should be put on the dishonest employee problem.

Go into candid details on internal theft problems with this group. Specific dishonest employee cases should be reviewed to show how they could have been prevented. Use photographs of the stolen goods to show how much damage is done by dishonest employees.

Find out how well the supervisor understands systems and controls. Are these controls effective in preventing employee dishonesty? Show how, in the past, supervisory failure resulted in dishonesty. Let him know that he *is* his brother's keeper. As a supervisor he is responsible for his people. Talk about his moral obligations. Tell him not to place anyone in a position of undue temptation to steal.

As a supervisor he is interested in people. What about the maladjusted employee. Of course he wants to know about such problems. Educate him. Explain the part that personal maladjustment can play in crime. Show him how psychological pressures and frustration can cause people to steal. Tell about cases in which personality maladjustments led to theft.

Tell him how he can detect these types of personnel problems. Particularly those that lead to crime.

Next, discuss with him another important part of his job. That of his leadership role. Tell him the example that he must set for his people. Remind him that today, more than ever before, people emulate their superiors. He must always keep himself above reproach. This includes not only personal honesty, but also means operating store systems without fear or favor. In his supervisory role he cannot cut corners or short-circuit store controls. He must be firm but kindly.

People will like and respect him for his integrity. They will take advantage of his leadership weaknesses, but they will not like him for being weak. No one wins popularity by being a lax supervisor.

Last, but also important, inform him how errors and carelessness lead to loss. Back this up with examples of actual errors. Use real saleschecks, marking tickets, transfers, or similar records to show how errors occur. You may find that "error control" is so important to your store that you will want to run a separate class on it.

Here, in a nutshell, are the objectives for a supervisor's training program:

1. Show how losses affect profits.
2. Hold candid discussions on the problem of employee dishonesty.
3. Complete his job description. "He is to prevent employee dishonesty."
4. Point out that he is keeper of store's systems and controls. They must be operated effectively. He is to administer them without fear or favor.
5. Give him a glimpse of the psychiatrist's couch. Reveal some things about the neurotic causes of theft. Show how mental psychological pressures can lead to theft.
6. Burn into his mind that he has a moral duty never to place people in a position of undue temptation to steal.
7. Point out that he has a duty to set a good leadership example for his people.
8. Show how carelessness and error cause shortages.

Tie all of this up in a package for him. The supervisor has a responsibility toward the security of his store, his department, and his people.

Top Management Executives

When you want to motivate top management people, your approach has to be more casual. Your goal in this case may be to gain support for your security department, or you may wish to set up stronger store policies.

Perhaps your budget for security is very slim and you want additional funds. Or you may want to expand the security department personnel or buy new equipment. All of these problems can become sticky. An educational program may be the solution, however.

Reports and memos should play an important part in your program for top executives. Your security department's monthly, semiannual, and annual reports can be helpful. They set up a statistical foundation that gives management the broad picture of the security operation. Put a covering memo of analysis on these routine reports. Interpret the figures; these men are too busy to read between the lines, so explain what these figures mean. Show crime trends. Point out your security needs. Now and then one of your memos will hit an open nerve, and you will get action.

How about your personal contacts with management? Did you make a point to tell Mr. Big about the case that involved large-scale thefts? Unusual cases, if reported in newspaper style and backed up with photographs of the stolen goods, can be extremely effective in the offices of higher management.

Does your store require a major policy change in order to improve security? Tie the suggested change to a recent case. Let the case illustrate dramatically the need for this particular policy change.

One story of an important case is worth a thousand opinions. Make your story exciting. Every executive likes Ellery Queen stories. Make it a whodunit that the top executive can tell to his corporation friends over a dry martini at the club. Let him thrill his wife and kiddies with it at his supper table.

Top management people live in a world of sledgehammer pressures. They have problems. Before you sell them an idea you'll need a loud gong to gain their attention. An important case is a loud gong. Especially if it points out a need. Dramatize your store's security needs!

Want to try another approach with top management? This one is good only once a year, however. Arrange a special meeting for a group of executives. Show slides or movies illustrating recent cases of interest at this meeting. Make your attention-getting techniques bright and make your story believable. Make sure that these cases relate to the company's security requirements.

Perhaps the store needs better security policies or tighter system controls. This special meeting can be a good time for getting the executives to consider such problems.

But in preparing this program for top management make sure that your goals are important to the store. Stay away from trivial problems. Ask yourself if the problem could be solved at a lower level of management? If so, don't present it.

Top executives are concerned with future plans, figures, and major problems—they are facing daily challenges. They have time only for important matters. They must look at proposals on a broad scale.

Although it helps to present your ideas with showmanship, they must stand on their own. In the end you must convince top management on the basis of your plan's merit. Top men tend to require more proof of need than do executives at a lower level. Once they are convinced that your suggestions are sound, however, action is swift, decisive, and effective!

Employment Department Personnel

You can direct a security training program for any department in the store. In one case you may use it for a high-shortage department to arouse interest in reducing losses. In another case you may be concerned with a department where numerous employee cases have recently occurred. You want to prevent more thefts. A program may be originated for any number of logical reasons. There are too many types of programs to list them all here. But let us look at one example of a program for store employment people. You can use it as a model.

Personnel department cooperation is important to security. At what point do all dishonest employees come into the store? They first pass through the employment interview. Before any employee can steal from your company he or she must be *hired*. This is why the employment interview is important. The employment office is the narrow corridor of entrance into your store. It is the one place where you have a chance for control. If the interviewers use care in screening new people, your store will benefit. They can save the firm thousands of dollars every year. How can you make this form of control more effective? The answer is to use educational programs to encourage security help from employment personnel.

How about a series of meetings sponsored by security with employment people? Review the store's dishonest employee problems. Use these meetings to examine the effect of losses on your store. Show how employee dishonesty reflects on the employment office in their selection of new people. Show how they can help to cut such losses. Be specific.

Show how the interviewer's ability at selecting employees decides the moral fibre of your store. Let them know an interviewer can weed out the dishonest person at the point of employment.

Use real employee cases to illustrate the problem. Show how these dishonest employees might have been spotted at the time they were hired.

In layman's language discuss the relationship between an abnormally psychotic person and crime. Get them to participate in the discussion. What test questions could be used to help the employment interviewer? Invite a psychiatrist to work with the interviewers and teach them what questions to ask and what the different responses mean.

Talk to the employment personnel about the delinquency test developed by Dr. Harrison Gough of the University of California. Explain how this test can locate the abnormally psychotic person. Show how he uses questions to reveal a person's attitude toward fear. Note that the abnormally psychotic person has little of the normal person's fears.

Furthermore, tell the employment personnel that if they can stop these abnormally psychotic people from getting into the store they will stop 25 percent of the store's dishonesty problems.

Whenever an employee is caught stealing, review the problem with the employment office. Try to talk to the person who interviewed the employee at the time he or she was hired. Your purpose is to find out how thieves can be prevented from getting into the store. With mutual discussion you can often find ways to spot these dishonest people.

Be fair and objective. Don't put the employment people in a position of unreasonable responsibility. They are human too. They cannot be held accountable for *all* bad employees. You want them only to be alert to the problem. Try to win them as your allies in your fight against crime. They are also interested in the welfare of the store. If you succeed in getting them interested in the problem, they will make a real effort to help you.

After Christmas Critique

Don't forget to hold a critique after the Christmas season. Go over the employees caught by security during the holidays. Temporary help accounts for 75 percent of a store's annual dishonest employee problem. The "after Christmas rehash" is held to answer the question—how could we have spotted this thief at the time of employment?

Merchandising Executives

An entirely different approach has to be used in designing a program for merchandise executives. Of course you want to arouse interest in security problems. But you also need to tell merchandise people how they can help improve store security. These executives are concerned with inventory shortages, stock controls, receiving, markdowns, ticketing, and similar things. This is your cue to the content of the training. Explore these areas from a security viewpoint.

Be strict with merchandise people for failing to take all their markdowns (a major cause of high shortage figures).

Every inventory shortage report is subject to questioning whether the loss is real or whether the buyer failed to record the markdowns. Direct buyers to keep accurate records. Go to work on psychological barriers to stop the buyer who is tempted to finagle.

Many buyers are in charge of a selling department. They act in the same capacity as a storeowner. With this power of control goes responsibility. One major responsibility is good inventory figures. Let the buyer know that top management is looking over his shoulder. If he has high losses, management will look to him to correct the situation.

Merchandising people are creative. They respond well to presentations about security. They also have a hard-headed desire to make profits. Shortages are a threat to profits and are a good line of attack when talking about security. Point out that losses drain a buyer's profits. Merchandisers listen intently when anyone tells them how to make more profit. Good security can increase a buyer's profits!

Don't make the buyer do the work of cutting losses himself. As an administrator, it is his job to delegate the work to the people in his department. The buyer has the responsibility for planning and control. He must see to it that the other people in his selling department carry out their duties in such a way that his department operates with good controls and accurate records. Hit hard at the cost of carelessness and error. Challenge the merchandiser to prove he can be a top-notch professional operator.

Buyers need to be reminded that they are part of a team, including members from the control division and the operating division. Tell them that they should conform to operating and control division policies. Retailing today is a job requiring *teamwork*. With their creative minds plus teamwork they can do a real job in cutting store losses.

High-Shortage Departments

Inventory shortages often get out of hand in some departments. The shortage controller and security department usually move into the high-loss area. Together they take steps to try to correct the situation. Part of this combined effort requires a security educational program.

One objective here is to get salespeople interested in spotting shoplifters. Talk to them about the store's award program. (Talk about protecting store merchandise but *don't* show them *how* shoplifters steal.) Get the selling personnel thinking about how to prevent and detect criminal activity.

Pamphlets and poster campaigns are a good follow-up for security meetings. Another good way to stimulate interest is to show what a thief stole in the department yesterday. When you arrest a shoplifter who has merchandise stolen from this high-shortage department hold a meeting. Show the salespeople the stolen goods. Let them see and touch the merchandise. Keep reminding these potential detectives to be alert for suspects. Could yesterday's theft have been prevented? If so, bring this out as part of your talk.

When an alert salesclerk finds a shoplifter, give her an award. Make this award presentation part of a departmental meeting. This gives the salesclerk a moment of glory. It also encourages other salespeople to try to show that they, too, can spot a thief.

A security program for a high-shortage department has other benefits. From group discussions you can pick up some good ideas about how to cut losses. These people who work in the area every day can often make excellent suggestions about how the store can prevent losses. They know many answers that are worth money to the store. But to get these suggestions you have to ask for them.

Motivational Research

Security educational programs of the future can use powerful new motivating factors. These are appeals that have not been used up to the present time. Where will we find these new appeals?

There is one very promising area of study, which if developed, could make security educational programs the most important element in crime prevention. This is true, not only for the retail store, but also for all of the community. The work that shows such promise is being done by people in *motivational research.*

Enlightened retail executives and far-seeing public officials should enlist the services of motivational research experts. These experts now apply their motivational studies to the problems of advertising. The same methods being used today to motivate people to purchase goods can be used to prevent crime!

Need for Study

Who are these motivational experts? What have they discovered? These are people who believed that advertising was not using effective motivational appeals. They decided to apply scientific methods to the problems of motivation in advertising.

They use techniques and theories culled from the various humanistic sciences. Their areas of study include sociology, social anthropology, social psychology, psychology, psychoanalysis, and psychiatry. They have discovered that the impulses that motivate people are hidden below the level of their conscious mind.

It has become increasingly apparent that some of the present methods of motivating people are totally ineffective.

Need to Relate to Reality

In the old days, the Greeks, in spite of their intellectual development, never worked out any real systems of science. They had one basic weakness in that they built elaborate systems of reasoning on a single key idea. This key idea came from logic or from common sense. Unfortunately, like the child's game of building a structure of matches, if the key idea were wrong, the whole structure would collapse. The early Greek intellectuals never bothered to find out if their key ideas were basically true in real life. We have a similar problem today. For example, people who believe that, because they use logic or common sense, the solution to crime is to put people in jail and that this belief is based on reality. The truth is we are quickly running out of prison space while the crime rates are continuing to soar upward.

Many people today still believe that you can motivate people by using logic and common sense. They fail to understand what motivates people. Even worse than this is their lack of curiosity about people. While engineers and scientists are doing outstanding research in the world of physics, we have done little to probe how the human mind operates. We think we already understand the human mind. We don't feel we need any further research. The truth is that today, more than ever before, we need to study motivation and communication. We need to study it as a science. Once we find the powerful motivating forces that cause people to act as they do, then we will have an effective way to fight crime.

Logic and Language Do Not Motivate

If we believe that we can sell people on an idea by telling them about its *logical* benefits, we need to remind ourselves that Coca-Cola has made a point in all of its years of advertising never to use a single benefit claim. They never give you a *logical* reason why you should buy Coca-Cola. Yet Coca-Cola has succeeded in motivating people all over the world. The advertising suggests that coke is desirable because it is "delicious" and "refreshing," though the advertising seldom says this in words. This communication is made on a level other than logic.

Words can never communicate anything unless they create images in our minds. People think in images. Words are meaningless abstractions unless they are translated into images. Coca-Cola advertising builds "fun" images in the mind.

Stress Emotional Appeals

In trying to motivate people, we have to change our basic thinking about persuasion. We have to recognize that logic and rational appeals are often not as effective as emotional appeals. Emotional appeals have impact.

We will win few arguments with logic. The people who believe that "if logic is on your side the case is won" are not dealing with reality. For many years people have worshipped at the altar of "logic." Today, however, people have begun to see that it is feelings that shape human judgments, for feelings form beliefs and behavior. People are not governed by reason or intellect alone.

To verify this all we have to do is reconstruct an hour of our own lives. We can ask ourselves why we acted irrationally. Our behavior is often influenced by habit and emotions. We often act because of prejudices. Often there is little mental thought in our behavior. Our emotions and feelings play a vital role.

To design a security educational program that will be effective, we have to see people as they truly are. We have to think in terms of emotional appeals. Appeals that will influence people.

The New Science

Motivational research is a new tool just now coming into its own. It is available for help in ferreting out mankind's powerful unconscious motivating drives.

Through various forms of mass communication, we have a new potential to change people. We can reach them at far deeper levels of the mind than that of rational understanding. We need to use suggestion, association, even fantasy, and many other methods.

In the real world virtually every problem is a blend of realism and fantasy. Sometimes one dominates and at other times the other, but both are almost always present.

Importance of Symbols

Every one of the five senses has an aesthetic capacity as well as a survival value. The sensations that we experience can affect attitudes and actions. Because the senses can be influenced, we can influence attitudes and actions.

The word *imagination* means, "the art of creating images in the human mind." When you stimulate imagination you have impact on the minds and actions of others.

The mind works with pictures and symbols. We grasp ideas only by cloaking them in symbols. Obviously, the mind does not operate with concrete realities; it doesn't need them. The image of a concept is sufficient. The mind thinks in pictures. It thinks in symbols. Because this is true, there are many ways of communicating. There are different systems of symbols peculiar to various communications needs.

The artist who paints uses one type of symbol, whereas the person who writes uses words as his symbol. When we apply motivational psychology, we plant preferences that will operate before reasoning takes place. Much of the material goes directly into the subconscious mind, which later programs actions at the conscious level.

There are not always words that can describe the meaning in symbols. Because we cannot define them does not mean that they are not powerful. No one can define electricity with any adequacy, but that doesn't prevent us from using it and recognizing its power. The same is true of television and many other things that we accept without understanding. If we use words for our security educational program, the arrangement of the words should create pictures in the minds of the listeners. Speaking and writing must generate far more powerful meanings between the lines than those that are perceivable in the words themselves. There must be a motivating thought behind the words used.

Appeal to Intuitive Judgment

It is in the abstract motivational appeals that motivation researchers deal. They are trying to reach the "inner ear" of the mind, the area of intuitive judgment. This is where real persuasion and conviction usually occur. To do this they seek to achieve meanings that exist entirely apart from the words used. Such meanings are often more significant than the literal language meaning. They are usually emotional.

Feedback

In order to find the materials necessary for motivational psychology, there must be feedback from an audience. We can't rely on our personal judgments to find the effective appeals. Each of us is a human being surrounded by our own individuality. Within this prison cell of our own subjective viewpoint, none of us can see the world as another person sees it. We may think we can but we would be wrong to feel that other people have the same motives we do. No one looks at the world the same way. Deciding what motivates us will *not* solve the problem of motivating others.

Group Influences

Each of us has a separate inner world of personal experiences and feelings. There is a constant interplay between our conscious and unconscious mind. And when it comes to decisions we are often influenced by our unconscious mind. We are also affected by the attitudes of our "group." We usually try to conform to the code of the group because we want to be accepted by others.

Social scientists believe that human behavior is the result of personal experiences. But these decisions to act in one way and not in another are arrived at in an essentially nonrational manner. Americans have been taught that logic, reason, and common sense are the "right" way of life. Because of this, many Americans are completely unaware of the real motivational systems that steer their actions and form their preferences. It never occurs to the average person that his personality is often controlled without his realizing it.

Hidden Reasons for Action

How can we find ways of gaining insight into people? How can our common-sense judgments be verified? How can we find out if emotional appeals are really effective?

Psychology as a science exists on two levels, observation of conduct and studying the unconscious. The second level is, of course, the most important because most motives come from the unconscious.

The unconscious mind is where we have our memory, our intuitive judgment, and our personality structure. It is the part influenced by suggestion and imagination.

A person reveals himself not so much by the things he says about himself as by the kind of questions he asks, the things he daydreams about, the goals he hopes to attain, and the role in which he pictures himself.

To find out about people we have to get a glimpse into this private inner world of thought and fantasies. We have to know what wishes are hidden behind the facade of the outer person. We are, of course, interested in the forces that apply to broad groups and to types of people, not just to an individual. People spend over half their time in a private mental world inside themselves. It is this world that contains the secrets for changing character.

Investigation Techniques

Motivational researchers use a number of techniques in trying to understand these hidden areas of the mind. These areas of the personality cannot be articulated and will not respond to direct questions. "Depth interviews" are one approach. These are free-wheeling conversations. They are pointed in the general direction of the problem under study and its various elements.

The idea here is to learn what is on a person's mind, to find out what feelings revolve around a specific question. Do any unguarded comments in the conversation contradict expressed attitudes? Rarely does the researcher take a person's first statements at face value. It is the unsaid things that are the most significant.

Another tool is the "projective test." There are many variations on this type of test. All of them are based on the principle of giving a person an unfinished situation that he is asked to complete. In completing it he unconsciously reveals the way he looks at the world. In other words, he projects his inner attitudes and feelings onto the story he tells.

Some of these projected tests are relatively easy to interpret. Others require extreme skill on the part of the person interpreting the results. One type of projective test is to have the person tell a story around a picture, with the picture being directly related to the problem at hand. Another variation of this method is to get people to fill in cartoon "balloons" in order to dig out seldom-expressed attitudes.

All of these approaches are relatively crude instruments. Yet they are illuminating. They push past the barriers of inarticulation and stereotyped responses. Motivation researchers are breaking gound in new frontiers. They are supplying broad directions for establishing a new framework for human understanding.

The advertising field was first to take advantage of the new science of motivational research. Isn't it a sensible next step to apply this new tool to the problems of crime?

Retailers are the logical group to tap the resources of the motivational research experts. They need to hire these experts to study motivational appeals that can prevent crime. In doing this they can contribute to research that has an important value for the community as well as the nation. From a purely selfish standpoint, such research can be a direct approach to cutting the heavy theft losses in retailing.

Advertisers have found out that motivational reseachers can show them powerful ways of persuading customers to buy goods. Retailers can take the next step and use motivational research experts to reduce store losses.

Some Final Warnings

There are hidden dangers in security educational programs. You want to *prevent* thefts. But can a security training program also create thieves? This is a danger that we have to face.

Have you ever walked into a store where there was a sign on display saying, "Shoplifters will be prosecuted?" What was your reaction? You probably hadn't been thinking about shoplifting at all until you read that sign. Now you look around the store. You start to ask yourself, "I wonder how difficult it *would* be to steal here." The germ of an idea has been planted in your mind. Probably *you* won't steal as a result of the thoughts the sign has brought to mind, but is this true of everyone? Could such a sign cause a person to think about stealing? Could such thoughts lead to theft?

A few years ago a movie called, "I Was a Shoplifter," played in New York City. The stores picked up numerous shoplifters in the weeks following the film's release who claimed they had never stolen before. All of them said they got the idea of shoplifting from the movie. It looked so easy that they tried it.

A magazine article showing how shoplifters conceal merchandise was published in a national magazine. As soon as the magazine was on the newstands, stores all over the country reported an increase in shoplifting cases. Many of the people who were caught stealing said they got the idea of taking things after reading the magazine article. Were thieves created by this movie or by this magazine article? Or was this only a lame excuse for a group of petty thieves who had actually been shoplifting from the stores long before the movie came out or the magazine was published?

One security manager wanted to know the answer. He gave lie detector tests to a group of shoplifters who claimed that they had been influenced by the film or the magazine article. What was the result of the tests? In every instance it was proven the person was telling the truth!

This danger is real. If we are aware of the problems, however, we can offset them. There are two things we can do when planning an educational program:

1. Try to avoid as much as possible pictures, demonstrations, or descriptions of *how* people steal.
2. If the methods of theft have to be used in the program, counteract the risk involved. Do this by combining strong deterrents to theft. Balance the program with dramatic evidence showing the penalties of theft.

By avoiding the problem or by counteracting the dangerous material with deterrent factors, we can avoid the dangers inherent in security programs.

Chapter 23

SECURITY EDUCATION: PART II

In order to institute an educational program we should first be good salesmen. It is imperative that we sell our security ideas not only to management but also to the entire store personnel. It is our responsibility to present educational programs in such an interesting manner that it will help to sharpen our employees' awareness of the shoplifting problems confronting our stores. It will also serve as a means to deter theft from within.

We are now ready to plan a security education program. Where should we start? What elements do we need?

In outlining a security education program there are five things to be considered:

1. *The Group*. For what group is your program planned? There are many groups where you can use a security education program. How do you decide which are the most logical groups with which to start?
2. *The Objectives*. After you decide on a group, you must decide what the goals of your program should be in relation to the group.
3. *The Media*. Next comes the decision on how to communicate your program. What method of presentation will be most effective for this particular group and the particular objectives you have in mind?
4. *The Motivation*. Your ability to pick good motivational elements will be the key to the success of your enterprise. Consideration must be given, therefore, to the motivational devices you intend to incorporate into your program.

5. *The Presentation*. Finally, you need a formula for your presentation, a proven pattern of presentation that fits the media you have chosen. This item will be discussed in detail in the following chapter.

(1) WHICH GROUP FIRST?

Before deciding which group you wish to direct your program, you must ask yourself what are the primary security problems at your store. A paper and pencil analysis will give you several leads as to what groups need security programs.

In selecting the first group to receive attention, you need to ask yourself what group can you most effectively influence. This may be determined by reviewing such things as the number of people involved in the group, the attitude of the people to be influenced, the communications media at your disposal, and so on. Your final decision will be a judgment based on a study of your store's needs, management policies, and similar considerations.

Plan for Other Groups to Follow

After deciding on the group your first security education program will service, it is also worthwhile to evaluate the other groups that you believe could be important in reducing losses in your store. You should rank these groups in the order of their greatest potentiality, which will give you a final listing of groups to which direct security programs in the order of effectiveness.

By starting with the most likely group, it will be easier to build the programs that follow. You will also receive better support from management by showing good judgment in your starting point. In the final plan you should include some type of security education training for all employees.

Plan for Year-Round Programs

Programs should not be limited to certain periods of the year. They should be used during the slow summer months as well as the months following the release of inventory figures. To be really valuable, security education programs should be used as a year-round psychological tool for the reduction of store losses.

Groups to Consider

In an earlier chapter we mentioned a few possible groups at which employee programs could be directed. Let's enlarge this group now, so that you can see how programs could be directed at many different types of store personnel:

1. New employees
2. Store supervisors
3. Selling personnel
4. Top management executives
5. Merchandise executives
6. High-shortage departments
7. Special departments
   a. Personnel department
   b. Charge office
   c. Bureau of adjustment
   d. Stock help
   e. Warehouse people
   f. Porters and maids
   g. Night employees
   h. Receiving and marking personnel
   i. Maintenance personnel
   j. Store's hospital staff
   k. Elevator operators
   l. Dock workers
   m. Delivery men
   n. Salespeople
   o. Cashiers
   p. Packers
   q. Display people
   r. Advertising personnel
8. Judges, prosecutors, or other law enforcement people
9. General public

Having once decided on the possible groups for your security educational program, let's now look at your objectives.

(2) WHAT OBJECTIVES?

Most security education programs directed at store personnel at any level should include eight basic goals. Special programs directed at outside groups, such as judges, prosecutors, or law enforcement people, and programs directed at the general public might have objectives of a different type. The objectives for these special groups will have to be determined by the individual store.

The Eight Basic Objectives

For most store people, however, the following eight objectives would normally be included:

1. Building psychological barriers in the mind of each individual to prevent theft.
2. Suggesting ways that each person in the group can help the store cut losses.
3. Gaining the interest and cooperation of the individual in detecting and reporting suspects to store security.
4. Showing the importance of errors and carelessness in causing loss.
5. Seeking ideas from the individual about how the store could reduce its losses.
6. Tightening store systems and controls.
    a. For supervisors this means better enforcement of store rules.
    b. For general personnel this means motivating them to follow store systems.
7. Informing the individual about the store's security department and its operation.
8. Educating store people about the effect of losses on the store profits, which should be the objective of the entire program.

Additional "Group" Objectives

In addition to the eight basic objectives of most security education programs, individual groups will have other elements of store security that can be added.

Following are some of the individual departments in which security education programs can have additional value. (The list of additional elements is, of course, only a starting point and is intended to suggest other possibilities.) Each store will have its own type of problems in any given area, and the following notes are intended only to suggest how you can include some of these things in your security training.

Personnel Department

Employment personnel can be alerted to the need for care in selecting new employees. They can be made aware of the importance of their job in preventing interior theft by eliminating the potentially dishonest employee at the point of employment.

Charge Office

The charge office personnel often interview customers whose accounts have been imposted. Such interviews, if carefully conducted, can be most useful to the security department investigation. A training program to instruct interviewers about what type of questions should be used and what leads can be developed will be worthwhile. In addition, special report forms can be provided for their use.

In the charge office the people who work directly with charge accounts should be trained to watch for credit balances on accounts. They can be instructed to use care when reporting on accounts so that they are sure that the facts they quote to security are accurate.

If you have people in this group who check charge account authorizations, they can be encouraged to be alert when checking on calls that are made to them about imposted charge accounts. Careful checks of authorization can result in the apprehension of fraud purchasers.

Charge account personnel should be instructed to use care in controlling charge plates, not only the new plates going out to customers but also the plates being turned in when people are closing their accounts. Some stores have had heavy impostor losses because these plates were not well controlled and fell into the hands of dishonest employees.

The charge office should also conduct its own educational program by issuing lists of names and addresses of accounts being used by impostors to salespeople.

Bureau of Adjustment

This area is particularly vulnerable to theft. Supervisors must be alert to watch out for adjustment credits that are not properly related to bureau of adjustment complaints.

They should use care to see that duplicate credits are not issued. In some stores the return goods room or the selling department may originate credits that are then unknowingly duplicated by people in the bureau of adjustment, thus causing a loss.

Bureau of adjustment personnel can alert security to customers who are receiving too many adjustment refunds or to people who request adjustment credits under questionable circumstances.

Nondelivery Complaints. One area in which the bureau of adjustment can develop leads helpful to security is when a customer complains of nondelivery of goods.

Nondelivery complaints may originate from many causes: failure of the selling department to fill the salescheck because merchandise was not in stock, mislaying the salescheck in the warehouse area so that the salescheck is not filled by a warehouse employee, or theft of the goods and salescheck at any point along its route of travel from the salesperson through the delivery driver. Only if nondelivery complaints are carefully investigated and the correct cause located can we accurately determine the reason for the complaint.

Nondelivery complaints that are the result of theft of merchandise are vital leads for the security department. A considerable drain on store resources can result if nondelivery complaints caused by theft are not recognized as such and are not brought promptly to the attention of security.

Because the bureau of adjustment serves customers who have complaints, credits from this department often fall outside of the normal pattern of credits. This means particular care must be used to see that all refunds issued by this department are authorized and carefully validated with supporting evidence of sale.

Return Goods. The return goods area in some stores comes under the bureau of adjustment. People in return goods should be trained to protect their goods. Merchandise coming back into the store as return goods is often vulnerable to theft.

Goods in this area should not be left unprotected overnight. The area itself should be screened off and protected at all times. When no one is in the room it should be locked. Your store should have tight controls on return goods merchandise. It should be checked into the area and checked back into stock.

Parallel records should follow the merchandise from the return goods room to the stock department. Points such as these can be used to train the bureau of adjustment and return goods personnel to reduce theft losses in these departments.

Stock Help

People who work in stock are often neglected when training programs come along, and yet stock help is an important part of every store's behind-the-scenes operation.

Stock people should be reminded that no one is to be allowed in a stockroom except people from the parent department. No merchandise should leave a stockroom without correct paper authorization.

The Protection of Stock. Stock people can use care to see that merchandise is not left in unprotected locations. If goods cannot be returned to stock during the day and have to be left out overnight, care should be used to see that they are protected. Stock people should be responsible for locking all stock areas where expensive merchandise is kept. This would be particularly true in the fur department and the expensive jewelry and radio stockrooms.

They should also be instructed to be alert for suspects. Dishonest employees as well as professional thieves from outside the store often go into stock areas to steal.

Stock people themselves have an unusual opportunity for theft. They work many hours, often unsupervised, in locations where they cannot be observed. They require training programs to build psychological barriers to theft. They must also be reminded to follow store systems, particularly the handling of employee packages and rules for leaving the building by the proper exits.

Warehouse People

Warehouses are often open to theft. Almost every large retail case has been a warehouse theft. Notice the next time that you read about a $100,000 retail theft and see if the crime wasn't connected with the store's warehouse.

Usually warehouses have several exits. The exits are often difficult to patrol. There are also many people coming in and out of the warehouse who may not be identified.

Watch for Unauthorized People. Warehouse people must be alerted to watch for unauthorized people entering the warehouse stock areas. They should be told not to leave doors unlocked and open unless they are guarded. The danger of people leaving and entering the warehouse across the docks should be stressed.

Salvage Merchandise and Saleschecks. The problems of salvage merchandise can also be acute in the warehouse. Therefore, warehouse people have to be informed about store policy on salvage merchandise. Another point to cover is the problem of unfilled saleschecks. Warehouse people should understand how such saleschecks can create nondelivery complaints and loss investigations for your store.

Porters and Maids

These people should be told to look carefully through wastebaskets and the rest of the trash for merchandise thrown away carelessly by sales and stock personnel.

In many cases expensive items have been recovered from store trash. For example, boxes that were apparently empty turned out to contain new merchandise or goods that fell off a counter accidentally sometimes landed in a wastebasket.

If these people are made aware of the need to be careful in handling trash, you will find that many items can be recovered that would have ordinarily been destroyed.

High Opportunity for Thefts. Porters and maids usually work early or late hours, outside of the store's regular hours. They have an opportunity to steal because they can leave the store through a customer door. Emphasis has to be placed on the fact that such personnel are to follow store rules. Warnings can be made about keeping personal packages in their lockers or workrooms.

These people are in a position where theft is easy. Many times they work in the hours prior to store opening when there is hardly anyone else in the store. They have access to goods in the departments where they normally work.

Because of these factors special work should be done with this group to show the penalties of theft and to indicate that they are constantly being checked by security. They must also know that failure to follow store rules will be decisively and quickly punished.

Night Employees

The people working at night also have special opportunities for theft. These people can be helpful in reducing loss.

Night workers should be encouraged to be alert for unauthorized people in the building after hours. Many good thieves stay in a store overnight. They often sleep behind a counter or some other hidden location. In the morning they leave the store via the customer door, loaded down with stolen goods.

Night workers who are aware of this problem can help security by checking on any unknown person seen in the building.

Special Rules. Because of the nature of night work, these people should be reminded to keep their conduct above reproach at all times. They should be requested to carry identification. They should not be allowed in unlighted areas and should not lift the cloth covers over goods on store counters. They should not enter any areas other than those in which they have been assigned to do work.

Night people can cause major losses; some stores have had cases involving thousands of dollars as the result of group dishonesty among night workers. Because of the potential dangers, the security program for night employees should emphasize store rules and the penalties for theft.

Receiving and Marking Personnel

In this area there are several things to emphasize. One is the need for error control. Merchandise should be checked in accurately. Retail extensions should be correct before the tickets are made out.

Count! Accurately! Receiving personnel should be encouraged to count the unit number of tickets printed to see that they match the units listed on the invoice. If there are any tickets left over when the garments are tagged, these leftover tickets should be reported to the security department. Failure of the tickets to match the number of the units of actual goods may indicate a theft of goods.

Receiving people should be alerted to the fact that no unauthorized personnel should be allowed in the receiving area. Unmarked merchandise is vulnerable to theft and should be protected. No unmarked merchandise should be allowed out of the receiving room. Merchandise executives requesting such merchandise should be asked to sign a form identifying the goods being taken.

Remarking Authorization. Receiving people should not allow remarking without paperwork to back it up. Many times a buyer may ask for a quick remarking and promise the paperwork later. Failure of the receiving clerk to follow this up can result in an inventory loss for the department since a markdown may not go through. This problem can be avoided by refusing to do any remarking without proper authorization.

Maintenance Personnel

These people, like night employees, porters, and maids, move about the building a great deal. They need to be careful that their actions are always above reproach. They should be told that they are not to touch merchandise at any time. At night they are not to go to any unlighted areas. The rules about salvage merchandise would also apply to this group.

Since they often work early hours they should be told about the necessity of leaving the store by the employee exit.

Maintenance people can be helpful in reporting suspects. If they find unauthorized people in nonselling areas they should report such people to security. If from the standpoint of the physical layout, they find weak spots that could result in theft, this information should be reported to their supervisors.

Store's Hospital Staff

Hospital doctors and nurses have an opportunity to help the store by being alert to people who show indications of psychological maladjustment.

Maladjusted employees often turn up in the hospital with various physical disabilities. Doctors and nurses who have an opportunity to talk to these people can detect psychological maladjustments. They should bring this to the attention of the store personnel department.

Specific Maladies to Look Out For. When nurses make home visits to employees who are ill, they should be alert to the problems of malingering. Such malingering should be reported. A person who will deliberately fake illness is a good lead for the security department.

When doctors examine new employees, the routine physical examination should include a check for narcotics addiction. A check should be made for needle marks on the arm of the applicant or any failure of the pupils of the eyes to dilate.

Finally, hospital people must be careful to control their supply of drugs and narcotics. Such medicines should be kept in a locked case whenever the hospital is closed. Failure to control drugs can have obviously serious consequences.

Elevator Operators

Like salespeople, the cooperation of elevator operators is important to the floor detective. Failure to cooperate with floor detectives can often result in a lost case.

Many times floor detectives have to follow shoplifters into elevators. If the elevator operator is not alert to the fact that the detective is following a shoplifter and does not let the detective into the elevator the detective may be shut out. As a result the store loses an apprehension.

Operators Should Know Detectives. Floor detectives should be known to all elevator operators. There should also be some type of code worked out between the detectives and the operators so that the operator will know when the detective is in a critical situation and needs to be able to get into the elevator no matter how crowded it is.

Elevator operators should be instructed that before or after store hours they should not leave their elevators except when they are relieved by another operator.

Pickpockets and sexual deviantes often operate in elevators. Elevator operators should have instructions about handling these types of people.

Dock Workers

Store and warehouse docks are an area where thefts often occur. Dishonest delivery men sometimes put several cartons on a receiving dock and after the dockman has given the cartons a receiving number, they put one carton back on their truck.

Delivery men can also deliver the order one carton short. If the store dockman does not know the correct carton count, the theft can occur without his knowledge.

Don't Allow Entry Across Dock. No employees or unauthorized people should be allowed to enter or leave the warehouse or store across the docks. Drivers and their helpers should not be allowed to pass into the building across the docks. No goods should be allowed to leave the store or warehouse without proper paper controls.

An alert dockman can be very helpful to your store security. He should be told that his job is a control point where heavy losses can occur and that he has a responsibility to prevent such losses.

Delivery Men

The men making deliveries for your store often take cash on C.O.D.s. They should be instructed carefully how to handle such money. C.O.D.s should be balanced out daily, and either the merchandise or the cash should be turned in by the driver.

Drivers can give leads on dishonest employees. They may find an employee on their route who is having an unusual amount of deliveries made to his home.

Drivers have a responsibility to protect the merchandise on their trucks. When leaving their trucks unguarded, they should be sure that the package compartments are carefully locked. They should also use special care in handling expensive items such as furs and fine jewelry.

Salespeople

Many programs have been designed for salespeople and most of the points to be covered are well known, but we will review them briefly here. In addition to raising the usual psychological barriers against personal theft, the salespeople should be encouraged to be accurate in their saleschecks and refunds.

Recording Errors. A salesclerk who makes errors in adding or in recording figures causes loss just as surely as does a thief. A study in one of the country's largest stores showed that 1 percent of all their saleschecks had a figure error. When projected over a year's time these errors showed a loss to the store of more than $100,000.

Most inventory losses are not the result of a single major problem but are rather the accumulation of small errors. Small errors on saleschecks or on refunds can lead to large loss totals.

Remarked Merchandise. Salespeople should be careful not to sell remarked merchandise without price tickets. Many times merchandise brought back by customers does not get remarked. This may be true in the jewelry department.

In one particular case returned merchandise was placed in a drawer and in selling the merchandise salesclerks *estimated* the value of the unit being sold. Shopping tests showed that whenever such estimates were made they always favored the customer.

Fitting Rooms. Salespeople working in departments with fitting rooms should limit the number of garments going into a fitting room. Some thieves will take in ten or twenty garments. They then ask the salesperson to take some garments out and bring others back until the salesperson is confused as to how many garments there are in the fitting room. This can be avoided by not allowing any customer to have more than three or four garments in the fitting room at one time.

Salespeople should be assigned specific fitting rooms which are to be kept clear of merchandise. Every salesperson should be instructed never to leave merchandise in a fitting room after the customer has left.

Many professional thieves steal by going down an aisle of fitting rooms looking for a fitting room where merchandise has been left by a careless salesperson. They then go into the fitting room and fill up their handbags or a cardboard box, or they may stuff the merchandise under the clothes they are wearing. Thefts of several hundred dollars worth of garments have occurred when a professional thief has spotted a fitting room where merchandise has been left by a thoughtless salesperson.

Good Service Prevents Thefts. Whenever a salesperson has a suspicious person in her department she should give good service to that person until security arrives. *Good service prevents thefts.*

Salespeople should be encouraged to cooperate with security. Many times a case can be made or lost by the attitude of the salesperson. If a detective requests a salesperson to stay away from a certain customer, the salesperson should comply.

Arrange Displays. Clerks can use care in displaying expensive goods and therefore reduce display losses. When a salesclerk works behind a handbag counter or similar area, she can display her handbags in a pattern, in groups of six or eight. In this way if a handbag is stolen she will be aware of it because there will be a hole in her pattern.

By reporting the fact that an article is missing from the display and by noting the approximate time that the loss occurred, the salesperson can begin to set up a picture of the theft pattern. This can help the security department. Many thieves develop habits like other people and may steal at approximately the same time every week.

Salespeople who sell in the perfume department should be encouraged to display dummy perfume bottles. In this way, if thefts do occur, they are not costly.

Salespeople should be careful in approving charge and take sales. They should be encouraged to check their impostor suspect list. Bank checks should also be handled according to the store system.

Refunds. When salespeople write refunds they should be careful that they are accurate. If identification is required on any transaction, for example, bank check, charge account, or refund, the salesperson should be instructed as to what types of identification are acceptable.

Salespeople should be told about special types of customers who should be kept under observation. When they have a suspect they should know how to obtain help from security.

No unauthorized people should be allowed in their stockrooms. They should not allow anyone to take merchandise from the department without a proper loan slip.

Modeling Store Merchandise. One last thought for salespeople is that they should not be allowed to wear store merchandise unless a loan slip has been filled out. Sometimes in certain departments the buyer will encourage the salespeople to wear jewelry, sweaters, or other articles in order to act as models for the customers.

If loan slips are made out and the merchandise is properly checked in and out, there is no harm in this practice. The tendency, however, is to wear the items without any loan authorization. A salesperson can forget that she has store jewelry on and discover it later when she arrives home. When this happens she has discovered the first step in how to become a thief. This type of thing should be avoided.

Cashiers

Cashiers are usually reliable people who have been thoroughly investigated prior to employment. They need to be encouraged to be accurate. Errors can be costly. In cashing bank checks, they should be instructed about what type of identification is required and they should be thorough in getting this identification.

Unusual Employee Activity. They should notice any unusual employee activity in relation to their job. If a supervisor occasionally brings a customer refund to the cashier, for cashing in a store where the customer cashes her own refunds, such irregularity should be brought to the attention of the cashier's supervisor who in turn should pass it on to the security department.

Holdup Precautions. Holdup precautions should be explained to the cashiers. The most important item in such instructions should be the fact that no one's life should ever be placed in jeopardy. It is helpful if the cashiers can be taken to the security offices to see what happens in the security department when such a call comes in.

Cashiers should be cautioned to keep their office neat at all times. Sometimes heavy losses have occurred because a careless cashier has knocked a pile of bills into a trash container without realizing it.

No personal items should be taken into cashrooms.

Packers

The packer is in a position to control large quantities of store goods. They can be very helpful in reducing losses due to carelessness and error. By encouraging packers to be careful in checking items against saleschecks many errors can be prevented.

"Packer-Error" System. One store has a "packer-error" system in which packers are given a form that lists a half dozen possible types of errors. When a packer dicovers that a salesperson has made an error on her salescheck, or if she discovers that the salesperson has given damaged merchandise to the packer to be sent to the customer, or any similar errors, she checks off the error on her packer-error form and the packer receives an award for reporting the error.

Interestingly enough, packers who have a system like this sometimes turn in as many as twenty or thirty errors a day. Errors can be costly to a store, not only in merchandise and money but also in customer goodwill.

Overgoods. Packers should be careful in handling overgoods. A control should be placed on the packer so that she is occasionally tested by deliberately giving her overgoods to see if she reports them. Packers should be told they will be "shopped" with this type of overgoods test.

Authorization Forms. No merchandise should be wrapped by a packer at any time without a salescheck or other authorized form. There should be protection for merchandise in the packing area before and after it is wrapped. If merchandise must be left to be wrapped on the following day, action should be taken to see that it is in a protected location.

The packer also has a responsibility to conserve packing supplies. No packing supply should be given to any employee or customer unless it is authorized by the department supervisor.

Your store can have losses in supplies that are substantial. Many times employees use packing supplies for personal needs such as sending Christmas gifts or for moving and other jobs that require boxes, wrapping paper, and twine.

Display People

Display, like the maintenance department, has free access to many areas of the store. There is very little supervisory control on their activities. Because of this, display people must be careful to keep themselves out of any situation that might appear questionable.

A security program directed at display people should build up the usual psychological barriers to theft. They should also be told that no merchandise is to be taken from any department for display purposes without a proper loan slip.

If merchandise is needed after the store has closed, then a security person should go with the display employee to get such merchandise. A temporary loan slip can be made out by night security to be replaced on the following day by a regular department loan form.

Return to Stock. Care should be taken in checking merchandise back into the selling departments after it has been used by display. Loan slips that are not properly checked are valueless. Any good loan system should have a point of control when the merchandise is checked back into stock.

No merchandise should ever be handled by display people after hours, except for display purposes. They should not go behind counters, into darkened areas, or lift up cloths covering goods on counters. Merchandise for display should be selected during regular selling hours and handled according to store systems.

Since display people often have early or late working hours they should be checked out of the building through the authorized employee exit. No salvage merchandise should be sold to display people. They should also not be allowed to store any merchandise in their working cubbyholes or in other closets not authorized for storing display goods.

Advertising Personnel

When the advertising department borrows merchandise for photographing and sketching it should be controlled. Instructions should be given that such merchandise be checked out on a loan slip. It should be returned on time and there should be a check-back system to ensure that all items are returned to their proper department.

Merchandise being held by the advertising department overnight should be protected. Special locked areas should be provided for this overnight storage of goods.

In Sum

These suggestions for education programs directed at individual departments will give the reader some idea of the potential for directing security education programs toward specific groups. From these partial lists your store can make further developments. Other areas can also be brought into your program along with those suggested here.

Remember that the *eight* basic goals of most security training programs should be a part of any specific departmental training outline.

(3) WHAT MEDIA?

Now that you have selected the group and determined your objectives, your next problem is choosing the media you will use to project your program.

Forms of Available Media

You have available, of course, numerous approaches to training people. All forms of communication are at your disposal. Some of the media often used in such programs are:

1. Talks
2. Photos
3. Slides
4. Movies
5. Demonstrations
6. Posters
7. Pamphlets
8. Memos
9. Exhibits

Media Choice Depends on Goals

When you consider one or more of these possible methods of communication, your decision as to which one to use will depend on whether your goals are minor or major in nature.

Do you intend your program to be short or long range? For example, if you have important objectives you will probably want to use more than one communication medium.

If you have a long-range program you may want to use a form of communication that lends itself to weekly or monthly repetition, such as posters, memos, or exhibits. Sometimes in a short-range program you may want to create a strong impact. In this case you would definitely use multiple media.

At another time you might feel that your objectives involve training in only one department. In this case talks may be the answer.

Is your program going to be highly personal? Is it going to revolve around the molding of the individual's attitudes and the setting up of psychological barriers? If so, you will need a direct contact with the people to be affected. Slides, movies, photographs, talks, and demonstrations fall in this group.

Demonstrations and Exhibits

Demonstrations and exhibits can be used in either type of program. Sometimes when you want to combine a long-range program and a program that is designed to have impact, you can use demonstrations or an exhibit as a weekly, monthly, or bimonthly type of presentation.

Let's suppose that you want to correct salescheck errors. To do this and also make an impact you can accumulate specific error saleschecks and each month issue a report showing photostatic reproductions of these saleschecks. This is a demonstration type of medium with considerable psychological impact.

Confidential Material

There may be some material that you might want to use in your program but would not want to have it appear in written form. For example, your store's profit figures, your actual inventory loss, or material for supervisors on dishonest employee problems.

There are many of these confidential areas in which you may want to use the information involved but not want the details to fall into the hands of someone else. This would mean personal contacts through talks, rather than using memos, pamphlets, posters, or similar media.

Consider the Group

To sum up, your choice of media is based on such factors as whether your program is short or long range. Also whether you want a fast psychological impact or to teach rules and methods.

In addition, your choice is governed by the attitudes and types of people to whom you are going to direct your training. It would be foolish, for example, to devise a very complex memo to be used in a program directed at warehouse dock workers.

Posters would be difficult to use in a program directed at only one department. Posters are usually used if you're working across the entire store operation. Although posters could be used in a program for elevator operators by periodically placing a poster in the elevator locker room, this would be a big expense for a relatively small group.

In making your final decision about media, ask yourself how effective this particular medium will be in relation to the group and the objectives of your security program.

(4) WHAT KIND OF MOTIVATION?

The final key to the success or failure of your security education program is motivation. How well you analyze the motivational needs of the people to be influenced, how carefully you choose your motivational techniques, and how effectively you apply these motivational principles will determine whether the other efforts put into your program will pay off.

Remember that the objective of your program is to persuade individuals in a group in order to attain specific goals.

When you learn the answer to the question—"How can you motivate people?"—you will have the know-how that will enable you to do a better job in any phase of your training program.

What are the latest psychological findings on motivating people? Everyone has several basic drives. These can often be used to motivate people to take predetermined actions or result in predetermined attitudes. These motivations should be chosen on the basis of individual needs. They should be applied through one or more of four persuasion devices. Let's look at these persuasion techniques.

Persuasion Methods

Acceptance of rejection of a program or policy is the fundamental aim of all persuasion. There are four simple devices that can be used to do this.

1. Virtue Words. First is the acceptance or "virtue" device that is used to cause people to accept through conditioned associations "good" words, symbols, and acts.

"Good" words or symbols flash pleasant pictures in our minds. We have all been conditioned to certain virtue words, intended to make us automatically approve people, things, and ideas associated with them.

Some of these typical virtue words are mother, home, fireside, childhood, friendship, sociability, neighborly, common sense, character, independence, integrity, truth, loyalty, honor, democracy, Americanism, freedom, social justice, and liberty. We accept people, things, or ideas associated with these words. You can use virtue words in order to sell security education.

2. The "Poison" Device. Next is the rejection or "poison" device, which causes us to reject something because of its association with "bad" words, symbols, and acts.

This method of persuasion, of course, is in direct contrast to the first method. With this device you apply a "poison word," bad name, or symbol that arouses a feeling of fear, disgust, or in some way makes us reject, shun, avoid, disapprove, or condemn a policy or program.

Words are used in both the virtue and poison devices to conjure up in our minds pleasant or unpleasant, or frightening or reassuring, pictures. We automatically react for or against the thing that the persuader wants us to approve or reject.

All of us have been conditioned since childhood to have specific responses to certain words. These words are stimuli to our reflexes just as Pavlov's dog was conditioned to react when a bell rang.

No device, of course, is good or bad in itself. It is only good or bad in the context of the purpose for which it is intended. The poison device, for example, has been used throughout history to save mankind from death, disease, or injury by causing people to automatically avoid harmful things.

It can be used in dealing with personnel to build up psychological barriers that cause rejection of criminal acts. The poison device, if honestly and correctly used, can save endless trouble and it can reduce losses for your store.

3. The Testimonial Device. This device is used to cause us to accept or reject something on the basis of the testimony or evidence of people we consider "good," "respectable," "successful," or inversely, "horrible examples."

In using this method you employ the voice of experience. The wisdom of authority is used to get others to approve and accept or disapprove and reject something. We use the testimonials of well-known public figures or the words of top men in national institutions to give sanction and prestige to our poison or virtue words.

The testimony device is often used in connection with the two word devices previously discussed. It improves their effectiveness.

4. The "Together" Device. This method unites people into a group. It's used to cause us to accept or reject things on a group basis.

Acceptance of ideas by a group will mold any people on the borderline of acceptance into mental acceptance of those ideas. Even a person who might start out by being negative toward an idea will be molded into an acceptable attitude if he is subjected to invisible group pressures.

To use this method, the persuader gets people together. You can get them to raise their hands in answer to questions, make demonstrations as a group, or do anything that is a group activity in order to mold the group together as a unit before applying the previous three devices of persuasion.

After they have taken action together, such as raising hands, they become a single powerful unit. They begin to react together. They are stirred by the same testimonials, moved to fear and hatred as a group by the same poison words, or given feelings of security and hope by virtue words.

The together device reinforces all other persuasion methods by causing the group to act as a unit. People like to be together. It expands satisfying feelings of brotherhood, security, and group strength.

Sometimes the together device can be used in what is called the "bandwagon" method. Here the theme is "everybody's doing it," with the implication that outsiders should get on the bandwagon and do it too so that they will be on the winning side and not subject to criticism.

This is successful because it has an appeal to the need for self-preservation, which can be accomplished best by group preservation. It exploits our natural desire to follow leadership.

When people have the same conditioned reflexes with respect to any given viewpoint, the together device works as a very powerful means of persuasion.

BASIC DRIVES

Having explored the persuasion techniques, let's now look at some of the needs that motivate people as individuals and as a group. All of us have several basic drives: the need for security, prestige, belonging, and self-development.

Two Motivational Drives. All motivation is dependent on two basic things. *First*, you must stimulate the person's natural drives. *Second*, you need to gain the acceptance of your ideas by using the person's previously conditioned reflex responses as triggers to action.

Modern psychologists list five broad groups of basic needs.

1. Biological
2. Security
3. Sociability
4. Prestige
5. Self-development

In examining these needs you must remember that any one person may not fit exactly into these slots but enough people do to make analysis worthwhile.

1. Biological

Food, drink, and clothing are needed to keep people alive. The ordinary American is not exposed to hunger and thirst, and therefore this drive is not pertinent to most training programs.

2. Security of Safety Needs

After people have been fed and clothed, they may begin to think about safety or security. Again, today's society protects people from obvious forms of violence such as fire, plague and proverty.

Security needs don't ordinarily come up except in an emergency but there are exceptions to this. Some people never get beyond a need to satisfy their feeling of security. A person who had lived through the Depression, for example, might very well have security as a prime need.

Symptoms of Security Need. A person with an excessive need for security shows some of the following symptoms:

1. His main goal is to stay out of trouble. He wants to play it safe.
2. His day-to-day objectives are to please the employer upon whom his job depends. He wants to please the boss—right or wrong.
3. He will give up pride, friendship, and even honesty as long as he can play it safe and take care of himself.
4. He doesn't like the new, the unfamiliar, or anything that suggests change. He never sticks his neck out.
5. He will frantically conceal mistakes and pass the buck in order to avoid personal blame.

6. Most people work hard to have a good job, to save some money, and to develop other goals. The security-minded person is more concerned with what he might lose. He does not necessarily think about additional things he might gain.

   Such people do not often appear in the top brackets of retailing management but they do appear often in the middle management group and frequently, of course, at lower levels.

   Security-minded people may become "yes men" and often are described by others as faithful and anxious to please. However, such people may ruthlessly double-cross someone if they feel that their own security is threatened.

   They are an important segment of any group toward which you direct a security program. Part of your program motivation material should be directed toward satisfying this security need.

   At some point in your program you must show how the individual employee, by doing the things that you want the group to do, will be more secure. The safety-first person will be motivated to constructive action when you stimulate his basic drive.

3. Belonging–Sociability

Most people want to belong to some team, group, or class. Everyone wants to feel part of the groups they admire. They want to be surrounded by a loving family and friends. They may want to belong to a country club or to the Masons. But what happens when a person's drive for belonging is stronger than normal? Three possibilities may result:

a. He may become a popularity seeker.
b. He may become an approval seeker.
c. He may reverse his position and become an authoritarian person.

Let's examine each of these in detail.

The popularity seeker. This person's first concern is to be liked. He speaks warmly to everyone. He tries to do things that will be liked by his boss, his subordinates, and his associates.

He becomes very disturbed if he is criticized and finds it hard to take a detached, objective view. He will often worry about the effect his actions have on his popularity. He is always in danger of choosing what will be popular rather than what ought to be done in business.

He can be a successful supervisor only if he is willing to take an unpopular stand from time to time. The difference between the popularity seeker and the prestige seeker is that the popularity seeker wants to be liked even if it means staying out of the limelight while the prestige seeker is willing to be disliked in order to get the limelight.

Handling this type of person is relatively easy. Show him a little warmth and let him avoid the jobs that are unpopular. His liking for people can be a plus factor in the security education program.

The approval seeker. This type of person very seldom reaches middle management, and almost never a top executive position. He is the "Milquetoast," the clerk who runs to the boss for a pat of approval every time anything happens. Such a person has to have clear goals to follow and has to feel he is doing what the boss wants done.

He can be motivated by giving him constant reassurance that he is doing a fine job. You should be careful never to tease or bully such a person; instead he should be helped and reassured.

The authoritarian. This person can often be a good subordinate but is very seldom a good person to work for.

He measures people on a scale of power. All those below him are inferiors to be pushed around. All those above him are superiors whom he worships and obeys while dreaming of the day when he will have their power. He cannot understand people who question authority.

This person can be useful in certain areas of security activity. He drives himself and others without slacking off. His standards are high and his discipline is ironbound.

Criticism doesn't bother him. He does not mind being ordered about. However, he has some faults.

Failures make him more suspicious and hardboiled. Success convinces him that ruthless methods are best. He thinks that patient and considerate people are weaklings, and he has no insight into people. He orders people around for the sake of feeling power, not for the good of the job.

When dealing with this kind of person, state your request, decision, or order in a firm, decisive manner and the authoritarian person will react by automatically carrying it out. A sentence that this type of person uses a lot is, "The boss wants it." Interestingly enough the same sentence works like magic when applied to him.

If you wish to have him take action in security programs tell him that "The boss wants it," and he will immediately respond. Never show weakness to a person of this type and never give him a chance to gain any sort of hold or leverage over you.

4. Prestige Needs

Everyone's need for esteem appears endless. People find satisfaction in knowing that they're doing a good job and they obtain triple satisfaction when their work is recognized by others.

This human reaction can be a powerful stimulant. It is based on the human desire for recognition. Sometimes the desire for prestige can become too great. Such a person can be recognized in the following ways:

a. He wants to be a star.
b. A compliment lifts him up, while criticism casts him down.
c. He dislikes men and women who are unenthusiastic.
d. He enjoys warm, enthusiastic people who show admiration and respect for him.
e. He wants publicity. If his picture appears in the store newspaper he is delighted. However, he can be depressed if his picture is not placed as prominently as that of someone else. He likes to see his name in print.
f. He enjoys titles and the symbols of power and position. He may want a big desk and his own water cooler. In his own eyes he is "the big shot."

   He cannot be happy until everyone around him agrees and keeps agreeing that he is the outstanding member of the team. He will accept a high sounding title with more speed than he will a raise.

On the good side, such a person can become an outstanding leader in middle management. He seeks responsibility, and he will fight hard to make a go of things. He is also a self-starter who is willing to be the boss.

On the bad side, in many cases he will be motivated by his own desire to be a star rather than by thinking of the good of the store. He wants to look good rather than to meet the standards of the business. He often cannot see when he should subordinate himself for the good of the team. He gives recognition to others only when it adds to his own luster.

This person has to be handled carefully. You should be careful not to puncture his vanity. You can use his vanity to gain certain constructive ends. By utilizing this need you can make him an important part of any security program.

5. Drive for Self-Development

This person is not overly dominated by a need for security, sociability, or prestige, but seeks to grow and develop his personality. He wants to become a better person.

He doesn't put on much front and doesn't adopt defensive poses. He doesn't feel a need to impress people. He is relatively calm and can work alone. He is sorry for people's faults but enjoys their good qualities. He is democratic without being a popularity seeker. He tries to do what is right and to avoid doing what is wrong.

He enjoys being creative. He also tries to avoid waste, to find new and better ways of doing things, and he does not overlook opportunities to help others as well as himself grow as workers and as human beings.

Such a person, of course, is a great asset in your security training program. If you have people of this type in the group they should be used as leaders to carry out security projects.

In Sum

This covers the persuasion techniques and the basic needs of the people who will be found in the groups with whom you will work. By applying these methods of persuasion you will inject the motivation necessary to get constructive and effective results from the people being influenced. If you leave out any of the basic drives you may very well find that some people will not respond to your program.

The care with which you choose your persuasion devices will be the most important single factor in the success of your security programs.

1. Determine objectives of the program
2. Choose the communications media
3. Decide on motivational appeals
4. Agree on the method of presentation
5. Choose examples of programs that apply to specific areas
6. Basic motivational drives
   a. Biological
   b. Safety
   c. Prestige
   d. Need to belong
   e. Need for approval

Chapter 24

SECURITY EDUCATION: PART III

In this chapter we look at some examples of security programs that have been used in various stores and suggest some variations of these ideas that you might use in your programs. We want to suggest ideas that can be adapted to your store's needs. We also will show how different kinds of communications media can be used in employee education.

Any program ideas that you may wish to use should be tested first against some of the program suggestions in the two previous chapters. Does the material contain the motivational factors needed to make it effective? Was the selection of the media correct for the application of materials? Most important, are there any inherent dangers in this particular program? All of these programs contain ideas that could be used in your store.

TALKS

New Employees

Some stores have a session on security for new employees. One store shows a film of the security department operation. It includes scenes illustrating how shoplifters steal.

In another company, demonstrations of the methods of theft are given to new salespeople by the security head. He also encourages members of the group to take part in role playing in his demonstrations.

In both of these cases, the material is interesting and dramatic, but it is of questionable value from a security education viewpoint. As we shall see later, there are dangers in certain types of security education.

Paging System

One large store installed a Motorola Paging System. To encourage the salespeople in spotting suspects and calling the security department, demonstrations were given of the Motorola Paging System.

The meeting, which covered several phases of the salesperson's responsibility toward losses, showed a series of placards in connection with the shortage controller's talk. These signs showed figures on store losses. They also showed how $125 worth of goods must be sold to pay for a single $5 theft (based on a 4 percent net profit).

In addition to the cards, a series of projected slides were shown. These were cartoon figures showing how salespeople can help prevent loss. One illustrated the need for keeping fitting rooms cleared of merchandise. Another pointed up the fact that no merchandise should leave the department without a loan slip, and so on. Tied in with the cards and the slides was a talk by the store's shortage controller on the problems of theft and carelessness.

Radio Receivers

At the end of the meeting radio receivers are handed out to the salespeople attending. At a prearranged signal, the receiver comes to life. The security head broadcasts from his office to the departmental meeting about the new communications system.

This demonstration comes to a dramatic climax and ends with a final request for help in control. It stimulates interest in finding shoplifting suspects. The demonstration shows how a salesperson's call for help will be broadcast over the air, which is a real ego-builder.

At the end of the session, a pamphlet listing specific things the salesperson can do to reduce loss is given to each attendee.

As you can see, this meeting combines five kinds of communication media:

1. A talk by the store's shortage controller
2. Poster cards to hold visual interest
3. Cartoon slides for memory impact
4. Radio receiver demonstration as a climax
5. The pamphlet as a lasting reminder

In a fifteen-minute meeting, all of these elements are combined to make a lively and effective presentation. Meetings were held in each selling department before the store opening.

Supervisors' Program

One large store found an unusual amount of rank-and-file employee dishonesty. Numerous employees were apprehended in a three-month period. It was felt that many of the employee thefts stemmed from supervisory failures. Supervisors had not set a good leadership example; they had failed to enforce store systems and controls.

A Talk and Slide Presentation

To educate all of the store's supervisors about the seriousness of these internal thefts and to bring home to them the responsibilities of their job, a talk and a slide presentation was arranged.

The executives and supervisors were asked to attend an auditorium meeting. The store's general manager gave a brief opening talk to set the mood for the security manager's presentation. The talk given was called "Ghosts."* The talk was made even more effective by integrating colored slides that showed the extent of the thefts involved.

The Slides

One woman had admitted stealing $5,000 in cash on sales. She worked in the candy department. To give her admitted thefts impact, a photograph of $5,000 worth of candy was shown.

In another case a salesclerk had stolen over 1,000 records. Few people can picture what the theft of so many records really means. A slide showing a photograph of 1,000 records brought the speaker's words into shocking reality.

The talk was also given emotional emphasis by photographing people (models) who had supposedly been the employees arrested for stealing. The photographs did not show faces; instead they showed people slumped over in their chairs with their faces in their hands. This was dramatic, pictorial proof of the shame and disgrace that these people had brought themselves by stealing from the store.

---

*See Appendix 7.

The talk was written to tell not only what had happened but also what could be done to prevent such personal tragedies in the future. It also contained strong, motivational material and is a good example for study to see how motivational factors can be woven into a talk of this type.

Presentations in the Community

Some stores use talks before community groups to educate parents in the community on ways of preventing retail juvenile crime. One store gives talks of this type before women's clubs, school teacher groups, "Y" leaders, church groups, and other service organizations. The store feels it is a constructive method for getting the community to help in fighting retail crime.

The security manager may also talk before professional groups. This can create interest in crime prevention. In one store, the security manager gives lectures before college groups specializing in police administration. Another store has the security manager give talks before organizations representing lawyers, judges, and law enforcement people.

DEMONSTRATIONS

How Thieves Steal

Some stores use demonstrations to educate personnel about the problems of shoplifting. One store, whenever a large case occurs, holds meetings in the departments where the thefts occurred. The detectives involved in the case act out for the salespeople the shoplifter's method of theft.

Unusual Theft Methods

In another store, trick boxes, unusual clothing such as trick coats, and similar paraphernalia used by the professional thief are shown at sales meetings.

There is danger in showing the methods of theft. While they are very interesting, they are too unique to be of practical value. A security detective could work on shoplifting cases for twenty years and never apprehend a thief using a trick box. It would seem better to educate store employees to look for the more usual methods of theft rather than for these unique techniques.

The old-time shoplifter is almost a relic from the past. Today the main concern centers on the compulsive thief. The few professionals still operating today know if they are caught using a trick box or similar paraphernalia, they are certain to be prosecuted.

We have to face the fact that the old-time shoplifter with oversized pants, coats with built-in pockets, and other fancy gimmicks is very rare today.

Created System Checks

This is a very effective educational device that can be used to improve any phase of your store's operation.

In a large store in Washington, D.C., it has been used to check on more than 200 phases of the store operation. Our discussion here will be limited to its use in security.

Checking Receiving Dock Vulnerability

One New York store with a branch in Manhasset, Long Island, was having trouble getting the branch store's receiving department to use more care in protecting the store during the early morning hours.

At 7:00 A.M. when the milk and bread men made deliveries of foodstuffs to the store restaurants, the receiving dock door was often left open. No one was placed at the dock entrance and the store was wide open for anyone to enter through the receiving area. There was very little danger of a thief being caught.

The Plot

To show the branch store management and, particularly, the receiving department personnel how vulnerable they were to theft, a created systems check was planned. A truck was rented and two men were dressed to look like delivery men. They took the rented truck out to the branch store early one morning. In the truck they carried a large carton of old phone books that they planned to "deliver." In return for this "gift" of old phone books, they were going to see how much merchandise they could take away in their truck without being caught.

They arrived at the store about 7:00 A.M. and found the receiving door wide open, as usual. In a few minutes they had delivered the carton of phone books and had made away with over $4,000 worth of new slacks.

The "Kick"

The truck driver and his helper, having successfully stolen the slacks, retired to a nearby diner to have coffee and await further developments. At 11:00 A.M. one of the truck men phoned the branch store manager.

"Are you missing anything from your receiving area?" he asked.

"Not that I know of," cheerfully replied the store manager.

"Well, we have $4,000 worth of your slacks on our truck," the truck driver replied just as cheerfully.

A loud gasp of disbelief was heard from the other end of the line. In a few minutes the driver had filled in the store manager on the plot. The truck driver and his helper brought the truck back to the store and unloaded the "stolen" goods.

Was This Lesson Effective?

Did it have an impact on the store manager and the receiving department's staff? You can be sure that it did; it had a profound effect.

After the men brought the truck back and returned the slacks, they got into the truck to drive back to the city. The truck wouldn't start. Investigation showed that the distributor rotor had been filched. It took the driver and his assistant two hours of fast talking before they could persuade the receiving department personnel to return the distributor rotor to the truck driver.

During the four years that followed this created systems check, spot observations were made of the receiving dock doors, and in the four-year period the docks were never again found unguarded.

Other Uses for a Created Systems Check

Do you want to know if your buyers are checking purchase journals as required? Test them by padding the purchase journal with a fictitious entry. See if the buyer catches the "error."

How is your store's transfer system working? Are you aware of any shortages that may be occurring? Find out by deliberately shorting a transfer shipment. Take four garments off a rack and see if the shortage is reported.

Are your packers turning in their overgoods? Plant extra merchandise in a sales order and see if the packer turns in the overgoods.

A Check on Employees' Packages

Some stores have a checkroom where purchases made by employees are examined and sealed. One store that had a checkroom of this type did a created systems check. They put store merchandise tagged at full price at the bottom of a paper bag containing old rags. An employee presented the bag at the checking counter and asked that the old rags be sealed so he could take the package home. The employee checker took a superficial look into the bag and put a seal on it.

Later this checker was called to her supervisor's office and the still-sealed package was handed to her. She was asked to open the package and empty its contents onto the desk. This dramatic method of showing her how careless her check had been was most effective. From then on, whenever anyone asked to check merchandise the bag was examined all the way to the bottom.

Testing Store Detectives

Even store detectives can be tested with a created systems check. One store was curious about how well their detectives could catch thieves in a ready-to-wear department. They employed people, who were not known to the detectives, to come into the selling area and attempt to steal merchandise.

To give the detectives a fair opportunity to catch the thieves, they notified them that the creative systems test was going to be made at a certain hour. The test showed that the detectives usually caught the thieves. However, when they were not notified in advance that a thief might come into the area, the chances of the thief's being caught were greatly reduced.

The Security Manager Learned a Great Deal

When a thief was caught without the detective knowing that the person was a "plant," the "thief" was treated as a usual apprehension. This gave the store security manager an opportunity to find out how his detectives handled the apprehension. How did they approach the thief? Were they rude? Were they aggressive? Did they attempt to start a fight in the street?

What sort of statements did they make to the "thief" as they brought her back to the security office? Were these questions related to the theft? Would they be useful if testimony in court would be required? Did they get an admission of theft from the thief at the time of apprehension?

These and many other questions that plague a security manager were revealed in the created test. This had a dual value in that in some cases it reassured the security manager about the operation of his people and in other cases, where the detectives had used poor judgment, these facts were brought to their attention and the errors corrected.

As soon as the detectives became aware that any person they apprehended might be a test, they handled all of their cases with more consideration and better judgment.

As can be seen from these few examples, the created system educational program has many possibilities. It can be applied in many different ways and is limited only by the imagination and ingenuity of the people who apply it. It can be one of the most useful devices your store can have. In the security area it can be a constant method of working at the problems of better supervision, tighter enforcement of systems, and the reduction of loss.

ROLE PLAYING

Charge Account Office

Use role playing to let people run through given situations when nothing is at stake. A person can learn how he or she will react when the actual situation occurs. Without a role-playing "rehearsal" it is often difficult for people to know what to do when an unusual problem or an actual crisis arises.

Role playing is an excellent method for helping people to learn by self-discovery. As we know, there is a wide gap between knowledge and learning. We can know a thing and still not be able to apply our knowledge to it. Once we learn a thing we then have it as part of our personality and we can use it. Role playing bridges the gap between knowledge and learning.

Interviewing Customers

People in your charge office are sometimes faced with the problem of interviewing a customer whose charge account has been used by an impostor. They may also, on occasion, have to interview a person who is suspected of being a fraud purchaser.

The objectives of these two interviews are quite different. In the first case, they are trying to find out information pertinent to the charge plate of a legitimate customer. They are looking for possible leads that can be used by security in tracing the person using the account. For example, did this person have any personal problems that might have caused someone to use the account to "get even?"

A variety of probing questions can be used to lead the customer into revealing something that can lead directly to the impostor. The problem here is to ask the right type of questions in order to gain the needed information.

Questions in black and white on paper are one thing but questions in an actual interview are something else. By giving charge account interviewers a role-playing situation they have an opportunity to transfer theoretical questions to the reality of a customer interview.

The interview of a legitimate customer whose account has been used by someone else can be quite delicate. It may very well happen that during the interview the customer will suddenly realize that her daughter has used the account. She may even have forgotten that she gave her daughter permission to use the charge plate.

This information can be quite embarrassing to her and she may be reluctant to reveal the facts to the interviewer. Therefore setting a permissive atmosphere to encourage the customer to reveal information of this type is quite important. There must be no antagonism to create mental blocks so that the customer cannot feel free to tell the interviewer the whole truth of the circumstances surrounding the loss or misuse of her charge account plate.

Interviewing the Impostor

In interviewing the impostor-suspect, there is even more at stake than with the legitimate customer. If the suspect is not positively proven to be a fraud purchaser, the interview is quite delicate. The suspect may have been given permission to use the account. Did the person use a fraudulent name? Did the person knowingly forge another person's name without permission?

There are many unusual but completely honest reasons why people use other people's accounts. The interviewer has to be especially careful not to jump to any conclusions. This interview should be role played over and over again with other interviewers acting the part of the customer.

In role-playing situations there is no danger to the store because there is nothing at stake. If the interviewer blunders the store will not receive a lawsuit for defamation of character. Let the interviewers make all their mistakes in role-playing situations. It is an excellent means of teaching the interviewer how to obtain information and how to avoid the pitfall of poorly stated questions or opinions. Some devices of interviewing will be helpful in drawing the truth from the suspect. There are also specific things an interviewer can do to pin down the suspect's identity and her right to use the charge account in question. All of these techniques are matters of training.

The Safe Way to Train Interviewers

Although sample interviews can be put into booklet form, a manual does not have the ability to come alive as does role playing an actual interview. These interviews are rare; therefore there is little chance to gain real interviewing experience unless role playing is used.

Because the first interview of this type is just as important as any other interview, that is, there is no room for error in any interview, the safest way to train the interviewer is to have him role play an interview. Give him an opportunity to discover how to handle this situation before he actually faces it.

Employment Office

It is important that the employment interviewer hire people with honesty and integrity and weed out people who are potentially dishonest. It is a real responsibility to avoid the maladjusted person who may later become a problem to the store.

This valuable judgment is made in the few minutes the interviewer spends with the applicant. Although the person's employment record does have some value, the applicant is judged during the interview conversation to the point of employment.

To the employment interviewer, role playing is almost a necessity in order to do a good job of weeding out the potentially dishonest person. Role playing is an excellent method of gaining experience without jeopardizing the store.

Department Manager

Supervisory people who work on the selling floor and deal directly with the customers also have a need for role-playing experience. They often have to deal with the problems of questionable refunds, suspected fraud purchasers, and similar security situations.

Because these problems occur only occasionally, the department manager does not have many opportunities to gain experience interviewing suspected impostors or customers involved in questionable refunds. The department manager has few opportunities to learn how to act in these situations in real life. Still the manager must know what to say and must have self-confidence when handling an unusual situation.

Questionable Refunds and Charges

Role playing gives the manager an opportunity to discover how it feels to be involved in the situation, what sort of questions the customer might ask, and how to handle these questions. Role playing can teach the manager how to handle a customer who may be using a charge account without permission. Role playing will also teach the proper order of questions when handling a questionable refund.

The manager will learn first in a simulated situation to ask the customer's name and address and, once the name and address are established, to ask for identification. If the customer has no identification, the manager then learns how to tell the customer that the refund will be mailed.

Even though the manager reads instructions about how to question a customer, it is not easy to do it until he has experienced the situation.

The Manager Needs Role-Playing Security

Role playing is just as important to a department manager in learning his job as it is for a professional actor. The actor spends many weeks in rehearsal and he knows his part perfectly; he knows what part he is playing and how he should act. There is little difference between acting on the stage and acting a part in a scene with a customer.

The problems are different, of course. In one case a script has been prepared in advance, whereas in the other case, the role playing is impromptu. In both cases there is a need for rehearsal. Both the store manager and the actor need the sense of security that role playing can give them.

How to handle critical situations cannot be learned overnight. The techniques cannot be packed into a brief training period. Role playing may have to be done every week for a period of time for a person to learn how to handle unusual situations.

Security Department Interviewers

People in the security department also require role playing. Good interviewers are difficult to find, but much can be done to develop the natural talent an interviewer already has. An interviewer can be taught the fundamental principles of interviewing if given the opportunity to apply these theories in interview situations through role playing.

Play Both Parts

It is good to have the person being trained to role play both parts, the part of the person doing the interview and the part of the person being interviewed. By playing the part of the person doing the interview, he'll learn how such an interviewer will feel in the situation, what type of questions should be asked, and how to handle himself. He will gain poise, self-control, and inner security.

By playing the part of the person being interviewed, he will learn how such a person feels. He will discover through personal experience what fears and doubts such a person experiences. He will find out what bluffs a thief may be tempted to make. Understanding how the person being interviewed feels and reacts will be a great aid to the interviewer later when he actually interviews someone in a similar situation.

It is also helpful in any type of role playing to have the session tape recorded so that it can be played back and reviewed. The person doing the interview has a chance to study what he actually said and how it sounded in the interview.

Fundamental Principles of Education

Good educational techniques are based on two fundamental principles. First, stimulating the trainee's interest and, second, allowing the trainee to "discover" the right answers.

We only truly learn the things we discover for ourselves. No one can *teach* us anything. People can *tell* us things and we can gain knowledge about things, but we never learn anything from the outside, only from within.

The best method of learning is to have situations in which the trainee can discover answers for himself. A theory is still a theory until it is put into practice.

Ouside of actual experience, role playing is the most successful teaching technique available today. It comes closest to simulating events themselves and it should be used in every security education program.

PAMPHLETS

Pamphlets for Salespeople

To help train salespeople Lord & Taylor printed a twelve-page pamphlet containing cartoon figures and short captions depicting methods of reducing shortages.

The booklet stressed such methods as giving good service to prevent loss, asking for identification on charges taken out of the store above the charge limit, and similar practices recommended to salespeople to help reduce shortages. The pamphlet was judged to be an effective tool for loss reduction.

Booklets on Inventory Shortage Controls

Inventory shortage control booklets are published by most large stores today to meet the needs of supervisors in all areas of the store. The booklet usually indicates causes of loss and suggests action needed to reduce losses. It also explains in simple terms how an inventory is prepared.

This type of booklet is generally comprehensive and contains material not relevant to a specific department. In other words, much of the material in the booklet would not be applicable to any one department using the booklet. For this reason there is a tendency to reject the entire booklet.

Sometimes too many checkpoints and too much material are assembled in one manual. Unless a person has a certain thoroughness of temperament, the booklet may be skimmed over in a general fashion and not used as part of a program for reducing losses.

If a store is conducting a campaign to reduce loss, the inventory shortage booklet can be useful as a reference if it is properly assembled.

MEMOS

Some years ago an interesting memo campaign was conducted at Lord & Taylor. It centered around a personable young guard named David.

The presentation began on a Sunday. Small cardboard cut-outs mounted on wooden stands and showing a photo of this guard were placed on each executive's desk throughout the store. With the cut-out photograph of the guard was "David Memo," and it was the first of a series of such memos dealing with various aspects of the store's shortage problem.

One memo, for example, dealt with the problem of carelessness. It said, "You will perhaps notice that the hand of carelessness has touched this memo," and in the lower right-hand corner of the memo was a set of smudged fingerprints. The memo went on to explan how carelessness may have touched other records on the executive's desk and brought out the point that carelessness can lead to errors and substantial loss for the company.

The David Memo campaign extended over a period of six weeks and aroused considerable discussion throughout the store.

A similar campaign was conducted more recently in another store. Only in this case the same principles were centered around the theme of "The Little Dutch Boy." This was the little Dutch boy who kept his finger in the dyke and prevented Holland from being flooded. The program stressed that the individual who takes personal responsibility to prevent loss in his store can very well be an important factor in protecting profits.

Use Distinctive Colors

An interesting technique used by the security department of a large store was to put all interdepartmental memos on pink paper and enclose them in a distinctive blue envelope. This combination gave every security memo special attention.

Whenever an executive had a security memo on his desk among his papers, he was always aware of it because of its color. Security memos were often given preferential treatment because they were recognized as being important. The color made this special attention possible.

Day-to-Day Memos

Memos used as part of security education on a day-to-day basis can also be effective. For example, memos that bring to the buyer's attention the fact that his showcases have been left unlocked at night, the memo that brings to the delivery department's attention an excessive amount of nondelivery complaints, or the memo that goes to the head of the selling force to show the number of refunds cashed without proper identification.

These and similar memos can be used continuously throughout the year and make an effective basic security education program.

POSTERS

Some stores have done a lot with posters. Security points to be stressed on posters should be applicable across the whole store organization.

Baby Pictures

One store used a series of cute baby pictures to emphasize the messages they wanted to bring to the attention of staff personnel. One, for example, showed a baby in tears and it said, "I'm crying because our shortages last year were $__________." Another poster showed a baby talking into a telephone. It said, "I'm calling security because someone just stole my diaper pin."

These baby posters were amusing to the store employees and served as good security propaganda. They got their message across in a painless manner.

"The Goop"

In another store, a poster campaign called "The Goop" was conducted. For two weeks prior to the first goop poster there were teaser signs throughout the store. They asked, "Who is a Goop?" "What is a Goop?" "Are you a Goop?" "You will find out what a Goop is on Monday," and so on.

Following these teaser cards, a series of posters ran one at a time for a week over a period of several weeks. On each poster there were two large photographs. One showed a sloppy, ill-kept looking salesperson doing something that was against the best interests of the store from a security standpoint. The photographs were of the "before-and-after" type. The "after" photo showed a good-looking, well-groomed, pleasant salesperson in the same situation doing the job correctly.

The top of the poster said, "Don't be a Goop." Underneath one picture the card said, "A Goop Does this—," and under the other picture was the caption, "A Good Salesperson does this—."

One example showed the Goop reading a magazine in a stockroom with a cigarette dangling loosely from her lips. The Goop was paying no attention to a woman who was stealing a coat off the rack beside her. In the other picture, the salesperson was shown asking the woman what she was doing in the stockroom area. Another poster showed the Goop helping a display person take merchandise out of the department, but there was no loan slip visible. The properly performing salesperson was then seen seated at a desk while checking off the display merchandise and listing it on a loan slip. This campaign was well received. No one wanted to be a "Goop."

Use Distinctive Paper

In another security campaign, a set of posters was made on small squares of blueprint paper. It made them distinctive. One set of blueprints was directed at packers. It noted such things as the need to check prices, to use care in handling of overgoods, and so on. There were many other similar points. This set of posters was put at packing desks throughout the store and was changed weekly. Later, the posters were made into a booklet that was issued to new packers when they entered the packing department.

Sketches Can Cause Resentment

Interestingly enough, making sketches of salespeople or packers for posters can be tricky. In one store, a set of cartoons depicted salespeople in a humorous fashion.

In one case, the sketch showed a salesclerk with a bun at the back of her head and a pencil stuck through it. In another case, a salesclerk was wearing a very worn and ratty-looking fur neckpiece.

When these posters were displayed, there was resentment among many of the salespeople. They did not like to see themselves portrayed, even humorously, in a critical way. The whole set of posters had to be redrawn. The salesclerk was changed from an amusing character to a sophisticated looking young lady.

The effect of the changed sketches was found to be very favorable. This, of course, illustrates how carefully any campaign must be designed. At no time should anything in your presentation injure the feelings of the people you are trying to persuade.

VIDEO TAPES AND MOVIES

Several stores have made motion picture films and video tapes to train their employees in security problems. When the films were presented, the security head read from a prepared script and added his comments along with the film as it was shown. These films showed many problems of employee and customer theft. One such film was directed almost entirely at supervisory personnel and dealt with the problems of dishonest employees. Another film was more general and showed some of the workings of the security department.

Another film used an ingenious idea. In one sequence a shopping bag supposedly taken from a shoplifter was shown; the security manager took an endless amount of goods out of the bag. Using a stop action camera technique the bag was made to appear as a bottomless pit holding an enormous amount of merchandise. No matter what things were taken from the shopping bag, more and more things continued to appear. It well illustrated the endless drain shoplifters make on every store.

One film dealt with inventory shortage problems. This film showed several methods of theft but concerned itself primarily with scenes of actual cases taken during the malefactor interview. These photographs were taken with a concealed camera and showed the faces of malefactors reacting to the discussion of their crimes. The point made by the film was that people who steal look like anyone else. The criminal does not outwardly appear to be different from someone's neighbor. It illustrates the fact that people of all ages and from all backgrounds can become retail criminals.

Shoplifters in Action

Another store made an interesting use of movies in a different way. They used them for training store detectives. One of the needs in training store detectives is to give them the experience of observing different types of thieves in action. "Still" photographs can help to supplement experience obtained on the job, but a still photograph does not give the same emotional effect as seeing an actual theft perpetrated.

New detectives are put with experienced detectives for a few weeks when they are being trained. This is done so they will learn to recognize shoplifters in a variety of cases.

Films in Training Programs

One security manager thought the floor training could be improved by showing movies that simulated theft situations in departments throughout the store. As a test, the store made a movie with thirty different kinds of thefts acted out in the settings where the detectives were going to work. The thief was played by an experienced store detective who had a good understanding of how a thief looks and acts while carrying out a theft.

Detectives who observed this film every day for a week during their training learned to spot shoplifters much more quickly than did detectives trained without the film. The film served as an indirect method of role playing. Although the detective's role was passive while watching the film, the detective still experienced the sensations and visual images identical to those seen later in real life. By using the same settings in which the detective would later work, the film became a practical process of automatic conditioning.

Motion pictures offer an unlimited opportunity for aiding security training programs. A film can be used in the training of new employees by insuring that needed motivational factors are always included in the presentation. It also insures the store that the orientation period for new employees is always handled the way in which the store wants it to be handled.

Films can also be used in almost any of the educational programs outlined in this chapter. Next to a live performance, films are the closest thing to real life in their educational impact. In many ways films are even better than a live performance because they can be edited and perfected. Film presentation has another big advantage in that any program that is going to be repeated over and over again for different groups of people is given consistency when it is on video tape or film.

TAPE RECORDINGS

Tape recordings have much potential value. People with imagination can use them effectively. They can supplement slides and add variety to security presentations.

One store used a tape recording about a dishonest employee case to educate supervisory people. After the tape recording of the case had been played, questions were asked by the group leader concerning the case. Then a group discussion was held about the factors that led to the theft.

Evaluation of the program indicated that the people attending felt they received much value from this approach. This particular session stressed the supervisor's responsibility in preventing dishonesty among his people.

In another case a tape recording was used for training security managers. At a conference of security managers from retail stores all over the country, a tape recording was played of an actual interview between a security manager and a professional refund operator.

The recording was used to show what techniques could be applied in interviews in order to gain admissions of theft. In this case, the person interviewed admitted stealing over $80,000 from the store during a six-year period.

This same tape recording was used in another way with the store management to stimulate them to make a study of the refund system. As a result of this study, the refund system was strengthened.

Tapes Combined with Visual Display

In another instance a stockclerk agreed to make a recorded interview detailing his thefts from a stockroom. This was then used as a training device. The stockclerk described his methods of theft and told about other people in his area who were stealing. He also discussed some of the lax practices of supervisors in his department.

The stockclerk had stolen over $4,000 of merchandise, which was recovered from his home. As a special training presentation, the $4,000 of stolen merchandise was set up as a display.

A series of meetings were then held with supervisory personnel. The supervisory people sat facing the display and listened to the recorded interview of the stockclerk. The impact of having the merchandise piled up in front of them combined with the reproduction of the interview as it actually occurred had considerable emotional impact. The results were far-reaching. Supervisory controls were tightened.

Tapes Used in Training Detectives

One problem of training detectives is to impress upon them the necessity for following common-sense rules of apprehension. Even though people may be aware that another person has stolen something it is still necessary to prove the intent to steal. Training detectives in this area of legal judgment is time-consuming and difficult.

In this store, detectives were trained in the rules of arrest by creating situations on tape and then asking the detectives what they would do about the simulated case. For example, this tape recording was played to a training group, and they heard a man saying:

> I was in your store yesterday afternoon about 3:00 o'clock. Luckily you didn't see me. I went into your wallet department and while I was there I succeeded in distracting your saleswoman, that short one with the dark hair.
>
> When she was looking through a drawer in the back of a counter for a special red wallet that I had requested, I was able to slip one of your wallets out of the display case. I quickly put it in my hip pocket. After looking at the red wallet, I told the saleswoman that I had changed my mind and then I turned and left your store. I went out the revolving door and up the avenue.
>
> Now I am wondering just one thing. If you had seen me take that wallet and put it in my hip pocket, would you have arrested me?

The tape recording was then stopped and a group discussion held in which the detectives stated whether they would or would not have arrested the culprit. In this case, of course, the correct answer should have been that the detectives would not have arrested the thief. By having put the wallet in his hip pocket, which is a normal place for a man to carry a wallet, it would have been very difficult to prove his intent to steal in court.

Similar problems were set up on tape and it was found that the detectives responded with enthusiasm to this technique of learning. Again, it is an adaption of the principle of role playing. The detective is sitting in judgment on a role-playing situation.

Using Tapes to Instill Safety

One store uses a tape recording in the delivery area where delivery men load their trucks. The delivery area has a public address sound system.

Every day while the men are loading their trucks, a personalized tape recording is put on the air between muscial selections. If it is raining outside, the tape recording may say,

> Say fellows, it's raining out today and the streets are pretty slippery. Let's be very careful going around the curves and be sure that we aren't going too fast when we enter school zones. Let's be careful that we don't hit a child.

Each day the message is varied to fit the weather or any other local situation. The messages are usually tied into the problem of safety and have been a big factor in improving the store's safety records.

NEWSPAPERS AND MAGAZINES

Many stores now use closed-circuit television equipment. Some stores have used the newspapers to publicize the television equipment. They do this for psychological benefits, hoping such articles will deter customers who otherwise might have been tempted to steal in their store.

Other newspaper stories are used to help security prior to Christmas. In one city the police department does a series on pick-pockets and handbag thieves. In another city there is a series done on the problems of shoplifting. Again, there is a tendency to illustrate such newspaper articles with photographs of people actually stealing. Unless there are strong deterrent factors included with such material, this can be very dangerous because it creates thieves.

Publicizing Prosecution Cases

One problem stores face is whether or not to publicize prosecution of cases. Some stores feel very strongly that cases should be publicized. They think there is value in such publicity in that it may deter other people from stealing. Stores concerned with their corporate image in the community, however, are afraid such stories may injure their community relationships.

Newspaper stories on cases show one small incident, implying that the odds are very much in favor of the store against the person. People have a tendency to favor the underdog, and those who are concerned about injuring the store's corporate image may very well have a good point in preferring not to have publicity about the prosecution of criminals.

It is also true, however, that if the store is obviously hard on people who steal, professional thieves may stay away from the store. The public, of course, has less sympathy for the shoplifter who steals from the store than they do for the employee who is prosecuted. Therefore, a solution to the problem might be to publicize shoplifter prosecutions, but not to release stories on internal thefts.

Publicity of Trained Dogs

Another application of newspaper and magazine publicity was done by two large stores about their trained dogs. Both stores did considerable work with newspaper and magazine writers, and numerous articles and photographs were published. A national magazine even ran a cover showing photographs of the dogs in action. The dogs became a widespread topic of conversation.

One company believed the publicity was a great deterrent to store prowlers. They had in the past apprehended nineteen or twenty prowlers in a single year; they found that following the publicity concerning the dogs, they had no prowler apprehensions. The dogs themselves were effective, but far more effective than the dogs was the publicity released to the general public, which frightened off after-hour thieves.

Certain material undoubtedly has strong deterrent effects and is an excellent choice for this communication media. The dog story is an example of a successful combination of security education program and communication media.

SPECIFIC ARTICLES

One magazine ran a very detailed story of a reporter's experience in observing a shoplifter from the moment of apprehension through a complete interview and psychological treatment.

Many articles contain hackneyed material dug up from old newspaper and magazine files centering around methods of theft and are not constructive in preventing dishonesty.

An exception was an interesting article that dealt with the problem of treating a maladjusted woman who was a shoplifter. The article showed an understanding of the suspect's illness and was a deterrent to crime because it strongly brought out the factors that may lead a person to steal. It also suggested that people who shoplift are apt to need psychological help.

The Employees' Publication

In talking about newspapers and magazines, we should not ignore the part that the store's employee publication can play in security education work. The store magazine can be a good persuasion tool. It can keep alive the problems of shortage and it can maintain interest in security problems.

Photographs and articles on new scientific equipment being used by the store can build psychological barriers to prevent employees from stealing. Articles and photographs of the people who won awards because they spotted a shoplifter and reported it to security can also be useful in giving recognition to these people. It also encourages other employees to lend their talents to the hunt for the thief in their midst.

The "Case of the Month"

One store ran a "case of the month" in its company magazine, in which they described an interesting shoplifter case and reminded employees to be on the alert for suspects.

Store magazines should stay away from any reference to the dishonest employee. In dealing directly with the problems of the shoplifter, the bad check operator, the refund artist, and the impostor, they have plenty of good material to arouse interest and gain help from employees. In stressing the award program, they indirectly suggest that awards are given for leads on dishonest employees as well as shoplifters. However, the main emphasis in awards should be on the dishonest customer, not on the employee.

Store magazines have shown photographs demonstrating methods of shoplifter theft. Others have presented detailed discussions of loss problems and what can be done about them. Some have tackled inventory shortage losses from the point of view of correcting carelessness and errors.

In every case there are things to be gained by using the store magazine. The programs designed for presentation in the magazine should be directed toward all store personnel. Care should be taken not to include any material that might create dishonesty.

Once these points are decided upon, the next thing is to decide what results you expect from the material presented. Unless you clearly define your expected results your material may be entertaining but not particularly useful.

EXHIBITS

Very few stores have done much with exhibits as a method of security presentation. However, there is much potential in this area. People believe what they see and the exhibit is really a form of demonstration. We'll look at only one exhibit in detail, one presented for the executives of Lord & Taylor.

An Executives' Exhibit

The store had had some severe inventory shortages, and it was decided to have an exhibit that combined the problems of theft with those of carelessness and error. It was assumed before the exhibit was constructed that the problems of carelessness and error were important and more likely to be the basic cause of the high-shortage figures than was crime. Emphasis was therefore placed on the error and carelessness factors.

The exhibit was set up in the store's board of directors' room to give it status, and it indicated to all store executives the endorsement of top management of the principles presented.

Motion Picture Film

When the executives entered the exhibit, they first went into a small room in which a continual showing of a motion picture called "Lord & Taylor Confidential," was held. This was a sound-on-film presentation photographed in the Lord & Taylor store, and it illustrated different types of people who cause loss through criminal activities. It showed that people of all ages and all types can be dishonest. The film also showed a few methods of theft but it dwelt primarily on the types of people who steal. After leaving the film, the executives followed a narrow roped-off path into a larger room.

Pamphlets and Photographs

On entering the exhibit room, the executive was given a pamphlet outlining the major points for controlling shortages.

In the first section of the exhibit he saw large panels filled with photographs of retail malefactors. On the panel were photographs of shoplifters, refund operators, impostors, bad check artists, and other people who prey on retail stores.

Next to this was a panel about eight by ten feet containing a photostatic blow-up of nearly 100 newspaper clippings dealing with crimes against the retailer. The title over the panel was "It Can Happen Here."

Phases of Loss Control

After the problem of retail crime as a cause of shortage had been emphasized, the remaining parts of the exhibit dealt with other phases of loss control.

The next section of the exhibit was devoted to salescheck errors. A large panel holding several hundred saleschecks, each containing errors, faced the executive. There were also two or three saleschecks blown up to a height of eight feet. On these saleschecks specific errors that led to loss were circled in red. One check contained seven such errors.

Following the salescheck exhibit, there was a frame with several earphones. The executive could pick up an earphone at random and hear a recorded message concerning shortage problems.

Then there was a booth with a curtained entrance. The executive, when entering the booth, found himself in a small dark room and to his left was a small opening into which he could peer. When he looked into the opening he saw a mirror that reflected his own face. Above and below the mirror was the message, "*You* are the cause of inventory shortage losses."

From here the executive continued around the room through a series of other exhibits showing carelessness and error. One exhibit, for example, had several clotheslines strung with safety pins and attached to them were hundreds of transfer errors. There was also a big washbasket full of transfer errors sitting underneath the clotheslines. A sign next to the exhibit said, "Some of our dirty wash."

In another exhibit a mannequin sat at a marking machine. The mannequin was turning out price tickets. On a board behind the machine was a blow-up of a price ticket error. The incident illustrated how several hundred articles were incorrectly marked because of an error in pricing.

Other parts of the exhibit dealt with problems of refund errors, packing errors, delivery errors, and so forth.

Visual Loss

At the end of the exhibit was a small room. When the executive entered it, he found himself in the presence of a mannequin policeman holding a submachine gun.

Piled about the room were many boxes labeled $25,000. These boxes were piled to the ceiling of the room and in the center of the room was a large open box containing several thousand dollars in actual cash. The exhibit indicated that in this room, represented by these boxes, was the actual amount of money lost by the store through inventory shortages during the past year.

After leaving the last room, the executive was handed an envelope. In it was fake money amounting to $120.70. A slip in the envelope explained that this was the amount of money the store had lost during the time the executive was going through the exhibit.

The Ingredients

This exhibit made use of almost all the different kinds of communication media, movies, demonstrations, photographs, slides, tape recordings, posters, pamphlets, and memos. The evaluation of the executives who attended the exhibit was that it was unforgettable and powerful.

As can be imagined, such an exhibit can be impressive. It is security education with tremendous impact. The success of such an exhibit depends on the care with which it is prepared, the investment in its presentation, and most important, the imagination used to make it effective.

MISCELLANEOUS

"Shrink MacShortage"

A store in Washington, D.C., as part of a campaign to "talk" shortages down, created a mythical character called, "Shrink MacShortage." They first introduced this character in posters and in cut-outs that were placed on executives' desks throughout the store. Later they developed the point further by hiring an actor and dressing him up in kilts so that he looked like a modern Sir Harry Lauder.

This mythical character, symbolized by the actor, would appear mysteriously and silently at the most unexpected times. If a staff meeting were being held he might come in unexpectedly, take a seat, and after sitting for a few minutes listening to the staff meeting, silently get up and leave.

At a training session he might wander in, take a seat in the front row, sit there attentively for a while, and then get up and leave. He appeared and disappeared throughout the store every day for a considerable period of time. He, of course, became a conversation piece and along with him went many discussions about shortages.

"Hey Rube!"

One security director, in order to get his entire store shortage-minded, used the store's weekly magazine to show various shoplifting methods in pictorial form. He also inaugurated a system called "Hey Rube" for all personnel.

The system was similar to the type used by the circus. When a protection problem comes up in a circus they can't contact their security department by phone, so they rely on a different kind of warning system. Their system is the "Hey Rube!" method. Whenever anyone in a circus hears "Hey Rube" he knows something is wrong and word passes from one person to another until it reaches a member of the circus police. This particular security director instituted a similar "Hey Rube" system to protect store merchandise and help control shortages. Instead of "Hey Rube," his signal was "212," which is the telephone line designated for the store's security department.

An Alert

He instructed employees who did not have a telephone handy to contact the security office when a shoplifter, pickpocket, or other person operated in their area to alert the nearest employee by quoting "212," "212." This employee, in turn, recognizing that this call was a warning signal, would immediately dial 212 and ask the security department for help. This system worked so well that in the months following this campaign he increased his shoplifter apprehensions by 25 percent.

Advertise

In order to publicize the special issue of the store's weekly magazine, *Echo*, which introduced the "Hey Rube" System, Mr. Murphy plastered the entire store with handbills two days before the issue. He also had security department personnel pass out these handbills as the employees entered the store in the morning.

The first handbill showed a picture of a circus train with only the number "212" on it. This aroused the curiosity of the store employees. Management was amazed at the number of employees who did not recognize "212" as the phone number of the security department.

On the following day a second handbill was distributed in the same manner. This one showed a picture of a telephone with the number 212 beneath it. A notation on the bottom of the handbill read, "We'll see you in the *Echo* Friday." That was the day the magazine was to be distributed.

In order to keep the theme of "212" alive, the security department continued a column in the weekly magazine that bore the heading "212." This column publicized the names of employees who had helped security in the apprehension of a shoplifter. They also used the column to instruct employees regarding the techniques of shoplifters, fraudulent charge account operators, bogus check people, and so forth.

Awards

This store does not give cash awards to employees but uses a special "awards club" as a motivating device. The requirement for becoming a member of this "club" is to give "Service Far Above the Line of Duty."

Each member of the club is presented with a scroll bearing his name and accomplishment at a tea attended only by top executives. Employees consider this a considerable honor.

The security director also holds weekly meetings with department personnel throughout the store and brings to the meeting an up-to-date rogues' gallery of well-known shoplifters, bad check operators, and con people who are operating in the area.

These meetings acquaint the salespeople with shortage problems, familiarize employees with the descriptions of active malefactors, and remind salespeople of their responsibility in security matters. The shortage control department also works to educate buyers, assistant buyers, and other merchandise people in ways of reducing shortages.

Follow-up

Security follow-up is not always thought of as educational, and yet, follow-up programs are educational.

Some stores do surprise register audits in the middle of the selling day. A security person and a member of the control division go into a selling department, take a drawer out of the cash register, and balance it immediately.

If the employee balances, everything is fine. If the employee is short, then an interview is held to see if the reason can be determined. These surprise audits have been successful in deterring people from dishonesty, and they have also resulted in the apprehension of several dishonest employees.

Follow-up interviews of employees with an excessive amount of overages or shortages in their register totals have proven to be a good educational technique.

Follow-up in All Areas

One of the most effective methods of follow-up can be used in connection with honesty shopping. Many times honesty shoppers shop salespeople and do not receive a sales receipt. However, a later check of the register tape shows that the employee was honest and did ring up the sale but was careless in not giving the customer a register receipt.

One store writes these policy violations up and turns the report over to the store's personnel department. They, in turn, call in the salesperson and conduct a corrective interview. It is felt that this type of follow-up often prevents carelessness and may prevent a person from eventually stealing cash from the store.

Follow-ups, of course, can be done in almost any area of the store. For example, follow-up on an expensive jewelry department to see that the cases are being locked at night, follow-up on non-delivery complaints, or follow-up on checking loan slips to be sure that merchandise on display is backed up by a loan slip.

Wherever loss problems develop, follow-up techniques can be used to check the area. They do an educational job and also act as a psychological barrier to carelessness, error, and theft.

Slogan Labels

One store uses stickers on company phones to remind personnel to be alert to theft problems. Such a sticker may say, "Security is everyone's responsibility," or it might say, "For security help phone Ext. 296." These gummed labels are put on and taken off weekly during the period of the security campaign.

A similar application has been done by stamping all mail going through the mail room with a security slogan.

Bulletin Boards

Posters, pamphlets, and even memos can be put on bulletin boards. Sometimes, however, the bulletin board can be utilized as an exhibit location.

For example, one store used the bulletin board carrying employee messages that is located outside of the employee cafeteria for a special security program. In this instance, the bulletin board contained 5 × 7 photographs of people who had won an award during the previous week. In addition to the person's photograph, there was a citation memo that told what the person had done and praised the person for his or her action. The memo was an enlarged reproduction of a memo written by the security department to top management. This board stimulated other employees to attempt to find dishonest customers.

Another store used an interesting technique to encourage people to earn awards. Whenever a person helped the security department, they gave this employee a small model of a policeman wearing a bright shiny badge. The figure is given out at a department meeting with much ceremony and is very popular with employees.

Safety Programs

This store uses the same principle in their safety program. The department that has the worst safety record for the month has a ceremony in which pallbearers bring a miniature coffin into the department and the department has to keep this coffin for a month or until another department has a worse safety record and is thus given the coffin. Both the little policeman and the coffin have been very effective as a stimulant to interest in security and safety programs.

The Unusual Case

Once in a while a very unusual security problem will arise and a security program can help to solve the case. For example, in one store a series of thefts had been occurring from the cash register in the housewares department. The thefts continued for several weeks.

Finally all the employees had been checked, with the exception of two women who had a day off when the theft occurred. It was assumed that one of these two employees had to be the person doing the stealing. The store decided to give these two people a lie detector test. The woman involved agreed and the test was given. The results showed that both women were innocent.

It was now clear that the store had a serious security problem. The security department by itself had not been able to solve the mystery of the thefts. It was decided to hold a meeting of the entire department and see if the salespeople could solve the problem.

An early morning meeting was held, coffee and doughnuts were served to the selling staff, and the store manager explained the problem of the thefts. He said the store was seriously concerned about the losses and the fact that these losses were occurring in the department where these people worked gave them a black eye. This suggested that one of them was dishonest.

The Proof of the Program

After the meeting the group returned to the selling floor determined to work out some plan of their own to catch the thief. It took only three days until the stockclerk who had been stealing the cash from the department's register was caught.

The salespeople had been on full alert. Before this the store had had no detectives in the area, but now they had a full staff of detectives working every hour the store was open. The salespeople had one objective—to catch the thief.

This is an interesting example of a security program. After several months of vain attempts by store management and store security to catch the register thief, the department itself caught the culprit within three days. Here is direct proof of the value of security education programs.

Educational Memos

Periodic memos to store personnel can be a good medium of communication to encourage all employees to help the store combat losses. The eight memos in Appendix 6 are an example of a series of security education memos that proved effective in soliciting the salespeople's interest and help in shortage problems.

Chapter 25

INVENTORY SHORTAGE PROBLEMS

Although it is not often realized, there is a great similarity between the problem of expense control and the problem of shortage control. Effective expense control represents a frame of mind—a determination in the organization that not one penny of excess expenditure or waste will be tolerated. Shortage control requires a similar consciousness and determination throughout the organization.

As a retailer you are probably having shortage troubles. Well, you're not alone. You are probably thinking for the first or tenth time—depending on how long you have been a retailer—that your losses are too high.

Your Losses "Are" Too High

What's more, you're right. Your losses *are* too high. Not because your store is any less efficiently run than other stores, but because efforts to solve store loss problems have not been adequate to do the job.

Your store, like every other store, will have its own way of handling loss problems. No matter what the solution, each store will feel that its way is the best. The truth is that you can always do more to reduce losses, and you can now have the consolation of knowing it can be done. But before we discuss cures, let's look at some of the things that cause shortages.

What Causes Inventory Shortages?

Trouble comes in many forms—faulty credit systems, receiving department problems, and others. Let's look at some of these trouble areas—things that are going to ruin inventory figures.

Marking

One wrong price ticket may not seem like much to be concerned about, but it's a starting point that may uncover large shortages. The value of small things can sometimes be deceiving.

One investigator was making a routine check of a lamp department. The department had a high shortage. He noticed two identical lamps, each with a different price tag. One lamp was priced at $17.95, the other at $6.95.

He asked a saleswoman, "What is the correct price of this lamp?" The saleswoman said it was $17.95. "And is this other lamp with the $6.95 price tag the same lamp?" he asked.

The saleswoman looked at the lamps. Yes, the $6.95 lamp was a wrong price. She smiled as she said, "We often have customers say we have the wrong price on our merchandise." This man did not stop at the one error he had found but did more checking. He found over *two hundred* incorrectly priced lamps.

A check of the department's marking system followed. In the end they had better controls. One price tag showed the way to cutting losses.

Receiving

A six-month inventory in one store's better dress department showed shortages of $32,000. This department sold dresses for $100 to $200 each.

At first the loss was dismissed as a "book loss." As is so often true with so-called book losses, a further check showed that the loss was real. A check of items flowing in and out of the area pinpointed the loss in the receiving room. It was found that the dresses were being stolen *before* they were marked.

The thief was a porter who cleaned the receiving room each morning before the store opened. This porter, working alone, had stolen over $30,000 worth of dresses in six months.

His method of stealing was simple. He stuffed two or three dresses into his shirt and pants each day. He then sold them for $10 apiece to a "fence" he met in a restaurant washroom when he went out for breakfast coffee.

In this case a reorganization of the receiving and marking departments was necessary. A system that a porter could easily beat was far from adequate.

Cash Thefts

Cash itself is interesting, for people can do a lot of things if they have money. And there are many ways of getting cash. Salespeople, for example, handle cash and know ways of getting it.

Recently, when the salespeople in a cosmetic department were "shopped," it was found that one saleswoman was keeping many of her cash sales. She put the money in her "bra" instead of putting it into the cash register.

In the interview, she said she had been stealing cash for some time. The security manager pressed her to find out the extent of her thefts. He found her in a boastful mood. "It's a bad day when I only get $10," she said. "An average day runs $20 to $25."

Backing up her story, she gave him a bank book with a balance of over $2,000. She told him this was part of the money she had stolen.

The dishonest employee problem should never be underestimated. A large chain store lost $1,400,000 in one year.

A cross section of the firm's employees were given a lie detector test to determine the extent of their thefts. It was found that 76 percent of these employees had taken $100 or more in merchandise or money in the six months prior to the test.

The moral in this case is not to think of your losses only in terms of merchandise. It may be that you are losing cash.

Poor Controls

An octopus has many arms as do loss figures; high shortages have multiple causes. For example take a recent jewelry department loss.

A check of the credit and remarking system showed that many pieces of jewelry were being wrongly marked when returned for credit. There was no sketch of the items in the price book to identify them for a new price tag.

In addition, the salespeople had been told by the buyer to model the jewelry during the day. No loan system was set up to handle the modeling. The result was that the salespeople—that is, the models—frequently forgot to take the pins and bracelets off before going home in the evening. The jewelry was worn home and not returned.

A further check showed that a large quantity of goods being sold did not have price tags. The salespeople were quoting whatever price they guessed the articles sold for. The prices they quoted were usually far below the actual retail value. As can easily be surmised, as a result of these factors there was a large inventory shortage.

Losses Can Be Cut

Let's not be defeatist in our thinking—losses can be cut. But to do so you must face the shortage problem without compromise.

You must also have a well-organized and flexible plan of checking and following through.

The flow of goods in and out of the problem department must be watched. Crediting, marking, and billing systems must be gone over to see if they operate as planned.

You must look over your customers and employees to see if any of them are causing your loss. A physical layout of the area should be reviewed with emphasis on the location of stockrooms, fitting rooms, and cash registers. Loan controls must be examined.

The refund and adjustment credits must be checked as well as the buyer's markup and markdown procedures. A daily check of the sales and credits must be part of the survey. The receiving room, stockroom, and packing department must not be overlooked.

You know that there must be a common denominator to the problem—and it's *carelessness*!

The fact that a shortage has occurred does not mean that a new system has to be devised. It may show that the present system is not being enforced.

There is no magic that will solve shortages overnight. You need constant work over a period of time to bring high losses under control.

Start with a Survey

To start work on your loss problems you first need a plan of attack. A survey of high-shortage departments is a good way to begin. Your inventory survey should be handled in two ways, indirect and direct.

During the indirect survey the personnel and operation of the high-loss areas should be observed without direct contact. Try to locate your dishonest customers and employees.

The second phase, that of the direct survey, needs an active investigator in the department itself. He should check the daily operation from every angle.

Your survey should be planned in advance—a plan made to apply to any high-loss area. No part of the operation should go unchecked.

The information you gather during the survey must finally be correlated and reviewed. The object of such a review is to locate sources of trouble and decide on needed changes in the operation to prevent future losses.

To do such a survey your store should have a capable group of investigators. These people can conduct inventory surveys in shortage departments on a year-round basis. Such a group is usually under the shortage controller, or it may come under your security manager.

Build a Competent Security Department

In the past, security departments were primarily concerned with shoplifters, but now they are coming of age.

The modern security department is headed by someone with a background in retail operations as well as security work. If he is given an adequate budget and the support of top management, he can give your store an effective security department.

Not only will such a security department be responsible for arresting shoplifters, forgers, impostors, and dishonest employees, but it will also prevent losses by improving the operation of many store systems.

A modern security department is capable of doing inventory surveys that will locate the sources of inventory shortages. It is also able to give constructive advice on designing your systems to prevent losses.

If you are a retailer who is constantly on the alert to increase your percentage of profit, one sure way is to cut your losses. You can do this by building a competent, hard-hitting security department.

Consider "Controls" and "Layout"

When shortages become so great that they begin to affect your profits, it's time to investigate the flow of merchandise and the physical layout of your departments.

Nobody knows for sure how much of the inventory loss is due to bookkeeping error, or to theft. It is usually a combination of these things that whittles down your profits.

One popular idea expressed today is that the shortage problem should be discarded on the theory that it is a "*bookkeeping error.*"

Practically speaking, this does not change your loss or solve your problem. If a shipment of dresses is marked incorrectly and sold for $10 below cost, an inventory shortage will result. This loss can be correctly called a *bookkeeping error* even though the loss to the store is still an *actual loss.*

When a shortage occurs, two questions arise. First, how much of your loss was due to inadequate controls and poor physical layout? Second, how much future loss can you prevent?

Merchandise Flow

One of the best starting points for a study of shortage problems is the *flow of merchandise.*

The store is a pipeline of moving articles, going from manufacturer to consumer. Shortages occur when there are leaks in this pipeline. At every point where a piece of merchandise is moved a point of possible loss occurs.

Every person from the store manager to the stockclerk is involved in the flow of merchandise. A competent system for controlling goods speeds up all phases of merchandise movement and protects it against loss.

Be Alert to Dangerous Areas

Mentally you should have warning signs to alert you to certain spots in your store's pipeline You have to be aware of these danger areas.

Basically, the danger points in your merchandise pipeline are at every point where goods change hands. The first place is where goods are *received* from the manufacturer. Next is the point where they are *opened* and *invoiced.* After that it is the movement to *marking*. From there to *stock*. Then to the *selling floor.*

Once the goods are on the selling floor, the danger points still continue. From selling floor to fitting room. Then from *salespeople* to *packer*. Then finally from packer to *delivery.*

If the goods reenter the store on *credit*, a new pipeline is set up with new danger points for loss. *Receiving* to *credit room.* Credit to *marking*. Marking to *stock*. Stock to *selling*, and so on.

POINTS OF CONTROL

What can be done to strengthen your pipeline against loss? The following three things should be done:

1. You need adequate, workable controls that parallel the movement of merchandise. These controls should keep contact with goods at all points where items change hands.
2. You should have physical layouts that keep the merchandise under control. They should help to prevent loss when the goods are at rest.
3. You must have competent supervision. You need this at every handling point to enforce your control systems. Systems must actually operate as they are designed in theory.

The stepped-up pace of retailing today often gives us so many current problems that the overall operation is neglected. We have to pay attention to the immediate work. But when shortages begin to increase, your overall picture of the operation must be reexamined.

Dishonesty Is Where You Find It

Before discussing suggestions for counteracting losses in merchandise flow, let's examine a few instances of how shortages occur at some of the danger points already mentioned.

Security people do not label any one spot as more likely to theft than another. Their motto is "Dishonesty is where you find it." But they do know that large-scale theft will occur from the spot that provides the best chance for loss.

Truck Driver Thefts

Do you ever think how the people who deliver goods to your store can also steal from you? One investigator making a routine check discovered a truck driver who, when delivering shipments of cartons from a manufacturer to the store, would unload all the boxes on the sidewalk at the store's receiving door.

He waited while they were checked and signed into the store by the receiving clerk. When the receiving clerk was busy checking another delivery, the truck driver would reload one or two cartons back onto his truck and drive off before the store could discover its loss.

This driver, like many others, had been contacted by a "fence" who agreed to purchase any goods the driver could salvage in his daily deliveries. The fence in turn operated an apparently legitimate wholesale firm.

He shipped the stolen merchandise given to him by the truck drivers to unsuspecting stores all over the country. When this case was finally broken, a quarter of a million dollars in stolen merchandise was found at the fence's warehouse. These goods were stolen from stores from Maine to Texas.

Many stores victimized by these truckers were not even aware of their losses. The weak spot here was at the point of receiving. When a carton of goods is stolen, the loss usually is several hundred dollars. Two or three cartons a week will create a substantial inventory shortage.

Carelessness

And what about that dragon, *carelessness*? Sometimes we can see carelessness in action, but more often it's a hidden cause of loss.

Honest employees may cause a shortage by careless handling of items. For example, take the case of a store that received a large shipment of jewelry intended for a big promotion. The jewelry was sent from the marking room to the jewelry department to be put in stock so that it would be ready for an advertised special. A careless stockclerk delivered it to the wrong department.

For nearly a year it remained in its dusty boxes unnoticed at the back of the hosiery department shelf. When it was finally discovered, the jewelry was no longer saleable as it had lost its retail value in a style-conscious market.

The store took a complete loss on the large shipment in addition to the cost of its advertising and the incalculable loss of goodwill from disappointed customers who had responded to the advertised promotion for "Carter for President" pins. Good controls on the movement of these Carter buttons would have prevented loss.

Parallel Controls

Emergency brakes on a car usually operate on a separate system from the floor pedal brakes. This gives double protection in case of an emergency. Parallel controls in a store can give the same type of dual protection.

Often a parallel control system will uncover a point of loss. One case of this type was that of an employee who was finally caught stealing expensive dresses from a receiving room.

"How did you find out I was stealing from receiving?" the arrested man asked. "Well," replied the security manager, "when we noticed large shortages we checked carefully all points along the route the merchandise traveled. One of the systems we then installed was a 'marking control'."

"Marking control? What's that?" asked the curious thief. "We made our price tickets from the original invoice independently of any count of the goods," continued the security manager. "Then when these tags were put onto the dresses, if there were any price tickets left over we knew dresses were missing. When we had price tickets left over it showed us the dresses were disappearing before they were marked. That narrowed the investigation and led to your arrest."

Protecting Fitting Rooms

Does the way you lay out and build your home have any effect on how well it weathers storms? Of course it does. Physical layout in a store can also affect losses.

For example, a professional shoplifter arrested with nearly $500 worth of dresses from a medium-priced dress department was asked why she didn't steal from the better dress department on an upper floor.

"Why should I make it hard for myself?" she asked. "Those fittin' rooms of yours upstairs have curtains on them that anyone can peek through, but the fittin' rooms in the department where I got my stuff have regular doors on them so no one can see you." Needless to add, the store had the fitting room doors replaced with curtains the next day.

Entrances

Groups of fitting rooms with more than one entrance are difficult to control. By redesigning fitting rooms so there was only one entrance and also by putting a checker at this entrance to conrol the flow of items in and out of the fitting rooms, losses were cut in six months from $6,000 to $200.

When the checker was removed, department losses again soared. The checker was returned to her post and losses are now kept to a minimum.

A men's clothing department that had several customer entrances at both the front and back was suffering heavy losses. The layout was redesigned so all entrances were at the front of the department. As a result, losses were greatly reduced and each customer received better service. He was met at the entrance of the department by a salesman and escorted back to the merchandise.

Sometimes You Have to Lock Up

If you have candy at home and you don't want your child to get into it, what do you do? You put it out of reach or you lock it up. Sometimes you have to do the same thing to protect the goods in your store.

By adding locks to packing chutes one store ended thefts by stockclerks who had been reaching into the chutes and removing packages coming from other floors.

Another store was not as lucky; a group of stockclerks drained of $80,000 worth of goods. This is the sort of loss that good controls can prevent.

Packing stations and stockrooms should be built so that the items are well protected. By removing expensive displays of small items near elevators and fire exit doors, display losses can also be cut.

Prevent Losses

Putting cash registers in active selling areas where they are easily observed by floor managers reduces employee thefts.

The dividing line between causing and preventing loss is often thin. It is usually determined by the efficiency of controls for moving goods as well as the physical protection of goods at rest.

Many loss problems are not criminal in the legal sense. On the other hand, the carelessness that creates shortages often leads to dishonesty.

The Basic Principles of Security

If you check the merchandise losses within any store, you will find individual security problems. They can often be solved by changing the physical layout and systems in that particular store. However, the basic principles of security are the same for all stores.

Here are the key protection points:

1. There must be a well-protected flow of goods. Every spot where goods move from one department to another should be protected.
2. Your receiving operation must be physically designed so that once goods are accepted from the manufacturer they cannot be stolen back by the truck driver.
3. A control system of signatures and numbers should start with the merchandise as it is received. This system should follow the goods step by step until they reach the customer. These controls should speed up the flow of merchandise and not in any way hinder the efficiency of transfer.
4. Displays, counters, fitting rooms, packing stations, and stockrooms must be designed to prevent theft when merchandise is at rest.
5. When goods are to be returned by the customer for credit, a well-designed credit room will prevent this merchandise from going astray.
6. At every transfer point the merchandise and the person it is transferred to should be identified on a record that is held until the movement of goods is completed.
7. Once a good, workable system for checking and handling merchandise is devised, trained supervisors must be always on the alert to see that the control system is kept in operation. Do not allow shortcuts. They will weaken your system's ability to prevent loss.
8. There are three things to check when shortages appear; (a) physical layout, (b) controls, and (c) supervision.

The flow of goods is the lifeblood of retailing. To prevent losses you must keep checking your store's pipeline. You have to find your points of possible leakage. If you'll do this and also keep your store personnel alert for the invasion of the "carelessness dragon," you can cut your losses.

Chapter 26

CONTROL SYSTEMS AND PROCEDURES

All stores or businesses have systems—for without them they could not function—yet without fail when shortages occur and large quantities of merchandise have mysteriously vanished, somewhere there has been a deviation from the established system. You then hear on all sides that we have this system or that system, which is fine, but who checks your system to see that it works?

Where Control Systems Originate

When we think of retail systems and controls we associate them with the store's internal audit and control division. This, of course, is where most store controls should originate. There are, however, some systems and controls that can be the *joint* effort of internal audit and the security department. There are others that can logically come under the jurisdiction of your store security area.

Each store should set its own patterns of job responsibilities. In some stores many of the controls suggested in this book will be under internal audit. Since the final objective is to reduce losses, it is of little consequence who originates the control as long as someone does so.

Security and Control Division Work Together

The security manager should be aware of all controls that can be useful to his store. By knowing about these controls he can check to see if they are in effect.

If the controls are not in operation, the security manager and the store controller together should discuss the application of the control. Between them they can work out a practical plan of responsibility.

Your store's security and control divisions are both concerned about the problems of loss. They are compatible departments and should work closely together in a daily exchange of information and aid.

Store organizations are designed for maximum efficiency. The organization plan is intended to serve the best interests of the store. Progressive store managements do not require slavish subservience to the white squares of an organization chart if it would cost the store efficiency and effective results.

Any type of systems or controls mentioned in this book can be handled with equal effectiveness in the store's control division or in the security department.

The decision as to where a control should originate is up to each individual store. Our objective here is to outline a complete plan of modern retail security. How to apply the plan is a matter for store management to decide.

A Partial List of Security Controls

Following is a list of security systems and controls. This list should not be considered complete or final. Certain things may apply in your store while other things may not. It is hoped that the list will stimulate your imagination and illustrate basic control principles. These samples are listed here only to suggest the potentiality of using this approach to store security. These controls show how security should be integrated into every area of your store's operation. Remember it is a *partial* list of controls. For example, one store in Washington, D.C., has a list of 200 systems checks.

Some of these controls should be a permanent part of your security operation. Others should be periodic checks done in cycles. Just as executives take annual physical tests to see in what condition their health is, so should a store make a periodic check of its operations to be sure there are no openings where profits can be drained off by malefactors.

1. Personnel Screening

Certain jobs in your store are key spots. People filling these jobs should get special attention when being screened at the point of employment.

For example, cashiers, packers, porters, and people who work at night need to be carefully investigated. In all of these cases, a special effort should be made to check out the person's references and background material.

Particularly in the case of cashiers, it is important for the security department to make personal contacts with their previous employers.

2. Averaging Cash Sales

Your sales audit department should periodically be requested to take some selling departments, such as cosmetics, and average the cash sales per salesperson over a three-week period.

From this comparative average you can determine if any of the salespeople in this department are low in *cash* sales. Such a person is a theft suspect who may be stealing cash from sales. This salesperson should be shopped three or four times to test his or her honesty.

3. Baling Room Test

Large-scale thefts from retail stores have been worked through the baling room. In one store the people who baled paper worked in collusion with the trucking outfit who removed the paper bales from the store.

This group stole thousands of dollars worth of men's suits. They put the stolen suits into the paper bales. Several miles away from the store, the truck driver and his helper took the suits out of the bales.

Your store can avoid this danger by making a test at least twice a year of your store's paper bales. This should be done after the bales have reached the truck. The bales should be opened by investigators and searched for any stolen merchandise.

4. Branch Store Transfers

Some stores keep separate inventory records for their branches. If the store fails to make accurate branch transfers, it can badly distort these inventory figures. Losses may appear to be in the branch store when they are actually in the parent store and vice versa. This causes problems for a security investigation if the losses are not correctly identified.

At least once a month an analysis should be made of the branch transfer operation. Check to see if the transfer merchandise is being properly recorded and the transfer control system is being operated as planned.

A created system check can give a quick answer on the effectiveness of your control. For example, security could remove several garments from a rack going out on a branch transfer before the rack reaches the transfer checkout point.

Will the four or five garments removed be noticed and reported missing by the person checking the transfer of goods? Is a unit count being made at both ends of the branch transfer operation? If neither end catches your created systems error, you will know that a reeducation program is in order.

5. Cash Bag Shortages

The head cashier should report any uncorrected cash bag shortages daily to the security office. Give special attention to shortages of even amounts. Also keep a record of any shortages that occur in the cash money room. Note on this record the name of the person reporting the shortage as well as the person against whom the shortage is reported.

6. Cash Overages and Shortages

Considerable attention has been given to this problem. Many dishonest employees have been detected by carefully studying records of daily cash shortages and overages. When salespeople are consistently short in their cash drawers they are investigated.

Much study is given to community drawer registers when a loss occurs. A check is made of days off, vacations, and illness. In this way the number of suspects can be narrowed down to one or two people. If there is only one suspect, this person is called to the security office for an interview. Admissions can be gained from dishonest employees by showing them the weight of statistical and logical evidence against them. (Normally it is *not* desirable to use "common drawer" registers because of the lack of accountability.)

Check your salespeople's records on overages and shortages. If you find patterns of irregularity, try shopping tests. If these fail to show any dishonesty, then a corrective interview should be held by the personnel office. Security investigators should pay most attention to *overages*, since people who are underringing quite often have a cash register overage.

7. Charge Accounts with Credit Balances

A quarterly analysis of your charge accounts to see what customers have credit balances can be useful. Many times it is found that customers' credit balances indicate weaknesses in the bureau of adjustment operations. Quite often customers are receiving duplicate credits, which can be very costly to the store. Only in the most unusual circumstances should a customer have a credit balance on her charge account.

8. Check of Cashier and Packer Stamps

If cashiers and packers have numbered stamps, it is important that they be carefully controlled. See that they are locked up at night and put in a central location where every stamp is accounted for.

During a cashier's or packer's lunch hour or relief period, the stamps should be locked in their money drawer along with their cash. Failure to control these stamps can be costly to your store because it permits a dishonest employee to authorize fraud saleschecks.

9. Charge-Taken Saleschecks

Regular examination of charge-taken saleschecks should be made by the security investigator. See if this store system is being properly followed.

Any saleschecks that fail to show proper authorization should be held out and the person handling the sale should have a corrective interview.

10. Close-Out Sheet

A weekly listing of all closed-out employees should be sent to security by the personnel department. In this way, security can eliminate anyone on the list from their suspect file.

Security can also check to make sure that any apprehended dishonest employees have been closed out of the company.

11. C.O.D. Control

Some stores are very careless in the control of their C.O.D. money. It is worthwhile to check, at least twice a year, to determine if open C.O.D.s are being properly investigated.

If there is no adequate follow-up on open C.O.D.s, your delivery drivers may soon begin to hold out C.O.D. funds. Substantial thefts have occurred when stores failed to control their C.O.D. system.

12. Created Systems Checks

Created systems checks are one of your best investigative tools. They can be applied to almost any area of the store. They can be used for checking on the efficiency and accuracy of people at all levels of your store organization.

By removing a few garments from a shipment coming into the store before the shipment is checked in, you can determine if your receiving checker is being accurate. By placing a fraudulent entry in your purchase journal you can find out whether the buyer will note the error. Is your buyer checking the purchase journal?

There is no end to the number of ways this particular investigative tool can be applied. Its use is only limited by your imagination. Created systems checks serve two purposes: (1) They determine whether your system is being operated properly as intended. (2) If the system is not being operated properly, they act as a dramatic lesson for educating the people responsible for the error.

13. Accumulative Credit Reports

The security department should examine each department's accumulative credit reports every month. Comparison should be made with the accumulative credit report of a year ago.

If there is any sharp increase in total credits, an investigation should be made. Someone may be writing fraudulent credits against that particular department.

14. Debit Credit Ledger Check

The debit credit ledger should be examined periodically. There should also be a control on payments taken off the debit credit ledger.

Dishonest employees can charge off money from this ledger for their own personal benefit. Because this is often an uncontrolled ledger, make a special effort to see that chargeoffs cannot be made without proper authorization.

15. Detective Tests

Floor detectives can be checked by using a created systems check. For example, one store hired people from the outside to come in at regular intervals and steal in the departments where the detectives were working. These tests showed whether the detectives were able to spot the "planted" shoplifter.

Sometimes such tests have been conducted without the detective's knowing that a test shoplifter was coming into the department. On other occasions, the detective was warned in advance.

In addition to determining the detectives' alertness, these tests give the security manager an opportunity to find out how his detectives handle apprehensions. He gets the answers to such questions as, "How was the malefactor approached?" "Was an admission gained on the street at the time of apprehension?" "Was the stolen merchandise taken away from the suspect by the detective immediately at the time of apprehension?" "Was the subject abused in any way?" "Was there any physical violence?" and so on.

Detectives usually enjoy the challenge of these created tests. It keeps them alert and helps to maintain a high standard of production.

16. Duplicate Delivery Records

When the original delivery stub falls off a package, a duplicate address label has to be put on. These duplicates should be carefully controlled. They are a potent weapon for a dishonest person.

Security should have a direct control on such duplicate labels. A copy of all duplicate labels should be forwarded to security daily. In this way such labels can be checked to see if any names and addresses repeat, and a check can also be made to determine if the names and addresses of any store employees appear on the duplicate labels.

17. Undercover Detectives

Most stores seldom talk about the use of "undercover" detectives and yet they are used in most stores. Undercover detectives are an important arm of the security staff. They are usually the only effective means of detecting dishonest employees in nonselling areas. They are most successful in stockrooms, and receiving, packing, warehousing, and delivery departments.

Some stores have more undercover detectives than floor detectives. This shows an intelligent appropriation of security budget funds. The dishonest employee is a much more serious loss problem to a retail store than is the shoplifter. Therefore the budget appropriations should express management's interest in internal thefts as compared to the problems of shoplifting.

The problem with using undercover detectives is usually in the selection of suitable people. Some stores obtain such people from detective agencies, but this is expensive. It has also been found that some detective agencies that furnish employee observers simply advertise in the paper for a person to work as a detective, and the person who comes into the store has no previous detective training.

Stores who use undercover detectives successfully usually select their own people and hire them for that particular job. The security manager is then able to train and direct these people. Since he also selects them, he is sure that they will fit into the store organization.

It is important that no one except the security manager and his immediate superior have any knowledge about the identity of these detectives. At the time of employment a signed agreement should also be obtained stating that the applicant is subject to immediate close out at any time. This is necessary because difficult situations can develop rapidly and require immediate elimination of such a person from the organization.

Undercover detectives should receive special training in the problems of employee dishonesty. Many detectives who have been hired by detective agencies give desultory reports on people who are late coming back from their relief periods or who are taking extra time on their lunch hours, and so on. This type of trivia is not the purpose of undercover detectives. Only the detection of employee dishonesty through theft of cash or merchandise should be of concern to such a detective.

Undercover detectives can be most effective when placed in departments where special problems are occurring. They are particularly useful if there is a suspect in the area.

Of all the methods of security detection, the undercover detective is by far the most effective.

18. Employee Package System

A strong control of employee purchases is vital if a store wishes to keep its losses down. Some stores today use numbered sealing labels to control packages. This can be effective if the labels are kept under tight control. However, if any employee is able to obtain these seals, they become an open invitation to theft. They become a pass for the dishonest employee, assuring his exit from the building without detection.

While investigating sealed package systems it has been found that a clever employee can slit the bottom of a sealed bag and insert stolen merchandise. The thief then glues the bag together and has an ideal container for stolen goods. Sealing packages can be a good control system, but a better system is to spot check employee purchases at the exit door.

In this system, a full salescheck is made out for every employee purchase. This salescheck is attached to the outside of the employee's bag. The bag is not sealed. As the employee leaves the building in the evening, he is subject to a spot check. The security department may pick out one in every three or one in every ten employees for an inspection. In each case, the person selected is asked to step out of the exit line to an examination desk. At the desk the contents of his package are emptied and compared against the salescheck that appears on the outside.

This spot examination creates a psychological barrier to theft. The employee never knows whether he will be checked or not. On occasion it also reveals a dishonest employee who has taken a chance.

As part of this control there should occasionally be a night when all employee packages are checked. When this is done, efforts should be made to see that no employees break away from the exit line and start to go back into the store. They may be trying to return the package they are carrying. By having detectives observe the line, such a person can be stopped and his package examined.

Good package control is vital to store security. Laxness in handling employee purchases can lead to severe theft situations.

19. Error Controls

Basic causes of any loss in a retail store are carelessness and error. For example, clerical errors and shortages in a study made by one store showed that in one out of every ten transactions in the parent store, there were one or more clerical errors with monetary consequences. The study showed that in a single year about 1,200,000 such clerical errors were made.

The most frequent error was charging the wrong sales tax. In terms of dollar losses, failure to ring a sale was most important. Sales amounting to over $420,000 were *not* rung up. There were fifteen possible types of errors in the study. Nine of these errors were found to cause a gross shortage of about $580,000 and a net shortage of about $440,000

One of the more interesting points brought out by the study was the fact that there was little relationship between inventory shortage figures calculated by the company and the figures revealed by the clerical error picture. The study suggested that a store would find it beneficial to measure clerical errors, pilferage, and net shortages independently and continuously so that they could be controlled and reduced.

They felt there were several other areas that also needed study. For example, do part-time salesclerks make more mistakes than full-time salesclerks?

They also recommended that the calculation of sales taxes, excise taxes, and employee discounts be checked by the auditing department.

Following is a list of the errors studied:

1. Wrong addition
2. Wrong multiplication
3. Wrong sales tax charge
4. Wrong excise tax charge
5. Wrong employee discounts
6. Mistake in recording in interstate transaction
7. Under- or overcharge.
8. Under- or overring.
9. Failure to ring up a sale
10. Wrong designation of transaction (mixing up C.O.D., will-call, and cash transactions)
11. Mixing up charge and cash transactions
12. Writing in the wrong department number
13. Ringing up the wrong department number
14. Recording over or under the amount of merchandise purchased
15. Wrapping a will-call or C.O.D. transactions as fully paid

Study Results

About 40 percent of all mistakes found were the failure to charge the correct sales tax. Eighteen percent involved mistakes in addition. The third most common errors were wrong multiplication, failure to ring up the sale properly, mistakes in the recording of interstate transactions, underringing or overringing, incorrect employee discounts, and incorrect excise tax charges. Each of these categories accounted for 6 or 8 percent of all mistakes. Wrongly designated transactions as well as under- or overringing were the *least* common errors.

It was interesting to note that some errors were more serious. For instance, although 40 percent of the errors were sales tax errors, from a money standpoint these errors were not as serious as were wrong additions, under- or overringing, or incorrect multiplication. Following is a list of the gross shortages found by type of error:

1. Wrong addition, $34,000
2. Wrong multiplication, $13,000
3. Wrong sales tax charged, $28,000
4. Wrong excise tax charged, $9,000
5. Wrong employee discount, $7,000
6. Under- or overringing, $70,000
7. Failure to ring up the sale, $420,000

   Total $580,000

Determining Loss Relationships

This particular study concluded that shortages and overages are composed of three factors: (1) clerical errors, (2) markdowns or markups not taken, and (3) theft.

It was felt that in order to measure shortages and overages, they would have to learn, with the help of a probability sample, what percentage of the clerical errors escape correction. Information obtained would help evaluate the success of controls and be an aid to the auditing department. It also would suggest points for improvement.

With the help of a probability sample, the magnitude of the failure to take markdowns and markups could be uncovered. Once these two elements were estimated, the difference between overall net shortages and the sum of these two factors would reflect thefts. Once the thefts were more correctly estimated, then the security budget could be related to the actual theft losses instead of to traditional practices.

Benefits of Error Control

Errors are an important part of your loss problems. Error control is important because failure to operate systems properly will lead to embezzlement, defalcations, and other forms of theft. If you have a good error control program you improve your store operation, reduce losses, and decrease opportunities for employee dishonesty.

Errors can be controlled by individual contacts, departmental meetings, retraining programs, and campaigns.

Definition of Error Control

Let's analyze the meaning of control and prevention. To control is to exercise a directing, restraining, or governing influence over others. To prevent is to stop or hinder, to bar the action in advance.

These two things go hand in hand in error control. Error control itself should be set up as an independent department. It should not be a training function because of the corrective and disciplinary actions that take place.

Any error control program should be a practical and realistic approach to the *prevention of error* at the source. It should gather data on individual errors in such systems as wrapping and packing, saleschecks, and cash registers. To cut down these errors, individual contacts should be made with the people involved.

Error data can be accumulated from sales audit, where salescheck errors and overages and shortages are listed; from delivery, where reports appear on labels and where the problems of wrapping and packing are known; and from layaway, where there are salescheck errors and wrapping and packing problems. The service building will also report salescheck errors. Accounts receivable, the cashier department, bureau of adjustment, and many other areas can contribute valuable facts to the error control center.

Floor supervisors should be held responsible for the daily corrections of errors. There should be monthly department error meetings as well as individual error interviews.

Types of Errors to Review

Here are some of the errors that could be recorded and followed up in an error control program:

1. Wrong address
2. Adjustment complaint
3. Amount wrong
4. Cash receipt envelope incorrect
5. Charge name or address incorrect
6. Classification wrong or omitted
7. C.O.D. procedure wrong
8. Customer's signature omitted
9. Delay in order
10. Denison card wrong or missing
11. Illegibility
12. Kind of sale wrong or omitted
13. Layaway procedure wrong
14. Mail order or telephone order procedure wrong
15. Merchandise short or over
16. Packed improperly
17. Pick-up procedure wrong

18. Salescheck incomplete
19. Salescheck not authorized
20. Supervisor's OK on credit omitted
21. Void incorrectly handled
22. Wrapped improperly
23. Overage or shortage of goods

Error records set up on a departmental basis can show:

1. Total number of errors by type and clerk number per department.
2. Total number of errors by type and department per division.
3. Total number of errors by type and division for a storewide report.

Individual interviews can be held with employees who have more than five errors or more than $5 net overage or shortage. These interviews should be conducted by the head of the error control department.

All errors involving procedure or policies should be explained thoroughly to the employee at the time of the interview. If an employee is interviewed for errors two months in succession he should be given a warning. If a third interview takes place corrective action should be instituted. For example, the employee could receive a 30-day warning, be transferred out of the department, or closed out.

When departments have ten or more errors of a single type in one month, arrangements should be made to hold a department meeting. If any unusual trend in errors continues in a particular department, a training program should be developed.

Special drives on errors as well as seasonal campaigns should be used as a means of building up enthusiasm and incentive to reduce errors.

The error control program supervisor should do these things:

1. Prepare monthly error reports.
2. Study causes and recommend methods of reducing errors.
3. Provide information on training needs of individuals or groups.
4. Conduct corrective interviews.
5. Schedule and hold departmental meetings.
6. Check on overages and shortages of $5 or more.
7. Correct saleschecks, credits, and refunds when necessary.

If your store does not have an error control plan you should consider adding such a plan to your organization. Its benefits are as follows:

1. Errors are reduced at the source, by holding corrective interviews.
2. Customer complaint problems are minimized.

3. Operating costs in such areas as delivery, wrapping, and supplies are reduced.
4. Theft losses are reduced because of increased controls.

20. Garnishees

Employees whose salaries are garnisheed become good leads for the security department, and their names should be reported to security immediately. If the employee is a salesperson, steps should be taken to shop this person for honesty. If the employee is in a nonselling area, a check should be made of the person's packages at the door and other measures should be taken.

21. Impostor Chargeoffs

Security should receive a copy of ledger chargeoffs because of impostor activity. In this way a check can be made to be sure security has been previously notified of the imposted charges. This chargeoff list acts as a control to insure that security is receiving a record of all impostor complaints.

22. Irregular Credits

The auditing department should report all improperly prepared credits to security. This includes unauthorized credits, refunds issued without proper saleschecks, and refunds issued on incorrect credit forms. Security should investigate the credits that appear to suggest malefactor activity.

23. Irregular Saleschecks

All saleschecks not properly signed by the authorizer should be referred to security for investigation. In certain cases department heads should be requested to discuss these irregularities with their salespeople at their regular weekly meetings. Irregular saleschecks should include even exchanges, voids, and so forth.

24. Loan System

A good loan system can go a long way toward preventing losses from display people, advertising personnel, comparison shoppers, and similar departments. A good loan system should provide for a method of checking the borrowed goods out and then back into the department at the termination of the loan.

A good system is to have one part of your loan slip sent to the security office when the loan is originated. When the loan is canceled and the merchandise returned to the department, the original loan slip is then forwarded to the security office and matched with the duplicate already on file.

It is important that security make regular checks to see that loan slips are available, that loan forms are being made out properly, and that control of loans is being followed according to the system.

If your system requires security to match the duplicate and original copies of the loan, then follow-ups should be made on any loan that goes past the date of termination.

25. Lost and Found Property

Local laws will determine what merchandise your lost or found department is required to report to the police. These laws should be followed of course. Merchandise returned to the police department should be handled by the security people in your division.

The security department should see that there is an adequate system for controlling items turned into your lost and found department. Merchandise that is unclaimed after 90 days should be turned over to salvage. Be certain that there is no leakage point for merchandise thefts at the lost and found control desk.

26. Merchandise Received Directly in Department

All merchandise coming into the store should enter through the receiving department. In this way it can be accurately checked and properly billed. Any exceptions should be recorded in the bill and order area, and a copy of these exceptions should be transmitted to the security department.

Departments with more than average exceptions should be investigated. Receiving merchandise directly into a department suggests the possibility of collusion between the buyer and manufacturer and may indicate manipulation of buyer records. Kickbacks and covering fraud markups may be the result. Any department that has frequent direct shipments and also shows inventory irregularities should be thoroughly investigated.

27. Missing Saleschecks

During the daily floor audit any missing saleschecks should be reported to the security department. Any series of missing saleschecks or anything that appears to be unusual should be investigated.

28. Nondelivery Complaints

The bureau of adjustment should make a monthly listing of nondelivery complaints. After there is a preliminary investigation, the listing should show the results of their findings and a record should be given to security.

Security should then attempt to pinpoint the problem. Was this merchandise that was not available? Did the salescheck get lost in the warehouse? Did the merchandise get on to the delivery truck?

Nondelivery complaints can be important leads. They are often a warning flag that indicates theft.

29. "No Sales" and "Void"

The auditing department should report to security any salespeople who ring more than two "no sales" a day on their register. Any salesperson having an excessive number of "void" transactions should also be reported. In both instances these people should be tested for honesty by shopping.

30. Overgoods

The security department should periodically check with the packing and wrapping department to see how overgoods are being handled. Listings and reports on the amount of overgoods should be turned over to security monthly.

A created systems check should be tried from time to time to see if packers are reporting their overgoods. If they are not, the store may be suffering losses from dishonest packers who are stealing overgoods.

31. Parcel Post Charges

In the parcel post weighing room, it is frequently found that customers need to pay more parcel post money than was originally charged by the salesperson. In these instances the parcel post clerk writes a salescheck for the additional amount, charging it against the customer's account. It is important that a record of such saleschecks be given to the security department.

This area usually has an uncontrolled salesbook. There should be only one salesbook in the parcel post room, and this book should be controlled by both the security and the auditing departments. As each duplicate check is written, it should be sent to the security department. All checks should be accounted for when the book is completed.

Failure to maintain control of this book can allow employees in the parcel post room to put new labels on customer packages and address them to their own homes. It is an easy method of theft.

32. Parcel Post Uninsured Losses

A listing of all parcel post uninsured losses should be given to security at the end of each month. If these losses get out of hand and appear to be too high, security should start an investigation in cooperation with the local post office inspectors.

33. Payroll Envelopes Undelivered

A control should be made on any payroll envelopes that are supposed to be returned to the paymaster. This includes pay envelopes for an employee who is on vacation, out ill, or absent for any other reason. If any of these undelivered envelopes fail to be returned to the paymaster, the security department should be immediately notified so that an investigation can be made.

34. Police Name Check

Make arrangements with your local police department for a name check of all new employees. Name, age, and address of new employees should be turned over to the police for a complete file check. Stores that do this have found as many as 23 percent of the people they were employing had previous criminal records.

When an employee is found to have a serious police record, it is advisable to refuse employment. A retail store is a great temptation to any person with a weakness toward crime. It is unfair to the individual to place him in a position of this type.

The police name check should be made within two weeks following the date of employment. Any longer period leaves the store open to theft losses and makes it difficult to explain why the new person is not being kept on as an employee.

35. Property Rooms

Security should make an occasional check of the comparison shoppers' property room and the models', display, and advertising property rooms. Any areas like these should be carefully controlled. There is a tendency to be lax in property controls, and this allows merchandise to stay in these areas longer than it should.

In one instance a store discovered 76 pairs of shoes laden with dust; they were being held in a closet by a careless display man. Many of these shoes were four and five years old, which made them no longer saleable. There is a danger of employee thefts occurring in these areas if they lack merchandise controls.

Sometimes people who are not directly concerned with sales are less concerned with the security of merchandise. By having a good loan system and a good follow-up plan for loans that pass the termination date, much can be done to prevent loss. It is important to insist that these departments provide locked protection for overnight control. Inspection should be conducted for housekeeping and fire hazards as well as for theft potential.

36. Refund System

One of the most vulnerable areas in a retail store is its refund system. In one store a mother and daughter team admitted, after being apprehended for shoplifting, that they had successfully stolen and refunded over $80,000 worth of merchandise in this store over a period of several years. Their practice was to shoplift one item on each floor of the store, going upward through the building. After reaching the top selling floor they started back down, refunding each item they had previously stolen, floor by floor. Their average take ran between $300 and $600 per day. They conducted this refund operation in the store on the average of three days a week.

Today many stores recognize that refunds are a vulnerable part of the retail operation. For this reason they require a salescheck or cash register receipt on all cash refunds. If the customer does not have proof of sale they *mail* the customer a refund check. There should be regular testing of your refund systems. Your auditing department should send out test letters each month. *The average-sized store should send out about 200 test letters a week.*

Refund Test Letter

The refund test letter or card is based on a policy of service to the customer. A sample copy is as follows:

> Dear Mrs. __________
>
> Our records show that on May 24, 19___, you returned to (name of store) a shirt valued at $8.50 for a cash refund.
>
> When one of our customers is put to the trouble of returning a purchase, we try to find the reason for this return so that we may improve our store's service.
>
> If you will fill out the enclosed self-addressed stamped card, giving a reason for returning the merchandise and any suggestions or criticisms you may have, it will be sincerely appreciated.
>
> Very truly yours,

The letter can be signed by the head of the bureau of adjustment. Of course, there should be no indication of a tie-in with the security department.

If a satisfactory reply is received, no further action is taken. If the letter is returned by the post office marked, "No such person at the address," or if the customer replies that she did not return the merchandise, then an investigation is conducted. As soon as a series of replies indicate irregularities on the part of any salesperson or department, a special investigation is conducted and a credit investigation case is opened.

Stores using refund test letters have found that they often uncover major instances of internal dishonesty. These test letters have also revealed the activity of shoplifting rings in which members were returning merchandise for cash refunds. In one instance a salesclerk worked a refund racket in collusion with five people from outside the store. She wrote refunds for these contacts daily when they came into the store. No merchandise was involved; she wrote a fraud refund, had it authorized, and then gave it to the accomplice for cashing.

Refund embezzlements can cause losses that run into the thousands of dollars. It is easy for a person to forge a refund if controls aren't maintained. Once a person discovers he can do this with little danger of being caught, the lid is off and his thefts skyrocket.

37. Returned Bank Checks

Bank checks returned by the bank should be turned over to the security department the same day they come back to the store, especially if they are marked "no-account," "account closed," or "signature unknown." These types of bank checks indicate an attempt to defraud the store. Insufficient funds checks or checks that are sent back because of a minor technicality would not be handled by security of course.

By getting these bad bank checks the same day they are returned by the bank, security has a better chance of obtaining a description of the check passer.

As soon as the check is obtained, the security investigator should attempt to interview the salesperson or cashier involved. An attempt should be made to get a good description of the person who passed the check. Even a day lost in getting a check back to the person who handled it may destroy the store's opportunity for getting a description. The first three days of a person's memory are best. After the third day recall drops more than 70 percent.

38. Surprise Register Audits

Many stores have found a successful control on salespeople was to make surprise register audits during the selling day.

Without advance notice, a member of the security department and a member of the cashier operation appear in a selling department. They go to a register, take the drawers out, and audit them against the register tape. If any substantial overages or shortages appear, the salesperson responsible is immediately interviewed in the security office.

Stores have found that the surprise audit has uncovered many dishonest employees. It has also been a deterrent to employee theft. If the audit is done frequently enough, salespeople feel there is too much risk in stealing cash from sales.

39. Salesbook Control

Salesbooks should be controlled. The security department should see to it that salesbooks are locked up at night and that the reserve stock of salesbooks is kept under lock and key. When salesbooks are issued, a record should be kept of the person using the book. No new salesbook should be issued to anyone until they turn in the cardboard back and stubs of the old book.

A dishonest employee can operate on a large scale if he obtains two salesbooks. He can write up his legitimate sales in one salesbook and write up the sales in which he steals on cash in the other book. He can also use the uncontrolled book for sending merchandise out to his home.

Control of salesbooks is important in protecting your store against loss. It is the security department's responsibility to spot-check this control and to be sure that it is being properly operated in all parts of the store.

40. Salvage Merchandise

Salvage merchandise can be a dangerous item for the store, especially if salvage goods are sold to employees. Salvage things are sold legitimately at first, but then employees deliberately put scratches on merchandise or cause minor breakage in order to obtain items at practically no cost. In the end the system breaks down completely and becomes a "cover" for dishonest employees who purchase new goods for a fraction of their value.

Many stores find it more practical to give salvage items to the Salvation Army or another charity, or to sell salvage goods outside of the store. They do not allow employees at any level of their store organization to have salvage goods.

If your store does sell salvage to your employees, be sure that you have a tight system of control, not only for the sale authorization but also for the money taken in for the sale of salvage goods. In one store it was found that the man in charge of selling salvage was making a lot of money by taking new merchandise out of stock and selling it to his friends at salvage prices.

41. Supervisory Check

Store security is only as good as the supervision that enforces systems and controls. Therefore a complete series of created systems checks should be worked out for testing supervisory controls in all selling and nonselling areas throughout the store.

A store that is interested in making its operations more efficient and its assets more secure should employ one or two people to make created systems checks on a full-time basis. If this is done, the operation of the store will be greatly improved and management can feel much more sure that figures, reports, and controls are being applied as they were intended to be used.

42. Use of Cash Register Drawers

Dishonest employees can steal cash from the cash register by not closing the drawer after a sale. To avoid this problem, security should have floor detectives make a periodic check of the store to see if any cash register drawers are being left open, if so, the salesclerk responsible should be shopped for honesty.

A survey of one store showed that on a given afternoon twenty-two cash register drawers were open throughout the selling areas. Subsequent honesty test shoppings resulted in the apprehension of nineteen dishonest salespeople stealing cash on sales.

43. Wrong Address Returns

When a package is sent to a wrong address and returned to the store, the merchandise is returned to stock if no correction can be made. The adjustment department should furnish security with a list of these saleschecks on a monthly basis.

They should be considered a part of the return mail. Just as in the case of an impostor salescheck where no account is used, it has been found in many cases that an impostor charging merchandise to a fictious name and address, if questioned, will simply say to the salesclerk, "send it." The duplicate saleschecks furnished to the security department from these wrong address returns should be checked against the impostor file.

Conclusion

As noted at the beginning of this chapter, this is by no means a complete list of the possible controls that can be used by the security department. It does, however, suggest the potential for tying the security department into many of the store's normal systems as a means of preventing thefts and detecting dishonesty. Many stores have systems that are not being used to their fullest potential because the findings of these systems are not being turned over to the security department.

The importance of a close relationship between internal audit, the shortage controller, and the security department is vital if the store is going to have effective security.

Chapter 27

SYSTEMS STUDY

How can a company do an effective systems study? The first step is to prepare a control systems checklist.

Control Systems Checklist

1. *List the key control systems*, both the systems now in use and any that are needed but do not exist at present.
2. *Evaluate the control systems* in terms of each system's relative value and importance to the company. (Misplaced emphasis and distorted priorities are often a basic cause of sluggish management practices.)
3. *Determine who is most familiar with a particular system.* This familiarity should be in two categories, first, in the original design and intent of the procedure, and second, in how the system is actually being operated as compared to the original blueprint.
4. Try to *determine which systems appear to be best designed and best enforced.* Next try to determine why the smoothly operating procedures are working well, and by contrast, why the less successful and downright poor procedures are not working as they should.
5. This study is actually a preliminary analysis of the magnitude of the systems problem so that you can reach decisions as to *what particular systems obviously need in-depth analysis for improvement.* This evaluation is important so you can put your emphasis and effort where you will get the most return for the time invested in the study.

6. *Keep an eye out for any systems overlap.* Is there any duplication in procedures that has relatively little value and could be painlessly stopped?
7. Finally, *determine if the duties of each job are listed in detail.* For each control procedure find out the *frequency of its occurrence*, the *time required* to handle it, and a *typical volume of use* to be expected from its application.

This checklist provides a starting point for your systems study. Before beginning your analysis you should accept as a basic premise of effective business control the philosophy that "Men should be held accountable—but are responsible only for those results they can do something about."

What is your next move? The logical next step is to *examine the operation to determine what can be controlled.* It is necessary (particularly in view of the above definition for placing responsibility) to separate what is controllable from what is not.

What Things Are Controllable?

Your list might include such items as receiving, transfers, overtime, training, supplies, direct administration, and other employee activities. In each instance, after deciding that a particular activity or process is controllable, you should evaluate the present situation to determine whether or not it is *now* controlled.

After separating the things in your business that are controllable, you then need a second list of the things that are *not* controllable.

This second list might include such items as planning, indirect administration, and salvage.

Once you have listed the controllable and noncontrollable activities, you need to dig out the historical data required to develop performance standards that are realistic and have satisfactory minimum and maximum tolerance levels. The controls usually applied to budgets indicate the type of controls also needed over handling, storing, and displaying of merchandise, protection of money, personnel, customers, and premises.

Naturally, in any attempt to develop a list of controllable activities you will find some borderline areas that must be discussed with key people, but these are not a major problem.

Once you have established a priority list for your study, you are then ready to begin the analysis of your first control procedure.

Studying a Specific System

First, *determine the objectives* of the particular control system you are studying. For example, for the refund control system it is obvious that two of the system objectives are to prevent shoplifters from being able to easily translate stolen merchandise into cash and to make it difficult for dishonest employees to embezzle money from the firm. They may do so by writing fraudulant refunds or by having their friends and relatives come into the store and receive phony refund payments made out by a dishonest cashier. These are two of the more obvious objectives of the control procedure, but the refund system also has other objectives. For example, it may involve dealing with a resource who has delivered faulty goods. Refunds also are related to store tax credits. Refunds may indicate faulty customer service, overselling, false promises, losses in delivery, and numerous other things.

List Objectives

To determine a complete list of objectives for the system you are studying, the following questions may be helpful:

1. What is it required to do?
2. What is it used for?
3. What is its outstanding requirement?
4. How important is speed of information?
5. What about the level of quality of records?
   a. How much accuracy is needed?
   b. What level of dependability is required?
   c. What is the cost factor?

Which Employees Are Involved in the System?

Next you need to know *who is assigned to work with this system.* Is the organization logical in relation to the accepted principles of accountability and responsibility? How many people work with the system? A key element connected to this point is what is the quality of these people? Define this in terms of competence, attitude, reliability, morale, training, intelligence, background, past experience, past performance, and how they are selected for this work.

Management Policies

Your study of a control system cannot be isolated from its relationship to basic management policies because these affect its design and use.

What policies are involved in this system?

- Pricing policies? (in a billing system)
- Customer policies? (in a system involved with customers)
- Management inventory policies? (in a merchandise control system)
- And so on

Chart the Procedure

Now you are ready to begin the process of analysis. First you should answer the well-known questions: *Who? What? When? Where? How? Why?*

Write down the answers so that you can visually and mentally see the problem in perspective once you've accumulated the facts. In some instances it is wise to *make a large chart of the procedure.* A rough chart of squares can show you problems in an instant while trying to untangle the same procedure by reading memos or a verbal analysis may simply make it seem more complicated and more difficult to solve.

Incidentally, the right way to chart a procedure is to chart it backward, for trying to chart it forward is a frustrating job. It is better to start with the final objectives of the system and then work backward step by step. In this way you will have to do far fewer revisions on your final chart.

The chart will indicate gross weaknesses at once and usually you will see immediate ways in which the system can be made more secure in terms of protecting the company's assets. More subtle weaknesses may be revealed only later as you continue your analysis.

Costs of the System

Although your primary objective is to determine whether the system meets its objectives successfully, the analysis is not adequate unless you also *determine the cost of the system* because costs are directly related to such factors as potential loss, usefulness of the control, and all the other objectives of the procedure. Excessive costs that drain off more money than a system saves may mean the company needs an innovative approach to the control problem.

How do you determine the cost of the system? This is evaluated by reviewing such factors as number of people involved, time spent on it, and salary ranges. In some instances, depreciation, rental of equipment, and duplication costs should be included. There is also the cost of forms. How many copies are made? Any that are not needed? Standard size? Then the system may have hidden costs in terms of space charges and other supplies.

Effectiveness of the System

Now you must be prepared to make some hard but important decisions. *What is the effectiveness of this system?*

1. Does it do what it was designed to do?
2. In the time allowed?
3. With adequate quality?
4. At optimum cost?

Because no system operates in a vacuum, you need to *determine the interrelationship of this system with other systems and other store operations.* Does the method of placing purchase orders multiply the work of accounts payable? Does the refund system unnecessarily harass the customer and hurt future sales? Does cash counting complicate timekeeping and payroll systems? And so on. Bear the domino effect in mind and be sure to determine what other activities this system interfaces with and how they are related before you make any recommendations for improving the control procedure.

Once you have determined how the system you are studying interacts with other store systems and activities, you are now ready to take a careful look at the forms, records, and reports being used for this control procedure.

Records and Reports

What about the records? Are they useful? Easy to read? Easy to understand?

1. Are these records used to spot problems needing attention?
2. Are they used to improve efficiency, prevent loss of future business, and secure company assets?
3. Do they raise a warning flag if losses begin to grow?

4. Are they used as a guide in planning, development, and growth of the business? Do they provide an adequate control of merchandise, money, and personnel?
5. Or are they only historical records, accumulated, stored, and forgotten? Are they stimulants to corrective action, or are they dust-gathering paper that clutters executive files?

Records Design

How about the design of these records? Are they efficiently designed?

1. Does the form prevent recopying of information or avoid recording meaningless, unneeded, or unused information?
2. Is the layout of the form designed to make it easy to fill in? Easy to understand and interpret? Laid out in logical sequence? Is there adequate space for recording information? Color coded? Does each copy carry adequate directions for filling it out and for movement of the document, distribution of goods, and so on. Are all carbons distinctly legible?
3. Does this form duplicate other documents?
4. Is it properly filed? Is there easy access to it (consider the time required to locate it) and is it easy to reconstruct the summarized information for analysis?
5. Does it use only figures or does it have written information as well? Can the writer be easily identified? Are signatures for authorization required? Is there adequate space for legibility?

Records: The Facts

Now we need to concern ourselves with the factual material required by the system. How thorough is fact gathering in this system? Are any significant facts being missed? If so, this may jeopardize the usefulness of the system or it might be a threat to the security of the operation it is intended to control.

Are the facts now being gathered for this system being held to those items *strictly* within the scope and purpose of the procedure? You do not want unrelated facts. Perhaps these facts are being recorded in the wrong document or perhaps they are not needed at all.

In retailing we are often too busy with the job of merchandising our store and serving customers to do a competent job of recording the facts about our business. This can make a flawed operation that eats into profits and can even, in the end, put the company into receivership. Recording the facts of your business is a vital part of the operation and needs to be emphasized more in retailing perhaps than in any other type of business.

What is the most important requirement in recording the facts of the business? *Accuracy*. Actually the most important requirement and the only important requirement is the use of extreme care in recording facts. What is clear today may be totally confusing a few weeks later when a problem requires analysis.

Are the facts in this system periodically checked out to determine the level of accuracy? This can be done either for the total system or on the basis of a sample.

Records: Completeness

The first rule of every form is to make the document a design that is clear and complete enough for someone else to understand. You want to have a form that avoids wasting time needlessly because of difficulties in summarizing information for later analysis.

Are records complete enough for competent analysis and review?

All the facts about a business are not found on the usual system work documents. When we talk about adequate recording of the facts related to a business, we are also concerned with questions such as these:

1. Does the company have an up-to-date organization chart by position?
2. Is there a job description for each position in the company on file and easily available?
3. Is there a personnel chart? A functions chart?

A review of the organization chart may reveal that with some rearrangement you can improve the ability to accomplish company objectives. A task chart reveals the jobs of each member of the store; it shows work distribution and can be an aid to analysis of operating data.

The value of records is directly in proportion to their reliability and accuracy. Therefore every supervisor should regularly spot check recorded facts related to his area of responsibility. Are the recorded facts the same as his actual findings? Are the recorded facts a true picture of the operation? Such an analysis can determine the completeness and accuracy of figures, and only with confidence in operating figures can a supervisor or top executive make scientific decisions about his operation.

How Do You Analyze the Facts?

Certain prerequisites are needed for proper interpretation of facts:

1. Are facts organized in a manner that relates them to the various major steps of the system?
2. Do they reveal the reasons why a system fails to achieve its objectives?
3. Are facts grouped according to the objectives of the system?

When properly grouped for analysis, the facts should reveal any external factors that may seriously affect the accomplishment of the objectives and the major steps of the system. They may show problems or reveal questions that need to be asked and resolved.

Once you have made this study, as you review the total system *ask yourself test questions* about it:

1. What would be the effect of eliminating "X"?
2. Could a random sampling be substituted periodically instead of laboring through the entire control procedure?
3. Where could I "beat" the system if I were a dishonest employee? A dishonest customer?
4. Where could the control be improved to give better protection from criminal attack on merchandise or money?
5. Do we need to know all this information?
6. Is there additional information we need but are not presently obtaining?
7. Can the time, cost, bulk, and complexity of the system be beneficially altered?

These and many similar test questions can be developed to help you make your final analysis and to help guide you in shaping your recommendations for tightening and strengthening the system so as to better protect company assets.

Analysis Is the Final Payoff

Whatever the system, the records must be organized so that they can be broken down into digestible proportions. The records must treat the most significant features of the control first.

This chapter has explained how you do a systems study. Every major control system requires periodic review. Only by doing this can you insure yourself that your control is not outdated or being improperly followed.

You must know at all times what is happening in your business. This is the "secret" of all successful, growing, and thriving companies.

The ultimate purpose of every system is to keep the key people in the company aware of exactly what is happening in the business. They must be armed adequately with facts so that they can take corrective action where needed and can continue to improve productivity, efficiency, and profit growth as well as shield the firm from major losses caused by poor judgment, carelessness, negligence, and dishonesty.

Chapter 28

RECEIVING

Effective receiving controls are vital to the well-controlled store. Nevertheless, I often find this fact overlooked by store managers and owners. I was reminded of this again recently while doing a security study of a chain of stores on the West Coast. In each store in the chain the job of receiving goods had been given to the youngest, and least competent worker on the staff. The reason was that it was considered one of the least desirable jobs in the company.

Yet this situation is not unique. I shudder to think how many stores have suffered heavy losses because they paid for merchandise they never received.

The Concept of Control

To manage means—to control. And we cannot escape the fundamental fact that *control can take place only where the action to be controlled occurs.*

What this means is that the receiving of goods cannot be properly controlled if all of the paperwork for the transaction is centered in the accounting office, nor can a store manager control what happens on the receiving dock while sitting in his office.

In fact, the only person who can control the receiving of goods is the person assigned to the store's receiving dock. He is the only one who can make sure that the company gets all the merchandise it pays for.

The employee assigned to the receiving dock is responsible for making sure that the correct quantity of goods ordered is received into the store before payment of the vendor's invoice.

During certain days of the week as well as particular hours of the day the receiving area may be an active, complex operation. At the point where there is the highest amount of confusion there is also the greatest possibility of heavy losses. The answer to control during peak activty is to minimize confusion. How can a store avoid confusion?

Schedule Receiving

Some companies reduce confusion in receiving goods by limiting receiving to specific hours of the day and insisting that their receiving schedule be followed by all resources. This not only limits confusion but also improves efficiency. It allows the company to staff heavily on the receiving docks, and lets management concentrate on the receiving function. Some larger firms decline to accept merchandise at the receiving dock except on a specified schedule. Smaller firms may not insist on a rigid schedule, but they can refuse to accept deliveries unless qualified employees are available to check in the merchandise properly.

Need for Competent Receiver

In either instance the importance of putting a competent worker in charge of the receiving operation is vital for effective control.

First, merchandise must be carefully checked to insure that the entire order is accounted for. Then (as soon as possible) the shipment should be brought into the store or warehouse and away from the vulnerable dock area. Leaving goods on the dock after they are checked in invites thefts. A resource driver can easily toss one or two cartons of an order back onto his truck while the receiving worker's back is turned.

If enough space is not immediately available inside to move the received goods to a point of safety away from the dock, then at least the more expensive and valuable merchandise should be moved away.

All merchandise may be tempting to a thief, but some items that are small in size and high in value are more likely to be stolen off the dock than items that are unusually bulky or heavy. It is wise to move goods off the dock on a selective basis, with top priority being given to the smaller, valuable items.

Counts Are Important

Naturally, losses can be expected if orders are not properly counted when received. These counts must be accurate. Two types of receiving count are involved here.

First is the carton or box count, which is done when the goods arrive on the receiving dock. If the number of cartons does not correspond with the receiving manifest, the receiving clerk should immediately fill out an exception report, which should be signed as well by the deliveryman.

The second counting process takes place after the goods are inside the store or warehouse. In this procedure the cartons are opened and the clerk counts the number of items of each kind of the shipment.

When making dock counts of cartons keep the "block counts" to no more than 25 cartons at a time. Experience shows that it is easy to mix up the totals when dealing with larger multiples. Try to keep distractions to a minimum during the counting process. A dishonest deliveryman may try to distract the receiver by interrupting his count with a comment or question. Receiving clerks should be aware of this trick and not allow such interruptions to destroy the accuracy of the count.

Watch for Short Shipments

Most drivers are honest and conscientious, but a few will not hesitate to withhold merchandise and give the company a short delivery if they have an opportunity to confuse the receiving clerk.

Some companies have the deliveryman make his own count. After the receiving clerk has made his count, he compares it with the count furnished by the driver. If the counts do not agree, the driver and receiving clerk recheck the load together until both of them agree that the final figure is accurate.

Improving the Receiving Operation

How do you improve your receiving operation? First, you make sure that a competent, experienced person handles the receiving of all company merchandise. Second, you require that all goods received be accurately counted and the count verified by checking it with the delivery manifest or receiving document. Third, you make sure that your receiving clerk understands that the company is legally required to pay the invoices for all merchandise for which he signs. He must realize his job is important and that errors are costly.

Weighing

Not only does the receiving clerk have a responsibility to accurately count incoming cartons of merchandise, but also the company should provide weighing facilities close to the receiving dock so that incoming freight, ordered by weight, can be properly checked.

Many retailers have found it wise to check the weight of incoming shipments against shipping charges to make sure that the company has not been overcharged. Some firms have recovered as much as $2,000 a week in freight overcharges. Even if the amount in your company is less, the initial cost of the weighing equipment is easily justified because cumulative shipping overcharges can be significant over a period of several months.

Dock Should Be Protected

When many stores are designed, there is a failure to recognize the importance of a protected receiving dock. The layout of a receiving dock is as important as the layout of a selling floor.

Keep in mind that receiving is a funnel through which *all* merchandise enters the store. It can be a vulnerable spot if it is not properly protected against thefts and weather.

Ideally, merchandise should be received on an inner dock protected against the weather. Losses frequently occur from wind and rain even in milder climates. Certainly receiving should not be done through a front door. A receiving dock should be at the side or rear of the store and hopefully as near the reserve stock area as possible. If no reserve stock area is included in the design of the store, then the receiving area should have direct access to the selling floor.

Avoid Front Door Deliveries

In large cities it is sometimes necessary to receive goods through the store's front entrance. This causes control difficulties because it's not always easy to supervise the deliveryman. In addition, resource drivers have access to merchandise in the selling part of the store. It has been a common experience that front door deliveries often result in a poor check-in of the goods and in heavy shoplifting losses by deliverymen.

Another problem has been the occasional injury of a customer by the deliveryman moving in large cartons of goods. Front door deliveries tend to interfere with customer traffic and if the goods are dumped into store aisles they can be hazardous to store patrons as well as giving an image of poor housekeeping.

Such confusion can also result in increased shoplifting losses since people tempted to shoplift find it easier to do so in a disheveled store.

Driver Tricks

The dishonest truck driver develops numerous techniques, some quite ingenious, for concealing his theft activities. Often his goal is to short the store's shipment. This can be done in a variety of ways.

One technique is to pile small cartons onto a pallett or hand truck so that the load appears to be solid, but is in fact hollow in the center. The cartons are stacked so that the receiving person will count the outside cartons and make his count by multiplying the number of outside units. Unless the pile is examined closely by removing a carton or two to verify that the inner core is the same as the outer stack of cartons, the receiver is easily misled into believing he has a full order. The driver may short the order by six to twelve cartons of merchandise depending on the size of the boxes.

Another trick of the thieving driver is to deliberately fail to unload all the cartons from his truck.

Sometimes the driver may use boxes from the incoming shipment to support the end of an unloading conveyor inside the truck. After unloading, these boxes are conveniently forgotten inside the delivery truck.

Naturally, a careful count by the receiver will spot the short shipment, but clever drivers may try to distract the receiver during his count. Or the receiver himself, because he has seldom or perhaps never noted a short count, may become careless and merely glance at the unloaded order, assume that it's about the right size for the quantity listed on his receiving manifest, and approve the stack of goods as being complete.

One method used by some stores is to provide spotlights on stands, with long cords, to flood the interior of the truck with light during the unloading process. This aids in efficient removal of the goods and reduces the risk of a driver carelessly "leaving" several cartons behind inside the truck.

I recommend the use of portable floodlights as standard receiving equipment on the dock to fully illuminate the interior of trucks as they unload.

Receive Away from Trash Disposal

In laying out the physical facilities for receiving, it is wise to consider the relationship of the receiving dock to outgoing shipments and to the way the company handles its trash disposal.

Too often I find in my studies that the receiving dock is also used for outgoing shipments of goods. This is a poor system. It allows for internal thefts across the dock to private cars or to trucks operated by confederates. It also makes it very difficult for management to determine whether merchandise on the dock is properly controlled, since goods found on the docks that appear to be questionable can be rationalized by the manager as an outgoing order.

Handling store trash across the receiving dock is an even worse theft hazard. Repeatedly I have uncovered major theft situations in which the method of theft was to conceal store goods in outgoing trash. This is one of the most common methods of employee theft. When trash and receiving merchandise are handled through the same dock door the problem of control is increasingly difficult.

The dishonest employee can allow incoming goods to linger on the dock so that they can later be moved with the trash into a trash pickup container. The trash covers the stolen goods until at a later hour, usually after store closing time, the dishonest employee drives his car to the back of the store and recovers the stolen goods from the trash receptacle. If the thief works in collusion with the driver of the trash pickup truck, he recovers the stolen goods later at a point remote from the store.

Control of store trash is vital to good security. The door used for trash disposal should be a considerable distance away from the receiving dock. When possible the receiving dock and trash door should be located on opposite sides of the premises.

If only one dock is available, you can separate it into two areas by using a portable fence mounted on wheels so that the fence can be shifted up and down the dock floor as needed. Some stores install rolldown steel doors that fasten and lock to the dock floor. When they are not needed to separate the dock area, these doors can be left in the overhead position allowing additional space for handling incoming shipments.

Multiple Store Receiving

Professional warehouse experts believe that centralized receiving at a separate distribution center provides the best control of goods in a multiple store operation. This central receiving area serves all stores and provides improved efficiency in handling incoming goods. It can also be physically designed for maximum security. The receiving staff is specialized and provides for a more competent operation than can usually be achieved by receiving at a variety of store locations.

Just as individual stores have various degrees of receiving expertise, so do managers of various stores also place different degrees of emphasis on receiving controls. Personnel used for receiving at the store level often are not as competent to handle receiving problems as are personnel at the distribution center. This is because personnel at the store level share a variety of responsibilities and also often receiving is considered an undesirable task and therefore is assigned to the new and less qualified personnel.

Receiving Documents

I am often surprised to find that some stores have no receiving documents. Such documents are needed to aid in counting and controlling incoming merchandise. Some firms use the packing slip inside the carton as a verification of enclosed merchandise. This is not desirable.

The packing slip is often illegible (it is usually a fifth carbon copy) and the numbers are difficult to decipher. Not only is the packing slip difficult to read, but also often the figures on this slip do not properly indicate either the quantity or quality of the merchandise. The shipping clerk who makes out the packing slip is often careless and such slips have many errors.

The receiver who used the packing slip as verification of a shipment is in effect agreeing to accept responsibility not only for any errors he and his crew might make, but also for any errors the shipper's personnel might have made.

Blind Counts

Many receivers believe that "blind counts" of incoming goods are desirable. The theory is that by counting the goods first and *then* comparing the count to the purchase order the receivers are forced to count incoming goods accurately. In actual practice this often works but it has also proven to be unreliable at times. Test controls with and without blind counts before deciding which system to use.

Well-controlled receiving docks have a copy of the original purchase order on file, often with all the information on it except quantities. This is then used as a receiving document. The problem with the packing slips is that the receiver often adjusts his count to the packing slip figures.

Resource May Pad Packing Slip

Unfortunately, when the packing slip is used as the receiving control document for receiving goods the store can be cheated. It has been found that a dishonest resource can deliberately short the shipment while providing a packing slip that indicates that the entire quantity ordered is in the cartons.

This is not the only form of trickery that some resources use when they know or suspect the receiver is accepting the packing slip as his control document. Some suppliers take advantage of the company by shipping extra merchandise that was not ordered. Since the store receiver has no copy of a purchase order he accepts the goods without question. This type of manipulation is seldom spotted, or if it is later uncovered, it is often too late to take corrective action.

The receiving clerk who unknowingly accepts merchandise not ordered by the company or who uses a packing slip as a receiving control without knowing what was actually ordered creates an error that most likely will not be discovered until the accounting office finds a discrepancy when comparing the purchasing orders with the receiving reports. By this time the incoming goods have been stocked and sold so that rechecking the in-store stock is futile and reconciliation is impossible.

Have Copy of Purchase Order at Receiving

With stock space at a premium in either the stores or warehouse, it is vital that the company coordinate its receiving operation with purchasing documents. This can best be achieved by providing the purchase order as the receiving control document.

Why is it that I often find store managers who seem to look upon receiving operations as a separate part of their organization?

Many stores keep purchase orders in an office filing cabinet or in the bottom drawer of a buyer's desk. This makes for inadequate control. A duplicate of the purchase order needs to be in the receiving person's hands where it can be used to check in the incoming merchandise.

Partial Shipments

Partial shipments are the curse of retailing. This means crossing off received goods on the purchase order and leaving undelivered items open for future receiving. The situation can be complicated by the fact that some resources who short ship back order automatically and others who short ship simply cancel the undelivered goods leaving it up to the store to reorder. A list of the firms that cancel undelivered goods should be held at the receiving desk so reorders can be written when these firms send partial shipments.

Some stores provide only one copy of the purchase order for the receiving person. If two copies are provided, however, the receiver can return one copy to accounting for comparison with the supplier's invoice and the other can be held or sent to the purchasing department.

Buyers Should Not Be Involved in Receiving

Do not use a system of control in which the receiving copy of the purchase order goes back to the buyer and is then forwarded by him to accounts payable. This system allows for the dishonest altering of receiving records prior to their being sent to accounts payable for payment.

Experience shows that such a weak control system often leads to fraudulent collusion between the buyer and his resources.

One copy of the receiving tally should be held at the receiving desk. A second copy of the receiving tally should go to accounts payable. Invoices should not be paid to suppliers unless they are supported by this copy of the receiving tally.

Spot Checks

Store managers are wise to make spot checks of received merchandise. They should make an unannounced visit to the receiving dock and make some counts of various shipments after the receiving clerk has signed in the merchandise.

This type of verification can uncover errors and careless receiving practices. It also puts the receiver on notice that the manager looks upon this operation as important to the company.

Audit Purchase Order Addresses

Audits should also be made from time to time of purchase orders to determine the address where the merchandise is to be shipped. The purchase order should include definite instructions as to how and where goods are to be shipped. The files of bonding firms are filled with loss claims involving dishonest employees who misdirected merchandise and had it delivered to their home addresses—the store paid for the merchandise. Make sure the goods you buy get into your store and not into the hands of a thieving employee.

In checking merchandise against the purchase order, the receiver must check to be sure that a resource that was unable to ship the exact goods ordered did not substitute a different brand or quality or otherwise alter the order. If substitute merchandise is discovered the receiver should contact the store manager immediately. The manager should discuss the situation with the buyer to decide whether or not to accept the substitute merchandise.

Overshipments Can Hurt Turnover

Overshipments are another device that some resources use. If you don't want to become a chronic victim of this ploy, it's wise to refuse to accept delivery of any excess merchandise. Otherwise the resources will soon learn that they can load up your store with goods that you will be required to pay for but may not be able to turn over very quickly.

Keep in mind that TURNOVER is vital in retailing. Overgoods tie up money that could be used to purchase goods with immediate sales value, thus increasing the turnover of your merchandise creating profits.

Overgoods pose another problem. Sometimes a receiving clerk may notice an overgoods shipment and put the goods into stock hoping the overage won't be noticed. Later the clerk will put this extra merchandise into his car or he will get a truck driver to take the merchandise to his home.

The random spot checks of the receiving operation by the store manager or his assistant can provide a psychological barrier to the theft of overgoods since receivers wouldn't know when incoming shipments might be audited.

Receiving Manipulation

Manipulation of merchandise at the point of receiving begins the moment management becomes careless about random spot checks of the receiving operation.

One method of manipulation can occur when merchandise is found short at the time of arrival.

For example, in one shipment a missing box of goods was valued at $35. Other boxes in the same shipment involved chain saws, small appliances, and items retailing for as much as $250. When the receiving clerk discovered that the shipment was short one carton he replaced the $35 cartons out of store stock and removed a carton containing an expensive appliance worth $165. This gave a higher value to the missing carton.

He then took the $165 carton home. In this instance the switch of packages was discovered because the resource truck driver remembered the specific article missing on the shipper's copy of the bill of lading. When the store claimed a credit for the "missing" $165 carton the driver was questioned by the resource company. By checking shipping bills of lading they soon uncovered the fact that the item actually short on the shipment was a fixture worth only $35.

An interview with the receiving clerk brought a confession not only of the switched package but also of previous thefts whereby he had drained off $2,700 worth of merchandise.

Bar Salespeople from Receiving Room

In some stores salespeople are allowed to rush into the receiving room to grab a "hot" item they need right away to sell to a customer. The store should have a rule that merchandise must be received, counted, checked, and marked BEFORE it can be moved to a selling department.

Failure to keep salesclerks out of receiving can lead to theft losses by a clever salesperson who realizes that the merchandise has not been completely checked in and a loss would go unnoticed.

Another problem that occurs when merchandise is moved prematurely to the sales floor is that the receiving count becomes confused and a shipment shortage can slip by unnoticed.

A clever truck driver who is dishonest can take advantage of stores with poor receiving controls. When everyone is busy and paying little attention to the driver's activities, he can throw cartons left unguarded on the dock onto his truck. Such driver thefts occur daily at numerous stores simply because many stores are careless in their receiving dock controls.

Collecting Claims

Collecting claims on damaged goods can be difficult and time-consuming. This problem can be handled easily if a few simple principles are followed.

First, have the receiving clerk make certain that the delivery driver signs the store's copy of the freight bill showing the incident of damaged goods.

Equally important to getting the driver's signature confirming that a damaged package was in the delivery is the need to discover the damaged goods in the first instance. The receiving clerk must know what to look for. He needs to be trained to watch for warped, punctured, water-stained, or broken packages being unloaded onto the receiving dock.

Another indication of damage is a container that looks like items were spilled against it while it was in the delivery truck.

Obviously a major reason why some stores fail to successfully collect on their damaged shipments is because they lack an orderly procedure for filing claims. Claims must be recorded at the time of delivery. They are too important to be postponed until some time later when the receiver has taken care of other work.

Failure to look for damaged goods when they come into the store and process claims for them at once will cause a company to lose considerable sums. Otherwise these goods slip past the receiving operation and end up unnoticed (until much later) in stock. By that time, there is usually no way to successfully lodge a claim against the resource.

Another control problem involves the movement of merchandise between units when a company has several stores. Some stores have good controls for receiving goods from an outside resource, but their controls become lax when it comes to the transfer of merchandise between stores. This sets the scene for collusive thefts by dishonest employees working on store receiving docks or driving transfer trucks. And it can be fatal to profits.

Careless handling of interstore transfers can stem from the belief that; "Our company is strick about controlling incoming shipments from resources, and therefore we are undoubtedly just as careful in handling the merchandise moved between stores." This belief is understandable, but in actual practice it can be a false assumption.

Once a dishonest receiving clerk realizes that the branch store will not count the transferred merchandise he knows he can short the shipment and steal merchandise without anyone knowing it. Employees often steal from transfers. This can be costly to profits and is a difficult type of theft to detect.

Personal Transfers Risky

We also see companies where it is an acceptable practice to allow the store manager or buyer to transfer merchandise. The manager will be observed loading his car or station wagon with merchandise he is taking to a branch store.

These armfuls of merchandise being carried out to the supervisor's car are supposedly being transferred from one store to another because of an immediate need for a particular item. However, this is a very risky practice!

If you do find it necessary to have personal merchandise transfers, by all means insist the proper documents are prepared by an authorized person other than the person making the transfer. Interstore shipment documents must show the specific items, quantities, and value of goods moved from one store and received into stock in another store. Be sure to have the goods signed for by an authorized person in the branch store. This control procedure is needed when "personal" transfers are made by private vehicle.

Failure to provide and enforce such procedures have cost many firms thousands of dollars.

The store manager or other executive who moves such goods in an uncontrolled operation takes little risk when siphoning off this merchandise for his own use or for resale. This is especially true if he or she knows that accountability is not being maintained by the company.

It is best to incorporate the following kind of clause into company rules: "No merchandise is to be transferred between stores except in the transfer trucks supplied for that purpose, and all such transfers must be processed through the store receiving docks and are subject to the same controls enforced on incoming shipments from company resources. Failure to follow this rule is cause for immediate dismissal and possible prosecution if it is found to have been done with criminal intent."

Personal Purchases

Another good procedure to have is a method for processing any resource merchandise received at the store but addressed to a company manager or supervisor.

If members of management object to having their merchandise packages opened they should have personal items sent to their home. Anything received at the store, whether it is for the store or for an executive in the store, should be opened, checked, and processed in the usual receiving manner. The goods can then be properly moved to reserve stock, the selling floor, or to the individual to whom they are addressed.

Invoices for store goods should be sent to accounts payable along with the receiving tally as evidence that the goods have been received. Invoices for privately purchased goods should be given to the executive who ordered them for his payment.

A recent audit of a store revealed that the store manager and his assistant had merchandise at their homes that had been received in the store but was invoiced to the company. The two supervisors claimed they intended to pay for the items but simply hadn't done so yet. The company terminated the two offenders for failure to follow proper procedures.

The executives in this situation may well have been telling the truth, and perhaps they had not gotten around to paying the company for the goods they were buying. But the situation is questionable at best. It certainly raises serious questions about the integrity of the executives.

The store acted wisely in this case since a manager or other executive is expected to set the standards of conduct for subordinates.

Paying Resources in Advance

Most retailers don't pay for merchandise in advance. One reason is because once the resource has received its money the effort to meet the store's specifications may not seem important. The store may also find it difficult to obtain repayment from the resource if the merchandise is damaged in transit or does not meet its specifications.

Some stores have an almost obsessive desire to obtain their anticipations (such as a 2-percent net discount offered for payment of bills within a limited period of time). To this end some firms make a practice of writing checks to the supplier in advance before the goods have been received. Even if the check is written before receiving the goods it is best NOT to send the payment until a receiving tally shows that the merchandise has been received.

When a shipment is received that is unsatisfactory because of the quality of the goods or because of their damaged condition, it is good practice to hold up payment on that part of the order that is unsatisfactory until an adjustment has been agreed upon between the company and the supplier.

Double Payment of Invoices

It is also a good policy to make payment only on the original invoice of the supplier. Be extremely careful of duplicate invoices or summarized vendor's statements, and *never* pay on the basis of a packing slip. If payment checks are written on duplicate invoices or vendor statements, the possiblity always exists that the resources's original invoice has been processed and paid and the duplicate invoice may result in a double payment to the supplier.

Suppliers will return a duplicate payment made in error, but often such an error is not caught by their bookeeeping department and neither they nor the store are aware that a double payment has been made.

Invoice Payment Safeguards

Three conditions must be met before an invoice is paid.

1. *You must have satisfactory evidence of purchase.* Compare the supplier's invoice with the accounts payable open-to-buy file to which the receiving report should be attached. The invoice, purchase order, and receiving report should be checked to make sure that they are in agreement as to all specifications of the merchandise shipped, quantity received, and the price charged.

2. *Verification of the receipt of merchandise* is the second requirement that must be met before paying an invoice. A carefully written, legible, receiving document provides proof that the goods have been received into the company. Never pay for goods not received.

3. *Finally, validation of the invoice order is necessary* before it is paid. The accounts payable clerk must make sure that the terms set forth on the purchase order are the same terms appearing on the invoice. Additions and extensions must be checked for mathematical accuracy to insure that the invoice is not being overpaid. Even the cost of freight routing should be noted. If the buyer asked for a specific routing and it was not followed and a higher delivery cost resulted, the company should hold up the invoice payment until adjustment of freight costs has been agreed upon by the supplier. If the resource has offered a cash discount, this should be verified and so noted on the invoice along with the net amount payable.

What if the terms of the invoice don't agree with the terms on the purchase order? In such a situation, the company should be governed by the purchase order.

Once all three of these requirements for payment are met, then all documentary verification should be stapled together and a form placed on the front of the assembled paperwork showing that the documents have been verified for accuracy. The person doing the job of verification should sign this form showing that he or she takes responsibility for the comparison and accuracy of the purchase order, receiving document, price, and extensions.

Perforate Paid Invoices

In some firms a rubber stamp is used to mark invoices as "paid." If such a stamp is used on the bottom edge or the corner of an invoice, it can be cut off and the invoice *resubmitted* for a second payment. In fact, I once uncovered a major larceny in which a store controller was taking paid invoices home and using ordinary ink eradicator from the dime store to wash off the "paid" stamp. He then submitted the invoices back into the system for repayment. He was able to steal these second payment checks and deposit them in a hidden bank account he opened in a nearby city.

Even if a "paid" ink stamp is properly placed in the center of an invoice, this is not adequate to insure that the invoice will not be paid a second time because the ink can be easily removed. The only safe way to prevent repayment of an invoice is to use a perforating machine that punches holes with the word "PAID" or "VOID" on the invoice.

Credit memos from suppliers should be processed at once through your accounting department. Deduct the credit from the next payment of a bill made to the supplier. If you don't use the supplier regularly send a letter requesting the shipper to forward a bank check for the credit by return mail.

The receiving function is a vital element in a sound store operation. It requires the best possible control procedures properly enforced. Receiving should be a continuing focus for management attention.

Improving receiving controls can substantially improve store profits.

Chapter 29

THE SECURITY VULNERABILITY STUDY

Complete security is not economically feasible in any business. It could never be cost effective in retailing where exposure to theft is greater than in any other type of business.

A glance through the index of any major work on retail security will show a listing of from several hundred to several thousand topics (an earlier book of mine lists 4,000 items in the index). Each topic usually relates to control issues, which are physical, procedural, or psychological. And each subject would require people, time, and money if it were to be implemented toward total company security.

Therefore, with possibly several thousand things that can be done to improve a store's security, it becomes immediately apparent that using all of the possibilities would be a herculean task. *Total* security control would simply not be cost effective.

Locating Major Control Points

What is the alternative? Obviously we need to know in a specific enterprise where the points of greatest vulnerability to theft losses occur. If we have a blueprint of the entire operation of the company in terms of not only physical facilities, but also the pipeline that moves merchandise in and out of the company, the way money is taken in and paid out, the style of leadership, the adequacy and professionalism of the security operation, and particularly how well accountability procedures are designed and operated throughout the enterprise, then we can soon determine the points of major security and shortage control vulnerability.

Once we know where we are most open to serious theft losses, we can then devise countermeasures to strengthen these key points of control and substantially improve company security.

The Security Survey

The security survey, or vulnerability study, is essentially an exhaustive sifting and analysis of operations throughout the entire company. Not only is it a review of the physical premises, but it also includes operational systems and controls, morale, supervisory competence, and the adequacy of the present security department.

The study is designed to determine the existing level of company security and to pinpoint high-risk situations and weaknesses in company defenses against losses from carelessness, errors, and theft.

The overall goal is to find everything that could be a threat to company assets, either at present or in the future.

An in-depth security vulnerability study actually does far more than merely pinpoint where efforts are needed to strengthen the security against thefts. It is intended to bring to light *anything* that may adversely affect the earnings of the company.

In a sense a security vulnerability study is a type of management audit. It is concerned with analyzing every detail of the business from security of the computer operations to the style of management used.

In the past security surveys have been much too narrow in scope. Some have been limited to the simple examination of locks, alarms, and other elements of perimeter protection. More complete studies have evaluated the shoplifting and employee theft problems as well as the adequacy of the security department. But even this kind of study is far from adequate.

The New Security Role

Today, business management recognizes that each firm is in a life and death struggle against strong cultural forces and equally difficult economic realities. In addition, most executives in top management are aware that each year businesses of various kinds, even major firms, are swept out of the marketplace, often because of a breakdown of controls or a failure to see weaknesses in policies, practices, or management philosophy.

As a result, modern security has a new role in the company. Today, security of the company must encompass all matters that might adversely affect present and future assets of the company.

A company's assets are far more than its building, merchandise, and money. They include its personnel, customers, reputation, and growth and development.

The modern retailer is caught in a complex web of daily operating problems. The simple concepts that were the basis of retailing several years ago are now no longer viable. It has become a complex business and it will become even more complex as the computer takes hold and changes the nature of retailing in many ways. And this new complexity challenges the retailer and gives him an exhilarating feeling of fast movement into the future but it also results in new and unexpected problems of security control. Assets become more vulnerable to attack, that is, to being drained off as the pipelines of operation become more multitudinous, more loaded with merchandise, money, and operating information.

As the complexity of business has increased so has the vulnerability of assets. And, paradoxically, the less able is the retail firm to see its own weaknesses. Parts of the operating body can bleed almost openly as merchandise, money, and profits are drained from the company and still the wounds may go unnoticed. Top management knows losses are occurring, for the inventory shortage sheets provide evidence that they are, but the daily pressures of immediate problems make it difficult to find the time or expertise to locate the sources of these losses and to develop effective countermeasures to control them.

Study Objectives

The security vulnerability study provides a professional, objective view of the company from all angles, not unlike a hologram. The study is three dimensional and can serve many ends as it is turned and looked at from a variety of angles.

The important points to be kept in mind are as follows:

1. A security vulnerability study should not be limited simply to problems of theft. It should encompass all phases of company operation related to total company security and shortage control. It must examine all elements of the business that may adversely affect the present or future profits of the company.

2. The study should develop recommendations to protect all present and future assets.
3. The countermeasures offered must be cost effective. Although the study may uncover several hundred things that could be done to improve the security of company assets, doing all of them would not be feasible. So the recommendations must be limited to those few problems (usually no more than six or eight) where a slight shift of emphasis can improve the security of the enterprise and substantially increase company profits.

Identifying the Problems

It is a truism that no problem can be solved until it is identified and analyzed. Only when the nature of a problem is understood can it be properly solved. The security of company assets requires, as a first step, the identification and analysis of security and shortage control problems. A security vulnerability study is undertaken to determine these danger points.

A company needs a systematic security analysis to reveal high-risk areas of operation. This can best be done with a professional survey.

When does a company need a security vulnerability study? First, it needs such a study if a similar effort has never been done in the past. Second, if it has never previously felt that security was very important. Third, if it has a small security department with limited authority. Fourth, if it is experiencing substantial inventory shortages. Fifth, if profits are declining. Sixth, if it is planning major steps of growth and development.

Who Should Conduct a Security Vulnerability Study?

Usually it is not wise to use company personnel to conduct a vulnerability study. It can be done, of course, but experience has shown that in-house studies seldom are unbiased and objective. It is a matter of being too close to the forest to see the trees.

In addition, the in-house survey team often takes certain situations and practices for granted and therefore provides an inadequate view of existing conditions. Because the people used for an in-house survey usually have other duties, the study sometimes becomes hurried or is shoved aside and can appear to be poorly directed or lacking in concrete plans.

Recommendations also tend to repeat recommendations made by members of the study team in the past. The suggested countermeasures are often outdated or limited in scope because the survey group tends to avoid critical matters or restricts its recommendations rather than risk possible reprisals by a disgruntled executive whose views are contrary to those of the survey team.

It is also self-evident that the in-house team must have at least one member who has the security background and the special knowledge necessary to evaluate the survey results and develop competent recommendations.

Outside Security Consultant

In the long run, the outside survey is usually more objective and more effective than an in-house study. The outside study will usually be conducted by a team of security specialists.

A security study is usually a team effort. A top security specialist heads the effort. On the team itself are specialists in such things as physical security of properties, computer security, control systems and procedures, and management techniques. These various specialists are given their assignments by the head of the team. Later their work is merged into a series of findings that are evaluated by the head of the team, who will also be responsible for the final survey report and recommendations.

Whoever is finally selected as the head consultant of the team, it is important that he have past experience in doing similar studies as well as knowledge and experience in retail security.

Management Liaison Executive

It is important that the company appoint a middle-management executive (who is well liked in the company and who has a wide range of knowledge concerning company operations) to work with the security consultant as a liaison between the survey team and the company. His role will be to work with the security specialist in planning the study. He will set times for meetings with various key people in the firm and coordinate the overall administration of the study.

The person in the company selected to work with the outside security specialist should not only be familiar with the company and its operations but also be highly skilled in human relations and be well liked by people at all levels of the firm. The acceptance and cooperation obtained by the outside security survey team will be largely determined by the selection of the company executive to work with the team in carrying out the program. His selection is critical to the final results of the study.

This company executive does not have to give full time to the survey. His cooperation and help will require only an hour or so a day at the most. The important thing is that he have the experience and ability to help the security consultant evaluate his findings, help direct him to needed information, and provide him with historical background on various phases of the company and its personnel. He also aids in planning the steps of the study and in setting appointments for members of the team as needed. He should also be available as a troubleshooter and problem-solver for the survey group when needed.

Planning the Study

After the security consultant and his in-company contact executive have been selected, the next step is to plan the study.

The survey must be planned in advance in order to (1) make the best use of personnel and (2) systematically study all phases of company operations.

The advanced planning, however, should be kept flexible. Everyone involved should recognize that as the study progresses certain findings will indicate a need to make shifts in the schedule. The in-house executive must realize that the original study plans probably will be altered from time to time and for a variety of reasons and that new plans and new time tables may be needed.

Planning will be aided by the consultant's experience, which was gained from doing similar studies in the past. Certain reports and figures made available to the consultant may also affect the plans.

The consultant will need the past few years of departmental inventory shortage results by percent to sales and by dollar figures. In addition, he will want to review a year or two of markdown and markup figures as a percent to sales to see how they correlate with various departmental shortages. Any major dishonest employee cases or investigations, whether they have been resolved by apprehension or not, should be provided for his review. He should also review any previous studies relating to shortage control or security matters in advance of the final planning.

Methods of Investigation

The methods to be used in obtaining needed information will be discussed and formulated during this planning stage of the study. At the end of this chapter I have included the opening pages of a final report prepared for a large retail chain after a security vulnerability study. This report reveals the methods of investigation undertaken to obtain information.

Included in the techniques for studying this company are one-on-one interviews, surveillance of operations, inspection of facilities, group discussions, outside investigations, questionnaires, and so on. The number of hours spent on the various activities is included, but it should be remembered that the methods and the time spent on various phases of a study always vary with the individual firm.

Company Study Goals

Early in the planning discussions the consultant and top management must agree on the overall goals of the study as well as the limiting factors. One firm may want only an evaluation of its physical security. Another may prefer a study to aid in setting a proper security budget. A third firm may want a study of its computer security. Another firm may want an evaluation of its security department, and so on.

But most companies will want a full-scale security vulnerability study because the benefits obtained from such a study invariably mean millions of dollars in additional profits for the company and the results are beneficial for many years. In some instances such studies have turned the company around and saved it from bankruptcy. Without exception the full-scale security study has always paid for itself several times over in immediate reduction of shortages and a related increase in profits.

Even in a full-scale study, the client company should have clearly stated areas of concern or interest it wants probed and evaluated. These company goals should be used by the consultant as a guide when planning assignments for the survey team.

It goes without saying that full cooperation is needed between the security consultant and company personnel. Employees need to be told that they must cooperate fully with the survey team members. Executives should be asked to be candid and open in working with the security consultant. Only if executives and the general staff are open and frank in answering questions can the security study be fully effective.

Steps in the Survey Study

A vulnerability study is a process that goes through several phases. First is planning and then the overall background of the company operations is examined. Finally, the individual departments and operations are reviewed in depth. The findings are collated, sifted, and evaluated, with minor or irrelevant material being discarded. Early in the study several specific areas of concern will begin to emerge. These will be given more examination and study than was originally intended. Some will be solved while the study progresses, whereas others will turn out to be serious areas of high risk.

The Presurvey

In a sense the vulnerability study is a two-part survey. First the consultant studies early findings to determine what will require in-depth coverage, and to what degree. This phase is almost a preliminary survey. It answers questions relating to what is now being done about security and about related controls throughout the organization. It seeks information about where the greatest control problems appear to be centered, what merchandise appears to be most tempting to thieves, where the major losses are now occurring, and other similar matters.

The answers to these questions indicate where the second part of the survey will place the most emphasis. This preliminary survey gives the survey group an opportunity to familiarize themselves with the company, its key personnel, and its problems. After this preliminary probing, the consultant is in a more informed position and is better able to plan the complete study.

Survey Checklists

The security consultant usually provides his team of specialists with checklists to help guide their analysis of various company operations. The checklists are not intended to be confining but rather are designed to stimulate the people doing the study to make sure that all pertinent data is obtained so few repeat visits to key operations will be needed. The lists do not include *all* the questions that are important in the study of a particular operation but they do create a grid that the individual team member can work with and enlarge upon.

Receiving

A typical checklist for the receiving department survey might include questions like these:

1. How is the paperwork flow charted?
2. Where is receiving done?
   a. On the dock?
   b. In the receiving room?
   c. On the selling floor?

   d. Some other place?
3. Do resource salesmen bring merchandise directly to selling departments?
4. Do outside salesmen remove merchandise from selling department for vendor credits?
5. If so, how is the direct receiving and crediting handled?
6. How is accountability established?
7. Who makes an independent verifying merchandise count?
8. How is merchandise checked into the normal receiving operation?
   a. Is a packing slip used?
   b. Does the purchase order show quantities?
   c. Is a separate receiving tally written?
   d. If so, how are copies distributed?
9. Does merchandise sit on the receiving dock unattended?
10. What happens if received goods are damaged?
    a. Who handles damaged goods?
    b. What is the paperwork involved?
    c. How are copies of the form distributed?
    d. What is done to verify that a credit is received for damaged merchandise?
11. What happens when the received shipment is short?
12. How frequently do shortages on shipments occur?
    a. Are there any dollar cumulative records?
    b. Is there any way of ascertaining whether some firms are repeatedly short?
    c. If so, what action is taken?
13. Who signs for received goods?
14. Is the "Key-Rec" system of receiving control used?
    a. If so, are master sheets sent to accounts payable?
    b. Does accounts payable check off the master sheet to verify merchandise delivery before paying the supplier's invoice?
15. What controls are used to achieve accountability when merchandise is moved:
    a. From receiving to marking?
    b. From marking to reserve stock?
    c. From reserve stock to the selling department?

Cash Register

A cash register survey checklist might have questions like these:

1. Does each clerk have her own cash drawer?
2. Does each clerk count her change bank at the beginning of her work shift?

3. What are all the steps followed in opening and closing the cash register at the start and end of each work shift?
4. Is the register detail tape pulled daily?
5. Does auditing review the detail tapes?
   a. On what basis?
   b. How frequently?
   c. What items are checked?
6. Does the relief cashier have her own cash drawer?
7. Does the relief cashier sign a detail tape when taking over the register?
8. Does the regular clerk sign a detail tape when returning to the register?
9. If point-of-sale registers are used, what are all the opening procedures used?
   a. What are all the closing procedures?
   b. How are all the different kinds of transactions handled?
      (1) Cash and take sale?
      (2) Charge and take sale?
      (3) Charge and send sale?
      (4) Credit?
      (5) Void?
      (6) Other?
10. Is the register locked when it is unattended?
11. How does the cashier receive change for the register?
12. What is the housekeeping like around the register?
   a. Is the clerk allowed to keep her personal handbag at the register?
   b. Does merchandise conceal the register?
   c. Is the indice window free of obstructing papers?
   d. Other?
13. What is the location of the register?
   a. Is it off the selling floor?
   b. Is it near an emergency exit?
   c. Is it near a stairway?
   d. Is it hidden from view by merchandise, a post, or another obstruction?
   e. Other?
14. Is money ever paid out of the register?
   a. If so, under what circumstances?
      (1) Credits?
      (2) Change from bank check?
      (3) Making change for another register, customer or employee?
      (4) Other?

b. How do you evaluate the controls and accountability for the register?

15. Does a floor supervisor oversee the register?
16. Are the register drawers closed after each sale?
17. Are surprise register audits made?
    a. When, by whom, and what are the findings?
    b. Is any alternative method of checking used?
18. Does the store use honesty shoppers?
    a. Are they from an outside firm?
        (1) Whom?
        (2) Number of tests made monthly?
        (3) Costs per test?
        (4) Results over past 12 months?
19. Who reads the register daily?

Accounts Receivable*

In some segments of the survey more general questions are used on the checklists because the information required is more detailed and voluminous.

Some of the following questions might be used on the survey checklist for accounts receivable:

1. What are the present billing procedures in accounts receivable? What is the design of the forms used and what are the verification authorizations required?
2. Would an employee be able to cash a check payable to the company?
3. Could a dishonest clerk destroy charge billing records for herself, a relative, or a friend?
4. Could billings be altered along with any supporting documents to show a lesser amount payable by the customer?
5. Would it be possible for a clerk to destroy all records of a billing after receiving a customer's check? Could this clerk then cash the customer's incoming check? Could it be done if collusion existed between two people?

*Fraud in accounts receivable often consists of pocketing customer payments on accounts and then applying one customer's payments to another customer's accounts while keeping ahead of the cycle billing (this is a form of "kiting"). Another risk is the ability to pocket cash payments on C.O.D. purchases. Less common but still a risk is the danger of a clerk destroying a customer billing and cashing the customer's submitted payment check. Explore each of these potential problems to determine the effectiveness of present cross-accounting methods.

Similar survey checklists are prepared for accounts payable, payroll, personnel, cash handling, purchasing, security, shipping, vendor returns, maintenance, warehouse, distribution center, transfers, company bank accounts, and all other operating, finance, merchandising, and selling departments.

Survey Overlap for Verification

In many areas of operation two specialists operate during the survey. One specialist in physical control would review a department from that viewpoint while another security specialist who is an expert in control procedures would review the same operation from the control systems viewpoint.

In some departments several specialists might make independent reviews. In the data processing operation, for example, the security specialist in premises and physical controls would make a review of the data processing department from the viewpoint of his expertise. Another and different study of data processing would be made by the expert in computer security. And a third study of the data processing department would be made by the security management specialist concerned about the style of management being used in the department, rate of employee turnover, types of people being employed in the department, policies and management procedures being used, and the interface between the data processing staff and other key people in the company. His evaluation would include looking for a possible risk of an alienated, hostile employee who might become excessively frustrated and might plan to sabotage the computer, destroy valuable programs, or damage the physical equipment.

Although three different members of the security survey team would be studying the data processing department from a variety of viewpoints, their questions might overlap.

Here are a few typical questions that might be explored by the security specialist in physical controls. Note: Several of these questions will overlap the questions to be examined by the computer security specialist. In this manner the various members of the survey team gain verification of findings from each other's work.

Data Processing

1. What financial programs are routed through data processing and what is the effectiveness of present auditing and verification procedures?

2. How are printouts of secret or confidential information handled? What is the adequacy of the protection of this information at the present time?
3. Does the company have duplicate computer tapes?
   a. A duplicate of key programs?
   b. Of financial information?
   c. Accounts receivables?
   d. Other?
4. How are duplicate tapes protected?
   a. Off the premises?
   b. In the vault?
   c. Underground?
   d. Is there radiation protection?
   e. Other kinds of protection?
5. Are stored tapes up to date?
6. Who is authorized to enter the computer operations center?
7. Can messengers enter the computer room?
8. Are there glass windows on any walls of the computer room?
9. What controls are there for fire and humidity? List them in detail.
10. How are programmers controlled in relation to computer operations?
11. Do computer operators do any programming?
12. What training in fire prevention is given the data processing staff?
13. What is the adequacy of protective devices and the protective program to physically secure the computer room against overt attack?
14. How is the computer protected from unauthorized acquisition of data?
15. How are program tapes and operating data protected from unauthorized access and use?
16. How secure are the locks used at all entrances of the computer area?
    a. Who has keys, lock combinations, or other access?
    b. What is the frequency of key audits?
    c. What is the lock change program?
    d. When was the last audit of the authorized list of key holders?
    e. Who controls the reserve keys?
    f. How are the reserve keys protected?
17. Who has access to the computer area after store hours?
    a. How is access after hours controlled?
    b. Is a log or other record kept?
18. Is there a fail-safe indicator of actual computer use?
19. Is a concurrent log kept of authorized use?
    a. By whom?
    b. Who makes an independent audit of it?
    c. How frequently?

20. Is an accountability cross check made of actual computer use and the concurrent log of authorized use?
    a. Who makes this cross check?
    b. How frequently?
    c. Are irregularities ever found?
    d. If so, what were causes?
    e. How was the situation resolved?
21. What are the access controls to the computer? List them in detail.

In the above checklist used by the specialist in physical controls, notice how the findings from some of his questions will provide information that will overlap the findings of the computer security specialist. The computer security specialist will make an independent study of the data processing operation using questions 1, 10, 14, and 15, for example. (Additional details about the methods used for developing the vulnerability survey are included at the end of the chapter.)

Once these findings are completed, the professional security consultant develops his report and recommendations together with his survey team. These are recommendations presented to management along with an oral review in which the consultant can add details and answer any questions.

Management Review of the Study

After management has hired a qualified security consultant to do the vulnerability study, the company's major decisions are held in abeyance until the report is submitted. Once the recommendations are submitted, management decides what recommendations should be implemented and to what degree.

At this time management should review the study to make sure that the consultant has adequately covered all areas of the company in his findings. The consultant's final report provides top management with an objective and professional overview of the company operations, which soon makes it apparent where company assets are threatened and what major security problems exist for the enterprise.

Recommendations

At first it is not unusual for management to find the survey recommendations are more than they expected. This is a normal initial response. But a careful review of the report in a technical manner can determine whether the recommendations are truly as excessive as they may seem at first.

Read the report asking yourself if the recommendations appear logical based on the survey findings. Will the recommendations work? The consultant's experience can provide factual input for this question. How much will they cost? Can alternative ways of achieving the same objectives be used that are less time-consuming or less costly? In each instance review the recommendation and answer these questions positively or negatively for the particular recommendation.

Production Level Review

Bringing in the heads of the departments related to the recommendations and discussing the recommendations with them can help management determine the practicality of implementing some of the recommendations. Management should be able to judge whether any negative answers by operations people are legitimate or merely a rejection of change.

The production level review of the suggested changes should include estimated dollar costs for putting the suggestion into use. This cost factor can be weighed by management with other elements. If operating department heads agree that the improvement is needed and would be wise and if they feel it will cost little to implement and will reduce losses, then management should weigh these positive reactions when making a final decision.

Costs Versus Benefits

This review should recognize that some security measures will entail one-time costs while others may involve ongoing expenses. Some suggestions may require changing only a particular business form or altering a particular employee's duties to a minor degree, either of which would add little or nothing to operating costs. But whenever costs are considered they should be looked at in light of the probable effect of the change on employee dishonesty and on company losses.

Some measures may seem prohibitively costly and yet may still need to be undertaken. A failure to limit dishonesty now may be far more costly to the company in the long run.

Costs will not be the only deciding factor. The overall effect of a change must also be considered. If implementing a certain recommendation causes improved honesty in one department, it will also improve honesty in other company departments. This is because all parts of the business interface, and creating a controlled working environment is a final effect that magically occurs when we close off high-risk situations, first in one department and then in another. Employees suddenly feel that the company is security conscious and that any violation of control systems and procedures, in other words, any dishonesty, will be detected. When employees see evidence of stronger security in one department they assume security is being strengthened in other departments as well.

Making it difficult or unwise to steal strengthens employee honesty.

Management decisions on the consultant's recommendations are determined by considering the costs of each suggested improvement, along with a weighing of the morale factors and the anticipated profit benefits in terms of increased profits from reduced shortages.

This situation is not unlike a company's decision to advertise. Known elements in the situation are analyzed and from that analysis it is decided that certain corrective actions will occur to produce added profits for the company and that profit improvement will also absorb the cost of these actions.

Implementing Recommendations

Once the survey report is in your hands you have an overview of the company's soft spots and you have a program of recommendations to improve the company's defenses against carelessness, errors, and thefts.

You may be pleasantly surprised to find that your present operations are already strong and that you need to make only a few minor changes in procedures or add one or two control elements in order to have a well-controlled working environment.

On the other hand, if the survey has been carefully done you may discover several high-risk spots in the company that need corrective attention. Several changes of a substantial nature may be involved if you are to achieve any degree of real security.

Scheduling

First you must decide how to implement the recommendations, putting them in one at a time or all at once within a short period of time.

The step-by-step method with a predetermined priority schedule is the method most often used when improving the company's security program. This has its advantages. It allows you to get into the new programs at your own rate of speed. You select a certain recommendation and implement it. In this way you install your systems one at a time. The initial cost is less, the changes won't be as apt to upset a large number of employees, and you can spend time in developing the new procedures so that they will run smoothly.

The Step-by-Step Method Has Problems

As good as this system sounds at first, it has some obvious flaws. It is essentially a reactive approach to the need for changes to improve security. It tries to outguess the criminals by deciding which of the survey recommendations are the greatest danger areas. If your guess turns out to be wrong and a major theft occurs because one of the other recommendations was not acted upon, this may result in a catastrophic loss.

Another weakness inherent in the step-by-step approach is that as time passes management becomes involved in other things and loses interest in the security problem. This apathy appears frequently after the first one or two recommended changes are put into effect and are operating smoothly. A satisfied management takes the position that some worthwhile benefits have stemmed from the vulnerability study, and they fail to support the installation of the other recommended changes. The company assumes a false sense of security because of the success of the first changes.

Once management loses interest in the program it is almost impossible to act further on the survey recommendations. Changes of this type require top management participation and support; important control changes cannot be implemented in the face of an indifferent management.

Short-Term Schedule Is Best

Experience has shown that implementing all the recommendations within a short-term schedule is far better than extending them over a longer period.

Some exceptions to a total approach occur, however. The total cost of implementing the entire program at one time may be prohibitive. Or the nature of the changes may be so demoralizing to a large number of employees that to do them all at once may be undesirable.

The relative degree of risk should also be considered. Some recommendations may not require instant action because the relative risk is not very great. The outside consultant should discuss these matters with the client and should indicate which recommendations are of vital immediate importance to the firm and which could be delayed for a reasonable period of time.

The consultant should also point out to management any proposed changes that need to be carefully made because of possibly upsetting the employees.

Heavy Administrative Responsibility

The main problem in installing all the recommendations within a short time is that during the early months the administrative load for these projects can be heavy. This difficulty can best be handled by hiring the consultant to also implement these programs. The consultant would continue to work closely on these programs with his liaison company executive. Because the consultant would be spending full time on the programs and also because he has considerable experience in such changes, the total approach thus becomes quite efficient and the study is immediately productive for the firm.

Training Workshops

Another important reason for retaining the consultant to aid in implementing his recommendations is that he can also be used to conduct security training workshops for supervisors and top management executives. These will help to sell his programs and will also provide insight on the nature of retail theft losses. For example, who steals, why they steal, and what the individual supervisor can do about it in his own department.

Usually the in-house security director is too heavily burdened with day-to-day problems to develop and present such security workshops and welcomes additional help.

In-House Implementation

If the consultant is not retained to implement the new programs, then the logical person to do so is the liaison executive who has worked with the consultant and his team during the study. Administratively, it may be difficult for him in the early months, but most of these difficulties can be overcome with proper preplanning.

Implementation requires that people who will work with the new controls must be trained to understand the control procedures; they must also be familiar with company policies relating to violations of procedures or other irregularities. Most improvements will involve some type of verification such as merchandise counts. To insure that accountability is being achieved, the person implementing the programs must make frequent independent checks in the early days to assure himself that the people involved in the new control are following procedures and making complete and accurate verifications as called for by the new system.

Accountability Controls and the Vulnerability Study

In the next chapter I discuss the use of a new concept called SAC (security accountability controls). This is a relatively new concept involving security department verification and monitoring of high-risk areas. The foundation of the SAC program is the security vulnerability study. This study provides the information needed to properly locate the SAC security monitoring procedures. Combining the security survey with the SAC program strengthens total company security and develops a controlled working environment.

Survey Review

It is wise to schedule a follow-up review of the survey by the consultant six months afterward. This six-month review should be part of the total survey costs and should be included in the initial arrangements made for the study.

At the end of six months the company should have put into operation the suggestions in the report that have been agreed to by management. The consultant's recheck study serves to provide an objective and professional evaluation of how well the company has understood the suggestions made. In addition, it allows the consultant and his survey team to check the effect of these suggestions on company operations.

The recheck can reveal minor adjustments required to improve document flow, relieve employee frustration, or make the particular operation more efficient. It is a reexamination and tightening of any small details that may not have been applied exactly as intended.

The review may also reveal that someone along the line has made a change in the recommendation that has reduced its effectiveness.

The recheck may discover that a suggestion was misunderstood or that the change may have unexpectedly opened a new security risk. At times someone in the line of command may have altered a proposed change and the trouble spot is more vulnerable now than it was before. The recheck survey spots such a situation immediately.

How well have the recommendations been implemented? How suitable are the control changes now that they have moved from the planning stage to actually being used? This second look by the survey team can answer such questions. They can also evaluate situations where the recommendations have not been acted upon and determine the possible future effects on the company of the failure to use them.

The resurvey gives both management and the consultant a chance to take a look at the changes and evaluate their effectiveness.

Periodic Resurvey

A resurvey once a year for the first three years following the initial vulnerability study is a good idea. It is in these first years that the company gains a revitalized security environment.

It is unwise to assume that improved security can be planned and then forgotten. The security director may become involved in other phases of his job. Perhaps he is putting his efforts into detecting shoplifters and is forgetting other phases of security. He may not have the time or staff to properly develop overall company security. His prior experience may be limited or he may not have the ability to implement a total security plan.

Many things can happen in any operation, some known to management and others not even guessed. Therefore for the first three years after the initial study it is best to have an annual resurvey. In this way the company's security performance can be periodically reviewed by an objective outside specialist.

A resurvey is also wise if major changes occur in the company, new stores are added, a new distribution center is opened, or changes are made in top management.

The yearly resurvey during the early years can insure a continued strengthening of security control throughout the enterprise. Even a good security director will allow small changes in conditions to accumulate until they become a major problem. For example, a new customer service department opens and someone fails to provide proper controls over the cash handling for this department which is under the stairs.

Or new cash registers are placed near fire exits or stairways and no one in security notices their vulnerability. Or an employee's lunch room with vending machines is provided in each of the branch stores but there is no security provided for stockrooms adjacent to the new eating room. Or rain washes the soil away from the corner of a fence that surrounds the distribution center, thus weakening the perimeter security of the building. These and many other changes will occur in even as short a space of time as a year. The periodic annual resurvey will update and revise the company's security program to cover such changes.

Soon the resurveys will be needed less frequently as the security staff gains experience and as other department heads become more involved in helping to develop a controlled working environment.

But even as the total company security program becomes effective it will be wise to periodically resurvey the company. All operating departments require a periodic outside review because no department—not even security—should be allowed to police itself.

After the first three years of annual vulnerability studies, the company should plan to have a resurvey every five years as part of its ongoing security program.

In Sum

The security vulnerability study by an outside consultant provides management with an up-to-date evaluation of the company's security situation and pinpoints the areas of high-risk requiring corrective action to insure proper protection of company assets.

EXCERPT FROM A SECURITY VULNERABILITY REPORT

The following is a short segment of a survey report recently prepared for a major retailing chain with nearly 250 stores operating in 12 states.

My reason for including these opening pages of the report are to provide the reader with some insight into such matters as:

- The purpose and limitations of the study
- How the assignment was carried out
- The kinds of reports reviewed
- The control systems that were analyzed
- How questionnaires were used
- Subjects discussed by company employees
- How probe sessions were used
- The number of stores physically studied
- Top management executives who participated
- Members of the survey team
- How a consultant's security study report differs from the usual auditing report

Linear Charts of Control Procedures

I have also included a sampling of the procedure charts to show how linear charting of a control procedure helps to visualize it. This visualization aids in comparing the charted plan with the actual procedure. Variations between plan and practice are noted and evaluated. Weaknesses in the procedure can be spotted and highlighted.

The exercise of translating written procedures into the form of a linear chart aids the systems analyst who has to clearly understand each step in the procedure before he can properly chart it.

After a set of charts such as these are prepared they are independently checked against the written control procedure by the consultant. Next, before evaluation and analysis take place, the charts are examined by company personnel who insure that they are correct. After this second verification the charts are duplicated so that members of the survey team will have copies for comparing actual operations with the charted procedure.

The charts can be easily changed as the control procedure is altered. A procedural change usually requires a simple deletion of a step in the procedure, or the addition of a square with the new step added to the system. When the vulnerability study is completed several sets of the charts are provided for the company. They serve as models for reviewing and adapting systems when new systems must be designed. In addition, they serve a long-term benefit as effective training tools for teaching procedures to new employees.

SECURITY VULNERABILITY STUDY INTRODUCTION

Purpose of the Study

The purpose of the study is to locate and identify high-risk situations in the company, to evaluate the present security department operation for adequacy and effectiveness, and to review all matters directly and indirectly related to the security and shortage control problems of the company.

In addition to reporting the security team's findings, this report interprets these findings and also provides recommendations.

Verification and Cross Checks

In developing the findings reported here, every effort was made to insure completeness and accuracy by employing cross checking, direct observation, and testing.

In preparation for this report all the survey team's findings were reviewed and evaluated. Only findings that indicated a high risk of substantial loss were included in this report. These areas of serious vulnerability, once isolated, provide the foundation for the recommendations designed to improve shortage control and security in the company.

Study Limitations

Unless a problem situation represented a potential for substantial loss it was not included in this report. In addition, when a problem situation was well known to management and was already under advisement, it, too, was not included.

During the presurvey study, a few situations were found that could have been labeled a security risk. Upon examination, however, it was determined that, although a risk existed, this risk was minimal and for this reason the matter was not pursued further.

By and large the study was limited to an examination of those departments, procedures, and locations that are related to retail security and shortage control and are recognized as posing a high risk if not properly secured.

What's in It for Me?

Neither a security study nor a report exists in a vacuum. As objective and impersonal as a report may try to be, it cannot escape the fact that people are involved. The executives who read the report invariably ask:

"What's in it for me?"

This is a logical question. My answer is that a lot depends upon what a company executive is looking for.

Obviously, the security study would not have been undertaken in the first instance unless management had some genuine concerns about the adequacy of the firm's present security and shortage control measures. Therefore, this report is intended to answer questions already in the minds of executives concerned about the adequacy of the measures being taken to protect company assets.

A large number of people have participated in the study and when you listen to their observations you will most likely gain fresh insights into many areas of company operations.

As in any retail establishment, when shortages appear to be increasing various top management executives have definite opinions about the adequacy or inadequacy of the company's shortage control and security departments. Top executives concerned about controlling runaway shortages also have their own ideas as to what should or should not be done about inventory shortage problems. Often they see situations from quite different viewpoints. It is not surprising therefore that executives may also not agree on what should be done about inventory shortage problems.

Once there is a lack of unanimity among the top management group as to how certain control situations are being handled and disagreement about what steps should be taken to effectively improve the company's security and shortage control programs, it is logical to turn to an outside specialist to clarify the situation for everyone concerned.

Objective View

The outside consultant and his survey team bring to the firm many years of security experience. They also have the benefit of knowledge gained in studies done in other retail firms concerned about losses like these.

Security experience and knowledge are important, of course, but equally important is the fact the consultant and his staff are not involved directly in the company. They bring a fresh eye to their task, and the type of perspective that only an outsider can have.

The work the outside consultant does indicates that he has at least average judgment, and probably he is well above average in his specialized field.

All these characteristics are assets to this kind of study. But probably the primary value of a vulnerability study is the fact that management receives an unbiased, objective report.

The interpretation and meaning of the findings as well as the recommendations are certainly open to discussion and disagreement. They represent the opinions of the security specialist based on his knowledge and experience, and opinions are always debatable. But the findings of the study are candidly and objectively reported and they are factual.

Professional Guidance

Even though everyone in top management may not agree with the consultant's interpretations of the survey findings, or fully accept some of his recommendations, the study nevertheless does tend to unify top management and stimulate cooperative effort in the right direction to solve control and security problems.

The report provides professional guidance for management and offers suggestions for improving control over the company and a better protection of all company assets.

The Bottom Line

As these recommended improvements occur, the total company is strengthened. Not only is security improved and inventory shortages reduced, but also the total company is favorably affected by the control changes that are initiated. In the end not only the executives at the top of the firm but also at all levels of supervision gain a pride of accomplishment as they see the improvements being made.

The bottom line on the operating statement is always profits. And a substantial increase in profits is the bottom line of the vulnerability study.

This means there will be more money available in terms of working capital, and therefore executives can develop new phases of the enterprise and can continue to further improve those elements of the company now in operation.

Security of Assets

One other benefit might be kept in mind—that is, the increased security of assets that will result from the actions taken following this report. With many firms and even giant chains failing in a highly competitive marketplace and with others in serious financial trouble, a company is wise to look after the protection of its assets.

The U.S. Department of Commerce reports that 33 percent of all businesses that failed in the country last year failed because of employee dishonesty. Keep that stinging fact in mind as you read the report.

And remember that the study is just what the name implies; it is a "security" study and improved security is what the recommendations in this report provide. And doesn't that mean better security for every executive in the company as well?

How Was the Assignment Carried Out?

In a company such as this, with more than 200 stores spread over a large geographical area and with seven regional offices and a large home office unit, one of the first problems was to gather information from a sufficient number of sources to insure the accuracy of the survey.

It was also important that the analysis of these findings avoid overemphasizing local store problems. The objective was to locate those shortage and security problems that are fundamental to the entire company.

In addition to identifying loss control problems, sufficient reliable information was needed to properly evaluate their relative importance and determine which problems should be resolved to provide a substantial return to the company.

To insure validity meant getting information from the home office, regional offices, and every store in the chain. Information had to be gathered from every unit and also from every organizational level within the firm.

Developing Information

To develop this information a variety of information-gathering approaches were used:

1. Reports of many types were requisitioned from home office files.
2. Procedural manuals for all major control systems were obtained.
3. Over a thousand questionnaires were sent to personnel in every store from regional to the home office and to every level of the organization from receiving dock worker to company president.
4. In five regions of the company probe sessions were held with store personnel from the branches located in that region.
5. On-premise studies were undertaken in 36 stores. One-on-one interviews were held with key personnel in each store and time was spent observing all phases of the store operations. Shopping, refund, ticket-switching, and other tests were conducted to determine each store's vulnerability to internal and external thefts.
6. A large number of former employees were contacted and interviewed.
7. At the consultant's request, the finance division of the company did an extensive mail test of the refund system and did other research studies on voids, bank checks, and other items requested by the consultant.
8. In addition to interviews with executives in five regional offices, many of the top executives in the home office were interviewed.

In addition to the above activities, confidential investigations to determine the answers to a variety of questions were conducted by professional investigators.

Some of the above items are self-explanatory, but several are worth additional attention.

What Kinds of Reports Were Obtained for Review?

One hundred and forty different reports, memos, and letters were provided to the consultant. They ranged from shrinkage reports, security budgets, computer readouts, and other topics covering the entire spectrum of shortage control problems. In addition, 70 major auditing studies were reviewed.

Reports were studied on everything from minutes of shrinkage committee meetings, regional and store meetings, reports on bank check losses, damaged goods, ticket-switching, security activities, layaways, price change problems, cancellation markups, and many more.

In addition, three years of polygraph test results were carefully reviewed.

An estimated 3,600 pages of reports, computer readouts, manuals, auditing results, and so on, were forwarded to and read by the consultant at his office.

Much of this material was valuable in providing needed background to the study. Many of the problems noted in the reports were much later confirmed by observation and testing at store level.

As this reading of reports was carried out, we also began to prepare for in-store studies, and for the probe sessions planned for all regions.

Former Employees Were Interviewed

Computer lists of former employees from all levels of the company were provided the consultant and the job of locating the former employees was started.

At the conclusion of this part of the study the survey team had interviewed 126 former employees, including former store detectives, store managers, assistant managers, cashiers, department heads, and receiving personnel.

These interviews were most productive. In many instances the interview was taped after permission to do so was obtained from the former employee. These tapes were transcribed by typists and the material used for further investigation into a variety of problem situations the interviews had brought to light.

The complete job of locating the former employee, setting up the interview, conducting it, and in many cases later transcribing it required 700 hours of work. Although it was a major undertaking, it provided important information for the work that was to follow.

Control Systems and Procedures Were Analyzed

Also providing background that was needed during the survey was the analysis of control systems and procedures.

From the company's procedures manual, the following seven controls were selected for analysis:

1. Cashier
2. Customer service desk
3. Receiving
4. Invoice auditing
5. Purchase orders
6. Retail price change system
7. Store report

In addition, 73 subdivisions of these basic controls were selected for detailed analysis.

The purpose of the control systems and procedures study was to:

- Determine how effectively the company's procedures book communicates the controls to store personnel who are supposed to follow them.
- Search for any serious loss loopholes that need to be corrected.
- Offer any suggestions for improvement that appear to merit consideration.
- Provide a systems manual to aid in training personnel using the charts as basic format.

The result of this work is a 150-page book with detailed charts of these procedures, laid out in linear fashion so we can comprehend how the controls function. See the appendix at the end of this chapter for the table of contents of this study and sample charts.

This reconstruction and charting of 73 procedures was done by M.T., staff analyst and charting specialist. It required 42 hours of study before charting. His first rough draft of the charts required 165 hours. The consultant took 18 hours to study the rough drafts, suggest changes, and insure accuracy of interpretation of the written procedures.

Then the final draft of the charts was done, a complete book in itself, which required 120 hours of work.

Once completed, the chart book and the original manual of procedures were given to a nationally recognized authority on control systems and procedures design. He reviewed the charts and provided a report on his findings. This evaluation required 32 hours.

The review charting, and final analysis of the control systems and procedures, required a total of 377 hours work.

Questionnaires Were Sent to All Stores

To insure input from all parts of the company and all levels of the organization, a program of questionnaires was initiated by the consultant. These questionnaires promised complete confidentiality and asked people (in all ranks of the company at every location) to provide the consultant with their views on the company's shortage problems.

Two questions were asked:

1. "What do you believe are the major causes of the company's inventory shortages?"
2. "What do you believe needs to be done in order to improve company operations so as to reduce inventory shortages?"

The questions were simple and open-ended to encourage spontaneous, honest answers. In addition, to aid those who hate to write, a letter, sent with the questions, offered the employee the opportunity to dictate a cassette or to arrange to make a phone contact with the consultant.

Basic sampling included questionnaires sent to the following employees of every store:

- Manager
- Assistant manager
- Security manager
- Head cashier
- Head receiver

Many questionnaires were also completed by receiving managers, cashiers, customer service managers, invoice auditors, operations managers, and other members of the store group. Questionnaires were also sent to all regional and district managers and to vice presidents, assistant vice presidents, and key people in the home office.

The response was overwhelming. We had nearly a 100-percent return. Many people wrote replies 10, 12, and even 15 pages long (often on both sides of the paper). We received 17 dictated cassettes and 217 requests for personal contact by telephone with the consultant. The 17 cassettes were transcribed (22 hours of typing), scrubbed clean, and then returned to the senders. Of the 217 phone calls, some could not be completed because of difficulty in making contact. But 107 were completed and resulted in 280 pages of typed notes from these conversations.

As to the questionnaires themselves, we received 1,371 replies from stores, regional offices, and the home offices.

The resulting paperwork was staggering: the 1,371 replies had a total of 6,125 pages (mostly handwritten). It took four people 23 hours just to collate these replies by store number, regional office, and home office and by position in the company.

Once collated they were edited by using three colored pencils. Red for examples, blue for explanations, and green for constructive suggestions for improvement. This editing and collating was the most difficult part of the reconciliation process and took 204 hours.

Once the underlining was done a rough draft of the underlined comments was typed. It was 1,245 pages long and took 313 typing hours (handwriting was often difficult to decipher).

A second editing was done by the consultant. This took a careful reading and 15 hours. Then the reedited material was again typed (now cut down to 917 pages). Next another editing and collation was done and the material catalogued into 49 subjects (requiring considerable cutting and glueing). This was typed into final form, a 604-page document of exceptional value to the company and the consultant. This final editing took 4 hours and the 604 pages of finished copy required 151 typing hours.

All told, this project required 893 work hours to shape the information into useful form. But the results were worth it. The document provides an unbelievably candid, intelligent, and meaningful insight into the problems of various parts of the company's operation and also offers worthwhile suggestions for improving many shortage and security situations.

What Subjects Were Explored by People Answering the Questionnaires?

When the reams of questionaire responses were finally boiled down to a 604-page document, we ended with 3,211 individual comments on the following 49 subjects:

Accounts Payable
Attitude and Morale
Bank Checks Losses
Carelessness—Cleaning
Cash Office
Cashiers

Communication Problems
Courtesy Card Program
Damaged Merchandise
Distribution Center
Employee Discipline
Employee Dishonesty
Employee Package Control
Equipment
Executive Visits
Housekeeping
In-store Transfers
Jewelry
Known Loss Report
Layaway
Merchandising
Miscellaneous
NOPOs
Organizational Structure
Overstocked Situations
Packaging and Display
Paperwork
Personnel
Personnel Changes
Physical Inventory
Policies and Procedures
Polygraph
Pricing
Priorities
Rain Checks
Receiving
Refunds
Salaries
Security
Sensormatic and KNOGO
Shoplifting
Shopping Tests
Staffing
Stanton Surveys
Supervision
Ticket Switching
Ticketing
Training
Unrecorded Loans

Probe Sessions Were Held in Five Regional Offices

When I first started consulting years ago, I used to go to each key person in a store, the manager, his assistant, the detectives, cashiers, receiving manager, and so on, and interview each person separately. Since it took one to three hours for each interview, this one-on-one process was time-consuming and made the consulting process costly.

Such an approach simply isn't practical when we need to touch base with a large number of managers and supervisors in many stores, as was the situation in this study. To make the process more efficient I developed a technique called "Probe Sessions." Here's how it works:

1. Fifteen people representing an equal number of stores meet with me for a two- or three-hour—no holds barred—off-the-record session.
2. Members of each group are always of the same management level so a subordinate does not have to talk in front of his boss.
3. The groups in this study were store managers, assistant store managers, group operations managers, cashiers, security leads, and a mixed group of the general staff. A session was also held

with the executives working in the regional offices. This last group also included district managers.

4. The discussion is open-ended and confidential. Everyone is free to say anything he or she wants to without fear of reprisal.
5. Some comments are obviously exaggerated, sometimes a unique situation is blown up out of all proportion, sometimes the person is speaking without personal knowledge of a situation, and often he or she may have poor judgment, but the consultant listens nevertheless. He selects the pertinent material and cross references it between groups, thus weeding out the chaff.
6. In addition, the groups themselves temper the situation by contradicting the person who exaggerates, is out of line, is personally teed off at someone or something, or is presenting a condition not typical to the stores as a whole.
7. In addition, as the consultant begins to see the same problems surfacing again and again in each group he begins to gain an excellent insight into the things that the various levels of supervision and the general staff are most concerned about.

   Since prior to the meeting, the consultant has already spent some time in several of the stores represented, he can identify with the employees. He knows their environment. As he gains insight into the problems common to all of the stores, the groups begin to identify with him. They also recognize he understands what they are saying.
8. The consultant requires that opinions be supported by factual examples and although everything is strictly off the record and no recordings are made of the session, the consultant does keep copious notes. He goes over these notes later and checks them against information from other groups previously talked with. He then formulates questions for the next session to help him validate the problems identified and to gain other factual examples of particular problems. He can then intelligently estimate the importance of any given problem situation.
9. These probes are a valuable part of the vulnerability study. They not only encourage important areas of concern to surface that are later investigated and verified by testing, observation, and other means, but also a rapport grows between the consultant and store employees so they know he and the company are on their side.

   The consultant tells the groups that he will do what he can to help them solve the problems they are dealing with daily on the job. This means that when final recommendations are made the people in the stores at the regional level are already in tune with many of them and are eager to see them implemented. Recommendations are dropped into an environment already conditioned to desire these changes and the resistance to proposed changes is low or nonexistent.

In fact, the questions at the end of every probe session were similar:

"How soon will your study be done?"

"How soon will your report be completed?"

"When can we start to look for these needed improvements?"

10. Every session raised some of the same topics. Many sessions produced excellent suggestions for correcting shortage problems, and every session also turned up new information, with different points emphasized and new viewpoints expressed. The regional office executives provided valuable insights into company operations and controls.

    Sessions often ran far over the two-hour period allotted. In one instance the building was locked up before the group was willing to leave. We discovered we'd gone past the four o'clock deadline and at six-thirty people still wanted to stay and talk.

Probes were run for four days at each of the five regional offices. The consultant also had the opportunity to spend some time in private interviews with the regional vice president, operations manager, and personnel director and these private conversations were also valuable.

The probe sessions totaled 106 hours along with the one- and two-hour private sessions held with each regional executive. This work resulted in 4,000 pages of dictated and transcribed notes.

No other single activity was as productive in terms of worthwhile security and shortage control information, material that could be validated by testing, cross referencing, and observations, as these open, candid, and intelligent discussions.

In Depth Studies Were Made of Specific Stores

Studies were made of 38 specific stores. Of this group, 8 stores in different cities were studied overtly. The consultant talked with the store manager, his assistant, security personnel, cashiers, and other members of the store staff.

A second group of 28 stores in 18 cities were visited by consultants who did not identify themselves but instead observed the store activities for several hours, conducting shopping tests, ticket-switching tests, and refund tests.

These investigations were done by the consultant and his survey team. Tests of cashier alertness in catching ticket switches, concealed merchandise, and merchandise not concealed going out the door were done to confirm the auditing reports in which similar tests were conducted. The findings of the internal auditing staff were confirmed throughout by these tests.

Top Management Executives Also Provided Input into the Study

In addition to the interviews at store and regional levels and the people talked with at the probe sessions, an important part of the study was a week spent in the home office talking with top executives of the company. During this week important insights that often added perspective on material uncovered in the field were gained. These interviews also helped explain the company's philosophy, policies, and goals.

Among those interviewed were:

- Chairman of the board
- Executive vice president and director of sales operations
- Executive vice president and general merchandise manager
- Senior merchandise manager
- Senior vice president and director of finance and treasurer
- Senior vice president and sales operation director
- Vice president, regional manager (region A)
- Vice president, staff finance
- Vice president, disbursements
- Vice president, senior merchandise manager
- Vice president, regional manager (region B)
- Vice president, distribution services director
- Assistant vice president, merchandise controller
- Assistant vice president, manager of business planning
- Assistant vice president, administrative services
- Assistant vice president, manager field sales operations
- Assistant vice president, manager of security
- Assistant vice president, manager of store operations
- Assistant vice president, financial controller
- Assistant vice president, manager of merchandise program development

Program Staffing—Who Made Up the Consulting Team That Conducted the Study?

Senior Analyst. *Bob Curtis*: Responsibility for direction, control, analysis, and reporting of the entire program.

Junior Analyst. *J.R.*: Head of own consulting firm located in Westport, Connecticut.

One of the nation's leading authorities on business penetration, terrorism, and espionage. Also expert in field of organized crime. Clients include major corporations in the United States and abroad. He also works with the U.S. State Department and INTERPOL.

Specialists. *B.M.*: Nationally recognized expert in control systems and procedures and specialist in computer security. Columnist, lecturer, and consultant.

R.N.: Owner of a security consulting firm in San Juan, Puerto Rico, with a branch office in Houston, Texas.

R.C.: For fifteen years was the security director of a firm with 66 stores in the United States and the Caribbean. Now a recognized retail security consultant in the chain store field.

D.L.: Security director of large chain of supermarkets in Puerto Rico. Also active in military security with the U.S. Air Force.

T.C.: Has done many organized crime investigations. Formerly commanding officer of the burglary larceny division of the police department's detective bureau in one of the largest cities in the United States. An expert witness before the U.S. Senate Select Committee on thefts from interstate commerce. He lectures regularly at the police academy and in 1971 was named state trooper of the year.

H.S.: Recently retired after 37 years in the U.S. Treasury Department. He served as assistant chief inspector for investigators of the IRS, and he ran the special rackets squad of the U.S. Customs Department for many years. He was a senior customs representative for the Far East, and he was assistant to the commissioner for foreign customs at the bureau's headquarters in Washington.

He was the first man to organize and direct the Sky Marshal program and served as the U.S. chief representative to INTERPOL.

M.T.: Staff specialist, responsible for control systems analysis and linear charting of procedures.

Colonel J.W.: Retired from the U.S. Military Intelligence where he was formerly the chief investigator for many years. He has served throughout the world on a variety of missions.

W.C.: Has served as a captain in the U.S. Military Intelligence. He has had a variety of intelligence-gathering responsibilities in various locations around the world. He is also the only training officer in intelligence collection for the U.S. Army Reserve. Before founding his own consulting firm he served as assistant security director for the Metropolitan Museum of Art.

H.K.: Heads his own agency in Atlanta, Georgia. His agency specializes in consulting services to retailers.

In Addition to The People Listed Above

The study also employed four secretaries and a clerical worker. They were an important asset to the survey team, for they worked into the late night hours and contributed encouragement and support along with typing, editing, and other office skills.

In Sum

The study was first discussed with the consultant on (date). The objectives, purpose, and scope were soon agreed upon and the actual study began (date). The study continued for 38 weeks over a period of 10 months. Every facet of the company operations was explored and every level of management as well as every store, regional as well as home office, contributed important information that helped the entire project.

What Exactly Is a Report?

A report should provide the solution to a specific and limited problem.

Keep in mind that a report is not a discussion. It is never argumentative. It must be objective, candid, and unbiased. It should show by the findings presented how conclusions are arrived at. The report should also contain new and useful information.

Why Is a Report Written?

Basically, a report is a written statement intended to lead to some type of action.

A Consultant's Report Is Not the Same as an Auditing Report

Often I find executives expect a consulting report to provide a detailed list of findings by investigators, the sort of items found in auditing studies. The consulting report is not at all similar to an auditing report.

The internal auditor does certain investigations, makes certain tests, and writes up his findings in accurate and complete detail. Personal comments are seldom made and auditing reports usually do not offer recommendations to solve the control problems uncovered.

A consultant's report, on the other hand, is not necessarily the documentation of a problem. It is not argumentative because it is usually a summary of his findings and primarily consists of the consultant's personal evaluations and judgments.

Hard facts are the major body of an auditing report. Facts are also a core element in the consulting report. The facts exist and have been recorded, but they have been summarized, evaluated, and interpreted by the consultant.

The security study consists of a sweeping exploration of the company for factual detailed information, but the consultant's report deals primarily in opinions.

A consultant is hired for his experience, judgment, and opinions. Of course, he must also be capable of gathering information efficiently, checking and cross referencing it for reliability. He must also be able to provide his clients with sound evaluations of his findings. Finally, his recommendations must not only be suitable but also cost effective and beneficial to the companies he serves.

A firm hires a consultant because he has experience and knowledge in a special field. However, he is also hired for his judgment. In the final analysis the difference between a good and a poor consultant is determined primarily by the soundness of his judgment. His ability to get the important factual information in analyzing a company's security and shortage problems is vital to a sound security study, but the material has little value unless it is interpreted with excellent judgment.

An auditing report is useful in terms of focusing on a specific control problem needing attention. But usually correction of the problem is left to someone besides the auditor.

By contrast, the purpose of a consultant's report is to solve the problem, not to talk about it.

Appendix

SECURITY VULNERABILITY STUDY: CONTENTS AND CONTROL CHARTS

CONTENTS

The Contents list is provided to show the many kinds of control procedures that are usually "charted" during a security vulnerability study. This index reveals the wide range of the study and the types of procedures investigated in depth during a security study.

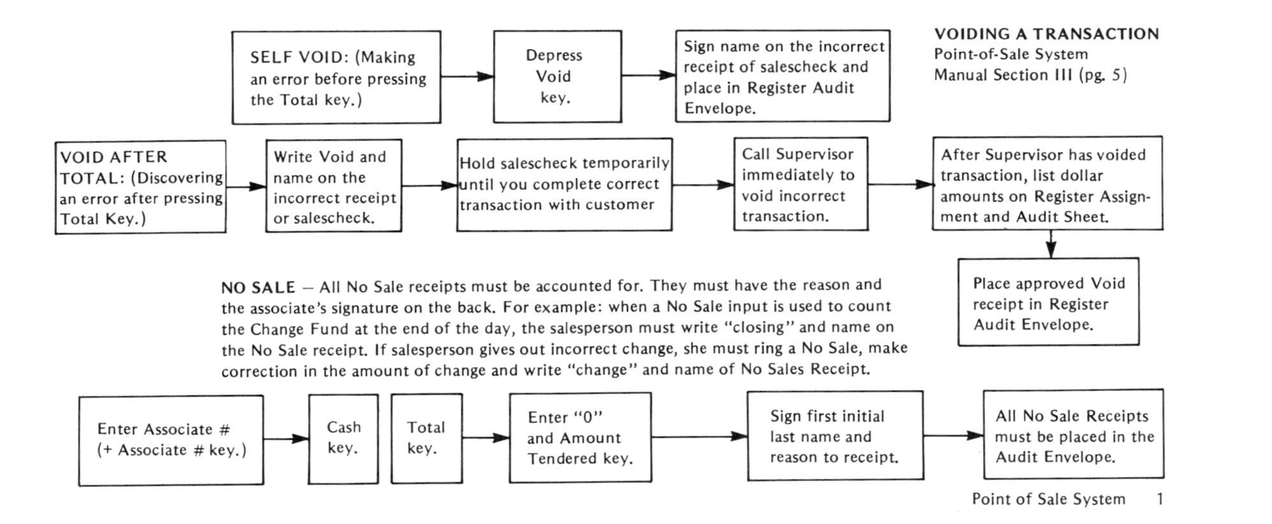

These sample pages from the report, show how control procedures are laid out in a linear format so the investigator can carry the chart with him, like a blueprint, and "walk" thru the procedure.

The original charts are printed on 14″ X 18″ pages for easy legibility. They are an accurate outline of the control procedures as "designed" in company manuals.

The investigator walks through the operation following his charts, step-by-step, looking for any "added" steps not in the original control system design and for any "modifications" that have worked into the system. He is particularly concerned about any control steps no longer being used. If the procedures are being followed as planned (charted) then only the quality of the control operation is of concern. But if deviations from the planned control system are in evidence, further work is necessary. Do the changes weaken the control. Are missing steps vital to good control? Or, has the system been strengthened and made more efficient by the changes? (all changes are *not* bad)

The charting of these opearting procedures is important in a vulnerability study because most store procedures were originally designed to serve not only a merchandise or money function, but were also intended to improve security of the enterprise.

The security specialist doing the study is concerned about the original procedural design. It is reviewed for any weaknesses or loss loopholes. Next he is concerned with how well the procedure is being followed, and the quality of the work done by those who are responsible for operating the various control steps involved.

Any need improvements in the procedural design, or a need to upgrade enforcement, will lead to recommendations in the final security study report.

ORDER CHECK OFFICE
ACCOUNTS PAYABLE

Responsibility:
1. Systematically matching all invoices with their orders
2. Logging of KEY-REC'S
3. Maintaining the "On Order" balance

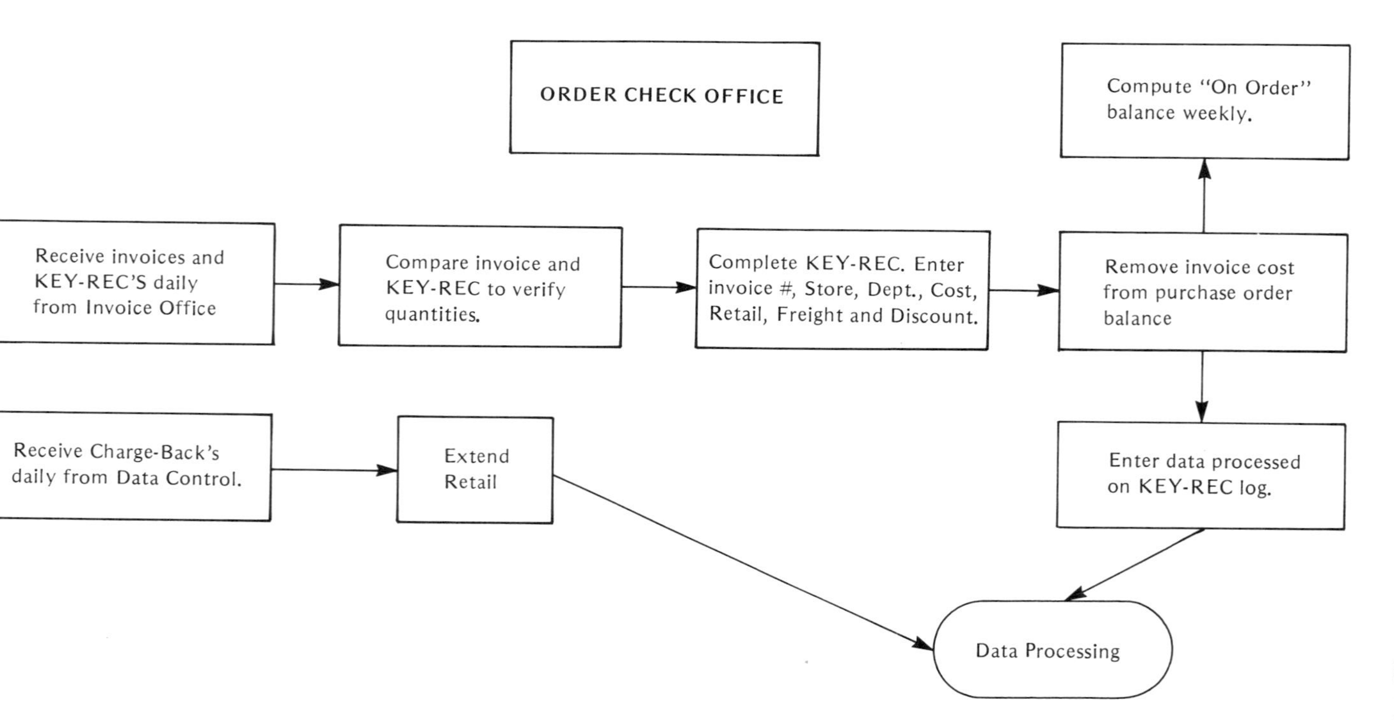

ACCOUNTS PAYABLE

ACCOUNTS PAYABLE
CONTROL DIVISION

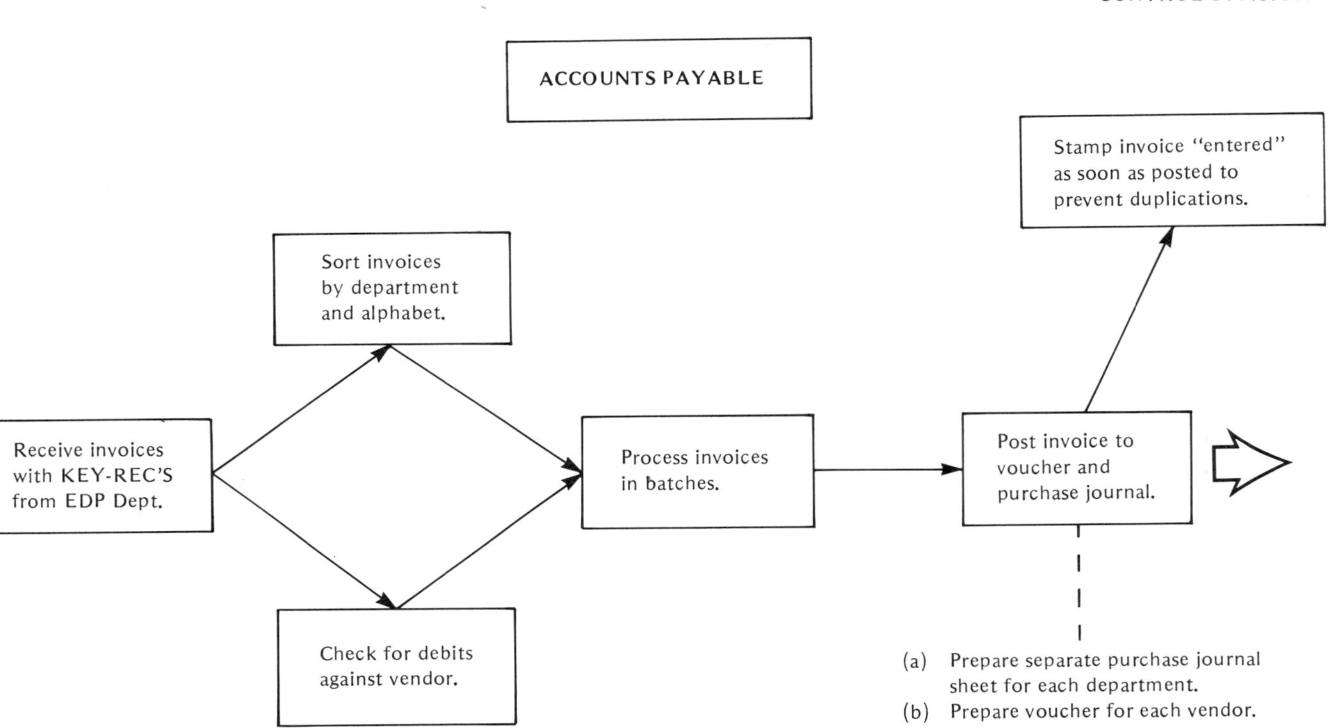

ACCOUNTS PAYABLE 2.

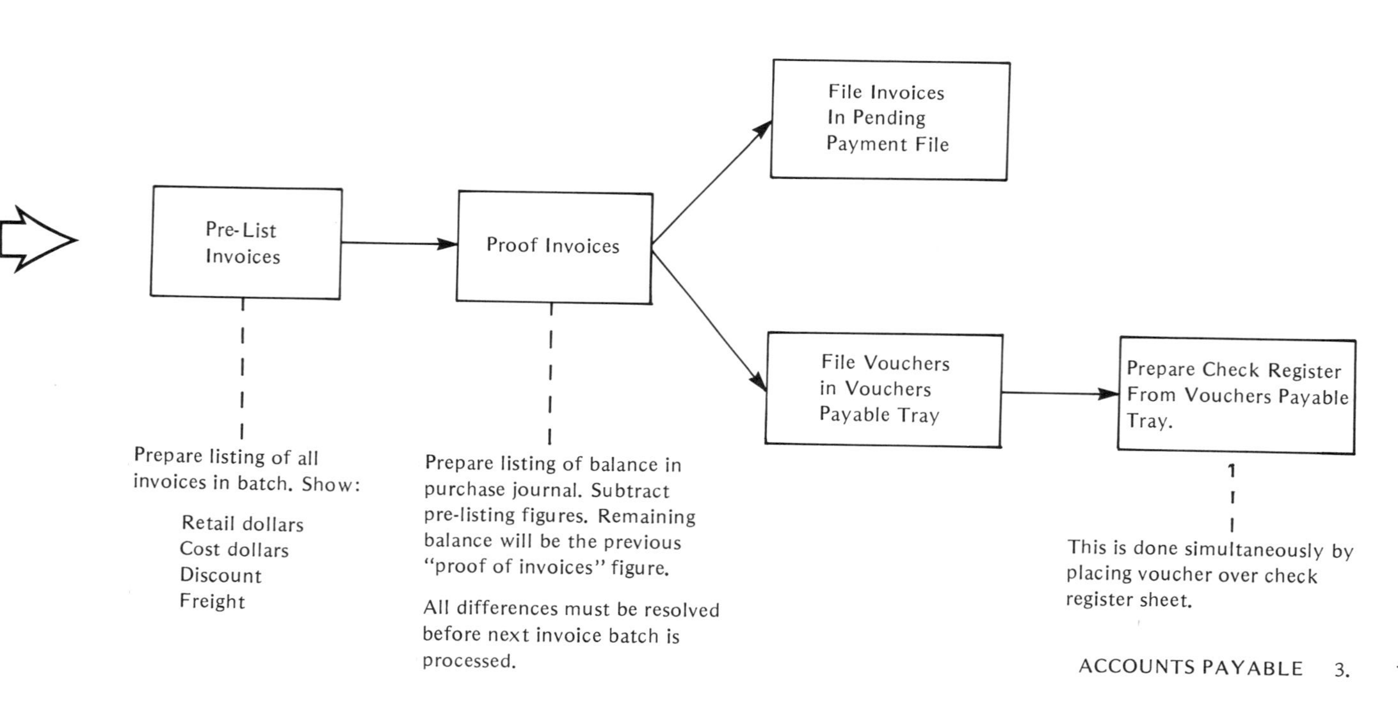
ACCOUNTS PAYABLE
CONTROL DIVISION
ACCOUNTS PAYABLE
Pre-List Invoices
Proof Invoices
File Invoices In Pending Payment File
File Vouchers in Vouchers Payable Tray
Prepare Check Register From Vouchers Payable Tray.
Prepare listing of all invoices in batch. Show:
Retail dollars
Cost dollars
Discount
Freight
Prepare listing of balance in purchase journal. Subtract pre-listing figures. Remaining balance will be the previous "proof of invoices" figure.
All differences must be resolved before next invoice batch is processed.
This is done simultaneously by placing voucher over check register sheet.
ACCOUNTS PAYABLE 3.

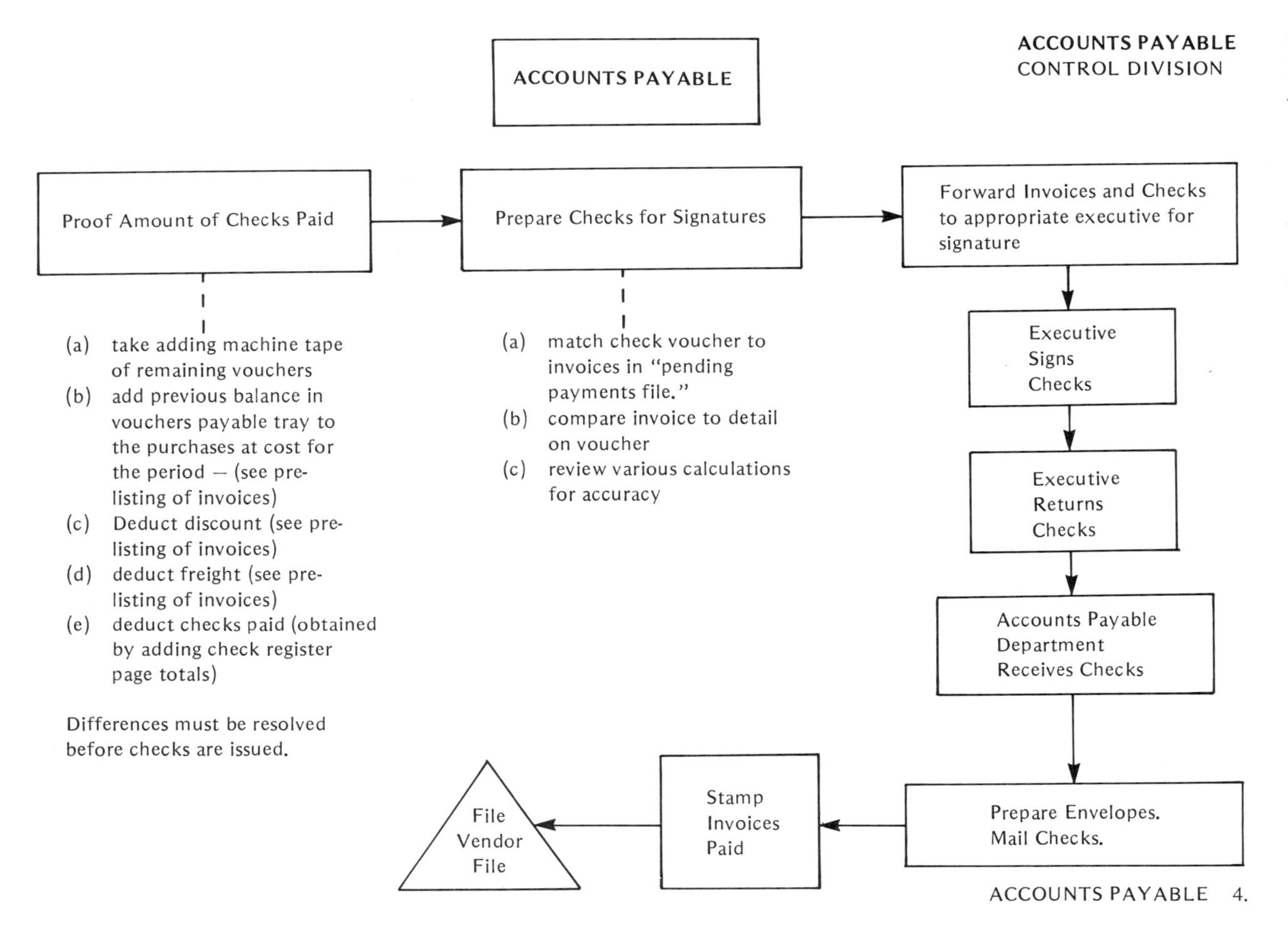
ACCOUNTS PAYABLE
ACCOUNTS PAYABLE
CONTROL DIVISION
Proof Amount of Checks Paid
(a) take adding machine tape of remaining vouchers
(b) add previous balance in vouchers payable tray to the purchases at cost for the period — (see pre-listing of invoices)
(c) Deduct discount (see pre-listing of invoices)
(d) deduct freight (see pre-listing of invoices)
(e) deduct checks paid (obtained by adding check register page totals)
Differences must be resolved before checks are issued.
Prepare Checks for Signatures
(a) match check voucher to invoices in "pending payments file."
(b) compare invoice to detail on voucher
(c) review various calculations for accuracy
Forward Invoices and Checks to appropriate executive for signature
Executive Signs Checks
Executive Returns Checks
Accounts Payable Department Receives Checks
Prepare Envelopes. Mail Checks.
Stamp Invoices Paid
File Vendor File
ACCOUNTS PAYABLE 4.

Chapter 30

SECURITY ACCOUNTABILITY CONTROLS

"Hey, Harry! Grab that rack of skirts and wheel it over to the elevator!" yelled the receiving manager directing dock activity on a busy Wednesday afternoon.

"How many skirts does the packing slip call for?"

The man holding the rack glanced at the packing slip pinned onto a garment, "It says 117 skirts."

"Okay, I got it," yelled back the receiving clerk as he marked the number on his receiving tally. "Take the rack up to marking and get back right away; we've got two other trucks coming in and I need all the help I can get."

"Okay," said the clerk and wheeled the rack of skirts into the freight elevator, disappearing from view as the door clanged shut.

The receiving record now showed 117 skirts received, the same number of skirts called for on the purchase order. Only one thing was wrong, the rack was short 12 skirts. If the receiving clerk had counted the garments as he was supposed to, he would have discovered the rack had only 105 skirts on it. His failure to do his job properly was costly for the store. Not only did the store pay $29 each for the 12 skirts that were never received, but the store also lost the anticipated profits on these skirts, which at a markup of 34 percent amounted to a loss of $118.32 in expected profits.

Total loss on this one failure to properly control incoming goods was $466.32.

Meanwhile, a buyer of auto accessories was huddled with a salesman for a company that manufactures car radios. The buyer had told his clerical to hold all phone calls and after closing his office door he and the salesman negotiated in hushed tones, aware that even the walls may have ears.

After some haggling, the two men finalized their deal. The buyer agreed to write a large purchase order for several hundred various styles of car radios at usual wholesale prices. The salesman in turn agreed to substitute various top of the line models with cheaper units, but the invoice submitted to the company for payment would be for the higher priced units. The difference in the actual value of the radios and the billed value would total $6,000. This extra money, it was agreed, would be split equally between them.

"What about the receiving man? Won't he spot the fact that less expensive radios have been substituted on the order?" asked the salesman.

"Not a chance, just make sure the packing slip calls for the same units as those on the purchase order. Those guys in receiving never count the merchandise coming in and never check the quality or styles of incoming goods against the purchase order. Nothing to worry about!" reassured the buyer.

"I'll have them shipped next Monday."

"Good enough," smiled the buyer. Silently they shook hands, and the deal was made.

While these events were occurring, a woman applying for a job as a store cashier was filling out a company application form in the personnel office. When she came to the lines asking for a listing of her past jobs, length of employment, and reason for leaving, she stopped writing for a moment, looked around the office, and nervously started biting her lip. What should she say about her last position? Should she leave it off the application? If she did that how could she account for her employment during that period of three years? Finally she decided to write the name of her past employer, "White's Discount Store." Length of employment as a cashier? Three years. Reason for leaving? Quickly she wrote, "reduction of staff." It was almost true. Stores never check on references anymore, she said to herself. She finished the application and turned it in, confident that the store would never find out that the reason she'd left White's Discount Store was because she was caught stealing cash on sales.

The unemployed cashier hoped she'd get a job soon, because she needed to get onto a cash register again. She had to steal the money she owed White's for restitution.

Accountability Is Key to Control

The core element of competent protection of store assets is accountability. When merchandise moves from the receiving room along the merchandise pipeline to the selling department, someone must be held accountable for the protection of that merchandise every step of the way.

The receiving manager is accountable for confirming that the merchandise received is the same quantity and quality as the merchandise ordered. Once this is certified, then other people must be held accountable for protecting that merchandise as it moves from receiving into the marking room, and again as it moves from marking to reserve stock, and so on.

This same need for verification is required at all steps in the purchasing process. The person buying the merchandise must not have access to receiving records, nor final approval for payment of resources. The isolation of functions, with each attesting to the accuracy of other functions, sets up a cross-accounting network that protects and controls all company assets.

Verification of statements made by a job applicant on the employment application to insure that they are complete and accurate is just as important as is the careful counting and documentation of merchandise received into the company.

To improve the security of company assets, a new concept is now being used in several progressive companies; it is called "Security Accountability Controls" or "SAC" for short.

Security Monitors Controls

SAC is a program of verification that is administered by the security department. Investigators called "monitors" are used to make independent checks of the enforcement of control procedures as well as the accuracy and completeness of control records.

Verification Objectives

In verifying merchandise controls, the security department monitors attempt to confirm that documents and facts match in such matters as:

- The number of items purchased
- The number of items put into reserve stock
- The number of items sold
- The amount of money paid for them

Independent checking is done at critical points of control, such as receiving, purchasing, reserve stock, cash registers, vendor returns, shipments, accounts payable, and credits.

Purpose Is to Prevent or Detect Major Shortage Problems

Initiating a SAC program should be done by the security department and it should be companywide. The overall objective is to create a controlled working environment.

SAC is intended to flash warning signals when any major shortages start to appear at any point throughout the merchandise and cash handling operations of the company.

Major losses are the objective, with other measures being used for petty dishonesty such as thefts of isolated items of merchandise that may go out under an employee's jacket or in a lunch box. Smaller thefts of this nature are handled with such things as surveillance, locks, or limited access to sensitive areas.

In a SAC operation, major thefts or shortages are spotted before they get out of hand, and the controls often identify the culprits involved. The verification process not only deters or detects thieves, but it also triggers warning signals when inventory shortages begin to exceed normal expectations because of errors or carelessness. And in these incidents, too, it will often single out the people involved.

SAC Keeps Employees Honest

SAC can protect the firm from even the most disgruntled, foxy, or delinquent employees because accountability is a barrier the thief cannot sidestep, overcome, or ignore. It keeps him honest, or if he is foolish enough to challenge the controls, it can easily catch him. Only the most foolish will even try to defeat the SAC system.

Control Documents Already Available

Bookkeeping records already exist in the store that can be used in this control system. They can serve a dual purpose. First, they perform their normal function as bookkeeping documents, and second, they serve as a basis for verification documents when independent checks are made of merchandise counts and procedures. They become a basic tool for cross accounting that establishes the accountability of each person involved in the procedure being verified.

The SAC program can cover a wide range of store activities. It can be used to verify merchandise counts, verify cash counts against sales tallys, or verify information on an applicant's employment card to determine if it is complete and accurate.

Control Locations Determined by Security Study

Where are SAC controls located? The decision about where the accountability controls will be most effective has to be determined for a particular company. These control points are best identified by having a security study made of the company. This study can identify the key points where the company will receive the greatest return for its investment in terms of reducing shortage losses.

Doing such security studies with company personnel carries certain risks. Usually the primary problem is that the in-house security analyst is too close to the operations to have a dependable overall view of the business. As experienced and capable as the in-house specialist may be he lacks the vital ingredient of perspective.

In some firms such a security study ends up as an exercise designed to enhance the prestige or power of an individual or a department. The tendency for staff to get back at line operations, or to want to have a say in line management decisions, often cannot be resisted and the security study becomes primarily a fault-finding exercise to discredit individuals or departments.

Benefits of Outside Consultant

When you use an outside consultant you eliminate political power plays or the danger of overemphasizing or underemphasizing the wrong things. You get an objective, unbiased view of the company through the eyes of a professional whose only interest in the firm is to isolate the problem areas where serious shortages are occurring and to develop a blueprint for improving security.

Temptation to Steal in Key Jobs

In many instances employees involved in major thefts never see or touch what is stolen. Because the employee is not walking out past the guard with an expensive shirt tucked out of sight in his pants, he is able to rationalize away the fact that what he is doing is really stealing.

It doesn't feel like stealing when you don't take anything out concealed on your person. In fact, many employees who would never think of physically stealing easily justify such larcenies as taking kickbacks from a resource, adding stolen goods to a friend's purchase, or switching an address label so that merchandise intended for a legitimate customer is misdirected to his home or that of a neighbor.

The clerk in the charge account office who tears up her family's charge purchase saleschecks so they won't be billed has a reduced feeling of guilt compared to the petty thief who hides merchandise in his lunch pail. Temptation in certain jobs is considerable, as in the case of the charge account file clerk whose job is to file customer charges into their account folders. Temptation in certain key jobs comes easier and the feeling of guilt is reduced because no direct theft is taking place. And yet these types of thefts are more damaging to the company because larger quantities of goods or substantial amounts of money are being stolen from the firm.

Nonmerchandise Areas of Control

Application of the concept of SAC to inventories and even to sales is easy to see, but many people don't realize it is equally applicable in areas where neither merchandise nor cash is involved.

SAC is just as applicable in the area of employment control as it is in controlling receiving of goods. To run a secure business it is important that every precaution be taken at the point of hiring to insure that the company employs honest people. Granted, honesty is a relative term that has to be defined in our modern society by the individual in terms of his lifestyle, and granting also that no foolproof system exists to insure that all dishonest people will be screened out at time of employment. We should, nevertheless, make sure that we have safeguards to keep out the obviously dishonest applicant.

How does SAC apply to the employment office? If you think of SAC as "verification" you will immediately see how it can be used in any phase of the business including the employment office.

Verifies Employment Application

SAC verifies the relative honesty of the employee applicant. Accountability starts with the application form. SAC verifies the information offered by the applicant on this form. SAC can also be used to assist in such matters as the screening of people being considered for promotion, or it can help a supervisor determine disciplinary actions of a punitive nature. The SAC records on the employee moving up to higher responsibility, or the employee being considered for punitive action, can aid in making sound and more scientific management decisions.

Benefits of the SAC Program

To sum up the benefits of a SAC program:

1. SAC prevents many employees who might be tempted to steal from doing so. Employees recognize it would be difficult to evade the verification network.
2. But if an employee or group of employees do develop a theft scheme, the SAC controls soon reveal that something is wrong, thus triggering a security investigation. Large-scale thefts cannot grow into major losses.
3. It is one of the few techniques that can uncover "kickbacks," a security problem that has long troubled many businesses.
4. Since the SAC program for the most part uses the company's present forms and records, initiating this powerful security control procedure throughout the firm is relatively inexpensive.
5. Many employees throughout the company are involved in the program and this develops a strong consciousness of shortage controls from front-line supervisors to top management.

Can Be a Challenge to Steal

Many company workers can function well in these difficult control jobs, especially if they have been carefully chosen for character and integrity and if the company has enlightened management methods so that the morale of workers is high. But to the substandard employee, or the bad apple who got into the firm because poor screening at the point of employment failed to uncover his true nature, the location in a critical control job can be a challenge to steal. The disgruntled, frustrated, or mismatched employee in a highly authoritarian organization with a martinet boss often looks on his job as a challenge to prove that he is smarter than the company and smarter than its security system.

Accountability Requires Verification

SAC means "verification." It requires that at key points in the company materials, merchandise, money, that is, things that are counted, are subjected to a *second* count at key points. This second count is independent of the first count. It is taken by other employees or at a different place. The counts are compared to verify whether the company still has all of its property.

SAC also means the verification of statistics in key top-management reports used for major decision making, and it verifies that the physical security measures now being used are really providing the security they are meant to provide. Many things other than materials and money are verified from a second, unrelated source. SAC verifies that statements on employment application forms are correct, that management people are living within their income, that the enterprise is receiving all the merchandise being paid for, that workers being paid overtime actually did work the overtime being claimed, and so on.

SAC is a control concept that can be used by the security department, internal auditing, shortgage control, or it can be part of the APD (Administrative Practices Division) operation. In whatever department the work is done the people doing it must be good at figures and have proven to be able to spot questionable situations as well as being good at digging into an investigation. Since dishonesty normally is a security department responsibility, it makes sense to put SAC under the security department operation. But keep in mind that people with specific investigative and statistical skills will be needed. If the security department does not have the type of personnel needed for SAC at the moment, then special people should be added to the security staff, possibly from the store's accounting division.

Try to Use Existing Records

Let me remind the reader that SAC should, wherever possible, use existing records and reports. Most of the counting reports that are needed for verification work are already part of normal operating procedures, although used for reasons other than security accountability. They are not presently checked against each other by an independent monitor.

Dishonest Maintenance Manager

Why do we need a security accountability system of control? Let's look at a simple example of what can happen without it. The maintenance department fills out a requisition for some supplies, in this instance 200 one-gallon containers of a special floor wax used on selling floors throughout the store.

The requisition for supplies is sent to the purchasing department where the purchase order is written and sent to the resource.

Maintenance hears nothing further about the requisition until one day the material is received in the maintenance department's stockroom.

Now in our imaginary company there are no Security Accountability Controls. When the purchasing department gets the maintenance requisition for floor wax, a purchase order is written for the 200 one-gallon containers as requested.

But let's suppose the purchasing agent is on the take. He has a secret arrangement with the supplier so that only 185 one-gallon containers of floor wax are actually shipped even though the invoice submitted by the supplier will be for payment of 200 containers.

When the shipment arrives the receiving manager checks the actual quantity received. He sends a receiving record to the purchasing department for 185 containers of floor wax. The order is short 15 containers.

Our dishonest purchasing agent has in his locked desk drawer a pad of blank receiving slips. They are identical to those used by people at the receiving door. The thieving purchase agent makes out a new receiving slip for 200 containers of floor wax; he destroys the legitimate receiving slip and clips his forged copy to the invoice. The false receiving slip and the invoice are sent on to accounts payable and the supplier gets paid for 15 gallons of floor wax that were never shipped to the store. Later the purchasing agent gets his split of the kickback payment, and life goes on without management being aware that anything is wrong with the controls on receiving of goods.

Control Uses Cross Check of Receiving Records

With SAC, accountability would be established by a cross check of receiving records. An independent copy of the receiving slip would be sent by receiving to accounts payable to be matched with the invoice before paying the bill. When the phony purchasing agent's receiving copy arrived in accounts payable, with the receiving slip (sent directly from receiving) attached to the invoice, the person authorizing payment of the invoice would have noted the disagreement between the two receiving records and the invoice would not have been paid for the full amount billed. In addition, security would have started an investigation that undoubtedly would have led to uncovering the dishonesty of the purchasing agent.

No new or different forms were needed to control this firm's receiving properly. All that was needed was that an additional copy of the form now being used be sent directly to accounts payable. Or the present number of copies could be used, but by changing the distribution of copies verification could be achieved and security accountability established.

Use Numbered Forms

Usually the records used in SAC should be prenumbered forms. Prenumbering provides strong control over forms so that misuse cannot be hidden. *The last copy of each prenumbered form should be filed in the department where it is prepared.* Even if the person who prepares the form usually doesn't sign forms, *this* form should be the exception.

These prenumbered forms should be signed by the person who makes the count or records the information. If this is not practical, the person responsible for the accuracy of the information should at least sign one copy of the form.

All Numbers Are Accounted For

Security monitors should inspect each numerical file of these control forms monthly and account for all numbers in the file. Voids must be so marked and all copies of the void must be in proper numerical sequence in the file. Never leave a loophole by having a situation where one copy of a form can be voided and the other copies used.

The security monitor, after making the monthly check for continuity of the numbered file, should *initial the last number checked* so that the next month's review will start at this place in the files.

What if a number is missing? First, security should check places where other copies of the form go. If all copies are missing this signals the need for a security investigation. If only the numerical file copy is missing then other copies must be checked for possible misuse. A substitute copy should be made and placed in the numerical file. This numerical accountability file should periodically be destroyed as the copies reach a point where they are of no further use. When the old numerical file is destroyed, a marker should be used to show where the new numbered series begins.

Proper control over the prenumbered forms means that there should be no gap in numerical sequence between the last number used in the old numerical file and the first number in the new one.

Missing Forms

If the reserve stock of these forms is missing any sequential numbers, security should be notified at once and *the missing numerical group should be posted wherever the various copies of that particular form are used and filed.* Security should also check places where copies of the form are matched with other records to make sure the missing numbers are missing from all places the form is used.

Random Spot Audits

The SAC monitoring process should be spot checked in many instances, although full monitoring may be needed in trouble spots or in certain extremely critical control points. But the monitors from security should not cause any delays in the normal work flow as long as no specific investigative problems exist.

Flexibility is the key to an effective SAC operation. The frequency of checking should increase whenever irregularities are found. Security monitors can make their own verifying counts at points where normal business counts are not made. Just the fact such counts are made is a deterrent to employee theft. Don't let the monitoring become routine. Don't always count the same things at the same places with the same regularity.

Check some things with frequent or irregular spot counts. Surprise checks are valuable; do them at random times.

Systematize the SAC Program

SAC has to be designed for your particular company. But whatever controls are used, they should be systematized in a manual. This manual should show the overall system, who prepares each form being monitored, how many copies are made, the distribution of copies, and so on.

People working with the forms being monitored need to be included in the system. They need to know their personal responsibility in the system. What are they required to do? How should it be done?

And the cooperation and effectiveness of the employees who work with the forms should be part of their regular rating evaluation.

Purchasing Accountability

Since we have already talked about how a dishonest purchasing agent could take advantage of a company that has inadequate accountability controls, perhaps we should take a further look at this high-risk area.

Diverting materials or merchandise and kickback schemes are related to purchasing security.

Diversion of material or merchandise before delivery is seldom given enough attention by retailers. This takes two forms. A dishonest resource driver is aware that the company's receiving operation is inadequately manned, poorly motivated, or indifferent to proper controls. Once he spots a receiving dock that is wide open because of sloppy receiving practices he delivers an incomplete order to the firm, retaining part of the shipment on his truck. He diverts the firm's goods for his own profit.

A more profitable theft situation is one in which a driver makes a deal with the receiving clerk who signs for short shipments and does not report the shipments as short. The driver sells the retained goods to a fence and splits the profits with the receiving clerk. These types of thefts by diversion are common but they are not likely to be large because large thefts would soon be noticed by buyers and by the lack of stock in particular departments.

Thefts by Diversion

Major thefts are usually the result of diversionary arrangements in which a supplier is paid a price higher than the quality or the market would normally sustain, or the supplier is paid for goods never shipped. This requires the cooperation between a supplier and a company employee. The dishonest worker may be the purchasing agent, the buyer, a person in receiving, or someone in accounting. The employee gets paid a kickback from the supplier.

The store employee in a kickback scheme is a person who can change a receiving record, or approve an invoice for payment. At the supplier's end a top executive is usually involved in the kickback scheme.

Nonmerchandise Kickbacks

A kickback does not have to involve merchandise. For example, the maintenance head of a large retail firm was in charge of subcontracting the painting of white lines on customer parking lots at the company's eleven shopping centers. The man getting this lucrative contract had to kickback 1/2 cent per line painted to the store's maintenance head.

Split Commissions

Another insidious method used by some salesmen to initiate a kickback scheme that at first appears harmless is for the salesman to offer to split his commission on the sale with the buyer.

At the start of such a plan the company suffers no loss (assuming of course that the quality of the merchandise is in line with the cost). The salesman merely promises the buyer part of his sales commission. To get this "bonus" the buyer need only switch to this new resource. Thus the supplier wins the important new account. Each time the salesman is paid his commission on sales to the company the buyer pockets his part of the cash from the split commission. Both buyer and salesman now profit from the transaction.

Why is such a scheme dangerous? Because it is a first step into the shadowy world of kickbacks, and once such a bribe is accepted it is a short step to the buyer's demanding and getting tribute from other resources he deals with. These kickbacks usually are no longer split commissions but are either excessive markup on the merchandise costs to the company or are manipulated approval of invoices for merchandise never received by the firm.

Easy money becomes a focus of the buyer's attention and soon the tricks to develop this kind of added income override the buyer's responsibilities to his employer.

Watch for Supplier Changes

Security should regularly review various buyer's accounts for any unexplained switches in suppliers where major purchases are involved. Also look for the buyer who makes a large percentage of his purchases from a single supplier. Accounts payable personnel can be trained to supply such information to the security monitors.

As many firms have learned, kickback schemes often cost the company far more in theft losses than the direct stealing of merchandise. Kickbacks are easy to start and once in operation they normally continue for many years without discovery. When they are uncovered it is usually by accident—unless, of course, a firm has established a program of security accountability.

Resource Gifts

The problem of gifts from suppliers has been faced up to in many companies. Buyers and purchasing agents throughout the firm are provided an ethical policy by top management that specifically forbids the acceptance of gifts of any size from suppliers or salesmen.

In one firm the gift policy tried to limit the value of supplier gifts to "such items as can be consumed in a single meal." This loophole allowed the buyers to continue to accept gifts without disturbed consciences because it suggested that the ethical policy was really only window dressing and the loophole had been left in it to indicate that gifts could still be accepted from salesmen but that the buyer should be cautious about publicizing the fact.

It is obviously better to have a management policy that absolutely forbids all gifts of any size from suppliers or salesmen. After all, any such gift is a form of a bribe or rebate and as such actually would belong to the company rather than the individual purchaser. It carries a message that the buyer has favored a certain supplier in the past and is expected to do so again in the future.

Letting resource people buy lunches for buyers should also be given attention. Much business is transacted successfully over a luncheon table. The problem is not to allow a supplier to turn the situation into one where the outsider always picks up the tab and eventually places the buyer under an implied obligation to return these social amenities with purchasing decisions favoring this particular supplier.

It is best to have a budget set up for buyers and purchasing agents so that they are encouraged to balance out these luncheon payments on a reciprocal basis. Encourage the buyers to reclaim lunch expenses by petty cash slips, or provide a special charge card for the buyer to use in luncheon situations. If a country club is used for business luncheons, or a regular restaurant, the company can often set up a company account at the restaurant for buyers to use to pay for these business luncheons. Being tight on the purse strings and making it difficult or uncomfortable for a buyer to get back payment of luncheon money will be a disservice to the company in the long run. A single buyer-supplier kickback deal resulting from luncheon obligations can wipe out many times over the investment in a budget for such luncheon meetings.

Merchandise managers should do a periodic check of luncheon expenditures to be sure that all buyers take advantage of this budget arrangement. In addition, the security monitor should spot check these expenditures as well. Where it is found that a purchasing agent or a buyer is not using the luncheon funds, it may be that he is doing a poor negotiation job with salesmen by allowing the salesmen to always pick up the luncheon tabs. Or it may be that he is unconsciously becoming obligated to the salesmen, which can mean serious problems ahead. In either case, the situation calls for an inquiry by the buyer's superior and the security monitor should give the situation some attention as well.

Thefts of Bulk Materials

Lumberyard operations or any business where raw materials are purchased can also be a weak spot in security control. The raw materials may be too low in value to warrant direct thefts, but although not subject to physical theft, failure to deliver the full order can be a most profitable manipulation of company funds. If there are frequent routine deliveries of bulk materials, these goods can easily be overmeasured without anyone being aware of the fact that the company is paying substantial sums of money for goods never received into stock.

Protection of such goods requires a SAC second verifying count of deliveries on a random basis to insure that the company is getting all the merchandise being paid for.

Rack Jobbers

Daily deliveries of milk and milk by-products from a supplier to a supermarket requires this type of periodic SAC verification count. So also do the deliveries by other rack jobbers such as the bakery deliveries and the direct floor deliveries of cigarettes. The removal of stale merchandise or of empty soft drink bottles for which the store is supposed to receive credits from the supplier need to have SAC spot verification counts done just prior to pickup. Later, these counts should be compared with the credits issued by the routeman for the goods or bottles removed from the store.

Theft of Gravel

Where weight of incoming raw materials is used as a receiving control, special care must be used by the SAC monitor. This problem is more common in factory operations, but some types of retailing also can get involved in bulk deliveries that are verified by weighing the incoming item. Let's say a lumberyard operation is providing large quantities of sand and gravel for building contractors.

The sand or gravel may be delivered periodically by truck. In one instance a lumberyard operation received several truck loads of sand and gravel weekly from a supplier. The company weighed the delivery truck when the first delivery was made. Once the bare weight of the truck was established, the full truck was weighed each time future deliveries were made and the weight of the bare truck was subtracted from the total weight, which left a net weight for the sand or gravel being received.

In this instance a foxy supplier, after the routine had been well established, concealed a 100-pound weight in the truck. From that day on every load delivered to the lumberyard was 100 pounds below the weight being recorded by the receiving clerk. The firm paid for 100 pounds of sand or gravel that was not being received. This type of diversion cannot occur if you have established accountability controls.

Protection in this case requires periodic verification by the security monitor. He makes a surprise visit to the receiving area periodically *and after a truck has emptied its load of sand or gravel he has the driver back the truck again onto the scales*. He then compares the truck's bare weight with the charted weight being used by the receiver to determine net weight of the raw materials.

If the monitor finds an empty truck overweight, it should be held temporarily in the yard until security can make a check of the truck for hidden extra weights. If the monitor establishes that a diversion of materials is occurring, then a security investigation is undertaken and in all likelihood it will be found that the supplier is the culprit. However, it is also possible that the truck driver has been doing this bit of stealing on his own and is selling the sand or gravel to another retailer.

In most cases of this type, however, investigation will show that the supplier and the receiving yard employee are in the scheme together. The supplier usually prefers to protect himself in such a diversionary operation by involving an employee of the lumberyard through a kickback arrangement.

The point to be made is that even raw materials of low value may require some attention from verification procedures.

Central Control

One of the important elements of purchasing control is that all purchases be funneled through a single general merchandising office or through a purchasing agent.

Even if a central control over all purchasing is established, a buyer will sometimes claim that the merchandise his department purchases is so unique that it is too special for regular purchasing procedures and that purchasing should be done only through the department head or department buyer. It will be maintained that only people in the selling department are competent to make purchases. This situation is often found in department store fur departments where the fur buyer deals with furs sent into the store on consignment. The fur buyer claims that the manipulation involved means he must operate outside the normal chain of purchasing procedures and thus he escapes the control provided by a central point of review for all buyer purchases. Such exceptions should not be allowed.

Security Should Investigate Exceptions

When a buyer makes such a claim of uniqueness he may sometimes sell management on this need for direct purchasing control and be provided purchase order forms as well as complete control over quantities, quality, and price of goods he buys. This arrangement in itself should be looked on by the security department as suspect, particularly if the department head can approve invoices for payment (loss of control over invoice payments is disastrous in terms of accountability).

Let's face it, *purchasing accountability requires centralized purchasing procedures* without regard to the specialized nature of the goods purchased. Technical assistance can be supplied the purchasing agent or the general merchandise manager approving all company purchases.

Verification of Purchases

Verification of purchases requires a copy of the resource's invoice, for then quantities and prices on the invoice can be checked against incoming goods. Accountability procedures verify the accuracy of billing and amount of goods received. The counts and comparisons are the method of accountability control.

Distribution of Forms for Accountability

Purchasing accountability requires two elements. First, approval of all purchases must be done through a central point of control, a purchasing agent or a general merchandise manager. Second, accountability also requires an independent and accurate count of goods received.

Copies of the independent count go to: (1) purchasing, (2) accounts payable, and (3) the stockroom where the goods will be held prior to sale. At these three points the counts join up with other records to provide the comparisons needed by the security monitor.

Proper forms usually follow this format:

1. A requisition form is made out by the buyer giving:
   a. Quantity
   b. Quality
   c. Other information needed to insure proper purchasing procedure
2. The purchasing agent uses the requisition to make up a purchase order with the three items needed for accountability:
   a. Quantity
   b. Description (type, quality, details)
   c. Unit price

   This purchase order is a prenumbered form. The person making out the purchase order should sign at least the numerical file copy that will be held in the purchasing agent's office.

   At least four copies of the purchase order are usually required. These are distributed as follows:
   a. Purchasing agent's working copy
   b. Numerical file copy to be filed in the purchasing agent's office
   c. Copy to accounts payable
   d. Copy to receiving department

   All copies are identical except one. *The copy sent to the receiving department must not show the quantities of the items being ordered.*

   To insure that the receiving clerk makes an independent count of the incoming merchandise, he should not know the quantities he should be receiving.

   Technically this is not a problem; the forms can be designed so there is no carbon paper where quantities are shown on the copy of the form provided for the receiving department. The receiving clerk will have all other needed information but he must make his own count.

Receiving Tally Form

The receiving department will have a separate receiving tally form. *This also will be prenumbered*, and at least four copies will be needed.

One copy of the receiving tally form is held in the receiving department in a numerical file.

The second copy is sent directly to the accounting department that keeps records of purchases and handles accounts payable.

Verification for security accountability is the result of bringing three important documents together at the point where approval of the supplier's invoice payment is made.

Accounts payable must receive *all supplier's invoices*, also copies of *all purchase orders*, and finally *a copy of the receiving department tally form*. Now the supplier's invoice is checked against the purchase order for price and quantity and against the receiving department's form for verification that the firm received the right quantity and quality of goods as ordered.

If the supplier's invoice is verified by these accountability verifications, the invoice can be approved for payment.

In the hands of accounts payable are the receiving report, the purchase order, the supplier's invoice, and the numbered voucher authorizing payment, *which make up a completed package that should be filed in the department's inactive files.*

Stockroom Merchandise Count

A second copy of the receiving form is sent along with the merchandise to the department's stockroom where a stock clerk can check to be sure that all goods received at the receiving dock have safely reached the stockroom. In many stores major pilferage occurs during the period in which merchandise is moved from receiving to the stockroom and this verification at the stockroom is vitally important for security accountability.

A third copy of the receiving tally form is stapled to the receiving department's copy of the purchase order and is forwarded back to the purchasing department. Purchasing compares the quantity received with the quantity on the purchase order and if these figures do not agree the purchasing department must investigate to determine the reason for the difference.

Split Shipments and Order Backs

In some instances a split shipment is involved, or in other instances some of the merchandise has to be back ordered. Whatever the situation, the purchasing department must take the steps necessary to insure that the complete order will be received before payment of the supplier's invoice. When the receiving documents show that the purchase order merchandise has all been properly received in the correct quantity and quality, *then the forms are stapled together and the purchase department files its completed order package.* Again, the final package is put into an inactive file.

What about back orders? If further shipments are to be made, a back order must be prepared. This back order form is prenumbered. It should be given the same distribution as the original order except that a copy need not be sent to the supplier.

Each back order must show the original purchase order number and any preceding back order numbers. This provides security accountability for tracing continuity from the original purchase order through to the receiving tally verifying the receipt of merchandise on the final back order.

Each time a back order is written, the preceding incompleted purchase order and back order package are stapled together and filed in the inactive file of the purchasing department.

If a back order must be made for unshipped balances of goods not received, that new back order is kept as the only open active record. Therefore purchasing has in its active files only records of merchandise that remains to be shipped.

Copies of the back order form are distributed the same as the original purchase order. And again, the receiving department copy of the back order should not record the quantity being shipped so the receiving department count can be made only by actually counting the goods received.

Write a New Back Order

Some firms prefer to retain the original purchase order and simply mark off the goods received, leaving the remainder of the shipment open on the original purchase order document. Experience shows that this causes confusion and errors and can lead to the concealment of serious shortages. To avoid such confusion and to have clean-cut accountability throughout this important purchasing, receiving, and payment process, it is wiser to *issue a new back order after each uncompleted shipment.*

The SAC monitoring of purchasing includes the numerical file check of prenumbered forms as described earlier. Any missing numbers, gaps, or misuse of the file should be investigated.

Employees Can Cause Control Breakdown

Remember that security must always be alert to the possibility that a breakdown in controls is caused by dishonest employees who cannot steal when the control procedures are working properly.

When employees seem unable to grasp the system of accountability and make mistakes, it is often not because they do not understand the procedures required for security accountability but rather because they know the procedures well enough so that they can deliberately throw a monkey wrench into the works.

In addition to monitoring the numerical files, security also will compare on a spot basis the completed order files in purchasing with the same order files in accounts payable to make sure there are no differences in quantities, quality, or price of the merchandise.

How often should such comparison be done? This is determined by the security requirements. The security study provides guidance as to the relative need for accountability checks at various points in the merchandise and money pipelines and this should guide the original frequency of such checks. Naturally, if problems are discovered, more intense and more frequent monitoring will be needed.

Danger Flags

Certain danger flags should be spotted by the security monitor. *Any changes or differences between forms attached to the same order in purchasing or in accounts payable should flash a signal that an investigation is needed. Particularly look for changes in price or quantity in one file. If you find anything like this, look for verification of these changes in the other file.* All differences should be verified as authentic by examining both files.

For example, if one receiving tally shows a changed quantity the security monitor must check to see that all other copies of the receiving tally show the same changes.

Receiving Tally Is Control Key

The main form that insures purchasing accountability is the receiving tally. Accountability can be effective only if the receiving records are accurate and are constantly checked for accuracy.

> The receiving record is part of the permanent record in purchasing, accounts payable, and in the selling department where the merchandise is finally deposited. A kickback scheme involving shorting of deliveries can operate only if this form is altered at one or more of these locations. Security monitoring of these forms as part of the SAC program can prevent or disclose kickback schemes because variations between the different quantities listed will be discovered.

In addition to the signed copy of the numerical file copy of the prenumbered forms used for accountability, it is desirable to have each employee who handles and processes a form also initial it to indicate who handled and processed it. If this is done, when a discrepancy occurs the point where the deviation occurred can be traced.

Final Accountability Step

Some companies believe that it is desirable to add one additional step to strengthen controls over purchasing of goods. This step is done by an employee in the accounting department, a person who does *not* have any connection with accounts payable. *This person makes a final independent audit of the purchase order packages before they are filed in the inactive file.* This extra audit is already done to check accuracy of price extensions and to catch errors in payments to a supplier. By adding one further step of verifying that all necessary forms are present and that figures on them are in agreement is a substantial aid to accountability controls.

Check That Procedures Are Followed

When reviewing the forms in an accountability system, the entire form should be examined periodically to insure that the total system is being complied with. Any deviation from established procedures should be investigated. Even if the security monitor finds that deviations are errors rather than indications of thefts, these errors should be brought to the attention of the department supervisor and the responsible employee. The SAC program is intended to create a controlled working environment. This includes an ongoing educational program so employees will know not only what the accountability procedures are but also will be aware that they are responsible for the completeness and accuracy of the records they are charged with processing.

It has been said that all you need for a kickback scheme are two dishonest people and a weak system of control procedures. SAC provides assurance that the critically important control procedures are complete and well designed, and most importantly that they are being applied. It also provides the prime ingredient of effective control in any business—security accountability—verification that the world of materials, merchandise, and money are in harmony with the world of records, statistics, and reports.

Receiving Department Is the Vital Link

Sometimes a single department may be a vital link to effective accountability controls in other departments. In the matter of kickbacks, the receiving department is this vital link. It illustrates the fact that accountability systems may overlap into other departments.

Receiving is an intermediate step between the ordering of merchandise and the selling of merchandise. Its function appears to be so mechanical that its importance is often overlooked by management.

The task of receiving is to record the receipt of incoming goods. The receiving form or tally that results from recording these receipts is the foundation on which purchasing accountability is built. For that reason it must be an accurate record.

The receiving form should be prenumbered and have at least four copies. In designing the form it is wise to make it easy for the receiving clerk to fill it in by hand. The receiving clerk should also be the one who signs the form, thus taking responsibility for its accuracy. *The form must also be cross referenced by the clerk to the purchase order copy previously sent to him.*

(Allied-Egry's "Key-Rec" forms are used by many companies because the patented system of overlapping forms provides an excellent document for efficient and accurate receiving.)

Example of One Company's Controls

Here is how one firm handles its receiving. Four copies of the purchase order containing all information except the quantities ordered are sent to the receiving department.

The receiving clerk counts the incoming merchandise and records the quantities and the data received on the purchase order forms.

This system saves time because only the date and quantities need to be recorded by the clerk. The rest of the information is already typed onto the original purchase order. This system also eliminates the receiving tally form, and therefore one copy of the prenumbered purchase order form is retained in the receiving department's numerical copy file using the purchase order number. *The receiving clerk thus always has all purchase order numbers accounted for either in his open file of unreceived orders or in his closed file of purchase orders.*

Copies of the receiving department purchase orders, after being filled in and signed, are sent as follows:

1. To accounts payable
2. To purchasing

3. To stockroom with the merchandise
4. Held in receiving department for the numerical file

Now, let's review the full circle of accountability controls from the original requisition for merchandise to the receiving of the merchandise.

The accounts payable copy shows the quantity of goods for which payment is authorized. It also shows quality and other information for comparison with data on the original purchase order.

The purchasing department copy of the receiving form is attached to the purchasing department's original purchase order form. Purchasing can then review the two forms to see if all of the order has been received or if a back order is needed. Purchasing can also verify that the quality of goods matches the original order. Although purchasing does not see the actual merchandise, a comparison of descriptions or stock numbers will make it easy to spot a material difference from what was ordered.

When the third copy of the receiving report is received in the department stockroom attached to the merchandise, it is wise to *have an immediate verification count* to be sure all the merchandise received has reached the selling department. If the order is complete this should be noted on the receiving document along with the name of the person who did the verification count. This document should now be attached to the department's copy of the original requisition record, the numerical file copy kept by the department's buyer, and refiled in the numerical file where the documents can later be checked by the security monitor.

If the stock count does not verify the receiving document, then the security department should be immediately notified of the discrepancy and an investigation undertaken.

As we can see, there are three places in the receiving cycle where the receiving record is compared with other forms:

1. The requisition copy
2. The purchase order copy
3. The supplier's invoice

Accountability occurs as long as at each of these three places, the receiving record is used properly for its normal business functions and with an eye to accuracy.

Security verifies that accurate performance is achieved by periodic auditing of the different copies of the same form at the various locations where they are used and comparing them.

The Packing Slip

The packing slip can be a major weakness in receiving control. Giving the receiving clerk the packing slip is as much a risk to proper accountability as giving him the quantities on the purchase order. Although the purchase order quantities can be kept from the receiving clerk, however, it is not possible to keep the packing slip out of his hands. As a result, additional security measures are needed.

The packing slip should be stapled to the numerical file copy of the receiving form. These copies are kept in the receiving room.

Without SAC, a receiving clerk can become part of a kickback scheme working with a supplier. All the supplier has to do is to invoice the company for the ordered number of goods and put into the merchandise shipment a packing slip with the number of items listed on his invoice. He then shorts the shipment so there are actually, say, twenty-five less items of merchandise than appear on the invoice.

The receiving clerk simply confirms the number of items on the enclosed packing slip as the number received. The supplier submits his inflated invoice and is paid for goods never shipped. He then kicks back part of the illegal profits to the cooperative receiving clerk.

Detection of Collusive Theft

How can such collusion between supplier and receiving clerk be detected? Since merchandise is usually purchased for a number of departments, it is highly unlikely that the receiving clerk will have kickback deals with all suppliers. The SAC program should include regular verifying counts of merchandise received. *These counts by security monitors should be done at the time the goods arrive into stock in the selling department. The actual counts can then later be verified against the receiving document with its attached packing slip in the receiving department's numerical file.*

In doing verification counts in the selling departments it is best to look for large regular purchases because they offer more opportunity for kickbacks. Kickbacks are less likely to occur in occasional large purchases of higher value. Regular purchases from one supplier tend to become a mechanical routine all along the line; they are done from habit with little or no attention to detail. Counts are carelessly done and irregularities less likely to be noticed.

Another problem with packing slips is that the receiving clerk may be pressed for time, be under a tremendous receiving load, or perhaps have a tendency to be lazy, and he may begin to take short cuts *by simply copying the packing slip onto the receiving tally without counting the merchandise.*

Experienced retailers recognize that packing slips are often grossly inaccurate, and the hard-pressed or lazy receiving clerk who takes the easy way out and copies the packing slip as a record of actual merchandise received can cost the company losses equal to deliberate thefts.

Check for Misspelled Words

When the security monitor examines the receiving records in the department's numerical files *it pays to look at and compare the wording on the packing slip with the wording on the receiving document. The lazy receiving clerk often copies the terminology from the packing slip instead of from the purchase order copy. He may also copy packing slip misspellings.* If the monitor finds that the clerk is copying information from the packing slips, chances are he is also copying the merchandise count. A minimum amount of investigation can soon determine this fact.

Discarding Files

How long should the numerical file copies of receiving records with packing slips attached be held in the receiving department file? Since the receiving records are the basis for controlling receiving and purchasing accountability, *the forms should be held until the final back order on a purchase has been received and processed.*

Because receiving records are critical to verification controls, they must be kept available until all possible use has been made of them by every department.

The receiving department should be isolated from trash-handling activities and it should also be physically separated from the company's shipping department.

Control Remote Receiving Areas

At times special receiving problems arise that may require that materials or merchandise be received directly in a selling department or at a location other than through the normal receiving room operation. Any decision to receive goods outside the regular receiving area should be cleared with security so that a system of SAC monitoring can be set up to protect this satellite receiving operation.

Stopping Shipping Losses

Accountability controls, often lacking in receiving operations, are almost always weak in shipping departments. Many stores ship goods to customers from their warehouse or distribution centers, and some retailers do a major part of their business through mail-order sales.

The salescheck, or sales order, lists the quantity, style, and price of merchandise being purchased. It is a form that authorizes transfer of the merchandise from the store to the customer for a certain sum of money. The salescheck simply notes how, when, and where this transfer of goods is to occur.

But at the point where the shipping process begins, the form of the salescheck changes from a scrap of paper to the actual merchandise itself. This change into a shipping process really starts when the order-filling section of the warehouse receives one or more copies of the salescheck or sales order document.

Blind Spot

To aid accountability, a blind spot must occur on the sales order just as a blind spot was needed to insure control over the receiving operation. In the instance of the receiving department, the quantities of items to be received are left off the purchase order. In the shipping process, *the sales order sent to the order-filling department of the warehouse should not contain the name and address of the customer making the purchase.*

The order filler must not know the name and address of the customer. He does not need this information to do his job. *A sales order number provides the best means of sales order identification.* The customer's name and address may be stored by computer and the computer can issue an order number to match.

A sales order number is anonymous. Using the customer's name and address can often be confusing to the order filler, particularly if the customer has more than one sales order being filled at the same time. With a sales order number this confusion is eliminated. More importantly, the number also eliminates the possiblity of dishonesty by an employee working in the order-filling department. Otherwise, this employee could pack additional merchandise into a customer's order.

In the past I have seen how easy it is for a dishonest order filler to overfill a standard package and bypass checking by the shipping clerk. Of course I have also seen massive merchandise thefts when the order filler and the shipping clerk were working together and stealing in collusion.

For security accountability, the customer's identity should not be revealed until the order is packed, sealed, and ready for delivery.

In a SAC operation, the order filler receives a sales order that has a number on it but does not reveal the customer's name or address. He fills the order and delivers the items to the shipping department. In the shipping department the clerk checks the merchandise against the quantities, price, and descriptions on the sales order. If everything is in order, he signs the form. It then becomes the shipping tally. The shipping clerk now packs the goods for shipment.

He puts the sales order number on each package and notes the weights and number of packages as well as any other pertinent information on the shipping tally. Once the tally is completed he sends it to the traffic office.

Shipping Authorization

The traffic office checks the sales order (or the computer) to obtain the customer's name and address matched to the sales order number. Then a bill of lading is prepared. Copies of the bill of lading along with a copy of the sales order which now contains the customer's name and address, are returned to the shipping department. The shipping clerk attaches the labels to the packages and the shipment is completed.

After shipment, a remaining form is returned to the selling department where it can be matched with a copy of the original sales order held in the unfilled order file.

When this matching is done a check is made to see that no variations have occurred between the shipping tally and the original sales order. If everything checks out satisfactorily the shipping tally, with sales order attached, goes to the accounting department. If it is a cash sale, the check is filed; if it is a charge sale, the sales order is sent to accounts receivable so that they can bill the customer.

Two Verifications

Verification of the contents of the send order have been done by two independent counts. First by the order filler and then by the shipping clerk, with neither person aware of the customer's name and address at the time.

Isolation of Functions

What we see here is that an important element in setting up accountability controls is to consider the need for isolation of the various functions involved in the operating process.

In this instance we find that isolation is achieved by observing five simple principles:

1. The order filler is *never* given the customer's name or address.
2. No shipping is done by the order filler.
3. The shipping clerk does not do any order filling.
4. The shipping clerk packs and seals the merchandise ready for shipment and prepares a shipping tally *before* obtaining the customer's identity.
5. Both the stockroom, where orders are filled, and the shipping department, where orders are made ready for shipment, are physically separated from each order.

Example of One Company's Controls

Let's walk through one firm's shipping procedures to visualize how the system performs. A salesperson writes a sales order (salescheck) for merchandise being purchased by the customer. Arrangements are made for payment of the goods either by cash or by putting the purchase on the customer's charge account. The sales order is next sent to the order-filling department.

In the order-filling department the clerks code each item of the sale according to class of product and warehouse location. Various warehouse locations are identified (in this instance) by different colors of order-filling cards.

Information not needed by the order fillers is left off the cards prepared for the order fillers. In this particular company, each order filler receives cards color-coded for his area of work in the warehouse. On the card he receives is the code number of the item to be picked, quantity ordered, and where he is to leave the merchandise for transfer to the shipping department.

After the order filler gathers the merchandise ordered and deposits it as directed, he initials and time-stamps the order-filling card. He turns in his completed cards as he picks up his next batch of cards for processing.

When all the cards on an order have been completed and turned in, the shipping and traffic departments receive other copies of the sales order that notify them that the merchandise has been gathered and is ready for preparation by the shipping department. These copies of sales orders contain all the information on the order except the customer's name and address.

The shipping department clerk matches the merchandise gathered by the order filler against the sales order to be sure that it is the same and then signs the copy of the sales order. It now becomes a shipping tally.

If shipping, however, finds that an item is missing in the order, or a substitute or wrong item has been included, this kind of error is turned back to the order-filling department for correction. It is the job of the order-filling department to verify that there is an error and to correct it.

When shipping finds a difference between the sales order and the merchandise presented to shipping by the order-filling department, shipping prepares a "difference" form noting the nature of the difference. One copy of this form is given to the order-filling department and one copy is sent directly to the security department. When the order-filling department has corrected the order it verifies this fact on the difference form and returns it with the correct merchandise to shipping.

The security department finds these shipping difference forms useful in two ways. First, if an incident suggests the possibility of illegal diversion of merchandise, an investigation is started. Or, second, if the differences were the result of errors, this fact is on file for future reference. If a pattern of such errors develops, corrective measures may be needed with the security department bringing the matter to the attention of the manager of the order-filling department.

Please note an important element of control in this company's program. They do not allow the shipping department people to go to a stockroom area to get merchandise to correct an order.

In firms where shipping clerks are allowed to wander in and out of stockrooms, it has often been found that these employees provided their friends with considerable company merchandise for which no one was ever billed.

In this company, as we can see, the accountability system is operating smoothly.

First, shipping verifies that the order-filling form matches the merchandise presented for shipment. The shipping clerk signs the sales order, thus turning it into a shipping tally. This tally in turn travels to the traffic department with all the information needed, such as the number of boxes or cartons, the weights of each, and other details needed to prepare a bill of lading.

Since the traffic department already has a complete copy of the sales order from the order typist, the clerk can compare this copy with the shipping tally. If he finds that they agree, he can then prepare the bill of lading. This bill of lading and a copy of the complete sales order including the customer's name and address are sent to shipping and provide the department with the authority to ship the order.

Multiple Use of One Form

In some firms sufficient copies of the sales order are prepared so that no new forms are needed throughout the order-filling and shipping process until the point where the bill of lading is prepared. Multiple use of one form cuts down the risk of errors in copying information and saves time and money. Keep in mind, however, that the copies of the sales order sent to the order-filling and shipping departments initially are blanked out where the customer's name and address would normally appear.

Three Basic Control Elements

It is a serious security risk to have bills of lading written in the shipping department. They should be prepared in the traffic department. *The bill of lading is another prenumbered form and one copy should be kept in a numerical file in the traffic department where the bill of lading originates.*

As we can see in reviewing the SAC program for controlling shipment losses, three basic principles are required for security. *First*, the order filler must *not* know whose order he is filling. *Second*, the shipping department personnel must *not* have access to the stockroom. *third*, bills of lading should *not* be prepared in the shipping department.

This isolation of functions is an important part of accountability controls and is a sound method for protecting the company from employee thefts.

Accounting Department

I have mentioned only briefly that SAC is used in nonmerchandise operations as well as where materials and merchandise are handled. I observed that the security monitors should verify key facts on the applications of people seeking employment in the company.

Money Controls

The accountability program should also extend to the accounting department.

Money must be controlled by the same kind of verification methods as I have described for the control of merchandise movement. Money is an important consideration in any security program. It is company property subject to the same principles of accountability as merchandise. Quantities must be verified by an independent count.

Actually money is easier to control than merchandise because businessmen have always recognized the need for accountability in the handling of money and as a result it is subject to constant inventory.

The problem is that in many firms the accounting people are primarily concerned with balancing accounts after they are established rather than paying attention to how the accounts were established or spent.

Cross Accounting

The key to good accounting control is cross accounting. This means that the person who approves payments cannot make the payments. The person who authorizes the employee paychecks does not handle the paying of employees. Bookkeepers do not handle cash and cashiers do not do the bookkeeping, and so on.

Payments of money require verification by independent audit. The auditor checks to be sure that invoices submitted for payment are authentic purchases and that receiving records act as verification and support for payment of invoices.

All elements in the money and merchandise pipelines are interlocked by parallel controls.

The two important principles governing accountability in the handling of money are:

1. One person should never have authority to approve payments and also make payments.
2. Accountability procedures should always require that all receipts and disbursements be independently verified before their records are filed away.

Security Department Accountability

Security operations also should be subject to verification. The monthly case report should periodically be compared to actual copies of arrest case histories and the case histories compared with the signed malefactor statements.

The cost-effectiveness of floor detectives should be reviewed to determine the cost of each case apprehended. Reviews of security department personnel, budget, and programs should be done by an independent analyst either from the accounting audit group or, better still, from an outside professional security firm.

In addition to the verification of counts, the comparison of control documents between departments, and the independent merchandise counts, security monitors should also oversee periodic testing of controls.

Created Systems Tests

Created systems tests are limited only by the imagination of the people who design them. In their simplest form, for example, to determine if a branch store is counting in a certain department's ready-to-wear merchandise at the receiving dock as they are supposed to, the security monitor can arrange to remove, say, 16 skirts from a particularly large shipment of skirts going to the branch store being tested.

If the branch store is counting the skirts at the point of receiving, a loss report on the missing 16 skirts will be phoned in at once to the company security department with a written loss report following. If no such reports are received it is reasonably safe to assume that the receiving crew at the store is not performing the merchandise count of incoming goods assigned to them.

A five-dollar overage planted in a cashier's daily bank to see if she is counting her bank when opening the register for the day is another form of created systems test. If the cashier does not report the overage and at the end of the day her receipts are over by five dollars, probably she is not following store policy of counting the daily bank before opening the register for sales.

Clerks hired to review invoices for extension errors can be tested by planting large errors in some of the extensions they are reviewing. Naturally, if they catch the planted errors they are probably doing a good job of catching extension errors. But if they fail to catch the planted errors, we must assume that they are not performing up to acceptable standards for the job assigned to them.

Conclusion

In sum, the concept behind the SAC program is to insure that merchandise, money, and information at critical danger points throughout the company operations are independently checked and verified.

Security acts as the monitor of the verification process to make sure that built-in verification controls are functioning as intended and that there is, throughout the business, a separation of functions. Only through such separation can a reliable system of independent verification controls be established.

Security monitors also make independent audits of merchandise, money, and records to be sure that documents that are supposed to agree actually do agree, that goods being paid for are received in the store, and that money taken in on sales is deposited in the firm's bank account.

This verification of documents, counts, and procedures under the SAC program will develop a controlled working environment in which many internal thefts will be thwarted. In addition, warning flags will indicate any minute major irregularities beginning to show in the operation pipelines. Honesty of employees is strengthened by the elimination of opportunities to steal, and thus management fulfills its responsibility to employees not to place them in positions of undue temptation.

As accountability begins to permeate all phases of the operations, employees will become more alert to irregularities and trouble spots will be quickly spotted.

The SAC program puts emphasis where it can return a maximum of increased profits for a minimum investment of time and money. It provides the foundation for a *controlled* working environment.

Chapter 31

STAFF AND LINE RELATIONSHIPS

What is the proper role of the staff specialist? How can the technical knowledge of the specialist be used effectively to help line management do a better job?

What are the proper activities of the staff specialist at the corporate level? How can frictions and frustrations between staff and line people be minimized?

What purpose do staff control records serve? What kinds of records are needed? How can they be used as a management tool to improve managerial performance at all levels of the company operation?

Many shortage and security problems represent an underlying problem in staff and line responsibilities and relationships. Before we can solve individual problems, however, we must resolve the matters of job definition, scope of responsibility, and relationships of line and staff.

The Staff Specialist

Staff work can be defined as that part of managerial work that is assigned to someone outside the chain of command. The aim of staff work is to help the executive manage.

We find widespread confusion about what a staff specialist is supposed to do because practices vary widely from company to company. Since there is no single pattern, management must design each staff position individually.

The work of the staff specialist can be defined in terms of the problems he covers, and what he does about them. But unless the staff specialist, his boss, and everyone he works with is able to understand the scope of his work, his activities may cause more trouble than help.

One constructive approach is to list the types of problems in his field and then decide how far the staff specialist is expected to go in dealing with them. If we analyze duties in this manner, we will go a long way toward eliminating misunderstandings about the use of staff specialists.

Characteristics of Staff Work

What features characterize almost all successful staff relationships?

1. *The staff specialist is first a representative of his boss.* He does things his superior would do if the latter had the necessary time and ability. He is an extension of his superior, advising, investigating, creating, encouraging, and following up on matters in his special field. His position gives him stature but also imposes an obligation not to misrepresent his boss. If he declares his own views when they are at variance with his boss, he should be careful to make this distinction clear, because people will normally assume that he reflects the thinking of his superior.

   And of course the boss must in turn spend enough time with each staff specialist so that they can establish a mutual and consistent point of view.
2. *The staff specialist must rely largely on persuasion to get his ideas acted upon.* He usually lacks the power of command and must rely upon the confidence in his opinions of those he deals with. He must be sufficiently sensitive to the situations and problems of the people he attempts to influence so that he can win their acceptance of his proposals by voluntary cooperation.
3. *A staff specialist must be a team worker.* He must be prepared to submerge his own personality and desire for personal glory to the welfare of the company as a whole. He must recognize that other operating executives will receive credit and praise for improved results. And he must be willing to see others receive recognition for accomplishments and ideas he may have subtly planted months earlier.

When consistently maintained, these three features of staff work go far in reducing the friction that arises when a third person is interposed in what is normally a two-person relationship between a line supervisor and his subordinates.

Staff Influence

How can the staff specialists bring about improvements in his particular area of responsibility? There are two basic approaches. First, he may make recommendations to his boss and then rely on his superior to issue the needed orders to put his plan into effect.

Or, second, he may try to secure voluntary acceptance of his ideas from other executives without the support of formal orders transmitted down the chain of command.

The Voluntary Approach

The second, or voluntary, approach is the most frequently used method because a top executive is either too busy to issue such orders, or he does not want to upset a pattern of decentralized control.

How does the staff specialist accomplish his mission under the voluntary approach? Why can the staff specialist expect to exert any significant influence?

First, *the staff specialist has the authority of knowledge*. People are inclined to accept the advice of the security specialist because he is a technical expert. Within his specialized field his word is usually taken as authoritative because of his specialized knowledge. Most operating executives will give careful consideration to the opinion of someone who speaks with the authority of knowledge.

Status is a second factor. When the staff specialist has an impressive title, reports to an executive high up in the company, and has an office that exhibits the symbols of importance, he enjoys status. His views will be taken seriously by reason of his status alone.

Skill in presenting his ideas is the most important way in which the staff specialist exercises influence.

A more subtle factor is the potential backing of his superior. If employees down the line believe that advice they have rejected is bound to return as a command, they often decide it is wiser to take the advice in the first place.

Finally, if a staff specialist's views may significantly influence salary increases, or promotions, employees tend to accord his recommendations with more than polite acknowledgment.

In sum, even though the specialist has no command authority, he may still gain acceptance for his recommendations if he is smart, persuasive, impressive, and influential. Obvious also is the fact that the potency of his influence depends on the individual person and the individual situation.

Defining Staff Authority

From experience we know that a militant staff tries to run the whole show. Line management then feels that staff management is trying to take over without being accountable. On the other hand, a conscientious staff person feels justified in demanding that line management comply with his recommendations. After all, isn't he the expert in his field? How can an executive resolve this basic authority conflict?

Compulsory Staff Consultation

Some companies follow a practice of compulsory staff consultation. Under this system, a staff person *must* be consulted before action is taken on a matter in his area of specialization.

An operating executive is not blocked from proceeding as he thinks best, but he is required to listen to advice from another point of view.

Compulsory consultation supplements a more general requirement for successful staff work, namely, that a staff specialist should have access to any information that relates to his field of interest. A directive is not the entire answer to this phase of the problem because in the end he can obtain such information only when he shares management's mutual respect and confidence. Nevertheless, it is helpful for management to make clear to store managers that they are to keep the staff specialist fully informed.

Concurring Authority

When staff control over certain operations is very important, management can strengthen the staff specialist's position by granting concurrent authority so that no action in his field of responsibility can be taken unless the specialist agrees to it.

Whenever we find this granting of concurring authority, we find a senior executive who wants to be sure that the staff specialist's viewpoint is incorporated into operating decisions related to his specialty.

This is a "safe" method of operation because store managers cannot take heedless action. But it slows action because if the staff specialist and the store manager do not agree, someone must appeal up the administrative line for a decision. In addition, although management can hold both the security director and store manager accountable for any actions they *do* take, both of them have the chance to pass the buck when they *do not* take action.

Probably concurring authority should be granted only when the point of view of the specialist is particularly important and when a possible delay in action would not be serious.

Functional Authority

In functional authority the staff specialist can give direct orders to operating personnel in his own name instead of making recommendations through his superior or to other operating executives.

Normally a staff specialist would have functional authority only over those areas where he has recognized technical competence and where his opinion would be accepted anyway.

In what circumstances would functional authority be used?

1. When only a minor aspect of the total operating job is covered, for example, if actions and plans do not substantially affect the bulk of operations one way or the other.
2. When technical or specialized knowledge of a type not possessed by operating executives is needed.
3. When uniformity, or consistency, of action in several operating units is essential. (A uniform policy on prosecutions would be one example.)

Obviously, functional authority moves farthest away from the purely assisting and counseling relationships. Compulsory consultation and concurring authority are intermediate positions.

In practice we often provide a different kind of relationship for different duties of a single staff specialist. But such composite sets of relationships are apt to be confusing. We will court the least trouble by keeping staff largely in an advisory role.

The Creative Staff Role

How can the staff specialist better serve his company?

He has to serve a role of catalytic agent who acts as a counselor to line executives, including first-line supervisors.

His job is to help executives in THEIR solutions to THEIR problems in THEIR work situations.

The staff expert in his creative role should not have operating responsibilities. His role toward that end is:

1. To make sure that problems that are important to the line management are solved, using the resources within the organization itself.
2. To give executives a chance to sharpen their management skills through on-the-job self-development.
3. To assure that the specialist and executive both profit from team work developed through opportunities of working together on mutual problems.

The staff specialist must take a "lawyer–client" approach; he must accept line executive authority as a prerequisite of his job. He must have the capacity and willingness to counsel executives on THEIR problems, both in individual and in group counseling, and to help THEM arrive at THEIR solutions.

Store managers in turn will have expert assistance on problems that they think are important; however, they cannot sit back idly while someone else works out a solution.

Define Results Staff Should Achieve

It is fundamental in designing any job that the results expected from it be stated. This rule also applies to staff jobs. Staff, too, must be responsible for results. Staff problems in some businesses result from the fact that the results staff is expected to accomplish have not been defined. Some managers say, "Staff is not accountable for results. They are simply to advise and consult with the line."

The results expected from staff should be clearly defined because every job should contribute to the overall objectives of the enterprise. Without a definition of results the staff specialist can never be held truly accountable. The tendency is to hold him accountable for his activity, which is subject to many interpretations.

In staff's advisory position it is natural to emphasize activity although this activity may not be harmonious with the results line management is trying to get. Line management may feel the staff specialist is working at cross purposes with them. On the other hand, staff may be busy with one project after another, and in many cases it is questionable whether these projects are helping secure better operation.

Line has a job to do, and staff is supposed to help it do this job better. From the point of view of results, staff and line always overlap. Staff is trying to expedite part of the results that line is held accountable for. The results expected of staff should be part of the results that line is attempting to get.

Staff Accountable for Results

After the results expected of staff are defined, they must be accountable by results. If not, they tend to glorify their function out of proportion to its value and to focus on special activities common to their field, whether or not these activities aid line management.

When staff people continually circulate reports on what they are doing, it often means they are accountable by activity, not by results.

It is natural for the staff specialist to do this. He is then relieved of accountability. He notified everyone! Since such reports tend to go to top management, they show up line people and defeat line cooperation. Executives at the top are burdened with these reports and memos because they have to separate the wheat from the chaff.

Need Is for Double Accountability

This leads to a fundamental principle for the accountability of staff—the principle of double credit.

Both staff and line should get full credit for any accomplishment of either the staff or the line in the area that the staff is set up to cover.

Application of this rule will encourage accomplishment from staff and line. They will be encouraged to work together because it is to the advantage of each of them.

It is unrealistic to hope that a staff specialist will be happy that he has made a slight contribution to the line even though he gets no credit for it. It is hard to get a creative person with initiative to assume this spineless, self-effacing role. On the other hand, it is also unrealistic to assume a line person will enjoy having a staff person involved in his activity unless he feels that if something works, he, the line person, will also get full credit.

As you can see we recognize here a complete overlap in accountability.

In staff areas there is never unique accountability. It is the staff person's job to help the line do its job better. But a line person must always be accountable for his total operation, including the parts where staff helps. A result expected of a staff person is only one of the results expected of the line person.

Planning Staff and Line Functions

The principle of the dual accountability of staff and line is an extremely important point for an executive to consider when setting up staff and line functions.

There are many areas where improvement can be measured and where mutual accountability for results can be established.

Records can establish performance in nearly all areas where security improvements is needed. In fact, if there is a staff function where it seems impossible to keep a record, this staff function may very well have no contribution to make.

Supervisors often do not learn how to use staff and must learn to accept and use them as part of their responsibility. The management climate must be one that encourages the acceptance of staff. Management must guide and train those below them in the line to accept staff functions, to explain the need for staff, to review staff objectives, and to aid in making smooth staff relationships. Planning is also needed to insure that staff and line have mutual objectives.

Fundamentally, it should be the job of the manager up the line to pave the way and educate his subordinates on the profitable use of staff. Part of this preparation for staff includes a careful analysis of the results to be achieved, because then the results expected of staff are in harmony with those expected of line.

Sound Authority for Staff Specialist

Earlier in our discussion we reviewed three types of authority that can be given to staff: consulting, concurrent, and functional. What is best for the security specialist?

I do not subscribe to the popular notion that regards the specialist as one who should have NO authority whatsoever except his "authority of knowledge." This view stems from the idea that only line should be accountable for results. We have noted that there is an overlapping accountability between line and staff and that both should be held accountable.

In companies where staff operations are making a valuable contribution staff has a certain kind of authority that is recognized and accepted by the line.

Authority can be given the security specialist if:

1. There is a need for a staff specialist, the work requires specialized knowledge or has interdepartmental (or interstore) implications, and where it is questionable whether line can do an effective job without technical, expert guidance.
2. Staff has been made accountable for results—results that are in harmony with line objectives—and where the staff specialist's sphere of activity has been carefully delineated.

Under these conditions, I would suggest the staff specialist have the following authority:

Within his own limited field, the word of the staff specialist holds unless proven wrong by line.

Under this arrangement, staff decisions (in his own field) would take precedence over line. What we are saying is, "The expert decides on the action."

Remember, there must be a need for an expert, and the staff specialist must be an expert, more experienced than anyone in line in his own specialty.

Line Can Appeal

Finally, line should have the right to appeal. If line disagrees with the staff specialist and cannot convince him, they may go to a higher executive to get the staff recommendation reversed.

In practice this would seldom happen. Why? Because of an important point—the staff specialist is now fully accountable for the results of the action. He is accountable for some of the same results expected from the line. He soon sees he needs the line's help to make his staff ideas work.

Under these conditions, staff will hesitate to be too autocratic and dictate to line when line feels an idea is not going to work. The staff specialist is inclined to solicit line's help and advice. He is apt to seek out the thinking of the store executive and to discuss a problem carefully with him to make sure he is coming to a wise decision. And line, under these conditions, is more apt to accept the decisions of the specialist because they know he is just as accountable as they are.

Let me emphasize that this does not erase the importance of the staff expert gaining most decisions through voluntary cooperation. His ability to persuade others to voluntarily adopt his programs is still his most effective method of operation.

The specialist should use this authority only as a last resort. But in today's work environment the staff specialist appears to need at least this kind of limited authority if management is to gain full value for the investment made in the specialist's technical skills.

What Should Line Expect?

How can the staff specialist know if he is operating effectively? One way is for him to put himself in the shoes of the executive he serves, that is, decide what he would want from a staff specialist if he himself were a line manager. Whatever programs and techniques the staff expert develops, line people (store managers and other executives the staff specialist deals with) should expect this approach from the staff specialist:

1. He tries to understand us, our operations, our problems, and what we are trying to do. He accepts our problems as a normal part of our jobs; we have not failed because we have problems. Above all he respects us.
2. He helps us get to the core of problems. He assists us in seeing the value of careful diagnosis as opposed to quick solutions. He does not take the problem away from us to solve it himself (even though we may at first have wanted him to do just that).
3. He helps us to see advantages in our working out solutions and resolving different points of view. He actively gives of his time, thought, and skills in aiding us to find positive means for resolving problems (although his persistence bothers us at times).
4. He helps us get our ideas into practical operation, not to get us to adopt his plans or techniques. He can see beyond his specialty to the larger matters with which we are faced.
5. He encourages us to clarify our thinking and our ideas, to work together as a team, to build for ourselves, and to check our solutions. He is not trying to "take over," to pull away our functions, or to establish special procedures to be handled by him.
6. We are more confident of ourselves and our management know-how, our ability to solve problems, and our skills in organization and administrative planning.
7. We call on him more and more because he has become a valuable source of staff help.

The Staff Specialist's Job

Here is a listing of activities that may *properly*, but not necessarily, belong to a staff specialist.

1. Gathering facts and information about technical or managerial problems of concern to line.
2. Drawing up policies, programs, plans, and procedures that depend for success on his specialized knowledge.
3. Accumulating and exchanging information on various company problems, especially between interested groups within his area of specialty and without direct line relationships.
4. Discussing all matters listed above with staff or line to secure advice or criticism that may be of value to line.
5. Obtaining approval for plans, usually by explaining them from the viewpoint of his own speciality.
6. Preparing written procedures and instructions (in cooperation with line) so that plans can be put into action. Such programs, of course, require line approval.
7. Explaining and interpreting plans, developing interest and enthusiasm (with line cooperation), and advising line on how to overcome difficulties related to his specialty.
8. Analyzing the operations of a plan and following up on its progress. Staff, because of its neutral character, can often do this more effectively than line.
9. Setting standards and establishing necessary controls in matters that relate to his specialty.
10. Collecting and analyzing results and measuring performance through reports and reviews—not usually on own initiative, but as requested by his superior.

Summary

1. Place responsibility for shortage and security control IN the store, not in a central staff operation.
2. Staff specialist's job is that of advisor and counselor (a lawyer-client relationship).
3. Staff gains acceptance and action through persuasion skills and authority of knowledge.
4. Consider giving staff limited functional authority in matters such as setting standards, policies, and procedures within the area of his specialized knowledge.
5. Staff should not have any routine operations.
6. Hold staff accountable for results:
   a. Set specific areas for accountability.
   b. Measure staff performance on basis of results, NOT on basis of activities.

7. Hold line management jointly accountable for accomplishment of staff objectives. Set dual accountability and give dual credit for accomplishment.
8. Emphasize that staff job is to help line executives with *their* problems, in *their* store, in *their* situation—*to help line do a better management job* and to SERVE line management.
9. Staff should not be looked on as an "enforcement" job. It should *not* engage in "policing" action but should develop constructive programs to help store management.
10. Staff's job, in sum, is to work *with* line toward a mutual objective—*TO GET THE JOB DONE.*

STAFF CONTROL RECORDS

Certain records should be gathered by staff to aid line management. What is the proper objective of these records? For whom are they prepared?

Staff Records Versus Accounting Records

These records are quite different from accounting records. They are management control records and should be designed to stimulate corrective action where it is needed.

The basic difference in accounting and staff control records should be understood when setting up such records. Accounting records, for example, give the overall situation—the total picture. But the staff control records *focus on departures from objectives.* What objectives? Those selected for a particular period of time.

To properly focus attention these staff records should point out only the departures from objectives that NEED ATTENTION. The purpose is NOT to present a report filled with various statistics. A store manager might, for example, receive only two or three figures a month from a staff specialist.

Staff Records Should Be Interpreted

These staff reports differ in another way; they should be interpreted. Keep in mind that *they are intended to stimulate corrective action*, and therefore the specialist should not merely report the facts but should also tell what these facts mean. And who should know more about the meaning of a set of figures than the person who puts them together?

Familiarity with the figures often causes the specialist to hit upon a significant item at once. He should pass this meaning on with his report.

Sometimes a one-line comment bringing into relief the implications of a certain figure can have more value than a ten-page report of untranslated statistics.

Records Should Cover Objectives

What records should the staff specialist develop? The answer is there should be records to cover all present objectives. That is the key. Since these records focus on improvement, they should emphasize advances being made.

Who Receives Staff Records?

Accounting records normally go to the executives UP the line, to higher management. In this respect the staff records are different, for they more often go DOWN the line, the reverse of accounting records. Although accounting records at times appear to pretend that first-line management isn't on the team at all, *the staff records do recognize first-line management's importance because the purpose is to encourage corrective action throughout the entire operation.*

In fact the staff records should normally report departures from goals directly to the management person himself, NOT to his boss. At least as long as the departure from the goal is within allowable limits for the executive—within the line executive's authority. After all, usually he is standing pat in the center of the spot where action needs to be taken. Top management sets the tolerance limits within which the line executive is allowed to act, but these authority limits must be broad. They need to be realistic. Departure from objectives should be SIGNIFICANT before it would be reported to the person's boss.

Normally, little would go up to senior management. This leaves the top executive freer to work on his broader problems. Still, he is assured that if a SIGNIFICANT DEVIATION occurs, it will be reported to him. In this way he retains adequate control over his operation.

Obviously this approach forces a decentralization of management and also makes a more harmonious working arrangement between staff and line. The staff specialist now is a helper instead of a critic. In fact it's his job to keep the line person OUT of trouble by letting him know when a deviation occurs so he can correct the situation.

He helps the line person gain recognition at the end of the period for sound achievement, helps him look good in the eyes of his superior.

Records Vary Annually

Although accounting records tend to stay the same year in and year out, and in fact are used for annual comparisons, the staff control records keep changing. They have to be flexible if they are to be effective. Staff reports should change whenever there is a change in objectives.

One year's reports may have no similarity with the past year's because the aims are different. These reports need flexibility, which is basic to the overall purpose of using these records to spur corrective action.

Staff and Line Accountability

In accounting we charge an expense to one department. It avoids confusion. This charge gets into all the reports and becomes traditional. But in staff control records this principle often does not hold because there is often dual accountability between staff and line.

A typical staff goal often overlaps with line in terms of the intended results. After all, the staff specialist is set up to help the line person do some part of his work better. In pointing up achievements of objectives or departures from objectives, the same item may be charged to two people, a staff person and a line person. Several people may get full credit or full discredit for a result.

This dual charge is needed to hammer home a full sense of accountability for final results. This makes it advantageous for people to cooperate with each other.

Of course a person should not be charged with any item he has no control over. This would be unfair and would reduce his interest.

Only Significant Deviations Are Reported

Accounting-type reports usually report ALL deviations—indiscriminately. This is one element that makes it difficult to use them to stimulate corrective action. They usually make no differentiation between items reflecting "random" deviations and items reflecting "meaningful" deviations. (Meaningful deviations are those with an underlying cause.) The difference between these two types of deviations becomes important when we want a report to stimulate corrective action.

By reporting random deviations, we upset people for no reason. There are normal fluctuations in every job and over a period of time they tend to balance out. If we call attention to them we cause the line person to worry about every small deviation and destroy the effectiveness of the staff records approach. What the line executive really wants is information on the meaningful deviations that he can do something about.

By pointing out significant departures from objectives, we encourage management-by-exception and the staff reports become a worthwhile tool for corrective action.

Reports Must Be Current

Staff reports should be current. They should report the situation as it is NOW. A report that is six or eight weeks old is not helpful. These reports should discuss present facts if they are to serve line management. But how current should they be? The answer is that a line executive should receive a report on any meaningful deviation from objectives—at once. At the first instance if possible, but certainly while the amount of deviation is still within the line executive's scope of authority.

Once the purpose of the reports is understood, the period of reporting will be determined by the objective. And some staff reports might be issued every month, every two weeks, or even daily. Keep in mind that the determining factor is that a meaningful deviation be reported while it is still within the range of the person's authority to correct the situation before it has to be reported to a senior executive.

Staff Reports Are Estimates

Again, unlike accounting reports, the staff records reports do not have to have a high degree of accuracy. Most management decisions are not based on data of extreme accuracy. All the line manager wants to know is that there is a meaningful deviation from the objective. Frequently crude estimates will be sufficient for this purpose. In some cases even an error of 10 to 20 percent is allowable.

This means amassing figures becomes an easier job. Even guesses (educated, that is) are satisfactory. At first it might seem impossible to develop rapid reports for this control system, but once it is realized that extreme accuracy is not needed such controls become possible.

Although staff supplies the facts and interprets the figures, the line person decides what the corrective action should be.

In addition, the figures should always reflect the line person's individual responsibilities. *Don't use allocated averages*, for the line person must have a major influence on the result reported to him if the report is to have any value. If a significant portion of the figure has been developed by general allocation, he does not feel that he can personally control such results.

Management Principles Are Involved

Several management principles are involved in this approach to staff control records.

In order to get people to take action there must be a realistic decentralization of authority. People down the line must be allowed to make the normal decisions, including normal errors, that would be required to accomplish the objectives set for them. If this is not the case, there is little point in reporting deviations to them because they are not in a position to take action anyway.

Permitting tolerance for the errors involved requires discipline on the part of other executives above. They must allow people down the line to take the action needed to correct the deviation reported by the control system. In effect, there must be a realistic recognition by top management of the management-by-exception principle in application.

Fundamentally the staff specialist must also be accountable by the action principle. Someone issuing a record report should be accountable for corrective action resulting from his records, not just for the accumulation of records or for the presentation of reports.

He would not be given credit for the number, size, or completeness of reports as is typically the case. In fact, these reports would be looked upon as expense items charged against him. The only way the staff specialist would get any credit at all would be by the action resulting from his reports.

In other words, the staff specialist should be tied very closely to the corrective action taken by the line people on whom he is keeping controls. He cannot shrug off his responsibility by saying, "Action is the responsibility of the line," because that would be shrugging off one of the greatest opportunities he has for contribution to the company welfare that is available through his use of staff control records.

This approach recognizes that the basic reason for staff records is to stimulate sound management action. The value of any such records can be determined by checking on the action that results.

Summary

1. Purpose of staff control records is to stimulate corrective management action.
2. Staff control records differ from accounting records, which provide a "general" picture, while the staff control records should focus on deviations from objectives.
3. Staff specialist should give interpretations of significant implications so that action can be taken by line management.
4. Records should cover all major objectives.
5. Records should focus on improvement.
6. Deviations should be reported to the line management person himself, NOT to his superior, as long as deviation is within the line manager's scope of authority (within previously set standards of tolerance allowable).
7. Only significant deviations beyond line manager's authority would be reported to upper management.
8. This forces decentralization of authority and improves relationship between line and staff. Staff is now a helper instead of a finger pointer. He is letting line person know that he has a problem so he can take corrective action.
9. Staff control records should be flexible. They should automatically change with changes in objectives.
10. In pointing up deviations these records may charge the same item of deviation to two or more people. Several people may be given full credit or full discredit for a result. This is based on staff and line having dual accountability for mutual objectives.
11. No person should be charged with an item that has no relationship to his work or that he is powerless to control.
12. Report only SIGNIFICANT DEVIATIONS. Do not report random deviations.
13. Staff control reports must be *current*. Such a report should indicate a deviation while it is still within the limits of the line person's authority.
14. Extreme accuracy is not important. The important information is that there is a significant deviation.
15. The decision about what kind of corrective action is to be taken is up to the line manager. But this line manager must know where

he stands. Records should reflect individual responsibilities, not allocated averages.

16. The underlying principle is management-by-objectives.
17. Objectives should be current and should be set by top management (based on recommendations of line and staff).
18. Top management must have tolerance for normal errors.
19. Staff specialist is not given credit for the number, size, or completeness of reports, but only for constructive action resulting from the staff control records.
20. Both staff and line must see these control records as directed to the stimulation of sound management action that can be determined by reviewing the results.

APPENDICES

Appendix 1

INVENTORY SURVEY

Checklist to aid the security manager in planning an investigation into the causes of a high inventory shortage.

I. RECEIVING DEPARTMENT

A. Receipt of "incoming" merchandise
  1. Receiving platform
     a. Method of checking incoming shipments.
     b. Protection of merchandise while on platform.
  2. Transportation to receiving point
     a. Type of truck used in conveying pilferable merchandise.
     b. Methods used in handling small packages to insure maximum protection.
     c. Freight elevator regulations and personnel.
  3. Receiving point
     a. Systems employed for safeguarding merchandise at receiving point.
     b. Possible accumulation of shipments with a view to speeding transfer to marking room.
  4. Parcel post
     a. Efficiency of personnel in following prescribed procedure.
     b. Physical protection of merchandise in parcel post room.
  5. Scout merchandise
     a. Methods of receiving scout merchandise.
     b. Special handling of valuable items.
     c. Facilities for protection of merchandise in office of merchandise scout.
     d. Methods of transportation to marking room.

6. Warehouse merchandise
    a. Methods of receiving merchandise transferred from store.
    b. Facilities for stocking and protecting merchandise in warehouse reserve.
    c. Control in transit of merchandise requisitioned by the store.
7. Comparison merchandise
    a. Methods of receiving purchases.
    b. Facilities for protecting merchandise in comparison office.
    c. Methods of marking and transportation to reserve or selling floor.

B. Checking and Marking
1. Marking area
    a. Location of marking section—entrance and exits protected.
    b. Facilities for marking and checking—adequate space and sufficient light.
    c. Personnel.
    d. Type of supervision.
2. Checking procedure
    a. Methods used in opening shipments and counting units.
    b. Verification of shorts by supervisor.
    c. Advisability of spot checks to test checkers' accuracy.
    d. Number of shorts reported per season.
3. Marking procedure (original marking)
    a. Marking methods
        (1) Unit marking—adequacy of ticket or stamp used.
        (2) Bulk marking—adequacy of marking materials from the viewpoint of legibility.
        (3) Premarking—accuracy of prices.
    b. Physical handling of merchandise
        (1) Advisability of providing locked cages for handling small expensive items.
        (2) Possibility of limiting number of employees who may enter cage.
4. Price change marking
    a. Authorized forms
        (1) Handling of two-part price change.
        (2) Three-part price change.
        (3) Markdown tally—order-filling units, possible abuses—selling department, possible errors in salesclerk entries.
        (4) Mark out of stock.
    b. Physical handling of merchandise
        (1) Advisability of remarking on floor in reserve.
        (2) Protection of merchandise in transfer to remarking unit.
5. Remarking
    a. Refunds and exchanges
        (1) Protection of merchandise in remarking area.
        (2) Transportation of refunds to remarking area.
        (3) Advisability of centralization of remarking.
    b. Merchandise returned for credit
        (1) Advisability of remarking on floor or in reserve.

c. C.O.D. returns
   (1) Necessity for remarking authorization.
   (2) Advisability of remarking on floor or reserve.
d. Department security
   (1) Methods of transportation.
   (2) Return of merchandise to stock.
e. Unmarked merchandise
   (1) Registry of signatures of executives authorized to sign remarking authorizations.
   (2) Proper issuance of remarking authorization.
   (3) Accuracy of prices.

C. Reserves
   1. Layout of reserve area.
   2. Control of exits.
   3. Facilities for storing merchandise.
   4. Restriction of number of persons having access to expensive merchandise.
   5. Sorting and binning of merchandise.
   6. Requisitions for merchandise—protection of merchandise during transit and control of number of units being taken from reserve.
   7. Advisability of securing signatures from selling department for receipt of merchandise.

D. Miscellaneous Procedures
   1. Returns to vendor
      a. Invoice returns
         (1) Accuracy of packers in verifying price, number of units, authorizing signature, and correct department information.
      b. Stock returns—check to insure that:
         (1) Price tickets and information on return coincide.
         (2) Number of units being packed corresponds with number listed.
         (3) Functioning of system provides for expeditious returns.
   2. Merchandise transfers
      a. Proper pricing.
      b. Remarking.
      c. Accuracy of counts.
      d. Departmental information on tickets and transfer sheets.
      e. Protection of merchandise in transit.
   3. Salvage
      a. Preparation of markdown sheet.
      b. Segregation of damaged items.
      c. Advisability of identification marks on salvage to prevent possible refund manipulation.
      d. Method of disposition of salvage merchandise.
   4. "As is" merchandise
      a. Type of ticket.
      b. Advisability of marking on floor or in reserve.
   5. Merchandise loans—other than interior display

a. Displays at remote points.
   (1) Method of controlling merchandise.
   (2) Adherence to prescribed procedure.
b. Loans for art work
   (1) Methods of controlling and protecting merchandise.
   (2) Enforcement of proper procedure.

6. Order filling
   a. Location of area.
   b. Facilities for protection of merchandise.
   c. Exclusion of unauthorized persons from area.
   d. Possibilities of manipulations by employees.
   e. Employee bonus and premium for detection of errors in filling checks.
   f. Staff rotation.
   g. Care in listing breakage.
   h. Care in listing price changes on tally price change sheet.
7. Customer's own repairs
   a. Adherence to store system.

II. SELLING FLOORS

A. Selling Area
1. Location
   a. Entrances and exits.
   b. Suitability for type of merchandise sold.
   c. Possibilities for seasonal expansion and contraction.
   d. Proximity to freight elevators.
2. Layout
   a. Facilities for floor reserve stock.
   b. Protection of merchandise in reserve—locks or chicken wire.
   c. Adequacy of fitting rooms.
      (1) Sufficient number.
      (2) Layout of rooms.
      (3) Checking of merchandise being taken into and removed from fitting rooms.
      (4) Possibility of observing customers' actions in rooms.
      (5) Type of job being done by checker.
   d. Arrangement of selling fixtures.
      (1) Blind areas.
      (2) Locking facilities.
      (3) Proximity to main traffic aisles.
3. Arrangement of stock
   a. Sorting and binning of forward reserve.
   b. Facilities for accumulation of damaged, mismatched, and unmarked items.
   c. Method of transferring to floor stock.
   d. Proper segregation or similar merchandise carried in adjacent departments.

4. Displays
    a. Quantity of merchandise on fixtures accessible to customers.
    b. Advisability of employing protective devices in display of pilferable items.
    c. Possibility of reduction of displays.
    d. Advisability of informing security department of planned expensive displays.
5. Service
    a. Coverage in department
        (1) Number of clerks.
        (2) Selling stations.
        (3) Type of instructions to clerks regarding:
            (a) Care of stock.
            (b) Protection of stock.
            (c) Selling at correct prices.
            (d) Removing unmarked merchandise from stock.
            (e) Segregating exchange items from regular stock.
    b. Salescheck system
        (1) Salescheck information corresponds with information on price tickets.
        (2) Department arrangements.
        (3) Authorizing signature on "as is" merchandise.
        (4) Authorizing signature on "new," "worn," "old," "sent," or "taken" transactions.
        (5) Tickets properly chopped in control departments.
    c. Wrapping
        (1) Clerk wrap
            (a) Indications of "pass-outs."
            (b) possibilities of sales at incorrect prices.
        (2) Merchandise checkers
            (a) Accuracy of check of price ticket and salescheck information.
            (b) Care taken in verifying matching tickets.
            (c) Possibilities for periodic rotation.
6. Supervision
    a. Section manager coverage
    b. Adjustments
        (1) Refunds, orderbacks, and exchanges.
            (a) Evidence of sale.
            (b) Misuse of remarking ticket.
            (c) Protection of these items in the department.
7. Security
    a. Adequate detective coverage.
    b. Cooperation among detective, section manager, and clerks.
    c. Instruction of section manager in the handling of suspicious refunds.
    d. Detective observations of system violations.

B. Manufacturing Services
1. Alteration rooms
    a. Control of items received for alteration.

b. Facilities for the protection of the items in workrooms.
c. Inspection and packing customers' own alterations.
d. Control of stock repairs.

2. Cleaning room
   a. Stock cleaning
      (1) Accuracy of check on items received and returned.
      (2) Facilities for protecting items received for cleaning.
      (3) Department follow-up efficiency.
   b. Customers' own cleaning
      (1) Control of items received.
      (2) Method of delivery to customer.
3. House repairs and engraving
   a. Authorizations for doing work.
   b. Protection of merchandise in workrooms.
   c. Control of valuable parts.
   d. Packing and shipping of sold and customers' own items.
4. Miscellaneous services
   a. Photo finishing.
   b. Upholstery and awning manufacturing.
   c. Initialing and embroidering.
   d. Special cutting.

C. Merchandising Function
   1. Handling of remarked merchandise.
   2. Pricing of unmarked merchandise.
   3. Handling of mismatched merchandise.
   4. Special orders.
      a. Placing.
      b. Follow-up.
      c. Advisability of physical handling by receiving department.
   5. Possible violations of established procedure for receiving and return of merchandise to vendor.
      a. Pickups by vendor on floor.
      b. Receipt of special or rush orders on floor.
   6. Control of breakage
      a. System for recording breakage.
      b. Proper disposition of breakage sheets.
   7. Control of merchandise loaned for display
      a. Use of merchandise loan book.
      b. Follow-up of merchandise signed out of department.
   8. Control of department items borrowed.

D. Miscellaneous Management Functions
   1. Style shows
      a. Method of securing merchandise from departments.
      b. Control and protection of items borrowed.
      c. Follow-up of return of items to proper departments.
   2. Supervision of floor stock personnel
      a. Close check on duties.

  b. Possibility of stock personnel carrying merchandise unauthorized out of the department.
  c. Adequacy of force.

III. PACKING

A. Packing Units
  1. Pickups by floor collectors.
  2. Protection of merchandise in transit to unit.
  3. Advisability of signatures for articles of high value.
  4. Protection of chutes and conveyors to packing stations.
  5. Protection of merchandise in packing unit.
  6. Control of "over goods."
  7. Analysis of shorts on orders.
  8. Security department observations in units.
  9. Breakdown of customers' nondelivery complaints and open C.O.D. records.

B. Merchandise Checker Coverage on Selling Floors
  1. Adequacy of space allowed.
  2. Location of packing desk.
  3. Possibility of customer theft of packed items.
  4. Advisability of instituting packing in department.
    a. As compared with clerk wrap.
    b. As compared with packing at remote point.
  5. Efficiency of merchandise checker job performance.
    a. Enforcing salescheck system.
    b. Avoiding shorts and overs on "sent" items.
    c. Checking prices and department numbers.
  6. Accessibility of stock merchandise to packing desk.

C. Shipping Department
  1. Transportation of merchandise to shipping point.
  2. Protection of merchandise in shipping area.
  3. Adequacy of system for controlling valuable items.
  4. Locking facilities in area.
  5. Advisability of protection bureau observation of shipping area.
  6. Control of stamps and insurance receipts.

D. Transfer Desk
  1. Packing area.
  2. Adequacy of method for accumulation of packages at this point.
  3. Number of duplications because of shortages.
  4. Possibility of employee manipulations in transfer area.

IV. DELIVERY

A. Sorting
  1. Protection of conveyors.
  2. Location of sorting stations.
  3. Accessibility of sorting points to unauthorized persons.

4. Type of personnel employed.
5. Possibility of eliminating breakages.
6. Adequacy of inspection of conveyors for lost packages.

B. Entering of Packages
1. System employed.
   a. "C.O.D." entry.
   b. "Paid" entry.
2. Possibilities of collusion between driver and entry clerk.
3. Breakdown of analysis of nondelivery and open C.O.D.
4. Type of personnel.
5. Special handling of valuable items.

C. Loading
1. Possibility of driver taking packages for which he is not charged.

D. On Load
1. Driver's care of packages.
   a. Locks on truck.
2. Driver's care of cash.
   a. Bank deposits.
   b. Limitation of money on person.
3. Control of C.O.D. returns.
   a. Switched merchandise by customer or driver.
4. Advisability of testing drivers with packages not entered.
5. Control of pickup items.

E. Depots
1. Advisability of sheeting transfer merchandise.
2. Protection of merchandise in transit.
3. Advisability of immediate entry of transfer merchandise at depots.
4. Method of protecting merchandise in depots.
5. Sorting and entering of packages.
   a. Danger of using drivers as entry clerks.
   b. Special handling for "value" items.

V. CONTROLLER'S OFFICE

A. Merchandise Control
1. Adequacy of control used by selling department.
2. Advisability of instituting register or unit control.
3. Efficiency of operation of unit control departments.
   a. Control of chopped stubs.
   b. Locking of chopping machines.
   c. Reporting of price discrepancies.
   d. Advisability of control inspection of white remarking authorizations.
   e. Competency of control clerical in attempting to reconcile apparent shortages.
   f. Possibilities of manipulation of control by merchandising executive.
   g. Frequency of "stock counts."

B. Auditing of Document
1. Department charges

a. Invoices
   (1) Possibility of charging invoices to wrong department.
   (2) Check on pricing of invoices—no price changes on invoice after merchandise is marked.
   (3) Incorrect extensions on invoices.
   (4) Special handling of consignment invoices.

b. Interdepartmental and affiliated store transfers
   (1) Possibility of charge to wrong department.
   (2) Figuring of transfer.

c. Customer refunds
   (1) Controller's office verification of department numbers.
   (2) Legibility and accuracy of figures.
   (3) Analysis of suspicious refunds.
   (4) Efficiency of control on order back and refund documents.

d. White vouchers
   (1) Control of vouchers by authorized signatures.
   (2) Possible manipulation by authorized people.

e. Charge tickets
   (1) Analysis of charge tickets.
   (2) Possibilities of affecting collection.

2. Department credits
   a. Merchandise transfers
      (1) Possibility of wrong department receiving credit.
      (2) Figuring of transfer.
      (3) Posting on journal.
   b. Returns to vendor
      (1) Possibility of credit to wrong department.
      (2) Extension of return.
      (3) Posting on journals.
   c. Sales
      (1) Controller's office report of missing saleschecks.
      (2) Crediting of sales incorrectly in departments.
      (3) Analysis of "no record" C.O.D. saleschecks.
      (4) Test check on salesclerk tallies.
   d. Markdowns
      (1) Correct department information.
      (2) Extension of markdowns.
      (3) Posting of markdowns on journal.
      (4) Memo markdowns.

C. Inventory Division
   1. Accuracy of stock listing.
   2. Reports of missing items.

D. Special Audit
   1. Findings of special audit on
      a. Customers' own merchandise saleschecks.
      b. Refund analysis.
      c. Salescheck analysis.

Appendix 2

PREVENTION OF STOCK SHORTAGES

A. Purchase Orders
   1. Write an order for every item ordered from vendors.
   2. Include only one department on each order.
   3. Indicate retail units clearly.
      This is especially important if the retail unit differs from the cost unit. For example, cost price may be per dozen whereas retail price is per item. On merchandise ordered by the case, indicate the number of units in each case.
   4. Indicate multiple price, if any.
      For example, if an item is sold singly at $1.00 but in units of three for $2.85, indicate both prices on the order; otherwise, inventory shortage will occur.
   5. Avoid changing retails on orders.
      You may change retails on orders without issuing a price change only if the price is changed before merchandise and invoice are received.
   6. Follow-up orders.
      Visit invoice office at least once a day to determine the status of orders, invoices, and unmatched entries.
   7. Cancel orders.
      Check through your purchase orders periodically. Cancel those that have not been delivered by promised date, or those with small remainders, etc., according to usual procedure.
   8. Notify branch store or warehouse of direct shipments.
      When you write an order for merchandise that is to be shipped directly from the vendor to a branch store or to the warehouse, notify the branch store or the warehouse immediately of your action by sending them their copy of the order.

B. Invoices

1. Visit the marking rooms and the invoice office daily.
2. Sign bills promptly.
   Do not allow invoices to accumulate. In the majority of cases, anticipation can be taken if bills are paid promptly. This benefits your department by increasing the dollar amount of your cash discount.
3. Check the department number on the entry.
   Do not sign invoices automatically. YOUR SIGNATURE MEANS that terms, transportation charges, costs, retails, etc., are correct.
4. Check that the merchandise for which your sign belongs to your department.
   This is especially important when the same merchandise is carried in two or more departments.
5. Check that correct retails for each item are entered opposite the corresponding cost figure.
6. Check that the retail unit is specified.
   This is especially important if the retail unit differs from the cost unit. For example, skirts and jackets may be billed separately but are to be sold as one retail unit.
7. Check that multiple prices, if any, are shown.
   For example, 35¢ each or 3 for $1.00. Both the single and the multiple price must be shown.
8. Check the entry.
   The entry is your notification that the merchandise has been received and that you are authorizing payment only for merchandise that has actually been received.
9. Check terms, etc.
   Check that terms, transportation charges, and who pays transportation and costs are according to your original order to your vendor, or if charged, that they are acceptable.
10. Make your notations legible and distinctive.
    Use a blue or green pencil for all notations that you make on the invoice or entry to distinguish them from notations by other persons.
11. Check reason for an auxiliary entry.
    When an invoice is attached to an auxilliary entry (one without the registry number printed in the right-hand corner), examine it carefully to determine the reason for the auxiliary entry. If in doubt, ask someone in the invoice office.
12. Avoid split invoices.
    Split invoices usually occur because department managers order for two or more departments on one order form. This causes unnecessary work and may cause errors in accounts payable. You can prevent split invoices by using one order for each department and by requesting your vendor to bill the store separately for each department.
13. Check split invoices carefully.
    When you do sign a split invoice, check that accounts payable has charged the proper protion of the bill to your department.

14. Check dummy invoices against actual invoices.
    When merchandise is opened on a dummy invoice, check the dummy carefully against the actual invoice before you sign the invoice. This will insure that you are charged for the quantity of merchandise you actually received.
15. Write "consignment shipments" on invoice.
    Write "CONSIGNMENT—DO NOT PAY" on invoice directly under the vendor's name.
16. Advise when to pay consignments.
    Check through consignment invoices periodically so that these bills do not become dormant. When advisable, to pay for such shipments, write "OK" on the entry or advise accounts payable in writing.
17. Check for carrier claims.
    When damages or shortages are indicated on the entry, the traffic department stamps, "claim pending," on the invoice and prepares necessary claims.
18. Check for vendor damages.
    When damaged merchandise is returned to vendor before it is marked and put in stock, the receiving department attaches a copy of the return invoice to the original invoice. Be sure the return invoice is attached so that it will be posted and deducted from the payment for this invoice.
19. Check for vendor credits (shortages).
    When a credit is being taken for the shortage or damage (without returning the merchandise), the receiving department attaches a copy of the charge credit to the original invoice so that over payment will not be made.
20. Check for vendor overages.
    If the vendor bills for more than the amount originally ordered, and if the overage is returned to the vendor, the receiving department attaches a copy of the return invoices to the original invoice so that overpayment will not be made.
21. Check for overages not billed on invoice.
    If you decide to return the "overage" to the vendor, have the receiving department prepare and attach a copy of the return invoice to the invoice. If you keep the "overage," have the receiving department prepare and attach a copy of the charge credit to the original invoice so that stock records will be accurate. Be sure the overage is not billed and paid on another invoice.
22. Check for overcharges.
    If the vendor overcharges, prepare and attach a copy of the charge-credit to the original invoice so that overpayment will not be made.
23. Invoices not accepted for payment unless properly received.
    Accounts payable will pay for merchandise only when it is RECEIVED OVER PLATFORM or shipped directly from vendors to customers in accordance with accepted procedures. When merchandise is picked

up by messenger at the vendor's business, send the messenger to the receiving platform so that the merchandise can be properly entered and receipted. Under no circumstances will merchandise be paid for when received in the department or by a department representative without going through the regular receiving procedure.

24. No payment on dummy invoice.
    Payment will not be made on a dummy invoice.
25. Change retails without price change only if:
    THE MERCHANDISE HAS NOT YET BEEN MARKED AND IF THE INVOICE IS STILL IN THE RECEIVING AND MARKING AREA. Both the department manager and the marking room supervisor must initial the invoice opposite the changed retail to verify that no merchandise bearing the original retails has left the marking room.
26. Issue a price change to change retails if:
    The invoice has been returned to the invoice office; issue a price change to change the retail even though the merchandise, either marked or unmarked, is still in the receiving and marking area.
27. Check on allowances from vendors.
    Make sure that the proper form has been issued to cover all allowances from the vendor. This includes allowances on purchases, claims, advertising, selling costs (e.g., demonstrators or extra commissions), or price reduction on merchandise in your stock.

C. Purchase Journal Sheets
   1. Examine purchase journal sheets carefully.
      The purchase journal sheet is the basis of your retail inventory. Examine these sheets carefully as soon as you receive them. Ask accounts payable to explain any entries that are not clear to you.
   2. Verify all entries.
      Verify that all invoices belonging to your department are entered on your purchase journal sheet at the correct costs and retails.
   3. Check claims.
      Check that all claims chargeable to either the vendor or the carrier are posted on your journal sheet.
   4. Check for returns.
      Check that returns to vendors are credited on your purchase journal sheet at the same costs and retails at which they were removed from your stock. Use tissue copies in your return book as a means of verification.
   5. Question entries dated prior to last inventory.
      If any entry appears on your purchase journal dated prior to your last inventory, challenge this posting with the manager of accounts payable.
   6. Review your unjournalized purchases monthly.
      At least once each month, review your outstanding unjournalized purchases in the accounts payable office. Unjournalized purchases are charged to your purchase account.

D. Receiving Merchandise
   1. Visit receiving areas daily.

Visit receiving areas at least once a day to answer any questions that the receiving checker or marker may have. Inspect the merchandise to make sure that you receive the quality and styles you ordered.

2. Only authorized receiving permitted.
   Merchandise may be received only at authorized points at the store, at a branch store, or at the warehouse. DO NOT RECEIVE MERCHANDISE DIRECTLY FROM VENDORS IN YOUR OFFICE, IN THE SELLING DEPARTMENT, OR IN RESERVE STOCK. Send the vendor's representative with the merchandise to the proper receiving point or to the receiving office.
3. Do not sign vendor's receipts.
   Such receipts will not be accepted for payment by accounts payable. Only the receiving platform or the receiving office is authorized to sign a vendor's receipt for merchandise.
4. Only receiving department personnel may open packages.
   Packages may be inspected and opened only by receiving department personnel. They are experienced in checking for damages and losses and in preparing necessary claims against the carrier or vendor.
5. Wait until entire shipment is checked and marked.
   Do not accept to take merchandise from the receiving department until the entire shipment is checked and marked, where marking is required. If, in an emergency, you must have some of the merchandise before the entire shipment is checked and marked, have the checker verify and note on the invoice the quantity that is being removed and make sure that it is properly marked.
6. Watch for sources of potential shortages.
   If you notice that merchandise in open trucks is left unguarded in any location, particularly back elevator corridors, customer elevators, etc., report it to the receiving department immediately. Make sure that receiving rollers are completely emptied before they leave your department. Do not put paper or other wrappings in the merchandise roller.
7. Spot check quantity received.
   Count merchandise you receive in the selling department frequently to make sure that you are receiving what you requisitioned or expected in the shipment. Report any shortages immediately to the suprevisor of the receiving department or reserve stock.
8. Check condition of merchandise received.
   Inspect the condition of the merchandise received from the receiving department or reserve stock frequently. If merchandise is received damaged or soiled, report it immediately to the manager of the receiving department. Wherever possible, a claim should be taken against the vendor or carrier. If that is impossible, issue a price change.

E. Marking and Remarking

1. Check that merchandise is marked when required.
   Do not accept unmarked merchandise unless it is on the approved nonmark list. Merchandise may not be sent to or accepted in the

selling department or in reserve stock until it has been released by the marking room.

2. Check the type of marking.
   Check that the marking room has used the type of marking that is authorized for your department and that all the information you need is included in the price markings.
3. Check prices for accuracy and legibility.
   Check that retails on tickets in each shipment are correct. If prices are incorrect or illegible, return merchandise for remarking.
4. Check the department number.
   Check that the department number on each price ticket is correct. This is especially important if the same merchandise is carried in more than one department.
5. Check retail unit.
   Check that the retail unit is indicated on the price tag or on the sign, when required; for example, $2.95 for a set of 4.
6. Check for multiple prices.
   Where merchandise is sold either singly or by multiple price, for example, 35¢ or 3 for $1.00, the price ticket or sign should carry both the single price and the multiple price. This is important for inventory purpose since multiple priced merchandise is charged to the department and inventoried at the lower retail.
7. Check for switched or changed price tickets.
   Inspect price tickets on merchandise frequently to make sure the customers, salesclerks, or other unauthorized persons have not switched or changed them.
8. Check for missing price tickets or signs.
   Train your salesclerks to report cases of missing price tickets or instances where signs are inadequate, etc., to you. Take necessary steps to have merchandise properly marked.
9. Investigate loose tickets.
   Investigate all cases of loose tickets found in the department without merchandise. Destroy them only if you are satisfied that no merchandise should be attached to them.
10. Train salesclerks to consult price ticket or sign.
    Train your salesclerks to consult the price ticket or the sign before quoting the price to the customer or recording the sale. Train them NOT TO GUESS but to consult you when in doubt.
11. Check unmarked merchandise against nonmark list.
    If you receive unmarked merchandise in your department, check that this merchandise is on the approved nonmark list for your department. This is one of the basic causes of stock shortages.
12. Provide signs for nonmarked merchandise.
    Both the price and the name of the merchandise on the approved nonmark list must be indicated on the sign. The sign should be equally readable to customers and salesclerks. Check regularly to make sure that the sign is adjacent to the right merchandise.

13. Inform salesclerks and wrappers of nonmarked merchandise.
    Post the authorized nonmark list for your department so that it is accessible to salesclerks and wrappers. Keep this list up to date. Spot check to see that the salesclerk or wrapper wraps unmarked merchandise only when it is on this nonmark list.
14. Issue a price change to correct price tickets or signs.
    If prices are incorrect, take the merchandise off sale. Check the invoice for the retail. If the correct retail is on the invoice, merely have the merchandise remarked. If the retails on the invoice are also incorrect, issue a price change to correct price and have merchandise remarked.
15. Only authorized persons may remark merchandise.
    The department manager is responsible for remarking merchandise. He should assign a limited number of people in his department to perform this function when remarking is done in the department. All price tickets, special remarking pencils, or marking machines must be kept under lock and key in the department manager's office.
16. Count quantity remarked.
    If merchandise is removed from the selling department for reticketing, because of a price change, missing price tickets, etc., check the quantity returned against what you originally sent out. Check that the remarked price is correct.

F. Price Changes

1. Price changes are vital records!
    Price changes are among the most important documents in adjusting book inventories to physical inventories. Scrutinize each change carefully.
2. Record every markdown or markup on a price change.
    Record every change in price either upward or downward in order to prevent stock discrepancies.
3. Account for each page in your price change book.
    The statistical department maintains numerical control over price change books. All pages of the book must be accounted for. Send all void pages to the statistical department promptly.
4. Take markdowns or markups before sale or merchandise.
    Issue a price change as soon as you decide that the price of the merchandise is to be changed. Do not wait until the merchandise is to be sold to issue the price change. This causes time lags that become serious as the end of the season draws close. Any exception to this procedure must be cleared through your merchandise office and through the controller's office.
5. Write the department number correctly and legibly on the price change.
    This is particularly important when you are supervising more than one department or when the same merchandise is sold in two or more departments.
6. Record quantity accurately.
    Count merchandise carefully before filling in the quantity on the price change. DO NOT GUESS at the amount. TAKE AN ACTUAL COUNT.

Do not depend upon your marker to count it for you. If your marker finds a discrepancy when he counts it, recheck your count with him. Both of your must sign the price change.

7. Reprice all stock used to fill saleschecks.

   Merchandise reduced for sale in the forward stocks must also be reduced in the reserve and warehouse stocks if saleschecks are to be filled from the latter source.

8. Notify reserve stock, warehouse, or branch stores of price changes.

   Send copies of the price change to the receiving department, to the warehouse, or to the branch stores, so that merchandise there can be similarly changed.

9. Changing price on only part of stock must be approved by controller.

   In case of a promotion, if you wish to change the price on only part of the stock—for example, only on merchandise that has been sold—you must obtain written approval from the controller's office to make this exception. Such exceptions are dangerous sources of inventory shortages, particularly for merchandise on the nonmark list.

10. Check statistics on price changes.

    Extend your price changes carefully. Arithmetical errors are frequently a source of stock discrepancies.

11. Price change is remarking authorization.

    Do not remark merchandise until a price change has been issued and distributed. Allow enough time so that the merchandise can be remarked carefully before it is returned to stock.

12. Check new and old retail prices on price change and ticket.

    Incorrect pricing of markdowns or markups causes inventory discrepancies. Check the new retail and the old retail carefully when you enter it on the price change. Make sure that the old retail and the new retail on the price ticket correspond to the old retail and the new retail on the price change.

13. Salvage damaged merchandise.

    All unsaleable damaged merchandise must be salvaged through the supply department. Take a markdown for the total value of the merchandise. Send the merchandise to the supply department for disposition.

14. Keep daily breakage reports where required.

    Instruct salesclerks to enter each breakage as it occurs on the daily breakage report. Issue a price change for all items listed on these daily reports.

15. Take markdowns for stolen or lost merchandise.

    Train your salesclerks and stockclerks to report all losses to you immediately. When you discover them, check first whether the merchandise has been borrowed by advertising, display, etc., or sent out for repair. If it is not found, take a markdown for the loss. Send the price change to the protection department for their information. The protection department will forward the price change to the statistical department.

16. Check prices of new shipments of same merchandise against previous shipments.

Where a new shipment is marked at a price different from that of previous shipments, issue a price change to mark the old shipment up or down.

17. Adjust prices of customer returns.
    If a customer return is placed back in stock at a price different from that at which it was originally sold and credited to the customer, issue a price change to take care of the difference in price.
18. Check on price adjustments to meet competition.
    When a customer complains that a competitor's price is lower or that we have reduced our price within seven days since she purchased the item, it is our practice to refund the difference in price, after verifying her statement. The department manager or the bureau of adjustment writes "MARKDOWN" at the bottom of the credit-refund voucher and the markdown is then taken automatically in the controller's office.
19. Record allowances to customers on price change.
    Record any allowance made to a customer at the time of sale on a price change. In departments selling piece goods, allowances may be accumulated on a daily allowance sheet and only one price change issued for all sales allowances that day rather than for each individual sale. No other deviations are permissible.
20. Take a markup if you sell vendor's free samples.
    If vendors give you free samples to test their saleability, issue a price change to get that merchandise into your stock and thus prevent stock discrepancies. Mark the merchandise from "0" to the price at which you are going to sell it.
21. Cancel markdowns after sales.
    If merchandise is to be sold at the regular price after the markdown sale is completed, issue a price change to cancel the markdown. Cross reference the cancellation to the original markdown. Include merchandise in all locations, which has been reduced to the sale price.

G. Sales

1. Report your daily sales accurately.
   Spot check your salesclerks' totals. Deduct federal taxes, if any. If your clerks intersell, make sure that sales are accurately reported for each department.
2. Make sales comparisons.
   Compare your total monthly flash sales with monthly audited sales on your weekly and cumulative merchandise report. Ask sales audit to explain and investigate any unreasonable differences in the figures.
3. Observe sales procedures.
   Check that the department manager who is responsible for supervising and instructing salesclerks in correct sales procedures is doing his job completely. Every transaction is a potential shortage. Therefore, it is wise to observe how salesclerks and the department manager handle different transactions. Give special attention to the handling of deposit receipts, memo checks, futures, holds, layaways, and other points mentioned below.

4. Take corrective action.
   If salesclerks are not handling transactions properly, ask the department manager to retrain them in the correct procedures. If at any time you feel that the department manager is not following procedures correctly, speak to him about it or call it to the attention of the controller and the floor superintendent.
5. Inspect cash register assignments.
   Examine cash registers—both the department key assignments and the tally envelope—periodically. Check that your department is receiving credit for the sales that belong to your department. This is particularly important when two departments use one register.
6. Observe cash sales.
   Notice whether salesclerks are ringing the correct amount of sales, including all taxes, etc. Every paid sale must be registered on the cash register or stamped by a cashier. Report any cases where this is not done to the protection department at once.
7. Spot check salesclerks' books.
   Examine your salesclerk's books periodically. See if the right salesbook is used and that the type of sale is clearly indicated. Check the department number on the salescheck. Check extensions and additions.
8. Check listing of items on saleschecks.
   Inspect saleschecks to see that items and units are properly indicated. This is especially important in departments where saleschecks are filled by stockclerks.
9. Look into wrapping operation.
   Spot check wrappers and clerks to see that only items listed on salescheck or purchased by customer are included in the package sent or taken by the customer.
10. Check on send sales.
    Inspect some send sales periodically before they leave the department for wrapping. Compare prices paid and items listed on salescheck with merchandise and price tickets.
11. Observe handling of cash register and salescheck voids.
    Observe whether salesclerks are handling voided sales correctly. Improper handling of voids can cause stock discrepancies.
12. Look into recording of taxes.
    Spot check the recording of all taxes and of federal taxes particularly. Tax records are carefully audited by government agencies. It is important to keep the tax separate from the price of the merchandise for stock and sales records.
13. Watch interselling operations closely.
    Interselling is highly desirable from a sales point of view in that it results in flexibility and better customer service. In order to prevent stock discrepancies, you must constantly supervise interselling operations. Spot check tallies to see that salesclerks are crediting sales to the proper department.

14. Fill orders promptly.
    Saleschecks must be filled as soon as possible. Do not allow orders to be held over unnecessarily. Delays in order filling lead to nondelivery complaints and may result in duplicate shipments or duplicate credits.
15. Check on control of held-over saleschecks.
    Saleschecks held over unfilled in the department should be carefully controlled, arranged, and followed up so that they may be filled promptly as soon as the merchandise is received.
16. Follow up on direct deliveries from vendors.
    When merchandise is to be delivered to the customer directly from the vendor, complete the proper order forms and send the vendor copies of the salescheck. Follow up to make sure that the vendor delivers the merchandise to the customer by the promised date.
17. Arrange merchandise neatly.
    Merchandise arranged in a neat and orderly fashion is much easier to control. Separate "sale" items from regular priced items. Make sure that signs show the correct price and are adjacent to the merchandise they promote.
18. Keep counters clear.
    Do not allow excessive amounts of merchandise, particularly higher priced items, to accumulate on counter tops. This safeguard not only improves the appearance of the department but also deters shoplifting.
19. Watch special sales events carefully.
    Be doubly careful in handling special sales and aisle table selling. Make sure that price signs are adequate and that the department number is correctly indicated.
20. Police fitting rooms.
    Since we do not maintain checkers at entrances to fitting rooms, it is important that these areas are constantly policed. Train salesclerks to keep track of the number of garments taken in and out and not to allow too many garments to accumulate in the fitting rooms. Keep fitting rooms clear of all merchandise except that which is being tried on by customers. Do not permit old merchandise to be kept in fitting rooms.
21. Spot check the recording of co-worker discount.
    Check on the authorized discount percentage for items in your department. Co-worker sales must always be recorded on a salescheck except in a few departments where a separate cash register key is set up for co-worker paid and taken sales. Failure to record discounts adds to inventory shortages.
22. Insist on sealing co-worker purchases.
    Laxity on the part of the salesclerks in sealing co-worker purchases can very easily lead to stock discrepancies. Check on the wrapping of co-worker purchases periodically. Do not allow co-workers to seal their own packages in their own departments.
23. Examine department shortage and overgoods report.

Examine shortage and overgoods reports periodically. They are good indexes of possible inventory discrepancies. Investigate them thoroughly or call the controller, particularly if they are unduly high.

H. Customer Returns

1. Spot check exchanges.

   Spot check salesclerks' handling of both even and uneven exchanges periodically. Check that the returned merchandise is saleable, that the correct department number is indicated, and that the returned merchandise is remarked, if necessary, and that it is returned to stock.

2. Check on signing of returns.

   The department manager or your head of stock should not sign credits unless the merchandise is actually received in stock, particularly in the case of calls.

3. Check department number.

   Spot check that the department number is correct. It is just as important to have returns charged to the correct department as it is to have sales credited to the correct department.

4. Inspect unticketed returns.

   The department manager should consult a competent department representative before issuing refunds or adjustments on merchandise returned without a price ticket. Have the merchandise remarked before it is returned to stock.

5. Check on the pricing of credits.

   Returned merchandise will normally be credited or refunded at the price at which it was originally sold. If, for some reason, the customer must be credited with an amount different from the price ticket, the reason for the difference must be clearly indicated on the credit-refund voucher.

6. Take markdowns on returns when returned.

   Merchandise must be remarked at the amount of the credit. If it is to be sold at a price different from that of the credit, issue a price change to record the difference.

7. Handle damaged returns carefully.

   Set up a procedure in your department so that all damanged merchandise is brought to your attention, regardless of the source of the damage. Follow standard store policy and procedure in reporting these damages, taking markdowns when necessary. Disposing of damaged merchandise without recording the amount of the damage on a price change can lead to serious stock discrepancies.

8. Amount of tax is itemized on credits.

   The amount of tax, both city and federal, must be itemized on the credit-refund voucher. In this way, the merchandise will be returned to stock at its correct price.

9. Discount on co-worker returns itemized.

   Merchandise returned by co-workers is credited or refunded at the discounted price. The original price and amount of the discount must be shown on the credit-refund voucher.

10. Look into adjustments.
    Examine adjustments made by the department manager periodically. Give special attention to those cases when no merchandise is returned—for example, nondelivery complaints. Duplicate adjustments sometimes occur in the case of nondelivery complaints, and such adjustments may result in inventory shortages.
11. Record allowances to customers on returns.
    If merchandise is not returned, or if it is not accepted for return, but an allowance is made to the customer (for example, $1.00 allowed for dry cleaning soiled merchandise), a credit-refund voucher must be issued for the amount of the allowance. The department manager writes "MARKDOWN" at the bottom of the voucher and encloses the department's copy in addition to the office copy in the credit envelope. The department's copy serves as the markdown authorization, and no price change must be served.
12. Investigate unusually high returns.
    If your return percentage suddenly increases sharply, investigate to determine the cause.

I. Repairs
1. Arrange for repair service.
   Arrange with our vendors or other agencies to handle the repair of either customer's merchandise (where it is the policy to give repair service) or merchandise from stock. Do not send merchandise out for repair before proper arrangements have been made.
2. Have repair invoices approved by accounts payable.
   Use memorandum repair invoice to send either customer's or stock merchandise out for repair. Take repair invoice to accounts payable for approval before sending out the merchandise.
3. Indicate clearly whether it is customer's own merchandise or stock merchandise.
   Failure to indicate whether the merchandise belongs in stock or is the customer's own merchandise can cause stock discrepancies.
4. Check that department number is correct.
   This is important for charging costs and will insure that the merchandise is returned to your department.
5. Check store return address.
   If merchandise sent out for repair is to be returned to the warehouse or to a branch store, insert the correct address on the return address label.
6. Follow up direct deliveries.
   If the repaired merchandise is to be delivered directly from the vendor to the customers, send the vendor copies of the salescheck for delivery. Instruct him to send us his invoice and the adjustment copy of the salescheck.
7. Follow up your repairs.
   You are responsible that an accurate record of outstanding repairs is maintained and also that the vendor returns repaired merchandise

promptly to use and delivers it promptly to the customer. See that your receiving quantity checker closes his copy of the memo repair invoice when the merchandise is returned to us. Also see that the corresponding copy is closed when the vendor has delivered this merchandise to the customer. Your tissue copy of the memo repair invoice is a convenient means of follow-up.

8. Returns from vendors must go through regular receiving procedure. All incoming merchandise must be received at the receiving platform or in the receiving office. So do not accept repaired returns from vendors directly on the selling floor. Send vendors or your messenger to the receiving platform with the merchandise.

J. Returns to Vendors
   1. Check with vendor first.
      Do not return merchandise to a vendor unless you have made previous arrangements with him to accept it. Merchandise refused by vendors leads to errors and confusion in handling.
   2. Use return room.
      Use a return invoice to list all merchandise returned to vendors. Send return invoice and the merchandise to the return room. If the return room does not receive this merchandise, there will be confusion. Never give or send it to the vendor without clearing it through the return room first.
   3. Count quantity carefully.
      Count the number of items carefully before you send the merchandise to the return room. If the return room finds discrepancies in price and quantities, recheck these discrepancies promptly with the return room clerical.
   4. Use same costs at which originally purchased.
      Cost price must be the same as that which you actually paid for the merchandise. Any change from actual cost must be approved by the controller's office.
   5. Check units.
      The unit designating the count must agree with the unit used to designate the cost. For example, if two pieces are being returned and the price is by the dozen, then the pieces should be listed as 2/12, not as 2.
   6. Check retails.
      Verify that the retails on the return invoice correspond to the retails on the price ticket. The return room removes and destroys price tickets or other markings before returning the merchandise to the vendor.
   7. Check department number.
      Check that the department number is correct so that your department will receive credit for the returned merchandise.
   8. Have return approved by accounts payable.
      Take the return invoice to accounts payable for approval before the merchandise is wrapped.

K. Retail Transfers
   1. Supply department issues retail transfers for supplies.

When you have to buy supplies from a retail department, go to the supply department where the retail transfer will be issued.

2. Use a retail transfer to transfer merchandise to another department.
   Have your merchandise office issue a retail transfer to transfer merchandise to another department. Your department is credited for the merchandise at cost and retail.
3. Check department number.
   Enter the correct department number on the receipt and indicate the department borrowing the merchandise.
4. Centralize control of borrowed merchandise.
   Merchandise may be out on loan for two weeks only. If an extension is desired, make sure that such extension is properly recorded on the receipt. If the merchandise is not returned within a reasonable time, have your merchandise office charge it to the borrowing department as a retail transfer.
5. Report unauthorized borrowings to the controller.
   If any merchandise is removed from your department by advertising, display, etc., without an authorized form, report it to the controller immediately.

L. Interstore Transfers

1. Use authorized form only.
   Use the interstore transfer to transfer merchandise to or from a branch store. Do not accept or send merchandise unless it is accompanied by proper copies of the interstore transfer. This form automatically transfers merchandise from the stock of the sending store to the stock of the receiving store.
2. Check and double check department numbers.
   Double check the department numbers on the interstore transfer. One of the most common errors in transferring merchandise to or from branch stores failure to record the proper branch number and the proper parent department number. Make sure that these numbers are correctly inserted at the top and on the stubs of the interstore transfer.
3. Use transfer room
   All transfers must go through the parent store transfer room or the branch receiving platform. If, in an emergency, merchandise is transferred personally, and it is inconvenient to clear it through the transfer room, send the original interstore transfer marked, "By Messenger," to statistics at once.
4. Record shortages or overages on stub.
   If more or less than the quantity listed on the interstore transfer is actually received, record the shortage or overage on the back of the stub before sending it to the statistical department.
5. Send stubs to statistical department.
   The stub is an important part of the interstore transfer for stock record purposes. Detach it and send it to the statistical department. The stub confirms the receipt of merchandise and the transfer of merchandise from the sending store's stock to the receiving store's stock.

6. Write interstore transfer for saleschecks sent to warehouse for order filling.
   When the branch store sends saleschecks to the warehouse or to the parent department for order filling, the items on each salescheck must also be listed on an interstore transfer. A copy of the transfer must accompany the saleschecks.

M. Reserve and Warehouse Stock
   1. Visit reserve stockrooms daily.
      Visit reserve stockrooms in the store daily. Cooperate with the supervisor to insure the best stockkeeping methods.
   2. Check to see if stock is clean and orderly.
      Check that stockclerks are keeping your stock in a clean and orderly manner. In this way, damages and losses can be prevented. If you are not satisfied with the method of stockkeeping, call it to the attention of the manager of the warehouse or the supervisor of the reserve stock.
   3. Visit warehouse stockroom weekly.
      Visit warehouse stockroom at least once a week. Check on stockkeeping methods.
   4. Check handling of fragile stock.
      Train your salesclerks and stockclerks to handle fragile merchandise carefully and to report breakage or damage to you.
   5. Take markdowns for damage or loss.
      Instruct your salesclerks and stockclerks to notify you of all damages and losses. Investigate the reason for such damages and losses. Take necessary markdowns to prevent stock discrepancies.
   6. Check on merchandise transferred to or from reserve stock.
      Check that the requisition for merchandise from reserve stock is properly completed. Check the department number and count the quantity. Check that the merchandise is either bulk-marked or unit-marked.
   7. Check on merchandise transferred to or from warehouse.
      Check that the warehouse transfer is properly completed. Check the department number and count the quantity transferred. Check that the merchandise is either bulk-marked or unit-marked. When transferring merchandise back to the warehouse, particularly after promotions, make sure that the merchandise is in good condition for resale. Do not return damaged merchandise unless it can be properly reconditioned at the warehouse.
   8. Inspect order filling.
      Inspect order-filling procedure at warehouse or reserve stock when it is the practice in your department to send saleschecks to these points for filling. Spot check items listed on salescheck against those included in the customer's packages. To simplify order filling, instruct your vendors to label cartons and packages.

N. Last Words
   1. Supervise selling floor operations at all times.
      You or your assistant should be on the selling floor at all times. In this way, you are aware of what is going on and can take corrective action on the spot. Do not wait until the end of the season to correct six months' operations.

2. Make salesclerks "shortage conscious."
   Train your salesclerks to assist you in preventing shortages. Explain departmental problems to them and instruct them on how they can help you to control and prevent shortages.
3. Report shortage incidents to the controller.
   Report any incidents that you feel might contribute to inventory shortages to the controller's office at once.
4. Call the controller for assistance.
   If you want to know more about the procedures outlined herein, call the controller's office. Feel free to call the controller's office at any time if you are in doubt in a particular situation.

And Last But Not Least:

5. Make every day inventory day.

Appendix 3

PLANS FOR INVESTIGATION OF A DEPARTMENT HAVING A HIGH INVENTORY SHORTAGE

Group I

A. All department members should be rechecked through the police for previous dishonesty records.
B. All sales personnel should be shopped.
C. The department should receive full detective coverage.
D. The department should have before- and after-hour coverage.
E. Credits of all types should be thoroughly investigated.
F. All stock areas should be sealed at night.
G. If practical, checkers should be used.
H. A check into the customer's own merchandise should be instigated.
I. The loan system and wrapping passes should be investigated.
J. An undercover operator might be added to the personnel.
K. Receiving procedures should be investigated.
L. Method of handling return goods and manufacturers returns should be investigated.

Group II

A. A daily spot check of merchandise should be made against unit control.
B. Sales personnel should be instructed on security principles.

C. Remarking of merchandise, especially markdowns, should be examined.
D. Refund test letters should be sent out on all credits.
E. Packing error slips should be examined.
F. Any complaints of nondelivery of merchandise should be investigated.
G. If department has cash registers, overages, shortages, and excessive "no sales" should be examined.
H. Are all departmental losses being reported to the security department?

Group III

A. Average departmental cash sales and check to see if any salesclerk falls below average to a marked degree over a period of three weeks.
B. How is salvaged merchandise disposed of?
C. Does the department have any suburban transfer errors?
D. Is unmarked merchandise removed from stock?
E. A daily floor audit of saleschecks should be instigated.
F. Check to see if any marking errors have occurred recently.
G. What control is there of merchandise sent to dry cleaning and alteration rooms?
H. How often does the buyer check the purchase journal?
I. Check employee delivery stubs.
J. Does any salesperson have an excessive number of "void" saleschecks?
K. Observe the department for possible "pass-outs." (Especially if department has a clerk wrap.)
L. Salesclerks should limit the number of articles of merchandise taken into the fitting rooms.
M. Are fitting rooms cleared after customers leave?
N. Do guards find any merchandise in fitting rooms at night?
O. How is individual employee morale?

Group IV

A. Are unissued salesbooks kept in a locked compartment?
B. Employees' hats, coats, and packages should not be allowed in the department.
C. Are packing supplies controlled properly?
D. Do packers work at the desk before and after hours?
E. Do packers wrap any merchandise without written authorization?
F. Do department's saleschecks show any erasures?
G. Department delivery stubs should be examined.
H. How well trained are department employees in store systems?
I. Is all reduced merchandise marked so that it cannot be returned for a full refund?
J. Is all remarking done in the receiving room?
K. How are telephone and mail orders handled?
L. Does the department have any handwritten price tags?

Group V

A. Have all employees sign a copy of the rules for handling cash sales?
B. How often is the tube station inspected and by whom?
C. Are "holds" handled only in the prescribed manner?
D. Should the layout of fitting rooms or organization of stock space be changed?
E. Does the department have enough sales personnel for the amount of traffic?
F. Are service manager's signatures being obtained wherever required by store systems?
G. How is merchandise of comparison shoppers handled?
H. Do any unsupervised personnel work in the department before and after hours?
I. Does the department have any interselling or intercrediting?
J. How does the department's percentage of credits compare with similar departments elsewhere?
K. Does the department have any merchandise in the warehouse? If so, how is it controlled?
L. Is any merchandise received by the buyer directly in the department?
M. Have any employee losses been reported?
N. Investigate even exchanges.
O. Analysis of credits issued by the adjustment office.

Appendix 4

INTERDEPARTMENTAL RELATIONS MANUAL

Modern retail security should integrate its operation with the following store departments.

A. Operating
  1. Personnel
  2. Training
  3. Store systems
  4. Service managers
  5. Accommodation desk
  6. Service desk
  7. Receiving department
  8. Delivery and packing
  9. Maintenance
  10. Adjustment department
  11. Supply department
  12. Mail and telephone orders
  13. Workrooms
  14. Service building

B. Finance
  1. Accounts payable
  2. Accounts receivable
  3. Addressograph
  4. Auditing
  5. Bill and order room
  6. Cashiers
  7. Charge office
  8. Collection department

9. Inventory
10. Mail
    a. Incoming
    b. Outgoing
11. Paymaster
12. Timekeeper
13. Statistical
14. Treasurer

C. Merchandising
1. Advertising
2. Comparison shopping
3. Departments—special precautions
4. Display—interior
5. Display—window
6. Fitting rooms
7. Interselling
8. Inventories
9. Loans
10. Markdowns
11. Models
12. Personal shopping
13. Promotions
14. Records
15. Employee sales (disposal of excess merchandise)
16. Sample room
17. Special deliveries
18. Stockrooms
19. Training assistant buyers

OPERATING

Personnel

1. Applications more carefully prepared.
2. Applications to include: full name, city of birth, previous address, and relationship of person to be notified in emergency.
3. ALL (even demonstrators) to be processed through reference bureau, and police record files.
4. Letters to be sent on out-of-town applicants.
5. Executives also to be cleared.
6. Retail credit bureau reports and improper references investigated.
7. Special investigations for cashiers (and cashier-packers).
8. Special investigations for teenagers, etc.
9. Appropriate notations on cards to those closed out for dishonesty.
10. Relatives and close friends of staff members not ordinarily to be hired.
11. All close-outs through personnel.
    a. Proper notation on card in suspected and proven cases.

12. Derogatory information not given.
13. Investigate cashier-packers.
14. Source of information not disclosed in close-outs because of unfavorable references or previous record except where it is a matter of public record.
15. Unfavorable reference investigated.
16. Misdemeanor to give false information on employment application.
17. Security to be notified of special employees (probationers, etc).
18. Control of extra's salesbooks.
19. Security will examine all employment applications.

Training

1. Company doors are to be used by all store members, so that packages may be properly inspected.
2. Store purchases must be left in locker or parcel room—not stored in department.
3. Personal packages brought into the building are subject to inspection and the same general conditions as store purchases.
4. Special permission is required to enter the building outside of regular business hours.
5. Each person entering or leaving building before or after hours is required to sign door pass.
6. Each regular staff member is assigned a locker. Lost locker keys must be reported promptly to security.
7. Special checking facilities are available to extras.
8. Purses may be taken to the floor, but only at the individual's responsibility. It is suggested that substantial sums of money be securely kept on each individual's person.
9. All accidents and conditions likely to cause accidents must be reported promptly to each person's supervisor. Emergencies will be reported to the telephone operator, who has been given instructions for immediate follow-up action.
10. Fire drills are held once a month. All staff members are required to familiarize themselves with the proper procedure to be followed in these situations.
11. Lost and found—when an article is found in the store, it is turned in to the accommodation desk without delay. Any customer reporting a loss is to be referred to the divisional service manager.
12. Keys for offices, stockrooms, etc., are to be turned in at a board maintained at each floor for that purpose. A master key board is always kept at the company door.
13. Customers or visitors acting in an apparently irregular manner are to be approached on a service basis.
14. Salespersons will never attempt to accuse or apprehend a person acting suspiciously.
15. It is suggested that salespersons observe customers of this type as carefully as possible, so that they can furnish accurate descriptions and, if necessary, be able to recognize and identify them at some future time.

Store System

1. Each transaction must be completed. The practice of accumulating sales is not to be permitted.
2. In charge transactions, proper authorization, identification, and signatures must be secured.
3. Salespersons may accept bank checks on purchase where:
   a. There is no change coming to the customer.
   b. The customer has been properly identified.
4. Service manager's signature is required for all unusual transactions.
5. Employees making purchases are to be treated exactly the same as customers. It is the responsibility of the person making the sale to see to it that a full check is written before delivering the purchase.
6. No delivered unwrapped purchases may be made without the approval of the service manager. On these purchases the entire original salescheck (including the address label) must be placed in the charge box.
7. Suspicious persons—all persons acting in a suspicious or irregular manner are to be reported to the service manager immediately. If the service manager is not available, the security office is to be called.
8. Sponsors—a special training program, including follow-up, is recommended for all sponsors. Salesperson should be able to refer all irregular transactions to them and service managers.
9. Basic sales instruction should be limited to only the most automatic types of sale. Salespersons should then be advised to refer all irregular matters to sponsors and service managers.
10. A training program is strongly recommended for all merchandising executives, particularly buyers, to acquaint them with the system required for their positions.
11. Forms must be unified. A general color scheme should be adopted to facilitate the accurate use of forms.
12. A systems and forms committee is recommended. Nothing new along these lines and no changes to be made without the approval of this committee.

Section Managers

1. Do not sign charge salescheck and credits all together at night—sign them individually at time of transaction.
2. Refunds—one book to a service manager.
3. Credit and adjustment books should have a definite location.
4. Blue-pencil signature is poor means of approval.

Service Managers

1. Provide service.
2. Provide supervision.
3. Interpret policy to customer.
4. Interpret system for salesperson.
5. Enforce regulations.
6. Responsible for physical appearance of department.

Accommodations Desk

1. Report losses where theft is possible, particularly where purse or expensive article is lost.
2. Where adverse claims for lost property, refer to police.
3. Report attempted refunds without salescheck.

Service Desk Training

Cash

1. Count change bank in morning.
2. Count bank before and after any cashier relieves at desk.
3. Count banks in evening.
4. On closing, bank should be picked up and turned in to proper cashier.
5. Any shortages in bank should be reported immediately to security.

Refunds

1. Head of service desk supervises.
2. A pink form must be used for a refund. It may not be used for any other credit.
3. No refund may be issued without a salescheck.
4. Saleschecks on which refunds are to be issued must have:
   a. "Refund"
   b. Amount in writing
   c. Section manager's signature
   d. Date
5. All refunds should be carefully checked for the following:
   a. Date issued
   b. Customer's name and address
   c. Department
   d. Sold by
   e. Salesbook and check number
   f. Article
   g. Amount
   h. Reason returned
   i. Person preparing
   j. Section manager's preauthorizing
   k. Customer's signature
   l. Section manager's amount in writing
   m. Section manager's signature
   n. Duplicate salescheck stapled to original refund
6. Refund books must be closely supervised at all times.

Customer's Own Merchandise

1. The customer's own merchandise salesbook is not to be used unless the section manager preauthorizes such action.
2. The person preparing the customer's own merchandise should place her number in the "sold by" box.
3. The specific article covered should be noted in the proper place.

4. The value of the article should also be noted.
5. The reason for the customer's own merchandise should be detailed explanation; order number, etc., should always be included.
6. The customer's name and address should appear on all customer's own merchandise.
7. The section manager signs the customer's own merchandise in two places.

Salesbooks

1. Salesbooks should be kept in a secure place.
2. They are issued only when backing of old book is turned in.
3. Salesperson must sign receipt.
4. Receipt is sent to security.

Closing of Desk (optional)

1. At close of business, duplicates of refunds issued that day are torn from book and arranged in numerical order.
2. Customer's own merchandise triplicates are handled in a similar manner.
3. Each refund and customer's own merchandise is examined.
4. If there are any errors, the head of the service desk checks the mistake, calls it to the attention of the person who made it, and then initials the refund or customer's own merchandise in the lower right-hand corner.
5. Pink envelope is prepared.
   a. Date
   b. Department (or floor)
   c. Number of enclosures
   d. Signature of service desk head
6. Refund duplicates and customer's own merchandise triplicates are then placed in pink envelope.
7. All parts of each void, refund, and customer's own merchandise are placed in pink envelope (it counts as only one enclosure).
8. Pink envelope is securely sealed.
9. It is then taken to security office.
10. A pink envelope is turned in every day, even if there are no enclosures.
11. Refund books, customer's own merchandise, and all extra salesbooks must be securely locked overnight. The key is turned in to the service manager.

Closing of the Desk

1. Refund duplicates are checked.
2. Refund duplicates are placed in the pink envelope.
3. Customer's own merchandise triplicates are checked.
4. Customer's own merchandise triplicates are placed in the pink envelope.
5. Return merchandise receipts are checked.
6. Return merchandise receipts are placed in the pink envelope. These are not considered as enclosures.

Merchandise

1. When merchandise is returned to each department, a receipt for it must be secured from that department.

2. These receipts are kept by department.
3. At the end of the day they are placed in pink envelopes. Periodic checks are made by the control clerk to see that receipts are secured for all of the merchandise credited.

Service Desk Physical Arrangements

1. Location
   a. Central
   b. Accessible
2. Appearance
   a. Attractive
3. Equipment
   a. Section manager's signal light
   b. Place for the location of returned merchandise
   c. Locked cabinet for salesbooks, refunds, etc.
   d. Telephone
4. Requirements
   a. Center of selling floor
   b. Section manager's signal light
   c. Entrance from back
   d. Hanger box
   e. Rods for returned merchandise
   f. Drawer space
      (1) Lost merchandise drawer
      (2) Change drawer (lock)
      (3) Supply drawer (lock)
   g. One chair or stool inside desk
   h. Well lighted
   i. Place for incoming mail
   j. Credit book shelf (lock)
   k. Place for fashion magazines
   l. Counter 3 feet from floor
   m. Several chairs for customers (outside desk)
   n. Telephone
   o. Room at least $20' \times 20'$

Instructions Given to Clericals at Service Desk Who Apply for Signature

1. Can sign:
   a. Credit (applied only)
   b. Nothing else (customer's own merchandise and refunds not to be authorized)
2. How to execute duties:
   a. Act as a receptionist. Always be pleasant.
   b. Secure authorization.
   c. Check authorization with merchandise for accuracy.
   d. Delegate assistant to prepare credit.
   e. Customer signs.
   f. You sign.

g. Attach authorization to credit.
h. Send credit and authorization to tube room.
i. Give only to customer.
j. File voucher.

3. Caution: *Do not* write out credit that you sign.

Receiving Department

1. Door
   a. Apron number used as control.
   b. Apron number carried through to delivery in department.
   c. Check for quantity in department
   d. Manufacturers' delivery clerks not allowed beyond certain control point.
   e. Guard for door.
   f. No receiving on street.
   g. Facilities to move things from door promptly.
   h. Receiving should be responsible to get merchandise to department.
2. Special Control
   a. Jewelry (expensive).
   b. Fountain pens.
   c. Fur coats, etc.
   d. Stock trucks covered and locked for small or expensive merchandise.
3. Price Tickets
   a. Preretailing to be encouraged.
   b. Securely fastened.
   c. All should have store's name.
   d. Remarking under receiving supervision.
   e. No tickets to be given to departments.
   f. Department number on all tickets.
   g. Ticket in conspicuous place on garment.
4. Manufacturer returns
   a. Should conform to salescheck sends as nearly as possible.
   b. Control on messengers.
   c. Should be under delivery—not receiving department.
   d. Discontinue accounts to payable authorization.
   e. On claims, this authorization should be done in department.
   f. Strict limitation on door pass approval (time included).
   g. Wrong address control.
5. Branch Transfer
   a. Hanging merchandise checked for number.
   b. Small articles in cartons.
   c. Errors to security.
6. General
   a. Control on merchandise received directly in department. (Important for executive to countersign—report exceptions to security).
   b. Jobs should be clearly defined.
   c. Sale of salvage goods disapproved.

d. Losses should be reported immediately.
e. Guard coverage at receiving door.
f. Special Christmas protection for receiving basements.
g. No apron may be issued unless the merchandise is actually being received at the time.

Delivery and Packing

Packing

1. Training department should train in system.
2. Special cashier at busy stations.
3. Physical setup of stations—locations.
4. No package to be wrapped without proper salescheck.
5. No one to wrap own merchandise.
6. Packing material not to be given out without approval.
7. Packer's number to appear on each package.
8. Number of enclosures noted.
9. Record of overgoods and shortages.
10. Small articles transferred in cloth bags.
11. Packers should cancel price tags.
12. Close check on receipt of supplies.
13. Price tickets chopped—not torn—when stubbed.
14. Packers not to handle bank checks, credit, and refunds.
15. Record and investigate cash shortages.
16. Cash stamps and boxes always locked when left.
17. Special Christmas precautions.
18. No erasures accepted.
19. Special check of job applicants—cashier and packer.

Delivery

1. Spotlight on delivery door at night.
2. Multiple sends need good authorization.
3. Customer's own merchandise authorization on address label.
4. No erasures accepted.
5. Duplicate delivery record control. Approval required.
6. Wrong address.
7. Special precautions—furs, jewelry, fountain pens.
8. Parcel post—control from store to post office.
9. Return goods need strong controls.
10. Manufacturer returns—see receiving.
11. Special protection on "hold" room—do not hold too long.
12. Control on uninsured parcel post losses.

Maintenance

1. Important that they report proposed physical changes—submit copy of all plans to security for approval.
   a. Cash register control.
   b. Cash register supervision.
   c. Porters not to handle money.

d. Check all who leave early.
e. Supervision of night porters.
f. Supervise physical changes.
g. Stockrooms—not to be shared—locked where possible.
h. Packing station: counter to separate packer and salesperson. Integrate cashier at busy stations. Use cash registers.
i. Fitting rooms: orderly layout.
   Curtains—not doors.
   Common exit and entrance.
j. Cashiers:
   Provision for relief drawer.
   Alarm button.
k. Service desk:
   Good location.
   Place for storage of merchandise.
   Place for refuse (wrappings).
   Signal light.
   Locked cabinet for credit books.
   Facilities for distribution of salesbook.
   Side entrance for attendants.
l. Executive office: not off hallways. Go through reception office first.
m. New departments: special provision for salesbooks and writing of saleschecks.
n. Have attendant at incinerator or in refuse room turn over merchandise discharged by mistake. Make created system tests.

Adjustments

1. Monthly report on wrong address returns.
2. Interview applicant for questionable refunds.
3. Monthly report on delivery shortages.
4. Wrong address—control issue—record follow up—don't hold too long.
5. All refund exceptions through adjusting; reported to security.
6. Unfair complaint file.
7. Refunds where improper deductions are made in charges against salary. Employees fail to take discount. (Manufacturing samples?)
8. Refund bank checks returned—wrong address.
9. Report payments on credit-balance charge account.
10. Control of adjustment credits.
11. Spot check of adjustment credits, particularly in departments with large shortages.

Supply Department

1. Control on issuance of forms.
   a. Refunds
   b. Merchandise credits
   c. Adjustment credits
   d. Duplicate delivery records

   e. Duplicate saleschecks
   f. Training saleschecks
   g. Customer's own merchandise saleschecks
   h. Manufacturer returns and claim books
   i. Suburban transfers
   j. Customer cash receipts
   k. Labels
2. No new forms or changes without security approval.
3. Setup for orders by purchasing department:
   a. Bid necessary over fixed amount.
   b. Records kept.
4. Special signature for payment of bills over $250.
5. System for disposal of salvage (not to be sold to employees).

Alteration Rooms

1. Employees arriving early in the morning should be checked.
2. Closer cooperation between security department and alteration room.
3. Workrooms not to be scattered.
4. Strict control of ornaments for dresses, etc.
5. Packing material not to be available.
6. One location for cleaning and alteration rooms.
7. Customer's own merchandise survey (periodic).
8. Have system of garment and salescheck control.

Service Building

1. Furniture delivery system.
2. Fur storage system.
3. Workroom plan system.
4. Building pass.
5. Direct sends.
6. Periodic inspection.

FINANCE

Accounts Payable

1. Control and check on the mailing of refunds.
2. Person who prepares bank checks should not receive the check again after it is signed.
3. Printed number on bank checks should be used as control.
4. Special check should be arranged to prevent duplicates to manufacturers.
5. Authorize manufacturer returns and claims.
6. Control of credit memorandum.
7. Bills for the payment of merchandise received directly in the departments should be approved by important executive.
8. Bank checks over a certain amount—when signature is necessary—should not be routine or informal signature.

Accounts Receivable

1. Bookkeeping uses the posting date and not the date of purchase.
2. Control to be placed on charge accounts so that excessive balances will be reported to security manager promptly ($400).
3. No changes or erasures are permitted in papers supporting bank checks.
4. Control on accounts with credit balances.
5. All impostor chargeoffs reported to security.
6. Charges against salary reported to security.
7. Debit credit ledger control.
8. Uninsured parcel post losses.
9. Security approval required for payment of bills in cases of short or lost shipments.
10. No cash taken off debit credit ledger without proper approval.

Auditing

1. Missing cash and C.O.D. checks should be referred to security at once. Preaudit would be helpful.
2. Need effective salesbook control renewal stub.
3. Salesbook to be opened from issue stub—not first check.
4. Weekly check for salesbook not used recommended.
5. Improperly authorized saleschecks, even exchanges, customer's own merchandise, voids, etc., refer to security department.
6. Control on missing triplicates to be referred to security as soon as possible.
7. Auditing has control of issuance of merchandise credit books.
8. Auditing has control of issuance of adjustment credit books.
9. Auditing controls issuance of customer's own merchandise books.
10. Auditing should have list of missing original house charges. Repeated offenders investigated.
11. Auditing reports to security irregular refunds for investigation.
12. Send refund test postcards and make other inquiries.
13. Record should be kept for shortages and overages of all cashiers. Regular report to security.
14. Stub for renewal of credit books.
15. Control for salesbooks not used in past week.
16. Improperly voided checks reported to security department.

Bill and Order Room

1. Monthly reports of merchandise received directly in departments.

Cashiers

1. Expense voucher control.
2. Returned bank checks inspected daily by security department.
3. Returned refunds reported daily to security.
4. Cashier daily reports periodically inspected by security.
5. Cash collections by guards of packers and floor cashiers of excessive money, especially during sales and Christmas and Easter seasons.
6. Cash bag variations reported to security daily.

7. Payroll shortages reported to security weekly.
8. Tube room report of claims to security department immediately.
9. Report all improper refunds to security department immediately.
10. Forward bank checks requiring change to credit office for approval.
11. Special investigations of all cashier personnel.
12. Payroll funds balanced by supervisor.
13. Forms should be controlled.
14. Money should not be transferred from one cashier to another.
15. Security department will make periodic checks for stamps not properly located when not in use.
16. Co-mingling of funds disapproved.
17. System of adjusting change bag errors often unsatisfactory; often makes overcharge one day and shortage another day.
18. All claims sent to security office the following day.
19. Voucher to balance on claim; when necessary must be approved by security.
20. Service manager responsible in connection with carriers.
21. Control of persons to whom payroll can be given.
22. Control of return of undistributed payroll envelopes.
23. Limited amount of money to be given to each person unless special arrangements are made.
24. Alarm in all cashier cages.
25. Payment on charge accounts, duplicate receipts—numbered control.
26. No direct entrance to cashiers' booths.
27. Periodic check on cash registers for lost money.
28. Investigation of persistent shortages and overages to prevent recurrence.
29. Periodic survey suggested of incoming mail, particularly the cashier part of it.
30. Good supervision needed of miscellaneous cashiers throughout the store.
31. Gift certificates—close control on issuance—no money refunded.
32. Payroll and service—gift certificates—printed amounts in different colors.
33. Limitation of change to be issued on gift certificates.
34. Control should start when book is issued.
35. Special night protection should be arranged for cashiers' cages.
36. System of basic rules should be set up for training program of miscellaneous cashiers.
37. Required space and equipment for each cashier's booth should be determined.
38. Relief drawer should be considered in this planning.
39. All cashier paperwork except bank checks should go to the auditing department.
40. Special care in branch stores.
41. Special arrangements should be made for the closing of the safes at night.
42. Payroll cashiers should report to the security office all persons receiving no salary.
43. A staggered system of paydays should be considered.
44. Shortages on registers should be reported to salespeople.
45. "No sales" and "voids" should be reduced to a minimum. Excessive number investigated.

46. Tube room should be reserved for unusual transactions.
47. Responsible person should be in charge of tube room.
48. Transfer or selling of cashier work undesirable.
49. IOU increase of bank recommended.
50. Change machines for customers recommended.
51. Cashiers should have some kind of control on expense vouchers.
52. Security manager to sign claims for payroll shortages.
53. Review cash register instructions.
54. Guards supervise locking of safes.
55. Security instructions posted in tube room.
56. Spot check, cashier's stamps. (Locked?)

Charge Office

1. Authorization: $50.
2. Identification: $50—first floor.
   $100—upper floors.
   Make proper record.
   Consider identification card.
3. Part paid and part charge transactions should be looked into.
4. $400 limit and excessive credit control—see bookkeeping.
5. Where charge account is closed—send letter to customer.
6. "No account checks"—secure as soon as possible for investigation.
7. All repudiated charges referred to security as soon as possible.
8. Repudiation statements signed before transfer.
9. Maintain bad bank check file.
10. Bank checks—cashing:
    a. Limit number of persons authorized to approve.
    b. Limit amount—charge account $50.00.
    c. Checks not cashed if no charge account.
    d. Do not authorize check for purchase.
11. Practice:
    a. Have customer sign or endorse check in your presence.
    b. Identify customer.
    c. Note identification on back of check near edge.
    d. Sign and date back of check.
12. Precautionary elements:
    a. Third-party checks.
    b. Checks on blank forms.
    c. Checks on out-of-town banks.
    d. Checks offered when banks are closed.
    e. Checks with identification from different places.
13. Action where precaution is indicated:
    a. Examine bad bank check file.
    b. Verify address given by customer.
    c. Check with bank.
    d. Notify security—check credit bureau—burns.
14. Bank checks—where change is being given.
    a. On purchases, all bank checks requiring change sent to charge office.

b. Cashier may give up to $25 change in payment of account.
c. Above $25 charge office must approve.
d. Routine on saleschecks:
   (1) Sent in tube to charge office.
   (2) Examine face of salescheck:
      "Bank check"
      Customer's name and address.
      Amount of salescheck and amount of change compared ($50 limit).
      Section manager's signature.
      Identification on back of salescheck.
      Face of bank check:
         Proper date.
         Name and address of bank.
         Amounts in figure and writing agree.
         Full signature of customer.
      Back of bank check:
         Cross reference (near edge).
         Endorsement if necessary.
         Charge office authorizer signs and dates back of approved bank check.
         Charge office authorizer returns both bank check and salescheck to floor.

15. Control employee charges against salary.

Inventory

Inventory—security must get prompt report of shortages.
Plan for taking inventory must be thoroughly prepared.
Comparison of count with book should be facilitated.
Record kept of shortage by department.

Stock Shortages

Actual

1. Unrecorded loans
2. Unrecorded losses
3. Price ticket lost—improper returns
4. Movement—small articles in cartons—spot check
5. Fitting Rooms
6. Employees—cover at night
   No coats in department
   Purchases checked
7. Inaccurate measure or weight
8. Manufacturer returns
9. Improper receiving in department
10. Breakage—short shipments
11. Interselling

Figure

1. Improper markdowns
2. Improper credits
3. Invoice errors
4. Salescheck errors
5. Sample errors

Mail

1. Incoming mail
   Cash control
   Returned store bank checks "unknown at address."
2. Outgoing mail
   Control of sample sending for executive accommodation.

Treasurer's Office

1. Check upon all employees.
2. Survey terms of general protection insurance policies.
3. Also check armored car service.

Timekeeper

1. Person who takes attendance not to handle salaries.
2. Need good timekeeping system.

MERCHANDISING

Advertising

1. Arrangements for disposition of used merchandise in advertising.
2. Special address labels have been provided for the use of the sending of envelopes containing pictures or samples through special delivery agencies.
3. Deliveries by advertising department should be closely supervised.

Departments—Special Precautions

1. Fur department—need good system of identification for fur coats. Special stockroom precautions should be enforced. Special arrangements should be made for the display of expensive furs. Special delivery control on furs.
2. Fur storage—make regular fur storage surveys.
3. Jewelry—showcase to be electrically locked. Same provision for jewelry in men's shop. Display restrictions should be enforced. Only the better trained salespersons should handle the more expensive jewelry.
4. Luggage—some kind of selling mark should be placed on luggage that is sold and taken unwrapped from the department.
5. Candy—the candy department offers special problems in its multiple Christmas sends.
6. Service building sends—service building sends require special control.
7. Every traffic department should be separated as much as possible and not bunched together.
8. Expensive merchandise—special registration.

Display—Interior

1. Special precautions for particular departmental displays. Wallets held by rubber bands—not displayed in groups. Gloves not displayed in bunches. Large displays of similar articles should have some order to them—for example, handbags displayed in groups of six.

2. Experience has shown that small expensive articles cannot be used in unprotected open displays or as accessories for special home furnishing displays.
3. Fixed responsibility for displays in departments.
4. Displays should be checked for price tickets.
5. Interior display department to be charged for lost or damaged merchandise.
6. Special arrangements to be made for the disposition of displayed merchandise that cannot be returned to stock—e.g., stockings—see employee sale section.
7. Greater use of cellophane covers for displayed merchandise.
8. Street floor counter displays should be removed at night. Showcases containing expensive merchandise should be locked.

Display—Window

1. Special protection for expensive displays:
   a. Lock windows—keep key
   b. Remove at night
   c. Special guard
   d. Fire protection
   e. Barriers

Fitting Rooms

1. Orderly arrangements of fitting rooms recommended.
2. Common entrance and exit for each bank of fitting rooms recommended.
3. Departments not to share fitting rooms.
4. In large volume departments where a comparatively small number of fitting rooms is available, it is suggested that rooms be assigned to particular salesclerks or groups of salesclerks for their use exclusively. Hold them responsible for merchandise clearance.

Interselling

1. Good interselling system suggested.
2. Accessory bars should be set up as different departments.

Inventories

1. Special fund put in control for constant delivery returns and manufacturer returns.
2. Special precautions for the distribution of used packing material in which merchandise is received. A great deal of merchandise is recovered from the incinerator room.

Delivery Shortages

1. Merchandise received in store should be at least spot checked into the department as well as in the return goods room and the receiving room.
2. Special inventory for each new buyer at the time he assumes responsibilities.
3. Odd amount prices used so that change will have to be given. Tends to decrease dishonesty by employees.

4. See provision against kickbacks in the penal law.
5. Special control to get all credits back to stock.
6. Unit controls and special stock counts used to check actual shortage (percentage can be estimated).

Markdowns

1. More care should be exercised in these cases.
2. Marking of merchandise for sales.
3. It is often possible to return reduced merchandise and secure full credit.
4. Markdowns checked against unit control.
5. Carelessness in "as is" sales dangerous.

Models

1. Special model supervision. Suggest model room be off buyer's office with curtain—not a door. Suggest closer supervision of models. Suggest uniform treatment of models throughout the store.
2. Informal modeling when necessary should be done on an I.O.U. loan basis only.

Personal Shopping

1. Suggest this service be tied in with mail and telephone orders.
2. Special training should be arranged for manager in these departments.
3. Hold personal shopping department accountable for losses.

Promotions

1. Special services and promotions should be carefully organized. This applies to the personal shopping, uniform shopping, brides shop, college shop, etc.
2. Follow-up on all loans of personal shoppers should be done regularly.
3. Whenever a new deaprtment is considered, a special survey should be made so that its services will fit in with the general system of the store.
4. Security department should be advised of special promotions. Arrangements should be made to handle traffic, etc.

Special Deliveries

1. Door passes required for manufacturer's samples brought into the building.

Stockrooms

1. Not to be shared.
2. Not too far from department.

Assistant Buyers

1. Take interest in merchandise from protection standpoint.
   a. Is stockroom securely locked after hours?
   b. Can physical arrangement of department be improved?
2. Report losses promptly.

3. Supervise:
   a. Stockclerks and other clericals
   b. Branch transfers
4. Spot check:
   a. Merchandise from receiving room
   b. Merchandise from return goods room (also prices)
   c. Loan book
5. Displays—adequately protected
6. Price tags—correct and secure
7. Credits
   a. Spot check merchandise credits
   b. Control for adjustment credits
8. Manufacturer returns—spot check shipments, shortage claims, and employee sales
   a. Send greatly reduced merchandise to employee store—do not give away in department.
9. Relieve section manager—be familiar with section manager's instructions.
10. Manufacturers
    a. Direct deliveries, *never*
11. Buyers of assistants are required to check monthly purchase journal.

Appendix 5

EMERGENCY ACTION

Following is an emergency booklet for your key executives. It tells them what to do if an emergency occurs. This booklet suggests basic principles to be followed whether the emergency is a wastebasket fire or an atomic bomb attack. This can serve as a model for a similar program in any store.

EMERGENCY ACTION BOOKLET

Introduction

Every year PANIC adds needless deaths to fires, floods, and other catastrophic events. Fear of the unknown suddenly triggers a group reaction of terror. This destroys self-control and impels people to frantic action. Such action is often self-destructive.

An unknown person on the night of November 28, 1942, pushed the PANIC BUTTON and 491 people died. This was in Boston at the Coconut Grove fire.

Such things occur every year. Many of them can be prevented. A calm, decisive leader who uses a plan of action worked out in *advance* can often prevent a major tragedy.

At any moment of any day a crisis situation may start in your work area. Customers and fellow employees will turn to you for help. How you act and what you do at that critical moment will be of vital importance.

As a Control Leader, you are one of the people who will be responsible for the human life and property within your store during this emergency.

These situations come in all sizes and types, but you must be prepared to deal with each crisis along lines carefully planned in advance.

You must know what to do if: A child screams and you see her small hand has been caught in the escalator belt.

A fire breaks out in a paper chute, and smoke fills the selling floor.

A sprinkler head breaks open and 50 gallons of water a minute pour over counters and merchandise.

A customer drops a perfume bottle she is examining and glass fragments, as well as liquid perfume, splash across the floor.

A woman reports that a windstorm has blown out a showwindow and glass litters the sidewalk outside your store.

A couple of overeager boys smash the glass in a revolving door, and one of them bleeds from a gash on his wrist.

An anonymous phone call reports a bomb has been planted somewhere in your store. It is set to go off in one hour.

A suicide leaps from an upper story window and panics the crowds of people on the street below.

There is a sudden power failure. Lights go out and elevators, as well as escalators, grind to a halt.

A customer falls and is hurt.

Word arrives that the city is under air attack.

Many of these things have already happened in our store. Many of them will occur again—today, tomorrow, or next week. You, as a Control Leader, must be ready to handle them.

In order to prepare yourself for the coming moment of crisis, here are three things you can do:

1. During normal periods, prepare yourself for the moment of emergency.
2. Be familiar with the contents of this book. Study it often to keep the material fresh in your mind.
3. Remember that, as a leader of people, you have a duty in times of crisis to set an inspiring leadership example. Remain calm—act with intelligence—be decisive.

One person who looks calm and goes about his duties in a businesslike way can do a great deal to avoid panic among hundreds of others. *Stay calm*—don't push the PANIC BUTTON!

General

We cannot outline in advance all of the actions to be taken in emergency situations. In the end it will be your own good judgment that will decide the actions to be taken.

However, you can prepare yourself, to a great extent, by knowing certain basic actions to be taken and by learning needed facts, such as the location of sprinkler turnoff valves, fire extinguishers, etc. These may be important in handling the crisis.

We will cover two types of critical situations: the *localized emergency* and the *evacuation emergency*. The first deals with problems that can be handled within your own area of control. The second deals with large-scale situations when a floor or entire building evacuation is required because of a major fire or air attack.

Localized Emergency

Most crises fall under this heading. Things such as escalator injuries, sprinkler-head leaks, small fires, power failure, etc.

The actions you take as the Control Leader are as varied as the problems themselves, but in all cases these basic points should be covered.

1. Take any immediate action needed to protect the customer or employee against injury or loss of life.
2. Take any immediate action necessary to protect your store's properties against loss, damage, or destruction. Return the selling area to normal as soon as possible.
3. Communicate with any other areas necessary to bring the situation back to normal, such as:
   Hospital
   Building maintenance
   Bureau of adjustment
4. Always keep management informed. Report any emergency directly to your supervisor.

In addition to these general guides, you should also know the following facts for the area where you work.

Know the location of:

1. Fire extinguishers
2. Fire alarm boxes
3. Sprinkler control valves
4. Wheelchairs
5. Teletalk system
6. Escalator shutoff buttons
7. Light control panels
8. Phones
9. Emergency lights
10. First aid kits

Communication

In matters of injury:

Phone the hospital

In matters of broken glass, spilled liquids, power failures, smoke, fire, sprinkler break, or anything pertaining to the building or property:

Phone building maintenance

In matters of torn or damaged customer clothing or loss or destruction of customer property:

Phone the bureau of adjustment

In matters of violence, crime or general disturbance:

Phone the security department

In matters of major catastrophe:

Phone the general superintendent

When several areas must be notified and when time is an important factor:

Phone the switchboard operator and ask her to notify the departments or the people concerned

Application of this Emergency Information

Let us see how this knowledge could be applied in specific problems.

Problem 1: A woman faints at the foot of an escalator.

Action to Be Taken: Applying fundamental principle number 1 (Take any immediate action necessary to protect the customer or employee against injury or loss of life), you would move the woman a few feet away from the escalator so that other customers coming down the moving stairway would not step or fall on the customer.

Next, following fundamental principle number 3 (communicate with any other department necessary to bring the situation back to normal), you would have someone phone the hospital, explaining the situation and you would act on their advice. If they said that the woman should be brought to the store hospital, you would direct someone to get the wheelchair located on your floor. (The location of the wheelchair would be known to you because of your advance preparation in learning the location of specific emergency equipment).

In a very few minutes you would have the customer in the hands of competent medical help and your floor emergency situation would be back to normal.

As a final action you would follow fundamental rule number 4 (always keep management informed by reporting any emergency situation directly to your supervisor) by contacting your supervisor and reporting all the facts concerning the incident to him.

Problem 2: A wastebasket catches fire behind a counter and flames leap up, causing items on the shelf above to burn.

Action to Be Taken: Following fundamental rule number 2, you would get the nearest fire extinguisher. (You would know where the fire extinguisher is because you would have learned this in your study of the location of special emergency equipment.)

While getting the extinguisher, you would delegate someone to phone the building maintenance department (fundamental rule number 3), and tell them what was occurring so they could send additional help to put out the fire and later to clean up the area. When the fire has been extinguished, you would notify your supervisor of the problem and action taken.

(Warning: If a fire is electrical, do not use a standard liquid fire extinguisher but the foam type designed for electrical fires.)

Problem 3: A sprinkler head suddenly breaks and a torrent of water pours out, dousing some customers as well as a counter full of merchandise.

Action to Be Taken: (Following fundamental rule number 1) you would immediately locate and turn off the sprinkler control valve to stop the water flow. You would then phone building maintenance so they could send help to clean up the area and fix the sprinkler valve. You would also phone the bureau of adjustment regarding the customers who got wet and have them escorted to the adjustment office, for example, if their clothes require cleaning, pressing, or replacement.

You would also, of course, report the entire matter to your supervisor (fundamental rule number 4).

Problem 4: A large portion of ceiling plaster falls, knocking down several customers and employees—it is immediately evident that this is a major emergency.

Action to Be Taken: Stay *calm*—don't push the PANIC button! Phone the switchboard operator and explain clearly and briefly what has occurred; instruct her to phone the general superintendent, hospital, building maintenance, and security departments.

While you are waiting for help to arrive, try to keep the customers and employees calm in order to prevent panic. Take whatever action you can to prevent further injuries and to help those people who have been hurt.

These examples have not been given with the intention of laying out any specific actions to be taken in a given situation—each emergency is an individual problem and must be dealt with in relation to conditions as they are at that time. Our intent here is only to illustrate how you can use the emergency principles.

We believe these "working tools," when combined with your own personal experience in handling people and your good judgment, can help you work out a constructive solution to any localized emergency situation.

Evacuation Emergency

In this section we will review the actions to be followed in case of a large-scale crisis, such as a major fire, explosion, or air attack.

You may never have to use the procedures outlined here, but you should study and learn them as if they would be needed tomorrow.

The following information will be directed primarily toward the problem of an air attack; however, it can be used as a basic plan for building evacuation. It is intended to serve as a *master plan* for any type of major emergency.

THE ALERT

In event of a major emergency, the alert will be sounded by sirens that are placed throughout the store and the warehouses. The signal will be THREE continuous blasts lasting 10 seconds each. ALL CLEAR will be one 30-second sounding of the sirens.

(The night superintendent is in charge of the emergency organization at night. All persons in the store during a night alert are to go to the first basement if at all possible. Since there will be no floor controllers at night, night personnel will receive individual instructions on what they are to do in case of an alert.)

Communication After the Alert

Teletalk System: A teletalk system has been installed with stations on each floor and at the warehouses. As soon as the alert is sounded, floor controllers will go at once to the emergency center on their floor. Each floor controller must know the location of the center for his floor and how to use the communication equipment.

Upon hearing the alert, all directors and alternate floor controllers will go at once to the area near the communication center to receive instructions from their floor controller.

Telephone Service: During the alert, store phones and pay stations will be for emergency use only by authorized members of the emergency control organization. On store phones, dial "0" for operator and tell her who you want to talk to. In case of breakdown of telephone or Teletalk, the superintendent's office will send persons throughout the store to instruct floor controllers.

Traffic Control

One of your important jobs will be handling employees and customers to insure their own safety. Thousands of people will be in the store during a daytime emergency and you must give them calm, intelligent leadership. This is vital in saving life and preventing injury.

In case of an air attack, it will be safer in the store or warehouses than on the street. It is URGENT that all areas near the outside walls be kept clear, for they are least safe. People may want to rush to the windows to "see what's going on." But on every floor, employees and customers are to keep away from the windows because of the danger from flying fragments of shattered glass.

Each floor controller will have a floor plan showing which areas on his floor are safest in an atomic attack and which elevators and stairways should be used to go to other areas, if necessary. Floor controllers should make sure that each member of their staff has a copy of the floor plan. Elevator operators have been instructed on procedure during the alert and will provide for movement of emergency control people and equipment.

Evacuate all people from the top floor of every building. Tell people to WALK. Except for the top floors, floors are about equally safe and nothing is gained by rushing to another area.

Floor Controllers:

1. As soon as the alert sounds, go to your station. Alternate controllers, directors, first aid crews, stairway and escalator guards, and entrance guards are under your supervision on the floor where they are assigned.
2. You are responsible for training of emergency control organization people assigned to you. All members of your staff should have copies of the plan showing areas on your floor which are safest.
3. Your staff must be complete at all times. Vacancies should be filled at once and reported monthly to the employment manager.
4. Know the "Six Survival Secrets for Atomic Attack" listed in the back of this booklet. Be sure every member of your staff knows them.
5. Regular check of emergency equipment on your floor is your responsibility.
6. Emergency conditions such as fires, leaks, shattered windows, etc., should be reported to Damage Control, Ext. ______. (In case of a power failure, use the Teletalk system). Summon additional first aid as needed from the hospital.
7. Make sure everyone in offices, washrooms, etc., has heard the alert.
8. Keep cool. Be firm. Your example will do much to keep order. You are responsible for human lives.

Alternate Floor Controllers:

1. As soon as the alert sounds, report to the area near the emergency center on your floor. Be ready to assist the floor controller in taking the instructions to your group.
2. Assist your floor controller in every way possible in training the emergency organization for your floor, in directing their work during an alert, and in any way that helps the efficiency of the group.
3. In the absence of the floor controller, you will direct the group on your floor.

Directors:

1. As soon as the alert sounds, report to the area near the emergency center on your floor. Your floor controller will send you to your assigned station or, if necessary, to another area.
2. Keep calm and direct people to the safest areas on your floor. Avoid crowding. Tell people to WALK.

Stairway and Escalator Guards:

1. As soon as the alert sounds, go to your station. Direct people to safe stairways if they are to move to another floor, and keep people from using stairways that the floor controller has declared unsafe.
2. Keep cool and set an example that will prevent panic. This is not easy in the face of an emergency, but it can be done.

3. After you have directed people to safe areas, go to the nearest safe area for your own protection.
4. After the attack, return to your station to see that no one returns to any unsafe area leading from your stairway or escalator. Remain at your station after the all clear until people have returned to their floors.

Entrance Guards:

1. As soon as the alert sounds, go to your station. You will, in general, be responsible for traffic coming in or going out of the store. Keep good order and prevent crowding. Tell people to WALK.
2. People who want to leave the store should be told that an air raid alert is in effect and that it is safer to stay in the building. They should not be prevented from leaving.
3. Basement entrance guards are responsible for light switches covering these entrances and will take proper precautions to prevent people from falling on the stairs.
4. After you have directed people to safe areas, go to the nearest safe area for your own protection.
5. After the attack, keep employees and customers inside the building until it has been declared safe to leave. There may be danger from radioactivity following an atomic attack.

First Aid

(Insert location of store hospital and emergency first aid stations.)

In the store there is an emergency water supply for use if the city water supply is cut off or contaminated. This water will be available for emergency use, including washing areas of the body exposed to radioactive contamination in an atomic attack. First aid crews will be notified as to the location of emergency water supply outlets.

First Aid Crews:

1. As soon as the alert sounds, go to your station.
2. Prepare all first aid equipment for immediate use if injured persons are brought to your station, or if you are called to assist in another area.
3. When the all clear sounds, return first aid equipment to its proper place in good order.

Emergency Equipment

There is emergency equipment on every floor at the emergency center. There are gauze bandages, antiseptic, sulpha powder, tape, and flashlights in the first aid box. Masks and other equipment will be in mobile units, to be sent to the areas where needed.

Special Information

Inspector Cashier Desks: When the alert sounds, cashiers will lock their tills and band them. Cashiers will keep keys on their person's during the alert.

Salespeople Operating Cash Registers: When the alert sounds, salespeople operating cash registers will lock their drawers and keep the key on their person during the alert.

Salesbooks and Tallies: Salesbooks are to be turned in to the floor manager at his desk as soon as the alert sounds.

Protection of Merchandise: Floor managers, buyers, and assistant buyers will do everything possible, with due regard to their personal safety, to protect merchandise when the alert sounds. Wherever possible, items should be removed from tops of counters and placed in stock cases to avoid damage and theft. Buyers should assign protection duties to each member of their staff for quick action in event of an alert.

Cars on the Road: Drivers of company cars or trucks will stop at the curb, turn out lights, lock the ignition, and set the hand brakes. Delivery trucks should be locked to protect the contents. Seek personal protection nearby until the all clear.

Machinery, Kitchens, Workrooms, etc.: When the alert sounds, operators will shut off all conveyors, presses, small tools, irons, sewing machines, etc. Turn off gas burners (except pilot lights). Steel doors at receiving and loading docks should be lowered.

Emergency Control Organization Personnel: Following is a list of personnel assigned to the emergency organization. The list will be revised and a copy given to you every three months. Keep this list up to date.

SIX SURVIVAL SECRETS FOR ATOMIC ATTACKS

1. *Try to Get Shielded*
   Should you be caught out of doors, seek shelter alongside a building or jump in any handy ditch or gutter.
2. *Drop Flat on Ground or Floor*
   To keep from being tossed about and to lessen the chances of being struck by flying objects, flatten out at the base of a wall or at the bottom of a bank.
3. *Bury Your Face in Your Arm*
   When you drop flat, hide your eyes in the crook of your elbow. That will protect your face from flash burns, prevent temporary blindness, and keep flying objects out of your eyes.
4. *Don't Rush Outside Right After a Bombing*
   After an air burst, wait a few minutes, and then go help to fight fires. After other kinds of bursts, wait at least one hour to give lingering radiation some chance to die down.

5. *Don't Use Food or Water in Open Containers*
   To prevent radioactive poisoning, select your food and water with care. When there is reason to believe they may be contaminated, stick to canned and bottled food if possible.
6. *Don't Start Rumors*
   In the confusion that follows a bombing, a single rumor might touch off a panic that could cost your life.

Appendix 6

SECURITY EDUCATION MEMOS

The following memos are intended to help bring the problem of losses to the attention of all employees who work in the store.

Although the memos are addressed to the department manager, the material is intended for all members of the department.

SAMPLE MEMO

Little Dutch Boy

To: All Department Managers

From: Inventory Shortage Control and Security Department

Subject: Security Is Everyone's Responsibility

We are all familiar with the legend of the Little Dutch Boy who saved Holland by holding his finger in the hole in the dike. The heroic action of this individual person saved a whole nation from disaster. This story of the noble Little Dutch Boy has an application in modern business because he set an example of personal responsibility which had a far-reaching effect.

Sometimes in a big store we feel that we can't do anything as an individual that will effectively help to reduce inventory losses. It is easy for each of us to use this excuse as a way of avoiding our responsibilities. The truth is, however, that it is the small things we do as individuals every single day which in the end results in lower inventory shortages for our store.

Here are seven possible leaks in the dike. By stopping up these holes you can help to hold back the flood of "inventory shortages."

1. Eliminate carelessness wherever you find it.
2. Give good service to prevent loss.
3. Report all losses to the Security Department immediately.
4. Keep fitting rooms cleared of merchandise at all times.
5. Question anyone in your stockroom who is not from your department.
6. Check and double check written records to be sure that they are accurate.
7. Be constantly alert to prevent shortages and report anything of a suspicious nature to the Security Department immediately.

Because you are an employee who wants to do a good job every single day—be like the Little Dutch Boy—assume personal responsibility to do your part in fighting inventory shortages every single day.

Be like the Little Dutch Boy—help prevent shortages!

SAMPLE MEMO

Little Dutch Boy

To: All Department Managers

From: Inventory Shortage Control and Security Department

Subject: Protect Expensive Merchandise from Theft

(Please convey this information to your staff.)

Theft from shoplifters can be greatly reduced if salespeople are careful to put expensive merchandise away after showing it to a customer.

Wherever expensive merchandise is shown on counters, the careful salesclerk should return the merchandise that is not being displayed to stock.

The problem of shoplifters stealing merchandise left carelessly about is even more acute in departments where fitting rooms are used. Salesclerks in these departments should give special care to return merchandise to its proper place in stock immediately after the customer leaves. Many shoplifters look for fitting rooms where merchandise has been left. A salesclerk who has been careless places the merchandise directly into the thief's hands. Merchandise left in a fitting room is in danger of being stolen. Merchandise returned to its proper rod in stock is "safe."

Think of it this way, if you just bought a new mink coat, would you leave it back in the fitting room where anyone wandering down the aisle could see it and stuff it in a paper bag or coat box? It is more likely that you would keep it out in the open on the selling rod where it could be watched.

Our merchandise is as valuable to all of us as a mink coat would be to you. You can prevent a lot of loss if you would return your merchandise to stock immediately after showing it to the customer.

Be like the Little Dutch Boy, assume personal responsibility to prevent shortages!

SAMPLE MEMO

Little Dutch Boy

To: All Department Managers

From: Inventory Shortage Control and Security Department

Subject: Good Service Prevents Loss

(Please convey this information to your staff.)

A shoplifter finds it difficult, if not almost impossible, to steal if she is given good service. There are cases, of course, where shoplifters have stolen while being waited on, but they are very rare.

Try to give good service to all customers, but to help prevent shortages, salespeople should give special attention to anyone of a suspicious nature who comes into their department.

The following should get special attention:

- A woman who enters the handbag department or glove department without a handbag or her own gloves, etc.
- Schoolchildren looking at merchandise.
- A man in a small-article department with a newspaper under his arm.
- A woman who takes identical pieces of merchandise into a fitting room.
- A customer who tears off price tickets, places packages over merchandise, or does anything else of a suspicious nature.
- Whenever you have a questionable customer prevent him or her from causing a shortage by giving *good service!*

Be like the Little Dutch Boy, assume personal responsibility to prevent shortages!

SAMPLE MEMO

Little Dutch Boy

To: All Department Managers

From: Inventory Shortage Control and Security Department

Subject: Report All Losses

(Please convey this information to your staff.)

Report all losses to the Security Department *immediately*! The proper way to report a loss is for the salesclerk to notify her department manager who, in turn, will report the loss to the Security Department.

A great deal of security work is based on observing specific areas at specific times. For example, if a salesclerk reports that she notices lipsticks being taken from her counter between 1 and 2 o'clock on Thursdays, the Security Department can assign a detective to observe this particular area every Thursday from 1:00 to 2:00 P.M. As a result the shoplifter who is taking the lipsticks may be caught.

Another problem that faces every retail store is trying to determine what amount of inventory shortages is theft loss as against losses caused by general carelessness. When a department shows a high inventory shortage and a check of the security records show no losses reported by that department during a period of 6 months prior to the inventory, the question immediately arises as to whether the loss is a theft loss or is due to general carelessness.

If it is felt that part of the inventory shortage is a theft loss, the fact that no report was turned into the Security Department may indicate that the people in the department are not as alert as they should be and perhaps are not taking as much interest in their merchandise controls as would be desirable.

This problem can easily be compared to the problem of disease. If a doctor gets an early diagnosis of a disease condition, the patient may be cured. If, however, the report arrives too late, the results may be disastrous.

If the Security Department gets an early report of a shortage condition, steps may be taken to prevent a more serious shortage. So, whenever a loss occurs, report it to your department manager immediately.

Be like the Little Dutch Boy, assume personal responsibility to prevent shortages!

SAMPLE MEMO

Little Dutch Boy

To: All Department Managers

From: Inventory Shortage Control and Security Department

Subject: Carelessness

(Please convey this information to your staff.)

As you can see, the soiled hand of *carelessness* has touched this Little Dutch Boy memo.

Carelessness often leaves its mark, though seldom as obviously as on this memo. Perhaps there are papers on your desk this very moment that have been touched by *carelessness*. It is a busy vicious elf, constantly at work undermining efficiency and creating loss.

Carelessness chortles with glee when:

- A salesclerk quotes a price from memory instead of having merchandise reticketed.
- Markdowns are inaccurate.
- A careless count is made of goods for branch store transfer.
- A packer fails to check the salescheck with merchandise for price and quantity.
- Figures are written hurriedly, so they become illegible.

And so, on and on in an endless chain of small errors the snowball rolls to become an avalanche of mistakes.

Almost all loss is caused basically by *carelessness*. High inventory shortages can be prevented by fighting this grimy little elf wherever you find him at work.

Let us make this a time to find every careless operation and correct it. Make those that work with you conscious of the part that carelessness plays in creating shortages.

Eliminate *carelessness* wherever you find it because *carelessness* leads to loss.

Be like the Little Dutch Boy, assume personal responsibility to prevent shortages!

SAMPLE MEMO

Little Dutch Boy

To: All Department Managers

From: Inventory Shortage Control and Security Department

Subject: Question Any Stranger Found in Stockrooms

(Please convey this information to your staff.)

Question anyone you find in your stockroom who is not from your department!

An alert salesclerk saw a man walking around in her stockroom looking at blueprints. A less alert person might have dismissed the matter as being none of her business, but this salesperson realized that no one had any business in her stockroom other than people from her own department.

So, she approached the man with the blueprints and asked if she could help him. He told her he was checking the sprinkler system, and at this time the salesperson had the good sense to ask him for his identification. He said that he did not have any but that she could check him by phone, which she agreed to do. As they started toward the office where the phone was located, he dropped his blueprints and ran out of the building.

Obviously, this man was laying the ground work for a major theft from a stockroom. Many professional thieves steal from stockrooms; therefore, it is up to all of us to be as alert as this salesclerk.

Question anyone you find in your stockroom who is not from your department. If for any reason you cannot identify them, notify your department manager at once. Anyone in your stockroom should be first approved by your department manager or some other executive such as the buyer, assistant buyer, etc.

Whenever you see a suspicious looking person in any of the back areas of our store, notify your department manager so that an investigator from the Security Department may be called to check immediately on the person, to find out who he is and what he is doing in the nonselling area.

Be like the Little Dutch Boy, assume personal responsibility to prevent shortages!

SAMPLE MEMO

Little Dutch Boy

To: All Department Managers

From: Inventory Shortage Control and Security Department

Subject: Double Check All Records

(Please convey this information to your staff.)

Check and double check all records! A record loss may be just as much an actual loss as a theft.

If a salesperson fails to charge the correct amount for merchandise, a loss occurs. If a buyer fails to take her markdown, a loss occurs. If the receiving room is not careful in checking incoming merchandise, a manufacturer may short change us. That again is an actual loss.

If a salesclerk hastily writes a charge salescheck illegibly, the customer cannot be charged for the article because the account cannot be found.

To reduce this type of loss, check and double check all written records, be sure that your writing is legible, and that the prices you quote are accurate.

Do not go under the misapprehension that every loss is a theft. Inaccurate records can cause as much damage as a shoplifter or any other malefactor.

Be like the Little Dutch Boy, assume personal responsibility to prevent shortages!

SAMPLE MEMO

Little Dutch Boy

To: All Department Managers

From: Inventory Shortage Control and Security Department

Subject: Report anything of a suspicious nature to the Security Department

(Please convey this information to your staff.)

If you see a man loitering on a stairway, if you find a stockclerk wandering through the executive offices, if you find an empty hanger behind a door or a price ticket torn from a garment, or if you notice anything that you think is questionable, report it at once to the Security Department. In many cases there may be a logical explanation for what you have observed, but you may also give us a clue that when investigated will uncover an important source of loss from our store.

So, no matter how far-fetched it may seem to you, if you find anything out of the ordinary, report it at once to the Security Department.

Let's review all of the points covered in our Little Dutch Boy memos.

1. Eliminate carelessness wherever you find it. Carelessness leads to loss.
2. Give good service to prevent theft.
3. Report all losses to Security immediately.
4. Question anyone you find in your stock room who is not from your department.
5. Keep your fitting rooms cleared of merchandise at all times.
6. Check and double check all written records to be sure they are accurate.
7. Report anything of a suspicious nature to Security at once.

Remember, the story of the Little Dutch Boy, his heroic action as an individual saved a whole country.

The small things you can do every day to help in the protection of your store will do a lot to prevent losses.

Be like the Little Dutch Boy, assume personal responsibility to prevent shortages!

Appendix 7

EDUCATIONAL TALKS FOR STORE EXECUTIVES

Security talks intended for executives in the store can prove valuable in winning cooperation and interest. When outlining such talks the caliber and intelligence of the executive level should be considered.

Following is an example of a talk given to store executives at the assistant buyer level and above. Note that it assumes the audience is imaginative and creative, and that strong emotional appeals are utilized.

The talk was combined with projected slides showing examples of the points discussed. Photos of specific malefactors showed men and women with their faces buried in their hands. The slides were all posed and had strong dramatic impact.

Ghosts: A Sample Executive Talk

Do you believe in ghosts? Perhaps you're thinking it's not the time of day to be talking about such things, or you're puzzled because you look on our store as only a business establishment where such things as ghosts have no place in the daily task of serving customers and earning profits. If you feel this way, you're wrong—and I'll tell you why.

What Is a Ghost?

Business, just like any other segment of our life, be it our recreation, our religion, our social activities, is the result of one common denominator—people. Business, like all of our other activities, is only the expression of human personality. And as soon as people are involved, we then leave the door open to ghosts as well. For what are ghosts but the memories of people no longer present?

What has all this to do with shortages? With store security?

Actually, as I think you'll agree, it has a lot to do with shortages. Because this morning gathered here in this room with us are the memories of 64 former store employees. They are the ghosts we are here to talk about today.

Only six weeks ago, they moved among us as our associates. We worked beside them, talked and laughed with them, knew them as we know each other. This morning they are here as ghostly memories—crowding about the room. All of you probably recognize some of their faces as they stand before you. Some shifting self-consciously from one foot to the other—some with tear-stained faces—some angry and defiant as they look directly at us—accusingly perhaps as though *we* had some part in the unhappiness that has come upon them.

And what did these dishonest employees do to our store? The place where they earned their living—did they do much damage? How badly did they hurt us? Perhaps you can see in their transparent pockets the money stolen from our cash registers—do you recognize the merchandise piled about their feet? Merchandise stolen from our counters, our stockrooms, our warehouses?

How Much Damage Can Ghosts Do?

What damage could 64 people do to a store like ours? These 64 people admitted they had stolen over $50,000 in cash and merchandise from our store. Does that seem like a lot?

How much merchandise must we sell in order to make up this $50,000? Over $3,000,000 worth. We must sell over $3,000,000 worth of merchandise just to break even for the thefts they have admitted.

And does this loss directly affect us? Of course it does, it affects the raise we are expecting, it affects our bonus, it cannot help but affect our future as an executive and as an individual because anything that hurts the store is going to hurt us. You and I *are* the store. A store is not only buildings and merchandise—it is people.

What Was the Cause?

But let's return to the situation itself. What has caused this widespread problem of internal theft? How did it come about? Who was responsible?

Profit is the life blood of our business. Is there any way we can stop the flow of this precious fluid out of the cuts and injuries made by people such as these?

Perhaps the answer can be found by an analysis of these 64 dishonest employee cases. That is why we are there today—to make such an analysis.

You and I are the leaders; in our hands alone rests the hope of solving this serious problem.

There are only four areas of search—where the thefts occurred—how they were committed—who did the stealing—and last—where was the area of responsibility? Let's take them each in turn.

Where Did It Happen?

First, where did these thefts occur? They occurred in 37 different departments throughout our store and warehouses. Candy, Records, Inspection, Art Supplies, Electrical Appliances, Cosmetics, Umbrellas, Dresses, Infants Wear, Men's Clothing, Interior Display, Monogramming, Return Goods, Warehouse Stock Rooms, and Cashiers, to name but a few.

They occurred throughout all areas of selling and throughout most areas of our nonselling operation. There is no pattern here except the one of prevalence. And this fact of prevalence alone is the most fearful pattern that could be diagnosed.

The disturbing fact is that the thefts were widespread, not limited to one or two areas. They cannot be isolated by location in the building or type of merchandise or kind of employee activity. This makes it immediately evident that we have no small problem here—no disease that can be suddenly cured tomorrow or the day after. This quick glance at where the thefts occurred suggests the gigantic task ahead of us—it shows that not one of us is in a position of immunity—that this problem of moral decay directly concerns every person in this room.

How Did It Happen?

And now let's turn to the methods of theft used by these 64 dishonest employees. We have prepared some slides to help clarify these methods. Members of the Security Department have posed for these pictures.

All together there were 16 methods of theft. Many of them used only one of these, but some used several. Let's examine a few.

Fraudulent Exchanges

One method was that of writing fraudulent even exchanges. A "friend" would come into the department and receive a package of merchandise made up by the dishonest salesperson, who would also make up a fraudulent even-exchange salescheck to cover the transaction.

Usually, the salesperson had a signature. Even though, she was not allowed to authorize her own saleschecks according to store policy, she would nevertheless sign her own check and give the duplicate with the stolen merchandise to her "friend." The accomplice would then leave the department with the package and another theft was successfully culminated.

How much merchandise was stolen this way? We have no way of knowing, but it was considerable. For example, one person admitted stealing over a thousand records by using the even-exchange method.

In case you might wonder how many records this is, in this picture there are a thousand records.

Let us ask ourselves how this salesperson was able to sign her own saleschecks for authorization when it is against store rules?

If we found one of our employees apparently purchasing fifteen or twenty records a day every day for months, would we have questioned her ability to make such purchases? Would we have noticed?

This problem of forged even exchanges was not limited to records; on the contrary, it was a method of theft used in many different departments.

Cash on Sales

Another method used was to steal cash on sales. Quite often the dishonest employee underrang on the register, and after accumulating several underrung sales, would take out the cash difference for herself.

Some of the dishonest employees ran up "no sales" and pocketed the cash. A few would take the customer's money and make change out of their own handbag.

Do such cash thefts become substantial? One clerk was here less than thirty days and stole $650—some admitted stealing $50 and $60 a day in this manner. Some individually admitted cash register thefts of over $5,000.

Doesn't this method of theft bring home with great impact the importance of insisting that *every* customer receive a cash register receipt on *every* sale? Have you ever noticed the cash register receipts lying about the floor that were *not* given to customers? Have you ever reflected that when we do *not* insist that the salesperson give a register receipt to the customer on *every* cash sales that we are tempting our people to become thieves?

"Special" Sales

One of the most vicious practices we uncovered during this series of cases was that of selling merchandise to "friends" far below its retail value.

This method of dishonesty was being conducted in almost all areas of the store and undoubtedly has cost our store many, many thousands of dollars. For example, in the Candy Department salesclerks treated their friends to 4 and 5 pounds of candy for a purchase price of 10 cents. Some employees made such candy purchases three and four times a week.

One candy salesclerk admitted that in addition to stealing $1,400 from the cash register on sales, she had also stolen and given to her friends over 500 pounds of candy.

How much candy is that? This picture shows 500 pounds of candy.

We also found salesclerks exchanging merchandise they sold for stolen merchandise in another department. As an example, one employee gave a pound of stolen candy in exchange for a pair of stolen cuff links and another exchanged stolen records for stolen gloves.

"As Is"

A variation of the selling below retail value theme was worked under the disguise of the month-end markdown or the "as is" pricing scheme.

A salesclerk would bring a $5.95 bowl to another salesclerk and ask her to give her a "break." The other clerk would sell the $5.95 bowl for 82¢ calling it an "as is" sale. In another instance, a new $22.65 broiler was sold "as is" for 65¢.

We found that some careless merchandising executives were allowing anyone and everyone to set "as is" prices and sell the merchandise immediately on the floor without any markdown being written prior to the sale.

Careless handling of month-end reductions by some merchandisers set up a pattern of operation that became a cloak allowing the dishonest employees to steal from the store.

Within the framework of this same general method of dishonesty, we found that failure to properly control blank price tickets had resulted in the dishonest employee writing her own "as is" price ticket of 10 and 15 cents for items retailing for $25 and $30.

Collusion

As an example of how lax this "as is" situation was, a dishonest employee in the warehouse would put a slip of paper listing a piece of merchandise and 50 cents into an envelope. He would then send the envelope by messenger to a salesclerk in the selling department. She would write an "as is" salescheck for the merchandise, ring up the 50 cents, and return the salescheck by the messenger to the warehouse employee.

He, in turn, got a piece of new merchandise worth $15 or $20 for 50 cents. Since he packed his own merchandise, he could add to the package anything else he wanted to steal.

The salesclerk did not get a merchandiser to approve the purchase—there was no markdown made—and an excellent system for theft was in operation.

Oftentimes, warehouse employees would purposely scratch or mar a piece of merchandise and then get the merchandiser to mark it "as is" it for them. One man purchased five bicycles in this manner; in another case, an electric mangle and a refrigerator were bought.

In some instances, rather than sell the merchandise below its retail value, the clerk would write up the sale for her "friend" for one article and put several articles in the package. The friend paid for one item and got the other stolen merchandise with very little effort.

Salvage

The salvage system, like the "as is" system, was also abused. Because we had no control on salvage receipts, an employee was able to set up an independent business within the store. This employee took new merchandise and sold it as salvage to unsuspecting employees, giving them a fraudulent salvage receipt and pocketing the money from his sales.

It is easy to become complacent about employee dishonesty. Suddenly we find we are involved in shortcuts, expediency, and carelessness, the three witches who cook a retribution as inevitable as it is destructive.

And here is another system that was used by these dishonest employees.

"Sends"

Accommodation saleschecks were used for sending stolen merchandise, much of which was obtained by sending it out on accommodation checks.

The accommodation salescheck is one of the most dangerous store systems. It is often used by dishonest employees as a method of theft and requires alert executive administration. An authorizing signature in the hands of a careful executive could have prevented losses such as these.

Overcharges

We also had dishonest employees defraud us by overcharging on services. This was done for years with immunity, and yet if any of the several people handling these slips had been alert, it could have been caught. For instance, in one case the charge for services should have been $15, but our store was charged $90.

Merchandise was also stolen by wearing it out of the building. One employee never got his shirts laundered. When his shirt became soiled, he put on a new one from stock and left the old one on a locker or in the stockroom.

Wearing a new jacket or a belt out of the building or putting small articles in the pocket is an obvious but successful method of theft. We can't combat this problem with systems. No, this requires something else—an intangible called "Attitude." Attitude is created by the "leader"—the supervisor—in which respect for merchandise is conveyed. The supervisor must set an example of integrity and character. We'll get into that problem of attitude further in a moment.

Additions

We also found dishonest employees who made a small purchase and added stolen merchandise to their package, using the salescheck so they could get the stolen merchandise out the door at night.

We. also arrested two former employees who came into the store before hours and stole.

This slide shows how much merchandise two boys were able to steal in only one day by coming in at 7:30 in the morning: $2,780 worth of merchandise. They packed the suitcases and wore the $220-dollar overcoats and $20-dollar hats. They also put merchandise in shopping bags and left it in the 4th floor public lockers where they picked it up about 2:00 in the afternoon.

Remember this picture if anyone ever tries to minimize the theft problem—two boys in only one day took out $2,780 dollars worth of merchandise.

There were other methods of theft too, but most were variations on those we have discussed.

What Can We Learn?

What can we learn about our problems from these methods of theft? Doesn't a lot of it tie in with careless supervision? There is also revealed a need for the strengthening of some of our systems and procedures; certain weaknesses became immediately apparent, such as the need for a better employee package system. But we must not be deceived into believing that improved systems are the whole answer.

Any system can be beaten by someone. No, the need is for conformity by everyone with existing systems so that the major amount of theft can be stopped.

Attitude

But what causes us to operate systems properly or poorly? One thing—and that is attitude. More than any other single thing, attitude must be changed before we can make any progress. If attitude is right, the rest will follow.

But what affects attitude? People, of course. We are back to that common denominator again. So let's take a look at the people who stole.

Who are they? These 64 ghosts? Was their age a factor? Were they all immature teenagers out for a lark? No, their ages ranged from teenage up to 65 years.

What about length of employment? Perhaps they weren't here long—they hadn't caught the store spirit. Wrong again; their period of employment covered from one month to twenty years.

Then the answer must be in the social group they came from. Perhaps they were all from the slums—wrong again. They ranged from poor up the scale to a former society matron.

Well, then, perhaps they just weren't our type. They didn't have those qualities we have always required in our people that make them outstanding. That answer is partly true.

Some of these dishonest employees were *not* our type and we will discuss them in a moment. But the majority of these people were no different from you or me. They were above-average, nice people, from good backgrounds, had families like ours, went to church every Sunday, and were just like the rest of us. What about them?

Well, we'll discuss them in a moment, but first let's look at some of the others who do not appear to meet the standards we set for our employees.

The Stockclerk

One young man who came with us as a stockclerk well illustrates the necessity for supervisors to get closer to their people so we can learn their problems. For often, it is the person who is very unhappy because of excessive problems who steals.

This boy lived in the worst poverty you can imagine. His family, a mother and five other children, lives in a shack on the outskirts of a village 30 miles from our city. The shack has three rooms, one large room combining living room, kitchen, and dining room, and two small bedrooms, each with only a single bed. Five cats and three dogs also roam the house, and when we went there, we found dog dirt on the floor of the cluttered living room. Dirty dishes were everywhere on the table, in the sink, and on the floor—disorder and filth were everywhere.

The family had no plumbing fixtures. There was an outhouse in the back. Water was pumped from a well—there was no bathtub and a single wood stove was used for cooking as well as for heating the house.

The boy's father had been a drunkard who had died 6 years before; the mother was on welfare. One brother, 11 years old, had a paralyzed leg—his worn metal brace was lying on the floor, part of the litter. Out of such a home came no clean clothes, and therefore the boy stole a clean shirt or a pair of clean socks or underwear whenever he needed it.

The boy himself, in his wrinkled, soiled suit and dishevelled hair, made a poor appearance. He had a speech defect, and when he spoke it was hard to understand his words. In conversation, he appeared mentally retarded with an intelligence quotient far below average.

It might be difficult to understand how he could have been hired originally. But once hired, if you had seen and talked to him, you could not have believed that he would be approved after his 90-day probationary period—or that he would be continued in employment.

This boy cost our store a lot of money. Not only did he steal very substantial amounts of merchandise as well as money from the cash register, but he also was directly responsible for the downfall of five potentially fine young men who came to work in his area—and who were led by him into similar habits of theft. As you know, one bad apple can rot a whole barrel of good apples.

The Alcoholic

Take a fellow we'll call "D," a confirmed alcoholic. He was 34 years old when he was employed as a stockclerk. It was known throughout his department that he loaned money to other employees for 50 percent interest. On lunch hours, he engaged a group of other stockclerks in daily gambling sessions. And, when they lost $40 or $50 to him, he would loan them the money at high interest that they had to repay him out of their weekly pay envelopes.

He often stayed out two or three days at a time when he was on an alcoholic binge. On one occasion he was arrested for a drunken spree.

Was he just a harmless drunk? Not quite—he stole large quantities of merchandise from the area he worked in—and he sold a lot of stolen merchandise to other employees. He also goaded honest employees who worked with him to steal.

And then there was the 44-year old woman who often came to work with the smell of liquor heavy on her breath. A frustrated woman who had always wanted a career as a ballet dancer, she was married to an alcoholic truck driver who was unemployed and couldn't get a job because of his drinking. She stole over $5,000 from the cash register because she said she had to buy whiskey and had to maintain her living standard.

Also, Mrs. B., a 34-year-old Canadian, in this country for 11 years, but who had never made any effort to become a U.S. citizen. Twice excluded from this country by immigration authorities because of poor morals—she claimed to have been married 15 times, but actually had never been legally married. Her present common-law husband was in the hospital and she was being sued for his bill so she obtained a $225 loan from our store to pay the bill. Instead, however, she used the money to buy a topaz ring for herself. This woman stole merchandise from our store.

Let's ask ourselves about these people. Can we lead people without getting close to them? Without getting to know them? Could their supervisors have learned about their problems? And, if they did know these things, then why didn't they take action to either help them or to remove these people from our store as unfit? Would we knowingly allow these employees to stay in our midst and contaminate and destroy the impressionable young people who came in contact with them?

Would we allow this because we didn't know the true facts about these people or would we allow it because we lacked the courage necessary to do our job properly.

All of the 64 were not employees such as these, however, no indeed.

The Minister

Let's take one we'll call "Mr. K."—he was a minister, his father had been a minister before him—and Mr. K. had come to our city to establish a branch of his church. He worked here temporarily while the church was being constructed. In less than two months this man was a thief. That's one to think about, isn't it?

There were many other people involved in these cases, like Miss "Y," employed here 17 years, a fine person, with a nice appearance and a pleasant personality. She was happily married with two children, one now in high school, the other planning a college career.

Or a young boy named "N" who was saving his money to study for the ministry—and after he was arrested, his mother offered to pay the restitution he owed. "N" kept her check and got a job in a filling station. After he earned the full amount he owed, he paid our store and tore up his mother's check.

Yes, the *majority* of the people we arrested were basically good people. They were people who had gone wrong—gotten off the track somewhere. Let's see if we can find out what happened to them—the ghosts that are still standing here with us.

What's Become of Them?

Some are now in debt for the rest of their lives because of their thefts. The tear-stained faces of many suggest the emotional and mental anguish they have gone through as a result of their experiences. In some cases their homes have been broken up. In many cases, they will never again enjoy the complete confidence and respect of those they love.

In some cases, they have even been sent to prison where they must now wait out the years in a small iron-barred room. All of them have undoubtedly thought a lot about many things—about what they've done, about our store, about us—and we, in turn, owe it to them to think a lot about them and the problems they represent.

These 64 people, this $50,000 tells us nothing about what has gone before. It does not foretell the future—and in no part does it include the cases Security is currently working on. Doesn't this fact suggest that like the giant icebergs that float down from the Northern wastes at this time of year to endanger shipping that the greatest part of our problem is beneath the surface—that it is still unknown in detail but is suggested by the part we now can see.

Responsibility

Don't these cases represent a warning of far greater problems still to be solved?

And how can any of this possibly be solved except by each of us taking on our share of responsibility?

You men and women in this room are a group of the finest retail executives in the country—this store and everything it stands for is a living proof of your ability—I could not find words to tell you how proud I am to be your associate.

But today we probably face one of our most difficult problems. I am confident we can solve it by applying the same idealism, the same fine abilities that have made this store so great—and I believe the solution will be worked out by the use of two fundamental truths with which we are all familiar. What are they?

The Philosophy

Well, first let me ask you if you remember a book called *One Life, One Kopeck*? It was an interesting title—translated, of course, it means "one life equals one cent." This is the philosophy of the totalitarian countries and it was the basic reason we have fought great wars. For we do not believe that a man or woman's life is cheap—that it is worth only a cent. We believe that human lives are the most valuable thing there is!

As a group, we, in this room and in this country, have had great pressures put upon us. As you know, we have been through the age of debunking. We have read books, magazines, newspapers, heard radio, seen television, movies—all of our propaganda mediums hammered at us day after day—ridiculing the fundamental beliefs—the moral codes—the truths that we believe in and have used to build sound and happy lives.

Much we have believed in has been called "corny," old-fashioned, outmoded—but truth still prevails. You know it and so do I. Suddenly we find the country returning to its churches—people moving to the suburbs to again establish family lives as a center of strength—a raising of moral standards.

Some have called the past few decades the "era of disillusionment," but the philosophies of our religions and the principles of goodness still survive; they will never be destroyed by debunking.

It is in these wise thoughts that have come down to us through the centuries of mankind's experience that we can find the answers to such problems as those we face today.

The Golden Rule

I feel that most of you will agree with me—that two great rules of life can solve this problem of *attitude* that we are facing here in this room. Number one is the fundamental belief that was used to found and build this store; it is, of course, the golden rule—"Do unto others as you would have them do unto you." Number two, another fundamental truth, is that "We *are* our brother's keeper."

You and I are responsible every minute of every working day for the lives of the people who work around us. It is part of that responsiblity to see that they are never put in a position where they are unduly tempted to steal.

Most people *want* to be honest. Once they have stolen they become very unhappy people—for once they have stolen, they feel quilty—and guilt feelings bring with them two witches called worry and fear. Ask any person who has stolen and they will tell you how they wish they could live it all over again and be *free.* They will tell you how they tormented themselves—of the sleepless nights, the nagging fears—how they were locked into the torture chamber of their own mind. We are indeed our brother's keeper.

Leaders Set Example

And now in summary, what have we found by analyzing these dishonesty cases?

First, that as a leader, *we* must set the example. Our people can only respond to the extent that we show them by *our* example.

We also must realize that we, as leaders, cannot buy popularity by doing "favors" that violate store systems and procedures. We can only build the lasting admiration and respect of our people with our own examples of integreity and character.

From these cases we can see that we must have the courage to weed out the unfit in fairness to the larger group of loyal workers.

Next, we must also examine our systems and procedures to discover weaknesses. Once we find such soft spots, we must strengthen them and build for tomorrow.

Prevention

And, we must all work together toward *preventing* dishonesty through our attitude, our systems, our people. Our program must primarily be one of preventive security and we will help you with such a program in whatever way we can.

In addition to such a program of prevention, however, you and I must search out dishonesty in our midst—there is no one else to do it. The purpose of the Security Department is not primarily to find dishonesty, but rather to prevent it and to deal with it after it is discovered. Security is like a fire department; when you discover a blaze or even a wisp of smoke—you call in the fireman to put out the fire. That is the way the Security Department works too—it is there to help you put out the blaze.

If you discover any indications of dishonesty among your people, turn this information over to the Security Department at once. Let these specialists handle the problem—don't try to do it yourself.

And now, before we dismiss these ghosts we've brought here today, I want to remind you that each dishonest employee we arrest represents a loss not measurable in dollars and cents, a loss that is far greater than money—the loss of a person. Perhaps this brief bit from a poem about ghosts by Norman Treadwell illustrates the thought we are trying to convey:

> Memories are dim ghosts of yesterday,
> Some pleasant, some sad and gray—
> and as these forlorn phantoms
> Move through our haunted halls
> About their ghostly figures
> A mist begins to fall
> Their grey shrouds of memories
> Give way to unborn dreams
> As tired, transparent fingers
> Etch upon our walls—
> The story of what might have been.

INDEX